A Mind of Her Own

A Mind of Her Own
The evolutionary psychology of women

SECOND EDITION

Anne Campbell

OXFORD
UNIVERSITY PRESS

OXFORD

UNIVERSITY PRESS

Great Clarendon Street, Oxford, OX2 6DP,
United Kingdom

Oxford University Press is a department of the University of Oxford.
It furthers the University's objective of excellence in research, scholarship,
and education by publishing worldwide. Oxford is a registered trade mark of
Oxford University Press in the UK and in certain other countries

First Edition published in 2002
Second Edition published in 2013

Impression: 1

Published in the United States of America by Oxford University Press
198 Madison Avenue, New York, NY 10016, United States of America

British Library Cataloguing in Publication Data

Data available

Library of Congress Control Number: 2013937761

ISBN 978–0–19–960954–3

Printed and bound in Great Britain by
CPI Group (UK) Ltd, Croydon, CR0 4YY

To Jamie

Acknowledgments

Books need researchers. Without frontline scientists doing research, there is nothing to write about. So my first debt of gratitude is to all the academics whose ideas and results have fueled this book. It is in conversations that nebulous ideas take shape and get formalized into words and hypotheses. For these, I thank my work colleagues and graduate students (especially Kate Cross, Helen Driscoll, Simon Hampton, and Lee Copping). Durham University undergraduates have also kept me on my toes with incisive and enthusiastic questions. Closer to home, thanks to Table 7 for the anecdotes, debates, therapy, and laughs.

Finally, I thank my family who have graciously shared their home with an "evolution" obsessive. In fact, my husband brought this on himself many years ago. I trace his responsibility to his disgusted expression when he learned that I was not familiar with (indeed had never heard of) the work of John Maynard Smith. There was no choice but to remedy my parochialism by reading about game theory. (From whence it was a short hop to Martin Daly and Margo Wilson, George Williams, John Tooby and Leda Cosmides, Sarah Hrdy, etc. . . .). All this set me wondering if the sole role of women in evolution was to vet male genes. After all, if women were all breeding at their maximum with little or no variation between them, that seemed the limit of their contribution. The innocence of this question is belied by the 18 years that I have spent struggling with it. This book is my attempt at an answer.

Contents

Chapter 1

The essential woman: Biophobia and the study of sex differences

Each of us lives only one version of a human lifetime. We live it as a man or woman. What would it be like to perceive, to think, and to feel as a member of the opposite sex? A few transgendered individuals may get a glimpse across that invisible wall but the sex chromosomes that we arrive with, whether XX or XY, are the ones we leave with. The psychological worlds of men and women have been a focal point of interest for scientists and feminists. But these two groups deal in different currencies. Scientists see an enigma and want to understand it. Feminists envision a social utopia and want to engineer it. During the latter part of the twentieth century, feminist ideology infiltrated science to such an extent that it was hard to tell the difference between the objective facts of sex differences and the political ambition to erase them. But the only way to find a path to a social goal is to recognize where we currently stand. Evolutionary psychologists knew this, but they had a fight on their hands. There were three camps that dominated the psychology of gender and that vocally opposed the application of evolutionary theory: social constructionism, cognitive learning theories, and social role theory.

Since 1970, over one million studies of gender and sex differences have appeared in academic journals. The zeitgeist of the post-war years profoundly influenced the questions that researchers posed, the methods they used, and the recommendations they made. In the West, incomes rose, educational opportunity increased, and women began to discern their very unequal standing in the world of work, professional achievement, and public recognition. These forces informed a belief that society was perfectible and that we should aim to equalize the standing of women and men. Quite right too. But the political ideology that drove this laudable quest for social equality began to drive psychological theories too. The only acceptable account of sex differences was one which explicitly acknowledged the socially constructed, arbitrary, and malleable nature of sex differences. Women's studies became steeped in a politically driven rejection of essentialism (the idea that the sexes differ at a fundamental psychological level) and committed on one hand to social constructionism (there is no objective truth "out there" only negotiable subjective representations) and on the other to extreme environmentalism (all sex differences result from factors external to the person). None of these roads took us very far toward an accurate understanding of why men and women differ.

Social constructionists effectively removed gender from the human mind and instead allowed it to float freely in an insubstantial ether as a "social construction," or an "emergent property," or an "interpretative repertoire." This is why it is possible to read statements such as the following, written in all seriousness: "Gender distinctions as dichotomous categories are perpetrated and maintained by social mechanisms and are socially constructed" (Epstein, 1997). The prevailing dogma was that the distinction between men and women is a collective and tyrannical fiction. There are no real biological or psychological differences other than ones that we construct through discourse. For these writers, questions about the causes of sex differences never rear their heads because positivistic science (with its traditional obsession with causality) is disparaged as simply another rhetoric among many—and an outdated one at that (Woolgar, 1996). Humans are the sole focus of interest and any comparison between our behavior and that of lower animals is unjustified, demeaning, and reductionist. This is because humans have language, language enables discourse, and it is through discourse that social reality, including gender, is constructed. (This is especially true of educated, middle-class Western humans judging by the disproportionate attention they receive.) The study of discourse is the study of implicit or received meaning and all meaning is subjective so there can be no single authoritative or "privileged" reading of a text. Although social constructionists recognize the implications of this observation for their own analyses, they nevertheless "deconstruct" (often in dense literary and psychoanalytic terms) the ways in which gender is created in social talk. To give a flavor of their approach to gender differences, I quote from one of the most frequently cited writers of this genre (Hollway, 1984, pp. 227–228):

> Hence recurrent day-to-day practices and meanings through which they acquire their effectivity may contribute to the maintenance of gender difference (reproduction without a hyphen) or to its modification (the production of modified meanings of gender leading to changed practices) . . . I am interested in theorising the practices and meanings which re-produce gendered subjectivity (what psychologists would call gender identity). . . . Gender differentiated meanings (and thus the positions differentially available in discourse) account for the content of gender difference.

In this article, Hollway goes on to explain how different discourses about sexuality locate women and men in different positions relative to one another. She writes of the "discourse" of the stronger male sex drive, the "discourse" of the Madonna–whore distinction, and the permissive "discourse" which appeared to (but did not) liberate women's sexuality. Now each of these topics is of some considerable interest to evolutionary psychology, as we shall see, but in that discipline rather than locating them as discursive fictions they are taken as answerable empirical hypotheses about which evolutionary theory makes clear predictions. Men's sex drive should be stronger than women's—and it is (Baumeister, Catanese, & Vohs, 2001). Women should experience a social cost if they gain a reputation for promiscuity—and they do (Cashdan, 1996). Women should find casual sexual liaisons less satisfactory than men—and they do (Campbell, 2008a; Townsend, Kline, & Wasserman, 1995). Nor are these findings exclusive to a single culture or language community—they exist independently of so-called "constitutive" discourse. For social constructionists the key question of the origins of these discourses is strenuously avoided:

> But to assume the mechanical reproduction of discourse requires asking how it got to be like that in the first place. And that question is in danger of throwing theory back into answers according to the terms of biological, Oedipal or social and economic determinisms. (Hollway, 1984, pp. 238–239)

In short, better not to ask the question if you think you may not like the answer.

But elsewhere in the social sciences some academics were indeed resorting to "social determinism." Sex differences come from outside the child. Babies are not born wanting to play football or dress dolls. These preferences are imposed by parents and the media, and then encoded into children's cognitive frameworks, magnifying and reifying the differences between masculine and feminine behavior.

Socialization explanations of sex differences were built on the foundation of the tabula rasa infant coaxed, rewarded, and punished until it conformed to societal demands for sex-appropriate behavior. They took shape in the era of behaviorism and learning theory. The account was a simple one. Parents treat boys and girls differently, reinforcing the correct behavior in each. Boys are encouraged to fight, climb trees, and play football. Girls are forced to wear dresses, play with dolls, and share. Despite the fall from grace of radical behaviorism, nobody seriously doubts that reinforcement can shape behavior. The question was whether it was strong enough to account for the worldwide patterns of sex difference that we see. The "Baby X" paradigm was hailed as conclusive evidence of socialization differences (e.g., Will, Self, & Datan, 1976). A six-month-old baby was wrapped in a blue or a pink blanket, identified as a boy or a girl, and then handed to a woman who was asked to look after it for a few minutes. When told it was a girl, the women more often offered a doll to the infant in preference to other toys. Surely this showed that parents treat infants differently as a function of their sex? But there was a problem. Despite many attempts to replicate the effect, it seemed even weaker than it had appeared on first sight (and recall the effect was found only for toy selection—there were no differences in social behavior toward the infant). It was certainly not strong enough to support the whole edifice of sex differences (Stern & Karraker, 1989). And even if parents give their children different toys, such a finding is trivial unless it can be shown that toys change the child's subsequent behavior.

But the real crunch came when Lytton and Romney (1991) collected 172 studies from around the world which examined the way in which parents treat their sons and daughters. Considering them all together, the evidence for differential treatment was virtually nil. Parents did not differ in the amount of interaction with the child, the warmth they showed, their tendency to encourage dependency or achievement, their restrictiveness, their use of discipline, their tendency to reason with the child, or the amount of aggression that they tolerated. There was, however, one area that showed a difference. Parents tended to give their children sex-appropriate toys. But sex-differentiated preferences for toys have been found in infants from nine months of age (Campbell, Shirley, Heywood, & Crook, 2000). Children play more with sex-appropriate toys even when their parents do not specifically encourage them to do so (Caldera, Huston, & O'Brien, 1989). It is quite likely that parents are not using toys to turn their children into gender conformists but are responding sympathetically to the child's own preferences. Anyway, if parents' behavior toward their children was guided by their desire to make them conform to traditional gender stereotypes than we would expect to find that the most sex-typed adults have the most sex-typed children. Yet studies find that there is no relationship between traditional household division of labor, parents' attitudes to sex-typing, their sex-typical activities, and their reactions to children's behavior on one hand and children's degree of sex typing on the other (Maccoby, 1998).

Following Skinnerian views came social learning theory which emphasized a hitherto neglected (but altogether central primate) capacity—imitation. No-trial learning. We can acquire a piece of behavior merely by watching it performed by others. But the trick was to co-opt this observation into an explanation of the acquisition of sex differences. This was done by proposing that children selectively imitate their same-sex parent. Laboratory studies were done in which children were exposed to adult "models" performing a variety of novel behaviors. If social learning theorists were right, then the statistical analysis would show a significant interaction between sex-of-model and sex-of-child—girls would imitate women and boys would imitate men. Dozens of such studies failed to find such an effect (Huston, 1983; Maccoby & Jacklin, 1974). Undeterred, Perry and Bussey (1979) devised a cunning experiment which avoided the pitfalls of the previous studies where children had only a one-off exposure to an adult model. They showed children a film of eight adults selecting a preferred fruit. In one condition all four men made one choice (e.g., orange) while all four women made the other (e.g., apple). In another condition, three men and one woman chose an orange while three women and one man chose an apple. In another condition half the men chose oranges and half the women chose apples. They found that the extent to which children copied an adult's preference depended upon the proportion of their sex that made that choice. In the first condition, there was a high degree of same-sex imitation, in the second a much smaller amount, and in the third condition, there was no significant difference between the girls and boys in their choices. This meant that children were not slavishly imitating a same-sex adult but rather judging the appropriateness of a particular (in this case wholly arbitrary) preference on the basis of the proportion of male or female adults who made it. These results helped to make sense of previous work which had already shown that children tended to imitate activities that they already knew to be sex typed, regardless of the sex of the model who was currently engaged in it (Barkley, Ullman, Otto, & Brecht, 1977). What was important was the child's internal working model of gender and behavior.

Until then, the differential treatment and selective imitation views had painted a thoroughly passive view of the child. There he or she sat, slowly being filled with sex-contingent reinforcement and exposure to adult models. Some developmental psychologists rebelled. They knew that children are active participants in their own development—Piaget had shown this. Now Perry and Bussey had put the child's own understanding of gender center stage. It was the genesis of *cognitive learning theory*. Martin and Halverson (1981) argued that children have a natural tendency to think categorically. They form categories about all sorts of things from animals to sports and it would be surprising if they did not, very early in life, form categories of male and female. Once these categories are formed, all incoming information that is gender typical gets shunted into the correct binary slot and over time a stereotype is built up about what males and females look like, do, and enjoy. It is this internal model or schema, not parental training, which drives the child toward sex-appropriate behavior. It was clear that Perry and Bussey, in their search for the mechanisms of imitation, had laid bare the process of creating gender schema. At the very same time that this proposal was being offered for child development, Bem (1981) was proposing an identical schema to explain adult differences in sex typing. She argued that the degree to which we "type" information as gender relevant is an individual difference variable. Women who strongly sex type information become more stereotypically feminine than women who are less inclined to tag information with gender labels. The cognitive revolution had come to sex differences—it was not a matter of behavioral training, it was a matter of mental categorizing, organizing, and recalling.

But the cracks soon began to appear. Children show sex-typed behavior before they are able to label the sex of other children (Ruble & Martin, 1998). Toy choice, play styles, activity levels, and aggression are found as early as two years of age (Brooks & Lewis, 1974; Fagot, 1991; Freedman, 1974; Howes, 1988; Kohnstamm, 1989; O'Brien & Huston, 1985; Roopnarine, 1986) but children are not able to correctly sort pictures of boys and girls into piles until toward the end of their third year (Weinraub, Clements, Sockloff, Ethridge, & Myers, 1984). Although children can point to pictures of boys and girls when instructed to do so somewhat earlier at about 30 months (Etaugh, Grinnell, & Etaugh, 1989; Fagot & Leinbach, 1989), for a gender schema to operate spontaneously and successfully, children should be able to categorize without specific verbal cueing to do so. Yet children prefer sex-congruent toys before they are able to say whether the toy is more appropriate for a boy or a girl (Blakemore, LaRue, & Olejnik, 1979). They prefer to interact with members of their own sex and show sex differences in social behavior before they can label either toys or behaviors as being more common among boys or girls (Serbin, Tonick, & Sternglanz, 1977; Smetana & Letourneau, 1984). Having gender labels at the age of two does not predict sex typing either at the same age or one year later (Campbell, Shirley, & Candy, 2004). Even where a cross-sectional study finds a behavioral difference between children who can label gender and children who cannot, it is found for only some behaviors not others, or for one sex but not the other (Fagot, Leinbach & Hagan, 1986). Children do not need the ability to discriminate the sexes or an understanding of gender stereotypic behavior to show sex differences. Even in later years, as children's gender stereotypes become more crystallized and peak at about seven years of age, there is no relationship between a child's gender knowledge and how sex-stereotypic their own behavior is (Martin, 1994; Powlishta, 1995; Serbin, Moller, Gulko, Powlishta, & Colburne, 1994). As Carol Martin (1993) ruefully concluded after 20 years' immersion in the field, "Seldom are individual differences in behavior and thinking explained by differing levels of gender stereotype knowledge."

But perhaps children really recognize gender at a much earlier age than experimenters' artificial requests to point to pictures of boys and girls reveal. Perhaps they lack the verbal or cognitive skills to execute such a task before the age of three. After all, animals seem to make no mistakes about the sex of their conspecifics and they lack the sophisticated cognitive machinery that we possess. Researchers turned to infants, using an ingenuous method to uncover their ability to categorize the world. Infants, like adults, get bored when they are exposed to the same thing for too long and they turn away—a phenomenon called habituation. Fagot and Leinbach (1993) showed a group of infants, aged between nine and 12 months, a series of photographs of different men's or women's faces. Every now and again, a face of the opposite sex would be shown. The infants would show a sudden recovery of interest when this unexpected face appeared. This suggested that infants had an implicit category of male and female for, if they did not, how could they detect the category shift when the "unusual" face appeared? This seemed to solve the cognitive problem—infants understand sex much earlier than we thought. But wait—the same type of study has also been performed in the laboratory using different categories such as animal species, rising and falling auditory tones, numbers, colors, and patterns (Bhatt & Rovee-Collier, 1996; Wagner, Winner, Cicchetti, & Gardner, 1981; Xu & Carey, 1996; Younger & Cohen, 1983). All these studies show that infants can habituate and then recover from habituation. Would we want to conclude, therefore, that six-month-old infants brought with them to the laboratory an acquired understanding of the difference between a zebra and a kangaroo? Given their limited exposure to such novel stimuli, how could they? Rather, we infer that during their time in the laboratory, infants develop (rather than reveal) categories for dividing up the perceptual world. So while infants can be experimentally primed to make a male–female distinction, this is not evidence that they have brought it with them from the outside world.

Even if they did have it, it would be of no use to them unless they knew to which sex they themselves belonged. Gender schema can only guide behavior when sex-of-self is incorporated into the schema. Children sort pictures of themselves correctly into the boy or girl pile at about the same time they sort pictures of others—around 36 months (Thompson, 1975; Weinraub et al., 1984). Indeed they do not seem to even recognize themselves in mirrors until about 20 months (Amsterdam, 1972; Campbell et al., 2004). (This is tested by surreptitiously placing a blob of rouge onto the child's nose and allowing them to view themselves in a mirror. If they try to wipe their own nose they have self-recognition. If they try to wipe the nose of the child in the mirror, they do not.) In any case, self-recognition is a necessary but far from sufficient condition for knowing which sex you belong to.

Gender schema theory was all too cognitive and the cognitive data would not fit the developmental time course. And there was the question too obvious to be asked—why do children socialize themselves to behave sex typically? Is the process one of simple social conformity? If so, is gender a special case or do children also schematize themselves in other ways (geeks, athletes) and strive to conform to these categories as much as they do to boy or girl? There lurks beneath cognitive theories a pervasive feeling that there is something special about gender, and that the engine that drives categorization and conformity is an innate propulsion—perhaps not to be aggressive or nurturing—but at least to realize oneself as a male or female.

At the heart of gender schema theory lie stereotypes. Initially crude and concrete (boys like trucks, girls like dolls), they become increasingly abstract and metaphorical with increasing age (men are more competitive, women more cooperative). We construct them from bits and pieces of observation—from the media, from watching others, from gossip and myths. And it is stereotypes that form the foundation for another explanation of sex differences—*social role theory*. According to this formulation, the division of labor in society, rather than the child's natural tendency to form categories, is the starting point for sex differences. Men occupy roles that require competitiveness, autonomy, and aggression. Women occupy roles that require nurturance, caring, and cooperation. These roles draw out of their occupants the commensurate qualities and skills. These in turn set up stereotypes that embody beliefs about the appropriateness of expected characteristics. "Expectancy confirming behaviour should be especially common when expectancies are broadly shared in a society, as is the case for the expectancies about women and men" (Eagly, 1987, p. 15). These expectancies are internalized psychologically, resulting in sex differences in both behavior and self-perception.

During the last years of the twentieth century, there was a significant change in the nature of women's labor as they moved into many arenas traditionally occupied by men. We might therefore expect to see a shift in both stereotypes and self-perceptions by men and women. No such shift occurred (Helmreich, Spence, & Gibson, 1982; Lewin & Tragos, 1987; Lueptow, 1985). Furthermore, we would expect to see a fair degree of cultural specificity with "traditional" societies showing more marked stereotypes than more egalitarian ones. We do not (Williams & Best, 1982). Social role theory supposes that sex differences follow stereotypes and hence that stereotypes should be more extreme and polarized than actual sex differences. They are not (Swim, 1994). We are left with the alternative suggestion that stereotypes are reasonably accurate assessments of the typical differences between men and women and that, rather than stereotypes causing sex differences, the reverse is the case. If this is true then we at least have a means of explaining the typical division of labor between the sexes (women prefer to spend more time than men do in parenting activities) which social role theory could not do.

Indeed its authors recognized that they must find a way to explain the origins of the sexual division of labor which, after all, formed the hinge pin of their whole theory. But there was a problem: in all cultures women assume the major burden of childcare while men (but rarely women) engage in warfare and violence. The most obvious candidate for explaining such human universals is evolutionary psychology, but this was not a route that appealed to Wood and Eagly (2002). Their radical solution was to divorce the mind from the body and allow evolution to work only on the latter: "Our biosocial model does not assume that any sexual selection pressures that contributed to physical dimorphism between the sexes are major influences on sex-typed psychological attributes" (p. 702). They acknowledged that men have greater size, upper body strength, and speed—this fits them perfectly for their "social role" in aggression and warfare. Women are capable of giving birth and lactating—this makes them good candidates for their "social role" as mothers. But the argument that bodily differences gave rise to the sexual division of labor begged some obvious questions. Where did these morphological differences come from? If they were not created by evolutionary sexual selection pressures, what caused them? And why do we share these physical dimorphisms with so many other species? Addressing these physical sex differences inevitably plunged Wood and Eagly into recognition of hormonal effects. They accepted not only that testosterone fosters muscle development, but also that it rises and falls in men in response to competition in order to direct men's "physical and cognitive performance." How did such a useful hormonal adjustment occur, if not through evolution? But if that were true, then Wood and Eagly would have to accept that competition was of central importance to male reproductive success and that selection had therefore acted on the male brain as well as male muscle. Perhaps more importantly, how does their acknowledgement of the psychological impact of testosterone square with their argument that evolution has had no effect on "sex-typed psychological attributes"? Endocrinologists have known for many years that testosterone, aromatized to estrogen, crosses the blood–brain barrier. Their neat disjunction between body and brain is not one that hormones or biological evolution respects.

With the "bio" side of their biosocial model addressed, the authors turned their attention to the argument concerning its social dimension: sex differences vary in magnitude across cultures. This results, they proposed, from differences in local ecology and technology which affect social role demands and hence the rigidity or plasticity of the sexual division of labor. Evolutionary theory, as it is caricatured by Wood and Eagly, stipulates that men but not women provide food. Why then, they ask, does the contribution of women and men to subsistence vary across cultures? Evolutionary theory predicts (and data confirm) that mothers everywhere spend more time with children than fathers—but why then, they ask, does the proportion of childcare contributed by men vary? Their conclusion: evolutionary theory must be wrong. But this rests on a profound misunderstanding of evolution and facultative adjustment. Evolution depends on the degree of fit between the organism and the environment. Because ecologies vary, so must the characteristics that are best suited to it. Evolution has built the ability to adjust, creating a kind of inherited intelligence. In plants, hardly noted for their sophisticated cognitive abilities, phototaxis causes them to orient toward the source of sunlight. In some species of teleost fish, the prevailing sex ratio causes some individuals to change sex. When we consider humans, with their unique ability to envisage hypothetical futures and to solve problems, the potential for a flexible response to the environment magnifies considerably. But I am getting ahead of myself.

Nobody can seriously doubt that environmental factors modify the expression of sex differences. The problem with socialization theories is that they ask the environment to do *all* of the work. They fail to recognize that the environment is acting on an evolved organ—the mind. Of course, forces such as reinforcement, imitation, cognitive schema, and conformity all modulate our actions. The pleasure of social approval, the ability to learn through observation, our internal representations, and the desire to be like others—these are part of human psychology everywhere. The question is whether these processes alone can explain the *origins* of the cross-cultural differences between male and female. Altering reinforcement contingencies for sex-typical behavior can temporarily change it: boys and girls will show cross-sex play where the environment is manipulated to encourage it and social approval is contingent on it. But when that intervention is removed, children revert to the same-sex preference that characterizes children everywhere (Serbin, Tonick, & Sternganz, 1977; Theokas, Ramsey, & Sweeney, 1993). Demeanor and language that used to be frowned on in young women as "masculine" is now unremarkable. But there is no link between girls' cultural approval of these new female behaviors and their level of aggression (Muncer, Campbell, Jervis, & Lewis, 2001): we have as yet seen no change in the universal tendency for men to be more violent than women. As new opportunities open to women, they eagerly accept them. Women's entry into hitherto masculine areas of achievement such as science, engineering, and entrepreneurship has been remarkable. Yet still, for the majority of women, occupational choice rests as heavily on the social as on the financial rewards and on the extent to which their work can be effectively combined with motherhood (Browne, 1995; Ceci, Williams, & Barnett, 2009; Geary, 1998).

Where we can open up new opportunities for women's self-expression, enjoyment, and achievement we should do it because it is morally right. But that is very different from saying that gender has no biological basis and that the nature of men and women is wholly constructed by society. The problem with such a position is that it fails to address the issue of why sex differences take the particular form that they do. If gender differences are arbitrary, it is a curious coincidence that they follow such a similar pattern around the world. Even if sex differences were driven by differential parental treatment, we would still want to ask why a trait is considered more desirable for one sex than another. If they were driven by selective imitation, we would still want to ask why children might show a preferential and untutored interest in the behavior of their own sex. If driven by gender schema, we would need to ask why sex-specific conformity is so attractive to children. If driven by the division of labor, we still need to explain the preference of men and women for different social and occupational roles. Social constructionist and environmental theories explain the transmission of the gendered status quo—but without asking where it came from.

Evolutionary psychology

Evolutionary theory addresses this very question. And the Darwinian algorithm is so elegant that it can be stated in five words: random genetic variation, non-random selection. Evolutionary psychology is the application of evolutionary principles to the study of the evolution of mind (Tooby & Cosmides, 1992). Natural and sexual selection pressures which shaped species-typical aspects of our anatomy (bipedalism, cranial capacity, gestation length) are assumed to have orchestrated the architecture of the human mind which in turn drives behavior. Evolutionary psychology holds that psychological attributes that conferred significant benefits in terms of survival and reproduction upon their bearer (relative to others who did not possess such attributes) are present today in the form of evolved adaptations designed to solve such specific ancestral problems as enhancing paternal certainty (Wilson & Daly, 1992), optimizing mate selection (Buss, 1989a), speedily acquiring language (Pinker, 1994), comprehending the mental state of others (Baron-Cohen, 1997), and weighting the costs of risky encounters (Campbell, 1999).

The distinguishing features of evolutionary psychology are fourfold. First, it is ultimately concerned with *mechanisms of mind* and not simply behavior. This distinguishes it from sociobiology in which comparisons are made between animal and human behaviors and implications are drawn about a common evolutionary pathway or about convergent evolution between species under similar selection pressures. Primate behavior is often described and discussed by evolutionary psychologists (and I will be doing this too) because many human adaptations are shared with other species and emerged prior to human speciation (Foley, 1996). Such behavioral comparisons are a starting point for attempting to locate the mental mechanisms which produce it. To do this, we need to ask questions about function—what does this behavior achieve? And to answer this we need a description of the circumstances under which the behavior appears and whether or not it solves an adaptive problem. But evolutionary psychology also asks about the relevant inputs to the mental device and the range of outputs that can appear. This is important in understanding flexibility of action—how the life stage and competencies of the organism, together with perception of the past and current environment, affect the strategy that is implemented. The same mechanisms can give rise to different manifest behaviors. Competition for resources, for example, can lead to combat, the formation of advantageous alliances, or dispersion to new ecological niches. The same mechanism can produce different manifest behaviors given different inputs; babies raised in China speak a different language from infants raised in England but that does not invalidate the existence of a universal mental device for acquiring the language heard in the local community. We are searching for the deep structure not only of language but of other universal human abilities including kin recognition, mate selection, and sexual jealousy despite the fact that their behavioral expression may vary.

Second, evolutionary psychology conceives of the *mind as an adapted organ*. Some have likened it to a Swiss army knife, equipped with many specific modules, each geared to the speedy and seemingly effortless processing and resolving of problems (Tooby & Cosmides, 1992). This view assumes that the environment of adaptation presented similar classes of problem again and again, resulting in selection of those specific mental abilities that were advantageous in solving them. The presence of a predator produces activity in the fear center of the amygdala at a pre-conscious level that triggers alertness and evasion even before we have consciously registered exactly what the threat is. (The path to the sensory cortex is slower and more roundabout than the direct pathway to the amygdala.) Fast-approaching objects on a collision course with us were a sufficient danger in our evolutionary past that infants today will fall backward when an object is made to "loom" (by simply increasing its size) on a screen in front of them. This reflex was sufficiently useful as an adaptation that it is now hardwired. The mind is a collection of modules that reliably develop in a wide range of environments. Some are simple reflexes, but many more are not. Humans have a tendency to commit various cognitive "errors" that have been successful rules of thumb in our evolutionary past. One is the availability heuristic—we judge the likelihood of events in terms of the ease with which we can recall instances of their occurrence. When asked whether accidents or cardiovascular disease accounts for more deaths in the United States, most people reply that accidents do. In fact, accidents account for 5 percent of deaths annually compared to 50 percent from heart attacks and strokes. Accidents are more vivid and memorable and their prominence in our memory misleads us (Tversky & Kahneman, 1974). In ancestral communities, only about half of infants survived to adulthood and many of these deaths would have been traumatic. The ability to attend to and recall such lethal threats (and consequently to overestimate their frequency) had advantages. For evolutionary psychologists, many human psychological abilities (controversially, some would say all) are hardwired and encapsulated mental modules—theory of mind; spatial orientation; numeracy; kin detection, face recognition, and a range of emotional systems including fear, disgust, and jealousy (Barrett & Kurzban, 2006).

The argument for this modular view of mind rests on three main points. The first is that specialized modules work faster and more efficiently than a general-purpose problem solver—they accept only certain kinds of input and are equipped with an algorithm that speedily generates a solution. Speed is of the essence in many situations of life and death, and these are the very situations on which natural selection operates most potently. A second point is what has become known as the frame problem. At any given moment in our lives our brains are assaulted by billions of bits of information. If an immediate decision is required (Shall I run from this tiger or finish eating this apple?), a general-purpose mind would first have to identify which of thousands of perceptual factors might be relevant to answering the question. (Is the sky blue? Is the species of tiger relevant? Is the ripeness of the fruit important? . . .) The reason these options sound ridiculous is precisely because our evolved mind is already furnished with a module that has solved the frame problem for us—it has automatically sifted out these factors as irrelevant. This computational efficiency is nowhere better exemplified than in language acquisition (Pinker, 1994, 1997). Babies acquire their native language in a couple of years. Yet to work out the rules underlying the grammatical structure of language in this period of time is impossible. The baby seems to arrive equipped with a program that directs it to correct linguistic constructions and allows meaning to be mapped to them. Finally, other bodily organs are not all-purpose designs: evolution appears to select for specific function so that hearts pump blood, kidneys maintain water balance, and so on.

Yet the massive modularity idea has proved controversial. It is relatively easy to accept that some lower-level brain functions are modular in the sense that they are sensitive to only certain inputs, encapsulated from other psychological processes, operate below conscious awareness, and automatically generate certain outputs (Fodor, 1983). Vision is a classic example. We have conscious access only to the products of the visual system, not to its processes. We see the world effortlessly and automatically. The modularity of the system makes it resistant to conscious interference—look around you now and try *not* to see your surroundings in three dimensions or in color. Emotional reactions have this same quality: when asked to eat a piece of fudge shaped to resemble feces, most people refuse because it is difficult to consciously override the automatic disgust module that has been so adaptive in our evolutionary past (Rozin,

Millman, & Nemeroff, 1986). But when we reach higher levels of cognition, can modularity still work? Cosmides (1989) believes that even something as apparently cognitively demanding as the ability to detect cheating on a social contract is a modular system. She asked subjects to choose which (out of four) pieces of information would be required to establish if a social rule was being broken (underage drinking). The speed and success rate was much higher than when the same task was framed as a decision that could be solved only by the application of formal logic.

Others are more skeptical. They go under the banner of dual-process theorists (Evans, 2008; MacDonald, 2008; Stanovich, 2004). They argue for two evolved systems. The reflexive system (sometimes more neutrally called System 1) is modular. It is unconscious, automatic, fast, requires little effort, and has a high capacity to process information. It is universal and does not depend on intelligence. Many evolutionary psychologists believe that this is an ancient system and one that we share with other species. The reflective system (System 2) is uniquely human, although elements of it can be seen in other primates. It is conscious, controlled, requires high effort, and has low capacity to process information. It is analytic, logical, and linked to language. The performance of this system is affected by individual differences in intelligence and working memory capacity. It is this system that allows us to play chess, and solve algebra problems—activities that are evolutionarily novel and hence for which we have no specific modular adaptation. It provides the cognitive "imagination" that allows us to envision the future and to engage in conditional and hypothetical thinking. This reflective system has an inhibitory role also: it suppresses the "automatic" behavioral tendencies generated by the reflexive system. We restrain the reflexive tendency to lash out when angry, to yawn during a conversation, or to laugh when we see a friend's pratfall. When evolutionary psychology first opened its doors, "massive modularity" was specified as an essential requirement of an evolutionary approach (Tooby & Cosmides, 1992). This is no longer the case. But whether the evolution of the human mind culminated in a set of discrete modules or whether these were complemented by a high-level general problem solver, evolutionary psychologists do not doubt the human mind is an evolved organ.

Third, evolutionary psychology *does not conceive of the mind as a conscious fitness maximizing device*. To appreciate this, the distinction between ultimate and proximate causes is crucial (Tinbergen, 1963). When we pose a "Why?" question about the causes of a behavior, there are at least two answers—both of them correct but in different ways. Why does a baby cry? At a proximate level, it cries to attract the attention of its caregiver. At an ultimate level it cries to increase its chances of survival and its future reproductive success. The ultimate causes of behavior are evolutionary and the proximate causes are the immediate mechanisms by which this larger goal is achieved. These mechanisms are adaptations that evolved incrementally over evolutionary time because individuals who possessed them (a baby who cried when hungry or endangered) survived more often than those who did not. These adaptations mean that animals, including ourselves, do not need to be conscious of the grand evolutionary picture because lower-level adaptations will automatically keep our actions on the right evolutionary path. Hunger makes us want to eat. Pain makes us avoid its source. Physical attraction makes us want sex. We have emotional responses that trigger evolutionarily appropriate tendencies to approach and avoid stimuli. Understanding the function of these adaptations and how they work is the focus of much evolutionary psychology.

It is also what distinguishes evolutionary psychology from its sister discipline of behavioral ecology, sometimes called Darwinian anthropology (Smith, Borgerhoff Mulder, & Hill, 2001; Tooby & Cosmides, 1990a). Behavioral ecologists focus on the way in which contemporary human communities optimize their interaction with others and their environment. Their subjects are usually peoples whose way of life corresponds to earlier human subsistence patterns; hunter gatherers, pastoralists, and agriculturalists. For example, optimal foraging theory is concerned with the net gain or loss in calories that are contingent on different organization of foraging. Their measure of fitness of a community's strategy is the extent to which it corresponds to statistical models of the most efficient means of calorie replenishment. Behavioral ecologists have been characterized as "baby counters" (Betzig, 1998). They examine which modes of kin and community organizations result in the highest yield of surviving children. The assumption is that humans do whatever they can to maximize their survival and success, and this entails the usually unspoken presumption that the mind is an all-purpose fitness maximizing device designed to operate adaptively in any environment in which it finds itself.

This focus on the optimization of current behavior is one way in which behavioral ecology differs from evolutionary psychology. Evolutionary psychology argues that much present behavior is a function of the *past* adaptive success of genetically encoded mental modules. Adaptiveness is a property of the past because that is where selection occurred. To know if a current behavior is adaptive we would have to return in several hundred thousand years, find what traits had gone to fixation, and trace the reproductive success of humans who had the necessary rudimentary adaptation compared to those who did not. Because the current environment differs from the one in which we evolved, it is quite possible that an adaptation is not currently adaptive. Men's fascination (some might say obsession) with sex stood them in good stead to take advantage of unexpected mating opportunities in ancestral times. Recently this adaptation has been exploited by 24-hour Internet pornography which not only threatens to undermine work productivity but may be creating a new form of behavioral addiction (Robinson, 2011). Our preference for fat and sugar was useful at a time when meat and berries were nutritious and rare. They are currently responsible for obesity and heart disease in an environment where sources are too plentiful. Indeed our appetite for sugar is so strong that, rather than simply refusing it, we go to extraordinary lengths to develop chemicals that mimic the taste while removing the calories. The question for any putative adaptation is "What did it do for us back then?" Although we can (and do) surmise on the apparent mismatches between evolved adaptations and current environments (Crawford, 1998), we cannot meaningfully speak of adaptations-in-the-making until the unknown future environment has a chance to make its genetic selection.

But the rise of dual-process theory brings evolutionary psychology and behavioral ecology much closer. As evolutionary psychologists recognize the evolution of the higher order and very human process of problem solving, they approach the territory of behavioral ecologists. The advantage of our creative intelligence is that it allows online adaptation to short-term fluctuations in our environment. We can imagine the different futures to which our current actions might lead and we adjust our behavior accordingly. We have become what Daniel Dennett (1997) calls "Popperian creatures" (in honor of the philosopher Karl Popper) because foresight means that our hypotheses can die in our stead. If a woman must make a decision as to the best foraging strategy, she can formulate the problem (food located at a minimum of two kilometers away), generate a number of possible solutions (the net utilities of various permutations of traveling alone, carrying the baby, leaving an older child at camp, traveling early before the sun gets hot, relying on leftovers from relatives), and select the most successful strategy. Now the chief difference between evolutionary psychologists and behavioral ecologists is reduced to the difference between explanations of individual minds and descriptions of group-level behavior. Evolutionary psychologists want to explain what mental processes are needed for decision-making and how such mechanisms evolved. Behavioral ecologists gather descriptive data from the field about how the ecology or social environment affects birth spacing, or longevity, or patrilocality. There is more and more scope for close cooperation between the two approaches.

Lastly, evolutionary psychology is chiefly concerned with *species-typical adaptations*. It seeks to explain the emotions, algorithms, and strategies that are common and central to all human experience (even though their behavioral manifestation may vary from one culture to the next and though they may only be activated given appropriate environmental input). This sets it apart from behavior genetics. Behavioral geneticists are engaged in a statistical attempt to explain differences between people in a population with respect to a given psychological trait. Using adoption and twin studies, they attempt to fit mathematical models that distribute the variance in a trait to environmental and genetic sources. The whole enterprise depends essentially on the presence of variance. But for species-typical traits, no variance exists. Because we have all evolved to have one heart and two lungs, there is no variability on this attribute (genetic abnormality aside). The trait has gone to fixation and falls out of the purview of behavior genetics. The very existence of a heritable component for any trait tells us that it has not reached fixation and is not possessed uniformly by every human being. Evolutionary psychologists are not uninterested in variability (and in Chapter 8 I shall have more to say on this) but to see the big picture of evolution we must dwell not on the noise but on the signal—those traits that were acted upon by selection to the point that they came to characterize the whole species.

We need a crucial caveat, however, when we talk of universality. Humans come in two distinct morphs—women and men—differentiated by the size of the gametes that they contribute to sexual reproduction. The bulk of selection pressures—disease, predators, famine—affected both sexes equally and no sex differences are expected in psychological mechanisms that allow us to cope with these threats. The majority of traits that were advantageous are passed on by sexual recombination to both daughters and sons regardless of whether they were contributed by the mother or the father. (Later in the book this statement will have to be complicated by the discussion of genomic imprinting—a process by which the expression of some traits depends upon the parent that contributed them.) Where the sexes differ, it is the result of sexual rather than natural selection. The strategies that enhanced reproductive success in women were not identical to those that enhanced it in men. Through sex linkage and sex limitation evolution has coupled genetically encoded adaptive strategies to the sex of the individual receiving them.

What evolutionary psychology offers is the hope of integration in the understanding of human behavior. Using the most powerful theoretical development of the last hundred years, we are finally able to address the "Why?" question and to ask it together with other disciplines that have long ago accepted the premise of adaptation. Psychologists must work with and depend on other disciplines if the enterprise is to be successful. We need primatology to help us understand the common and unique paths of adaptation in the anthropoid line. We need paleoanthropology to track the evolving size and shape of the brain. We need archaeologists to describe the man-made tools and art that were part of the early emergence of *Homo sapiens*. We need anthropology to describe and document the varieties of human solutions to ecological and social problems. We need geneticists to map the genome and tie complex psychological traits to their even more complex interacting genetic loci. We need biologists to identify the mutual paths between genes, hormones, and environment. We need developmentalists to document the trajectory and constraints on the successful emergence of human capabilities. We need neuroscientists to identify the evolution and modification of structures that govern specific human emotions and actions. We need pharmacologists to help us understand the actions of neurotransmitters and their relationship to subjective experience. As psychologists, our contribution is to identify the characteristics and parameters of the mental mechanisms that drive behavior. It will be a long and cooperative undertaking if it is to be finally successful.

The meteoric rise of evolutionary psychology has been impressive—but it has not gone unchallenged. Its birth in the 1990s was greeted with disapproving howls as feminists attacked its politics and its scientific status—and sometimes both simultaneously.

Bad politics?

Sociobiology functions as a political theory and program. (Bleier, 1984, p. 46)

Evolutionary psychology is not only a new science, it is a vision of morality and social order, a guide to moral behaviour and policy agendas. (Nelkin, 2000, p. 20)

. . . the biological accounts of male-female difference and male dominance that have emerged since the mid-nineteenth century have merely used the language of science, rather than the language of religion, to rationalise and legitimise the status quo. (Bem, 1993, p. 6)

Nevertheless, the social construction of the categories "woman" and "man" has been historically justified by reference to biological differences, and the modern tendency to provide essentialist and reductionist explanations which include the effects of genes and hormones can be viewed as a contemporary manifestation of this long-standing tradition. (Muldoon & Reilly, 1998, p. 63)

Sociobiologists are . . . constructing a framework of ideas about what is natural and what is not. Women who enter professions that are typical of men are therefore seen as unnatural and going against their biology; so too are men who take up professions using abilities considered typical of women. These "unnatural" women and men are considered to threaten the fabric of society, as seen and maintained by those (scientists, politicians, business leaders and the general public) who see genes as paramount in causing sex differences in behavior. (Rogers, 1999, p. 49)

Ought science to be seen as truth-telling, or as politics by other means, or can it be both things at the same time? (Fausto-Sterling, 1992, p. 58)

As these quotes show, one line of attack has come from those who are more concerned with the political implications of evolutionary psychology than with its truth value. As they see it, any attempt to identify a universal human nature and to posit a biological basis is equivalent to abandoning all hope of social progress. For them, evolutionary psychology is about the maintenance of the status quo and the rejection of a liberal agenda. Some go further, viewing evolutionary psychology as a right-wing conspiracy (see Segerstrale, 2000), despite the fact that evolutionary psychologists share the same left-of-center views as other branches of psychology and are considerably less conservative than average Americans (Tybur, Miller, & Gangestad, 2007). Many of the most vehement objections come from feminists who have been particularly offended by the proposal that universal sex differences may have a biological basis. But let's unpack their arguments and take them one at a time.

Charge 1: Evolutionary theory is biological determinism. Evolutionary theory is certainly biological. It argues from the premise that the genes associated with phenotypic characteristics that increase survival and reproductive success will increase over generations. For feminists, the real issue is whether there are other biological differences between males and females aside from the somatic changes that are triggered by the 23rd chromosome pair. In short, are some psychological traits sex linked (carried on one of the sex-determining chromosomes) or sex limited (carried on autosomes and triggered by the presence of male or female hormones)?

Most feminists agree that there are two sexes possessing different reproductive organs and that the two sexes also differ on average in height, strength, and fat distribution (Lewontin, 1994). However, some writers do not even concede these facts—Muldoon and Reilly (1998, p. 55) believe that "the objectivity of 'hard science' in this area can be questioned, so much so that the biological definition of sex itself becomes untenable." They suggest that there is no biological basis for our belief in male and female as "dichotomous, mutually exclusive categories" (see also Bem, 1993). Notwithstanding these authors' uncertainty, most feminists broadly agree that there are two discriminable sexes. Indeed most feminists are even willing to acknowledge that biological differences are the result of evolution—provided that biology stops at the neck (Bem, 1993; Wood & Eagly, 2002). Even though the brain is the most expensive organ in the human body in terms of calorie consumption, and even though feminists accept that hominid brain size itself was a result of natural selection, feminists reject the notion that evolution could have had an impact on the minds of men and women. Though successful reproduction is the reason for our existence today and though the sexes play vital and different roles in that process, feminists reject any notion that their minds may have been sculpted by millions of years of evolution to pursue different strategies.

Most five-year-old children also agree that people are either male or female. They will also tell you that boys are rougher and fight more than girls do. They are correct. The sex difference in physical aggression is evident in naturalistic studies of playgrounds, in experimental studies of undergraduates, in psychometric inventories, and in criminal justice statistics (Eagly, 1987; Hyde, 1986; Kruttschnitt, 1994). This sex difference is cross-cultural and trans-historical (Daly & Wilson, 1988). There are no human societies in which women commit more violent crime than men. We also know that in animal species like our own, in which females provide the bulk of parental investment, the same sex difference exists (Geary, 2000). We have seen too that children show sex differences in aggression before the age at which they can correctly label the sex of others or sort photographs correctly by sex. Together these facts strongly suggest a very fundamental difference between the sexes in aggression and one that, however biologically mediated, may be traced back ultimately to differential evolutionary pressures on the two sexes. It is important to bear in mind that evolutionary theory predicts sex differences in only a few psychological domains—those that are relevant to male and female roles in sexual reproduction. There would be no evolutionary reason to suppose that men and women should differ on average with regard to sociability, intelligence, sense of humor, or openness to experience (to name but a few) and they do not. There is every reason to think that they should differ in nurturance, hostility, and assertiveness and they do (Feingold, 1994).

The "determinism issue" relates to the erroneous belief that genes alone direct development and behavior. Patently, this is not the case—although it is a straw man that is frequently used to bait evolutionists. Take three examples culled from many dozen similar pronouncements:

> Sociobiologists argue that these strategies are given by biology and thus imply that they are eternally fixed features of human sexual relations. (Sayers, 1982, p. 60)
>
> By reducing human behaviour and complex social phenomenon to genes and to inherited and programmed mechanisms of neuronal firing, the message of the new Wilsonian Sociobiology becomes rapidly clear: we had better resign ourselves to the fact that the more unsavoury aspects of human behavior, like wars, racism, and class struggle, are inevitable results of evolutionary adaptations based in our genes. (Bleier, 1984, p. 15)
>
> [Genes] are therefore seen as the source of human behaviour, including sex differences in monogamy and polygamy, aggression and the perception of beauty. This is clearly a reductionist position. Of course, genes have a part to play in the development of sex differences and other behaviours, but it need not be any more important than other influences from both inside and outside the body and the part played by genes may not be separable from these other influences. (Rogers, 1999, p. 44)

Where are these evolutionary psychologists who allege that genes operate without reference to hormones, experience, or environment? Wherever they are, I have not been able to locate them. Rather it is environmentalists who set up mythical distinctions between nature and nurture in order to maintain a clear line between the politically correct and incorrect. As Margo Wilson and her co-workers (1997, p. 433) explained:

> "Biology" is the study of the attributes of living things, and only living things can be "social". So whence this idea of antithesis? . . . The irony is that developmentally, experientially and circumstantially contingent variation is precisely what evolution-minded theories of social phenomenon . . . are all about.

Surely it is evident that the ultimate success of a given individual in evolutionary terms depends upon manifest behavior which in turn derives from a particular gene–environment complex. Smuts (1995) provides a good example of this. Cooper and Zubek (1958) took strains of maze-bright and maze-dull rats that had been so successfully bred that there was no overlap in their maze performance. They then reared a new generation under normal, enriched, or impoverished conditions. All of the rats who were raised in the enriched environment performed as well as the maze bright rats that were reared normally. All the rats raised under impoverished conditions performed as poorly as maze dull rats reared normally. Behavior depends upon the confluence of genetic disposition and environmental influences.

The environment interacts with genetic predispositions in a variety of ways (Buss, Haselton, Shackelford, Bleske, & Wakefield, 1998). Some environmental parameters are necessary for the emergence of adaptations—absence of contact with a language-using community can severely disrupt the development of language and early close contact with a reliable caretaker seems to be important for later social and emotional functioning. Early developmental events may channel individuals into different pathways by setting different expectations about the environment. Father-absent children are more inclined to pursue short-term mating patterns with the expectation that paternal investment is a statistically rare event. Families and communities characterized by high levels of competition and hostility set children on a more aggressive life course than those whose early interactions are more stable and cooperative. Other genetic tendencies are expressed only if the environment provides the necessary trigger—nicotine addiction has a high genetic component but whether it is activated depends upon environmental (and sometimes chance) factors such as exposure to peers who smoke. Environmental experiences can alter the expression of adaptations—sexual jealousy seems to be activated only when people experience a deep and exclusive attachment to a romantic and sexual partner. The emergence of one strategy rather than another depends upon a variety of contemporaneous factors such as the life stage of the individual, the prevailing sex ratio, the number of alternative avenues of action, and her behavioral and psychological competencies. Humans are characterized by facultative responses to the demands of their environment. Differences between societies and between individuals are seen by evolutionary psychologists as environmentally induced variation in the expression of similar genotypes.

In evolutionary theory, genetic predispositions orchestrate universal trends in human psychology and behavior and thus create what is often called human nature. It also directs particular male and female natures in some psychological modalities. However, superimposed upon these, we must take into account the impact of the environment in both development (nutrition, education, opportunities congenial to the development of particular abilities) and facultative adaptation (the particular environmental input that inform decisions about behavioral strategies).

Charge 2: Evolutionary theory is simplistic and reductionist. Evolution is the process of selection which causes differential survival and reproduction of individuals as a function of their performance in a particular ecological niche. I can think of few other theories that can be expressed so succinctly. Yet pejorative accusations of "simplistic" notwithstanding, it is apparently not simple enough to escape misunderstanding. Fausto-Sterling (1992), a biologist and vocal critic of evolutionary psychology, correctly explains the evolutionary premise that the sex which makes the lower parental investment (typically males) tends to display greater promiscuity in its mating habits. She then points to female promiscuity in phalaropes (sea snipes) exclaiming "You name your animal species and make your political point." The non-political point which she completely misses is that in the phalarope it is the male not the female that makes the greater parental investment. Hence this example is entirely consistent with evolutionary theory and merely demonstrates what the theory has always argued—it is parental investment not sex per se that drives mating strategy.

The truly remarkable thing about evolution is that, although the theory itself is simple, it leads to highly varied and often counter-intuitive hypotheses. An evolutionary analysis of incest developed by Edvard Westermarck argued that people develop an aversion to sexual contact with individuals with whom they spent their infancy and childhood years (normally siblings). One counter-intuitive prediction was that children raised in kibbutzim should avoid marriage with their kindergarten peers despite their non-relatedness. This prediction turned out to be true (Shepher, 1983). A different strand of evolutionary thought has been concerned with homogamy (the tendency for like to mate with like). Together these two pieces of work can explain reports that siblings separated at birth and then reunited in adulthood tend (often to their distress) to find one another sexually attractive. This seems to me to be simplicity at its best—a simple theory that is able to explain apparently unrelated and unexpected findings in the real world. There was a time when simplicity used to be called elegance and constituted one of the criteria for explanatory quality—if the data equally support two theories then the simpler one is the better one.

The charge of reductionism comes in two forms. The first objects to the "reduction" of complex human behavior to the action of genes and we have already discussed the fact that no serious evolutionary psychologist believes that genes can operate independently of the environment (although many feminists apparently fear that they may). The second highlights a failure to include the full range of variables that are needed to account for a given behavior. No scientist really wants this contrived simplicity, any more than her critics do. We would all love to offer complete theories that account for the full range and diversity of human behavior. But reductionism is a necessary evil. It is a stepping stone that allows us to work toward the truth by first decomposing the explanation into its constituent elements. If (as many feminists prescribe) we reject reductionism and take on the full complexity of a phenomenon as it appears in the real world, we are faced with an insurmountable problem. Every event is determined by multiple causes and no event is ever exactly repeated. So without "reductionism" (the identification of causal factors and their interaction) we can offer only a description and nothing more. We cannot generalize beyond the historical moment and the actors involved. Feminists, like Gestalt psychologists, argue that the whole is more than the sum of the parts. So if as scientists we remove or introduce variables to observe their effect, we have "committed reductionism" by accepting the decomposability of what we study. Many feminists are happy to reject scientific method. But in making that choice, they become historians (not psychologists) describing (but not explaining) non-generalizable and unique events by the use of a subjective interpretation (that is itself the product of a particular moment in history, geography, and culture).

Charge 3: There are no human universals and hence no such thing as human nature. If something is universal, it may reflect a fundamental human nature and, if such a thing exists at a biological level, then attempts to ameliorate the status quo are doomed. This is the shaky reasoning that underpins the enormous kudos given to anthropologists who return from their travels with reports of novel and bizarre behavior in exotic locations. Obvious hoaxes such as Carlos Castenada's dissertation on Don Juan or the discovery of the Tasaday (who were inventions of the Marcos government) were eagerly and, for many years, uncritically embraced by cultural anthropologists. Especially welcomed was Margaret Mead's (1935) challenge to the traditional equations of masculinity with aggression, and femininity with gentleness. She conveniently found, within a hundred-mile area, three tribes in which these equations broke down; the Arapesh (both sexes gentle), Mundugumor (both sexes aggressive), and the Tschambuli (sex role reversed). Since that time, her claims have been discredited by other researchers and these have been carefully documented by Freeman (1983). Her determination to demonstrate the existence of these three anomalous permutations of sex and temperament lead her to some strange interpretations of her observations. Though she argued that among the Mundugumor both sexes are violent, the men express it through murder, rape, and head-hunting raids, while the women express it by serving tastier dishes than their co-wives. Among the allegedly gentle Arapesh, young men were not initiated into adulthood until they had committed homicide. Among the sex-role reversed Tschambuli, the make-up worn by men celebrates their killing of an enemy and the "aggressive" women were frequently beaten by their "gentle" husbands. Anthropologists vocally encouraged reports of cultural difference rather than cultural similarity (Geerz, 1984) and this no doubt affected the way in which field workers interpreted the behavior that they had witnessed.

Critics often seem confused about just what is meant by human nature. Consider the following quote from Sandra Bem (1993, pp. 21–22): "As a biological species, human beings do not have wings, which meant that it was part of human nature to be unable to fly. But now human beings have invented airplanes, which means that it is no longer part of universal human nature to be unable to fly." Now the idea that sitting in flying machine 30,000 feet above the ground constitutes an alteration of "human nature" is an odd distortion of the concept. The evolution of wings might indeed have led to a radical alteration of human nature but we have not evolved them. Has air travel in any way lead to an alteration in our physical morphology? Do we seriously suppose that airplane passengers show a different psychology or physiology to those who have not flown?

It is equally hard to know what to make of Fausto-Sterling's (1992, p. 199) claim that "there is no single undisputed claim about universal human behavior (sexual or otherwise)." Presumably even the most ardent cultural relativist would accept that everywhere; people live in societies; they eat, sleep, and make love; and that women give birth and men do not. The arguments seem to arise when we move from basic universals to their specific behavioral expression. Though everywhere women are the principal caretakers of children, the fact that there may be variation in how that task is fulfilled leads some anthropologists to conclude that mothering is not universal. This is analogous to arguing that because people eat different food in different parts of the world, eating is not universal. Evolutionary psychologists do not argue for cultural invariance in the expression of evolved adaptations. As Tooby and Cosmides (1992, p. 45) put it, "manifest expressions may differ between individuals when different environmental inputs are operated on by the same procedures to produce different manifest outputs." At a behavioral level, the expression of the mechanism may vary but that does not question the universality of the generative mechanism itself.

Fortunately Donald Brown (1991), trained in the standard ethnographic tradition, has documented the extent of human universals. The list is astoundingly long but here is a taste of the hundreds that he finds: gossip, lying, verbal humor, storytelling, metaphor, distinction between mother and father, kinship categories, logical relations, interpreting intention from behavior and recognition of six basic emotions. Of special interest to the study of gender we find: binary distinctions between men and women, division of labor by sex, more child care by women, more aggression and violence by men, acknowledgement of differences between male and female natures, and domination by men in the public political sphere.

Now this last observation (that men predominate in positions of power) provides a nice example of the extreme reluctance of cultural anthropologists to acknowledge universals. In 1973, Steven Goldberg wrote a book documenting the universality of patriarchy. He was inundated with letters informing him that he was wrong and pointing out counter-examples. (Other feminists were more willing to accept his premise, see Bem, 1993; Millett, 1969; Rich, 1976.) Over the next 20 years, he carefully examined the available ethnographic documentation for each putative counter-example and in 1993 authored a second book in which he was emphatic that no society had yet been found that violated his rule. There are societies that are matrilineal and matrilocal and where women are accorded veneration and respect—but there are no societies which violate the universality of patriarchy defined as "a system of organisation . . . in which the overwhelming number of upper positions in hierarchies are occupied by males" (Goldberg, 1993, p. 14). Such a state of affairs is deplorable but mere denial of the facts will do nothing to alter it—women's engagement in the political arena will.

Charge 4: Evolutionary psychology is used to naturalize and legitimize the status quo. Evolutionary psychology has considered a number of highly charged and socially relevant issues including infanticide, sociopathy, wife abuse, and rape. In these areas, feminists (e.g., Fausto-Sterling, 1992) have objected that such work opens the door to frivolous exonerating pleas in the criminal justice system ("I beat my wife because it is in men's nature to experience extreme sexual jealousy due to internal fertilization and concealed ovulation"). The misuse of scientific research by defense attorneys is doubtless widespread but it is certainly not confined to evolutionary theory. Indeed, environmental factors are far more commonly implicated. Parental abuse and neglect, inadequate educational opportunities, and drug addiction are all used to mitigate criminal guilt and reduce sentences. The issue here is not evolutionary theory but the prevailing legal philosophy of responsibility and free will.

This objection also charges that an evolutionary explanation of, for example, patriarchy will allow policymakers to view it as "natural" and therefore benign. It is deeply ironic that evolutionary psychologists have been the ones to argue most forcibly against the naturalistic fallacy—the belief that what is natural is morally right or desirable. This is not a post hoc attempt to make their position politically correct but flows from the very nature of the theory itself. Natural selection operates as a sieve allowing some genetic variants to pass through and others to die. This sieve knows nothing of good or bad, kind or cruel, desirable or unacceptable. It does not result in progress in the form of the survival of "better" species or individuals. Humans have proliferated exceedingly successfully and one feature which we possess is a large brain relative to our body size. That does not make a species with high intelligence better than one with low intelligence, although it did make it a useful adaptation for *Homo sapiens* trying to survive in a particular ecology several hundred thousand years ago. If intelligence was "naturally" good, then ants and spiders would have developed an enormous cortex or would have become extinct—neither of which has occurred. It is vital to make a distinction between what we as humans hold to be morally desirable and what natural selection has retained as an adaptation. Malaria, tuberculosis, and death in childbirth are "natural" but we hardly regard them as good. Indeed we have poured enormous (positivist) scientific effort into their eradication with considerable success. Our vision of a more perfect world cannot be found in evolutionary theory which tells us only about the selection pressures of the past, not about our moral aspirations for the future.

Charge 5: Culture and technology have so changed the environment that we are freed from natural selection. Evolutionary psychologists hold that evolution has provided us with "fitness tokens"—desires, pleasures, aversions, and goals that mold our preferences and behavior. Teenagers do not attend discos in order to increase their share of the future gene pool—they go there because browsing the potential mate pool exerts an untutored fascination for teenagers everywhere. A teenage couple who have sex after such an event are not seeking to increase their reproductive success—if they were, they would not employ contraception. Consensual sexual contact is inherently pleasurable (evolution has seen to that) and they are simply enjoying that evolved pleasure. Natural selection worked to make sexual contact enjoyable because in ancestral environments contraception was not available, so sex eventually led to pregnancy and increased reproductive success. The principal aim of evolutionary psychology is to understand the origins and the parameters of these mental adaptations. Such adaptations have not magically disappeared with the advent of new technology or social institutions in the past one hundred years.

But, some argue, the world today looks nothing like the environment of evolutionary adaptation (EEA). Population density is greater. Social and political structures are more complex. We live in parts of the world that would have been uninhabitable then. International conflicts, air pollution, and multinational companies dominate the world. At first glance, there is an enormous gulf between the hunter-gatherer societies in which humans spent 99 percent of their existence and the contemporary societies we now inhabit. But these changes have been wrought by the human mind and this mind was adapted in the EEA. As Crawford (1998, p. 291) points out, we have not created a world "designed for individuals who can fly, who choose mates indiscriminately, who have litters of offspring, who have fur to protect them from the cold, who make little investment in infants once they are born, who do not mind being cheated in a social contract, who do not value close relatives and so on." Cultures everywhere value altruism, reciprocity, fairness, and in-group solidarity. Cultures devalue selfishness, cheating, theft, and in-group violence. Cultures which endorsed mass suicide or abstinence from sex would not last long.

However, it is true that adaptations now engage with a range of environments that are richer and more diverse than those they evolved to deal with. Activity in the dopaminergic reward pathways of the brain feels pleasurable and supports our appetite for important adaptive behaviors such as sex and food. But these same dopamine receptors can be directly stimulated by illegal and addictive drugs. Today, some ancient adaptations have been recruited in the service of leisure activities: the pleasure that soccer brings to millions may derive from our natural fascination with inter-group conflict, with male–male competition and with the demonstration of young male strength and agility. The universal enjoyment of gossip is exploited in soap operas. Despite knowing that we are watching miniature representations of human beings (as pixels on an electronic machine) who are pretending to be people they are not, we still find our emotions engaged in the drama of these people's lives even though they are so artificially presented.

The mind and body that we have today exist in their current form because we come from a long line of individuals who survived past puberty and successfully reproduced. Many did not. We are fortunate to live in cultures where medical advances have enhanced the survival of severely premature infants and have brought cures for diseases that would have been lethal in the EEA. We have seen significant increases in longevity in the past decade. Infertility treatment has become widely available, as has contraception. When medical and technological advances can be used to give and take life, we have created the instruments of our own selection. We would do well to keep a watchful eye on those who exercise that judgment on our behalf.

Bad science?

Another set of objections has come from those who question the scientific status of evolutionary psychology. We begin with the most radical critiques from those who regard the scientific enterprise in general as androcentric and who accuse those women who engage in it as "sleeping with the enemy." Their wrath is not specifically directed at evolutionary psychology per se but at any use of the hypothetico-deductive method.

Charge 6: Evolutionary theory, as part of traditional science, fails to recognize that there can be no objective truth. Many feminists have objected that the very questions posed by scientists are laden with tacit political agendas and that the scientific method itself can never be value-free (Fausto-Sterling, 1992; Harding, 1991; Hubbard, 1990; Keller, 1992). The solution they offer is for researchers to announce their politics at the same time as their results so the reader is made aware of possible bias in their data collection, analysis, or interpretation. Of course, this has the side effect of allowing readers to pick and choose articles in terms of the author's politics and to be prejudicially positive to articles that gel with their own ideological agendas. Fausto-Sterling (1992, p. 212), for example, writes of the difficulty that she has in distinguishing between "science well done and science that is feminist." She is also surprisingly honest about the double standard that she employs in evaluating data which is not congenial to her ideological position: "I demand the highest standards of proof, for example, on claims about biological inequality, my high standards stemming from my philosophical and political beliefs in equality" (Fausto-Sterling, 1992, pp. 11–12). Theories that are not consistent with a feminist viewpoint often fail to achieve this high standard. Feminists are keen to promote high-quality research—but this aim is compromised by their inability to distinguish between feminist science and good science. Many feminist journals will refuse to publish data that are unacceptable to their ideological position. This state of affairs has already inhibited open expression of ideas by those who fear incurring feminist wrath and, if it continues, will seriously jeopardize academic debate.

There is a more liberal possibility. Traditional scientific method is a cyclical loop joining theory and data via hypotheses. It is a system that requires explicit and coherent reasoning at the level of theory building, and honesty and clarity about the method and results of data collection (but not about the ideological position of the authors). It also crucially depends upon the endeavors of many scientists working separately and together. The scientific system allows freedom of politics to individuals, is self-correcting (unsupported hypotheses are modified or abandoned), and open (replications can be undertaken by detractors as well as supporters). Though hypotheses, or even whole theories, may be laden with tacit ideology, the data that they require for falsification are collected from ordinary people who have no axe to grind. Scientific method can be the antidote to hidden agendas.

Charge 7: Evolutionary theory does not resonate with women's experience. Two strands of contemporary thinking have come together to create a new criterion for the acceptability of an explanation: it must reflect women's lived experience—it must "feel" subjectively true. The first strand (which I wholeheartedly endorse) is the feminist demand that researchers should address women's experiences, recognizing them to be potentially different from those of men. The second strand is the post-modern rejection of grand theory (feminist theory excepted, of course) which prioritizes qualitative description of experiences and discourses that are contextually and historically bound. This effectively replaces theory with subjectively interpreted description. Since there are multiple possible descriptions of any event and no objective criterion for deciding amongst them, the best one is the one that resonates with the feminist reader's own experience and intuition. (Parenthetically, it should be noted that the rejection of any objective set of truths necessarily excludes men's oppression of women as a historical truth.) This emphasis upon personal resonance has been endorsed by feminists who encourage women to "transcend" positivist empirical method and seek alternative ways of knowing that are true to their own life experiences (Belensky et al., 1986). But this personalized approach to knowledge places resonance with the reader above the truth, generality, or coherence of the argument.

For many women, evolutionary psychology does not resonate with their own experience. They do not "feel" that parental investment impacts upon their emotions or behavior. It does not "feel right" that differences in gamete size could create differences between men and women's behavior or interests. But intuition is not a reliable guide to the quality of an explanation. Children do not "feel" as if their bodies are composed of 65 percent water. People do not "feel" that solid matter is made of atoms. "Feeling right" is equally controversial with regard to psychological truth. Psychotherapists can persuade clients that they are secretly in love with their father. Palm readers can persuade clients that they are destined for greatness. In an influential article, Nisbett and Wilson (1977) demonstrated that participants in psychology experiments perform no better than chance in guessing the causes of their behavior when these are manipulated in experiments. Although we have conscious access to the products of lower-order processes (recalling our mother's name or the ability to speak in grammatical sentences), we do not have access to the processes themselves (we do not know how our memory or language production systems work) except by the formal knowledge gleaned by psychological science. Evolutionary theory is concerned with how the mind was shaped in the environment of evolutionary adaptation approximately 150,000 years ago. We cannot have any "feel" for what the selection processes were or even what it felt to be an early human at that time. What are available to us are the psychological products of evolution. We like the taste of sugar, feel sick in the first trimester of pregnancy, experience fear when we look out from a tall building, see three-dimensional images in stereograms, enjoy sexual contact, and feel anger when our child is threatened. Evolutionary explanations have been offered for all these experiences.

There are many feminists working in the evolutionary sciences. They have misgivings about the way in which women have been systematically excluded in their discipline both as objects of study and as collaborators (see Hager, 1997). However, few evolutionary feminists want to see the abandonment of empirical techniques. Instead, they seek to identify the evolutionary problems faced by women but ignored by male researchers such as patriarchy (Hrdy, 1997; Smuts, 1995) or male infanticide of infants (Hrdy, 1981). Others highlight the selection pressures that operated specifically upon women such as the care of slow-maturing, altricial young (Lancaster, 1991) or the infant's greater dependence on maternal rather than paternal survival (Campbell, 1999). They believe that their work is important because it can illuminate the evolutionary basis of sexual inequality and, in so doing, complement mainstream feminist work to inform a more solidly grounded agenda for change. Evolutionary feminist research on wife abuse and male proprietary jealousy; on brutal techniques for increasing male paternal certainty (such as clitoridectomy, infibulation, and claustration); on polygyny and the gendered inheritance of wealth are a few examples of how evolutionary theory and feminism can work together to improve the status of women.

Other critics of evolutionary theory, far from wishing to see the abandonment of scientific method, argue that evolutionary psychology is not scientific enough.

Charge 8: Evolutionary theory is tautological. In principle, this objection can be leveled at any functional explanation in the social or natural sciences. Some radical feminists argue that (male-dominated) governments allow the production of pornography in order to objectify women and to keep them in a state of fear about the possibility of rape. This is a functional explanation. It seeks to explain why the status quo is the way it is. The simple question "What is this for?" is the driving force of most scientific enquiry that goes beyond mere description or classification. When directed at evolutionary theory, the objection takes the form of allegations of the Just-So Story: the invention of plausible but unverifiable stories about how an adaptation occurred (Bleier, 1984).

In fact the methods of evolutionary psychology have been clearly explicated by Tooby and Cosmides (1992) and others (Andrews, Gangestad, & Matthews, 2002; Halcomb, 1998; Sherman & Reeve, 1997). Broadly, evolutionary psychology proceeds by: (1) identifying an adaptive problem that proto-humans would have faced in the environment of evolutionary adaptation; (2) developing a description of the module that is suggested to have evolved in response to this problem, including the range of inputs that would have activated it and the impact of its outputs in terms of differential survival and reproductive success; (3) formulating a description of the current environment and a map of correspondence between the ancestral and present conditions that allows specific hypotheses to be generated about the current activating inputs; and (4) undertaking tests of these hypotheses which, where appropriate, allow comparison with alternative (evolutionary and non-evolutionary) accounts.

An adaptation is identifiable by evidence of special design such as complexity, economy, efficiency, reliability, precision, and functionality (Williams, 1966). The eye, for example, is so manifestly and complexly suited to the function of tracking the environment and allowing an animal to orient itself that nobody could seriously doubt that it evolved to serve that function (Dawkins, 1986). The ability to interpret the mental states of others also evidences special design—it is fast, accurate, automatic, follows complex rules, rarely makes errors, and bestows obvious advantages on its bearers. Language also has these trademark features. But to make the techniques of determining an adaptation more concrete, let us take a different example. Let us posit for a moment that individuals everywhere prefer to avoid, rather than seek out, situations in which they are cheated or exploited. Universality is taken to suggest (but not prove) that the trait may have an evolutionary basis. The next step is to ask what purpose it might have served in the EEA about 300,000 years ago. The fossil record provides information about where we were living (on the savannah plains of sub-Saharan Africa) and roughly how (in small hunter-gatherer bands). We were highly social and our survival depended as much on regulating social relationships as on ecological pressures. We can posit that it would have been important to detect social cheaters—those who failed to repay altruistic acts. If we could not do so, we would find our generosity exploited in the service of someone else's reproductive success. Let us hypothesize that one module of the evolving mind might have been devoted to detecting cheats.

Cosmides and Tooby (1992) made such an assumption and tested it on the Wason card task which goes like this: A person is presented with four cards; on one side is a number and on the other is a letter. The upturned cards read

D F 3 7. They are then given the proposition "If a card has D on one side, it has 3 on the other," and the person is asked which cards they need to turn over in order to determine whether this proposition is correct. This is a standard philosophical P-not-Q problem. They ought to turn over card D (to verify the conditional) and then a second card bearing a number that is not 3 (to disconfirm the consequent). Most people find this task quite difficult. But then Cosmides changed the task slightly. The subject is presented with a cheater detection problem. They are told that they are a barman and that they must ensure that nobody under the age of 18 is unlawfully drinking alcohol. They have four cards before them: One side of the card tells them the customer's age (26 or 16) and the other side what they are drinking (beer or cola). As before they are asked which cards they need to turn over. Most people rightly realize that if the person is 26 years old it does not matter what they are drinking and ignore this card. They also rightly realize that if a person is drinking cola, it also does not matter what age they are. Correctly, they turn two cards: Age 16 and Drinking Beer. The identical problem when translated into cheat detection becomes easy. And it is not just the fact that the problem was made social rather than abstract. The cheater problem also seems to be activated only when a rule of exchange has been broken. If we alter the situation to "If a person eats chili peppers then they drink beer" people seem as flummoxed as they were before because although the problem is still social, no rule violation is involved.

The environment of evolutionary adaptation has become a particular source of concern to some. We have no time machine so we cannot visit it and we must rely on archaeological and paleoanthropological reconstruction. Because we believe that savannah living was the lifestyle that shaped our species, there is a tendency to caricature the EEA as something akin to an African hunter-gatherer community. This is can be misleading if we fail to recall that evolution is deployed over vast stretches of time and that different characteristics evolved during different time periods and conceivably in different ecologies. For example, humans' tendency to live in kin groups can be traced back over 25 million years to a common ancestor shared with other anthropoids. Meat-eating may have evolved about two million years ago. The evolution of language is traced to a mere 300,000 to 100,000 years ago (Foley, 1996). There were a variety of adaptively relevant environments. And every adaptation comes from a statistical aggregate of selection pressures spread over time—the environment presented the same problems over and over again with sufficient regularity to make a problem-solving adaptation a distinct advantage. The uncertainty that must surround the details of life at the time of each adaptation does not preclude the generating and testing of adaptational hypothesis. If adaptations evolved, they are part of human nature and will manifest themselves today over a wide range of cultures given the appropriate environmental inputs. Some have argued that the study of contemporary human adaptations will help to build a more accurate picture of the EEA (Tooby & Cosmides, 1990a). Even if it does not, the status of current adaptations is not dependent on a complete account of their genesis. It is dependent on their ability to offer elegant and empirically supported explanations of contemporary human behavior. Adaptations exist as part of our nature—from the infant's Moro reflex to our fear of heights—and a psychology that denies the available evidence in favor of a wishful world where humans are formless clay waiting to be molded by cultural practices may serve politics but not truth.

However, tests of evolutionary predictions will never satisfy critics if they insist on moving the evidentiary goal posts. The standards of proof that are required from evolutionary theory are far higher than those demanded for social environmental theories. The interpretative constructionism espoused by many feminists is subject to the single standard of "plausibility." Ironically this is the very standard that feminists reluctantly agree that evolutionary psychology meets. Fausto-Sterling (1992, p. 187) admits that "At one level it all seems quite plausible" and Bem (1993, p. 30) acknowledges " . . . the consistent pattern of sexual difference and dominance that not only appears to exist across time and place but that a theory like sociobiology appears to so elegantly explain."

Charge 9: Evolutionary theory is riddled with disagreements. The "modern synthesis" brought together Darwin's nineteenth-century insights about natural selection with our twentieth-century understanding of genetic transmission. Together they have inspired an ever-increasing body of empirical work that seeks to test and refine these ideas. In so doing, the modern synthesis has brought together biologists, anthropologists, geneticists, developmental and social psychologists, and neuroscientists who, for the first time, have a common language with which to communicate. Notwithstanding this remarkable integration, Fausto-Sterling (1992, p. 169) asserts that "arguments continue to rage" within evolutionary theory. The arguments to which she refers are the objections offered by Steven Jay Gould, an ardent Darwinian, which have been greeted with delight by many critics of evolutionary theory. His critiques are not rejections of adaptationist thinking but proposed modifications and cautionary admonishments to his fellow Darwinians (Sterelny, 2001).

First a possible modification—Gould believes that the trajectory of evolution is discontinuous rather than smooth (see Eldredge & Gould, 1972). He believes that the normal equilibrium of evolving life is punctuated by dramatic events that select for new macromutations before the pace slows again. His claim is far from radical—there is no reason why evolution should proceed at a constant pace and periods of stasis when species were freed from dramatic environmental change were probably commonplace (Dawkins, 1986; Dennett, 1995). Failure to find evidence of intermediate forms of life that evolved and were extinguished in a matter of a few hundred thousand years is not especially surprising. For a species to be identified as a unitary entity some degree of stasis has to be involved—we would not even entertain the idea of a species, whether alive or extinct, unless all of its members shared common attributes over some space of geological time. Whether the emergence of new life forms happens "momentarily", as Gould proposes, largely depends upon one's definition of a moment. The punctuated equilibrium argument depends upon the scale on which one draws evolutionary change. Gould himself appears to recognize this and agrees that "Our theory entails no new or violent mechanism, but only represents the proper scaling of ordinary events into the vastness of geological time" (Gould, 1992a, p. 12). In this matter, he hardly seems to part company from Darwin himself who wrote "the long periods, during which species have undergone modification, though long as measured by years, have been short in comparison with the periods during which they retain the same form" (see Dennett, 1995, p. 290). So, for many evolutionists, Gould's thesis hardly constitutes a major threat to Darwinian ideas.

Gould also argues that chance can be an important component of evolution—and again this is far from heretical. It is universally acknowledged that evolution (defined as a change in the relative frequency of genotypes over time) can be the result of things other than natural or sexual selection (Majerus, Amos, & Hurst, 1996). However, only these latter forces can produce adaptations—by which we mean a feature of design that becomes common by the differential success of phenotypic variants in previous generations. Mutation, migration, and differential mortality due to chance events can all change the gene pool—but not adaptively. Although random catastrophic events may cause the extinction of a whole species (for example, dinosaurs from a meteor strike) they do not cause systematic changes in the gene pool of an existing species. This is because such events, by their definition and nature, are random. Every year people die as a result of being struck by lightning. The people who die take their genes with them. But the genes that are eliminated are a random selection from the human gene pool. Chance does not systematically retain and reject different variants. Some critics appear to believe that the mere existence of such chance events is a serious challenge to the whole theory. For example, Fausto-Sterling offers a hypothetical example of an island of birds, composed of blue and speckled variants, in which the speckled variants are blown onto a neighboring deserted island. She points out that this is an example of evolution by "a chance natural event, not natural selection" (Fausto-Sterling, 1992, p. 172). But the example is flawed because the probability of the wind carrying only one color of bird by chance is vanishingly small. A chance event would be unselective about what color of birds it affected. When a natural event (wind) selectively affects one variant (speckled birds) while not affecting the other (blue birds) then it is most likely for a reason—perhaps the speckled birds weighed less than the blue ones. This made them more likely to be blown away and would constitute a clear case of natural selection. To give another example, imagine a community of people who vary genetically in their tendency to store fat. A famine occurs and those with low fat reserves perish before the rains come. The genes for low fat reserves will be selectively culled. Although the famine was a chance event, its effect was systematic selection. Chance events that do not distinguish their targets can have evolutionary effects, notably the extinction of whole communities and species, but only chance events that have systematic effects on different variants can generate adaptations.

Gould and Lewontin (1979) coined the term "spandrel" to describe epiphenomenal aspects of natural selection. They borrowed the term from architecture. In cathedrals, notably the Basilica di San Marco in Venice, spandrels are ornately decorated and give the appearance of having been put there specifically for this aesthetic purpose. But as Gould and Lewontin note, they are simply a by-product of the design—they had to exist as soon as the architect decided to join two rounded arches at right angles and thereby created a tapered triangular space. Gould's point was that we must not assume everything in nature to be a functional adaptation. Some apparent design features are merely side effects of selection for something quite different. Bones are white and we might be tempted to pose the question "What is the evolutionary advantage of the whiteness of bones?" if it were not for the fact that bones just happen to be made out of calcium which happens to be white in color. Blue or purple bones could do the job just as well and the color is of no evolutionary significance (although bones themselves are). Because most genes are pleiotropic (they have multiple effects), some natural phenomena are simply side effects that have survived because they tagged on to an adaptive gene complex and were not so detrimental as to outweigh the beneficial impact of the other phenotypic effects. As Dennett notes, daisies float in water but no sensible person would ask what the adaptive significance of their buoyancy is.

> The thesis that every property of every feature of everything in the living world is an adaptation is not a thesis anybody has ever taken seriously, or implied by what anybody has taken seriously, so far as I know. If I am wrong, there are some serious loonies out there, but Gould has never shown us one. (Dennett, 1995, p. 276)

Gould (1991) has also introduced another term—the exaptation—to describe "any organ not evolved under natural selection for its current use—either because it performed a different function in ancestors (classical preadaptation) or because it represented a nonfunctional part available for later co-optation." His example is bird feathers which originally evolved to conserve heat but were later exapted for use in flying. This example highlights the co-option of a functional feature from one role to another but his definition also includes the co-option of spandrels (non-functional features). In one sense it is misleading to coin a new term for this process because all current adaptations arose from previous states of the organism and genetic mutation can only use available components to engineer change whether they were functional in some other realm or not. In birds, feathers happened to be available and, along with a host of other mutational changes, were exploited for flying purposes. But Gould's writing has had the effect of generating confusion about the agency that is responsible for co-option. In places, he implies that natural selection does the work, while in others he seems to suggest that it is the human mind. If he means the former then there is nothing very new being added to the concept of adaptation. But if he means the latter, then we are talking about a different process. Reading and writing are human abilities that are too recent to have evolved by natural selection and may well represent exaptations of existing human abilities (language, symbolic communication, manual dexterity, representational thought). The human ability to creatively exploit our mental and physical capacities in new ways deserves study in its own right but cannot (yet) be examined in terms of natural selection.

There we have it. The pace of evolution, the role of chance, and the status of spandrels and exaptations constitute the full extent of the "raging disagreements" in evolutionary thought.

Let us now turn to the extent of unanimity in feminist theory. Though the term is widely used, it is hard to pin down a definition. The nearest I have been able to find is this: "Feminist theorists are concerned with how gender (which is the social construction of characteristics associated with sex) affects individuals' access to control of their own and other people's lives, power, and resources" (Gowaty, 1992, p. 218). This certainly defines the subject matter of the discipline, but where is the theory? Theories are usually taken to be higher-level explanations from which local hypotheses can be drawn—but explanation is absent from this definition. Even a more direct statement of feminist theory such as "The belief that women have been oppressed by men" is essentially a statement of historical fact rather than an explanation. The absence of agreement about just what constitutes feminist theory is perhaps not surprising when its own proponents acknowledge that "There seem to be many kinds and varieties of feminism, as many kinds and varieties as there are individual feminists with individual desires, notions and conceptions of what we are and want" (Gowaty, 1992, p. 225). Indeed, we are chastised for expecting consensus: "Individuals unfamiliar with feminism or women's studies often assume that feminist theory provides a singular and unified framework for analysis" (Rosser, 1997, p. 22).

At least nine brands of feminist theory have been identified (Percy, 1998; Rosser, 1997). *Liberal feminists* argue for the advantages of psychological androgyny, the establishment of a gender-blind society with equal opportunities for men and women, and are unique among feminists in continuing to accept traditional scientific method. *Marxist feminists* argue that gender oppression can be traced to capitalism and to the power structures reproduced by class in capitalist societies. *Socialist feminists* integrate material, social, and unconscious processes in explaining how race, gender, class, and sexuality produce power relations that disadvantage women. *Afro-American feminists* reject the Eurocentric approach to knowledge embodied in individualism and positivism. They maintain that race is the primary oppression and that gender is secondary to this. *Radical feminists* believe that men's oppression of women is the most fundamental and widespread oppression in society. They urge women to reject all theories developed by men including Marxism, psychoanalysis, positivism, and existentialism. Women can gain true knowledge only by using and reflecting on their own personal experiences and those of other women. *Essentialist feminists* argue that women by virtue of their biological and psychological qualities are equal or superior to men. Originally rejecting biological differences as "a tool for conservatives who wished to keep women in the home," they have now rethought their position "with a recognition that biologically based differences between the sexes might imply superiority and power for women in some areas" (Rosser, 1997, p. 29). *Psychoanalytic feminists* use neo-Freudian theory to argue for the unconscious internalization of female powerlessness. They trace male dominance to the fact that women are the chief caretakers of infants and children, resulting in boys distancing themselves from their mother and adopting independent and autonomous styles while girls become enmeshed in over-dependent relationships with their mothers. *Existential feminists* emphasize the ways in which women are raised to see maleness as the natural human state in which women are the objectified "other." *Post-modern feminists* reject the notion of a stable and unified self. They also reject the idea that women can speak with a unified voice. They reject grand theoretical narratives and argue that gender, like the self, is neither real nor fixed but variously socially constructed in different contexts. (I thought this was a comprehensive list but three more brands of feminism have appeared, see Maidment, 2006, and the more discriminating take the total number of feminisms to 20, DeKeseredy, 2011). However, I am sure you get the general idea. Intra-disciplinary diversity on this scale leaves plenty of room to chastise outsiders as naive and uninformed, and to hide from critics: "It is though erroneous to view feminism as a monolithic enterprise, which is frequently done in attacks on feminist research and theories" (DeKeseredy, 2011, p. 298). In most of the examples given, it is clear that the political agenda of feminism or a putative description of the status quo has superseded "theory" as it is normally understood. It is a surprise to many evolutionary psychologists to find themselves accused of internal wrangling when faced with the bewildering disarray of feminist theory.

Time for reconciliation?

After the flurry of attacks and rebuttals that greeted the arrival of evolutionary psychology, things have quieted down considerably in the new millennium. Feminists and liberal social scientists have begun to recognize that biology need not be equated with destiny or determinism (Vandermassen, 2005), and feminist journals have hosted special issues on evolution (e.g., Eagly & Wood, 2011). Evolutionists have widened their horizons to encompass higher-order cognition and cultural evolution. They have increasingly engaged with the origins of conflict between the sexes (Borgerhoff Mulder & Rauch, 2009). The theoretical debate is more measured now. Less raucous and acerbic, it takes place in the most prestigious academic journals (e.g., Archer, 2009; Eagly & Wood, 2009). Indeed, the invention of a new term—"evolutionist feminist"—might seem to signal a truce (Liessen, 2007). Surely it finally dispels the artificial gulf between support for feminist political goals (equal opportunities for all irrespective of their sex) and acceptance of Darwinian theory (that humans evolved through a process of natural and sexual selection). Yet, things are not quite that simple. The olive branch of rapprochement is not held out to all Darwinians:

> Over the past 25 years, evolutionary approaches and feminism itself have complemented each other, offering insights into female behavior and the relationships between the sexes. In fact, those subfields that have roots in sociobiology—*evolutionary biology, behavioral ecology, primatology, and evolutionary anthropology*—have built strong bridges with feminism, and feminist insights have also been well received within these fields. (Liessen, 2007, p. 62)

Notice Liessen's conspicuous omission of evolutionary psychology—and this is not a mere oversight. Why? Because the disciplines that are acceptable to feminism "are interested in behavioral outcomes, whereas evolutionary psychologists are more interested in the *psychological processes* that lead to reproductive decisions" (Liessen, 2007, p. 62). This rather enigmatic explanation of evolutionary psychology's exclusion (shouldn't psychologists be interested in psychological processes?) is based on the argument that evolved psychological modules remove "flexibility" from human behavior. This is why Liessen endorses a convenient silence on the question of how the human mind makes decisions: "Unlike evolutionary psychologists, behavioural ecologists are not concerned with the actual mechanisms (genes or psychological mechanisms) that lead individuals to their adaptive solutions" (Liessen, 2007, p. 63). By ignoring proximate mechanisms, behavioral ecologists cannot be accused of determinism because they do not take a position on how genetic and psychological processes produce optimal behavioral choices. Their silence on the "determinism" issue makes them more acceptable to feminists. Oddly, while evolutionary psychologists are accused of ignoring human plasticity (Liessen, 2007, p. 55), they are simultaneously credited with believing that "humans have evolved underlying psychological mechanisms . . . that are sensitive to the environment, interactions with others, and what we know about ourselves" (pp. 54–55). Here she is quite correct. Evolved modules are responsive to specific environmental inputs and depend upon them for their normal development and their functionality. The life history strategy pursued by an individual is shaped by her circumstances: high rates of local mortality and family disruption signal an uncertain future and, in response, individuals move to a "faster" life tempo with less secure emotional attachments, more intense competition and earlier reproduction (Belsky, Steinberg, Houts & Halpern-Felsher, 2010; Chisholm, Quinlivan, Peterson, & Coall, 2005; Wilson & Daly, 1997). The local ecology also modulates mate preferences: Where the chief dangers to offspring survival are famine and drought, women prefer long-term relationships with high-investing men. Where the chief risk is disease, women select men on the basis of their genetic quality because children's survival depends most strongly on their inherited ability to fight pathogens (Gangestad & Simpson, 2000).

But putting aside the specifics and accuracy of these feminist criticisms, it is useful to remember Robert Benchly's pithy remark: "There are two kinds of people in the world: those who divide the world into two kinds of people and those who don't." Feminists seem to specialize in dividing people up (Twenty kinds of feminism? And now five types of "evolutionist feminist"?). Others see such an activity as divisive and counterproductive. The disciplinary nameplate on a departmental door is considerably less important than the quality of thought and research that goes on behind it. There is plenty of room for everyone in our attempt to understand the behavior of men and women, from those working at the level of population statistics to those examining cellular responses to hormones. But it is not reasonable for feminists to demand that psychologists ignore the human mind for fear of finding something politically uncongenial in there.

Three questions

Are there inequities between women and men in society? Where did they come from? How shall we change them?

The first question is a straightforward empirical one that we can answer with respect to a variety of criteria including relative income, likelihood of promotion, leisure time, voting rights, participation in political life, public recognition of achievement, and so on (while holding all other variables apart from sex constant). Most people would agree that such differences do exist and in the main women fare less well than men.

The second question is the subject matter of this book. I will map some of the domains of women's lives that are characteristically different from men's and offer an interpretation of them from the viewpoint of evolutionary theory. I will be addressing the distal causes of male–female difference stemming from disparate pressures on men and women over several hundred thousand years. But these evolved differences can also set up a dynamic of their own. If fewer men than women excel in the field of interpersonal sensitivity and if fewer women than men excel at spatial navigation, we can be misled into categorizing these activities as "male" or "female." But the differences between men and women are differences of degree not kind. The overlap on the statistical distribution is great. Even in the most male-advantaged tasks (running a marathon or weight-lifting), there are always some women who do better than the less able men (and vice versa). This is even more true of most psychological characteristics. We must avoid restricting opportunities on the basis of crude stereotypes about what men and women are able to do. My concern with stereotypes is not so much that they drive people to conformity—I have already explained that stereotypes are more likely the product rather than the cause of sex differences—but that they may cause us to debar entry on the basis of sex. For example, denying women the opportunity to be firefighters or police officers is rationalized on the grounds of women's lesser strength or endurance. But this is clearly wrong. The criteria should not be sex but the individual's actual ability to perform the tasks that the job entails. Capable women should be given entry not in the belief that they will act as role models to other women but because to deny them the right to take up a job for which they are qualified is a basic human injustice.

Whether or not we want to alter the status quo is not a matter for psychologists, but for society at large. The last half-century has shown that there is a public will to do so. But social engineering without a firm scientific understanding of sex differences is like a surgeon operating with a blindfold (Tooby & Cosmides, 1992). In promulgating the belief that gender is socially constructed and is without any psychological basis, we are already in danger of developing policies that are not in women's best interests. We are told that women's nature can and should be the same as men's. Psychosexual neutrality is applauded. We are told that there is nothing special or privileged about the bond between a mother and her infant. As a result, single mothers have been financially coerced into putting their children into day care and returning to work. Employed mothers' feelings of loss and guilt are concealed because they are incompatible with effective performance in the workplace (Hrdy, 1999). Women employees who do not show the ruthless drive of their male counterparts are disparaged as poor role models and blamed for their sex's failure to break through the glass ceiling. Girls who resist the contemporary educational pressure to take science subjects are viewed as academic also-rans.

But if we were to accept that women and men are different, we can think about a society that breaks down the barriers between children and work, that does not force women into competition with one another, and that allows women to capitalize on their natural advantages. If evolutionary theory is correct, we cannot design twenty-first-century woman from scratch. Ideology, social policy, law, and the media cannot make women into something they are not. What governments can and should do is to give people choices that allow them the maximum freedom to be whoever they want. With that freedom, women's nature can take its own course.

Chapter 2

Mothers matter most: Women and parental investment

Ask a child why mothers matter and there will be no shortage of answers: they make costumes for the school play, they organize birthday parties, they look after you when you have chicken pox, they do the school run, they make up the beds so friends can stay overnight, they take you to kids' movies that bore most grown-ups, and so on. Fathers do not lack the competence to do these things yet they do them less often. For many social scientists the reasons are to be sought in patriarchy, constricted gender roles, and maternal guilt. But evolutionary theorists step further back to look at the biological basis of reproduction because that is the wellspring from which these other more proximate social and psychological causes spring.

Sexual, not natural selection

When we think of evolution we tend to think of natural selection—the competition for survival. But Darwin knew that there was more to the process of evolution than this. Survival without reproduction is a genetic dead end. An animal that survives but does not reproduce leaves no genes behind. Our forebearers may not necessarily have lived a long life, but we know that they successfully reproduced and ensured that their progeny reached reproductive age. Darwin (1871) named this second strand of evolution sexual selection; "the advantage which certain individuals have over others of the same sex and species, solely in respect of reproduction."

So the prize is not necessarily to survive to an old age but to reproduce. After reproduction, natural selection is indifferent to us, even callous. Genes that enhance youthful reproduction will flourish even if, as a side effect, they happen to cause earlier death. Cancer and heart disease are immune from natural selection, as long as they do not kill people too early in life. Death is the result of an absence of selection pressure on the diseases of old age because our death is of no consequence in the grand scheme of things. Sex differences derive from sexual rather than natural selection. If women were more vulnerable to death—if they made easier prey or succumbed more quickly to the effects of food shortage—women (and the whole species with them) would have become extinct. In fact, if we look at average age of death, women survive longer than men. If there is an imbalance it seems to work against men rather than women. For every 100 girls born, about 105 baby boys arrive. Because males take more risks, are more vulnerable to violence, accidents, and suicide, and experience more developmental difficulties such as attention deficit hyperactivity disorder, autism, and conduct disorder, we need to begin with a surplus of males in order to end up at maturity with an equal representation of both sexes.

Inclusive fitness is the sum total of the genes that we leave behind in all of our blood relatives including children, grandchildren, and great grandchildren. This number is probabilistically related to our own personal reproductive success. The more children we have, the more grandchildren we are likely to have. Each child will carry one half of our genes and each grandchild one quarter. Any genetic trait that has the effect of increasing the number of children that we rear will be expressed in more future bodies than a genetic trait that puts us at a disadvantage in reproductive competition. But the traits that assist men and women in carrying their genes forward are not identical. A good strategy for a man may be counterproductive for a woman. Over evolutionary time, we begin to see a sex difference appear. Baby girls receive those genes that selectively help females to become reproductively successful, while baby boys receive a slightly different complement of genes that in the past have helped their fathers and grandfathers.

There are a number of ways in which these genetic sex differences can be carried between generations. Some traits may be sex limited: here the genes are carried on autosomal chromosomes (ones that do not code for anatomical sex differences) and are only activated in the presence of sex-specific hormones such as testosterone. Or they may be sex-linked—carried on the X or Y chromosome that determines the child's sex. An added wrinkle to this pathway is the increasing number of genomically imprinted traits that are being found. In this process, whether or not a gene is expressed depends upon which parent donated the gene. For example, recent work suggests that girls' greater social intelligence is mediated by genes received from their father not from their mother. The X chromosome that the father contributes carries the critical genes. The homologous genes on the X chromosome that the mother contributes are silenced. This may explain why boys, who receive only the mother's copy of the X chromosome, are more vulnerable to disorders of social cognition and language, such as autism (Skuse, 2000; Skuse et al., 1997). Studies of rodents suggest that a similar process may operate for maternal behavior—the mother's tendency to retrieve straying pups and return them to the nest is mediated by the X chromosome of her own father.

Whatever the pathway used, each sex receives the genetic instructions most useful for building a mind that will enhance the body's reproductive success. So sex differences are expected only where they have a direct influence on sex-specific reproductive strategy. Biology can point to the sexual strategies of men and women that lie behind evolved psychological differences.

Anisogamy: The start of parental inequity

Sexual reproduction is not obligatory in nature. There are plenty of ways to reproduce that do not require the fusion of gametes from two individuals. In parthenogenetic species, no mating is needed. North American whip tail lizards are all female and, in the breeding season, they produce about 10 unfertilized eggs that hatch carrying 100 percent of their mother's DNA (Fisher, 1993). There are plenty of advantages to this strategy—these females do not waste time and energy on finding mates, they do not expose themselves to predators while copulating, they do not have to compete with others to impress the opposite sex with their desirability, and most importantly they do not dilute their genetic legacy by 50 percent. But it is this last factor that paradoxically becomes an advantage in mating. Sexual reproduction creates novel and unique individuals and this has a threefold implication. First, because offspring differ from their parents and their siblings, they can occupy a variety of different environmental niches and so create less competition with their kin, while increasing the odds that at least some will survive in the face of unpredictable local hazards such as sudden climatic changes. Second, each offspring's unique genotype means that it has a unique immune system—when parasites take hold they may prove deadly to some of the brood but others will survive. Another advantage of sexual reproduction is genetic repair. A strand of DNA is composed of sequences of the four nucleotides C, G, T, and A. When an error occurs—CG?—the best way to find out what should really be there instead of the ? is to examine the second copy of the sequence on the complementary strand of DNA. But it will do no good if the second strand has come from the same genetic line as the first because there is a good chance that it will carry the same error. In sexual reproduction, the enzymatic "proofreading" machinery of the cell consults the corresponding sequence on the strand provided by the second, unrelated parent and fixes the error (Williams, 1996).

So two biological parents can be better than one. But why have an egg and a sperm? An egg is about one million times bigger than a sperm and far more costly to make. It carries not just its DNA message but the metabolic machinery and nutrients to supply the zygote until the tiny bundle of cells can attach itself to the uterus and set up its own supply line through the placenta. A sperm is little more than a DNA-containing nucleus with a tail to propel its search for a free genetic ride in an egg. Why not have more equality—two parents who each contribute equally to the zygote?

Multicellular algae do this. Each alga releases cells into the surrounding water that fuse with cells from another alga creating second-generation compound cells. All that is required for basic sexual reproduction is organisms that are capable of releasing haploid gametes (ones that contain half the adult number of chromosomes) that can join with a gamete from another organism to form a viable zygote. The story of the evolution of sperm and egg begins with just such an egalitarian scenario (Parker, Baker, & Smith, 1972). Each gamete carried half the nutrients needed by the about-to-be-formed zygote. But then came variability; some gametes carried less than their fair share of nutrients and others more. Imagine that every individual made a thousand gametes for every milligram of material devoted to reproducing (Williams, 1996). Each gamete was worth one microgram and when they fused they created a two-microgram zygote which made it strong enough to be viable. But now some cheating begins, thanks to the random process of mutation. Some mutants produce not 1,000 but 1,100 gametes even though each one is slightly smaller (only 0.9 microgram). If each one fuses with a normal, non-mutant gamete, the zygote will weigh a little less (only 1.9 micrograms) but that will be compensated for by the fact that there will be 10 percent more of them. As long as the net disadvantage is less than 5 percent, the mutant form will still be ahead of the game. When two mutant gametes meet, the zygote drops to 1.8 micrograms so now the mutant forms lose their net advantage, preventing the whole species from adopting the cheating strategy. But the situation could stabilize favoring ever larger and smaller gametes. Organisms producing small gametes can make a larger number of them and hence a larger number of offspring but they have the disadvantage of small size and lower viability. Organisms producing larger gametes make fewer of them but they are better equipped and more likely to survive. Gametes have to achieve two objectives—they must find a partner and create a well-resourced, nutrient-equipped zygote (Low, 2000). Small gametes do best at the former— sperm are cheap to make, light, and motile. Big gametes do better at the latter—eggs carry the nourishment that the growing zygote needs to survive. Intermediate-sized gametes have neither advantage and so lose out to both. Once anisogamy (the size difference between egg and sperm) began, the gulf between them could only get bigger. Sperm that were designed to move fast and carry only the minimum fuel out-competed slower, fatter sperm. Eggs that carried the most nutrients and conserved their energy could survive longer and create stronger zygotes and so they became more numerous than thinner, more active eggs. So the process continued until the giant quiescent egg dwarfed the stripped-down searching sperm. The consequences of this gametic "cheating" have been almost unimaginably far-reaching for the two sexes.

> The sperm will have to compete for the limited number of eggs available, and will therefore retain the locomotor mechanisms (long propulsive tails in most species) needed in the race for fertilisation. The eggs can leave the work of finding a partner to the sperm . . . When egg-producers reproduce, they must bear the entire nutritional burden of nurturing the offspring. By contrast, the sperm-makers reproduce for free. A sperm is not a contribution to the next generation; it is a claim on contributions put into the egg by another individual. Males of most species make no investments in the next generation, but merely compete with one another for the opportunity to exploit investments made by females. (Williams, 1996, p. 118)

Thus were females first exploited by males at a purely biological level. But the egg and sperm distinction did not end there. The greater gamete size and cost that females incurred was only the beginning of their greater lifelong commitment to infant care.

It was Robert Trivers (1972) who spelled out the key reproductive difference between the sexes. He called it parental investment and defined it as "any investment by a parent in an individual offspring that increases the offspring's chance of surviving (and hence reproductive success) at the cost of the parent's ability to invest in other offspring." It is absolutely central to an evolutionary analysis of sex differences. The more time and effort an individual channels into any single offspring, the fewer offspring they will ultimately produce. This simple principle amounts to a distinction between offspring quantity and quality (MacArthur & Wilson, 1967; Promislow & Harvey, 1990). Animals who have taken the quantity route are called r-selected (or fast) species. Insects lay thousands of eggs but invest very little time or energy in any of them. Instead they move swiftly on to the creation of a new batch. K-selected (or slow) species, such as primates, give birth to one baby at a time and spend several years feeding and protecting it. Some animals, like cats, steer a middle course giving birth to multiple offspring but yet providing milk and care to all of them for a limited time. The point is that there is always a trade-off—the more time devoted to one offspring, the less time to produce more.

The fast–slow distinction seems to hold for men and women also. The minimum biological costs of reproduction are greater for women than for men. Each month about 20 ovarian follicles prepare their oocytes for possible ejection: one is chosen, ripened, and released into the Fallopian tube. Meanwhile the endometrium of the uterus must be engorged in preparation for the arrival of a fertilized egg (even if one fails to arrive which, as we will see, is usually the case). These twin processes are so time-consuming and costly in terms of calories that they take about 14 days (half a menstrual cycle) to achieve. If pregnancy occurs, the woman's body is occupied for nine months with gestation. After the birth, lactation requires even more calories than were necessary to sustain the pregnancy (almost double a woman's normal daily requirements) and, in the ancestral human environment, lactation would have continued for up to four years. For every mother, each baby represents a very large investment of time and energy, to say nothing of emotion.

Compare this with a man's minimum investment. He can ejaculate several times a day. Admittedly, the number of sperm produced falls with each emission from a high of 300 million on the first occasion to a low of a mere 30 million after a three-hour interval. Nonetheless, pregnancy only requires one sperm in the right place at the right time. Once a man has gallantly donated his sperm, any further contribution on his part is optional rather than biologically mandatory. It does not require a mathematical genius to realize that under optimal conditions a man could father half a dozen infants in a day, while a women would take 30 years to do the same.

A host of psychological differences between males and females, as we shall see, derive from the fact that women's biological parental investment is greater than men's. It is important to recall that the crucial factor that drives these sex differences is not maleness or femaleness per se, but the degree of parental investment (and in some species competition for mating opportunities, see Clutton-Brock, 2007). In our species, it happens to be women who invest more heavily but in other species like pipefish, sea horses, and teleost fish, it is fathers who make the greater investment. And this seems to result from the mechanics of reproduction in these species (Dawkins & Carlisle, 1976). Out of 49 species of fish where paternal care is found, 48 reproduce by external fertilization (Trivers, 1985). Because gametes evaporate in the air, earthbound species copulate using intromission of sperm to keep them in a safe host environment. Among fish, however, the sea water protects them from evaporation. Because of this, a female lays her eggs and they are then fertilized externally by the male—he must wait until she spawns because his sperm are lighter than her eggs and are more likely to be carried away by passing currents. Because the female finishes her part of reproduction before the male, she can then desert knowing that the male will be forced to take responsibility for the brood. Of course, the male could desert also but there would be no selection pressures for abandoning viable offspring. A male who continued to do this would leave no progeny behind and so deserting last is not an adaptive choice. In any case, the real bonus of external fertilization for the male is that he is certain of his paternity and this means he can be equally certain that the effort he devotes to the egg batch is going to his own offspring, rather than a rival male's (Trivers, 1985). In humans and other mammals, however, fertilization occurs within the female's body and the fertilized ovum remains there, developing, for several weeks or months. This gives the male ample time to desert leaving the female holding the baby. Because deserting first offers the advantage of further copulations with new and unencumbered partners, it would have been selected for and, because of internal fertilization, this would lead to the evolution of a male strategy of seeking multiple sexual partners (for a more complex treatment of sex-role divergence, see Kokko & Jennions, 2008). Because the tendency to desert is related to future reproduction prospects, desertion will be less likely among females than males because their future prospects are always lower than males—in human females that time window of potential reproduction is especially truncated by menopause and because each infant demands such a very long period of maternal care.

Why has natural selection favored this long period of parental care? After all, if infants were born ready to cope with the world by themselves, humans could produce several times the number of children that they currently do. Many mammals arrive in the world able to find their feet (quite literally) and, within weeks, to feed themselves. The answer is our unusual intelligence. Compared to our hominid ancestors, *Homo sapiens* has an extraordinarily large brain—about three times the size of *Australopithecus* (McHenry, 1994). Brains are very expensive: they consume more calories than any other organ of the body. The benefits of their steadily increasing size must have been a consistent advantage at every evolutionary step. They gave us a better memory (capable of storing massive amounts of information), representational thought (the ability to perform safer off-line "thought" experiments rather than costly trial-and-error learning), consciousness (the ability to represent ourselves in our internal model of the world), language (and hence speedy information transmission), a theory of mind (the ability to accurately impute mental states to others), and meta-cognition (the ability to reflect on what we know and how we know it). A brain capable of doing these things needs to be big. It was the increasing size of the brain that posed special problems for women (Lancaster & Lancaster, 1983: Rosenberg & Trevathan, 1996). Humans were walking upright and enjoying all the benefits that came with this ability. But bipedal locomotion requires a small pelvis and, as the infant's head became bigger, a smaller pelvis meant a more difficult childbirth. Babies born any later than nine months were simply too big to get through the pelvic bones. So nine months became a compromise gestation period. Any longer and the baby could not be born, any shorter and the baby would be too immature to survive. But, as any woman who has given birth knows, natural selection pushed gestation time to its upper limit. During childbirth, the four plates that compose the baby's skull are forced over one another leaving the newborn with a visible and vulnerable soft spot, the fontanel. Human infants are born too early in a maturational sense. The first three months of extra-uterine life have even been called the "fourth trimester." Infants are helpless, totally dependent on parental care, and have another 13 years before they reach bodily maturity.

Men and the attractions of polygyny

The optimal condition for male reproductive success is access to as many fertile women as possible. If a man remains with a single woman throughout his life and is completely faithful, he can only produce as many children as his wife can give birth to. Her intensive period of investment in each child places a ceiling on his success also. But a man with two women can double his reproductive success. With a harem, he can increase it a hundredfold. In fact, under such "perfect" conditions, a man's sexual performance would be even further enhanced because novelty increases sexual arousal. (This "Coolidge effect" is named after the president's famous remark on being shown around a chicken farm. His wife, when informed that the cock copulated several times a day, asked her host to tell the president about it. When told, her husband asked if it was always the same hen. "No, Mr President, it is a different one every time." "Tell that to my wife" he allegedly replied.) Concubinage was aimed at precisely this kind of maximization of male reproductive success. Ismail the Bloodthirsty of Morocco (1672–1727) is reputed to have had 500 concubines at any one time (they were recruited at puberty and ejected at the age of 30) and to have produced 888 children (McWhirter & McWhirter, 1975).

Most men are not so fortunate but that does not alter the basic fact that for several thousand years men's reproductive success was directly related to their number of sexual partners. Staying with one woman may have had advantages but it had a definite cost too. Any man who took advantage of the occasional opportunity to have sex with other women had a definite reproductive edge. There is much evidence that this strategy of at least mild polygyny was (and continues to be) a strong theme in human evolution.

The evidence comes from comparing sex differences in humans to those that are evident in other polygynous species. Polygyny is strongly associated with differences in size and strength between the sexes. Because the ratio of adult males to females is about 1:1, any male who monopolizes or impregnates more than one female leaves another male without a mate. This means that males must compete with one another to gain access to extra female partners and this selects for ever larger and stronger males over the generations. (Big males have many children, half of whom will be sons who carry their fathers "big" genes. Small males have fewer children and so fewer sons carrying "small" genes. Over generations, male size increases.) The size difference between human males and females was very marked indeed in our hominid ancestors. *Australopithecus* males were between 50 and 100 percent larger than females (Geary, 2000). Though the magnitude of the sex difference has diminished—probably as a result of less intense male competition resulting from an increase in paternal investment and a consequent decrease in polygynous matings—it has remained relatively constant over the last 300,000 years with males being about 20 percent larger than females (Geary, 1998; Hrdy, 1999). At puberty, boys' height shoots up and men's extra height is largely attributable to their longer leg length. They also develop larger skeletal muscles, and a greater capacity for carrying oxygen in the blood and neutralizing the chemical products of physical exercise. Men have about twice the upper body strength of women (Browne, 2006). They can run faster, grip harder, and jump higher than females (Tanner, 1990).

In polygynous animals, puberty occurs earlier in females than in males. At reproductive maturity, a young male must enter the ferocious male–male contest for mating opportunities. The bigger he is and the greater his experience of preparatory rough-and-tumble contests, the greater his chance of success. So there is an advantage for males in delaying puberty, even though it means that they must wait longer for their first reproductive opportunity. In polygynous species, the female pubertal growth spurt starts earlier and peaks more quickly than in males (Leigh, 1996). This is true of humans also and boys reach puberty at the age of about 13–14, approximately two years later than girls (Tanner, 1990).

Males in polygynous species also tend to die earlier than females. The Y chromosome instructs the formation of testes and so begins the production of testosterone. At adolescence, the surge in testosterone production energizes youthful sexual and competitive behavior—but at a cost. In the long term, testosterone is believed to compromise the immune system leading to men's earlier death relative to women (Folstad & Karter, 1992, but see Roberts, Buchanan, & Evans, 2004).

Another piece of biological evidence adds to the picture of ancestral human polygyny—testes size (Harcourt, Harvey, Larson, & Short, 1981). Animals that have no need to compete for females, like the solitary harem-holding gorilla, can manage with modest testes. But animals that mate with many females must produce copious quantities of sperm to compete with other males who are also seeking mating opportunities. Admittedly, human testicles look rather undersized in comparison with promiscuous chimpanzees but they are considerably more impressive than those of the gorilla.

A final requirement of the successfully polygynous male is a strong sex drive. A male must be ready and eager to have sex at every possible opportunity and this seems to be marked feature of human males. The data are unequivocal. In a review of 177 data sources (Oliver & Hyde, 1993) men had a far more positive attitude toward casual sex than did women; they had intercourse more frequently; and the biggest difference of all was in incidence of masturbation—an activity enjoyed more often by men as a substitute for sex with partner. Men experience sexual fantasies and sexual arousal about once a day compared to about once a week in women, and men more often fantasize about someone with whom they have not yet had sex while women tend to re-run past sexual encounters (Ellis & Symons, 1990). Men want sex more often than women and with more partners. They are less willing to forego sex and more willing to make sacrifices to obtain it (Baumeister, Catanese, & Vohs, 2001). Because of this disparity in motivation, the frequency of intercourse for a couple depends upon the woman's rather than the man's willingness (Baumeister et al., 2001) This is demonstrated by the very high rate of sexual contact among male (but not female) homosexuals where there is no female partner to gate or suppress high male sexual drive (Symons, 1979). An ingenious study in the United States documented undergraduate men's willingness to avail themselves of additional sexual partners by using a male and a female confederate to approach students on campus and invite them back to their apartment for sex (Clark & Hatfield, 1989). Predictably, 75 percent of men, but none of the women, took up the offer. One psychological mechanism that may give rise to this sex difference is the standards that men and women apply to casual sexual partners. Men, more than women, are willing to relax their standards very markedly for a short-term sexual partner compared to what they expect in a spouse (Kenrick, Sadalla, Groth, & Trost, 1990). Though men may have paired with a single long-term partner, it seems as if nature fitted them to take advantage of sexual opportunities whenever they arose.

Women as choosy investors

Biologically speaking, men's investment is completed at conception and they are free to move on to pastures new. But women, unlike men, are quality not quantity specialists. Their investment is not limited to a few moments' pleasure—they are committed to the reproductive consequences and women produce only a limited number of offspring. In hunter-gatherer societies, birth spacing is about four years and a woman typically gives birth to four or five babies in her lifetime. Each one is precious and each one must be carefully nurtured to adulthood. So great is the commitment demanded by every child that women's bodies and minds are exquisitely crafted to invest only in the highest-quality child that they can produce. This fussiness is all the more remarkable since menopause drastically shortens a woman's reproductive career relative to a man's, yet still she will not invest in an infant that has a poor chance of survival.

First, she must ensure that her body has a reasonable chance of sustaining the pregnancy. Menstruation is the first casualty of a poorly resourced environment. Malnourishment signals that a pregnancy under current conditions would not be viable. Athletes and dancers, who put considerable physical demands on their bodies while maintaining a very restricted diet, lay down little fat and have later menarche than other girls (Angier, 1999). Although women with anorexia deliberately choose to avoid food, the body does not distinguish between an active choice and an environmental scarcity, so first ovulation and then menstruation ceases. When food is scarce before the harvest, women in Zaire lose weight and show a drop in progesterone levels and ovulation. After the harvest, their fertility returns to normal (Ellison, 1994, 1996). The same relationship between abundance and fertility can be detected by examining birth rates around the world in the wake of periods of famine or plenty. Nine months after a food shortage there is a significant drop in births (Betzig, 1997a).

Stress is a warning that the body is under strain. That strain may result from resource shortage in the outside environment or from problems in the immune response inside the body (Nepomnaschy, Sheiner, Mastorakos, & Arck, 2007). In many cases, the two are linked. High levels of stress can suppress ovulation and menstruation because the stress response system (hypothalamic–pituitary–adrenal axis) is closely connected to the system that regulates reproduction (hypothalamic–pituitary–ovarian axis). The body shuts down the reproductive system and waits for a better time to start a pregnancy (Baker, 1996; MacDonald, 1997). Acute stress, rather than chronic stress, seems more likely to trigger ovulatory shutdown. Among women who live in unrelentingly harsh environments, external stressors are consistently high and, if the body responded by shutting down ovulation, women would hardly ever reproduce. In circumstances of chronic stress, it makes sense to produce more offspring in the hope that some at least will survive the adverse environmental circumstances. Stress is relative. A woman living in more favorable circumstances may inhibit ovulation in response to acute stress: her body, through cortisol release, signals that she should wait for a more favorable moment to conceive. Yet her current circumstances might well seem like a life of luxury to a street beggar in India.

When circumstances are propitious, the time is right for possible conception. But a woman's body should be fussy about which man she will allow to take a free genetic ride on her costly parental investment. Evolution has shaped two ways to assist her—concealed ovulation and sperm competition.

During a normal ovulatory cycle, a woman is capable of conception for only a very narrow band of time. That fertility window lasts from five days before ovulation to 12 hours after it, with peak fertility occurring precisely 48 hours before ovulation. The problem, of course, is that neither she nor her partner knows for certain when she is ovulating. It happens 14 days before her next menstruation but, because she cannot see into the future, a woman has to rely on a retrospective estimate based on the date of her last period. This is notoriously imprecise as cycles can vary by several days from one month to the next. The function of concealed ovulation has been a source of fascination for evolutionary thinkers. In many (but by no means all) primates, the female's fertile period or estrus is signaled very clearly through genital swelling. Females and males are rather indifferent to sexual opportunities outside this time and save themselves a lot of wasted energy by engaging in sexual athletics only when it will have a reproductive pay-off. What is the point of concealing ovulation? There have been plenty of suggestions.

Perhaps this concealment is designed to fool the woman herself. And they do indeed seem to be fooled—even the minority of women who claim to know when they are ovulating are far from accurate (Sievert & Dubois, 2005). If ancestral women were capable of knowing when they were fertile and equally capable of observing the pain (and possible death) associated with childbirth, they might use abstinence as a contraceptive measure. Women who recognized their own ovulation would produce fewer children than their less sensitive peers and there would have been selection for ignorance (Burley, 1979). But this explanation credits ancestral women with a rather sophisticated understanding of reproductive biology. It was not until the 1930s that researchers realized that ovulation occurs at mid-cycle rather than during menses as they had previously believed. Even as late as 1923, women were advised to abstain from sex during menstruation as a contraceptive measure (Thornhill & Gangestad, 2008). Although hunter-gatherers know that intercourse is connected with pregnancy, they believe that conception occurs immediately after menses (Marlowe, 2004). No wonder people have been confused: after all, most acts of intercourse do not lead to pregnancy, the latency between intercourse and the awareness of being pregnant can be lengthy and some (infertile) women never become pregnant despite plenty of sex. The more obvious biological consequence of concealed ovulation is that it creates uncertainty about who the father of the child might be. And that leads directly to three very different hypotheses about its evolution based on female strategies of pair bonding, polyandry, and a blend of both.

A well-advertised estrous (think of those swollen hindquarters of baboons) means that a male can copulate with a female at the "right" time and need only guard her against rival males for the few days of her estrous. But when estrous is cryptic and a woman is continuously receptive to sex, there is no signal to the man (or indeed the woman) of the "right" time. This means that repeated intercourse over at least a month is needed for a possible pregnancy and this creates opportunity costs: the costs of all the other activities that a man must forego—including sex with other women. When a man makes post-copulatory investment in the woman and her offspring, as humans typically do, he must be sure that the offspring is indeed his. This entails mate guarding to ensure her fidelity and avoid cuckoldry. Continuous sex had the added bonus of holding a man's attention and cementing the pair bond. Recent research reveals that both oxytocin (a neuropeptide associated with increase trust and decreased fear) and dopamine (a neurotransmitter associated with desire and reward) are triggered simultaneously by copulation in monogamous species. Their co-action is thought to underlie partner preference and pair bonding (Young & Wang, 2004). So, according to this scenario, women evolved concealed estrous to keep their male partners around.

But the uncertainty of paternity introduced by concealed ovulation had another and rather opposite effect: it allowed women to take multiple mates and, because each man believed he was the father of her offspring, he would act paternally toward it (Hrdy, 2000). The original impetus to this hypothesis was Sarah Hrdy's (1979) discovery of the high rate of infanticide in langur monkeys that often accompanied the takeover of the group by younger, incumbent males. Infanticide effectively cleared out the genetic legacy of the previous males, wiping the slate clean to begin again. The costs to females were extreme. Perhaps then, women used concealed estrous and continuous sexual receptivity not to capture one man's interest but to ensure many men's paternal tolerance. Among the Ache of Paraguay, three types of fathers are recognized: the man to whom the pregnant woman is married, the man with whom she had sex just prior to her pregnancy, and the man whom she believes is responsible for the pregnancy. About 63 percent of babies have multiple fathers or "partible paternity," and the average number of fathers is just over two. Because the Ache sometimes dispose of a child whose father dies, children with multiple fathers have an important advantage. Among the Bar of Venezuela and Columbia, a woman who claims multiple fathers for her unborn child runs a lower risk of miscarriage and of perinatal death, presumably because all the fathers ensure that she is well supplied with food throughout the pregnancy. The child also has a greater chance of surviving until the age of 15 because it has the support of two fathers. These unusual cases notwithstanding, not everyone accepts the partible paternity hypothesis. Its plausibility depends on exactly how strong human paternal certainty must be to ensure investment in the offspring and on whether that investment is graduated by the degree of paternal confidence. If a man's certainty of paternity has to be high before he will invest (and men's acute sensitivity to women's infidelity and the frightening strength of their jealousy suggests this is likely) then trying to convince multiple men that they may be the child's father ought to be doomed to failure because each of them would have sufficient doubt to prevent their investment. This would argue strongly for the mate-at-home hypothesis of concealed ovulation. But it may be that, under some ecological conditions, a modicum of care from several men outweighs full investment from one. This depends upon paternal investment being graduated according to certainty rather than being an all-or-none affair. Men who harbor a hope of their possible paternity will make some efforts to protect the child—as long as the cost is not too great. Even if they simply refrain from harming it, the child's survival chances may be enhanced.

Diamond (1997) suggests that both hypotheses are correct but they apply to different points in our evolutionary history. By examining the family tree from which humans descended (Sillen-Tulberg & Moller, 1993), it is possible to find at least 20 points at which changes in ovulatory advertisement occurred. If we look at those species which shifted from advertised estrous to concealed ovulation, we find that the vast majority were promiscuous or harem structured (where a newly established alpha male might well pose a threat to infants). This seems to suggest that concealed ovulation developed originally to confuse paternity rather than to enhance monogamy. But we can turn the question around and ask what the prevailing estrous conditions were in those species that went on to develop monogamy. Monogamy never evolved in species with advertised ovulation and was largely confined to those species that had already developed concealed ovulation. This suggests that concealment was a female strategy to retain the attention of a single male. If we put the pieces of the puzzle together, the primate data suggest that concealed ovulation arose first in promiscuous or harem species in order to confuse paternity and prevent infanticide. Then once it had evolved, the species switched to a monogamous mating system in which concealed ovulation worked to keep a single male at home. Given the flexibility of human sexual strategies and our ability to fine tune our behavior to different circumstances, it may be that women exploited these two benefits under different circumstances, depending on the quantity and quality of available men.

A third possibility, championed by Thornhill and Gangestad (2008) is that concealed fertility allowed women to simultaneously have their cake and eat it. A good strategy for women might be to find a long-term provisioning mate, while at the same time engaging in extra-pair copulations with more genetically desirable partners. Given that the strategy depends on secrecy, it is difficult to get reliable data from women themselves. Contemporary non-paternity rates vary between 1 percent in affluent Switzerland (Sasse, Müller, Chakraborty, & Ott, 1994) and 20 percent in impoverished neighborhoods (Cerda-Flores, Barton, Marty-Gonzalez, Rivas, & Cakraborty, 1999). According to Thornhill and Gangestad, women's mate preferences change in a predictable way around midcycle when they are most fertile. They prefer men who exhibit more masculinity in their face, body, voice, and scent. They prefer men with greater bilateral symmetry, indicative of high-quality genes, an efficient immune system, and developmental stability. Women who are partnered with men of low genetic quality, show a more marked estrous preference for these "good gene" qualities and feel less committed to their partner at that time. Married women are more likely to be unfaithful at this time in their cycle and are less likely to use contraception when they are with a lover (Baker, 1996). This argument remains controversial. Thornhill and Gangestad define estrous in terms of a woman's enhanced (but selective) sexual interest when she is most likely to conceive, and maintain that "women's estrous is not concealed from themselves" (p. 275). But the evidence of increased sexual desire during ovulation, as the authors note, is far from supportive. If women's sexual desire is not enhanced, what motivates them to actively seek extra-pair partners at this time? If the illicit garnering of high-quality male genes is the aim of concealed ovulation, then why are women's extra-pair copulations relatively rare? After all, by definition, only one woman in the world is mated with the optimal man. Despite uncertainty about the origins of concealed ovulation, one thing we can be sure of is that it did not work to men's advantage—it evolved to benefit women (and their offspring).

When it comes to the act of intercourse itself, women do their best to make life (at least the creation of it) difficult for a man. The more demanding and tortuous the achievement of fertilization, the greater the chance that only the best sperm will succeed. Let us view this Olympian feat from a sperm's perspective. Before our sperm can even enter the arena of the female reproductive tract, he has journeyed from the testes into the epididymis where he sits for two or three weeks before he is capable of self-propulsion. When his turn comes, he enters the vas deferens awaiting the orgasmic contractions that will shoot him from the scrotum via the penis into the woman's vagina, traveling in the seminal fluid that has been collected at the prostate gland. He does not travel alone. A man releases between 100 and 300 million sperm in each ejaculate. This sounds like a lot, but as many as 40 percent are defective or fail to swim properly. The vagina's usual acidity, designed to control bacteria, is thoughtfully relaxed a little as ovulation approaches. The mucous, normally impenetrable, becomes thinner and forms channels like swimming lanes to guide the sperm upward. The sperm seem to be attracted to the heat of the upper Fallopian tubes and also by chemical signals. (Q: Why does it take so many sperm to fertilize an egg? A: Because they won't ask for directions. Thanks to signals from their female host, maybe they don't need to.) But the journey is slow: although they must travel just 10 centimeters, their swimming speed averages only three millimeters per minute. It is also tortuous: the sperm have to avoid the crevices and blind alleys of the reproductive tract, and attack by the woman's white blood cells. After 10 minutes or so, some of the first sperm have passed through the cervix and entered the uterus, with their slower companions arriving there in the next 72 hours. Only 1 percent of the original band will have made it this far. Now, hyperactivated and able to fertilize after their immersion in their host's body, a mere 1,000 remaining sperm swim into the Fallopian tubes pushed forward by uterine contractions. About 100 of the strongest sperm reach the egg and use enzymes to digest the cell's outer membrane. But only one of them can penetrate the oocyte. When that first heroic sperm enters, the tail which has served it so well is left outside. The newly formed zygote slams the door shut by forming a thick wall to keep the slower sperm out. Fertilization finally takes place.

A woman's body subjects the hapless sperm to such an obstacle course as a form of quality control. A woman does not want to share her costly egg, loaded with expensive nutrients, with just any old sperm. A man's sperm are pitted against one another in a race to find the fastest, strongest, most active, and most viable. A whole area of evolutionary biology is devoted to the study of sperm competition (Birkhead, 2010; Parker, 1970a; Shackelford & Goetz, 2007). In species where females mate with multiple males, sperm competition takes place between rival males. In these species, females have lengthened their oviducts to make the sperm's trip more hazardous and so impose stronger quality criteria (Anderson, Dixson, & Dixson, 2006). It is a form of sexual selection that operates after, rather than before, mating. Male intrasexual competition moves from direct combat and extravagant display in the world outside, to tests of sperm speed and strength inside the female body. In many species, males go to considerable lengths to ensure that theirs are the only sperm in the competition—at a cost to the female. In seed beetles, for example, the male has a large barbed penis that tears the female tract during mating. The pain deters the female from re-mating with any rival male who might fertilize her eggs. The damselfly's hooked and horned penis is designed to remove the sperm of previous male suitors and it seems to be a useful adaptation: if a female mates with two males, it is the second male who fertilizes 90 percent of her eggs. A similar function may explain the structure of the human penis: the coronal ridge removes an estimated 90 percent of vaginal contents, as opposed to only 35 percent in an unridged penis (Gallup & Burch, 2004). The spiny penis of chimpanzees is not found in humans (for which women everywhere give thanks). It absence has been traced, serendipitously, to a segment of non-coding DNA near the male's androgen receptor gene (McLean et al., 2011). Monogamy, it seems, eased competition between men with happy consequences for their penis structure and their partner's comfort.

Sperm competition does not mean that a female is a passive spectator to male attempts to exploit her reproductive facilities. A key lesson in evolutionary theory is that for every gambit there is an equal and opposite gambit—the co-evolutionary game. Just as predator and prey are locked in an arms race, so are males and females. (We'll return to this in Chapter 8.) We can see this best in the avian kingdom. Among wildfowl, low-status males occasionally bully females into unwanted copulations behind the back of the dominant male. She retaliates by ejecting the offending sperm before the upstart male has even dismounted. She rarely does this after a tryst with the desirable dominant male (Pizzari & Birkhead, 2000). And the females do not have to depend on visual recognition of the offender; the sperm alone provide the information they need. When a female wildfowl is inseminated with a cocktail of semen from two males (one more dominant than the other), she disproportionately ejects the sperm of the subordinate (Birkhead, Chaline, Biggins, Burke, & Pizzari, 2004).

In humans too, about 35 percent of sperm is lost from the vagina within 30 minutes of intercourse. This is what biologists rather indelicately term "flow-back." As yet we do not know whether women, like birds, can bias their retention of sperm from different partners through this form of cryptic choice. If they can, it may be linked to orgasm timing (Baker & Bellis, 1993). If a woman experiences a copulatory orgasm one minute before and up to 45 minutes after her partner ejaculates, she retains between 50 and 90 percent of his sperm. If the woman does not climax at all or does so more than one minute before her partner, she retains 0 to 50 percent. During orgasm (in fact shortly after she psychologically experiences it) her cervix gapes open, widening the mucus channels, dipping down into the seminal fluid and allowing more sperm to pass through. The contraction of uterine and vaginal muscles creates a pressure change which sucks the semen more effectively through her cervix. The orgasm also expels old sperm from the uterus creating space for new sperm to enter. Women are more likely to experience orgasm with an attractive rather than an unattractive partner (Shackelford et al., 2000; Thornhill, Gangestad, & Comer, 1995) and with a lover rather than a husband (Bellis & Baker, 1990). (The same seems to be true of female Japanese macaques who orgasm more frequently with dominant males, Troisi & Carosi, 1998). So orgasm may act as a mechanism that enhances the probability of a pregnancy from an act of intercourse. But this view remains controversial and female orgasm may have no functional value at all: Perhaps it is simply a by-product of the fact that male and female genitals develop from the same underlying structure (see Barash & Lipton, 2009; Gould, 1992b; Lloyd, 2005). The presence of testosterone turns the embryo's genital tubercle into a penis; otherwise it becomes a clitoris. Some argue that orgasm is important for male sexual excitement and fertilization, but it is just an added but unnecessary "bonus" for females. After all, females can be impregnated without experiencing orgasm at all.

Even after sexual intercourse, women have ways of controlling whether or not conception will occur. Failure to conceive can result from a shortening of the normal 14-day interval between ovulation and menstruation which reduces the chance of a fertilized egg implanting. It is in this time window that a number of embryos are ejected without the woman's awareness. Only about 60 percent of fertilized eggs succeed in implanting themselves in the uterus. Of these a further 60 percent will not survive to the 12th day of pregnancy and the woman experiences what she may believe to be an unusually heavy period. Of those that make it through the 12-day barrier, about 20 percent will be miscarried in the first trimester (Baker, 1996). The majority of these pregnancy failures are a result of genetic abnormality in the embryo or highly stressful maternal events. Miscarriage rates increase with the outbreak of war or with the death or infidelity of a woman's partner.

Even when a pregnancy is established, women still exercise choice about its continuation and even about whether to care for a child after it is born. If a fetus or infant is not viable then a woman is better off abandoning it as early as possible. Trivers (1972) argued that this was because the longer she continued to invest in a child, the more time and effort she had wasted when it ultimately died. This was christened the Concorde fallacy by Richard Dawkins and Tamsin Carlisle (1976). They drew an analogy with Britain's sustained and economically disastrous commitment to the supersonic airliner which was driven by the logic that so much had already been spent that it was unthinkable to abandon it. Dawkins and Carlisle pointed out that this retrospective view of "investment to date," however intuitively appealing, was incorrect. They argued, and Trivers (1985) later came to agree with them, that the true explanation of early abandonment lay in the amount of prospective investment that remained. A woman who abandons a non-viable fetus saves herself 15 years of future wasted investment, while a woman who abandons a 12-year-old saves herself only a further three years of investment. These interpretative arguments notwithstanding, the evolutionary predictions are identical and are not in dispute. The cruel truth is that from the point of view of her own genetic success, a woman who spends time and effort in raising a child who is a poor reproductive prospect or who will be born into an environment too harsh to sustain normal development curtails her chance of investing in other more viable offspring. Natural selection should favor female bodies and minds that are profoundly selective about which infants deserve the mother's scarce and valuable investment.

In many contemporary cultures, women have the option of terminating the pregnancy. We would expect that this decision would be related to whether or not the mother would do better to wait for a more propitious time to bear the child and to the currently available resources for rearing the child. The decision to have a child now—rather than waiting for better emotional and material circumstances—is closely related to the mother's age. Younger women have a longer reproductive career ahead of them and can afford to wait for a more optimal time. Statistics confirm that the rate of voluntary abortion is high among young women aged 20 or less, with approximately three-quarters of 18–19-year-olds choosing to terminate their pregnancy (Hill & Low, 1992). Young women can afford to wait not only in terms of their biological clocks but because they have a better chance of finding a male partner to assist in child-rearing in the future. Younger women have a much higher probability of marriage and remarriage than do older women, and childlessness increases their likelihood of finding a marriage partner.

Material, personal, and interpersonal resources also play a role in the decision to abort. Fathers make a contribution to the economic and emotional welfare of the mother and child, and statistics confirm that the best predictor of abortion is whether the father is willing to commit himself to the mother. In the United States, 65 percent of pregnancies among unmarried women were terminated compared to 10 percent among married women (Hill & Low, 1992). A study of 300 middle-class American women asked them to estimate the probability of terminating a pregnancy (Essock-Vitale & McGuire, 1988). The estimated probability was 0.07 for married women but 0.64 for unmarried women. Fathers are less likely to contribute to the care of a child who is not their own and, when married women were asked about the likelihood of abortion given uncertainty about who the father was, the probability rose to 0.57 in line with the figure for no supporting male. Fathers are not the only source of possible support. State aid may be meager, but it is better than nothing. In a study of teenage girls who made different choices about their pregnancy, the provision of state aid decreased the abortion rate to 42 percent compared to 71 percent among those without such aid (Leibowitz, Eisen, & Chow, 1985).

A woman's own psychological resources are important too. Women suffering from psychological instability may lack the social, emotional, and physical resources not only to rear a child but also to retain a long-term male partner. In a comparison of women suffering from anxiety and depression with a non-clinical control group, the clinical group was less likely to have ever married (70 versus 94 percent) and far more likely to have divorced (87 versus 38 percent). These women had a 0.39 probability of abortion compared to 0.07 for the control women, although the two groups did not differ in their likelihood of ever having been pregnant or in the probability of miscarriage or stillbirth (Essock & McGuire, 1989).

Infanticide is an act that not only excites feelings of revulsion but one which at first sight seems wholly incompatible with evolutionary theory. Yet given the extreme time and resource commitment demanded of human mothers, we should expect infanticide to be a line of last resort when circumstances militate against continued investment. Although abortion has effectively removed the need for infanticide in many societies, in others it may be the only avenue for a woman who bears a child that she cannot support without severely compromising her existing children. In the United States, infanticide is mainly confined to young women who effectively deceive themselves (and others) into believing that they are not pregnant at all. After giving birth alone and in secret, the young woman disposes of the child and may even convince herself that she has done nothing wrong. Some believe that the child "belongs to them" and as such they have a right to decide upon its life or death without state interference. In other cases, the woman convinces herself that the child was stillborn and that she has not committed any offence (Pearson, 1998).

From the point of view of evolutionary theory, we would expect to see more frequent infanticide when the infant's health is so poor as to cause doubt that it can survive to reproductive age. Daly and Wilson (1988) consulted cross-cultural evidence from 60 societies around the world, noting in each case the reasons that were given to explain the use of infanticide. Twenty-one societies indicated that deformity at birth or serious perinatal illness would be grounds for infanticide. Fifty-six societies recognized infanticide as a response to the absence of male support for the child and economic hardship. Twins place an extra burden on the mother and on the available economic resources. Usually one rather than both of the twins are sacrificed and infanticide is less likely in societies where the mother can give up arduous work because she has female relatives or friends to help her. An infant that is born too soon after a previous birth is also more likely to be killed. The mother must decide between the older child's need for her milk and that of the new arrival—in line with evolutionary predictions, the favored child is the one in whom she has already invested most. If the child is the product of a clandestine extramarital affair, the chances of infanticide rise in line with the potential threat that the infant poses to the continued provisioning of older children by her husband. Contemporary data from Canada and France (Daly & Wilson, 1988) support the idea that infanticide is related to the mother's evaluation of her current economic and social situation as well as her future likelihood of giving birth.

From the woman's reproductive condition before the act of intercourse to her emotional attachment of her newly born infant, there are many points at which a less-than-optimal conception can be unconsciously or knowingly prevented or halted. Once the baby is accepted, the women commits herself to nearly two decades of care, protection, and concern—small wonder that such an investment is carefully made.

Women as heavy investors

Those mothers who were good carers and protectors had more surviving offspring and psychologists are beginning to understand how evolution has crafted a "maternal brain." This knowledge has come from studies measuring changes in the key neuromodulator oxytocin during pregnancy and beyond, and from imaging studies which show graphically the changes in the mother's brain that occur in the weeks after giving birth.

Oxytocin has received a lot of media attention and become popularly known as the "trust" hormone. Some enterprising, if misguided, companies have even tried to market it as a kind of scent. Despite its sudden rise to prominence, versions of oxytocin have been around for 700 million years and its homologues are present even in insects. Though its precise function varies across species, oxytocin in mammals has long been recognized as important in the birth process where it triggers the smooth-muscle uterine contractions needed for delivery. Doctors use a synthetic version, pitocin, to induce labor. It is also involved in the milk let-down reflex necessary for breastfeeding.

But oxytocin has psychological as well as bodily effects. The bodily effects occur because it acts as a hormone traveling through the bloodstream to reach many parts of the body. After being synthesized in the hypothalamus (the magnocellular neurons of the paraventricular and supraoptic nuclei), it travels to the pituitary gland where it is released into peripheral blood circulation. But oxytocin has another route taking it to many parts of the brain. This starts in a different part of the hypothalamus (the parvocellular neurons of the paraventricular nuclei) which projects to ancient "old brain" limbic sites (hippocampus, amygdala, striatum, hypothalamus, nucleus accumbens) and to the brain stem. In short, oxytocin looks like a good candidate for orchestrating mothering at a psychological as well as systemic level.

The early research that pursued this idea was on rodents (see Broad, Curley, & Keverne, 2006; Insel, 2000; Kendrick, 2000). In pregnancy, triggered by rising estrogen levels, oxytocin receptors are upregulated in the brain as well as the uterus. The vaginal stimulation of birth activates the hypothalamus to release oxytocin to many brain areas responsible for maternal behaviors such as nest building, pup retrieval, licking, crouching, and maternal aggression. A stunning experiment demonstrated just how powerfully oxytocin could affect mothering (Pedersen & Prange, 1979): when oxytocin was infused directly into the brains of virgin rats (who normally give pups a wide berth) they began to behave like mothers. And it worked the other way around too: if an oxytocin antagonist (a neurotransmitter that blocks oxytocin's access to its receptors and therefore renders it ineffective) is given to a new mother, it prevents the normal onset of maternal behavior (Insel, 2000).

In humans too, prenatal and postpartum oxytocin appears to enhance the mother's initial bond with her infant and reduce her stress levels (Neumann, 2008). We cannot see the chemicals inside a human brain, but we can use spinal taps to measure the contents of the cerebrospinal fluid in which the brain is bathed. During childbirth, these central levels of oxytocin rise and postpartum plasma levels are correlated with positive feelings and reduced anxiety (Takagi, Tanizawa, Otsuki, Haruta, & Yamaji, 1985). Immediately after birth and prior to their first feeding, infants massage the mother's breast causing oxytocin levels in her blood to rise and remain high during feeding (Matthiesen, Ransjö-Arvidson, Nissen, & Uvnäs-Moberg, 2001). Oxytocin lowers maternal stress and increases feelings of calmness. According to women's own reports, breastfeeding lowers subjective stress and negative mood states (Mezzacappa & Katkin, 2002). This is evident at a biological level too: lactation is associated with lowered activity in the stress response system (the hypothalamic–pituitary axis), visible in lower levels of cortisol and other stress hormones (Amico, Johnston, & Vagnucci, 1994).

Recently researchers have begun to examine the emotional and behavioral effects of oxytocin. In one study, researchers tracked oxytocin levels in women's blood during the first and third trimester of pregnancy, and then during the first postpartum month. A stronger attachment between the mother-to-be and her fetus was associated with a pattern of increasing oxytocin during pregnancy (Levine, Zagoory-Sharon, Feldman, & Weller, 2007). Higher oxytocin levels in early pregnancy and postpartum also predicted attentive mothering including more attachment-related thoughts, gaze at the infant, affectionate touch, and frequent infant checking (Feldman, Weller, Zagoory-Sharon, & Levine, 2007). Unlike rodents, human maternal behavior does not critically depend upon oxytocin: after all, high-quality infant care is given by adoptive mothers, by mothers whose babies have been carried by surrogates, and by other relatives and adult caretakers. But oxytocin does appear to play a supplementary role in enhancing bonding in the early weeks. What remains to be understood is where and how oxytocin is affecting the brain.

We can gain some ideas from neuroscientists who have trained their sights on motherhood. They use scanning techniques such as magnetic resonance imaging (MRI) to map the structure of the brain. (Lying in the scanner, the subject is surrounded by a giant magnet. This produces a magnetic field that aligns the protons of hydrogen atoms in the brain. They are then exposed to radio waves that cause the protons to spin out of alignment and, as they resume their previous position, they emit radio waves. These are used to construct an extremely detailed the image.) In one study, structural changes in the brain were assessed by examining mothers' gray matter volume (regions of the brain containing cell bodies and dendrites)—once when their babies were two to four weeks old and then again when they were three to four months old (Kim et al., 2010). Every brain area that they investigated showed a significant increase between the two testing times. The more the mother experienced positive thoughts about her baby, the greater the increase in volume of a cluster of midbrain regions including the hypothalamus, substantia nigra, and amygdala. Animal studies indicate that the hypothalamus is associated with maternal motivation (if it is lesioned, mothers have a higher risk of infanticide) and its enlargement is correlated with the amount of interaction between mother and offspring. The substantia nigra is part of the "wanting and liking" reward system of the brain associated with the neurotransmitter dopamine. These regions are particularly activated when mothers view a picture of their smiling infant (Strathearn, Li, Fonagy, & Montague, 2008). The amygdala is involved in consolidating emotional learning about the infant. Other brain areas showed enlargement too, especially those that process somatosensory information (the smell, feel, sound, and sight of the infant) and the prefrontal cortex (the executive function of the brain that plans and executes new behavioral repertoires). What is surprising is not that these areas are more active after giving birth, but that they show changes in structure: a new maternal brain is being built.

Other researchers have used functional MRI (fMRI) to investigate the specific activation of different brain regions in response to different baby-related stimuli. (fMRI works much like regular MRI but it exploits the fact that when an area of the brain becomes active, blood vessels dilate to attract fresh oxygenated blood. This causes a change in the magnetic field which the scanner reads as the blood oxygen level-dependent (BOLD) signal.) In one study, mothers and fathers were interviewed and scanned two to four weeks after the birth of their baby and again at 12–16 weeks (see Swain, Lorderbaum, Kose, & Strathearn, 2007). In the scanner, they heard their own infant's cry as well as that of a strange infant and a control noise. Mothers of very young infants showed selective increased activation to their own babies in the midbrain, basal ganglia, cingulate, amygdala, and insula. These latter areas are associated with emotional alarm, threat detection, and arousal; the former with obsessive–compulsive thinking. These effects were much less pronounced in the new fathers. By the time the baby was four months old, these "old brain" emotional regions had become less responsive and instead prefrontal cortical areas which modulate emotional reaction and organize planful behavior became more active. The new mothers seem to be shifting from an anxious emotional over-reaction to their infant's distress to a calmer more thoughtful behavioral response. Other researchers have used visual rather than auditory stimuli such as photographs of the infant and other unrelated babies (see Swain, Lorderbaum, Kose, & Strathearn, 2007). When viewing their own infants, mothers showed greater activity in dopaminergic brain reward areas; in the fusiform gyrus, a part of the brain dedicated to processing and discriminating faces; in the hippocampus, involved in episodic memories of events; and in areas of the brain that are sensitive to the neuromodulator oxytocin. This link between central oxytocin and brain activation is an important avenue for future research.

Neuroimaging studies are prizing open the doors to understanding the brain–mind nexus but at present they are far from definitive. Findings can vary depending on which stimuli are compared, and which brain regions are chosen for investigation. Because we are only beginning to identify the functions of different brain areas, interpreting the results of fMRI studies is still fraught with difficulties. For example, amygdala activation has been variously argued to reflect fear, threat detection, stimulus salience, or a range of positive and negative emotions. Locking region to function is made even more difficult by the fact that increased blood oxygen merely tells us that a region is engaged—but that region may be excitatory or inhibitory in its effects. For now, all we can safely say is that there are postpartum structural changes in the maternal brain and that mothers become uniquely attuned to their own infant's appearance, smell, and sound. Women may or may not have a maternal "instinct" that makes them want babies, but they do seem to have a maternal adaptation for caring for them. There is a considerable overlap between neural sites implicated in parental and romantic love—and oxytocin is involved in both. The new mother effectively "falls in love" with her baby: she focuses on it exclusively; has intrusive thoughts; idealizes it and worries obsessively about possible harm; is distressed when separated; checks on it frequently; and engages in soothing, repetitive rituals (Leckman et al., 2005). The transition to motherhood is a strange mixture of love and anxiety. The baby is "perfect" and yet helplessly dependent—creating alarm about anything that might harm it and prompting compulsive monitoring.

And a mother who tends and cares is vital because the juvenile period is "a great selection funnel into which many enter but from which few emerge" (Lancaster, 1989, p. 65). Among carnivores only about 10 percent of animals born survive to adulthood, that figure is about 25 percent for non-human primates. Among human hunter-gatherers, half of the babies born survive to reproductive age. A critical factor in ensuring their survival will be the mother's ability not just to defend and feed her offspring but to ensure her own survival too.

Without a mother, the life expectancy of infants is cut tragically short. As Mealey (2000a, p. 341) succinctly puts it, "Desertion by one's mother means almost certain death, whereas desertion by one's father generally means only a reduction of resources."

Animal behaviorists have observed the fate of orphaned primates in the wild. Jane Goodall (1986) followed the life of Flint who was born to an ageing female called Flo. He persisted with nursing until the age of five despite his mother's attempts to wean him and he refused to give way even when a younger sister, Flame, was born. When Flame died, Flint became even closer to his mother, sharing her nest at night in the trees. When he was eight years old, Flo died. Flint sat by his mother's body for hours and became increasingly inert and depressed over the next few days. Despite attempts by his older siblings to coax him into activity, he developed gastric enteritis and peritonitis and three weeks later he was dead. A systematic study of Japanese macaques (Hasegawa & Hiraiwa, 1980) followed the fate of a number of orphans. Seven out of nine who lost their mother in the first year of life died. The older orphans fared somewhat better. Of the 25 who lost their mother between one and five years of age, five disappeared or died.

For humans in the West, medical advances mean that maternal death during childhood is a rare tragedy. When it does happen, the existence of monogamy, relative affluence, and welfare provision mean that the father, other relatives, or the state will assume the role of caretaker. But in the environment of evolutionary adaptation in which humans evolved, such safety nets were not always present. We can gain some idea of the fate of motherless children by examining the ethnographic and historical record. Several studies have gathered data on child mortality following parental death in societies with little or no access to medical care. Some come from contemporary hunter-gatherer or farming societies, others use data from early Europe.

Examples of the first are studies in Paraguay and rural Gambia. When anthropologists first arrived to study them, the Ache of Paraguay were still forest-living, and on every occasion when a mother died in the first year of an infant's life, the child died also. Even at later ages, the best predictor of child mortality was maternal mortality—at all ages, motherless children were five times more likely to die than those whose mothers were alive and they were four and a half times more likely to be killed. Later when the Ache moved to a reservation, far fewer adult deaths occurred. However, of the four children who lost their mothers, two died before maturity while of the handful of fatherless children none died (Hill and Hurtado, 1996). In rural Gambia, Sear, Steele, McGregor, and Mace (2002) focused on parent and child mortality up to the age of five. The death of the father had virtually no effect on the likelihood of his child's survival but children who lost a mother were massively more at risk. If they were under the age of two, these children were between 11 and 13 times more likely to die than those whose mothers were alive. Ostfriesland is a north-west German coastal region. The births, marriages, and deaths of the citizens who lived there between 1668 and 1879 were recorded in church documents. Voland (1988) focused on 870 families in which the last born child either survived the death of one of its parents during the first year of life or was born alive after the father died. He examined how many went on to survive until their first and 15th birthday. One-quarter died in the first year and 45 percent died before the age of 15. In the first year of life, child mortality was twice as high when the mother died (33 percent) compared to the father (18 percent). Overall, 52 percent of motherless children failed to survive until 15 years of age compared to 38 percent of fatherless infants.

Sear and Mace (2008) brought together information on the effect of maternal death from 28 different populations. In every case, it was associated with higher levels of child mortality. As they note, "The consequences of losing a mother in very early life are catastrophic" (p. 5). If the mother dies during childbirth between 1 and 25 percent of infants survive. (This latter figure was from Bangladesh in the 1980s.) Up to 50 percent survive if her death occurs in the first year of life. Nevertheless, a mother's death increases the odds of her baby dying in infancy by a factor of six, in toddlerhood by a factor of four, and in childhood by a factor of two (see Pavard, Gagnon, Desjardins, & Heyer, 2005; Sear et al., 2002). A stunning fact that emerged from Sear and Mace's overview of studies was the small effect that fathers' deaths had on child mortality: in 68 percent of cases, a father's death had no impact on the survival chances of his child. In 32 percent of cases, it actually improved the child's odds of surviving. But we will return to this tantalizing riddle later.

So mothers matter most in the early years and it is not hard to see why. The Gambian toddlers who lost their mothers weighed significantly less than their peers. In our evolutionary past, a mother breastfed for up to four years and her infant's life literally depended upon her ability to sustain lactation. The mother's supply of breast milk was, and in many places still is, the best predictor of whether an infant lives or dies (Hrdy, 1999). To feed her baby, she required 600–700 additional calories every day creating a situation where she had to forage regularly and successfully to meet these basic needs, to say nothing of the extra calories required for carrying the growing baby who accompanied her on these expeditions. The composition of breast milk itself provides one of the strongest clues that she took her baby with her. Unlike the fat-rich solution of animals who leave their offspring when they forage for food, women's milk contains only 3–4 percent fat and is 88 percent water. To sustain an infant on such a weak mixture, the mother must have carried it with her and fed it for several minutes every hour during the day. At night, she may have fed the baby (or more likely the baby latched on to the nipple and fed itself) three or four times. Beastfeeding is a positive feedback system—the more milk the baby takes, the more production is stepped up. In this way, the baby effectively calls the shots, ensuring the correct amount of nutrients for its weight and growth.

Lactation carried benefits for both the mother and baby. For the mother, by suppressing ovulation, it ensured optimal birth spacing between children. Effective suppression depends upon many small feeds and those that take place during the night seem to be especially important. These trigger prolactin surges that are up to six times more intense than those that she experiences during the day and it is prolactin that is responsible for the suppression of ovulation. The three- to four-year gap between children in hunter-gatherer societies was doubtless a result of the mother's continual breastfeeding. With agriculture and more predictable food availability, mothers could grind grain and cook it to create an easily digestible food for infants which reduced the age of weaning to as early as six months. But this meant that mothers became pregnant again after shorter intervals and were placed in the evolutionary novel situation of caring for multiple dependent young at the same time. While we consider the low birth rate of Western populations as anomalous, Hrdy (1999) points out that 100,000 years ago, women produced as few as four children in a lifetime and this low birth rate seems to have been at the root of our very slow growth as a species. Anthropologists estimate that in the Pleistocene the human population was probably not more than about 100,000 people. It took 15,000 years for that population to double in size compared to our current doubling rate of 50 years (Hammel, 1996). The investment costs of children have always been high and it is a wise woman who judges her timing well.

For the baby, breast milk brought the advantages not just of perfectly tailored and digestible nutrients but a second survival boost—immunological protection (Cunningham, 1995). During pregnancy the fetus receives antibodies through the placenta from the mother. After the baby is born and before milk proper arrives, the mother produces colostrum, a thick cream-colored mixture that is rich in antibodies. By the fourth month of lactation, the baby receives as much as half a gram of antibodies each day. Because mother and infant are bonded together day and night by lactation, they are exposed to the same pathogens and the mother is able to supply exactly the antibodies that the baby needs. Mothers' milk is especially geared to attack antigens that cause dysentery and diarrhea, the most dangerous of potential infant killers.

For mother and baby, breastfeeding brought with it prolonged and pleasurable skin-to-skin contact. The infant's suckling stimulates the release of oxytocin in the mother, generating feelings of warmth and contentment that may be passed back through the milk to the infant (Hrdy, 1999). Both mother and child seem to be soothed by feeding and this sense of well-being may be as much to do with oxytocin as with the infant's full stomach and the mother's relief at dispatching the heavy load of milk she has accumulated. This special kind of relationship with the infant was exclusively reserved for mothers. Though males of some species deliver food to their young and some male birds produce crop milk (a mixture of partially digested food and mucous produced in the throat), males do not lactate. The female-specific nature of lactation with the massive demands it makes on energy and time was a natural consequence of a woman's certainty of genetic relatedness and the huge investment that she had already made in that baby.

First love

The bond between mother and infant is the primary social relationship (Fedigan, 1982) and it extends far beyond milk provision. This is as evident in chimpanzees as in humans. Like us, chimpanzees are slow to mature. They are weaned at the age of four or five, with the females reaching sexual maturity at 11 (though, because of adolescent sterility, the first pregnancy does not occur until about 13 years of age). The males may be able to produce sperm by the age of nine but are not sexually mature until about 14 years of age. Childhood then is long and is spent in an intimate relationship with the mother. Despite intense curiosity about the newborn shown by community members, the chimpanzee mother prevents any of them from touching the infant during the first six months of life. She provides milk and in later years she shares fruits, nuts, and honey freely with her offspring. She fishes for termites and dips for ants, showing the offspring how to create and use the tools they need for this. She protects them from the volatile temper of adult males and is constantly watchful when they are close by. A band of chimpanzees may be composed of between 15 and 80 individuals, but during waking hours they travel in smaller parties. Mothers usually travel alone with their offspring, coming together with the community at night to make their tree nests. During daylight hours, the mother seeks out areas that have sufficient food resources for herself and her infant, and this means that adult females spend relatively little time together compared to the males. The mother–infant bond is strong and is broken only when her adolescent daughter must emigrate from the group to seek mates among neighboring groups.

Observations of mother–infant interactions among chimpanzees show a three-phase development from infant dependence to juvenile autonomy (Marvin, 1997). In the first stage, lasting until about 10 months of age, the infant has poor locomotor and communication skills and is unresponsive to adult attempts to communicate. Because of this, the mother maintains very close proximity, suckles the infant frequently, and protects it from other troop members. This corresponds to the human age range from birth to about 15 months during which human infants are equally socially inept and mothers in all cultures perform the same tasks. In phase two, which for chimps extends from about six months to four years, the infant begins to eat solid food, becomes more adept at independent locomotion, masters communication skills to keep in contact with the mother over a longer range, and begins to communicate with other members of the troop. During this time, a secure attachment between the two becomes evident. The mother is used as a base for exploration. The infant leaves the mother occasionally for short excursions, it plays with other youngsters and practices communicative signals, it becomes responsible for reinstating contact with the mother (although she maintains close visual monitoring of the infant), and the two reunite immediately when danger is perceived. At last, in the juvenile phase, the mother has a new infant to care for and the youngster is independent of the mother in terms of feeding and locomotion. It possesses all the receptive and expressive communication skills required for integration into the social group. The juvenile travels with the mother but spends increasing time with other troop members and becomes more responsible for its own protection (though the mother may still intervene in an emergency).

This whole pattern shows strong parallels with human youngsters. John Bowlby (1969), in his explicitly ethological theory of human development, describes the human infant's emotional attachment to the mother, the use of the mother as a safe base from which to explore, and the child's internalization of a working model of the mother as a source of security in her absence. Human mothers and infants form close bonds from the beginning of the infant's life. Just 48 hours after birth, a mother can distinguish the cry of her own infant (Wiesenfeld & Klorman, 1978). Her baby reciprocates by distinguishing the sound of its mother's voice (Field, 1985) and the unique features of her face (Bushnell, Sai, & Mullin, 1989). During the first six months, mother and child engage in mutual imitation, smiling, and vocal turn-taking. Between two and four months, studies using forehead temperature change demonstrate a positive emotional reaction to the mother and a negative response to strangers (Mizukami, Kobayashi, Ishi, & Iwata, 1990). Between seven and 11 months, the infant is able to display behavioral evidence of this specific attachment by responding with distress to the disappearance of the mother (Schaffer & Emerson, 1964). For the majority of children, the mother is the principal attachment figure (Kotelchuck, 1976) and, when upset, children are far more likely to seek comfort from their mother than their father (Cohen & Campos, 1974).

Mothers take the primary responsibility for child care worldwide (Brown, 1991; Ember, 1981; Geary, 2000). In many hunter-gatherer societies, like the ones in which humans evolved, women provide the majority of the calories consumed and they share their food only with their family, unlike men who share meat from successful hunts throughout the group. Most of the food consumed comes from foraging expeditions undertaken by women, carrying their infant on their back, two or three times a week. The infant is in close proximity to the mother at almost all times—they sleep, eat, and travel together. Among the Kung San, noted for their egalitarian society, fathers provide less than 7 percent of child care (West & Konner, 1976). Aka fathers in the Central African Republic have been hailed as among the most paternally minded, holding their one- to four-month-old infants for 22 percent of the time when they are in camp. But this looks fairly modest when we note that, on a typical day, a father holds his infant for an average of 57 minutes—compared to his wife's 490 minutes (Hewlett, 1988). The greater involvement shown by the mother rather than the father is not limited to infants. Between the ages of three and six years of age, children spend between three and 10 times more time with their mother than with their father (Whiting & Whiting, 1975) and by the ages of four to 10 years, they are with their mother two to four times longer than with the father (Whiting & Edwards, 1988).

In the West, even in this liberal era, mothers do the majority of child care. This has been found in observational studies in the home when parents are visited at early evening—a time when many mothers have been at home all day and fathers have only just returned. Mothers perform routine caretaking chores (such as feeding and changing) between two and four times more often than fathers and spend up to twice as much time holding, touching, or playing with their child (Belsky, Gilstrap, & Rovine, 1984). At infant ages of one, three, and nine months, mothers more than fathers respond to the child, care for it, and offer stimulation and positive affection. As the authors of this study noted, "The only thing that men did more of than women was engage in personal leisure activity (i.e. read / watch television)!" (Belsky, Rovine, & Fish, 1989, p. 142).

This differential attention to children is not merely a function of the fact that mothers are more frequently in the home. In Israel, where children are cared for during the day in nurseries while both parents work, mothers are still far more frequently involved in child-care duties and spontaneous interaction with the child at the end of the day than fathers (Sagi, Lamb, Shoham, Duir, & Lewkowicz, 1985). Lamb, Frodi, Hwang, Frodi, and Steinberg (1982) took advantage of innovative Swedish legislation that allowed *either* parent to take nine months of paid leave after their child's birth in order to examine child-rearing under the most liberal of gender role conditions. The leave could be divided between the parents as they wished. The take-up of this opportunity was revealing. Between the introduction of the legislation in 1974 and data collection in 1979, less than 15 percent of fathers took leave and the majority of those that did took one month or less. Most fathers took this leave at the same time as their wife and the extent of their actual contribution to child care is hard to ascertain. The researchers originally identified 52 couples, half of whom planned to take paternal leave for one month (the "non-traditionals") and half of whom had no plans for paternal leave. At re-contact one year after the birth, only 17 of the original 26 "non-traditional" fathers had actually taken the month of leave. The researchers reclassified the families on this basis and analyzed observational data that they collected in the home. In both traditional and non-traditional families, mothers more often than fathers displayed affectionate behavior, vocalized, smiled, tended, held, disciplined, and soothed the infant.

Of all the factors that have contributed to the central importance of the mother over evolutionary time, perhaps the most critical is male reproductive strategy. Men's quest for novelty and variety in their sexual life increases their chances of both death and desertion, leaving the mother firmly holding the baby. In animal species, polygyny is associated with earlier death among males. In part, this results from the dangers of male–male competition and from the generalized risky behavior of young men. In England and Wales, the male-to-female ratio for deaths from external causes is at its most extreme at ages 15 to 24 years when it reaches nearly four to one (Office of Population Censuses and Surveys, 1995). However, even males who survive past their peak reproductive years still die earlier than do females and it is the mother who must shoulder the full burden of infant care. About 7 percent of children living in single parent homes in the United States do so as a result of the death of one parent (Weinraub & Gringlas, 1995).

But men's polygynous inclinations more often increase the likelihood of desertion than death. Even in officially monogamous societies, men seek more pre- and extra-marital affairs than women (Daly & Wilson, 1988; Fisher, 1993). Men's preference for youth and physical beauty in sexual partners means that as their wives age, younger women become increasingly attractive and divorce more likely. After divorce, men are more likely than women to select younger partners, to remarry, and to produce further children in their second marriages (Buckle, Gallup, & Rodd, 1996; Johanna, Forsberg, & Tullberg, 1995; Jokela, Rotkirch, Rickard, Pettay, & Lummaa, 2010; Kaar, Jokela, Merila, Helle, & Kojola, 1998). When divorce happens, the burden of parental care is almost always taken up by the mother—in no country do mothers abandon their children at the rate which fathers do (Geary, 2000). In the United States, custody is awarded to the mother in over 85 percent of cases (Furstenberg, Morgan, &

Allison, 1987). (When fathers remain the principal caretaker, it is usually the result of the mother's incompetence or desertion: it is rare for fathers to contest the custody of the child; Greif, 1985.) After divorce, only one in six fathers maintains regular contact with his child and about half of absent fathers fail to pay monetary support for their upkeep. Men do not always wait until after marriage to desert. In 2008, 41 percent of births in the United States and 44 percent in the United Kingdom were to unmarried women (Center for Disease Control and Prevention, n.d.). About one-third of these births were to lone women, while the remainder were to cohabiting couples. It is estimated that 43 percent of cohabiting parents (compared to 8 percent of married parents) will separate before their child's fifth birthday (Kiernan, 1999). Sometimes men choose to desert and sometimes they are pushed because they can make no meaningful financial or emotional contribution to the household. Either way, the fact remains that unmarried fathers who seek custody of their children are rare in comparison to the number of men being pursued by government agencies to provide financial support for their abandoned children. Twenty-six percent of children in the United States live in a single-parent home. Nationally, about 12 percent of American households are female-headed, a figure that pales into insignificance compared to figures from Belarus (54 percent), Eritrea (48 percent), and Haiti (44 percent). Rates of female-headed households are a proxy for a nation's poverty but, at an individual level, they are a testament to a mother's commitments to her children through the worst of times.

For all these reasons, nature has crafted a special emotional attachment between mother and child that functions to increase the chance of an infant achieving independence, adulthood, and reproduction. Fathers contribute in their own way to a child's safety and provisioning—although, because good fathers tend to marry good mothers, some of the apparent advantages accrued by their children may have as much to do with his wise choice of mate than with his direct contribution to parenting (Amato, 1998; Geary, 2000). Mothers know that a good partner is worth having. But through our evolutionary past from an infant's viewpoint, mothers have always been essential while fathers have been an optional extra.

Pursuing half the point

Sexual selection is at the very core of Darwinian theory. The difference between men and women in their parental investment was the key that opened the research doors to the study of human reproductive psychology (and academics poured through them). The reproductive task can be broken into two stages and two kinds of problems: finding the right mate and raising offspring to maturity. Males direct a greater part of their energy to the former, females to the latter.

The study of mating drew far more research attention than the study of parenting. It is tempting to think that this was the result of the predominance of male researchers whose interest was understandably in their own sex. But it was also something to do with the way that sexual selection was defined, predominantly by male researchers (Campbell, 2009). They focused on competition for mating opportunities using a definition that Darwin employed in his earlier work: "the struggle between males for possession of the females." This is a more restricted definition than Darwin used later with its focus on differential reproduction: "the advantage which certain individuals have over others of the same sex and species, solely in respect of reproduction." Reproduction is a much bigger concept than copulation—it includes birth and parenting and so accords a much more critical role to women. As (Hrdy 1999, p. 81, original emphasis in italics) puts it so aptly, "Unless mating results in the production of offspring *who themselves survive infancy and the juvenile years and position themselves so as to reproduce*, sex is only so much sound and undulation signifying nothing." Raising offspring is as critical to reproductive success (if not more so) as sexual athleticism. Yet women's capacity to perform this feat—lasting over years, costing them dearly, constraining their own life choices, shaping the next generation—was taken as unremarkable. While studies of mate preferences loomed large in evolutionary psychology research, decisions about birth spacing, breastfeeding, weaning, and alloparenting took a back seat. Until the arrival of Sarah Hrdy's exceptional book *Mother Nature*, mothering was taken for granted as a straightforward and unproblematic exercise. Hrdy (1999, p. 69) was forced to underline again and again the critical importance of the mother:

> For species such as primates, the mother *is* the environment, or at least the most important feature in it during the most perilous phase of any individual's existence. Her luck plus how well she copes with her world—its scarcities, its predators, its pathogens, along with her conspecifics in it—are what determine whether or not a fertilization ever counts.

I think that an important reason for this neglect derived from the way parental investment was portrayed. Females, with their heavy parental investment, were the prizes for which swaggering males competed. The image is irresistible—a female sits on the sidelines, passively awaiting the arrival of a male who, by demonstrating his dominance over his rivals, has won the undisputed right to her reproductive favors. It was male competition—risky, desperate, and tinged with sexual anticipation—that became the attention-grabber. The long hard road that lay ahead for the female—mundane, time-consuming, repetitive—seemed so much less exciting. And the focus on male winners and losers informed a belief that women, and the mothering that they did, was all much of a muchness. There was little to choose between women either in the strategies they used, or the quality and quantity of children that resulted. The number of offspring that a male could sire ranged from a stunning zenith in the hundreds to a catastrophic zero. Males were brilliant success stories or dismal failures, while women took a moderate middle road steadily producing as many offspring as their circumstances would allow. A female's life was portrayed as a predictable cycle: enter estrous, copulate, get pregnant, lactate, and begin again. If this were true, there would be no variability in female reproductive success and so little of interest to discover about differences between females in their choices and strategies. And if there were no differences between women in their reproductive output, there could be no selection and no adaptation. The driving force of evolution would be *men's* success or failure: women were relegated to the role of convenient sperm receptacles and breeding machines. Females' contribution to evolution in this scenario could only be as choosers of male gene quality.

But we now know there is considerable variability between females in their ability not just to produce children but to raise them. The variance may not be as great as between males but that is irrelevant because *females are not in competition with males, they are in competition with other females*. If you die leaving six grown children behind and I leave one, you leave six times as many of your genes in the next generation as I do. Women were choosy investors alright, but to opt out of the competition altogether was no more an adaptive option for a female than it was for a male. The difference was that females were forced to carry out their competition in a much less overt way (for reasons I will discuss later). So it was the dramatic life-or-death quality of male competition that grabbed researchers' attention. Risk taking and bravado were the routes to the winner's podium where males strove to secure the glittering prize of reproductive success.

But, paradoxically, the preoccupation with male competition obscures a critical fact—males compete so ferociously because their lives are *less* important than females in the reproductive process. Males may seem to be the stars of the show, but we should bear in mind that they are essentially freeloading on females' efforts. Consider this: If we knew our planet was about to be struck by a meteor and only 100 people could be saved in an underground bunker, what proportion of men and women would you put down there? My suggestion would be about 10 men and 90 women. Ten should be able to do an adequate job of impregnating all the women and the fewer the men, the fewer the calories they would consume and the lower the competition between them would be. But imagine if we had made the opposite choice—90 men and 10 women. What kind of hope would we have for the future of the human race? The fact is that the majority of men are, biologically-speaking, dispensable but when the number of women drops, our future looks bleak. In the real world, the sex ratio remains roughly equal and as long ago as 1930, Fisher explained why. When there are too few males, the lower intensity of same-sex competition means that any boy that gets born does very well indeed, reproductively speaking. Genes that bias toward son production rather than daughter production will start to spread. But as the sex ratio reaches equality, the reproductive advantages of producing sons begin to diminish. The same logic holds when there are too few females. Eventually the sex ratio stabilizes at a near equal number of sons and daughters. But in some species extraordinary sex ratios can occur and when they do, it comes as no surprise that they are female heavy. In some insects, there are 20 females born for every one male (Hamilton, 1964).

In Chapter 3 I will try to convince you that men's greater willingness to take life-threatening risks is a testament not just to the reproductive gulf between male winners and losers but to men's smaller contribution to parental investment. Men hold their lives less tightly in their hands because they have been more marginal than women in ensuring the successful survival of their offspring.

Chapter 3

High stakes and low risks: Women and aggression

The proposition that men are more aggressive than women is hardly a contentious one. A glance at criminal statistics from any nation in the world confirms that men are more likely to engage in criminal violence. Ninety percent of criminal violence on our planet is committed by men (Kruttschnitt, 1994; Simon & Baxter, 1989). But this is the visible and extreme end of aggression. Do these sex differences trickle down to more mundane aggressive episodes? Many hundreds of psychological studies have examined sex differences in aggression using a range of techniques including laboratory experiments, observation, personality assessment, and self- and peer-reported behavior. The results have been summarized using a technique called meta-analysis that determines just how big the sex differences are when they are weighted and averaged across many studies. The results fit a clear pattern. The more dangerous and risky the form of aggression studied, the larger the sex difference (Archer, 2009; Campbell, 2006). For physical acts such as hitting, punching, and kicking the effect size is large: up to 82 percent of men are more aggressive than the average woman. For verbal acts such as abuse and threats, the effect size is somewhat more moderate: 70 percent of men are more verbally aggressive than the average woman (Archer, 2004; Eagly & Steffen, 1986; Knight, Fabes, & Higgins, 1996; Knight, Guthrie, Page & Fabes, 2002). Acts of indirect aggression include spreading nasty rumors, excluding people, and stigmatizing them. Because the aggressor can remain anonymous and the possibility of retaliation is consequently reduced, these acts are much less dangerous and here the sex difference virtually disappears (Archer, 2004).

The traditional question has been: Why are men so willing to risk their lives in violent confrontations? A convincing account was provided by Daly and Wilson (1983) and rests on men's polygynous mating strategy. The desire to mate with multiple females causes intense male competition. The operational sex ratio (the number of reproductively available members of each sex) is always skewed toward too many men because when women are pregnant or lactating they are effectively removed from the pool of prospective mates. If 10 percent of men have a monopoly on 50 percent of the available female population, other men are faced with the possibility of going to their graves childless unless they fight for their share of reproductive opportunity. So men have been pitted against one another to win a larger share of the next generation's gene pool than their rivals and the route to that prize was to compete for as many mating opportunities as possible. The disparity between male winners and losers is great. Men who win, win very big. Those who lose, leave no descendants whatsoever. To put it more technically, the variance in reproductive success among men is greater than that among women. Emperor Moulay Ismail's 888 children outstrip the women champion's total of 69 by a considerable margin. Even today under official monogamy, the disparity between the sexes in reproductive success continues: the variance in the number of children produced is 10 percent higher in men than women because, after divorce, they more often marry younger spouses, a strategy of serial polygyny. Men with three wives during their lifetime have 19 percent more children than those who stayed with one, but additional husbands make no difference to women's output of children (Jokela, Rotkirch, Rickard, Pettay, & Lummaa, 2010). Bigger prizes warrant greater risks. Males engage in risky physical aggression because the possible reproductive returns offset the risks.

Remember that we are not speaking of men consciously and deliberately vying with each other to inseminate women. Male sexual competitiveness was forged long before the advent of our species because aggressive males left behind a bigger share of their genes than their more restrained peers. In primate species, including our own, male competitiveness does not always appear to be about females (although a remarkable number of assaults between men are directly connected with romantic triangles) but they are about achieving dominance over other males, which is associated with greater reproductive success. In these days of contraception, some people find this whole notion preposterous. Victors of Saturday night brawls, even when those fights are about women, rarely have impregnation in mind. Contraception has effectively severed the link between sex and reproduction. The fact that we have welcomed contraception so warmly is evidence that human reproductive success was a product of our enthusiasm for making love, not for making babies. As long as sex naturally led to pregnancy, selection only needed to ensure a keen interest in sex. Effective and easily available contraception has been with us for barely a century and this is insufficient time to upset several hundred thousand years of evolutionary pressure. The fact that men desire women (and lots of them) and are willing to fight for them is part of male evolved psychology.

With mating opportunities center stage, it seemed that women had little reason to compete. If they wanted sex, men would be only too happy to accommodate them. As Symons (1979) rather tersely put it, "I trust no one believes that women compete for opportunities to copulate." Because of men's sexual eagerness, women were assumed to breed at their maximum rate (Daly & Wilson, 1983). If so, there should be virtually no variance in female reproductive success. But we now know that this is incorrect (Stockley & Bro-Jorgensen, 2011). Females vary in their ultimate reproductive success because some are better than others at the twin challenges of motherhood: feeding their children and protecting them from danger. You and I are here today because we came from a long line of successful mothers. And, when resources are scarce, motherhood means competition. But the intensity of that competition is constrained because, as we saw in Chapter 2, mothers are so vital to the survival of their progeny. Raising offspring to maturity means avoiding injury and death. So female competition does not look the same as men's, a fact presciently noted by primatologist Sarah Hrdy over 30 years ago:

> Women are no less competitive than other primates, and the evidence will be forthcoming when we begin to devise methodologies sufficiently ingenious to measure it. Efforts to date have sought to find "lines of authority" and hierarchies comparable to those males form in corporations. No scientist has yet trained a systematic eye on women competing with one another in the spheres that really matter to them. The difficulty is not simply narrowness of vision and the mistaken assumption that female competition will take the same form as competition between males, but also the subtlety of interactions between females. . . . How do you attach a number to calumny? How do you measure the sweetly worded put-down? (Hrdy, 1981, pp. 129–130)

In this chapter, I will turn the traditional evolutionary question on its head. My question is not why men compete so ferociously, but why women don't. Women do not lack the motivation to compete—they need resources as much as men and more so when they have dependent offspring. But the extreme dependence of infants on their mothers meant that ancestral women who avoided exposing themselves to injury or death raised more surviving offspring. The evolutionary message to women was clear: at all costs, stay alive.

The aggression equation

Darwin, as did Malthus before him, observed that in nature there are rarely enough resources to go round. Food, mates, shelter, and safety are needed by every organism and when they are in short supply, competition ensues. This is, of course, the basic tenet of natural selection. Competition can take two forms depending on where and how the resources are distributed in time and space. Resources that are spread out over a spatial area give rise to scramble competition because they cannot be defended by a single individual. For example, if a group of individuals fish in a single lake then a declining stock affects everyone and each person can only scramble to get what they can. In other cases, there is contest competition when the resource can be held and defended by a single individual or group. The winner drives off the competitors and takes the prize for themselves. Aggression is a form of intense contest competition. It is about gaining and defending a resource. Psychologists often distinguish between proactive and reactive aggression. Proactive aggression (sometimes known as instrumental aggression) is a means to securing some extraneous goal or resource. Reactive aggression (sometimes known as hostile, angry, or defensive aggression) is responsive to the takeover bids of others. From an evolutionary perspective, these are two sides of the same coin. If you have a resource that I want, then I will use proactive aggression to take it from you. You, most probably, will respond to this by using reactive aggression to hang on to it. In either case, it is about who controls the valued resource.

Aggression is a tactic best used sparingly. It is risky and potentially fatal. In the animal kingdom, deaths from contest competition are rare although not unknown. This is because, although both parties have something to gain (a resource), they also have something to lose (their life). For this reason, in many species contests have a ritualized form that reduces injury. Unlike predatory aggression which is designed to kill a prey with maximum efficiency, intraspecific contests often involve a warning period in which contestants size each other up, allowing time for one to back off if their odds look poor. Even in a full-blown fight, attacks are often directed to robust parts of the anatomy such as the flanks. The aim is to establish dominance and cause the opponent to withdraw, rather than to kill them. But the dangers of sustaining injury and occasionally death, are real. What kind of mental mechanism has evolution crafted to govern the decision as to when a fight is worth it? And how does this explain sex differences in aggression?

The rewards and costs of aggression (and other forms of risky behavior) differ for males and females. In net terms, aggression is more beneficial for males than females because male reproductive success can be increased by dominating same-sex rivals and gaining additional copulations. Women, with their higher burden of infant dependence, can increase their reproductive success by staying alive and protecting their young. But reproductive success is the distal cause of aggression, responding at a macro level over hundreds of generations of selection pressures. Psychologists are interested in the ways that these long-haul sexual selection pressures are realized in the brain—the proximal causes of aggression. Feelings run high in aggressive encounters and this suggests that its evolutionary roots are likely to be buried deep in lower-level brain structures governing emotion. We share these ancient neural structures with other species. In humans, they form the evolutionary bedrock with which our higher cortical processes interact in guiding our behavior. Yet for many years, economists and psychologists who studied risky decision-making (including aggression) did so in terms of expected utility theory stressing its cold cognitive basis. Human rationality, they assumed, made us different from other species. Our decisions resulted from an expectation-based calculus, which researchers modeled in algebraic terms. Prospective rewards and costs were anticipated and suitably weighted by their probability to arrive at an objective judgment. *Homo economicus*, a Spock-like fiction, dominated research obscuring until recently the role of emotion in decision-making (see Loewenstein, Weber, Hsee, & Welch, 2001). Rewards and costs are not conscious entries into a cognitive balance sheet: they are instantiated at a deep emotional level that we share with other species. Emotions, evolved over hundreds of thousands of years, act as "whisperings within" that guide our action (Barash, 1981). Emotions are designed to help people make approach–avoidance distinctions and these lie at the heart of aggressive behavior. What emotions might feed into this evolved decision-making calculator?

On the one hand, anger acts as an impelling motivation, spurring us forward with righteous indignation. ("How dare she?" "Who does she think she is?"). The emotion of anger is the accelerator pedal for aggression. On the other hand, fear holds us back ("She looks mean." "She's massive."). The emotion of fear acts as a braking mechanism. So the probability of aggression depends on the relative strength of anger and fear. Aggression = anger–fear. In situations of threat, anger and fear can and do co-occur. In some situations, the scales are tipped strongly in favor of anger so that fear barely registers as an emotion. In other situations, despite our fury, fear overpowers us and we retreat. Men and women are capable of experiencing both emotions but the relative balance between them is tipped more strongly in favor of overt aggression in men. Is this because men experience greater anger? The sex difference might be mediated by men's stronger anger, part of an approach system resulting from their sex's intense competition for mating opportunities which selected those most willing to enter the aggression arena. Or is it because women experience greater fear, an avoidance motivation resulting from greater offspring dependence and the crucial importance of maternal survival? A difference in the threshold for experiencing one or both of these emotions might explain the sex difference in aggression.

Anger

Anger is a universal emotion. It is recognized in all cultures and is visible very early in life. We see facial anger in primates also. But what is the evolutionary function of anger? It signals what psychologists call goal blockage: someone or something impedes our ability to achieve or maintain some desired goal. That goal may be to keep our self-respect ("How dare she treat me like that?") or our resources ("She stole my boyfriend."). When the goal is sheer survival and safety, we get even angrier ("She punched me."). The important thing is that it triggers approach motivation—it drives us forward to take action.

This may not surprise you, but it certainly surprised many non-evolutionary minded psychologists. The study of emotion was for many years dominated by the "valence" approach. The spectrum of human emotions was split in two according to the pleasantness or unpleasantness of the experience (e.g., Forgas, 1995). According to this view, emotions such as sadness and guilt are "negative" emotions that we dislike; while others, such as happiness and serenity, are "positive" emotions that we enjoy. But for an evolutionist, this makes no sense. Natural selection is driven by functionality, not by our emotional preferences. The route to understanding emotions is not through their valence—whether hedonic (pleasant or unpleasant) or moral (right or wrong)—but through the behaviors that they motivate. Emotions evolved to provide speedy and efficient guidance about how to react to events, and evolution is quite indifferent as to whether we happen to like the experiential information we receive. For example, disgust warns us to avoid a stimulus and serves to put distance between us and pathogen-carrying substances such as decaying meat or human feces. Pain tells us about bodily injury or malfunction, ensuring that we reduce our mobility and divert our energy resources to healing and immune system activity. Disgust and pain may be "unpleasant" experiences but they do their job very effectively. According to the old valence view, positive emotions were associated with approach motivation and negative emotions with avoidance motivation (Davidson, 2000; Lang, Bradley, & Cuthbert, 1992; Watson, Wiese, Vaidya, & Tellegen, 1999). Because anger is experienced as unpleasant, it should be associated with avoidance. Yet there is much evidence that this is not the case (Carver & Harmon-Jones, 2009). To persuade you of this, we need to make a brief excursion into the two hemispheres of our brain.

Over 70 years ago, psychologists noticed that patients who had received damage to their frontal lobes (sadly a relatively frequent event because car accidents often propel passengers head first through the windscreen) showed different moods depending on whether their right or left hemispheres had sustained the damage (Goldstein, 1939). Later this finding was followed up by experimental work (e.g., Alema, Rosadini, & Rossi, 1961) in which the barbiturate drug amytal, which suppresses brain activity, was infused into one hemisphere or the other. Injecting amytal into the left hemisphere—so that only the right hemisphere is fully functional—produced feelings of depression and withdrawal. Knocking out the right hemisphere, so that the left remains functional, produced feelings of euphoria and engagement. These experiments were confirmed by more systematic studies of patients with lesions to the two hemispheres. Left hemisphere damage causes depressive symptoms associated with avoidance, while right hemisphere damage produces a manic approach tendency. The same pattern occurs in primates too (Hopkins, Bennett, Bales, Lee, & Ward, 1993). In humans, this hemispheric lateralization is seen most clearly in the prefrontal cortex, located immediately behind the eyes. We can access electrical activity in this area fairly easily with electroencephalography (EEG) by using electrodes placed on the scalp. People are presented with stimuli designed to trigger approach (such as delicious food) and avoidance (such as diseased bodies). Over 70 studies show that approach is associated with greater left-side frontal activity and avoidance with greater right-side activity (Coan & Allen, 2004). Even infants at a few days old show more left-side activity when given a drink of sucrose rather than water (Fox & Davidson, 1986).

Now, being critical, it could be argued that what we are seeing here is not the brain indicating whether we should approach or avoid something but simply responding to pleasant or unpleasant emotions. And that is why anger is such an interesting emotion. The valence camp suggest that it is an unpleasant emotion and should activate the right hemisphere but the functionality camp believe that it signals approach motivation and so should activate the left hemisphere. The results are clear—anger is an approach motivation (for reviews see Carver & Harmon-Jones, 2009; Harmon-Jones, Gable, & Peterson, 2010; Murphy, Nimmo-Smith, & Lawrence, 2003). For example, Harmon-Jones and Sigelman (2001) brought participants into the lab and, after taking baseline EEG measures, asked them to write an essay about a current events issue. The essay was ostensibly evaluated by a second unseen undergraduate participant. Some received provocative feedback giving very low ratings to the essay's quality and adding a gratuitously insulting comment ("I can't believe an educated person would think like this. I hope this person learns something while at the University of Wisconsin"). People in the control condition received good ratings and the comment "I can understand why a person would think like this." After this, EEG readings were taken again. The participant was then allowed to respond to their critic. The experimenter asked the participant to make up a drink for the second student as part of an experiment on taste in which they were told it was important for the experimenter themselves remained "blind" to the taste condition. They were asked to dilute some water with another substance which they could choose from a group including sugar, apple juice, lemon juice, salt, vinegar, or hot sauce. These options form a nice scale running from pleasant to unpleasant, and so constitute a measure of the participant's aggression toward their critic. The insulted participants showed greater left frontal activity than the control group. Within the group of insulted participants, the strength of left hemisphere activation correlated positively with how angry they reported themselves to feel and with the unpleasantness of the drink they concocted.

Evidence that anger is approach motivated comes from other types of study too. Transcranial magnetic stimulation (TMS) is a way of changing the polarization of neurons in certain areas of the brain. Slow repetitive pulses can reduce brain activity so when repetitive TMS is applied to the right hemisphere, the left hemisphere increases its activity. When this is done, participants show increased attention to pictures of angry faces (d'Alfonso, van Honk, Hermans, Postma, & de Haan, 2000). There are other less intrusive ways to increase left-brain activity. A simple way of producing hemispheric differences in activation is to make a fist with one hand: contracting your right hand increases left hemisphere activity. Those participants whose left brain was made more active (by squeezing their right hand) gave longer and louder punitive sound blasts to another participant who had previously insulted them (Peterson, Shackman, & Harmon-Jones, 2008). Beyond the laboratory, anger correlates positively with psychometric scales measuring a person's approach motivation and negatively with their avoidance motivation (Harmon-Jones, 2003; Smits & Kuppens, 2005). At a physiological level, anger increases muscle tension, heart rate, blood pressure, muscular blood flow, and body temperature. These are the familiar components of sympathetic nervous system activity preparing us for exertion and combat.

So, do men simply get angrier than women? There are different data source we can consult but they all converge on the same answer: no. Some information comes from the study of anger as a personality trait which is measured by paper-and-pencil multi-item tests. Respondents rate their agreement with statements that describe a general tendency to experience anger such as "Sometimes people bother me just by being around." Archer (2004) brought together 46 of these studies in a meta-analysis and the results were clear. There was no sex difference at all (see also Kring, 2000). Perhaps men experience anger more frequently? Some studies find that there are no sex differences in frequency (Brebner, 2003; Simon & Nath, 2004) with both sexes experiencing anger about six times a week (Frost & Averill, 1982). Others find that women experience anger more often than men (Mirowsky & Ross, 1995; Ross & Van Willigen,

1996). Perhaps then, men's anger is more intense? Experimental studies, which elicit anger through the presentation of film clips or slides, do not generally find sex differences in reported anger intensity (Kring & Gordon, 1998; Wagner, Buck, & Winterbotham, 1993). Experiments that elicit descriptions of hypothetical or remembered emotional reactions to provocation also find few overall sex differences in anger intensity (Manstead & Fisher, 1995; Milovchevich, Howells, Drew, & Day, 2001) and, where they do appear, they favor women (Brody, Lovas, & Hay, 1995; Fischer & Evers, 2011; Harris, 1994). International surveys also find no sex difference (Brebner, 2003; Fischer, Mosquera, van Vianen, & Manstead, 2004). Where a sex difference is found, it is women's anger that is more intense (Brebner, 2003 (Australian sample); Simon & Nath, 2004). So, if anger is not the source of sex differences in aggression, could it be that the sexes differ in their braking mechanism—fear?

Fear

Like anger, fear is a fundamental emotion that we share with other species. Joseph LeDoux (1998, p. 128), who has spent his life studying the fear response, encapsulates its function perfectly, "Fear is designed to detect danger and produce responses that maximize the probability of surviving." His studies on the architecture of the fear circuitry reveal the critical role of speed in getting us safely away from threats. When danger presents itself, the information is dual tracked to key brain areas. The "fast" route takes the crude sensory information that has arrived at the thalamus from the eyes and ears, and delivers it within 50 milliseconds to the amygdala, a small almond-shaped structure buried deep in the temporal lobe. Once activated, the amygdala's connections to a variety of other brain structures cause increases in heart rate, blood pressure, respiration, vigilance, cortisol secretion, and cortical arousal. Behaviorally, it triggers freezing and withdrawal in order to stop forward motion and pull the organism away from immediate danger. While this is happening, a second "slower" system delivers more detailed information to the amygdala from the sensory cortex. This allows a more finely discriminated recognition of just what this threat is. The amygdala communicates with the frontal lobe that sends back commands for behavioral and physiological adjustments that may correct the initial "automatic" response.

The whole process is a marvel of evolutionary engineering. Imagine this: You are sitting watching a late night film on television, absorbed in the plot. Someone tries the front door handle. Even as you hear it, you freeze—your heart speeds up, your breathing quietens, your senses are on massive alert and highly sensitized. A split second later, your frontal lobes integrate more information:

Your hippocampus sends memory information that your husband was out and should be returning about now. Your senses catch the sound of a key—burglars don't have keys. Panic over. You can breathe again and your heart rate returns to normal. This kind of apparent over-reaction may be physiologically wasteful, but the fear system works on the fire alarm principle: better too many false positives (threats that turn out to be harmless) than a single false negative (an undetected threat that kills you).

I have highlighted the fact that, for good evolutionary reasons, fear is an avoidance motivation. The evidence on brain lateralization confirms this. People who normally have higher right hemisphere activation report stronger negative responses to fear-inducing films, as well as other avoidance-motivated emotions such as disgust (see Harmon-Jones, Gable, & Peterson, 2010). Using TMS to increase right frontal activity causes participants to avoid pictures of angry faces which they had found engaging when their left hemisphere was activated (d'Alfonso, van Honk, Hermans, Postma, & de Haan, 2000). Individuals who are high in avoidance motivation show a stronger EEG response in the right hemisphere when viewing negative stimuli (Peterson, Gable, & Harmon-Jones, 2008).

But is there evidence that the sexes differ in the frequency or intensity of fear? If women's reproductive success depends on their own survival, we would expect that they would have highly sensitized fear reactions. And it appears that they do. In infancy, girls express fear earlier than boys (Nagy et al., 2001). They show more hesitation in approaching novel objects and greater distress (Gartstein & Rothbart, 2003; Martin, Wisenbaker, Baker, & Huttunen, 1997; Rothbart, 1988). Around the world, parents report that boys show stronger approach behavior than girls (Carey & McDevitt, 1978; Hsu, Soong, Stigler, Hong, & Liang, 1981; Maziade, Boudreault, Thivierge, Caperaa, & Cote, 1984). Sex differences increase through childhood (Fredrikson, Annas, & Fischer, 1996). A Canadian study plotted developmental changes in personality identifying one group of children that showed a profile of high and increasing fearfulness: the group was dominated by girls (Cote, Tremblay, Nagin, Zoccolillo, and Vitaro, 2002).

Among adults too, women experience fear more intensely than men (Brody & Hall, 1993; Crawford, Kippax, Onyx, Gault, & Benton, 1992; Fischer, 1993; Gullone, 2000; McLean & Anderson, 2009). International surveys have found significant sex differences in the intensity and duration of fear (Brebner, 2003; Fischer & Manstead, 2000). Women express their fear more intensely than men, both verbally and non-verbally (see Madden, Feldman Barrett, & Pietromonaco, 2000). While women are superior to men in accurately identifying all emotions, they show the greatest accuracy of all for decoding fear (Hall, Carter,

& Horgan, 2000). One of the five key personality factors is anxiety or neuroticism: women exceed men on this trait across the world (Costa, Terracciano, & McCrae, 2001; Feingold, 1994).

Fear has been taken into the laboratory in experiments that exploit the potentiated startle response. The paradigm goes like this: Participants watch slides that elicit different emotions, including fear. As they watch, a sudden blast of noise is delivered. This causes an automatic startle reaction (a marked eye blink) which is more pronounced when the participant is viewing a negative, fear-inducing image. (Much like in the cinema when a sudden gunshot or ghostly apparition is more frightening when the mood is tense than when it is more relaxed.) The startle reaction can be detected by electrodes placed near the eyes, and other electrodes record negative facial expressions in the corrugators muscle (the muscles between your eyes that contract when you frown). Women and girls show more corrugators muscle activity than men when watching negative images and a stronger blink response to the noise blast delivered during the fear-inducing pictures. They also show greater sweating on the palm, indicating higher anxiety (Bradley, Cuthbert & Lang, 1999; McManis, Bradley, Berg, Cuthbert, & Lang, 2001).

A phobia is a marked and persistent fear of specific objects or situations which the sufferer recognizes to be excessive or unreasonable. The Fear Survey Schedule, designed to measure this sensitivity to phobic objects, shows that females score higher than males (Arrindell, Kolk, Pickersgill, & Hageman, 1993; Gullone & King, 1993). To rule out the possibility that this was caused by factors such as gender role conformity or differential willingness to admit to fear, these were measured and their effect statistically removed from the analysis (Arrindell et al., 1993; Arrindell, Mulkens, Kok, & Vollenbroek, 1999). Sex still remained a strong predictor with women scoring higher than men on each of the five types of fear (social; agoraphobic; bodily injury, death, and illness; sexual and aggressive scenes; and harmless animals).

The fact that sex differences in fear have a fundamental biological basis and are not simply the result of the way we socialize boys and girls has recently received further support from studies of testosterone. In a series of innovative experiments, testosterone was orally administered to women. Neither the woman nor the experimenter knew whether she had received testosterone or the inert placebo solution. Following this, the women were tested for alterations to their fear threshold. To examine whether testosterone would make women less attentive to threat, the experimenters used a task called the emotional Stroop test (Van Honk, Peper, & Schutter, 2005). A series of faces is presented on a monitor, each with different facial expressions (neutral, happy, and fearful). The exposure time is so brief that participants are not consciously aware that they have seen anything at all. Each photo is colored to appear red, green, or blue. The participant's task is to name the color of the photo. Psychologists have established that the more strongly our attention is engaged by a picture, the longer it takes us to name the color. So, as expected, these researchers found that participants were faster in identifying the color of the neutral faces. When exposed to fearful faces (but not happy ones), women who received testosterone were much faster at color naming, indicating that they were less emotionally engaged and threatened than the placebo group. To follow this up, another study used a version of the potentiated startle paradigm described earlier. Participants were periodically startled by white noise delivered through headphones and their eye blink response was measured (Hermans, Putman, Baas, Koppeschaar, & van Honk, 2006). At the start of the experiment, electrodes were attached to their wrists and they were told that they would receive electric shocks. They would receive three electric shocks of increasing intensity but they would never be shocked when the word "Safe" was visible on the monitor screen. (In fact, only one shock was actually delivered.) Over the next trials, the experimenters measured their eye blink reaction to white noise blasts, both when "Safe" was on the screen and when it said "Danger." They expected that the "Danger" signal would potentiate the startle response—and it did. Eye blink responses to noise blasts presented when "Danger" was signaled were much stronger than when participants believed they were "Safe." But when women had taken testosterone, their eye blink reaction was significantly reduced in the "Danger" condition. In another study, testosterone administration was associated with heart rate acceleration to images of angry faces—a cardiac pattern associated with low levels of fear and a willingness to attack (Van Honk et al., 2001).

So surveys, experiments, and physiological responses all suggest that women are higher in fear. And this may explain why men make riskier decisions than women (Hersch, 1997). This sex difference in risky decision-making becomes larger when the risks involved are potentially life threatening and when researchers study real-world risky behaviors (such as turning across oncoming traffic with barely time to make it) rather than cold hypothetical choices ("Would you prefer a 50–50 chance of winning $100, or a 100 percent certainty of winning $45?"). This is why psychologists have come to realize that "*fear* responses may explain gender differences in risk taking more adequately than the cognitive processes involved in the reflective evaluation of options" (Byrnes, Miller, & Schafer, 1999, p. 378). Traditional theories of risk assessment have overestimated the role of cognition and underestimated the impact of fear (Loewenstein, Weber, Hsee, & Welch, 2001). While cold rational cognition can be useful for making impersonal and detached decisions, emotions are central to urgent decisions about approach or avoidance (Frijda, 1986). Unlike objective cognitive risk appraisals, fear does not work on probability estimates such as likelihoods or odds. It works on an emotional all-or-nothing principle: fear is sensitive to "the *possibility* rather than the *probability* of negative consequences" (Loewenstein et al., 2001, p. 276). If something just might be dangerous, avoid it. Fear favors cautious, risk-averse decisions (Lerner & Keltner, 2000, 2001) and, like that fire alarm, it errs on the side of false positives.

Anger, fear, and aggression

What happens when anger and fear are experienced simultaneously? Relevant studies are few and far between. Winstok (2007) studied them together in the context of hypothetical aggressive conflicts. He presented participants with vignettes in which they imagined they were approached by a male stranger in the street. The danger that he presented was varied in terms of the stranger's demeanor (easily scared, not scared, or ruthless), his actions (verbal aggression, threatened physical aggression, or use of physical aggression), and his likely reaction to the respondent's counter-aggression (by backing off, escalating, or trying to kill). This created a sliding scale of dangerousness, running from low to high. Participants rated how angry and fearful they would feel, as well as how they would respond behaviorally. As the attacker's aggression became more severe, the respondent's decision as to how to respond depended more and more upon the emotional intensity they were feeling. As we would expect, feelings of anger were particularly important in guiding decisions in low danger situations, while fear was the more influential emotion when danger was high. The study's conclusion is that "anger functions as aggression facilitator whereas fear functions as aggression inhibitor" (Winstock, 2007, p. 131).

The tragedy of the World Trade Center provided an unexpected opportunity to examine the effects of anger and fear in a more naturalistic context. In the weeks after the 9/11 attack, a nationally representative sample of Americans participated in a survey about risk perception (Lerner, Gonzalez, Small, & Fischhoff, 2003). They were also asked how angry and how fearful they felt after the terrorist attack. Fear increased risk estimates and plans for precautionary measures while anger had the opposite effect, decreasing risk assessments and increasing support for an aggressive policy of deporting foreigners. Women reported significantly higher levels of fear and gave higher risk estimates than men. Between 60 and 80 percent of the sex difference in risk assessment was explained by these differences in the strength of fear and anger.

There is also evidence that fear explains the magnitude of sex differences in experimental studies of aggression too. Eagly and Steffen (1986) asked 200 judges to rate descriptions of 63 experimental studies in response to the question "How much danger you would face if you enacted this (aggressive) behavior?" Female judges rated the danger of using aggression significantly higher than male judges and the actual sex differences found in the original aggression experiments were stronger when the sex difference between the male and female judges was larger. In fact, the judges' estimated danger ratings were the strongest predictor of the sex difference in aggression actually found in the studies. This was confirmed in another meta-analysis by Bettencourt and Miller (1996) who found the same sex difference in danger judgments and once again, the size of the sex difference in aggression was correlated with the extent to which female judges perceive greater danger than males. As they note, in experimental studies the ethical safeguards mean that the actual danger is very small indeed. Yet faced with the same low level of objective danger, women found the situation more threatening than men and this predicted their lower level of aggression.

Some research even suggests that fear has stronger effects on women than men. Edelyn Verona and her associates (Verona & Curtin, 2006; Verona, Sadeh, & Curtin, 2009) conducted a series of laboratory studies of aggression. In one such study (Verona & Kilmer, 2007), strong or weak air blasts were directed at the throat of participants as they attempted to complete a reaction time task. Participants' reports confirmed that these air blasts caused fear. Following this they were allowed to deliver electric shocks to a second "participant" whenever they made errors on a recall task. No surprise that men gave higher shocks than women but, when the results were examined within each sex, a pattern emerged. Women in the high air blast condition gave lower intensity shocks than their counterparts in the low air blast condition. Among men, air blast intensity was not related to shock delivery. Fear reduces aggression in women significantly more than it does in men.

Emotion and the brain

How does the brain cope with information about provocation and danger from the world outside? Unfortunately, most neuropsychological studies of emotion focus on the experience of just one emotion at a time. But in the real world we often experience different emotions simultaneously. With jealousy can come sadness. Bittersweet films can make us feel happiness and sorrow at the same time. And of course, I have suggested that we often feel anger and fear together. How can the balance between the two emotions be evaluated and weighted so that they are capable of informing our behavior? I have stressed that much of the everyday decision-making that drives our behavior has a strong emotional input. Neuroscientists are beginning to uncover the brain regions that may be involved. And we are beginning to see where the sex differences may lie.

Le Doux's pioneering work made it clear that the amygdala was involved in the registration of fear. But since then, things have come a long way. We now know that it is also involved in the processing of a wide range of emotions, both positive and negative (Sergerie, Chochol, & Armony, 2008). Its role seems to be to rapidly detect stimuli that are biologically relevant (Sander, Grafman, & Zalla, 2003), especially where they may require an immediate response which is often the case when they are unexpected, threatening, or dangerous (Adolphs & Spezio, 2006).

The amygdala sends this alerting information to a region of the frontal cortex: the ventromedial prefrontal cortex (VMPFC; Figure 3.1) and its partner, the ventral anterior cingulate cortex. (I should say that I will include studies of the orbitofrontal cortex (OFC) here also. This may dismay purists but there is some controversy as to terminology in this region with some researchers distinguishing the OFC and VMPFC and others including OFC as part of the broader area

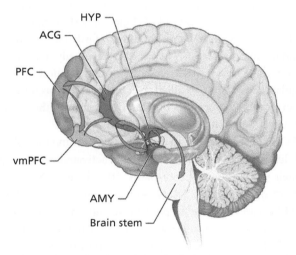

Figure 3.1 Emotion and emotional regulation in the brain. ACG = anterior cingulate gyrus; AMY = amygdala; HYP = hypothalamus; PFC = prefrontal cortex; vmPFC = ventromedial prefrontal cortex (lying toward the central underside of the brain). The dorsolateral prefrontal cortex (DLPFC) is not shown separately but is part of the prefrontal cortex: it lies toward the exterior and side of the skull.
Reproduced from Tost, H., & Meyer-Lindenberg, A. (2010). I fear for you: A role for serotonin in moral behaviour. *Proceedings of the National Academy of Sciences of the United States of America, 107*(40), 17071–2, figure one © 27 September 2010, *Proceedings of the National Academy of Sciences*, with permission.

of VMPFC.) There is still a fair amount of debate as to the exact functions of these areas but they are certainly implicated in the experience and control of emotion, and in our seemingly "automatic" or prepared responses to these emotions.

The VMPFC acquires and stores knowledge about the reward and punishment probabilities associated with the emotional information that it receives from the amygdala and sensory areas (Grabenhorst & Rolls, 2011). It can therefore predict the value of approach (when the stimulus is rewarding) or avoidance (if it is likely to be punishing). Sometimes this information is straightforward and the amygdala requires little additional input from the VMPFC. When it is more complicated, the VMPFC intervenes. For example, psychologists have long been aware of a phenomenon called the "framing" effect. Imagine I award you some "free" money ($50) and then ask if you want to gamble with it. I make you a proposal: "You can either keep $20 of it or you can gamble on keeping it all" (the Gain frame). Sometimes I make a different proposal: "You can either lose $30 of it or you can gamble on keeping it all" (the Lose frame). Of course, from a purely rational perspective, there is no difference. Yet people show a fairly consistent pattern: they prefer the sure thing in the Gain frame but are willing to gamble in the Lose frame. This represents the most common decision pattern and when participants make this kind of choice they show heightened activity in the amygdala. They seem to be responding to fairly basic signals about approaching and avoiding risk. But when they occasionally make the much less natural decision to gamble in the Gain condition, they show activation in the anterior cingulate cortex (an area allied with the VMPFC), as if this structure is working to correct the "natural" inclination they felt from their amygdala (De Martino, Kumaran, Seymour, & Dolan, 2006).

The VMPFC is able to talk back to the amygdala, turning the volume of emotions up and down. For example, the VMPFC is activated when people actively try to alter their mood (Cooney, Joormann, Atlas, Eugene, & Gotlib, 2007) or suppress it (Levesque et al., 2003). But as well as regulating the intensity of emotion, the VMPFC can intervene to prevent the automatic behavioral inclinations that are generated by strong emotions (Beer, Knight, & D'Esposito, 2006; Ochsner et al., 2004). Callous-unemotional syndrome is a subtype of childhood conduct disorder involving acts that are frequently aggressive. These aggressive children show structural and functional problems in the VMPFC: specifically they show a weaker connection between the amygdala and the VMPFC, suggesting that an inability to suppress emotion and inhibit automatic responses may lie at the heart of their problems (Rubia, 2011). Normal adolescents with decreased OFC volumes have a stronger tendency to argue back at their parents during disputes (Whittle et al., 2008) and in adults, an underactive VMPFC and OFC is associated with impulsive aggression (Best, Williams, & Coccaro,

2002; Blair, 2004; Coccaro, Sripada, Yanowitch, & Luan, 2011). The involvement of the OFC was demonstrated in an innovative neuroimaging study by Pietrini, Guazzelli, Basso, Jaffe, and Grafman (2000) who asked 15 men to imagine four related situations. In the first (a control condition), they imagined themselves taking an elevator ride with their mother and two unknown men. After this, they imagined watching as the two men assaulted their mother while they took no action (cognitive restraint), then they imagined trying to attack their mother's assailant while they were restrained by the second man (physical restraint), and finally they imagined hitting the two men with all their strength (unrestrained aggression). Compared to the control condition, all three aggressive images were accompanied by a decrease in blood flow to the OFC. This was the only frontal region affected and the largest deactivation was associated with unrestrained aggression. It seems that the OFC which normally restrains the expression of emotions was deactivated when the participants were encouraged to imagine the expression of behavioral aggression. The results gel with another imagery study in which participants thought about experiencing extreme anger: They showed increased activity in the OFC, supporting the idea that this area was involved in restraining their spontaneous inclination to lash out (Dougherty et al., 1999). In short, the VMPFC and OFC seem to be a kind of "hot" decision-maker, taking emotional inputs and speedily initiating the "best bet" behavioral strategy. In situations of aggression, it can compare the strength of experienced fear and anger, and the positive and negative consequences if one or the other predominates. It can enhance or suppress the strength of each. It can open or close prewired behavioral channels. In short, it can act like an approach–avoidance calculator (MacDonald, 2008; Siever, 2008)

Evidence is beginning to accumulate about sex differences in this calculation system. Most of these studies examine emotional responses at quite a general level, rather than specific emotions such as fear and anger. Women's amygdala responds more strongly to aversive pictures compared to men (Domes et al., 2010). At a purely structural level too, the OFC and the VMPFC areas are larger in women than men, after correcting for differences in overall brain size (Goldstein et al., 2001; Raine, Yang, Narr, & Toga, 2011; Wood et al., 2008). Consistent with a stronger ability to modulate emotion, the ratio of the volume of the orbitofrontal cortex volume to the amygdala is greater in women than men (Gur et al., 2002). Indeed the sex difference in VMPFC volume completely explains sex differences in the ability to reappraise and suppress emotion (Welborn et al., 2009).

The OFC also seems to be particularly responsive to threat in women. Women show greater activation than men in the amygdala and OFC to pictures of threatening faces (McClure et al., 2004). The OFC and VMPFC not only register emotional experiences, they decide whether these emotions will be given free reign over our behavior. In both sexes, antisocial behavior is more frequent among those with a smaller OFC volume: the sex difference in the size of the OFC region explains two-thirds of the sex difference in antisocial behavior (Raine, Yang, Narr, & Toga, 2011).

There is also evidence that the male hormone testosterone is associated with both OFC underactivity and aggression. The OFC contains receptors for androgens and, in response to threat, testosterone is responsible for changes in neurotransmitter turnover and activation in the OFC (Hermans, Ramset, & van Hon, 2008). This has been examined in a series of studies using the Ultimatum Game as a way of generating anger and spiteful aggression. In this game, one player is given a sum of money (say $10) to split with a second player. The first player makes an offer which, if it is accepted, is honored. However if the second player refuses the offer, neither player receives anything. Unfair offers ("$9 to me, $1 to you") are typically rejected. Rejecting an offer seems illogical: surely $1 is better than nothing? But that ignores the emotional factor. Usually the second player is sufficiently angered by the derisory offer that they are willing to sacrifice the small monetary gain for the psychological satisfaction of penalizing their opponent. Individuals with high testosterone levels are especially likely to reject unfair offers (Burnham, 2007) and so are people with damage to the OFC (Moretti, Dragone, & di Pellegrino, 2008; Koenigs & Tranel, 2007). These two findings suggest that testosterone might be having its effect on aggression through its action on the OFC. To find out, Mehta and Beer (2009) obtained testosterone levels from participants' saliva before scanning their brains as they played the Ultimatum Game. Aggression (rejection of unfair offers) was associated with underactivity of the OFC and also with higher testosterone levels. But, more impressively, the relationship between testosterone and aggression was explained by the testosterone-driven decrease in OFC activity.

Another study looked explicitly at how testosterone affects the strength of the connection between the amygdala (with its basic registration of emotion) and the OFC (with its ability to modulate amygdala input and control behavioral responses). Women received either testosterone or a placebo and then viewed a series of angry and fearful faces on a monitor screen. After testosterone administration, women had a stronger connection between the amygdala and the incoming low-level sensory information from the thalamus. They were more emotionally reactive to the visual signals of anger and fear. But at the same time, the women's brains showed reduced communication between the amygdala and the OFC. Testosterone was prioritizing emotional information in their amygdala and at the same time liberating it from higher control (Van Wingen, Mattern, Verkes, Buitelaar, & Fernandez, 2010).

The impulsivity problem

If the OFC and VMPFC control our impulses, perhaps there is a simple message from all these studies. The sex difference in aggression results from a sex difference in impulsivity. But when the word "impulsive" enters the discussion, things get complicated. Most psychologists and lay people would agree with a broad definition of impulsivity as a "tendency to act spontaneously and without deliberation" (Carver, 2005). But that still leaves things wide open. Does it mean a failure to plan? A lack of perseverance? Adventurousness? A lack of self-discipline? Susceptibility to boredom? All of these and more have been taken to be aspects of impulsivity.

We performed a meta-analysis of sex differences in impulsivity, analyzing the most inclusive range of studies we could find (Cross, Copping, & Campbell, 2011). We included every study we could locate which claimed to be about "impulsivity" and which had measured sex differences. We analyzed 741 samples of participants from 277 studies. We first looked at studies that had used general paper-and-pencil measures of impulsivity. These questionnaires ask a series of very broad questions such as "I plan trips well ahead of time" or "I often say things without thinking." What we found initially surprised us. There was virtually no sex difference. Then we turned our attention to some very different measures that psychologists have subsumed under the umbrella heading of impulsivity: sensation seeking and risk taking. Here the sex difference was marked: men scored higher than women.

What could explain this mixed pattern of results? The answer lies in the difference between two systems of impulse control that have been identified by neuropsychologists. So far I have described only the first: the VMPFC and OFC areas, sometimes called the reflexive system because of their automaticity, regulate *emotion* and its behavioral responses. But another part of the frontal cortex is involved in regulating *cognition*: the dorsolateral prefrontal cortex (DLPFC), sometimes called the reflective system. The DLPFC sits above the VMPFC at the front of your brain behind your forehead. It is the seat of what psychologists call executive function. Unlike the VMPFC, it has no direct connection to the emotional information in the amygdala (Lieberman, 2007). It is the overarching "thinking boss" that allows us to make a plan, carry it out, stay focused, resist distraction, maintain awareness of events around us, monitor the plan's success, and adjust it if necessary.

Imagine you have to do the weekly shop on a Saturday. On Friday night, your executive function rolls into action. Your prospective memory tells you that tomorrow is shopping day. You develop a plan: to make a list of what to buy. You decide to structure it by dealing with fresh produce first, then meat, then drink, then staples. For each category you check the cupboards and see what is needed. Your short-term memory holds the information until you can write it on your list. Your child appears wanting a drink. You break off and supply it, then your executive function reminds you where to pick up again on the list you were making. You overhear an interesting news report on the television next door and feel an impulse to go through and watch it. But your executive function holds you back—you can catch it later on the late night news show. You notice that there is no kitchen roll on the counter. But that doesn't fit the category scheme. Does that count as a "staple"? If not, you need a new category on your list. Executive function is a godsend—keeping us anticipating the future, making plans, and staying on-track despite competing bids for our attention.

Executive function is a top-down processes, recruiting various lower centers (like motor areas, memory, and attention) to carry out goal-directed tasks. The regulation exerted by the DLPFC has been called the "cool" cognitive control system (in contrast to the "hot" emotional control system of the VMPFC). Recall that conduct-disordered children show problems with the VMPFC "hot" system and it results in emotional and impulsive angry outbursts. When children have difficulties with the DLPFC we see a different symptom profile. They cannot maintain attention on tasks, they are fidgety and restless, they disrupt others in the classroom, and as a consequence they often do poorly at school. This is attention deficit disorder (Barkley, 1997; Rubia, 2011).

Now recall that general impulsivity questionnaires ask rather non-specific and unemotional questions about planning, premeditation, perseverance, and acting without deliberation. These questions seem to be tapping the cold control system: executive functions. There is little evidence that there are adult sex differences in this domain. It is true that in childhood boys exceed girls in the prevalence of attention deficit hyperactivity disorder. But boys are more vulnerable to a range of childhood pathologies and their over-representation may reflect a developmental advantage that girls have in effortful control in childhood (Else-Quest, Hyde, Goldsmith, & Van Hulle, 2006). By adulthood, there is little evidence of a sex difference in the planning, attention, working memory, or cognitive inhibition (Campbell, 2006).

Questionnaires that measure sensation seeking ask about the respondent's preference for scary, exciting activities (such as parachute jumping) over safe but tedious ones. Risky activities are undertaken because they are fun, at least for some people. They are associated with a "hot" attraction to emotional intensity, not a miscalculation by the "cold" executive system. When parachute jumpers jump from planes, it is not because they have failed to plan. On the contrary, they plan carefully, checking their equipment, drop site, parachute, and timings. At an empirical level too, there is reason to doubt that sensation-seeking is the same as general impulsivity because the two concepts frequently emerge as separate factors in correlation analyses. Sensation-seeking, novelty-seeking, and risk-taking scales cluster together as a single factor and one that is only loosely associated with scales measuring "cold" cognitive impulsivity (e.g., Depue & Collins, 1999; Flory et al., 2006; Whiteside & Lynam, 2001). Sex differences appear in areas that are linked to an emotional attraction to risky experiences, not in failures of effortful planning and organization.

What kind of *emotional* difference might exist between men and women that could feed into this reflexive risk-taking preference? We looked at studies of sex differences in emotional sensitivity to reward and to punishment because both have been linked to impulsivity in different ways. Impulsive behavior could reflect an over-attraction to the rewarding aspects of behavior ("What a thrill a bungee jump would be") which prevents reflection on the possible negative consequences. Or it might reflect insensitivity to punishment ("Danger? What danger?"). We found a marked sex difference in one but not the other: women were much more sensitive than men to possible punishment.

It is not that women do not enjoy the excitement of risk; it is that they are more acutely attuned to its possible dangers. For example, women's lower participation in extreme sports is best explained by their stronger anticipation of possible negative consequences and by their higher ratings of the severity of those consequences should they occur (Harris, Jenkins, & Glaser, 2006). We see the same effect writ small in the laboratory (Gabriel & Williamson, 2010). In the Balloon Analogue Risk Task, respondents are asked to inflate an on-screen balloon with a series of pumps. With each pump, the balloon gets bigger and increases in monetary value. However it can explode at any time and, if it does, all the money is lost. Participants have a choice of opting out by "banking" their winnings at any time during balloon inflation. To some participants the experimenter emphasized the possible monetary losses, to others the possible gains. Drawing attention to the losses had no effect on men but a strong effect on women: it caused them to take the safe "bank-the-money" option much more frequently. Women's heightened punishment sensitivity also explains why they suffer higher rates of anxiety and depression than men at both a non-clinical and clinical level (Costa et al., 2001). Anxiety is associated with prioritizing attention to threatening stimuli (Mogg et al., 2000). These orienting responses occur before the nature of the stimuli is consciously registered, indicating the involvement of low-level reflexive processes which are automatic and unconscious (Bar-Haim, Lamy, Pergamin, Bakermans-Kranenburg, & van Ijzendoorn, 2007). Among people suffering from depression, women ruminate about negative life events more than men. Rumination not only demonstrates their preoccupation with impending punishment but also exacerbates depressive symptoms (Rood, Roelofs, Bogels, Nolen-Hoeksema, & Schouten, 2009). In short, stronger punishment sensitivity amounts to a lower threshold for experiencing fear. And this gels with the argument that women have evolved to be especially attuned to dangers that would jeopardize their own survival and that of their offspring. Stronger fear keeps women away from dangerous aggression and out of harm's way.

Indirect aggression

I chose my words carefully in that last sentence. Women may stay out of dangerous confrontations, but that does not mean they don't compete. Women need food and shelter not only for themselves but for their children. Most importantly, in highly social species such as humans, alliances are an important resource. Friends who can be depended on for support are essential. Social exclusion or, worse still, expulsion from the group means death: humans are not built to be solitary animals.

It was a research team in Finland that first identified a particular form of aggression that they called "indirect" (Lagerspetz, Björkqvist, & Peltonen, 1988). They defined it as "a type of behavior in which the perpetrator attempts to inflict pain in such a manner that he or she makes it seem as though there is no intention to hurt at all" (Björkqvist, Lagerspetz, & Kaukiainen, 1992, p. 118). (Later, others used the terms "relational" and "social" aggression to describe essentially the same phenomenon, see Archer & Coyne, 2005.) Sometimes it involves acts in which the aggressor cannot be identified, such as nasty gossip behind the victim's back, spreading rumors about them, and breaking confidences. At other times the behavior may be direct and apparent, but too ambiguous to be defined as intentionally aggressive: giving the victim the silent treatment, excluding them from social events, or refusing to be friends any more unless certain conditions are fulfilled. Indirect aggression in the workplace can take the form of hurtful criticisms that can be made to appear rational if challenged ("I was only trying to help you"). Or it can be a strategy of dismissing others' opinions or piling extra work onto them. Indirect aggression requires social intelligence because its successful deployment depends on the ability to understand the state of mind of others, and to manipulate their mental states. Because of this, it starts to appear around the age of eight and rises in frequency with age, overtaking direct verbal and physical confrontation. It can damage self-esteem, destroy social standing, jeopardize friendships, and lead to stigmatization and social isolation.

The perpetrators of indirect acts are often hidden so that even if a victim becomes aware of a scurrilous rumor that is circulating about her, she is unable to pin down the source. ("I didn't start it—*everyone* is saying it.") Or if the act is more direct, there is enough ambiguity about its motive to make a challenge appear aggressive or paranoid. ("It's not that we didn't *want* you to come to the party, it's just that the restaurant put a limit on the numbers.") It means that retaliation is far less likely than when a direct attack is made. And this makes it an especially useful tool for females given their reluctance to expose themselves to danger.

Early research suggested that girls were specialists in indirect aggression and there was much excitement about the discovery of a form of aggression on which girls outdid boys. Thirty years on, we know that the sex difference is much less impressive than we thought. In children, its magnitude depends on how it is measured. Girls are less willing to admit to this kind of behavior so self-report data show a slight difference in favor of boys (Card, Stucky, Sawalani, & Little, 2008). But when children are asked to nominate other children in their class who use indirect aggression, there is no sex difference: it seems that boys and girls come equally to mind. When children are asked to think about every class-mate in turn and rate their use of indirect aggression, girls are rated higher. An even stronger female bias is found when mothers and teachers act as unofficial observers and is strongest of all when trained behavioral scientists observe and record playground behavior (Archer & Coyne, 2005). Sex differences, apparent at the age of eight, become stronger and appear to peak in the mid-teens. However, boys catch up and, by adulthood, there is virtually no difference between men and women (Archer & Coyne, 2005). These findings of parity between the sexes are less dramatic than the early claims of a sex difference reversal, but they underline my point that, as the form of aggression becomes less confrontational and dangerous, girls become more willing to use it.

And do not underestimate the effects of indirect aggression. The social ex-clusion and sense of personal rejection have short-term and long-term effects. Initially the shock causes an emotional blunting, creating a sense of numbness similar to that found in pre-suicidal states (Baumeister, 1990). Time seems to slow down, there is a sense of lethargy and pointlessness (Twenge, Catanese, & Baumeister, 2003). In the longer term, social rejection is painful in the most literal sense: the same brain regions that are active when people experience physical pain are also active when they feel rejected (Eisenberger, Lieberman, & Williams, 2003; MacDonald & Leary, 2005). When social rejection is tem-porarily manipulated under laboratory conditions, the shared brain regions are those associated with the *emotional* aspect of pain—distress. But when individuals are asked to relive a real-life rejection, such as the break-up of a close relationship, the pain also activates centers associated with pain's *sensory* qualities—"ouchness" (Kross, Berman, Mischel, Smith, & Wager, 2011). In fact,

the painkiller acetaminophen which acts on the central nervous system can reduce both self-reported emotional pain and brain activation in areas associated
with social rejection (DeWall et al., 2010).

The stress associated with the social rejection of indirect aggression may be
especially powerful for girls and women. Girls say they find indirect aggression
more harmful than boys and even worse than direct aggression (Galen & Underwood, 1997). At a biological level too, women showed higher cortisol production than men in an experimental manipulation in which they are gradually
excluded from a three-person interaction (Stroud, Salovey, & Epel, 2002). The
reason seems to lie in the nature of women's friendships which we will examine
more closely in Chapter 5. Girls' intimate and intense friendships are a major
source of support during times of stress. The loss of these friendships can be
devastating and is associated with increased levels of depression among young
women (Hankin, Mermelstein, & Roesch, 2007). Ironically, friends are both
the cause and the cure for depression in girls. Girls' friendships involve strong
emotional inter-dependency and girls disclose far more personal information
to their friends than boys do. This means that a break-up is not only more hurtful in terms of the loss of close social support but the ex-friend carries away
with them a considerable amount of personal information that can be used as
a source of gossip to others. Girls' friendships also play a special role in coping with negative life events. While boys respond to adversity through distraction and social activities ("Forget about it—let's go play football"), girls tend
to co-ruminate with a friend about the source of their problem ("Let's go over
it again—tell me exactly what she said") (Eschenbeck, Kohlmann, & Lohaus,
2007). In short, social exclusion is a triple whammy for girls' depression: they
lose their best friend, their secrets can now become public knowledge, and the
very person who would normally have talked them through these depression-
inducing events has gone (Kochenderfer-Ladd & Skinner, 2002). Social exclusion is a powerful weapon yet the aggressor remains invisible, shielded from
retaliation. The hurt has been delivered but without the danger of a face-to-face
confrontation.

Maternal aggression—a predictable paradox

I have argued that fear is functional for females. It restrains them from exposing
themselves to possible injury or death which would have disastrous implications for their young. But this emphasis upon the costs of aggression to females
always has to be balanced against the prospective benefits. It is true that given
identical pay-offs, females should be less willing to expose themselves to danger
than males. But there is one clear situation where the pay-offs for aggression are

much larger for a female than for a male—saving her child's life. That life has cost the mother dear in terms of time, effort, vigilance, and protection. In polygynous species, that same life has cost the father a few million easily-replaceable sperm. The cost of replacement for the mother is measured in years while for the father it is measured in minutes. Though animal mothers rarely go as far as sacrificing themselves for their children, they are more willing to tolerate the risks of aggression for the sake of offspring survival than for any other reason.

Maternal aggression has been documented in many species from lemmings to lions and it occurs when another animal approaches or interferes with one of her offspring (Maestripieri, 1992). The species in which it has been most widely documented are those where male infanticide is a serious threat to female reproductive success. The mother's attack is ferocious and immediate. In many primates such as macaques, vervets, and baboons, males avoid infants and display fear when one approaches them. Females in these species are extraordinarily vigilant to males' proximity to their infant and, when an infant shows distress, a nearby male may be attacked even if he has displayed no overt aggression (Smuts, 1987).

Some researchers have been skeptical about the function of maternal aggression arguing that females may be defending food located at the nest site rather than protecting their infant, or even that it functions to test the mate quality of an attacking male. But the pattern of maternal aggression is too closely tied to the welfare of the pups to support these views (Maetsripieri, 1992). If territorial defense of food sites were the reason for aggression, we would expect animals to defend food sites away from the nest, which they do not. If the goal of the aggression was to test the ferocity of the male intruder then it is hard to explain why females are more reluctant to challenge large males compared to small ones. It is also theoretically unsatisfactory to propose that a female would readily abandon her current infant and prefer the uncertain possibility of mating anew with a strange male. The costs of repeating this kind of behavior during a lifetime would be a severely reduced number of progeny.

In rodents, maternal aggression begins during pregnancy and continues through lactation (Rosenblatt, Factor, & Mayer, 1994). It lasts for the period when the young are most vulnerable. It disappears when the pups are removed for five hours but is restored five minutes after the pups are returned. If the pups are attacked and killed, maternal aggression switches off immediately. Females discriminate between the danger posed by different intruders reserving their most ferocious attacks for those males who are most likely to harm the offspring (sexually naive, newly arrived, and recently-mated males) rather than paternal males or other females. The severity of maternal attack is directly related to the size of the litter that she is protecting.

Does maternal aggression work? Natural selection would only have favored such a life-threatening act if it enhanced reproductive success in the long run. In the Southern elephant seal, orphan pups are bitten three times as often as those with mothers present and the most aggressive mothers rear the largest pups. In Northern elephant seals, mothers whose offspring survive to weaning show more aggression than those whose pups die. Their pups are less often bitten or shaken, and the frequency of these attacks is negatively related to maternal aggression. Maternal aggression has been shown to effectively drive off intruders among polar bears, lions, mice, and rats.

Primates provide a different slant on maternal aggression because, in some species, threats to the infant may come from other females as well as infanticidal males. Pulling, rough handling, kidnapping, and direct aggression against young come from unrelated females in a number of primate species (Maestripieri, 1992). In macaques, 90 percent of infant attacks are by females (Troisi, D'Amato, Carnera, & Trinca, 1989) and pre-emptive maternal aggression (interrupting the attack before it can get underway rather than punishing it afterwards) is associated with a reduced probability of infant harassment. In these species, females display a linear dominance hierarchy that is based on matrilines. This leads to a distinct pattern of maternal protection of young that depends on the females' standing in the group (Maestripieri, 1994). Low-ranking mothers protect their infants by restraining them—they prevent the infant from breaking contact with them by holding its tail or leg. High-ranking females have little to fear from lower-ranking females and they can count on the support of their equally well-placed kin. So they accord their privileged offspring much greater freedom. When a low-ranking mother is forced to attack an abusive higher-ranking female, she is more likely to be counter-attacked. Despite this, these low-ranking mothers are more willing to attack a high-ranked female to protect their infant than for any other reason. The value of saving their infant outweighs the costs of potential injury. In the face of the ultimate danger to their reproductive success, females attack and they attack severely.

But what mechanism accounts for this? If fear is a critical regulator of female risky behavior, as I have argued, then fear reduction should be implicated in maternal aggression and most scientists think that it is. Immediately after giving birth, rat mothers show a host of maternal behaviors, and they also show a significant drop in fear combined with heightened aggressiveness toward intruders (Erskine, Barfield, & Goldman, 1980; Ferreira, Hansen, Nielson, Archer, & Minor, 1989; Fleming & Luebke, 1981; Hard & Hansen, 1985; Ostermeyer, 1983). Their increased aggression is attributable to their reduced anxiety (Miczek & O'Donnell, 1980; Mos & Olivier, 1989). This chimes with other facts about aggression. Mice from genetic lines that show high levels of aggression also show lower levels of anxiety (Parmigiani, Brain, Mainardi, & Brunoni, 1988) and a high level of anxiety is inversely related to the probability of showing maternal aggression (Maestripieri, Badiani, & Puglisiallegra, 1991). Lesions to a brain site that result in increased maternal aggression to a threatening male also result in reduced fearfulness (Lonstein, Simmons, & Stern, 1998).

During lactation, the normal hypothalamic–pituitary–adrenal (HPA) response to stress is downregulated. The HPA system is headed up by the hypothalamus. In response to messages of threat from the amygdala, the hypothalamus sends corticotrophin-releasing factor (CRF) as a messenger to the pituitary gland which lies adjacent to it in the brain. The pituitary uses adrenocorticotropic hormone to communicate via the bloodstream with the adrenal cortex gland sitting above the kidneys. The adrenals trigger the release of cortisol in humans and corticosterone in rodents. These hormones increase glucose metabolism, causing a burst of energy to prepare the body for dealing with threat. Cortisol and corticosterone are useful indicators of fear. When exposed to stressful experiences (like electric shock), lactating rodents show a much weaker stress reaction as measured by corticosterone secretion. This is because, following parturition, there is downregulation of CRF which controls corticosterone secretion (Lonstein, 2005; Neumann, 2002, 2003) and we see the results in the new mother's reduced fear and anxiety. In rats, it is possible to experimentally infuse CRF directly into the brain and so artificially increase the stress response: doing this significantly diminishes maternal aggression while leaving other maternal behaviors quite unaffected (Gammie, Negron, Newman, & Rhodes, 2004).

Because maternal aggression coincides with parturition and lactation, a useful place to search for the mechanism that causes this fear reduction is with an examination of a hormone that is specifically associated with birth and milk production (Campbell, 2008b, 2010). Oxytocin, as we have seen, is a neuropeptide made in the hypothalamus that stimulates the contractions that expel the infant from the uterus, and precipitates the milk "letdown" reflex. The more the infant sucks, the more oxytocin is produced. The frequency of these oxytocin pulses is correlated with the amount of milk produced and with maternal calmness. Administering oxytocin to rodents and humans inhibits CRF neurons, decreases corticosteroid release, increases parasympathetic functioning, and results in lower levels of fearful behavior (Dreifuss, Dubois-Dauphin, Widmer, & Raggenbass, 1992; McCarthy, McDonald, Brooks, & Goldman, 1996; Uvnäs-Moberg, 1997; Windle et al., 2004). Oxytocin also reduces activity in the amygdala which registers fear and we are beginning to understand how this works, at least in rats (Huber, Veinante, & Stoop, 2005). The central amygdala controls autonomic fear responses through its connections to other parts of the brain including the hypothalamus. Within the central amygdala, there are two distinct populations of neurons; one is activated by oxytocin receptors and a second is inhibited by oxytocin but excited by a sister neuropeptide called arginine vasopressin. Vasopressin is structurally similar to oxytocin but the two appear to have almost opposite effects. Vasopressin excites neurons in the medial part of the central amygdala that stimulate fear arousal and responses. Oxytocin activates neurons in the lateral and capsular portion of the central amygdala which counteract the fear-inducing effects of vasopressin via an inhibitory neurotransmitter called GABA (gamma-aminobutyric acid). At very high levels of fear, with no escape route, both humans and rodents respond with freezing or tonic immobility (Blanchard, Hynd, Minke, Minemoto, & Blanchard, 2001; Moskowitz, 2006). The expression "scared stiff" captures this behavioral effect, which appears to be reduced by oxytocin, permitting maternal attack.

The stress-reducing effects of oxytocin are among the widely recognized of its effects in humans. Magnetic resonance imaging studies suggest that these anxiolytic effects are realized both by reducing amygdala activation and by downgrading the connection between the amygdala and brain stem areas responsible for sympathetic nervous system activation (Ferguson, Young, & Insel, 2002; Kirsch et al., 2005). Administration of oxytocin to men and women drastically reduces their production of stress hormones (Heinrichs et al., 2001; Light et al., 2000). In new mothers, stress hormones similarly fall during bouts of breastfeeding when oxytocin synthesis is high.

Despite the wealth of circumstantial evidence supporting oxytocin's role in stress reduction and maternal aggression, attempts to study the phenomenon *in vivo* present insurmountable ethical problems. We cannot ask new mothers to witness or even contemplate a threat to their newborn. (Interestingly, despite the extremely low objective probability of infant kidnap or attack, these concerns remain disproportionately high in the minds of new parents.) However, a recent study came as close as it could to examining aggression in mothers: groups of breastfeeding, bottle feeding, and nulliparous women were compared on their willingness to deliver aversive sound blasts to a hostile experimental confederate. Breastfeeding women delivered significantly louder and more aggressive retaliation than the other two groups. And this was associated with lower levels of fear, as measured by lower systolic blood pressure reactivity. Those women with the lowest systolic blood pressure were the most aggressive overall (Hahn-Holbrooke, Holbrooke, & Haselton, 2011).

This viewpoint contrasts with another model of women's response to threat proposed by Shelley Taylor and co-workers (Taylor et al., 2000). Although they concur with my argument that a mother's life is more central to offspring survival than a father's, they reach a very different conclusion about the implications for women's aggression. They suggest that women and men respond to threat in different ways. While threat triggers a "fight or flight" response in men, they propose that in women it triggers a "tend and befriend" reaction: women aggregate together as a group, seeking safety in numbers and focusing their efforts on quieting their children until the danger has passed. Although the HPA stress response is very similar in males and females, they propose that testosterone channels male behavior toward attack or flight, while oxytocin produces sedative effects in women that depress both of these behavioral responses. Because either fighting or fleeing would put offsprings' lives in danger, oxytocin enhances infant tending and affiliation with other women. But a clear problem with the model is that it cannot explain the existence of maternal aggression. Although Taylor et al. (2000, p. 414) briefly acknowledge that mothers fight ferociously for their offspring, they treat it as an unexplained anomaly, noting that "female physical aggression appears to be confined to situations requiring defense." But responses to threat are always forms of defense whether that response is attack, withdrawal, or, as they propose, inaction. The phenomenon of maternal aggression is far from anomalous—in mammals it is the most frequent and most ferocious form of female aggression. And for good reason: it has been selected over evolutionary time because it has kept infants alive. In situations of life and death, inaction is not a viable option.

While Taylor et al. argue that the sedative and calming effects of oxytocin inhibit aggression, I argue that its effects are twofold. It simultaneously supports maternal love and a willingness to fight for her infant's life (Campbell, 2010). Oxytocin increases a mother's attachment to her infant, promoting the feeling of love that makes her infant valuable to her. It also suppresses the fear that would normally cause her to back off from threat. Recent research has provided initial support for this twofold effect—albeit in the context of a much less significant relationship than that between mother and child. After administering oxytocin or a placebo, De Dreu et al. (2010) randomly assigned male strangers to groups. In response to threat of losing money to another group, those men who had received oxytocin showed increased aggression in defense of their group. The authors suggest that the "tend-and-befriend" slogan be recast as "tend-and-defend." I agree. Women reserve their most dangerous attacks for the defense of their offspring, and that bellicosity is a far cry from the tend-and-befriend picture of cowering women, each hoping that by chance the attacker will victimize someone else's baby. Such a passive strategy hands the probability of infant survival to sheer luck and we know that chance cannot cause directional selection. If infant survival was random, there could be no selection for effective mothering, including the fierce determination to keep infants safe. Throughout our evolution, some women kept more infants alive than others. It is their genes that proliferated: we all come from a long line of mothers who were more than just lucky—they were fierce.

Females, fear, and fitness

The difference between men and women in their willingness to escalate from conflict to violence is tied to the reproductive strategies of the two sexes. For men, the advantages of polygyny encouraged direct competition for mating opportunities and a greater disregard for their own safety. Aggression performed two interlinked functions. It intimidated other men and, in doing so, it won status. The more successful a man was, the greater power he had not only to attract fertile females but also to monopolize other disputed resources. These twin benefits increased reproductive success in direct and indirect ways. Directly, other males were more inclined to withdraw from conflicts over sexual rights to women. Indirectly, his ability to claim the lion's share of food and to use his status to protect mates increased his attractiveness to females. He became a more desirable mate. So for young males, physical aggression brought rewards that made even noble failure preferable to abstaining from the competition.

For females, aggression had costs that males did not have to face. With mothers undertaking the bulk of parental care, a male's death need not compromise his current reproductive success. But for females, injury or death meant the loss of her current offspring. Such a price counseled conservatism and risk-aversion. Avoid unnecessary conflict and stay away from physical aggression—both threaten the huge investment a woman has made in rearing her dependent young. I believe that the mechanism that underlies this sex difference is fear.

For males, low levels of fear open the door to extravagant displays of bravery that can be used to achieve a reputation in the community. The prize is status and all the benefits that come with it. But wouldn't status be useful for women too? Might high-status women not gain better mates, more food, and stronger support from allies? If status is as valuable to women as to men, why are so few of them leaders of multinational corporations and governments? Does the glass ceiling, erected by men, simply stop them? Do they prioritize raising children over running banks? Or could it be that status doesn't provide big enough rewards to outweigh the costs?

Chapter 4

Who does she think she is?
Women and status

Status is a matter of some importance to men—a point that has not escaped most women's attention. Certainly not that of poet Wendy Cope (1992):

> One man on his own can be quite good fun
> But don't go drinking with two -
> They'll probably have an argument
> And take no notice of you.
>
> What makes men so tedious
> Is the need to show off and compete.
> They'll bore you to death for hours and hours
> Before they'll admit defeat.*

From an evolutionary point of view of course, men engaged in status competition are far from taking "no notice of you." Women are the limiting resource for men and it is reproductive access to women that drives men's quest for status. The more dominance a man can gain, the greater his chances of securing the most attractive women. Nobody is suggesting that men consciously know this. In fact, as Cope rightly observes, male–male status jockeying often seems to exclude women completely. But 100,000 years of sexual selection has shaped the male mind to be especially sensitive to slights that call into question their social standing and they respond less than philosophically to other men's attempts to assert their superiority.

Why men want dominance

Before turning our attention to the complexities of human status striving, it is helpful to look at how dominance functions among our nearest primate relatives. The Darwinian predictions are clear: males strive for high rank because it benefits their reproductive success in two ways—it means that they can dominate rival males in competition for resources (including access to fertile females) and because females have a preference for highly-ranked males. In humans, this female preference may be based on a man's resource-holding potential which indicates his ability to provide for the woman and her offspring. In non-human primates such as chimpanzees, females mate promiscuously and males offer little in the way of provisioning so female preference for high-status males reflects selection for good genes: a male who can achieve and maintain dominance, with its associated costs in physiological stress and frequent male–male antagonism, is a male with a strong constitution and robust genes. So we would predict that these males do better in the mating market than their subordinates.

For many years, this hypothesis was tested by counting copulations. It was never a satisfactory method. Primate males sometimes mate with females outside their period of receptivity and even with pregnant females. Some copulations do not end in ejaculation and even those that do are no guarantee of pregnancy. The fertilized egg may fail to implant or the male's sperm may be beaten by those of another male who copulates with the female afterwards. When young females first reach maturity, they have anovulatory cycles and cannot become pregnant. In other words, the male who achieves the greatest number of copulations may not be the one who fathers the most children. But in the last 20 years, it has become possible to establish paternity with much more certainty using biological techniques. Paternity exclusion analysis can rule out as a possible father any male who lacks a particular allele carried by an offspring but not its mother. DNA fingerprinting compares and matches bands of DNA appearing in the infant with both its mother and possible fathers. These methods allow a more accurate assessment of the true relationship between dominance and paternity.

For many primate species, there is a positive relationship between rank and paternity (see Bradley et al., 2005; Ellis, 1995; Gerloff, Hartung, Fruth, Hohmann, & Tautz, 1999; Launhardt, Borries, Hardt, Epplen, & Winkler, 2001; Widdig et al., 2004). But the relationship is not perfect and it does not always conform exactly to the "priority of access" model (Altmann, 1962) which predicts offspring number from male rank taking into account the number of male competitors and the number of receptive females. According to this model, for example, in a group of five males and two receptive females, the two highest-ranking males should each gain access to one female each (Wroblewski, et al., 2009). This model gave good predictions for the West African Tai population of chimpanzees (Boesch, Kohou, Nene, & Vigilant, 2006) but not at the East African Gombe reserve where, although dominant males sired a disproportionate share of offspring, lower-ranking males sired more offspring than the model predicted (Constable, Ashley, Goodall, & Pusey, 2001; Wroblewski et al., 2009). The same was found at Mahale reserve in Tanzania where two dominant males sired five out of the 10 offspring, with the remaining paternity spread across five other males—two of whom were low ranking (Inoue, Inoue-Murayama, Vigilant, Takenaka, & Nishida, 2008). It seems that dominance is a reasonable but far from perfect guide to reproductive success.

How are these lower-ranking males achieving mating success? Chimpan-zee males use three main mating strategies (Tutin, 1979). The first of these is possessiveness or mate guarding. Here alpha males gain a clear advantage because they can successfully drive away other suitors and coerce copulations from a female during the 10 days or so that she is in estrous. They can also enlist the support of allies (younger, ambitious males) in mate guarding. Alpha males choose the most desirable females who, unlike our own species, tend to be the older females with established fecundity and mothering experience, enhancing the probability of long-term reproductive success (Muller, Emery Thompson, & Wrangham, 2007). But there are other routes to copulations that depend much less on rank and tend to occur when the group gets sufficiently large that the dominant males cannot monitor and control their subordinates (Newton-Fisher, Thompson, Reynolds, Boesch, & Vigilant, 2010; Wroblewski et al., 2009). Some males are able to gain "sneak" copulations behind the back of the dominant male or they may take a female away from the group on a consortship—a kind of chimp honeymoon (Constable et al., 2001). These tac-tics usually depend on a willing female partner and that introduces the element of female choice (Stumpf & Boesch, 2006). Females sometimes appear to defy Darwinian logic by showing a liking for medium- or low-ranked males. They are inclined to especially favor male "friends" who have spent time grooming them. The females are also either strangely prescient of leadership qualities or they are king makers in their own right because they mate more often than expected with young males who later go on to achieve dominant status. Despite this perturbation in the system arising from the fact that females have prefer-ences of their own, dominance works reasonably well for chimps. Males in the top tier do better than their subordinates and, further down the ranks, males have to scramble and charm their way to reproductive opportunities.

Among our own species, status depends upon much more than the crude ability to physically dominate others. Social and cultural success may involve the accrual of material goods (wealth), the achievement of recognized power over others (in organizations or government), or the possession of specially val-ued knowledge and competence (doctors, athletes). Cultural success can be rec-ognized by the deference we accord to certain members of society. The routes to cultural success in a meritocratic society depend upon a host of personal factors including natural ability, determination, and social intelligence.

Looking back through history, there can be no doubt of the extraordinary reproductive success of men whose wealth and power allowed them to keep multiple wives and harems (Betzig, 1986; Dickemann, 1979). Julius Caesar was happy to find that a bill had thoughtfully been drawn up legitimizing his union with "any woman or women he pleased—for the procreation of chil-dren" (Betzig, 1997b). His great nephew Augustus, renowned for his humility and common touch, nevertheless was supplied with women by his wife Livia as well as by his friends. "His friends used to behave like Toranius, the slave dealer, in arranging pleasures for him—they would strip mothers of families or grown girls of their clothes, and inspect them as though they were for sale." In China, emperors kept royal harems of 1,000 women. The system was managed by female supervisors and the women were brought to the emperor on rotation according to a calendar that guaranteed that they were at mid-cycle. One Indian potentate fathered four children in one week and nine more the following week. The key to this kind of unimaginable reproductive success was simply power. Kings with limitless resources could afford as many concubines as they liked and like them they did.

But were the benefits of dominance confined to despots who had absolute power to organize social arrangements to their own advantage? Does the link between dominance and reproduction survive in societies that have much smaller wealth and power differentials? The most egalitarian societies that have been described are hunter-gatherers and foragers. These people live on the edge of survival in the sense that they cannot accumulate food but subsist on their daily excursions to hunt meat or gather vegetation. This hand-to-mouth existence evens out differences in rank that accrue from resource surplus and trade. Hunter-gatherers are rarely polygynous for the simple reason that men cannot acquire enough resources to support two wives. The Ache of Paraguay live in this way and their egalitarian lifestyle is exemplified in their food sharing. Small mundane nutritional packages, such as vegetable and insects which are gathered daily, are shared only with close kin (Hill & Kaplan, 1994). But more exotic, desirable, and unpredictable foods such meat and honey are shared across the whole band. When a monkey has been killed and prepared for consumption, it is cut up and distributed among all the family units. On any given day, 90 percent of hunt food that is consumed by any given family is actually killed by a non-family member. This works to reduce day-to-day variation in food intake by evening out the difference between good days and bad days for each hunter. Nonetheless hunters vary in quality. Some do much better than others and a key question is why successful hunters tolerate (even reward) the poor performance of others by feeding them. Why don't they give the food selectively to their own families since, on average, they do better than other men?

A number of solutions have been proposed. Under the tolerated theft theory, a man might as well share a large piece of food rather than allow it to rot or waste his effort fighting for it. Under the cooperative acquisition theory, individuals share in order to maintain cooperative bonds that they will need in the future. But an intriguing proposal has been made which has implications for both dominance and reproductive success (Hawkes, 1990; Hill and Kaplan,

1994). First, by sharing with others, a good hunter makes himself indispensable to the group. The kudos of his hunting may make other band members particularly indulgent to him as a way of ensuring his continued loyalty. This elevation in status has direct implications for the welfare of his wife and children because they receive better treatment from others. But his generosity and derived status has more carnal payoffs. Although they do not differ from poor hunters in the number of children born to their wife, good hunters are more often taken as extra-marital lovers, have more illegitimate children, and both their illegitimate and legitimate children have a higher chance of survival (Hill & Kaplan, 1994). This pattern also seems to hold for other groups such as the King San, the Hadza, the Ifaluk, and for pre-twentieth-century European populations (Hawkes, 1993; Hill & Kaplan, 1994; Perusse, 1993). In a recent study of the Tsimane in Bolivia, the researchers defined "dominance" in terms of the ability of inflict costs and measured it as a man's ability to win an aggressive confrontation. They also examined "prestige" which refers to the attribution of status by others and was defined as a man's influence within the community. Both dominance and prestige were associated with greater intra-marital fertility and with more extra-marital affairs (Von Rueden, Gurven, & Kaplan, 2011). In a survey of nearly 300 cultures, Gregerson (1982, p. 84) concluded "For women the world over, male attractiveness is bound up with social status, or skills, strength, bravery, prowess and similar qualities."

But something strange has begun to happen in the West over the last hundred years. Wealthier families do not differ from low-income families in their number of children and in some cases have *fewer* children (see Chapter 9). The relationship has been found by plotting fertility against family income in a variety of Western societies. How could this be? Does this not show that something is seriously awry with evolutionary theory? Daniel Perusse (1993) decided to find out. He collected data on the sexual, reproductive, and economic histories of 1133 French Canadians. He wanted to know if this "demographic shift" was a result of the imposition of monogamy or the use of contraceptives. First of all he confirmed that there was no relationship between the social class of the father and the number of children ever born to him (by his current wife, ex-wives, or unmarried partner). Then he computed the number of potential conceptions that could have occurred if contraception had not been used—he derived this from a measure of the number of partners the man had had and the number of sex acts that took place with each of them. Here he found a positive correlation—if contraception had not been available, the men with higher social status would have fathered more children. But, he reasoned, this relationship was based on all the men in the sample, including married men. These men are constrained by monogamy and so unlikely to seek multiple sexual partners.

When he analyzed the relationship again, examining only unmarried men he found it was even stronger and did not vary markedly with the age of the man. So it appears that both monogamy and contraception reduce the variance in male mating success and that both have the effect of diminishing the relationship between a man's status and his reproductive success. But the imposition of monogamy and the easy availability of effective contraception have been recent events in evolutionary terms. Contemporary social arrangements have not had yet altered the evolved male interest in dominating other men and impressing women.

Dominance in men's interpersonal style

There are two important classes of social behavior that have appeared and re-appeared in a variety of psychological studies. Although they were derived in different ways and given different names, the actual content of the categories is remarkably consistent. On one hand, we have agency (also called instrumentality, dominance or masculinity). Agentic people strive for individuation within the group. They seek independence and autonomy. They believe in meritocracy and the value of competition. They see rules as a necessary means for regulating competition and are concerned with fairness more than compassion. On the other hand, we have communion (also called expressiveness, nurturance, or femininity). High-communion people strive to be part of a larger whole, to merge themselves into the group. They view relationships in terms of meeting others' needs rather than a tit-for-tat exchange of favors. They believe in equality rather than equity. They value intimacy and mutuality in their relationships and define themselves in terms of their close friends. We all recognize ourselves in both of these descriptions and with good reason. They are independent dimensions that are uncorrelated with one another. A person's score on one does not predict their score on the other. We are all a mixture of both. Nonetheless, sex differences have been reliably found on both dimensions (see Campbell, 1998).

We can trace the twin themes of agency and communion back as far as Confucius (Wiggins, 1991). But more recently, psychologists have re-invented them, not as philosophical notions, but as measurable aspects of personality. The dimensions form the vertical and horizontal coordinates of the circumplex model of personality (Freedman, Leary, Ossorio, & Coffey, 1951; Kiesler, 1983; Wiggins, 1979; see Figure 4.1) that was developed using factor analysis to distill a large number of self-rated traits into two manageable dimensions. Their analysis suggested that interpersonal behavior can be seen as a circle with north–south indicating the trait of dominance versus submission and with

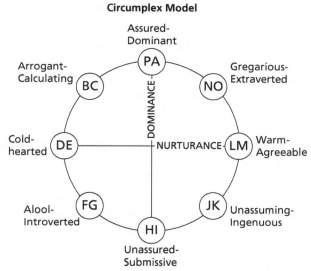

Figure 4.1 The circumplex model. Reproduced from Kiesler, D.J. (1983). The 1982 interpersonal circle: A taxonomy for complementarity in human transactions. *Psychological Review*, *90*, 185–214 © 1983, American Psychological Association. <http://psycnet. apa.org/journals/psp/59/4/images/psp_59_4_781_fig1a.gif>

east–west identifying the complementary trait of nurturance versus hostility. (As we move around the perimeter we find blends of each two contiguous styles so that, for example, between nurturance and dominance we find extroverted gregariousness.) There are significant sex differences with men scoring higher on dominant traits, such as self-confident and assertive, and women higher on nurturing traits, such as kind and tender-hearted.

Dominance and nurturance are highly correlated with Bem's (1974) dimensions of Masculinity and Femininity. Bem asked 200 judges to rate the desirability of 200 adjectives to men and women. From the resulting data, she selected the 20 items that were most stereotypically associated with men (such as forceful and individualistic) and with women (such as compassionate and warm) and used them to create the Bem Sex Role Inventory (BSRI) on which subjects were asked to rate how well each adjective characterized them. She found that the two dimensions were statistically independent of each other (as had been found for dominance and nurturance) and that there were significant sex differences in how subjects rated themselves. Men rated themselves higher on traits such as self-reliant, assertive, willing to take risks—a dimension she called Masculinity. Women rated themselves higher on adjectives such as loyal, affectionate, and sensitive—which she called Femininity. But subsequent work on the BSRI has revealed problems. Most importantly, she included as items on the questionnaire the two adjectives "masculine" and "feminine." These items are very highly negatively correlated. Someone who describes themselves as extremely feminine will almost certainly describe themselves as not at all masculine. This suggests that masculinity and femininity are opposite poles of a single dimension, rather than being independent of one another as we would expect. Furthermore, these two items do not load on the Masculinity and Femininity dimensions extracted from the other adjectives. The extent to which you describe yourself as feminine is not highly correlated with whether or not you rate yourself as warm or compassionate. People's essential sense of their own sexual identity treats masculinity and femininity as two opposite qualities, but how feminine or masculine they feel overall is not reliably predicted by the number of feminine or masculine stereotypic traits they endorse. This led to Janet Spence (1985) to critically re-examine her own work that had been undertaken at the same time and in the same way as Bem's. Her Personality Attributes Questionnaire scales showed an extremely high correlation with Bem's scales and, like Bem, she also found significant sex differences. However, she argued that neither of them had measured what they thought they had. They had believed that they were capturing the essential nature of masculinity and femininity but in fact they had uncovered two dimensions of social behavior on which the sexes differed. To prevent further confusion, Spence argued that these dimensions should be called instrumentality and expressiveness and that we should clearly acknowledge that how a person scores on these two components of personality is distinct from their private ineffable sense of themselves as masculine or feminine beings. Dominance or agency is the personality dimension that is most relevant to understanding sex differences in status (see Cross & Madson, 1997). We shall take a closer look at communion in the next chapter.

Growing up competitive

Sex differences in dominance behavior begin early and continue into adulthood. Boys have been found to be more assertive than girls at 13 months of age (Goldberg & Lewis, 1969). Between the ages of two and four, boys more often attack people, fight, and destroy things than do girls (Campbell, Shirley, & Candy, 2004; Campbell, Shirley, & Caygill, 2002; Koot & Verhulst, 1991). At preschool ages, boys dominate girls (Pellegrini & Perlmutter, 1989) and, as we shall see, this is an important reason for the sex segregation that children spontaneously develop from about the age of three years (Maccoby & Jacklin, 1987). Boys are insensitive to the negative way that girls react to their style of behavior and girls find themselves overwhelmed by the abrasive and dominating tactics of boys (Maccoby, 1990).

When given a choice, boys prefer to compete while girls prefer to cooperate (Ahlgren, 1983; Boehnke, Silbereisen, Eisenberg, Teykowski, & Palmonari, 1989; Charlesworth & Dzur, 1987; Moely, Skarin, & Weil, 1979; Strube, 1981). This preference is reflected in the play styles that the two sexes adopt. Lever (1978) distinguished between play (a cooperative activity in which there is no winner and no clear end point) and games (competitive interactions governed by rules aimed at achieving an explicit goal). Boys spend 65 percent of their free time in games compared to 35 percent among girls. Boys choose directly competitive zero-sum games while girls prefer turn-taking games such as skipping or hopscotch where the form of competition is more indirect. In fact, girls seem to dislike situations where one person's win means another person's loss (Curry & Hock, 1981). When children are explicitly told to compete against all the other players, boys are happy to do so but girls still form small non-competitive friendship cliques (Hughes, 1988). In fact boys seem to spontaneously relish competition for its own sake. Roy and Benenson (2002) put children into same-sex groups of four to play a game. Each child was given a vertical stick on which they could thread beads. The aim was to collect enough beads to reach a red line drawn at the top of the stick. Each player rolled a dice to determine how many beads they could add to their stick. They then had a choice about where to take their beads from: they could choose to take them from another player's stick or from a common bowl of beads. The game was played under two conditions. In the direct competition condition, the first player to reach the red line got the prize. Here girls and boys did not differ in how often they took beads away from a peer because this was clearly a winning tactic. But in the indirect competition condition, all players who reached the red line received a prize. Here taking beads from another player did not advantage the bead-taker, it was essentially competition for competition's sake. And this is where the sex difference was apparent. Boys gratuitously took beads away from their peers while girls did not. In fact, the boys said that unless they took beads from each other the game would be "no fun at all."

While girls play in dyads and small cliques, boys prefer large groups in which they can play team sports such as football and baseball. Throughout history, men have predominated in team sports that depend upon coordination, speed, and agility (Craig, 2008). Boys' enjoyment of team sports has not altered over the last three decades (Sandberg & Meyer-Bahlberg, 1994; Sutton-Smith, Rosenberg, & Morgan, 1963). Although there are plenty of arguments during the game, boys resolve these by reference to commonly agreed rules. Of course, there are disagreements about their relevance ("That was never offside") but boys rarely take these disputes personally and seem to enjoy the verbal cut-and-thrust. Girls, by contrast, will abandon a game if it causes arguments (Lever, 1978).

Boys' love of sport may result from their stronger preference for gross motor behavior and propulsion, which is evident cross-culturally from infancy onward (Eaton & Enns, 1986; Eibl-Eibesfeldt, 1989; Lever, 1978; Whiting & Edwards, 1988). But boys also seem to enjoy the active competitiveness of sport and derive particular gratification from the approval of their teammates. Sports provide the opportunity for individual excellence in a public forum. And this does not seem to be imposed on them by adults. Benenson, Apostoleris, and Parnass (1997) created groups of six same-sex children who were allowed to play relatively unsupervised in a room furnished with animal puppets and foam balls. Five out of six groups of boys divided themselves into two teams and played out war games. They used the puppets and balls only as weapons. From time to time, they would have an unofficial truce to allow both teams to regroup and discuss tactics before returning to the fray. None of the girls groups engaged in team games, let alone aggressive ones. They played with the toys but spent much of the time just talking.

There is a marked difference between the sexes in their involvement in rough-and-tumble play: chasing, capturing, wrestling, and restraining. This sex difference is evident by the age of three years, with boys engaging in rough-and-tumble three to six times more often than girls (Maccoby, 1988). In one study, groups of three same-sex children were allowed to play freely in an experimental trailer equipped with a punch bag, trampoline, plastic ball, and pillow (DiPietro, 1981). In all of the 43 schools visited, boys' groups were more likely to launch playful attacks on one another, wrestle, and repeatedly hit the punch bag. This sex difference is as visible in hunter-gatherer societies as in Western nations. From Kalhari Bushmen to Brazilian Indian tribes, boys enjoy wrestling, chasing, and making toy spears and arrows to emulate the grown-ups (Gosso, Otta, Morais, Ribeiro, & Bussab, 2005). Despite its superficial resemblance to fighting, rough-and-tumble play lacks true hostility. Boys do it more with friends than with non-friends, move easily from a playful wrestling bout to other forms of play with the same partner and, if injury occurs, it is usually accidental. Boys not only seem to enjoy this kind of high-propulsion body contact, but they also accord it more social significance than girls. Boulton (1996) found that boys more than girls can tell who is strongest in rough-and-tumble play, think it is important to win, try to win in order to show that they are tougher, and think it is also important to be good at real fighting.

This kind of rough play seems to be important in establishing status in the group. Hierarchical dominance relations can be found in boys' groups from the age of six and once established, disputes are chiefly between individuals who are adjacent to one another in the pecking order. Boys rate the importance of social dominance higher than girls (Jarvinen & Nicholls, 1996). Athletic ability, strength, and early maturation are all associated with dominance in boys (Tanner, 1978; Weisfeld, Muczenski, Weisfeld, & Omark, 1987) and at high school age, girls are attracted to athletic boys (Closson, 2009). These status enhancing abilities seem to be established early and a boy's dominance at age six predicts his dominance nine years later (Weisfeld et al., 1987).

In a summer camp study in the United States, Savin-Williams (1987) examined the formation of boys' dominance hierarchies. Once dominance was established, it was remarkably stable over time and across different settings. The best predictors of a boy's overall dominance rank were his use of overt acts such as physical assertion, verbal directives, and threat. Those who ranked high in dominance tended to be athletic, fit, physically larger, and more attractive. The flavor of a dominant position in the camp is nicely conveyed by Savin Williams (1987, pp. 77–78):

> Perhaps because of his status position, Andy usually received what he wanted. On Day 1 he let it be known that he was going to sit beside SW during meals and he maintained that position throughout camp. On Day 10 Delvin had a choice of passing the cake, and hence decide who would grab the second largest piece, to Andy or to his best friend Otto. He passed it to Andy. When Gar suggested on Day 16 that perhaps the defense and the offense could switch for one day, Andy ended the egalitarian effort by retorting "Hell, no one is going to stick me on defense!" When Andy was in the top bunk, Gar frequently complained that his feet were hanging over the side of the bed in his face. Andy's usual response was "Tough! Move your face." After they switched positions at mid-camp, Gar quickly moved his feet when Andy complained they were in his face.

Savin-Williams found that there were five ways in which the boys used speech to assert their dominance; giving orders, calling people names, threatening or boasting, refusing to obey orders, and winning arguments. Maltz and Borker (1982) also found that boys use speech chiefly to assert a position of dominance, to attract and maintain an audience, and to assert themselves when another speaker has the floor. They emphasize that dominant boys are not simply verbal bullies. The important thing is not the content of the speech, but what successful boys can achieve with it. Speech is about claiming, holding, or disputing status. For boys, maintaining an audience is a real skill because, unlike among girls, the speaker cannot count on a patient and sympathetic audience.

> Storytelling, joke telling and other narrative performance events are common features of the social interactions of boys . . . The storyteller is frequently faced with mockery, challenges and side comments on his story. A major sociolinguistic skill which a boy must apparently learn in interacting with his peers is to ride out this series of challenges, maintain his audience, and successfully get to the end of his story. (Maltz & Borker, 1982, p. 208)

By adulthood, men more than women describe themselves as competitive, independent, dominant, self-sufficient, and powerful (Simmons, 1987; Wylie, 1974). Men rank relationships as less central to their sense of identity than do women (Thoits, 1992). Men's self-esteem, but not women's, can be predicted two years in advance by how strongly independent they feel (Stein, Newcomb, & Bentler, 1992). As they enter adulthood "Young men with high self-esteem seemed self-focused and defensively critical, uneasy, and unready for a connection with others" (Block, 1993, p. 28). Status can be enhanced by comparing oneself to less successful peers and men's self-esteem seems to derive from just such comparisons "The less positively men view their peers, the higher their self-esteem" (Goethals, Messick, & Allison, 1991, pp. 170–171). Even in childhood, boys are more likely than girls to be friends with children who are less competent than themselves on important tasks (Tesser, Campbell, & Smith, 1984) and to distance themselves from siblings who are better than them at school or in sports (Tesser, 1980). This use of comparison to bolster self-esteem extends even to romance: men who believe that their romantic relationships are superior to those of their peers express greater satisfaction with the relationship than men who think that their relationship is of similar quality to others. When it comes to close same-sex friends, both men and women prefer similarity in areas such as academic success and romance, but outperforming friends seems to upset women more than men and they believe that their friends would be more likely to dislike them because of it (Benenson & Schinazi, 2004).

Men's concern with status differentials has implications for their intimacy with friends. Because an element of competition always exists between them, men are wary about self-disclosure to other men. As Derlega, Durham, Gockel, and Sholis (1981, p. 445) put it, "if men do not disclose personal information, other people cannot understand, predict or control their behavior." Although men may disclose facts about themselves, they are much less willing than women to share emotions. One male respondent explained to a researcher why men's friendships are different from women's: "Well, there's a lot more sense of competition between a lot of men. A lot less openness about personal matters" (Walker, 1994, p. 250). They are particularly unlikely to share negative emotions that reveal vulnerability such as depression, anxiety, and fear (Snell, Miller, Belk, Garcia-Falcone, & Hernandez-Sanchez, 1989). Men's conversations with other men tend to focus on shared activities or on depersonalized topics such as politics and sport (Aries & Johnson, 1983). Compared to women, they are more likely to define intimacy with other males in terms of shared activities rather than shared emotional experiences (Caldwell & Peplau, 1982). Relationships with women are different: here men make emotional disclosures more often and regard these relationships as more meaningful, intimate, satisfying, and pleasant than male–male relationships (Derlega et al., 1981).

Men and women differ too in the political attitudes they hold. Men support group differentiation and group hierarchies: they hold more positive attitudes than women about conservatism, racism, militarism, and violence. They are more favorable to defense spending, stationing troops in foreign countries, and the death penalty but less favorable to spending on social welfare and to minimum wage legislation. These political views derive from what Pratto (1996) calls a stronger social dominance orientation—a preference for group hierarchy over group equality. Sex differences in attitudes to specific political issues (such as gender, gay/lesbian rights, and social welfare spending) are all explicable in terms of the different orientation that the two sexes have toward the basic principle of between-group equality (Lee, Pratto, & Johnson, 2011). Men see inequality as a natural result of competition and are unfavorable to policies designed to dilute or mitigate that competition.

As leaders, men operate in a more autocratic style compared to women (Eagly & Johnson, 1990). They more often emerge as leaders in newly-formed groups, especially when the leadership role involves organizing members' contribution to a group task (Eagly & Karau, 1991). This tendency for men to assume task leadership is found no matter how leadership is assessed—whether by analyzing verbal behavior, by tallying group participants' votes, or by task productivity. Traditionally, the qualities that we expect in leaders are the ability to take responsibility, assume control, and make decisions (Koenig, Eagly, Mitchell, & Ristikari, 2011). This leadership stereotype is highly masculine involving as it does typically agentic traits such as autonomy, decisiveness, and dominance.

Men's competition colors their sense of identity and their relationships with others. Too much intimacy with other men can be dangerous—it reveals vulnerability that weakens their claim to autonomy and gives away information that might later be used against them. Men crave closeness with other men and achieve it often, but they do so without revealing their private feelings—this they reserve for women with whom they need not compete. Men's relationships are more like alliances in which they support one another and share their interests, but always with an element of wariness. One drink too many and even the best of friends can find themselves competing to tell the best story, to argue a stronger justification for their political views, or to challenge the superiority of the other person. The end of a friendship, which is often devastating to women, does not prompt the same sense of loss because deep inside men are always on their own against the world. To lose an ally is not the same as to lose a soulmate.

What female dominance buys

We have seen why dominance matter to males. As Daly and Wilson (1983, p. 279) put it, "They wheel and deal, bluster and bluff, compete overtly both for valuable commodities and for mere symbols. Ultimately these male machinations reflect a struggle for access to female reproductive capacity." Note that what males struggle for is mere "access." As we have seen, copulations do not inevitably lead to pregnancy (and if they do, there is no guarantee of paternity), pregnancy does not inevitably lead to live births and live births do not inevitably lead to the production of an adult capable of reproduction in their own right. So the whole edifice of male status competition is built around the mere *opportunity* to leave a genetic legacy.

Given that the genetic connection between mother and child is certain, that female reproductive variance is lower than males, that maternal investment is high, and that only a fraction of infants survive—should we not expect to see even greater concern with status among females? The advantages of dominance for females are not measured in mere "opportunities" to produce young but in the survival of existing young in whom females are already invested. Should competition for status not be *more* rather than less intense among females? To answer this question, we have to begin by looking at the rewards for dominance in females.

Remember that females are not in general competing for copulations. Female primates do sometimes interrupt another female who is mating with a male but this is a way of decreasing a rivals' likelihood of pregnancy rather than competition for copulations per se (Stockley & Bro-Jorgensen, 2011). Even if they did routinely compete for mating opportunities, primate studies have generally concurred that males do not show a strong or systematic preference for high-ranking females, so female rank does not guarantee better quality partners (Loy, 1971; Packer, 1979; Small & Smith, 1985).

What females need most is a regular and ample food supply, and dominance could provide this. One explanation that has been offered for females' low levels of direct competition is that a single piece of food is not worth risking a life for (Kahlenberg, Thompson, & Wrangham, 2008; Smuts, 1987). But what if there were a way to guarantee continuous and permanent priority of access to any disputed food? Surely this benefit of dominance would be worth fighting for? Regular food intake is vital in a number of ways (Stockley & Bro-Jorgensen, 2011). Accumulated fat stores can carry a female through periods of famine. Low body weight is associated with infertile cycling and in primate studies that have provided food to free-ranging populations, the additional calories increase the number of offspring born. Food is necessary to sustain gestation and lactation. After weaning, food requirements increase even further in species like chimpanzees where the mother provides solid food for her young as well as feeding herself. Food intake accelerates growth so that juveniles attain puberty earlier. For female apes, access to adequate food resources is the key to greater reproductive success (Emery Thompson, Kahlenberg, Gilby, & Wrang-ham, 2007; Pusey, Williams, & Goodall, 1997). Dominant females have access to more and better quality food than subordinates, they expend less energy in obtaining food, their feeding is less often interrupted, and they are able to drive subordinates away from the best feeding sites (see Stockley & Bro-Jorgensen, 2011).

Dominance may have other rewards too. High-status animals are not sub-ject to harassment: indeed they are usually the ones who inflict it on others. High-status females harass subordinates to induce reproductive suppression. Sometimes this is done as a series of direct skirmishes by female coalitions and, at other times, by indirect signals that communicate their dominance. The re-sults are impressive and important: the victim's stress level rises (Hacklander, Mostl, & Arnold, 2003; Young et al., 2006) and, in response, the reproductive system closes down. Victims fail to enter estrous, refuse to mate, experience implantation failure or spontaneous abortion. The stress associated with har-assment can even reduce the victim's life span. By contrast, dominant females are more likely to have allies who will support them in a dispute. Their infants are less likely to be handled, kidnapped, or killed by other adults. And if rank is heritable, then their young will themselves grow up to experience all these rewards.

Does dominance increase female reproductive success? Ellis (1995) measured reproductive success in females from a range of species using key indicators such as number of offspring born, number of offspring surviving, the age of the female and the point in the breeding season at which first conception occurred. In addition, he also examined the length of between-birth intervals, infliction of reproductive suppression, number of copulations, strength of bonds with males, harassment of others during copulation, and the length of the females' life span or reproductive career. Among lowly rodents, it is clear that higher status is associated with greater copulation frequency, more offspring, a higher percentage surviving to maturity, and more reproductive suppression inflicted on rivals. Among other mammals, the data are more mixed but there is a gen-eral trend toward increased reproduction by higher-status females. Studies that have looked at cercopithecine monkeys usually find that higher rank is associated with earlier maturity and earlier age at first conception, shorter birth intervals, healthier offspring, faster growth, and about three-quarters of stud-ies find that rank increases the number of offspring born (see also Silk, 2009). Macaques are the species that has been studied most extensively. Although less than half of the studies found that maternal status was associated with more births, about two-thirds of the studies found that high-status females had greater infant survivorship and an earlier age at first birth. Among baboons, studies generally find an association between status and number of offspring born and about half showed that higher rank predicts infant survivorship, age at first birth, and freedom from reproductive harassment. Among chimps, higher-status females have greater offspring survival, reach sexual maturity earlier, live longer, and have a larger annual production of infants surviving to weaning age (Pusey, Williams, & Goodall, 1997).

Across species then, it appears that the relationship between rank and reproductive success is less clear among females than males. But that statement needs some qualification. Females are quality not quantity specialists and counting babies may be less informative than counting how many offspring survive and successfully reproduce. And establishing female rank is far from straightforward as we shall see. Rank disputes are rare and much less evident in female primates, introducing error into any attempt to correlate rank and reproductive success. Females' general level of aggressive interactions with one another is much lower (among chimpanzees, adult male aggression is 20 times higher than among females, de Waal, 1993). Female dominance relations are vaguer and less linear than among males. This kind of unreliability in the measurement of dominance diminishes the likelihood of finding significant associations for females.

The costs of achieving dominance

Looking at non-human primates, we find that female linear dominance hierarchies are confined to only some species—chiefly those that are *female-bonded* (Jolly, 1985). In female-bonded species (such as lemurs, vervets, baboons, and macaques) females remain in their natal group throughout their life, rather than transferring to a new group at sexual maturity in the way that chimpanzees do. A maxim of primatology is that social relationships depend principally on females since they act as a limiting resource on reproduction. Males go where the females are and so the way that females disperse gives rise to different forms of male organization. Females go where the food is and attempts to explain why most primate species are female-bonded have been driven by examination of the feeding patterns of different primate females (van Hoof & van Schaik, 1992; van Schaik, 1989).

If food occurs in well-defined clumps that can be monopolized by a few animals, females will strive to take control of it, increase their food intake, and so enhance their reproductive success. In these circumstances, dominance is important and a female can increase her power by having relatives with whom she can form alliances. These allies indirectly benefit because they share genes with the dominant female and hence her reproductive success is linked to their own. In addition, allies benefit from assistance from the dominant female when they need it. Dominance relationships tend to be consistent and linear—if female A outranks B then she also outranks C, D, and E. Groups of females feeding in this way will have a high emigration threshold—females should be unwilling to leave the natal group. If a female were to emigrate, she would be forced to enter at the bottom of the new group's hierarchy and she would have no allies to assist her. So where food competition is intense and food patches must be defended, females remain with their kin who make the best allies and they show a steep dominance hierarchy. Once the hierarchy is established, aggression over food is frequent but low-key and has been described as "mild bickering" (Walters & Seyfarth, 1987, p. 308). Hrdy (1981, p. 106) notes, " . . . females rarely inflict serious damage on one another in their quarrels. Even though female-female quarrels are more frequent than fights between males in most species, encounters between adult males are much more likely to result in one animal being wounded." Seyfarth (1976) found that among baboons the ratio of approach-retreat interactions to bouts of overt aggression was 20:1 for females and 1.7:1 for males. We have seen in Chapter 3 why females should be unwilling to risk severe assaults.

But how did the alpha female ever succeed in achieving her high rank? Are the dominance hierarchies found in female-bonded species an exception to my proposal that females generally avoid outright aggression? Are these females risking their lives and those of their offspring in their fights to achieve high rank? No, they are not: in female-bonded species, dominance is inherited not achieved. Everything depends upon which matriline you are born into (Kawai, 1958; Kawamura, 1958). Matrilines can be ranked with respect to one another with virtually no overlap so that all members of matriline A dominate all members of matriline B and so on. There are just three rules that predict a female's rank (Chapais, 2002). First, daughters inherit their mother's rank relative to other members of the group. There is no requirement for direct combat. Second, mothers dominate daughters for life. Daughters can rise to their mother's position in the matriline only upon her death. Third, in adulthood younger sisters dominate older sisters. This latter rule, which is consistently found, may be the result of mothers favoring the daughter with the highest reproductive value (Chapais, 2002) or it may be a strategic maternal decision. To prevent her daughters from forming an alliance against her, she operates a divide-and-rule favoritism so that the younger daughter cannot improve her rank by forming a coalition with her sister (Horrocks & Hunt, 1983). The rule-governed system of female rank inheritance is a million miles away from how rank is achieved by males. Male chimpanzees stay in their natal group, just as female macaques do, but rather than passing rank peacefully from one generation to the next, it is strenuously and dangerously contested. Challenges are occasionally lethal and nearly always damaging. Adult males frequently carry severe wounds from past dominance contests.

In female-bonded species, consider the benefits that could accrue to a female who broke the rules and successfully challenged a dominant female. Not only would she immediately increase her food intake, freedom from harassment, and reproductive success but all of these advantages would be passed down to her daughters. Unlike male chimps, her payoffs would not last merely months or years but through several generations. This makes it all the more remarkable that matrilines are extremely stable over time. Walters (1980) found that a juvenile female's rank at the time of her birth correctly predicted her adult rank in 97 percent of cases. In a 400-day study of yellow baboons, Hausfater (1975) found not a single instance of an agonistically induced change of status among females. Among capuchins, the female hierarchy is inherited, linear, strong, and stable over 22 years (Bergstrom & Fedigan, 2010). Female gelada baboons also show strong and stable linear hierarchies: over a four-year period, there was no alteration in rank position despite the disruptive potential of births, deaths, fissions, and male takeovers (Le Roux, Beehner, & Bergman, 2011). To examine the circumstances that might promote a challenge to rank, Chapais (2002) experimentally established a number of female groupings. He concluded that:

> . . . although competition for rank does occur, it also appears somewhat constrained. In all of the 58 experimental subgroups, actual relative power was in favour of subordinates, i.e. the latter were either larger or more numerous than the single highborn female. Despite this, subordinate females outranked the single dominant female in only 56 per cent of the 148 dyads tested. It is noteworthy that they outranked them only in situations where the power asymmetry (relative size or relative alliance power) was pronounced. This was referred to as a "minimal risk strategy" of competition for dominance. (Chapais, 2002)

So in species where food distribution induces competition, we see that females remain with their relatives to increase alliance support from their matriline. Their rank in the stable linear hierarchy is determined by their birth rather than by direct combat, and day-to-day aggression over food rarely results in injury because individuals know their relative position in the group and defer when threatened by a higher-born animal. Unlike male chimps (who also remain in their natal group) they do not show political maneuvering and complex alliance formation to usurp the dominant animal. Such tactics are dangerous and females are rarely willing to risk their life even in pursuit of long-lasting benefits. Even though the payoffs for a revolution from below are enormous, they are very rarely undertaken.

Our closest relatives are chimpanzees and they are not female-bonded. When adolescent females move to a new group, they have no kin support with them.

Non-female-bonded species feed on food stuffs that are spread out rather than clumped together. This leads to the dispersal of the females over a wide area and reduces direct conflict over food because it cannot be monopolized. Animals "scramble" for food rather than vying for control over food patches. Because of this, there is little advantage to having kin allies and this may be why females are willing to leave their natal group. Matrilines do not exist and individual dominance relationships are unstable and inconsistent (Emery Thompson, Stumpf, & Pusey, 2008). Female relationships are often described as egalitarian (de Waal, 1993).

This pattern is clear in wild populations of common chimpanzees. Females spend more than half of their time alone with their infants. While male chimpanzees spend much of their day grooming, patrolling, and hunting with other males (Gilby & Wrangham, 2008; Muller & Mitani, 2005), females are less gregarious. In fact, it was thought until recently that they rarely formed social bonds with one another. When female friendships were documented (Wakefield, 2008), it was believed that these dyads were simply a by-product of females foraging in contiguous territories, which happened to bring them into mutual proximity (Gilby & Wrangham, 2008). Recent observations suggest that female friendships, although they are associated with neighboring feeding areas, are not explained by them. They arise from genuine social affinity (Langergraber, Mitani, & Vigilant, 2009). Aggressive conflicts are rare because each animal occupies her own feeding territory and, when conflicts occur, they are about the control of high-quality feeding sites (Pusey et al., 2008). Female dominance relations are described as ill-defined, weakly-developed, egalitarian, and unstable (Van Hoof & van Schaik, 1992). It is often impossible to assign ranks to females because "dominance behavior in stable groups or stable pairs of females is uncommon and is never observed among some dyads" (Pusey et al., 1997). Females can sometimes be placed in rough "bands" or groupings according to patterns of deference they show to one another but there is little evidence of the clear linear hierarchy of female-bonded species. How female rank is achieved remains poorly understood but aggressive interchanges are extremely rare.

Studies of captive chimpanzees show the same absence of vertical structure. De Waal (1989, p.53) describes female relationships this way: "[T]he female hierarchy is rather vague. Since status communication is rare among females, it is difficult and almost useless to assign them positions on a vertical scale. The same is true of feral chimpanzee females." Over a six-year period, he witnessed not a single instance of female status ritual. Captive females form close affiliative bonds that are based on personal preference and shared history. These kinds of friendships may be more intense than in the wild where females are forced to spend much of the day alone with their infant, searching for food.

Once formed, these female friendships can be extremely stable. However, when antagonisms do develop, females are less conciliatory than males. Reconciliation occurs after only 18 percent of female fights compared to 47 percent of male fights. De Waal (1989) attributes males' greater willingness to reconcile to the male dominance hierarchy which depends upon political maneuvering and alliance realignment. Because females do not enter into such power-mongering alliances, they have less pragmatic motivation to forgive and forget. Their relationships seem to be based upon emotion rather than strategy.

Bonobos (pygmy chimpanzees) share an ancestry with common chimps from whom they split about one and a half million years ago. They are fascinating and highly intelligent animals but what makes them especially interesting is that the social relationships among females are very different from those of common chimpanzee and, as we would expect, this difference seems to have arisen from their feeding patterns (Sommer, Bauer, Fowler, & Ortmann, 2010). Common chimpanzees are found north of the Zaire River where the ancestral environment was harsh and changeable. Food was sparse and spaced out which resulted in mother–infant pairs foraging alone, separated from other females. Bonobos, however, found themselves in a Garden of Eden. They had an abundant supply of plant food in the forest, both up in the trees and down on the forest floor. Fruit is plentiful and one of their favorites, the Treculia fruit, grows to a weight of 30 kilograms—nearly the same size as an adult bonobo. So bonobos face a very different situation than chimps. They do not have to split into mother–infant dyads to find food. They have far more time to devote to their social relationships and these ties are especially strong among the females. Studies that compute grooming indices find a stark contrast between bonobos and chimps (Furuichi, 2009). Grooming rates are extremely high among bonobos, while among female chimps grooming bouts are 20 times lower than between males. One remarkable way that bonobos bond with one another is through sexual encounters. A female will approach another and stare fixedly into her face—a sign that she is soliciting sex. One of the two will then lie on her back while her partner mounts her and they rub their genitals together—a pastime dubbed G–G rubbing. (Who lies on top rather than below is arbitrary and unrelated to social seniority.) The clitoral stimulation seems to delight both of them and this may be the reason that bonobos unlike other primates typically copulate facing one another. Females are continually sexually receptive (though not continually fertile) and this may have evolved to harmonize social relations in the group. Although shallow (non-despotic) hierarchies have been found among females in captivity (Stevens, Vervaecke, de Vries, & van Elsacker, 2007), among wild bonobos females show no clear dominance ranking. Kano (1992, p.193) describes their relationship like this:

Older influential females do not perform dominance displays to show off their high position. (I call them "influential" because we do not use the word "high-rank" with respect to females.) These older females solicit various social contacts from their followers such as grooming, GG rubbing and copulation. They seldom receive threats or attacks from others (including males) and also rarely display aggressive behavior. They are respected out of affection, not because their rank is high.

The egalitarian relationship between bonobo females and the relative abundance of food means that females live peacefully together. Out of 325 recorded episodes of aggression, only nine occurred between adult females. In fact, female coalitions are sometimes strong enough to combat male coercive aggression, leading some researchers to argue controversially that bonobos are a female-dominant species (see Furuichi, 2009). The more equal relationship between the sexes seems to result from the very strong bonds between females that give them the power to contest male control and coercion.

Primate studies confirm the evolutionary prediction that competition between females is chiefly about food. The intensity of competition depends on the abundance and spacing of the food supply. If food can be monopolized, then dominance has advantages. But the achievement of dominance is rarely worth fighting for because the risk of injury or death is too high. So dominance is decided by inheritance and age. These tight rules prevent females from having to engage in the sometimes lethal competition seen among males. When food is spaced out, females adapt by foraging alone or with their infant. This spacing avoids the need for competition and its accompanying risks even though the price is a solitary existence with few female friends. When food is abundant and competition relaxed, as it is among bonobos, females become strongly bonded with one another despite the fact that they share no genetic relationship. Female fights are rare and much less lethal than those of males. Primate females do not show the scheming, shifting alliances and mob-handed attacks that males use to pursue dominance. The risks that accompany this kind of behavior are simply too great. Dominance brings advantages and, if it can be had without risk, females will take it. But if the price of status is bloodshed, females have good evolutionary reasons to stay out of it.

Women and status

Anthropological surveys of traditional societies show that, like apes, humans have generally favored male patrilocal residence which means that females transfer from their home group and lose the advantages of living with genetic relatives (Ember, 1978; Foley, 1987; Leakey & Lewin, 1979; Murdock, 1967; Rodseth, Wrangham, Harrigan, & Smuts, 1991). Together with this, consider van Hoof and van Schaik's (1992, p. 363) conclusion that "we consider the low rates of aggression and agonistic support and the weakly expressed dominance hierarchy as diagnostic of non-FB (female bonded) groups." Taken together, these facts suggest that women should show less evidence of dominance hierarchies than do men.

In childhood, we have seen that boys show a preoccupation with dominance in their styles of play, their preference for competition, their love of rough-and-tumble fighting, and the language that governs their social interactions. By contrast, girls in almost every culture are less competitive than boys (Strube, 1981). When given a choice, girls prefer cooperation to competition and there is a marked rise in this preference at the time of puberty (Ahlgren & Johnson, 1979). Girls are concerned with developing shared norms and cohesion within the group (Eder & Sandford, 1986) and more often resolve conflict through discussion (Eder, 1990; Youniss & Smollar, 1985). Girls use speech styles to create and maintain relationships of intimacy and equality, to recognize others, and accurately interpret what they are saying. They interrupt less, express agreement more, and more frequently acknowledge what another girl has said before beginning to speak (Maltz & Borker, 1982). Collaborative interchanges are most common in girls groups while domineering exchanges are more common in boys groups (Leaper, 1991). Girls are more likely to influence others by suggestion rather than by giving direct orders.

> In brief, the boys' structure their directives to emphasize differences between group members. Girls, on the other hand, share decision making during the task activities and formulate directives as proposals which include themselves as parties who are obliged to perform the action at issue. Their directive system during task activities tends to minimize differentiation among group members. (Goodwin, 1990, p.135)

Savin-Williams (1980) reviewed research on adolescent groups and came to four main conclusions. First, girls are less likely to form stable and consistent peer groups. Second, girls' groups are typically cliques composed of dyads or triads. Third, group structure is harder to discern and fourth, the female group serves to develop and support interpersonal skill and sensitivity. Later, in his detailed study of summer camp, he concluded that:

> Boys were more likely to physically assert themselves, argue with others, and, to a lesser extent, verbally and physically threaten and displace cabinmates. . . . The dominance structure among the early adolescent girls was not obvious to either group or non-group members . . . Dominance does not seem to appear to have been a highly desirable or discernible trait to them. (Savin-Williams, 1987, pp.124–126)

But this reluctance to engage in direct status competition goes beyond simply abjuring it. Girls seem to actively resent other girls who see themselves as superior. Girls who "stick out" attract a kind of negative halo—they are seen as egotistical and likely to betray friendships. Witness this interchange between teenage girls discussing their acquaintances (Brown, 1998, p. 136):

AMBER: I know someone who is really pretty, but her attitude is blown way out of proportion . . . is right out of it . . . Yeah, a major attitude problem.
STACEY: Snobby.
PATTI: Yeah, people who have attitudes . . . Nosy.
DIANE: What do you mean, like stuck up?
STACEY: Yeah, two-faced.
AMBER: Personality plays a big part in it.
DONNA: You've got to be able to trust them . . . A person that doesn't take over in a group.
STACEY: Oh, yeah. They are trying to be the center of attention.

Goodwin (1990) also found that inner-city girls criticized and rejected other girls who sounded too sure of themselves or whose behavior implied that they felt themselves superior to other group members:

> Girls differ from boys not only in terms of the criteria they employ for making comparisons but also in their attitudes towards the activity of ranking itself. Boys seem to openly encourage statements about relative ranking (although they of course may argue about them). However a girl who positively assesses herself or explicitly compares herself with others may be seen as showing character and attitudes that the other girls find offensive. Girls constantly monitor each other's behavior for displays that might be interpreted as showing that a girl is trying to differentiate herself from the others in the group. (Goodwin, 1990, p. 44)

In adulthood too, this reluctance to appear superior sets the tone of female friendships. Not only do women avoid bragging about their accomplishments, they actively work to understate them.

> Most women are well aware that failing to downplay their own success may arouse hostility and personal criticism and may cost them friends. Furthermore, many who are more successful than their friends—or are successful in different ways—feel guilty about the disparity, as though they were showing them up. Thus, women have good reasons to succeed in silence: not merely to protect other women from feeling bad or feeling jealous, but to protect themselves from other women's negative reactions . . . But self-deprecating appeasement doesn't really forestall competition. Rather, it reverses the usual direction; Nadine competes to lose, not win. Between women this form of downward competition is as habitual as the cycle of complaint and commiseration from which it takes its form. (Fillion, 1997, p.51)

Tannen (1996, p. 146) deconstructs the conversational ritual between women through which they actively ward off any suggestion of personal superiority. The "one-down-womanship" gambit is tacitly understood by both partners (at least if they are women) and the listener can be counted on to raise the speaker's status back up again: "Conversational rituals common among women involve each saving face for the other. One speaker is freed to take the one-down position (ritually, of course) because she can trust the other to, ritually again, bring her back up. Neither has to worry too much about casting herself in the best possible light because everyone is working together to save face for everyone else." Women recognize that another woman's understatement of her ability or success is not to be taken as a serious assessment, but as a polite social ritual designed to assimilate her into the group. The problem is that men often fail to understand this. A ritual female gambit such as "I was so lucky to get into college" will evoke "Nonsense, you've always been the clever one" from a woman but "Never knock luck" from a man.

This need to avoid appearing more able, decisive, or knowledgeable than others may explain why studies of leadership reveal that women are much more likely to become social leaders, responsible for maintaining good relationships in the group by expressing agreement and showing solidarity, rather than task leaders responsible for delegating jobs and assigning roles (Eagly & Karau, 1991). This may also explain why women who assume leadership roles prefer to use a democratic style that downplays their own authority in favor of engaging all group members on an equal footing (Eagly & Johnson, 1990). When women use an autocratic leadership style, they are evaluated less favorably than autocratic men—especially by other women (Eagly, Makhijani, & Klonsky, 1992; Statham, 1987). In a study of medical personnel, Tannen (1996) found that nurses were willing to accept an authoritarian style from male but not from female surgeons. Female surgeons who were most successful at enlisting cooperation from nurses were those who refrained from giving orders and instead emphasized the need for teamwork. Aries (1976) found that women who spoke more than average at one group discussion intentionally diminished their contribution at the next meeting in order to avoid appearing dominating.

To make it to the very top of the corporate world requires a particular constellation of traits: decisiveness, self-assurance, assertiveness, ambition, and willingness to take risks (Browne, 1995). Many of these are of course the very traits that are used to measure dominance or agency. Indeed one study found that a woman's score on this dimension was more predictive of career achievement than any other background information (Wong, Kettlewell, & Sproule, 1985). (Her score on communion—including adjectives such as yielding, loyal, sensitive to the needs of others—was *negatively* correlated with career success.) Because the prevailing view of leadership continues to emphasize its stereotypically male qualities, it puts women leaders in a Catch-22 situation. If they conform to this masculine leadership style, they violate their gender role and are disliked. But if they employ a democratic and inclusive style that is more congenial to women's natural way of interacting, they are not perceived as effective leaders (Eagly & Karau, 2002). This is all the more surprising because the democratic leadership style that comes naturally to women has emerged in many evaluation studies as more effective than autocratic styles (Judge & Piccolo, 2004). Yet the top echelons of business remain male dominated. Women who make it into these ranks have to compete on male terms. Top female executives develop many of the same qualities as their male peers—they are aggressive, ambitious, strongly career oriented, and willing to take risks. Small wonder then that, despite the lower pay and restricted career prospects, so many women avoid the fiercely competitive arenas of the private profit-making sector in favor of public or non-profit-making institutions. Women managers are most often found in departments where the emphasis is upon interacting with others in a supportive way (such as human resources, corporate communications, community and government relations), rather than positions where competition to make the best sales figures or departmental profit is intense and overt (Browne, 1995). Women care less than men about visible status differentials in the workplace such as money, status, and power (Rhode, 1991).

Many women see dangers in dominance. As Australians say "The tall poppy gets cut down" (Besag, 2000) or as the Japanese out it "A nail that sticks up gets hammered down." To be dominant is to incur the wrath of other women and to risk their intense and intimate friendship.

The popularity paradox

The picture of women's sympathetic and egalitarian relationships that I have painted is too rosy. We all know that, as Orwell might say, some women are more equal than others. Certainly some are more popular than others. Donna Eder (1985) was one of the first researchers to examine popularity. She worked with middle-school teenagers in the United States. Eder realized that female popularity was more complex than she had supposed when she found that the very girls who had been nominated by others as the most popular were also among the most disliked. Clearly, for teenage girls, "popular" meant something other than likeable.

Researchers measure "likeableness" by asking every member of a class (or group) to rate how much they like every other member. Each individual gets a score that shows how often she is chosen by others. Well-liked girls have the expected set of positive traits; they are prosocial, kind, academically competent, and they exhibit low levels of aggression and social withdrawal (Newcomb, Bukowski, & Pattee, 1993). But a rather different picture emerges when researchers ask students to rate their peers for popularity. The correspondence between the liking and popularity scores can be quite low (Parkhurst & Hopmeyer, 1998).

Popular students of both sexes embody a mix of positive and negative qualities: they are cool, rich, smart, well-known and fun to be with. But they are also conceited, powerful, influential, arrogant, exclusionary, manipulative, and aggressive (Adler & Adler, 1998; Closson, 2009; Lease, Kennedy, & Axelrod, 2002).

Popular girls are seen as having nice clothes, being physically attractive, and sociable. But they are also mean, snobby, rude, indirectly aggressive, intrusive, and teasing (Closson, 2009; Lease, Musgrove, & Axelrod, 2002). Girls, much more than boys, associate popularity with negative behaviors (LaFontana & Cillessen, 2002). This negativity emanates most strongly from those lower down the popularity totem pole. Highly popular girls think that popularity means being liked, whereas averagely popular girls think popularity means being mean, snobby, and conceited.

In Eder's (1985) study, the popular girls were members of high-status cliques and the chief criteria for entry were attractiveness and being a cheerleader (which also depended in large part on physical appearance). When girls first joined the ranks of the cheerleaders, they experienced a brief rise in social kudos and many other girls wanted to be their friend. But the chosen few began to ignore overtures by non-clique members and rapidly came to be seen as rude and snobbish. The same pattern is reported by Brown (1998) in her study of junior high school girls in Maine

> LYN (Interviewer): What bothers you so much about them? I mean, other than . . .
> LYDIA: I hate whiners.
> KIRSTIN: They're conceited.
> JANE: They treat us like we're nothing.
> KIRSTIN: They're so conceited, they think . . .
> LYDIA: They're like the kings of the school
> KIRSTIN: They're so much awesomer than us. They're like . . .
> LYDIA: "You're stupid," or . . .
> KIRSTIN: "Get away, you're a scrub. We're better." They don't say it, but they imply it so heavily it's disgusting.

The abandonment of their old friends from the lower-status groups was driven by the popular girls' awareness that association with non-cheerleaders would seriously jeopardize their membership of the elite group. In fact, they had to monitor their behavior just as carefully even within their own exclusive clique of friends:

> If one group member failed to acknowledge or was not especially friendly to another group member, she was frequently accused of being stuck up. The considerable anxiety surrounding the use of this label was evident when one girl would tease another and jokingly accuse her of being stuck up. In most cases, these accusations were taken seriously and denied rather than treated in a light and humorous manner. . . . Girls who were thought to be better than other group members were also accused of being stuck up, even when they had little control over this perception . . . In general, it appears that girls strongly uphold an egalitarian norm and view members who are better or worse than other group members as less desirable friends. Consequently, girls are concerned about being more successful than their friends and about being less successful. (Eder, 1985, p.162)

So there is little evidence of girls striving for individual prominence within these "popular" groups. Indeed, girls seem to actively work at negating their own superiority in order to avoid being seen as a snob and being ejected from the group altogether. It is true that the cliques of popular girls are more visible than others but this visibility is not the same as being liked or accepted—in fact, quite the reverse. When a girl is promoted into a high-status clique, she loses her old friends. This creates even greater pressure for solidarity within the new clique and an even greater need to debase her own qualities in the interest of equal relationships and continued membership. So even in areas where we might most strongly expect to see status striving, it looks very different from that of males. The aim is to belong but not to excel, to blend in rather than stand out, to be attractive to boys but not to alienate other girls. Brown (1998, p. 138) captures the image held by teenage girls of the perfect young woman: "beautiful, tall, long hair, perfect skin, pretty eyes, nice figure. This girl must also be talented and get good grades; *she is humble, modest and liked by everybody*, with a personality to match her looks."

The epigenesis of sex differences: Biology and social development

So far I have used evidence from primatology, anthropology, and psychology to illustrate men's preoccupation with dominance and women's reservations about its costs. But skeptical readers will by now be wondering how evolutionary psychologists could so willfully ignore the power of stereotypes in driving gender differences. Everyone knows how men and women are "supposed" to behave and our natural tendency to conformity pushes us to live up to these images from childhood onward. Hence, men are more interested in dominance than women because dominance is a characteristically masculine quality.

Evolutionary psychologists do not dismiss stereotypes but they interpret their relevance in a very different way. The stereotype has had a bad press. The *Oxford English Dictionary* defines it as "an unduly fixed mental impression" and in everyday usage we treat stereotypes as evidence of over-simplified and prejudiced thinking. Stereotypes are bad—we want to eradicate them. But psychology suggests that we may have a hard time doing so because schema provide an important mental shorthand for understanding the world. The ability to form schema—to categorize persons, objects, and events into natural groups—allows us to anticipate how they are likely to behave and how we should react. Consider the mental representation ("stereotype" if you will) of a house. When we think of a house in the abstract, our core representation contains the features that typify houses—walls, a roof, doors, windows, and an understanding that it is a place where people live. Although any given house—such as an igloo or a teepee—might violate our core stereotype, we still recognize it as a member of that group. Stereotypes may be "fuzzy sets" but they are handy for anticipating the unknown. As far as gender is concerned, stereotypes have taken a lot of flak. We are told that these simplified fictions of maleness and femaleness drive our expectations of sex-appropriate behavior and the way we socialize our children. Stereotypes are not merely useful interpretative mechanisms but, some argue, they have a causal status in the social world. They drive conformity and so ensure that maleness and femaleness become self-fulfilling prophecies.

What is the evidence that stereotypes are, as the dictionary defines them, "unduly fixed"? If we take such a phrase to mean unchanging over time—plenty. Consider women in the 1950s and 1990s. They came all the way from stay-at-home mothers to power-dressing executives. Yet our stereotypes of women (and men) did not alter over those years (see Lueptow, Garovich, & Lueptow, 1995). We continued to believe that men are more authoritative, ambitious, domineering, and competitive than women. With so little change over time, we can only suppose that structural changes in society had no impact upon gender stereotypes: stereotypes stumbled on with a life of their own blind to the changes that the personalities of women and men had undergone. Stereotypes lost contact with reality.

But did they? Other studies have investigated not stereotypes (people's view of the typical man and woman) but men's and women's actual ratings of their own qualities (Lueptow, Garovich-Szabo, & Lueptow, 2001). Here, people are given a list of adjectives (with no reference made to gender) and simply asked to indicate how well each adjective describes them as an individual. Again we find sex differences and no change in their magnitude. This stability is equally evident in standardized psychological tests of masculinity and femininity. It also appears on psychometric test norms for sex-linked traits such as "tender-minded" and "assertive" measured in 1955 and 1992 (Feingold, 1994). Could it be that while roles, responsibilities, and incomes have altered, the basic nature of men and women has not? Evolutionary psychology would be surprised indeed to find that evolved traits had undergone such a change in a period as short as 50 years. The fact that women work is no reason to suppose that they have altered their personalities. From an evolutionary point of view, the oddity is that there have been historical periods when women did *not* work. Without the calories that women provided through gathering tubers, vegetables, and honey, families would have starved. What marks our present-day environment as special is not the fact of women working but of women having to leave their children in order to do so (Hrdy, 1999).

It looks very much as if stereotypes are reasonably accurate appraisals of the differences between men and women. Alice Eagly (1995, p.154), whose own theoretical position has been strongly influenced by the notion of stereotype conformity, goes further noting that "the idea that gender stereotypes exaggerate reality has yet to receive convincing empirical support." If, as some have proposed, stereotypes drive conformity then we would expect that they would be much stronger than actual sex differences. After all, the argument is that gender stereotypes are idealized and overblown caricatures which we strive to approximate in our own behavior. Swim (1994) carried out a revealing study that took advantage of the known differences between women and men that had been revealed by hundreds of experimental studies. She asked her subjects to estimate the size of the difference between men and women over a variety of traits. Given that the participants in the study could not have met every man and woman in the country, they must have relied upon stereotypes to guide their responses. Her results showed that these stereotypes were actually underestimates of the real differences. Rather than presenting idealized exaggerations of gender, stereotypes slightly underestimate the differences between the sexes.

Then there is the developmental question: if sex differences in behavior arise from children's knowledge of gender stereotypes, we should expect to see sex differences only after children know what boys and girls are "supposed" to be like. By gender stereotypes, we mean not simply the ability to tell the difference between a girl and a boy but to make inferences about how girls and boys typically behave. We performed a longitudinal study to examine which came first— gender knowledge or sex-typed behavior—by measuring the same children at 24 and 36 months of age (Campbell, Shirley, & Candy, 2004). During that year, the children became markedly more successful at identifying the stereotypic toys and games that each sex liked. (Games were the most difficult and even by the age of three most children were unsuccessful.) The children also showed an increase in sex-typed behavior with boys engaging in more antisocial and dominating behavior (grabbing toys, resisting attempts to grab them, and pushing one another around) while girls showed an increase in spending quiet time in close proximity with their parent. Both sexes showed the expected increase in preference for same-sex playmates. But the really interesting finding was that gender stereotype knowledge at 24 months did not predict later sex-typed play preferences at 36 months. The message is clear: gender differences can occur without knowledge of stereotypes. Reviews of hundreds of studies conducted by developmental psychologists have converged on the same conclusions: "The literature does not support the proposition that concepts about gender (gender stereotypes) precede preferences or behavioral enactment" (Huston, 1983, p.409; see also Martin, 1993).

Then what can be causing sex differences? One possibility is that even by the time they are born girls and boys are already different in their interests and preferences. A poignant case study can illustrate this (Colapinto, 2000; Diamond & Sigmundson, 1997). In 1966, a pair of identical twin boys aged seven months were scheduled for circumcision to remedy problems with urination that were being caused by tightening of the foreskin. During the operation, one of the boys suffered severe burns to his penis from the electric cauterizing needle that was used. What was left of the blackened penis dried up and broke into pieces over the next few days. Seven months later the boys' parents spoke to a psychologist specializing in gender issues at Johns Hopkins medical center. He recommended surgical creation of female genitalia and raising the child as a girl. He was confident that if this physical and social change of sex could be done before the child was three (and achieved gender identity), there was every reason to believe that she would develop quite normally. Gender, he believed, was simply a matter of how a child was socialized. At 22 months, what remained of the penis was ablated and reconstructive surgery created labial folds and a cosmetic vaginal cleft. The child henceforth was named Brenda and her parents were instructed not to reveal any of the previous events or convey parental doubts that might make her question her status as a girl. Such was the pressure to conform to the doctors' instructions that in their letters to the hospital her parents emphasized her feminine behavior. By the time Brenda was seven, academic papers and books proclaimed that she had completely accepted her status as a girl. The tabula rasa principle of gender socialization appeared to be vindicated.

But Milton Diamond, an endocrinologist who had argued forcefully that sex-typed behavior is established prenatally by fetal androgens, was unconvinced. Since Brenda had experienced the normal surge of testosterone during the second and third trimester *in utero* and for two months after birth, he was astonished that her later behavior bore no signs of her original sex. Every year, Keith Sigmundson who had overseen Brenda's psychiatric treatment, noticed an advertisement in the American Psychiatric Society journal asking whoever was treating the twins to get in touch, but he did not respond. At last, in 1991, Milton Diamond contacted him and persuaded him to discuss what had become of Brenda.

Together they published a full account of the events up until her marriage at the age of 24 based on interviews with Brenda, her twin brother, parents, and teachers (Diamond & Sigmundson, 1997). Her twin brother described their childhood like this:

> I recognized Brenda as my sister but she never, ever acted the part. She'd get a skipping rope for a gift and the only thing we'd use it for was to tie people up, whip people with it. Never used it for what it was bought for. She played with my toys: Tinkertoys, dump

trucks. Toys like this sewing machine she got just sat. . . . When I say there was nothing feminine about Brenda, I mean there was *nothing* feminine. She walked like a guy. She talked about guy things, didn't give a crap about cleaning house, getting married, wearing make-up. (Colapinto, 2000, pp. 9–11)

A child guidance counselor noted "Brenda's interests are strongly masculine. She has marvelous plans for building tree houses, go karts with CB radios, model gas airplanes and appears to be more competitive and aggressive than her brother and is much more untidy both at home and in school" (Colapinto, 2000, p.11). At puberty, she was given female hormones to encourage breast development. She was miserably unhappy. When she was 14, after a session with her psychiatrist, Brenda's father could tolerate the deception no longer. He told her the whole story of what had happened. Brenda's reaction was not tears but relief: "Suddenly it all made sense why I felt the way I did. I wasn't some sort of weirdo." He immediately changed his name to David, switched from female to male hormone therapy, and had surgery to remove the breasts and construct a rudimentary penis. He later married and acquired two step-children. He bravely went public with his story in a bid to help other intersex children but his story did not end happily. In 2004, he committed suicide.

David's brain had been hormonally masculinized and no amount of socialization as a girl could alter that fact. His interests and his interpersonal style of relating to others had been set down very early, even before birth. After a male fetus develops testes, the production of testosterone begins and testosterone levels are particularly elevated between eight and 24 weeks of gestational age and for the first six months of independent life. When testosterone is aromatized into estradiol (an estrogen), it is capable of crossing the blood–brain barrier and affecting the chemistry and the wiring of the brain, shunting it along a male trajectory. (Genetic females are saved from the paradoxical masculinizing effect of their own estrogens by a protective mechanism that binds estrogen to alpha-fetoprotein and thus inactivates it.)

David's experience of a mismatch between brain and body arose as a result of an unforeseeable accident. Other children have similar experiences but from anomalous hormonal overdoses rather than bungled surgical procedures. Congenital adrenal hyperplasia (CAH) is one such condition which occurs when the developing fetus produces large quantities of androgens—a masculinizing hormone—from the adrenal glands. One child with CAH is born for every 5,000 to 15,000 live births. This excess of male hormone is often undetected in infant boys, but in girls it can be recognized by masculinization of the genitals at birth. Typically the condition is "corrected" by surgery to feminize the external appearance of the genitals. But this surgery cannot correct the organizing effects that androgens have had on the brain. In consequence, these girls as children show more "tomboyish" behavior than their peers (see Berenbaum, 1999, 2006; Berenbaum & Beltz, 2011). They enjoy masculine activities such as athletics and rough-and-tumble games, they choose male-typed toys, and prefer boys as friends. They show decreased interest in feminine clothing, cosmetics, dolls, and infant care. These differences are sustained into adolescence with CAH girls showing higher levels of aggression, greater interest in male activities (such as football, model building, working with engines), lesser interest in female activities (such as reading fashion magazines, cheerleading, keeping a diary), and more interest in typical masculine rather than feminine careers.

So before birth there are biological forces at work shaping the interest and activities of boys and girls. But these early differences are further canalized by a powerful social force. And that force is not parents but peers. There is a positive feedback loop that exaggerates these early sex differences through a very social amplifier—children's preference for associating selectively with their own sex.

As we have seen, boys' characteristic play style is boisterous. And it assumed a central place in the thinking of Eleanor Maccoby (1998) who struggled to understand the mechanisms that underlies sex segregation—why is it that boys and girls the world over prefer to associate with their own sex? Despite adult attempts to encourage cross-sex interaction, when children are given a free choice they pick their own sex as preferred partners (Serbin, Tronick, & Sternglanz, 1977). This is as true in Africa and India as it is in the United States and Europe (Dunn & Morgan, 1987; Omark, Omark, & Edelman, 1973; Whiting & Edwards, 1988). With these preferred partners, children seem to have a more enjoyable time—they engage in genuinely interactive play, rather than merely playing in proximity or passively observing (Serbin, Moller, Gulko, Powlishta, & Colburne, 1994). When three-year-old children are randomly assigned to play with a peer, twice as much social behavior is directed to a same-sex than a cross-sex partner (Jacklin & Maccoby, 1978; Lloyd & Smith, 1986). The same-sex preference is quite visible by the age of three and increases in magnitude until, by the age of six, children are spending as much as 11 times longer with same-sex than with opposite-sex peers (Maccoby & Jacklin, 1987). Maccoby believes that the force driving this is a kind of chain reaction that is initially triggered by the different play styles of boys and girls. Boys' behavior is more active, unrestrained, and rough, while girls' interactions are more modulated, harmonious, and less physical. Although children might be drawn to their own sex by their shared preference for the same kind of toys, studies suggest that it is not toy choice but interaction style that explains same-sex preference (Bukowski, Gauze, Hoza, & Newcomb, 1993; Serbin et al., 1994). Boys who show the most rough-and-tumble play and who are regarded by teachers as the most disruptive and active are the same boys who show the greatest preference for playing with other boys. Girls who are regarded as being the most socially sensitive and controlled are the ones who most often associate with other girls. This initial preference for others who enjoy the same ways of playing is then enhanced by a positive feedback loop—boys playing with other boys display higher levels of activity and increased amounts of threats, challenges, and competition (Fabes, Shepard, Guthrie, & Martin, 1997). Both sexes are responsive to the reactions they provoke in their own sex and relatively unaffected by the reactions of the opposite sex (Fagot, 1985). This has the effect of increasing the different kinds of interaction in girls' and boys' groups. Boys—especially in a group—are boisterous, unrestrained and rowdy. Girls avoid them, sensing and withdrawing from boys' dangerous inability to control their wild activity level. Sex segregation is seen first in girls as they avoid their over-excitable male companions but, after a year or so, it is boys who take the lead in sex segregation and refuse to take part in girls' games.

Once formed, boys and girls groups become increasingly distinctive. A new dynamic begins—in-group allegiance and out-group hostility. Psychologists have recreated this phenomenon in the laboratory by simply allocating people to different groups on the flimsiest of reasons, such as their preference for one of two paintings (Tajfel, 1982). Once formed, groups reinforce their identity by comparison with the other group. They attribute to the out-group ("them") a range of undesirable traits that differentiate them from the in-group ("us"). Furthermore while the in-group is seen as richly differentiated in its membership ("We are all different from one another"), the out group is homogenized as well as denigrated ("They are all the same"). These processes lie behind the formation of social identity. If researchers can generate these dynamics in the laboratory, imagine how much stronger is the impact in groups that spend every day at school together. The perceived distinctiveness of boys' and girls' groups is apparent in the way children describe them. Between the ages of five and eight, girls think that boys "scratch, fight and wear trousers," boys are "naughty" and "horrid." Boys believe that girls are "dumb," "rubbish," "horrible," "a little bit soppy," and "teacher's pets" (Abrams, 1989, pp. 65–66).

So strong are the between-group dynamics that by middle childhood, there are rules that govern association with the enemy (Sroufe, Bennett, Englund, Urban, & Shulman, 1993). Fraternization is permissible only under clearly defined circumstances. First, if the contact is accidental (if you bump into a member of the opposite sex). Second, if the contact is incidental (you have to line up next to members of the opposite sex in order to get a drink at the water fountain—conversation is not allowed). Third, if contact has a necessary purpose—you may ask a member of the opposite sex to pass something to you provided that no personal interest is expressed. Fourth, contact is acceptable provided that neither sex is alone—two boys may speak to two girls as long as same-sex contact is more evident than cross-sex contact. Fifth, interaction is acceptable if it is accompanied by disavowal—a child may verbally insult or physically intimidate a member of the opposite sex.

What lies behind these strictures on cross-sex interactions? Remember that by adolescence, these same interactions will not only be sought out but become a central part of most teenagers' lives. An intriguing suggestion has come from Daryl Bem (1996). He took on the task of trying to explain sexual orientation and his answer involved a five-step chain of causal links. Rather than arguing that for a direct genetic basis to sexual preference (Hamer & Copeland, 1994), he argued that the principal genetic effect is upon childhood temperament, especially boys' aggression, rough-and-tumble play, and activity level. Temperament affects the kinds of activities and games that children like and draws children together with others who share those preferences. In the majority of cases this is same-sex peers. Once in these groups, children develop a strong feeling of being different from the opposite sex. While Maccoby sees this step as a social psychological one involving group differentiation, Bem conceives of it as a less social and more personal experience. He notes, for example, that among adult homosexuals 71 percent of gay men and 70 percent of lesbians retrospectively recalled feeling different from their same-sex peers (see Bailey & Zucker, 1995). (Among heterosexuals 51 percent of men and 38 percent of women also said that they had felt different. But unlike the homosexual sample who cited anomalous gender-linked preferences as the factor that made them feel different, heterosexuals cited reasons that were unrelated to gender-typing such as differences in intelligence, extraversion, or physical attractiveness.) Now comes the step that gives it name to his theory: "Exotic becomes erotic." He argues that, at sexual maturity, we experience sexual arousal in the presence of peers that we see as different from us. For heterosexuals, this is the opposite sex and for homosexuals their own sex. How does this occur?

One answer is sexual imprinting, a phenomenon originally proposed by Westermarck (1891). He noted that individuals who had spent their childhood together tended to avoid sexual intimacy in adolescence and adulthood. In Taiwan, it was the practice for families to "buy" a girl child who would live in the family and provide domestic labor until she reached adolescence, when she would be married to the son of the family. These marriages had a high rate of failure, non-consummation, and childlessness. In a similar vein, children raised in communal nurseries on kibbutzim do not later marry (Shepher, 1971). For evolutionary psychologists, such a finding strongly suggests that operation of an evolved module geared to incest avoidance. The peers with whom we would normally be raised would be siblings and hence such a mechanism would ensure that we did not feel attraction to them at puberty. The fact that sexual attraction is diminished in "simpua" marriages and kibbutzim suggests that the module is triggered by extensive early contact rather than by some form of kin-recognition system. In a sense, the incest avoidance module is "fooled" by the input. This same mechanism, however, can be exploited as an adaptation for eroticizing the opposite sex if it operates under a general psychological mechanism of causing disgust at the idea of having sex with our childhood peers. We would only be attracted to individuals with whom we had not spent extensive time as children, and in the majority heterosexual case this would be the opposite sex.

If Bem is right, then pre-adolescent cross-sex interaction might be seen as indicating either homosexuality or precocious sexual interest. On the first point the literature is clear—sex role rigidity is far stronger for males than for females and boys suffer the consequences of "being different" more extremely (Archer, 1992). Boys who prefer to play with girls or enjoy feminine games are subject to considerably more ridicule than girls who show masculine preferences. Tomboys are acceptable but effeminate boys are not. By adolescence, this intolerance is most marked among male peers (Duncan, 1999, p. 108):

> CARL: There is no way I'd be mates with a poof.
> ND (Interviewer): What about you?
> CARL: If he was queer? I'd slap him, I would. I would not have him coming near me.
> ADIE: It's right. I would do the same, not hit him, but tell our mates and we'd probably all get him. Let him know.

Boys reject feminine boys quite brutally—ridiculing, shunning and referring to them as "girls" (Thorne, 1986). These boys are positioned far down the boys' status hierarchy (Best, 1983). Fathers, as well as male peers, are alarmed by evidence of a boy's inappropriate gender role behavior, concerned that he may grow up to be homosexual. Adult homosexuality is seen as a likely outcome of effeminate boyhood, but boyish behavior by girls (being a tomboy) is seen as a temporary phase. Fathers are more likely than mothers to refer their sons to psychologists and psychiatrists about gender-atypical behavior (Archer, 1984, 1992). A follow-up of boys who were referred to a gender clinic program in California suggests that these paternally forecasted outcomes were often accurate: most boys referred at the age of 12 or younger for effeminate behavior developed homosexual or bisexual preferences within the next 10 years (Green, 1987; Zucker, 1990).

But alternatively, early cross-sex interaction might signal precocious sexual interest. If it is not subject to "gay" teasing, it often provokes "they're in love" teasing. Many cultures have their own versions of the kiss–chase game in which members of one sex must tag a member of the other and then kiss them. The game seems to generate a frisson of excitement and taboo, despite the fact that boys particularly are inclined to treat a kiss from a girl as a form of contamination ("catching a cootie," Thorne, 1986). Any cross-sex encounter—even the most innocent—is liable to be interpreted as romantic interest. A boy who entered a girls' tent at summer camp when retrieving his radio was greeted with taunts from his friends wanting to know if he had been kissing them (Sroufe et al., 1993). A boy who harasses a particular girl too much (chasing, pushing, or calling her names) is equally likely to be accused of being attracted to her—a form of behavior that has been eloquently named "pushing and poking courtship" (Schofield, 1981). As Maccoby (1998, p.69) explains: "Children themselves seem aware that a declaration of 'hating' a given child of the opposite sex is by no means a denial of interest in that other child, and indeed can be very close to 'liking.'" Cross-sex encounters seem to both attract and repel children, combining the anticipatory pleasures of future romantic intimacy with the recognition that at present they are too young to fully enter this sexual minefield.

As well as maintaining the social separation needed for later eroticization, sex-segregation sets the scene for close peer scrutiny of sex-appropriate behavior. Years of research have made it clear that peers are more influential than parents in children's social development (Harris, 1995). And with good reason—peers are drawn from that generational cohort in which future allies, enemies, and mates are likely to be found. The childhood peer group is salient to children for the same reason that the adult peer group is salient to adults. Social success is about relationships with our own cohort. Just as adults do not slavishly seek acceptance by their child's peer group, no more should we expect children to care about their popularity with adults. Children may acquire underlying sex-typed preferences from evolution and biology, but the specific ways in which they are expressed is likely to be molded by their peers. Sex segregation both enhances the differences between boys' and girls' groups and minimizes variability within each group. The ways in which masculinity and femininity are expressed change across time and culture and much of this "fashion setting" is done by peers. Boys in contemporary Western culture prefer four-wheel drive cars to chariots, guns to lances. Girls prefer Barbie to rag dolls, and toy microwaves to cauldrons.

The trigger for this process of sex segregation (and all that follows from it) seems to emerge from the boisterous and exuberant behavior of boys focused around the establishment of a dominance hierarchy—one that girls neither seek to be part of nor to replicate within their own sex. Yet that very quality which girls abhor—superiority at the cost of reciprocity, conspicuousness at the cost of intimacy—is something that will later prove peculiarly attractive to them in the opposite sex.

Why winning is dangerous

Dominance brings rewards—deference from others, the pick of the best resources, and freedom from the daily stress of appeasing others and hustling for a share of leftovers. The rewards are just as great for females as for males—arguably greater. We would all opt for dominance if it cost nothing. But dominance is a zero-sum game that creates winners and losers. To win you have to compete and competition means conflict. Among primate males, these conflicts are dangerous and can be deadly: alpha males do not give up without a fight. We have seen why females should be especially reluctant to risk their own life and those of their young to attain dominance.

In female-bonded primates, a few females have found a way to have it all. Rank is inherited rather than fought for. The benefits of dominance are a happy accident of birth, not a result of bravery. But what of those who are born to low-ranking mothers? Why is there such extreme reluctance to challenge this despotic and unfair system of privilege? The answer is fear. The costs of a failed revolution are too great and only under the most extreme conditions—when they massively outnumber the opposition—will low-status females risk the little they have for a larger share.

In common chimpanzee groups, adult females have no kin allies. They forage independently and their closest relationship is with their offspring. If that offspring is a daughter, then she too will leave them one day to seek her fortune in another group. Daughters return now and then, as if to acknowledge their tie to a mother who has sacrificed so much for them. Though females show evidence of special friendships with one another, the demands of daily foraging constrain the frequency of their interactions with one another. This lonely lifestyle may be hard but it is better than risking life and limb to fight with other females over each piece of food. Bonobos also leave their natal group but nature has been kinder to them. They feast on the fruits of the forest and need not compete for the resources they need to survive. Because they have time to spend together, they forge very close female friendships. Unlike males, these friendships are not shot through with squabbles about dominance. Though some individuals are more influential than others, such influence comes through age and personality rather than fighting ability.

The common thread for females from different primate species (including our own) is their reluctance, compared to males, to engage in direct competitive aggression. Girls' development is marked by this avoidance of physical combat. But more than this, it is marked by a greater indifference to public status and an active aversion to flaunting dominance over others. The emphasis upon egalitarianism is so strong that girls and women manage their self-presentation to minimize the possibility of being seen as stuck-up or snobbish. To incur the resentment of others is to risk conflict, and conflict might lead to confrontation. Although in today's society outright fighting is rare, this aversion to conflict is an inherited adaptation that was forged in an environment much harsher and more ruthless than the one we currently inhabit.

But conflict carries with it another danger too—banishment and exclusion. A woman who thinks she is superior to the rest, risks becoming the victim of the specialist female strategy of indirect aggression. She is ignored, shunned, and rejected. Social isolation provokes a special fear in an obligately social species such as humans. In Chapter 5 we shall try to answer another evolutionary puzzle—what made women so dependent on their friendships with one another?

---

* Reprinted by permission of United Agents and Faber and Faber Ltd on behalf of Wendy Cope.

Like a sister: Women and friendship

Women's friendships are deeply enigmatic for evolutionary theory. Our species evolved in a pre-history in which women left their relatives to live with strangers in an unknown community. Yet despite the lack of blood relationship between them, women became friends. Indeed they became more than friends, they became intimates. They forged not just equitable relationships with one another ("I'll help you if you help me"), but something stronger than this—they forged an emotional interdependence that went beyond mutual back-scratching. Their relationships were intense, trusting, and communal. In this chapter we will explore how and why this happened. But first let's look at the key differences between the friendships of men and women.

The intimacy/size trade-off

Women's friendships have a different flavor to those of men both quantitatively and qualitatively. From childhood on, girls prefer to have one or two intimate friends while boys play in larger groups (Rose & Rudolph, 2006). This is not to say that boys never engage in two-person interactions. In one study, boys and girls spent about equal amounts of time in dyadic interactions but for girls these exchanges occurred with a fewer range of people and were more extended in time. Boys moved from one partner to the next, spending less time with each of them (Benenson, Apostoleris, & Parnass, 1997). In a study of young people at summer camp, researchers examined network density: the proportion of a child's friends who were friends with each other (Parker & Seal, 1996). Boys and girls began with the same network density but by the end, boys' network densities were considerably larger than those of girls. Over time, boys' circles of friends expanded leading to greater interconnection while the girls' networks became increasingly restricted. Girls' friendships are more exclusive and more intense.

A key part of the intensity of female friendships is their intimacy. As one teenage girl put it "girls can talk to each other, boys just keep things into themselves, they don't tell no one nothing" (Brown, 1998, p. 50). For women, intimacy means self-disclosure—confiding private details and experiences to another person. Self-disclosure can be broken down further, however, into descriptive self-disclosure (in which we share facts about our lives) and evaluative self-disclosure (in which we reveal the emotional impact that these experiences have had on us). Men's friendships seem to include a comparable degree of descriptive disclosure but less evaluative disclosure than women's (Cross & Madson, 1997). Men are especially reluctant to disclose negative emotional experiences such as depression, sadness, anxiety, and fear, whereas discussion of these vulnerabilities is the mainstay of close female friendships. This sex difference does not seem to be linked to different motivations—men express just as much interest and desire to have close relationships as women do. But studies of their actual patterns of self-disclosure suggest that they reserve it for women rather than sharing it with men (Dindia & Allen, 1992). In men's friendships, intimacy revolves around experiences that are relevant to their shared interests. They discuss public-domain issues that they have in common such as sport, business, and government. Men believe that these common interests and activities are the most important factor in their friendships. Women are more likely to talk about personal topics such as feelings, relationships, and problems (Bischoping, 1993; Caldwell & Peplau, 1982).

When things go wrong, girls and women turn to their friends for emotional empathy and advice. Women provide a sympathetic ear and are more focused on supportive listening than on problem solving. Men react to stressors by distracting themselves or putting the problem out of their mind: "A problem shared is a problem doubled" seems to typify their view. To men, unburdening to a friend not only advertises an inability to solve their own problems but entails divulging errors of judgment—weaknesses that gave rise to the problem in the first place. But women's reliance on female friends carries its own hazards. When faced with a problem, women find it hard to resist co-rumination; they re-run and re-analyze the stressful incident from every possible angle, entertaining different solutions and different possible futures. This tendency to dwell on negative incidents contributes to women's higher rates of depression (Hankin, Stone, & Wright, 2010; Rose, 2002).

Women's intimate conversations establish and depend on mutual trust (Dindia & Allen, 1992). A best friend knows all of a woman's secrets and this intensity breeds a need for exclusivity. Once such a relationship has been established, it is jealously guarded as Eder and Sandford (1986, p. 293) describe:

> Tami at one point interrupted her story to ask Heidi if she had been combing Peggy's hair the other day. Heidi denied it but Tami persisted saying "Yes, you had." Heidi denied it again and just then Peggy happened to walk by. Heidi asked her if she had been

combing her hair and Peggy said, "no." Then Tami said to Heidi, "Well, whose hair were you combing?" Heidi said "I wasn't combing anybody's hair!"

To spend too much time with a third party is to threaten the exclusive bond and much gossip between girls revolves around who is "best friends" with whom. Because girls reveal so much of their private lives and personal feelings to one another, the loss of a best friend threatens not only loneliness but also the betrayal of the confidences that have been made. The importance of trust runs through the literature on girls' and women's friendships and the greatest betrayal is the abuse of trust. It is trust that distinguishes a best friend from other friends:

> I probably trusts her the most of anybody and she trusts me. I mean, of course people have told me things that they don't really want anyone else to know, and I've told someone else and everybody does that. But something Jane tells me I couldn't tell anyone else. Something that I told her, I hope she couldn't tell anyone else . . . Like Nicky [another friend] and me are very close but I couldn't trust her at all. We're basically not very alike. She doesn't really know how much something means to me when I tell her something, and, I mean, she's very bitchy behind my back. (Lees, 1993, p. 76)

Best friends hold a special status for women. These relationships can endure for many years and partners are privy to each other's most personal experiences and innermost emotions. As Fillion (1997, p. 5) describes one typical female friendship:

> They entertained and sustained each other, sharing even the most mundane details of their lives—especially their love lives—and remembering to ask how each other's big meetings had gone. Both were successful, but disaster was the staple of their conversations: men who said they would phone but never did, mothers who turned every phone call into an inquisition about their marriage prospects, male colleagues who got the promotion that would have been theirs if they too had been given the opportunity to bond with the boss on the golf course. The anecdote of failure became something of an art form between them; the narrator usually depicted herself as a hapless naif, bumbling through crisis with gallows humor. But there was always a feel-good ending: the more they confessed, the closer they felt. . . . One night by way of concluding a baroque tale about an unreliable ex-boyfriend, Anna sighed and said, "I think I've given up on men. Too bad you're a woman, we'd make a perfect couple." Of all the possible subtexts to her remark, Julie thought the most important one was this: men come and go, but women friends last forever. Monogamy was not the label she attached to her expectations, but it fit. The best friend is, after all, singular by definition.

Because time and energy are finite, all of us face a necessary trade-off between the size of our friendship group and the intensity of each friendship (Geary, 2010). But women and men have solved it in different ways. Women have opted for intensity and men for size. When asked to make a direct choice between their preference for a larger number of friends or a higher level of intimacy with each of them (defined as emotional support and willingness to help solve personal problems), men go for number significantly more than women (Vigil, 2007). Men report having more friends than women, while women invest more time in their fewer friendships; they spent longer than men talking to their best friends, specifically about personal feelings and relationships. Make no mistake: men need and value friends. The preoccupation with dominance discussed in Chapter 4 does not mean that men are social isolates (Baumeister & Sommer, 1997). Nor is there anything second-rate about male friendships: boys and men report just as much satisfaction with their relationships as women (Lempers & Clark-Lempers, 1993; Parker & Asher, 1993). But they reflect a different set of priorities.

For men, dyadic friendships are less important than the group as a whole. The greater size of men's groups contributes to the structure they assume: dominance hierarchies become an organizational necessity as well as a means of striving for power, resources (and women). The jockeying for status—and the shifting alliances used to achieve it—mean that men are more tolerant than women of interpersonal conflicts. Yesterday's antagonist can easily become tomorrow's ally. An argument that would devastate a female friendship is just part of the cut-and-thrust of social competition for men. But the verbal sparring and humorous (and not so humorous) one-upmanship between men fades away when their group faces a threat from the outside. There is nothing like a common enemy to bring men together. Men's intergroup rivalries seem to be universal whether in political factions, gang hostilities, or competitive team sports. In one experiment, male and female undergraduates were put into six-person groups and each member was awarded a sum of money (Van Vugt, De Cremer, & Janssen, 2007). They could choose to keep the money or invest it in the group. If at least four of the six members chose to donate it to the group, all members would receive twice their original allocation in return. If fewer than four people donated, then no bonuses were given and those who had contributed lost their money. Then came the experimental manipulation. Some groups were told that the same experiment was being run at 10 different universities and the results would be compared. This was enough to produce a significant sex difference: men contributed significantly more than women when an element of intergroup rivalry was introduced. Men rally together impressively when challenged by another group (Bugental & Beaulieu, 2009; Pemberton, Insko, & Schopler, 1996). Nowhere is this more dramatically demonstrated that in men's stories of wartime experiences. Months and years can be spent together living at very close quarters, on inadequate rations, poorly clothed, and wholly dependent on one another for the will to survive and succeed. This ability to close ranks in the face of external threat gave men power and this power may explain a great enigma of human prehistory: why women and not men left their natal group to live among strangers.

The puzzle of female friendships: Female exogamy

Women often describe their closest friend as being like a sister to them. But of course they are not. They are one-time strangers who became so close, trusted, and dependable that they began to feel like members of the same family. But in the animal world the rule is that we are closest to our blood kin. In a fight, they will back you up; when in trouble, they will help you; when you are hungry, they will feed you. It is in the interest of any animal to remain with its own kin because they make the most dependable allies and, in a social species, allies are the key to survival. Kin care about one another because they share genes. By saving kin, we increase the probability of saving a proportion of our own genes. If you save a sister or a daughter, you save 50 per cent of your own genes. If you save a niece or a grand-daughter, you save 25 per cent. Kin are loyal because they are genetically intertwined.

But one sex must always give up the comfort and safety that kin provide. Sexual reproduction requires the mixing of unrelated genes. Inbreeding increases the rate of harmful genetic mutations so, to keep the gene pool fresh, some members of the group must leave home. In most primate species, females stay with their kin and the males, after reaching juvenile status, have to leave and find a new group of females within which to seek mates. Because females are a limiting resource for males, they are obliged to fit in with the females' plans.

But among a few species, males won the right to stay home and females dispersed. This pattern occurs in hamadryas baboons, red colobus monkeys, chimpanzees—and humans. In a world survey of human societies, Murdock (1967) found that two-thirds were patrilocal and less than a fifth were matrilocal. In hunter-gatherers, whose lifestyle typified human communities for many thousands of years and who are among the most egalitarian of all societies, 62 per cent involve female transfer (Ember, 1974). Female transfer becomes increasingly common, rising to 71 per cent, as societies move from hunter-gatherer lifestyles (in which women make a major contribution to food production) to more formal economies involving agriculture, division of labor and trade (Hawkes, O'Connell, Blurton-Jones, Alvarez, & Charnov, 1998). The predominance of male philopatry has been confirmed by DNA analyses. The non-recombining section of the Y chromosome passes only from fathers to their sons while mothers contribute mitochondrial DNA to their offspring of both sexes. These twin facts, combined with DNA analysis of contemporary populations, can help us to reconstruct migration patterns of ancient men and women. These analyses show that men were less likely to migrate into new populations than women (Hamilton, Stoneking, & Excoffier, 2005; Langergraben et al., 2007).

Remaining with kin confers significant advantages, so it is unlikely that women readily agreed to it. "Philopatry, consanguinity and cooperation tend to coincide" (Rodseth, Wrangham, Harrigan, & Smuts, 1991, p. 230), so it would be a foolish animal that gave up these advantages without a struggle. Chimpanzee females transfer with understandable reluctance. One day when a young female is in estrous and near to a neighboring group of males, she will leave and join her new group. But she is likely to be on the receiving end of considerable aggression from her new female companions (who resent the additional competition for resources that she presents) and she may return temporarily to her natal group as if seeking comfort or reassurance (Pusey & Packer, 1987). Why did females simply refuse to emigrate? As yet we have no definite answer. Male philopatry is likely the result of males banding together cohesively and forcing females out. To achieve that kind of solidarity, some ecological force must have acted to increase males' in-group cohesiveness and decrease their internal squabbles. That force was probably an enemy.

Humans and chimps are territorial. Control of a territory means food, water, safety, and stability. An established territory is worth defending at all costs and new territory is worth fighting for. Bigger and better territory attracts immigrant females to join the group. And if the females are not tempted by the resources, they can be forcefully kidnapped, abducted, and raped (Chagnon, 1983). Male chimpanzees patrol the boundaries of their territories, challenging individuals from adjacent areas and early humans did the same: "Only two animal species . . . have a system of intense male-initiated territorial aggression, including lethal raiding into neighboring communities in search of vulnerable enemies to attack and kill. Out of four thousand mammals and ten million or more other animal species, this suite of behaviors is known only among chimpanzees and humans" (Wrangham & Peterson, 1996, p. 24). Because of the value of territorial control, male bonds became strong and, coupled with men's greater size and strength, juvenile females may simply have been forced out. This hypothesis is supported by comparing chimps with orangutans. Both have the same diet and the same range size, but orangutan males do not cooperate in territorial defense and consequently have less reason to remain together. In this species, it is the males who emigrate (Pusey & Packer, 1987). In human evolutionary history, the necessity of holding and expanding territory against a common enemy was the basis of male group-level alliances. Warfare is dangerous. It requires a willingness to lay down one's life and, in evolutionary terms, this is a reproductively successful strategy only if the recipients of this benefit are genetic kin. (Even in early twentieth-century warfare, British conscientious objectors were tested by asking them how they felt about failing to defend their mothers from rape and murder.) Men's willingness to risk their lives depended upon remaining with their own kin. And this may have been the reason for enforcing female exogamy.

But how did males succeed in establishing such a high degree of group cohesion when, within their own group, they were natural competitors for mating opportunities? How did group level commitment develop in the face of within-group male competition? Surely, competition for females stood in the way of males achieving the kind of common interest they would need in order to form coalitions with one another? Even chimpanzee brothers will dispute access to an estrous female despite the fact that they share 50 per cent of their genes (though the disputes are less fierce than among unrelated males). But it is from observations of chimp political maneuvering that we can begin to see how it might have happened. Males form alliances to challenge the dominant male, although these alliances are opportunistic and shifting. Having overthrown their mutual enemy, two allies would not hesitate to fight one another with the loser entering another alliance to start the cycle again. Often male allies use their power to coerce females into copulations, both within their own group and beyond it, making females vulnerable to the threat of attack not just by one but two angry males (Goodall, 1986).

During human evolution, men became increasingly successful at sustaining alliances with one another in the face of the competitive tension between them. Men's capacity to set aside individual conflict over reproductive opportunities may have been enhanced by their increased ability to engage in strategic planning which freed them from the immediate short-term imperative of competition. Long-term planning may also have been the driving force that moved humans away from despotic rule by a single, privileged male and toward democracy and power sharing (Henrich, Boyd, & Richerson, 2012). Dominant men began to recognize that the best way to ensure faithful and committed followers was to give up their monopoly of female reproduction and encourage monogamy. To keep other men pacified and loyal, it was wise to ensure that they could meet their basic needs and the most basic of all was reproductive opportunity (Betzig, 1986). In this way, male–male competition for mates was mitigated and men were able to act in concert to launch territorial takeovers against neighboring groups which had the twin benefits of extending their food supply and acquiring additional women. During times of peace, women were exchanged in marriage to foster alliances between groups while blood-related males stayed together (Berndt, 1964; Hayano, 1973). Women were commodities—gifts to cement ties between groups or trading tokens between friendly bands (Levi-Strauss, 1969). But this kind of expropriation and bartering in female lives could only appear after men were able to develop strong in-group alliances and so unite against other groups.

So, under female exogamy, women found themselves cast out at adolescence alone in a new community, deprived of the strong kin ties that had protected and supported them. This is what makes the pattern of strong female friendships so paradoxical. These women, to whom the immigrating female had no blood ties, nevertheless became a kind of pseudo-kin. Yet when female gorillas and hamadryas baboons leave their natal group, they develop only the most rudimentary relationships with other females. Instead they concentrate their social efforts almost exclusively upon the breeding male in the group—and wisely so. Hamadryas baboons live in groups composed of a single male and several females. These breeding units associate together in bands which include some unattached males who are eager to seek copulations. The breeding male constantly herds his females way from such interlopers and, if a female strays too far away, her male partner targets her with threatening stares. Should she fail to instantly move back toward him, he launches an immediate biting attack on her neck to discipline her. The female is less concerned about bonding with other females than avoiding attacks by the male—which is a pity because some sisterly solidarity might make him think twice.

For many years, we were told that female chimpanzees were asocial. But recently systematic studies reveal that this is not always true. Although males are the more sociable sex, females are far from social isolates. At some sites, females socialize with each other as often as with males (Lehmann & Boesch, 2008) and some female best friends spend more time together than male dyads (Langergraber et al., 2009). But, as we have seen, bonobos take female friendships to new heights. Having left her natal group at the age of eight years, a young bonobo is firmly established with her new friends by the age of 13 (Kano, 1992). She will spend two-thirds of her time in body contact with other females, grooming and playing (Parish, 1996). Despite their lack of kinship ties, bonobo females are among the most amicable, supportive, and mutually protective of all the primates. When the females act in concert, they can and do dominate males (White & Wood, 2007).

Why women form close friendships

And so we come to the critical question: Why in our species did women form these exclusive and intense relationships with other women to whom they were not related? The answer remains uncertain because female relationships have only recently come under scrutiny. But for evolutionary psychology, an important place to start is by considering what kin relationships offered females before they were forced to leave their natal group. Whatever benefits they obtained, it seems reasonable to guess that they were and are trying to recreate them in their new group. But first, a newly arrived female had to overcome a less than hearty welcome.

A female immigrating into a community is a stranger. She has no allies and many potential enemies. Other females resent the arrival of this young unknown who represents yet another competitor for limited resources. Look at bonobos. A newly-arrived adolescent female is careful to avoid unpleasant interactions with her new female companions. She does not become involved in others' disputes, does not initiate any aggression of her own, refuses to counter-attack if picked on, and rarely vocalizes. She does, however, show a lively interest in the older established females. She initiates friendships by "peering"—staring directly at the face of the other female. This behavior is a prelude to sexual activity and signals her willingness to engage in genital rubbing. Afterwards, she takes her food away and feeds quietly on the outskirts of the group. Later she may approach older females to groom them. She seems to be actively working at "making friends."

Imagine a hunter-gatherer society like the one in which we spent the majority of our species' history. A newly-arrived woman brings many threats and no obvious benefits. Her novelty and youth make her a powerful sexual rival given what we know of men's mate preferences. Her presence means that food must be shared across one extra person. Her youth and inexperience mean that she can contribute only in a limited way to foraging and food preparation. She is unknown and therefore unpredictable: Is she stable and trustworthy? Will she reciprocate any kindness we show her? Will she injure other women's children? A newly arrived woman will find it in her best interests to establish the warmest relationship she can with her new comrades in order to avert social isolation (at best) or aggression (at worst). If she can persuade these strangers that she represents no threat to them, or even better that she is a trusted ally, she may be able to persuade them to accept her.

Establishing trust takes time. For female primates, time spent together depends on resource distribution. Where resources are patchy, females must separate in search of food, spending much time alone or with their infants. Females whose food patches are close together can spend more time with one another and develop stronger attachments. In captivity, where food is provided, these bonds can become very strong (de Waal, 1993). Bonobos, famous for their intense female bonding, inhabit an ecological niche where food is abundant and where its distribution can support large numbers feeding together. Groups of females acting together are able to defend these food resources and drive males away. This cooperative activity further enhances female bonds and allows them to increase their reproductive success. As well as augmenting their food intake, cooperation gives them crucial leverage over male aggression. Neither infanticide nor forced copulation has ever been reported among bonobos. Females can dominate males but only when they act in concert so each one has to be sure that she has back-up before she risks an attack. Only numbers can prevail over the greater size and strength of a bonobo male. A female who goes forward to find herself deserted by her friends, is staring injury or death in the face. Bonobo females have to be certain that their friends will support them and that certainty comes from trust. Mutual grooming and genital rubbing maintain the affectionate ties between females. Bonobo females do not have dominant females who harass subordinates—females' aggression toward males and their friendly sexuality toward one another are based upon equality. When unrelated female primates have the chance to spend time together and where there are benefits to mutuality, they can form powerful sisterhoods.

Securing food plays a strong role in human hunter-gatherer societies also. Women contribute by foraging for plants, nuts, and honey, and although this is often a solitary activity, women still spend about 90 per cent of the day at camp with other women. The more calories men supply by hunting, the less time women have to spend foraging (Waguespack, 2005). And this extra time is not wasted: women's work involves cooking, laundry, weaving, pottery, butchery, house building, rope making, hide working, basketry, and burden carrying. The key thing about all these activities is that they can be combined with round-the-clock child care and can be performed close to home (Hurtado, Hawkes, Hill, & Kaplan, 1985). In these communities, women spend much of the day in each other's company giving ample time for mutual surveillance, cooperation, and gossip. New arrivals have plenty of opportunity to ingratiate themselves and establish friendships.

Friendship and safety

Friends also mean safety. Humans are vulnerable animals and there is greater security in numbers. Flocking by birds, which looks like a coordinated group activity, is driven by the selfish desire of each bird to work its way to the center of the group where the risk of predation is lower. Safety from predator attack may also explain female grouping (Dunbar, 1988; Taylor et al., 2000; van Schaik, 1989). Living as we do now, it is hard to appreciate the vulnerability of early humans. Our species cannot outrun big cats and we lack the strength of many of our primate relatives. Predatory attacks might have been rare but they were often fatal, and this is the kind of strong selection pressure that produces adaptations. We retain the vestiges of those early pressures in children's spontaneous fears of monsters, especially at bedtime (Boyer & Bergstrom, 2011). Childhood fears are remarkably consistent across the world from South Africa (Muris, du Plessis, & Loxton, 2008) to Italy (Salcuni, Di Riso, Mazzeschi, & Lis, 2009). In ancestral environments, nighttime brought the band together for safety and babies slept close to their mothers. Small wonder that infants today object to finding themselves alone in a darkened room, without protection from the potential threats that the night holds.

There were dangers from our own species too. Men's intergroup hostilities included the abduction, rape, and killing of women and children. Though it is men who initiate the wars that are responsible for the deaths of nearly half of young adults in hunter-gatherer societies, women are as often the casualties of violence as men (Hill, Hurtado, & Walker, 2007). Hrdy (1999, p. 242) gives us one woman's account of the calculated violence of Karawetari warriors against Yanomamo children:

> ... the men began to kill the children; little ones, bigger ones, they killed many of them. They tried to run away, but [the Karawetari raiders] caught them, and threw them to the ground, and stuck them with bows, which went through their bodies and rooted them to the ground. Taking the smallest by the feet, they beat them against the trees and the rocks. The children's eyes trembled. Then the men took the dead bodies and threw them among the rocks, saying "Stay there, so that your father can find you and eat you."

The vulnerability of children would be all the greater when the able-bodied men were away on a hunt. How could women protect themselves and their children? Shelley Taylor and her coworkers have offered a suggestion: tending and befriending (Taylor et al., 2000). Because fight or flight would endanger both mother and child, women adapted to threat by soothing and quieting their infants, and by affiliating with other women. Many hundreds of studies of how men and women cope with stress have confirmed a very strong sex difference. Men respond to stress by seeking solitude; women respond to stress by seeking proximity to other people. And not just anyone—they prefer to be with other women. As we noted earlier, women turn to other women for support and sympathy in times of trouble. But they receive something more fundamental than a listening ear and constructive advice. The neuropeptide oxytocin, released under stress, enhances affiliation. Because oxytocin reception is upregulated by estrogen, it is particularly relevant to understanding female behavior. Contact with others during a stressful event reduces our physiological stress reactions, including sympathetic system arousal (heart rate, muscle tension) and the hypothalamic–pituitary axis (cortisol release, glucose availability). Women's friends matter—especially in times of stress. From an enemy or a predator's viewpoint the easiest victim is a lone individual: defenseless and easily targeted. Groups present more of a problem. A group is better able to detect approaching danger, and their sheer numbers hint that an attack might be met with counter-attack. So a clear and important benefit of having friends is safety.

But having *good* friends is even better. When a group of women crowd to-gether against predators or enemies, they are showing cooperation—every member of the group benefits equally. But what about situations where some-thing more is called for? An act of genuine altruism—an act that benefits the recipient and costs the donor. This kind of support is needed when the threat comes from within the group and especially from a woman's male partner. In all biparental species, males exhibit marked concern with ensuring paternity and avoiding cuckoldry. Men are acutely sensitive to the possibility that they may be investing their hard-won resources in another man's child (Buss & Duntley, 2011). The independent development of adultery laws in the Mediterranean, the Far East, the Andes, Mexico, Northern Europe, and Africa all converged in defining adultery exclusively in terms of the marital status of the woman involved (Daly, Wilson, & Weghorst, 1982). In criminal law, the "justifiable" rage of a sexually-betrayed husband provides mitigation for his violence and the Anglo-Saxon law of torts specifies adultery (as well as loss of consortium, enticement, criminal conversation, alienation of affection, seduction, and ab-duction) as wrongs for which a husband may seek compensation (Wilson & Daly, 1992). In hunter-gatherer societies, as in the West, murders of wives are often prompted by husbands' suspicions of adultery (Hill et al., 2007). Men who abuse their wives are often convinced that she is having an affair, or that she plans to leave them, or that she seeks a more independent lifestyle that will diminish the husband's ability to monitor her whereabouts. The exercise of this kind of male control depends upon isolating the wife from her support network and this process often starts in courtship. Ironically, women sometimes inter-pret this as deeply romantic—her fiancé wants to know where she is at all times, never wants her to be with anyone else, phones her often, meets her from work, and seems besotted with her. Only later does she realize that this behavior is not love but a desire to isolate and control her (Browne, 1987; Pagelow, 1984; Walker, 1979, 1984). Such men not only cut the woman off from friends but are equally eager to isolate her from her family—both can offer an escape route. This sense of effective house arrest is captured by one Scottish woman:

> We were two miles from the village. He allowed me half an hour to go up to the village and half an hour to walk back and ten minutes to get what I needed from the shops. That was what I was allowed, an hour and ten minutes. If I wasnae back inside that hour and ten minutes I got met at the door saying where the f----- hell have you been. . . . I used to marvel at women that could go down shopping, you know, and their friends

say, "Oh, come in for a cup of coffee." And they spend an half an hour chatting and having a cup of coffee and then come home. But I couldnae do that. (Dobash & Dobash, 1979, p. 129)

What protection can a woman find? State intervention, orchestrated by men, has waxed and waned over the years depending upon the prevailing political attitude to the family and, by extension, to men's right to control women by force (Pleck, 1989). Families offer a more dependable source of support than the state and women attempt to maintain kin relationships even after exogamy if they are able to do so (Rodseth et al., 1991). In contemporary society, women more than men make active efforts to maintain contact with kin (Hogan & Eggebeen, 1995; Schneider & Cottrell, 1975) and know more about their own family genealogy (Salmon & Daly, 1996). Married women depend upon the advice, help, and support of their natal family, especially their mothers (Komarovsky & Philips, 1962). Daughters, more than sons, keep in contact with their family of origin when they leave home and are more likely to stay in touch with maternal rather than paternal kin (Salmon, 1999). Friends can offer a proximal substitute for the kin that matter so much to women. In a study of 300 Californian women, respondents were asked about help they had received during the preceding year (Essock-Vitale & McGuire, 1985). Friends were nominated by 35 per cent of the sample and were an even greater source of immediate help than blood relatives (19 per cent).

When women are in danger from men, a woman's best hope lies in allies. But these allies must be more than fleeting or pragmatic acquaintances. Since her safety may depend upon them, she must create bonds of trust that are as strong as those she feels with her own family. In a Milwaukee study in the United States, 43 per cent of battered women obtained help from family and 52 per cent from friends (Bowker, 1984). Social support can be an important determinant of coping and readjustment (Janoff-Bulman, 1985). Friends can challenge the aggressor, provide sympathy and shelter. But perhaps the main help from friends is preventative. Friends join a woman to a wider community and close friends are those with whom a woman can share her most private experiences. They can render semi-public events that would otherwise be private. In this way, they can act as an effective deterrent to abuse.

Friends and mothering

But in addition to keeping each other safe, did ancestral women go further and actively boost their friends' reproductive success? In recent years there has been much interest in the idea of humans as cooperative breeders and in women as "allomothers" (providing maternal care to children other than their own).

This idea is immediately appealing: the overwhelming responsibility and steep learning curve that most women go through after their first birth is manageable mainly because of supportive female friends and family. Where else did expressions such as "It takes a village to raise a child" come from? But when we look more closely, the evidence for human allomothering is mixed.

Hunter-gatherer societies vary greatly in the extent of such child care assistance. Among the Kung, babies are held by people other than the mother for between 20 and 25 per cent of the time (Konner, 1975). Among the Efe, non-mothers provide 60 per cent of physical contact time when the baby reaches four months (Tronick, Morelli, & Winn, 1987). But the main providers of this care are kin relations; fathers, grandmothers, sisters, brothers, and aunts (Clutton-Brock, 2009; Konner, 2010). Essentially then, this kind of allomothering is simply an instance of kin selection: relatives are genetically invested in the baby and have good reason to want to assist. From an evolutionary viewpoint, this is far from revolutionary. The more strongly genetically related individuals are, the more they gain by assisting. (In wasps and other hymenoptera species, sisters share three-quarters of their genes and it is this high genetic relatedness that explains why they are willing to forego their own reproduction and encourage their mother's production of more sisters instead.) But if genetic relatedness predicts assistance to the mother, the fact that women married out of their natal group becomes even more mysterious. Because maternity is certain, maternal grandmothers know that their grandchild is unarguable related to them and are especially willing to assist in raising them. And it seems that where a couple resides has consequences for who provides help with child care, at least among Aka foragers (Meehan, 2005, 2008). Here it is customary for a young couple to live with the bride's parents early in the marriage so that the husband can provide bride service. Later, they move to the groom's family although they may relocate several times in their life. Aka mothers prefer to reside with their own kin and here they receive more help from juvenile and adult women. Women in the father's camp are less likely to hold infants but the husband increases his involvement so that the total amount of assistance received does not vary significantly. The main message of the study is the adaptability of women's child care assistance. Could that flexibility extend to allomothering by unrelated female friends?

Cooperative breeding is not common in the animal kingdom—it is only found in 3 per cent of mammals. And where it does occur, it is not so democratic and communal as it might sound. In fact, "despotic" mothering might be a better term than cooperative. Meerkats live in groups of between three and 50 animals, but 80 per cent of the pups born come from a single alpha female. She produces a litter of pups up to four times a year. If any other female in the group gets pregnant she will be driven out or, if she manages to stay and give birth, the alpha female will cannibalize her pups. The threat of infanticide seems to be responsible for subordinates shutting down their own reproductive careers. The same is true among other cooperative breeders such as hyenas, dingoes, and wild dogs. But humans are different. Even Sarah Hrdy, a champion of cooperative breeding, notes: "Nothing in the ethnographic literature for hunters and gatherers suggests that a single dominant woman monopolizes breeding opportunities" (Hrdy, 2009, p. 204).

Nor is there much support in terms of phylogenetic patterning. Our closest cooperatively breeding relatives are marmosets and tamarins (Callitrichidae), and they are New World monkeys. They may be anthropoids like us, but they are far removed from the Great Apes to which we are most closely related. As with meerkats, only a single dominant female breeds: she shows the same infanticidal attitude to upstart females with the temerity to give birth and her helpers are usually her genetic kin. Our closest relatives, chimpanzees and bonobos, show little evidence of trusting unrelated females with their offspring.

And no wonder—allomothering is often much less benign than it sounds. In many primates, young nulliparous females are especially interested in babies and eagerly try to carry them off. Whether they intend to harm them is unclear but often they handle the offspring roughly and abandon it when their interest wanes, leaving it alone and undefended—an enterprise rather sinisterly known as "aunting to death." And in our nearest relatives, the chimpanzee, infanticide by unrelated females is a special threat. One episode was vividly described by two ethologists who encountered a young injured female, with her week-old infant, screaming and running from six attacking females (Townsend, Slocomb, Thompson, & Zuberbuhler, 2007). The attackers caught her and, as she shielded her infant, they pounded her back. They wrested the infant away from her, and after competing for it one female delivered a lethal bite to its head and neck. The mother was not seen again. Nor was this an isolated incident (Pusey et al., 2008). The researchers believe that it was a systematic attempt to reduce competition for feeding sites after the community nearly doubled over a 10-year period due to immigrant females with dependent offspring.

Perhaps we should not sentimentalize the death of a baby chimpanzee: after all, half of the infants born will die before they reach the age of six. But from a mother's perspective, infanticide is a serious hazard not only emotionally but in terms of replacement costs which directly affect her ultimate reproductive success. Unlike death from disease or infection, it is a threat over which she can exert some control and surely the most basic preventative tactic would be to avoid leaving her infant alone with other adults. No one else will value that infant's life as highly as she does and, when competition for resources intensifies, non-mothers may be tempted to remove one of the competitors—preferably one small and weak enough that it cannot fight back. Infants themselves seem to be tacitly aware of this threat. While it is true that infants can and do form attachments to consistent caretakers, they also display an untutored fear of less familiar adults that begins at a few months of age. This universal adaptation suggests that non-kin have been a source of danger to children, as we saw in the case of the slaughter of Yanomamo infants. Even securely attached infants show signs of distress when their mother leaves them and this seems to sit badly with the argument that humans have adapted to a prehistory of allomothering.

Yet there are reasons to suspect that women did share childrearing—at least to some extent. For one thing, our species is unusual in the combination of a remarkably long period of infant dependency combined with a mother's need to care for more than one child at a time. This places an unusually high burden on them and the short interbirth intervals that characterize our species must have evolved because a woman obtained assistance in caring for her children. In many primate species, allocare reduces interbirth intervals, and infants grow faster and are weaned earlier (Ross & MacLarnon, 2000).

An obvious source of support is the father of the child. After all, the children (probably) carry his genes as well as the mother's. It has long been thought that fathers are important because they assist the mother, provision the family, and protect their children. Yet the data do not wholeheartedly support this (Sear & Mace, 2008). A father's presence has no impact on his child's survival in two-thirds of societies studied. Nor do the data suggest that children do better when fathers are more committed to their families. Among the Hiwi, children are raised in nuclear families and the father provides meat and child care— yet the death of a father has no impact on child survival. Compare this with the Ache where marriages are unstable, fathers offer little direct child care, and where meat is widely shared throughout the group. Here the death of a father significantly reduces his child's survival. In any case, women would be foolish to rely on fathers, even the best of them, because in our evolutionary past the likelihood of them remaining around was far from certain. Among the South American Hiwi, 36 percent of all adult deaths are the result of violence or warfare (Hill et al., 2007). In contemporary Western populations men between the ages of 18 and 30 are far more likely than women to die from external causes including accidents that are often the result of risky behavior (Owens, 2002). They are twice as likely to die as a result of homicide. Men are also more vulnerable to death from parasitic infections: testosterone, valuable for youthful ambition and competition, compromises the immune system in the middle years possibly through its effects on energy allocation, carotenoids, or free radicals (Muehlenbein & Bribiescas, 2005; Owens, 2002). And supposing he survives? Every year that passes diminishes his wife's sexual novelty and youthful attractiveness, while the husband increases in status and resources—both extremely attractive to younger women. The evolutionary conclusion that fathering is facultative rather than obligatory in our species embraces all these risks and the consequent need for mothers to find a back-up helper.

At present, we do not know for certain the role played by unrelated women in raising children. But my threefold suggestion would be this: (1) other mothers helped with child supervision but probably not until the child was over two years of age, (2) this child care arrangement was reciprocal, and (3) allomothers were extremely close friends. Below the age of two, babies are extremely vulnerable, very labor intensive to care for, and reluctant to leave their mother. Models of the human life cycle indicate that fitness is most sensitive to survival threats between the ages of zero and four years (Jones, 2009). This is the age range of real danger, creating a survival bottleneck. Once through this perilous period, a child's chances of reaching reproductive age improve considerably. This fits neatly with the finding that a mother's survival is most crucial to the survival of her children when they are very young. For example, in nineteenth-century Sweden only 1.6 per cent of infants survived to age five if their mother died in childbirth. But as they grow older, particularly after they are weaned, they fare better. Sometime after the age of two or three, mothers become less critical (Sear & Mace, 2008). This, combined with the fact that children show decreased fear of strangers and increasing willingness to spend time away from the mother as they become mobile and are no longer breastfeeding, suggests that allomothering by non-kin might start about then. Much has been made of the fact that, in some hunter-gatherer societies, babies much younger than two years of age are passed around the group for inspection and cuddling. Among the Efe and the Aka, other women will even nurse the infant until the mother's own milk comes in (Hrdy, 2009). Members of the Efe will pass pre-masticated food into the mouths of infants as young as three to four months. But there is nothing here to suggest that the mother is absent. When the mother is present, babies will tolerate interaction with a variety of strangers, using their mother as a social referencing point (Walden & Ogan, 1988). The real test of a mother's trust is whether she will leave her child alone to be cared for by a non-kin allomother.

Children's natural tendency to enter the wider social world as they leave infancy has been explained in terms of group socialization theory (Harris, 1995). Harris' theory was designed to answer a question that has dogged developmental psychologists: why parents' childrearing seems to explain so little variance in their children's subsequent behavior. Aside from genetic factors which explain about half the variance, the other importance source of individual differences between children is the unshared environment (the environment not shared by siblings raised in the same family). Harris argued persuasively that this un-shared environment was to be found in the children's own peer group. For any social organism, the key players—their future allies, enemies, and mates—are same-age peers. Children and young people care much more about social integration in their peer group than with fitting into the adult world of their parents. (And parents, if they are honest, care more about how much their friends like them than how popular they are with their children's peers.) All of this makes good evolutionary sense. So from toddlerhood, children become interested in their peers and this moves their attention away from the mother, making them considerably less demanding. They are now mobile and no longer need to be carried which eases the burden of parental care. They are weaned and can eat the same foods as adults. All these developments mean that they are less dependent on the mother and more willing to have others step into a caring role. A mother's friendship circle can provide baby-sitting services: a mother who is keeping an eye on her own child can also keep an eye on her friend's child.

Now this will come as no surprise to those of you who (like me) were children before the trend toward hyper-protective parenting began 20 or so years ago. Children spent most of their free time outside the home with friends. They played in neighborhood streets, or in one another's gardens. They ate (far from elaborately) in whichever parental house they found themselves in when hunger struck. When they misbehaved, they were reprimanded freely by mothers or by adult neighbors. This comes much closer to the kind of environment that characterizes many hunter-gatherer groups and that gave rise to the saying that it takes a village to raise a child. In these societies, there is much less distinction between the family and the village: the privatization of the home is a Western development that has occurred within the last 400 years (Hareven, 1985). This mutual system of child care depends upon a strong adult peer group: a network of mothers who interact frequently and know each other well. In Western society, these maternal support networks are typically composed of about six adults (Melson, Ladd, & Hsu, 1993). Their friendships are typically of long duration, averaging six years. A mother's satisfaction with her support networks is associated with a warmer and less intrusive style of interaction with her children (Jennings, Stagg, & Connors, 1991) and with stress reduction especially in vulnerable mothers (Colletta & Lee, 1983). Social isolation is depressogenic for mothers: perhaps this is why most mothers work hard to establish friendships with other women when they move to a new town. Jointly, through mutual trust, mothers create a safe environment for their children.

The key word here is "trust." A mother should only relinquish her child to another's care if she is certain that they would not harm it. Ideally women prefer their children to be cared for by genetic kin but, where that is not possible, close female friends come second. But what sort of relationship would provide women with that degree of trust? To answer this, we need to examine the bigger evolutionary questions of friendship and help-giving. These two domains are usually considered separately, but in the real world our willingness to assist others is closely bound up with the kind of relationships we have with them. The kinds of friendships that men and women prefer correspond to an important distinction that psychologists have noted between communal and exchange relationships. And these two forms of friendship map on to a distinction that evolutionary theorists have made between different kinds of altruism. By examining these in more detail, I want to suggest that women's friendships are an attempt to recreate a particularly close bond of communion that mirrors the kind of relationship most often found among blood relatives.

Kinds of friendships

One type of relationship is called communal sharing (Fiske, 1992), interdependence (Cross & Madson, 1997), or mutual aid (Kropotkin, 1972). Here, people's individual identities are merged into a greater whole. The driving motive is "From each according to his ability, to each according to his needs." People are given assistance without regard to their ability to repay it. Goods are held in common and used as they are needed. At a party, for example, the guests drink out of a communal punchbowl without anyone keeping track of how much each individual has consumed. When it is applied to work relations, people work collectively without assessing individual inputs and the product of the joint labor is a collective resource. It typifies the spirit in which people will dig out survivors of a collapsed building—they work until the job is done without apportioning specific amounts of work to one person or another. In group decision-making, communal sharing is expressed in a search for consensus, unity, and conformity. Contributions are about finding a joint solution that will transcend the separate attitudes of the participants, rather than claiming special authority by one person. This requires a degree of humility and a desire to please other participants. The over-riding motivation is not to be different from others, not to draw attention to one's self as a unique or special individual. We see it most evidently in very close attachments such as between lovers or between a mother and child. The greatest fear is the loss of this closeness. But communal sharing also has its less attractive aspects. People can lose a sense of individual identity and be unable to separate themselves from others, leading to a personally destructive dependency.

In communal relationships, friends feel mutual responsibility for each other's welfare and provide benefits to each other in response to need or to show their concern for one another. The aim is not to selfishly get something out of the relationship or even to ensure that both parties receive an equal benefit but rather to meet the other person's needs. Clarke studied communal relationships experimentally, by leading subjects to believe that the stranger whom they had just met was likely to become a close friend (Clarke & Reis, 1988). She found that when such an expectation was in place, people paid little attention to how much each of them had contributed to a joint task. In fact, if their partner tried to immediately recompense them for favors they had given, they felt insulted. Even when they gave help but received none in return, they did not feel exploited.

I suggest that this kind of close, interdependent friendship maps closely to the evolutionary concept of kin altruism. Altruism presented a real problem for Darwin because it was unclear how such a trait could evolve. Let us suppose that one person in a community behaves altruistically; she places a greater importance on the lives of others than on her own. She spends her time helping others at her own expense while they take the benefits but incur no costs at all. Her genes will die out and theirs will survive. Yet we see acts of altruism all around us, from small generosities to life-saving heroics. William Hamilton (1964), armed with knowledge of genetic transmission which Darwin did not have, solved the altruism problem not only with great elegance but in a way that changed our whole approach to evolution. He pointed out that the unit of genetic transmission is the gene and the same gene can reside in many bodies. It is especially likely to reside in the bodies of close relatives. He built his theory on Wright's (1922) coefficient of genetic relatedness which is the probability that a particular gene will be identical to another because they share a direct ancestry. This relatedness (r) value is 0.5 for parents and their biological children, 0.25 for uncles or aunts with nieces and nephews, and 0.125 for cousins. Hamilton argued that natural selection would favor altruism toward kin where r was greater than the cost to the altruist divided by the benefit to the receiver (both measured in units of prospective reproduction). In short, altruism is more likely between those who are closely genetically related than between strangers. We are more likely to donate a kidney to our child than to someone we have never seen. In short, we feel a close interdependence with our kin (or those we treat as kin) so that what hurts them hurts us, and we are willing to go out of our way to avert that hurt.

A very different kind of relationship has been described that is based on exchange (Clark & Reis, 1988), equality matching (Fiske, 1992), or reciprocity (Polanyi, 1957). Here the focus is upon balancing the net utility for both parties in the relationship. With acquaintances or colleagues, to whom we are not emotionally close, we tend to follow a rule of equality: we strive to keep the rewards and costs that we both obtain from the relationship fairly balanced (Deutsch, 1985; Mikula, 1980). If I agree to act as chauffeur on one evening out, then it is only fair that you forego the alcohol the next time we go out. My current cost has to be balanced by your later cost. And your current reward of being able to have a glass of wine tonight has to be repaid to me sooner rather than later. Exchange relationships depend upon a close monitoring of who is benefiting most at any given time. When the costs become too great for one partner, the relationship will begin to show the strain and eventually may dissolve. Clarke's experimental studies confirmed that in exchange relationships people forged relationships governed by principles of equity. They liked it when they received immediate pay-back for favors given and when their partner requested immediate return of favors that they themselves had received. On joint tasks, they carefully monitored every input and felt exploited when their contribution was not appreciated and reciprocated. In exchange relationships people like to know where they are and want to avoid feelings of both obligation (so they repay debts immediately) and exploitation (when another person does not immediately return a favor).

Anthropologists have noted that exchange principles also regulate some working relationships—in farming communities neighbors will assist in threshing your grain on the understanding that you will do the same for them at a later date. The underlying notion of fairness or balance also guides co-worker relationships so that people feel aggrieved if they have a greater workload than their equally-paid colleagues. When one party receives a favor, they feel obligated to return it. This back-and-forth symmetry can be seen in the way that we send Christmas to one another, or our feeling of obligation to return a dinner invitation. Exchange relations are so universal that they carry with them both a moral force (sufficiently binding as a principle that a violation requires some apology or explanation) and a norm (a regularity of behavior that people expect of one another). Gouldner (1973) in a classic paper argued that the norm of reciprocity is universal and no societies have been found so far in which it is absent. The aim of social exchange is to do as well as the other person and to avoid coming out worst. The underlying principle of exchange relationships is fairness, regardless of the particular individuals involved (Rawls, 1971).

This kind of relationship bears strong similarities to another form of help-giving in the animal kingdom that can occur between unrelated individuals and even between different species. Robert Trivers (1971) was fascinated by the behavior of fish at underwater cleaner stations. Here small cleaner fish enter the mouths of larger species and feed on the ectoparasites within. This is a simple case of cooperation, rather than altruism. Both fish benefit immediately—the small fish gets a meal and the host gets a free dental cleaning. What seems to require explanation is why the host fish does not end the encounter by simply swallowing the cleaner. Essentially the larger fish foregoes this benefit in order to save the small fish's life. Indeed the host goes to some lengths to carefully signal to the smaller fish that he is about to close his mouth and his guest should leave. It even chases off other fish that represent a danger to the cleaner. But why? Trivers argued that it was because the two species of fish have a long-standing relationship with one another. The cleaner is worth more alive than dead. If the big fish ate the cleaner, it might be unable to find another or at least one that was equally good. It would certainly encounter some expense and danger in seeking a new cleaner at a different location. Although the big fish's behavior appears altruistic, it is actually acting in its own best interest. Trivers speculated that humans and other animals evolved "reciprocal altruism," as he called it, because it was in their own best interests to do so. Reciprocal altruism occurs because the benefit received by one individual is greater than the cost of the act to the donor. If you are starving and I am replete, the piece of food I give you benefits you greatly but costs me little. And at some future time you will reciprocate in a way that costs you less than it benefits me. This kind of mutual back-scratching is especially likely to flourish in communities where the population does not disperse too widely: if I help you and you promptly move to another group, I will never be repaid. It is especially valuable in species with long lifetimes, since there is ample time for such altruistic acts to be given and returned. A good long-term memory helps (to keep track of debits and credits) and a particular ability to discriminate and recognize faces. These are all qualities that humans have in abundance.

But wherever there is an adaptation, there is a counter-adaptation to challenge it. If most people are altruists then a cheater can flourish. Cheaters can benefit from being helped by others, while not having to risk their life or expend energy for anybody else. Psychopaths (who are predominantly men) are classic examples of cheaters who serially exploit others (Mealey, 1995). Psychopaths, cross-culturally, rarely constitute more than 4 per cent of the population of the male population. The fact that they can exist only in small numbers suggests that the rest of us have specially evolved mechanisms for detecting their presence and avoiding them (Cosmides & Tooby, 1992). Trivers suggests that reciprocal altruism has also been responsible for a range of universal emotions designed to regulate it. Anger is a reaction to injustice and failure to reciprocate: it controls levels of cheating by inducing fear in the cheater. Guilt (an emotion conspicuously absent in psychopaths and other cheaters) motivates us to repay acts of altruism. Gratitude alerts us to the fact that we have received help. Sympathy may be a way of calibrating how needy another person is of our help. For Trivers, friendship and liking are emotions that regulate long-standing patterns of reciprocal altruism between people. We are more altruistic to those that we like.

The friendship continuum: How long is the trust leash?

These two forms of altruism (Hamilton's kin and Trivers' reciprocal) have often been seen as complementary accounts relevant to different social relationships—kin and non-kin. But in many ways they are overlapping. From an evolutionary viewpoint, there is reason to believe that reciprocal altruism evolved out of kin selection. Kin selection was a necessary precursor to reciprocal altruism for a very simple reason. Reciprocal altruism cannot get started as a strategy in a population of individuals who exploit others. Imagine a hypothetical community of people in which 95 per cent refuse to act for the good of anyone else and indeed take advantage of anyone who does. The few altruists rarely encounter one another so any help-giving move toward another group member is met by steadfast non-reciprocation. Eventually, as Darwin saw, the trait of altruism is pushed into extinction. In order to survive, altruism must reach a critical mass where altruists meet each other often enough to increase their pay-offs and improve their chances of survival. Where might such a critical mass of altruists be found? The answer is among individuals who are genetically related to one another. If you have a genetic tendency to altruism, there is a good chance that your sister has it too. Since reciprocal altruism is advantageous, we should expect that individuals in such altruistic families would be reproductively more successful than others and in this way the tendency for altruism might spread. In the end it might be present in the whole community. Once that happens, altruism has a second advantage. Altruists flourish when they are in the majority. But for cheaters the opposite is true: they do not benefit from being in a majority because they keep meeting others like themselves. As Wright (1994, p. 200) puts it, "Simple conditional cooperation is more infectious than unmitigated meanness."

There is another reason why we should not view these two forms of altruism—Hamilton's kin selection and Trivers' reciprocal altruism—as distinct. A moment's reflection reveals that, although we will go far out of our way to help a sibling in need, there is always a limit to that beneficence. Even among kin, altruism is not infinite. On the other hand, there are some relationships with non-kin that seem to stretch the bounds of reciprocation very far indeed. We continue to care for a terminally ill friend even though there is no possibility of later reciprocation. Adoptive parents exhibit staggeringly high levels of care for their acquired children given the absence of genetic relatedness. Among married and cohabiting partners, the degree of emotional closeness may approach or exceed that which we feel for genetic relatives.

The two forms of altruism shade into one another, forming a continuum. It is as if our "kin responder mechanism" can be fooled by particularly close, trusting, or long-standing relationships so that we act altruistically without expectation of repayment. Even our linguistic usage blurs kin and non-kin relationships as in "Brother, can you spare a dime?" (Daly, Salmon, & Wilson, 1997; Haslam, 1997). Individuals, rather than being discretely demarcated into kin and non-kin, can be graded in terms of intimacy ranging from true and close genetic relatedness (a sibling) through extremely close friends (that fictive "aunt" who was in fact your mother's best friend), to acquaintances and strangers. These relationships map on to a continuum of altruism that ranges from kin selection in its most extreme form (as in a mother toward her child where no element of reciprocation is anticipated) to reciprocal altruism at its most extreme (where payment of a plumber is immediate, business-like, and without any expectation of further interaction).

There is some ambivalence among evolutionary psychologists about a continuum of this sort. The notion of psychological modularity has been taken to imply that we have discrete modules that "fire" to specific stimuli and hence that people should be automatically sorted into kin and non-kin categories in order to evoke the appropriate degree of caring or altruism. For example, Haslam (1997, p. 302) claims that relationships are governed by "discrete cognitive structures and do not simply represent poles on continuous relational dimensions." Yet he admits that "many relationships are governed by some combination of two or more [relationship categories]." Likewise, Daly, Salmon, and Wilson (1997, pp. 271–272) claim that "cognitive structures do not merely locate relationships in a space defined by a couple of dimensions such as 'intimacy.' They distinguish relational categories." But they also go on to say that "A long-standing mateship becomes increasingly like a genetic relationship . . . " (p. 278). This determined preference for categorical distinctions (in the light of an irritatingly continuous perceptual world) derives from a commitment to locate and describe evolved psychological modules. These separate modules (for cheat detection, for sexual jealousy, for taste preferences, and so on) are thought to be activated by specific external stimuli (potential cheaters, signs of infidelity, sugar). Some evolutionary psychologists believe that the notion of a dimension destroys this categorical input. But does it? Take color perception. It is true that everywhere in the world people discriminate the boundaries of colors at the same point in the wavelength spectrum, suggesting discrete categorization (Lumsden, 1985). But that does not mean that they are perceptually unable to tell the difference between a green that is nearly blue and a green that is nearly yellow. When we say

"She is like a sister to me," we are not distorting the objective input in the sense of really believing that we share genes with that person but we are redefining the position of that friend toward the kin end of our emotional continuum. While evolutionary psychologists are happy to endorse the fact that we discriminate between fine degrees of genetic relatedness (as Hamilton's theory requires), they are less happy to acknowledge that we discriminate equally fine degrees of friendship. It would seem on the face of it to be grossly maladaptive to suggest that we treat all non-kin in the same way. Indeed, Trivers has noted how emotions such as gratitude and guilt serve to modulate, discriminate, and refine our behavior between members of the "friend" category. Over time, friendships can gradually move from a Tit-for-Tat exchange relationship into a communal "pseudo-kin" closeness. We are more likely to implicitly consider people as kin when they share similar attitudes (Park & Schaller, 2005) and we feel a sense of emotional closeness with them (Korchmaros & Kenny, 2001).

And it is along this continuum of closeness that men and women seem to differ in their friendships. Women's friendships are more communal and men's more exchange oriented. What is especially paradoxical is that women formed kin-like relationships with non-kin, while men who shared genes with other men in their group often behaved more like reciprocal altruists.

Friendships: Male and female

Let us take men's friendships first. Status striving, as we have seen, is greatly facilitated by alliances. These are often of a shifting and short-term nature as we can see in chimps (de Waal, 1982). A dominant male's enemy may be a subordinate chimp's most useful ally because they both have something to gain by deposing the alpha male. But if the ally now assumes dominance, his erstwhile partner will seek a new ally to overthrow him. Furthermore, if our status-seeking chimp finally achieves dominance, he will likely find his two prior allies lined up shoulder-to-shoulder against him. All this Machiavellian strategizing means that there is little room for trust—if we define it as a continued willingness to show altruism (such as coming to the defense of a threatened ally) when there has been no immediate pay-back of a previous good turn. Males then should be keenly aware of reciprocation and less willing to endure long periods of self-sacrifice without seeing a return on it. There is no advantage to a male of risking his life for an ally again and again when that partner not only fails to reciprocate but achieves dominance at the altruist's expense. Given the shifting and opportunistic nature of these alliances, males should also be careful to conceal vulnerabilities. An ally who knows your weak spots is one thing—an enemy who knows them is quite another. Better to rely on exchange relationships than communal relationships where intimacies and weak spots are revealed. But among male philopatric species such as chimps (and humans), surely this tendency for mutual distrust ought to be diluted by their kin relatedness? If a senior brother achieves dominance and sires many offspring then his younger sibling increases his inclusive fitness also. Why should not the younger brother bask in the reflected glory and the accompanying, vicarious genetic success? The answer seems to be that, while chimps may share less valuable resources such as food with relatives, the value of reproductive dominance is simply too great to be compromised by kinship.

Reciprocal altruism (with its debit/credit emphasis) has the paradoxical quality of opening the door to very unequal relationships. The more resources an individual can accrue, the greater is his ability to help others. Recall that, under reciprocal altruism, the cost to the giver is lower than the benefits accrued by the receiver. In the long run, costs and benefits should average out because, although one individual may be rich in food today (and can be generous at low cost to himself), another may be oversupplied tomorrow and so able to return the favor. But in human society where rewards are chronically unevenly distributed, those at the top have more "giving power" than those below. Debtors who cannot repay in kind must repay in some other currency, such as respect and deference. Perhaps this is why men think twice about incurring the kind of debt they cannot repay—a man who offers to find a job in his company for his friend's son uses his status to perform a favor of such magnitude that the beneficiary may never be able to repay it fully. We call unwillingness to accept such a large debt "pride." (Women often see it as stubbornness because it penalizes the needy child in order to salvage the father's self-esteem.) The same premise explains the curious "round buying" ritual seen in British pubs. Men will carefully monitor who bought the last round of beer and whose turn it is now, despite the fact that the monetary sums involved are relatively small. What the men are doing is ensuring equality of status among friends. People who "flash their money" by buying round after round of drinks are not popular—quite the reverse. Their behavior is read as an attempt to pull rank by creating indebtedness in others. Men who cannot afford to "stand their rounds" often stay away from the pub altogether rather than become beneficiaries of a largesse that is interpreted not as generosity, but as a status display. At the same time failure to buy rounds is equally heinous: cheapskates are social cheaters who exploit the altruism of others by failing to reciprocate.

With colleagues and acquaintances, women also behave as reciprocal altruists. They are aware of their debts and credits. When they say "It's my turn for the next dinner party," they demonstrate this sense of fairness. But there is something special about the one or two women that are singled out as best friends. Here the relationship is characterized by a much longer leash of trust—a willingness to extend credit for a long period of time based upon assessment of another person's need. This trust is meted out with care. It may take years of intimacy to achieve and it is rarely extended beyond one or two close friends—a mistake can be costly. But such a friendship can afford a sense of solidarity and closeness that men may experience only with a spouse. If women are trust specialists, we would expect considerable selectivity about the beneficiaries of trust. Among primates, kin altruism is glued together by the mutuality of genetic relatedness: blood is much thicker than water. Relatives can be trusted because their genetic interests overlap to a large extent with your own. A friend who is like a sister—a friend who can be trusted to care for your own child—must be selected with care.

Recall that evolutionary theorists have suggested that altruism beyond the kin group must have depended upon selecting beneficiaries who were trustworthy. One such mechanism is to choose friends who are similar to yourself. If they resemble you in other respects, then there is a better than average chance they also resemble you in their tendency to provide help when it is needed. And this idea is corroborated by one of the most robust findings in social psychology—the tendency of friends to resemble one another. (Though this may seem obvious, many years were spent working on the hypothesis that friends were selected to be complementary rather than similar. If you are an introvert you might compensate by becoming friendly with an extrovert that could widen your social circle. This would not have been the prediction of evolutionary psychologists and they were right.) Now if reciprocal altruism depends upon similarity, how much more true this should be if we are speaking of "pseudo-kin" altruism where trust takes the place of immediate pay-back. And, as we would expect, women's friendships depend more than men's upon similarity of personality and attitude (Cross & Madson, 1997). Men like other men who share the same interests so that they can focus their activities and discussions on things that are satisfying for both of them. Women are less concerned with common interests than with common character.

Are women more likely than men to treat their friends as psychological kin? The answer appears to be, yes. In one ingenious experiment, participants were paired with a good friend, a family member, or a stranger (Ackerman, Kenrick, & Schaller, 2007). Each member of the pair was seated at separate computers and asked to complete an online exam. Afterwards, they were told that because the researchers were interested in group processes, only the pair's average score would be considered. All the pairs were told that they had scored in the 93rd percentile and then each member was asked which of them was most responsible for the impressive score. Men and women did not differ in how much credit they gave to their partners when they were paired with a stranger or a family member. But when paired with a friend there was a very noticeable difference: women gave more credit to their friends than men. In fact, women gave just as much credit to a friend as to a family member. Women also reported stronger feelings of closeness and similarity to their friends. As the researchers concluded " . . . assuming ancestral patrilocality, the establishment of supportive social alliances with nonkin may have been especially beneficial to women, and this could be facilitated by a psychological inclination to perceive nonkin as kin" (Ackerman, Kenrick, & Schaller, 2007, p. 372). The term "fitness interdependence" has been used to describe the mechanism underlying the selective tendency of unrelated individuals to form strong communal bonds with one another (Brown & Brown, 2006). And the term perfectly describes the relationship between women who, isolated from their kin, depended on one another for safety, support, and child care. In short, for survival and reproductive success.

The ups and downs of communal relationships

Communal relationships depend on sensitivity to social cues that signal another person's state of mind. In an exchange relationship, a failure to successfully analyze another's mindset is less critical because the chief requirement is knowledge of the current debit/credit balance and this can be calibrated directly from memory of past behaviors. Unreturned favors clearly indicate that the relationship is in potential trouble and help can be withdrawn until the debtor makes good. But with a long leash of trust, incorporating heavy past investment and a willingness to provide help in response to need, it is important to understand a partner's state of mind.

The evidence is clear that women more than men are relationship specialists. Women's interpersonal sensitivity has been examined by looking at the ability to read non-verbal information from other's behavior such as posture, vocal inflection, and facial expression. Many studies have examined sex differences in accuracy and the results clearly favor women (Hall, 1984; Hall, Carter, & Horgan, 2000). This difference in the efficiency of facial expression processing is already apparent in infancy (McClure, 2000). As well as decoding emotion, women seem to be more effective senders of signals that foster intimacy and closeness. In conversations, they demonstrate greater involvement in the interaction and a greater interest in tracking the state of the other person's mind: women smile and gaze more than men, they express their own emotional state more clearly in their facial expressions, they use more hand gestures, and approach others more closely. In short, women seem keen to establish closeness in their conversations by engaging and monitoring their partner's state of mind.

Nowhere is the difference in sensitivity to another person's mindset more evident than in the sex ratio of two related disorders—autism and Asperger syndrome. Autism is an impairment of social development with deficits in communication and imagination, the presence of narrow, restricted interests and repetitive activity. The overwhelming majority of those affected are male— official figures put the ratio at about four to one (Rutter, 1978). Three-quarters of those affected also have mental handicaps and, if we take only those cases where intelligence is unaffected (Asperger syndrome), the ratio rises to nine males to one female (Wing, 1981). One ability that is prominently affected in autism is "mind reading." Despite the terminology, there is nothing mysterious about it. It is simply the capacity to accurately infer the desires and beliefs that lie behind another person's behavior. In normal children, this ability manifests itself quite spontaneously by about the age of four. A typical diagnostic task is to show the child two puppets (Baron-Cohen, Leslie, & Frith, 1985). One of them, Sally, places a marble in a basket and leaves the room. While she is away her partner puppet changes the location of the marble from the basket to a box. The child is asked simply where Sally will look for her marble when she returns. The answer to this deceptively simple question lies in understanding that the absent puppet cannot have known what occurred when she was not in the room despite the fact that the child herself knows. It requires an ability to recognize the differing perspectives of the puppet and herself. Autistic children show a specific impairment in this task compared with both typically developing children and a control group of learning disabled children. Yet they excel in some tasks at which normally developing children fail such as identifying hidden objects embedded in larger pictures. They have a specific difficulty with understanding other people's minds although they have a fascination (bordering on obsession) with non-social stimuli such as trains, cars, or numbers. They are object-oriented and have little comprehension of others' motivations, which leads to deficits and inappropriateness in their social behavior. The sex difference in autism is so marked that it has even been suggested that it represents a pathological degree of "maleness" (Baron-Cohen & Hammer, 1997).

Mind reading is a cognitive ability and it finds its emotional parallel in empathy. (Autistic children, as we would expect, show very little response to the distress of another child.) Empathy can be defined as an affective response to the emotions of others (Jordan, Kaplan, Miller, Stivey, & Surrey, 1991). If women engage in more communal relationships where another person's emotional needs must be tracked, we would expect women to show higher levels of empathy. It has even been suggested that the tendency to empathize has different motivations in the two sexes (Ickes, Robertson, Tooke, & Teng, 1986). Men tend to adopt a partner's perspective infrequently and usually in order to gain instrumental control of the interaction, while women do so frequently and are motivated by the intrinsic satisfaction of sharing the other person's mental state. Men can also "switch off" empathy more efficiently than women in line with their more exchange-oriented relationship. In one study, both sexes showed activation of similar brain areas both when experiencing pain themselves and when witnessing it in others: but among men only, this effect was absent when they witnessed pain delivered to someone who had acted unfairly (Singer et al., 2006).

Sex differences favoring girls have been found in the response of infants to the sound of another baby crying (Hoffman, 1977). At preschool age, girls respond to the distress of another child with greater emotional arousal reflected in their facial expression, statements of concern, and gestures (Zahn-Waxler, Radke-Yarrow, Wagner, & Chapman, 1992). In adulthood also, there are large differences favoring women where self-report measures of empathy are used or where facial expression are analyzed in response to interactions eliciting sadness, sympathy, and distress (Baron-Cohen & Wheelwright, 2004; Eisenberg & Lennon, 1983; Eisenberg, Fabes, Schaller, & Miller, 1989). However, when physiological measures such as changes in heart rate, sweating, and blood pressure are taken while participants watch a stranger's distress, the evidence for a sex difference becomes mixed. Perhaps then, women simply report or display greater empathy, rather than truly co-experiencing other people's emotions? Yet evidence from a brain imaging study suggests that men and women do indeed process other people's emotions in different ways. In one study, men and women were shown photos of faces displaying fear and anger under two conditions (Schulte-Rüther, Markowitsch, Shah, Fink, & Piefkea, 2008). In one, they were asked to think about their own emotional state and in the other, the emotional state of the person in the photograph. When focusing on another's emotions, women showed a stronger response than men in the right inferior frontal cortex. This area is implicated in the human emotional mirror neuron system (Gallese, 2003). This system was first identified when it was found that moneys showed matching activation in their own motor areas when they viewed another monkey perform a reaching task. It seemed that witnessing the action caused a corresponding firing in the observer's own nervous system that might function to allow the observer to assess another's actions and intentions. It has been suggested that the mirror neuron system may be the neural basis for empathy and in the fear–anger study, activation in the mirror neuron system was correlated with a questionnaire measure of empathy. Interestingly, men in this experiment showed more activity in an area called the temporoparietal junction which is responsible for distinguishing between our own experiences and those of others. Perhaps men may experience a greater separation between their own and other's emotions.

So women are more sensitive to the non-verbal cues of another's state of mind and seem to experience greater empathy with them. But this social sensitivity—and the close female relationships to which it gives rise—has its downside. Failure in friendships can have negative consequences for mental health. Self-esteem for women, but not for men, is correlated with the strength of close personal relationships and how highly a woman values her relationships predicts her self-esteem two years later (Stein, Newcomb, & Bentler, 1992). Self-esteem is more damaged by relationship stress in women than in men (Moran & Eckenrode, 1991). Women report that not being forgiven by a friend whom they had hurt would have a greater effect on their self-esteem than men do (Hodgins, Liebeskind, & Schwartz, 1996).

Girls and women are more prone to depression and anxiety than men (Brody & Hall, 1993). But depression can be more finely differentiated. One form, called interpersonal depression, appears more often in people who are preoccupied with personal relationships and fear abandonment by others. This of course bears a close correspondence with communion (with its emphasis on connectedness to others) and as we would expect, there are significant sex differences in this form of depression. For example, among third- to 12th-grade students, girls more often endorse interpersonal symptoms of depression including loneliness, not liking themselves, and wanting more friends (Leadbetter, Blatt, & Quinlan, 1995). (Self-critical depression on the other hand is seen more commonly in people who are preoccupied with issues of self-worth and are particularly concerned about failing to meet personal goals or appearing incompetent. Predictably, men show greater depressive vulnerability in this area than do women.) People who are vulnerable to interpersonal depression also place an intense value on emotional closeness and are preoccupied by fears of being abandoned or neglected in relationships. Because relationships are so highly valued, their loss is a severe blow. Girls report more stress than boys in connection with close relationships (Gore, Aseltine, & Colten, 1993) and display stronger associations between these stressful relationship events and behavioral problems (Cohen, Gotlieb, Kershner, & Wehrspann, 1985).

But the pain associated with the loss of a friendship may be relatively mild compared to the pain of ostracism by the group. Evolutionary psychology has drawn attention to our obligatory social nature. Unlike some species, we cannot survive as solitary animals. So imagine this: You are a young female living with a group of strangers. You try to forge good relationships but one day, apparently without reason, your new companions shun you. In the normal course of events, you would turn to your family for comfort and support but they are miles away. You are alone and isolated. Nobody will cooperate with you in child rearing or food sharing. It is a short step before they drive you from the group and, if that happens, death will follow. Ostracism is a powerful weapon and one that has only recently been appreciated as evolutionarily significant. Within any group there will be individuals who refuse to pull their weight or who act in antisocial ways to other members. Evolutionists have debated at length the sanctions that could be brought against them and pondered the "commons" problem: why should any single individual take on the risk and burden of retaliatory punishment for the good of the larger community? There is a simple route which does not involve the risky use of force and should therefore be especially appealing to women—ostracism (Guala, 2012).

It is not for nothing that solitary confinement is considered one of the worst forms of punishment in our species. The destabilizing impact of social isolation has been shown in an analysis of high school shootings in the United States: chronic social rejection was the major contributing factor in 87 per cent of cases (Leary, Kowalski, Smith, & Phillips, 2003). This kind of extreme and violent response is rare and largely confined to men. In both sexes, rejection can trigger hostility, avoidance, and emotional numbing. But a more frequent effect is to increase attempts to reintegrate into the group, especially among women. In one study, participants played a ball-tossing task in which they were excluded by the other two participants who were actually experimental confederates (Williams & Sommer, 1997). Following this experience, they joined a group and were asked to work on a task under two conditions. In one condition, their individual contribution could be evaluated and, in the other, the group was evaluated as a whole. Ostracized men made more other-blaming statements and, in both conditions, they tended to engage in more social loafing (letting other do the work). Women who had been ostracized made more self-denigrating statements and worked harder in the collective condition. Whatever behavioral response it evokes, rejection is painful. It damages self-esteem, and reduces feelings of acceptance, personal control, and meaningful existence. When people are asked to recall a physically painful event or an incident of ostracism, they report higher pain levels for the latter (Williams, 2007).

Women have always been especially vulnerable to the effects of social exclusion. We see it today in girls' and women's acute response to indirect aggression (see Chapter 3). This evolved sensitivity stems from an evolutionary past of female exogamy and the loss of natal kin which placed a premium on establishing close friendships in their new group. These friends offered support, assistance, and protection especially during times of stress. Women's sense of self-worth came to depend on these relationships but their very centrality to women's lives meant that their loss can plunge a woman into depression. How much worse then, is the threat of collective exclusion by the whole female group?

But Lord help the sister . . .

In this chapter, I have argued that female bonding requires an explanation in its own terms. It is tempting to see it as simply the result of female's lack of interest in dominance—if individuals are not engaged in status struggles, surely friendship is bound to ensue? For many years, evolutionary psychology with its special interest in the male of the species, accepted this "default option" for females. When attention finally turned to the intimate quality of women's same-sex relationships, explanations were sought in their reproductive function. Their capacity for mothering was uncritically generalized to their peer relationships. For example, MacDonald (1995) suggested that, because of their high parental investment, women have a greater elaboration of affective and caring mechanisms than men. But what this proposal amounts to is the suggestion that because mothers unconditionally love their infants, they unconditionally love everyone else too. This is deeply problematic from an evolutionary perspective, because individuals should tailor their behavior quite sensitively to the specific individual with whom they are interacting. If women displayed unconditional, need-responsive love to everyone around them, they would have little time and energy left to devote to their own lives and reproductive success. We have already seen that females are quite capable of aggression when there is a threat to their infants and, in Chapter 6, we will see how competition for male partners can incite considerable hostility between women. In this chapter I have argued that the intensity of women's special friendships means that they are more exclusive than those of men. Throughout human evolution, female friends have assumed the role of pseudo-kin, assisting one another not only emotionally but practically—by offering safety in numbers, protection from male aggression, and mutual child care. But lest we become too idealized in our view of these friendships, we now examine the forces that threaten the bonds of affection even between the closest of friends.

Chapter 6

But she that filches from me my good name: Women and mate competition

What a man and a woman look for in a mate is critical not only to understanding male–female relationships but to understanding within-sex competition. A high-quality man (and we will discuss what he might look like shortly) is a valuable asset because, by definition, the best are in short supply. Women must compete to attract and retain them. But the focus of women's efforts—the qualities on which they try to outdo one another—is determined by what such a man values in a prospective female partner. First we must step back and look at the evolutionary basis of mating strategies in the two sexes, before we can understand why men and women value particular traits in the opposite sex. Then we can see how (and about what) women compete with one another.

The power of female choice

In southeast Asia, thousands upon thousands of male fireflies sit in a group of mangrove trees in the forest and flash in synchronous rhythm through the night. The effect is so dazzling that it is used as a navigational aid by ships and aircraft. The fireflies care not a jot about the safety of passing humans but care deeply about how attractive they are to firefly females. They gather together to flaunt their brilliant lights and so to entice females to visit and select the very best of them for mating. Females are more likely to come and survey a group of males rather than a lone "flasher" and they know where to come because the display ground is passed from generation to generation.

This type of communal male display is called a lek and is common in species where males and females meet only for the purpose of copulation. Among birds, the lek site is situated apart from the usual nesting or feeding territory. Four hundred or so male North American sage grouse occupy a hectare or more of land during the mating season. Each bird monopolizes his own area that can vary from 10 to 100 square meters. But only the males at the very center of the lek are attractive to females. Because of this, about 10 percent of the males achieve 75 percent of the copulations. The males are naturally very competitive about who will gain the best real estate, and the young males do better and better with each passing year. When a prospective female "buyer" arrives, the male inflates his chest sack, tilts his body forward, and holds his head high. He erects the plumes on the side of his head and expands the yellow combs above his eyes. Then he performs a noisy, two-second ritual. After making a brief cooing sound, he extends his wings forward and then backward over his chest, raises and then abruptly drops his chest sac to reveal two bare yellow patches of skin on his chest. The second time he does it, the sac is compressed and air is released into the pockets of yellow skin which inflate forward like balloons and then collapse. The whole operation produces two sharp snapping sounds which can be heard several hundred meters away. It is his territory that initially makes him attractive to the female but, among the centrally located prime males, it is the strength and grace of the chest display that clinches the deal for one male or another. After several days of window shopping, the female crouches down before her chosen mate and he obliges with the only gift she will ever receive from him—his genes.

Darwin firmly believed in the importance of female choice. It was not a popular idea in Victorian England, relinquishing as it did so much power to the "second" sex. Many of his followers were less confident, preferring instead to highlight the importance of competition between males: elaborate displays were to intimidate opponents not to seduce females, they argued. Indeed, more than 100 years after Darwin, Donald Symons (1979, p. 203) wrote that "Human physical sex differences are most parsimoniously explained as the outcome of intrasexual selection (the result of male-male competition) and perhaps natural and artificial selection, not intersexual selection or female choice." Yet female choice has now been demonstrated unequivocally in a wide variety of different species (Andersson, 1994). The biology textbook maxim that females' higher parental investment makes them the limiting sex, acknowledges that it is females who determine which males breed.

The sage grouse lek seems, on first sight, a rather arbitrary way for a female to select a mate. Yet it serves the female's purpose well. She is not choosing a husband but a set of genes. She is not interested in finding a good parent: male parental care is rare—it occurs in only about 5 percent of species. The male will play no part in defending, feeding, or caring for the offspring. Whatever a female grouse wants it is not long-term commitment, so what makes one male better than another?

Darwin was vague about why some characteristics were preferred over others. Colorful plumage or flamboyant displays were thought to "charm the female" as a result of some innate sensory bias toward the particular trait. So for

Darwin, female preference came first and preceded the appearance of the trait in males. There is evidence that he may have been right. Male Tungara frogs display a trademark "chuck" noise at the end of their mating call that is not found in related frog species. Yet when played a sound recording of this call, females of these other species displayed a distinct liking for the sound by hopping eagerly toward it (Ryan, 1991). So it may be that there are inchoate female preferences and successful males simply "discover" and exploit them. In this view, female preferences are essentially frivolous—they are not geared toward any particular advantage. This approach, championed by Fisher (1930), came to be known as the "sexy son" hypothesis. Once a female preference begins—however arbitrary it may be—it takes on a dynamic of its own, called runaway sexual selection. If most women prefer men who are tall, then any woman that bucks the trend and goes for short men will be less likely to produce tall sons herself. She will also be less likely to produce daughters who share the normative female preference for tall men. She loses on two counts—her sons get fewer mates and her daughters, like herself, choose undesirable mating partners. The dynamic of contagious female choice can be seen at a lek: female grouse are more likely to mate with a male who has just finished mating with another female. In some fish species, females prefer a male who they have just seen courting another female rather than swimming about solo. In humans also, women's ratings of men's attractiveness are influenced by other women (Graziano, Jensen-Campbell, Shebilske, & Lundgren, 1993). It is hard not to see teenage girls' contagious hero-worship of a rock star in much the same terms. It is a kind of market forces model—the more people buy a given commodity, the more desirable it becomes to others. Nothing succeeds like success and fashion creates its own dynamic. The only cost to females in this scenario is the likelihood of becoming so picky that they waste valuable time that they could be spending in reproduction. The lek offers a perfect solution to the problem of comparative shopping. All the goods are on display at the same store and the female does not have to waste her time trudging from shop to shop.

Among peacocks, the female preference for huge decorated tails led to the evolution of ever-more enlarged tail displays until at some point natural selection (greater male vulnerability to predators as a result of the slower running speed caused by the weight of a large, if unfurled, tail) countered the sexual selection pressure. At some point, tall men cannot get taller without incurring a risk of weakened bones and fractures. There is line beyond which the advantages that accrue from mating success are offset by the disadvantages of compromised survival. This nicely explains why female choice cannot push male decorations to ridiculous extremes. But the sexy sons hypothesis faces a theoretical problem called the "lek paradox" and it is this: if females all want the same thing, they will only mate with males who possess the desired trait and refuse males who lack it. After a few generations, all their sons will have the trait and all their daughters will want it and there will be no male variability left for females to choose from. At this point, female choice becomes meaningless. The solution to this conundrum was the realization that genes are always subject to random mutation and mutations are, in the main, bad news. The more complex the trait for which genes code, the less likely a genetic mutation is to improve it. Most mutations are harmful. They have the effect therefore of introducing variation into an otherwise "perfect" genotype and over generations they maintain variability (Pomiankowski, Iwasa, & Nee, 1991).

And this suggests a more utilitarian and less capricious basis for female choice. Perhaps it is not so arbitrary after all—perhaps females focus on particular male qualities for a good reason. This view is called the "good genes" approach. This camp argues that the traits that females prefer are true indications of the genetic quality of the male—which after all will determine 50 percent of her offspring's own qualities. Certainly sons will inherit their father's sexiness but offspring of both sexes will also inherit a host of other traits that will fit them for survival to a greater or lesser extent. In this view, male ornaments are designed to advertise the fitness of the bearer. And the very trade-off between sexual and natural selection that had troubled Fisher's theory became a central part of the good genes theory in the form of the handicap principle. Zahavi (1975) reasoned that peacocks' tails represent a distinct disadvantage in terms of survival. Peacocks would be better off without them. For sexy son theorists, they emerged to satisfy females' whims. But for Zahavi they emerged because what females want is good genetic quality and what a brilliant blue tail says to them is that this male, who has been subjected to even greater predatory threats than his less colorful peers, has nevertheless survived. He has proved his genetic superiority by staying alive despite the massive threat posed by possession of that tail.

What females use as an index of genetic quality may be more than the presence of gaudy plumage. It may also be its quality. Parasites represent a constant threat to health and survival. Fortunately animals are equipped with resistance to many parasites. But parasites replicate asexually at a rate which far exceeds that of their hosts and in each generation they find new ways around their host's defenses. They have speed on their side. Animals can counter parasites' advantage by reproducing sexually and creating unique offspring, because their young will vary in their resistance to different strains of parasite. If females select males on the basis of disease resistance, and if the biggest threat of disease comes from different parasites in different generations, then females will always be selecting for effective resistance to whatever parasites happen to be flourishing at the time.

The question is: How do females manage to read male healthiness simply from inspection? Hamilton and Zuk (1982) found that the most brightly colored and ornamented bird species also carried the greatest load of blood parasites. The quality of ornaments that a male could maintain in these species might be a good way of establishing his health. They proposed that male health could be read from the state of his secondary sexual characteristics. Hamilton and Zuk tested this idea experimentally by infecting young jungle fowl with a parasitic worm. These males grew more slowly and, when they matured, sexually-selected traits were more affected by their poor health than were other bodily characteristics. The parasite made their comb smaller and less brightly colored, but it did not affect other neutral traits like ankle length to which the females were indifferent. Compared to non-diseased males, the parasite group was selected only half as often as mates by the females. In male grouse also, spots painted on the air sac to mimic the effect of lice infestation, causes reproductive success to drop (Boyce, 1990). Many other studies have found that parasite infection is associated with deterioration of sexually selected characteristics, poorer survival, lower female preference, and inferior infant survival rates (Moller, 1994; von Schantz, Wittzell, Goransson, Grahn, & Persson, 1996; Wedekind, 1992).

Another line of research which supports the good genes approach has come from studies of symmetry. Symmetrical bodies are harder to grow than asymmetrical ones: any slight error in genetic translation or an environmental perturbation such as stress or malnourishment causes development to become uneven. Females searching for high-quality males would do well to pay attention to their symmetry. Barn swallow males have long symmetrical tail feathers. These feathers are a handicap to the male in terms of food foraging, but they are a good predictor of his speed of mating, likelihood of producing a second brood in a single season, number of extra-pair copulations, the quality of his mate's parental investment, and his reproductive success (Moller, 1994). Tail feathers are an index of parasite load and physical health. The female chooses her mate by establishing his health which she reads principally from his tail feathers. And this relationship between symmetry and reproductive success has been found in 78 percent of the 41 species studied, including humans (Moller & Thornhill, 1998).

In male ornaments, symmetry is a sign of good genes and so is size. If the good genes argument is correct, symmetry should be greater in larger sexually selected characteristics. The sexy son position, however, argues that these characteristics tell the female nothing about the quality of the bearer and so there is no expectation that symmetry (health) should be associated with size (sex appeal). To examine this, Moller (1992) artificially shortened or lengthened the tail feathers of different male barn swallows, as well as tinkering with their symmetry. Those with long tail feathers mated sooner and produced more offspring. But regardless of whether their tail feathers were short or long, symmetrical birds were more reproductively successful than asymmetrical birds. Because they were preferred by females, they mated sooner and their mates were quicker to lay their first egg clutch. In an ingenious study, Moller (1990) switched some of the nestlings fathered by long- or short-tailed males so that half were raised by adoptive rather than biological parents. He infected half of the nests with a parasite. The best predictor of the nestlings' resistance was the length of their biological father's tail. So it seems that male ornaments are an honest signal of genetic quality and females are acutely attuned to these differences between males.

Females are able to read genetic quality not only from a male's physical appearance but from his extended phenotype—the artefacts that he produces. Bowerbird males build elaborate bowers of twigs and ferns decorated with brightly colored flowers or objects to attract females. A special favorite of the females is a rare bright blue feather. Once a male has found or stolen one, he must guard it jealously for his rivals will attempt to steal it. What the female seems to be doing is selecting males who are brave enough to capture and hold the feather against rivals—a useful sign of his genetic quality (Diamond, 1991).

Among primates, social status seems particularly important in female choice. When primates live in social groups, the males with whom a female might mate are likely to be around her for some time and she has the opportunity to check them out. Her choices depend upon ensuring not only genetic quality but a safe environment for herself and her offspring. One general rule of thumb is that females prefer mature males and, although they may rather disinterestedly tolerate juveniles' attempts to mate, they limit this tolerance to the beginning or the end of sexual cycles when they are least likely to become pregnant (Small, 1993). A second rough rule is that they tend to prefer more dominant males. The advantages of choosing a dominant male lie partly in gene quality. A male who is capable of subduing other males and resisting challenges to his power is one who must be strong, healthy, and vigilant. He will pass these qualities on to his sons—but only if they live long enough to reach maturity. Dominant males are in a better position to protect the female and her infants from attack by other group members. Among chimpanzees chivalry is not the norm—males attack females twice as often as they attack other males (Goodall, 1986). Some attacks occur in disputes over food, some in sexual encounters (or attempts at them) and some male attacks have a distressing "kicking the dog" quality in which the male simply takes out his irritation on a passing female. In olive baboons also, males attack and can severely injure females. Her offspring are vulnerable to being kidnapped by both males and females so a female's choice of mate may be driven by her need to ensure a defender who will protect the pair (Dunbar, 1984; Smuts, 1987). Dominant males can offer such protection but not all females choose them as mates. Sometimes they are forced to accept them, whether they like it or not, by the sheer crude force of male pressure. The power, brutality, and selfishness of dominant males can be seen in the disturbing phenomenon of infanticide. When a new dominant male enters the group, he may kill existing offspring in order to replace them which his own. At the very moment when we would expect the female to repel his mating attempt most vigorously, she acquiesces (Hrdy, 1979). The logic is simple—a male strong enough to take over the group and kill her off-spring is a male with whom she would do well to cement a relationship. Whether she does so out of fear, respect, or a simple desire to ensure the survival of her next offspring is not known.

But primate females do not always choose the most dominant male. In her search for a safe haven for herself and her offspring, a female may develop a special friendship with one or two males. Baboon females demonstrate clear preferences for some males by following them, sitting next to them, and groom-ing them (Smuts, 1985). Often these friendships are with a dominant male, but not always. On 90 percent of occasions when a female or her infant were de-fended from attack, the assistance came from a male friend. The male friend regards these relationships as special: although he rarely goes near the young of other females, he will spend time playing with his special friend's infant even if he is not the father. But there is a downside too: male friends can be jealous and attacks on the female are not uncommon if she strays too far away from him. What the male gains from his friendship seems to be a sexual relationship with the female. They are far from monogamous but males copulate with their female friends twice as often as they do with non-friends and are more likely to ejaculate during these copulations.

And females also have a liking for strangers. In one group of chimpanzees, 50 percent of offspring were fathered by non-group males (Wrangham, 1997). This preference may be strategic. Females have been known to mate with mem-bers of hostile neighboring groups. Sometimes it is in the female's best interests to anticipate a forthcoming takeover, with its concomitant risk of infanticide, and make a pre-emptive sexual strike. Females can also use their sexuality to influence whether or not outside males are allowed to enter the group. Gelada baboons live in harems of about 10 females and one male. If a new male has ambitions to take over the group, he can operate by stealth (following the group as a subordinate while he develops grooming relationships with the females and infants) or he can launch a full-scale junta. In either case, his success depends critically on the amount of female support and allegiance that he can muster (Dunbar, 1984).

Short-term relationships: What women want

In many human societies, both sexes have short-term as well as long-term sexual relationships. I am afraid that evolutionary psychologists have been guilty of creating a rather unnatural division between the two. In their research studies, they typically ask respondents about the qualities they would find attractive in short- or long-term mates. This makes it possible for the researchers to link human mate preferences with those of other species, both promiscuous and monogamous. But humans are rather more complicated. Women can and do reproduce with and without the assistance of a co-resident male. Some relationships endure for a lifetime, some for a few years, and others do not make it past the first hour. Babies are born to lone and separated women, as well as happily married wives. When we are first attracted to a man, it is impossible to say whether this will turn out to be a short- or a long-term relationship. That being the case, the idea that the two forms of relationship depend on different selective criteria is problematic. It is more likely that we move through a progressively refining filter system. Our initial attraction is based on visible qualities that can be quickly evaluated. If the relationship sustains itself past initial sexual attraction, we begin to examine less obvious but more important qualities that suggest a good long-term partner. Is he kind and generous? Does he have the ambition to acquire and share resources? Will he make a good ally?

The advent of contraception means that our choice of short-term mates does not carry the potential reproductive consequences that it once did but contraception has been available only for a century even in the West—a blink of an eye in evolutionary terms. The criteria we use to initially evaluate male quality have probably not changed drastically in such a short space of time. And when we speak of women's short-term preferences as reflecting attention to male genetic quality, it is important to realize that there is no implication that women, any more than females of other species, consciously realize the link between a man's attractiveness and the quality of genes he will contribute to his offspring. When a woman's attention initially homes in on a man—whether it turns out to be a one-night stand or the start of a lifelong partnership—she is responding to his observable qualities. What is it that captures her attention?

Of course, and perhaps tautologically, women like attractive men. For years, attractiveness was considered to be too subjective (different people have different preferences) and too culturally variable (different countries and ethnic groups vary in their preferences) for serious scientific study. In fact, different judges' ratings of people's attractiveness show near perfect agreement (Langlois et al., 2000). Even when people judge the attractiveness of people from ethnic groups and cultures different from their own, the agreement remains just as high. We view attractive people more positively than unattractive people (we think they are better at their jobs and at relating to others) and in the main, we are right (Eagly, Ashmore, Makhijani, & Longo, 1991; Feingold, 1992a). Attractive people are indeed more successful at work, more popular, have better social skills, enjoy better physical and mental health, and obtain more dating and sexual partners.

But what makes a man attractive? Attractive men are taller than the average. In a study of personal ads, 80 percent of women who mentioned height asked for a man who was six feet or taller (Lynn & Shurgot, 1984). Ideally, their bodies form an inverted V-shape in which the shoulders are wider than their hips (Barber, 1995; Lavrakas, 1975; Singh, 1995a) and the waist is slightly smaller than the hips—a 0.9 waist-to-hip ratio. Male models and mannequins are usually about six foot two with a 42-inch chest and 30-inch waist (Etcoff, 1999). Women like men who appear tall and powerful—features that signal a man's strength relative to other men.

Women, like men, prefer symmetrical features. Galton was the first psychologists to blend photographic images to form composites—in his case he wanted to create a stereotypical criminal face by fusing photos of robbers, burglars, and killers. The surprise was that the average face turned out to be better looking than any of the specific faces that had been used to compose it. Contemporary psychologists have followed his example and produced digital images of composite faces (Grammer & Thornhill, 1994; Langlois & Roggman, 1990). And the results follow a simple rule: the greater the number of faces that are blended, the more attractive the composite becomes and the lower the likelihood that any one of the faces will be more attractive than the "group face." Merging many faces removes random and deviant examples of bilateral asymmetry creating a more symmetrical face. And symmetry is attractive.

Recall that among animals symmetry was argued to reflect both good genes and strong disease resistance. Low (1988, 1990) developed the ingenious hypothesis that if men lived in an area with many parasites, only the genetically superior males would be able to develop symmetrically and this would cause large differences between men in their attractiveness to women. Gangestad and Buss (1993) confirmed that women in high-parasite cultures rated the importance of physical appearance in a mate as more important than did women in more parasite-free societies. This should mean that some men would be unacceptable as husbands. Women should avoid them and be prepared to accept a polygamous marriage to a healthy male in preference to a monogamous marriage to a less healthy specimen. Examining 185 cultures, Low found that the number of pathogens in the environment was strongly related to the degree of polygamy.

Fluctuating asymmetry, as it is called, can be assessed by careful measurement of bilateral body and facial features such as eyes, ears, and wrist size. Symmetrical males are perceived as healthier and they do indeed report fewer minor illnesses and lower levels of anxiety and depression than less symmetrical males (Jones et al., 2001; Thornhill & Gangestad, 2006). They also have lower metabolic rates, are more muscular, taller, heavier, more vigorous, higher in social dominance, and have a slightly higher IQ than their peers (Furlow, Armijo-Prewitt, Gangestad, & Thornhill, 1997; Gangestad & Thornhill, 1997; Manning, 1995; Manning, Koukourakis, & Brodie, 1997). Not only are they healthier but, as we would predict, they are preferred as mates. Symmetrical boys have sex three or four years earlier than their peers and as adults have twice as many sexual partners (Thornhill & Gangestad, 1994). They bring their wives to orgasm more often and, even though symmetry is associated with bigger, taller, and more muscled bodies, it is their symmetry over and above these factors that predicts orgasm frequency. Symmetry is a stronger predictor of women's copulatory orgasms than their partner's ratings of their love and commitment to the relationship, their frequency of lovemaking, or the amount of past sexual experience (Thornhill, Gangestad, & Comer, 1995). Male body symmetry is also positively correlated with sperm number per ejaculate and sperm motility (Manning, Scutt, & Lewis-Jones, 1998).

But what about masculinity and dominance in male faces? Do women prefer men with the classic hallmarks of masculinity—rectangular faces, strongly etched cheekbones and brow ridges, and prominent chins (Mazur, Mazur, & Keating, 1984; Mueller & Mazur, 1996)? Here the evidence is far from clear. These features develop during puberty and are dependent on levels of circulating androgens (Tanner, 1990). Levels of testosterone can be depleted by stress hormones resulting from a poor environment or from parasite infestation and this has the effect of "de-masculinizing" these facial features (Thornhill & Gangestad, 1993). Men with masculine faces are healthier, less vulnerable to disease, experience fewer developmental problems as children, and are physically stronger (see Little, Jones, & DeBruine, 2011). So it originally seemed to researchers that women should find dominance attractive.

Women certainly seem to be attracted by dominant behavior in men. Sadalla, Kenrick, and Vershure (1987) experimentally manipulated social dominance in both sexes (through body posture and position, as well as active rather than passive behavior) and found that, although dominant women were not rated as especially attractive by men, women's judgments of attractiveness were strongly affected by social dominance. But when it comes to facial features, dominance seems to be a two-edged sword. Advances in digital technology means that photographs can be manipulated to increase or decrease facial masculinity.

Features and outlines are marked onto facial photographs of men and women to establish where the average differences between the sexes lie. These differences are used to manipulate new images to make them more or less masculine or feminine. Although feminized women's faces are more attractive to men, the converse does not seem to be true. Exaggerating sex-typical male features does not create the highly attractive "supernormal stimulus" that it does when women's faces are feminized. Men with masculine facial features are rated by women as high in strength and dominance but they are also rated as lower on warmth, emotionality, honesty, and cooperativeness (Perrett et al., 1998). Most significantly, they are rated as less likely to be good parents. It seems that too much dominance may make a man attractive as a short-term mate but raises the specter that his very good looks may make him an unreliable long-term partner.

An intriguing spate of recent studies has found that women are attracted to these dominant male faces only at a certain point in their menstrual cycle—the follicular phase when they are most fertile (Thornhill & Gangestad, 2008). Why should this be? Some studies find that this cycle effect is exaggerated when women are specifically asked about short-term mating or when they are in a steady relationship. This suggests that women specifically seek good genes rather than good fathers at this time. In short, women find these masculine men attractive as lovers but correctly, if unconsciously, recognize that they are unlikely to stay around. Women already in long-term relationships may be employing a deceptive reproductive tactic colloquially known as the Madame Bovary strategy: find a reliable providing man, then furtively seek a better genetic partner on the side and deceive the male provider into raising it as their own. But, as we noted in Chapter 2, there are problems with this argument. An alternative explanation, that has the advantage of applying to unpartnered as well as partnered women, has been offered by Roney (2009). He argues that women in ancestral environments only rarely experienced fertile cycles with elevated hormone concentrations. These fertile cycles could occur only when energetic conditions were favorable to sustaining a successful pregnancy and they would be disrupted, not only by current pregnancy and lactation, but also by weight loss, calorie restrictions, elevated energy expenditure, and stress. The rise in estradiol associated with ovulation is "telling" a woman that she is experiencing a rare and important high-fertility cycle and directing her amorous attention to prime examples of the opposite sex. This brings women into line with other species, even those without pair bonds, where estrous enhances females' discrimination of the quality of prospective mates. While the Madame Bovary hypothesis predicts that women's mate preferences should be tied to the fertile window in their monthly cycle, Roney links these preferences to variations in estradiol level. He performed an ingenious critical test between the two explanations: during the luteal phase of her cycle, a woman cannot conceive but her estradiol level is likely to be higher during more fertile compared to less fertile cycles. As predicted by Roney, levels of estradiol sampled during the luteal phase predicted women's preference for the faces of high-testosterone men.

When it comes to short-term relationships, women's preferences have the edge over men's. Men are very accommodating to a woman looking for sex which puts her in a strong position to be choosy (see Chapter 2). A highly desirable man may not be willing to commit for life but he may well be prepared to commit for a few hours. But the blurred line between short- and long-term relationships, which has not been carefully examined by researchers, raises questions. If a woman is explicitly and only looking for sex, then she can probably find a fairly high-quality man. But male fantasies notwithstanding, this is not a typical scenario. Women who behave in this way on a regular basis may pay a price in retribution from other women, as we shall see. And though they enhance their short-term popularity with men, there is often a reputational cost that will haunt them when they move into the market for a long-term partnership. For most women, short-term relationships are not carefully planned in advance. Rather they become "short-term" de facto after it becomes apparent that this relationship is not going to progress any further. Perhaps a man passes a woman's initial short-term criterion but fails to meet her long-term criteria—he turns out to be selfish, mean, humorless, or abusive. Or, more painfully for her, a woman may fail to meet a desirable man's threshold for long-term commitment. Men become much more choosy when they tie their reproductive future to a single member of the opposite sex.

Biparental care and two-way sexual selection

When both parents remain together to raise children jointly, evolutionary researchers predict that females want more from males than good looks and good genes. What women should be evaluating is the resources that a man can offer and the degree to which he is likely to commit those resources exclusively to her. There is strong evidence that this prediction is right.

In cultures as widely spaced as the Kipsigis of Kenya (Borgerhoff Mulder, 1990) and the Yanomamo of Venezuela (Chagnon, 1988), the richest men are preferred as husbands. David Buss (1989a, 1989b) began a now-blossoming line of work on mate preference by surveying 10,000 men and women from 37 cultures. He asked each of them to rate various qualities they would look for in a long-term partner. Women rated the importance of good financial prospects higher than men in all cultures, and the importance of ambition and industriousness higher in 34 of the 37 sites. Whether from the United States,

Japan, and Russia, women place a higher value on success, earnings, and status than do men (Hatfield & Sprecher, 1995). Feingold (1992b) performed a meta-analysis of 26 questionnaire studies of mate preference conducted on 82 independent samples. The results strongly confirmed the idea that women place a much higher value on qualities such as socioeconomic status and ambition. His analysis of men's and women's lonely hearts advertisements showed the same pattern—women more than men stipulate a desire for high income or status in their prospective partners. In a representative sample of Americans, irrespective of age or race, women wanted husbands who were better educated and who earned more money than they did (Sprecher, Sullivan, & Hatfield, 1994). This preference for resource-rich men pays off. Compared to women who select young or less educated men as husbands, women who marry older and better educated men have more children, are less likely to get divorced, and report greater marital satisfaction (Bereczkei & Csanaky, 1996).

But money alone is not enough. Women also seek men with signs of warmth and character that are associated with making a long-term commitment to her and her children. In fact, Buss found that women placed a higher value on a man who was kind, understanding, and intelligent than a man who was financially successful but had none of these softer qualities. Feingold's meta-analysis also revealed that women place a higher value than men on the character of their mate. Dunbar (1995) analyzed personal ads placed by men and women. He found that 45 percent of women (compared to 22 percent of men) stipulated traits that signaled commitment and parenting qualities such as loving, warm, good sense of humor, family-minded, gentle, and dependable. Men who are prepared to invest heavily in their children are likely to try to impress women with their resources but they are also more likely to offer her help, give her things she likes, be sympathetic to her troubles, and emphasize their fidelity (Cashdan, 1993). If women are seeking men who demonstrate commitment, then we would expect men more than women to engage in deception about these qualities in an attempt to sell themselves to the opposite sex. Men not only exaggerate their dominance and resources but also their sincerity, trust, and kindness. They admit to saying things to "butter up" the opposite sex by pretending to be more humble, polite, trusting, and considerate than they really are. They also feign disinterest in immediate sex and pretend to be interested in starting a long relationship when they are not (Tooke & Camire, 1991).

So women on the lookout for a long-term relationship pay attention to status, resources, ambition, and commitment. But they may not always get it. Under monogamy, it pays a man as well as a woman to be choosy in their choice of partner. If all a man contributes is sperm, he relaxes his standards quite considerably. If he expects only a sexual one-night stand, a man will lower his more stringent marital requirements for intelligence, friendliness, kindness, excitingness, health, easygoing temperament, creativity, emotional stability, sense of humor, educational attainment, and social status (Kenrick, Sadalla, Groth, & Trost, 1990). But while women's preferences differ between short- and long-term partners, what men find attractive remains relatively consistent—it is the threshold of acceptability that changes. Men raise the bar considerably when they give up the potential mate quantity of polygyny for the mate quality of monogamy. As we shall see, what men want drives the features that women seek to advertise about themselves.

A universal feature of men's preferences is age. After reaching menarche at about the age of 12, girls experience anovulatry cycles for up to two years and it is not until they are 18 that they attain full reproductive function. After this period of adolescent sterility, women become most fertile between the ages of 20 and 25 from whence their fertility declines until it reaches zero by the age of about 45 to 50. Thus when adult men are asked about age preference they consistently choose someone who is younger than themselves and marriage patterns indicate that the typical age gap is about three years (Buss & Schmitt, 1993; Kenrick & Keefe, 1992). But this three-year gap is not constant; as men age, they prefer younger and younger women. By the age of 60, they prefer women who are on average 15 years younger than themselves. Teenage boys, by contrast, rate a woman five years older than them to be the perfect partner (Kenrick, Keefe, Gabrielidis, & Cornelius, 1996). The data suggest that what men are trying to do is to capture the most fertile women that they can, regardless of their own age, and for men who marry at the normal time that means a woman about three years younger than themselves. But in addition to immediate fecundity, a younger woman has more years of future reproduction. This residual reproductive value is important when men choose just one woman to be the sole bearers of their children.

Men place a greater premium than women on physical attractiveness (Buss & Schmitt, 1993; Feingold, 1990) and this is closely bound up with age and estrogen levels. Across the world, from the industrialized West to the Ache and Hiwi of Central and South America, men prefer women with feminized facial features (Rhodes, 2006). Relative to men's faces, feminine faces have underdeveloped jaws and chins, and less defined brow ridges which make the eyes appear larger and more open. During puberty, estrogen inhibits facial growth leaving the face smaller and more neotenous. In young women, current levels of estrogen correlate positively with observer ratings of femininity, attractiveness, and health (Law-Smith et al., 2006). (Interestingly, this association is not found when women wear make-up suggesting that cosmetics can successfully deceive observers about women's underlying attractiveness.) With increasing age and number of children born, women's lower face becomes elongated, the brow ridges more prominent, and the lips smaller. They lose the key markers of femininity which are closely age-related. Women become less desirable to men as they age, unlike our chimpanzee sisters where the males particularly favor middle-aged females who have successfully given birth several times.

Estrogen levels are associated not just with women's faces but with their bodies—a conspicuous region of male interest. Women carry more fat than men: fat accounts for only about 14 percent of young men's weight but more than a quarter of women's. Following puberty, women's store of fat doubles and gynoid fat is conserved for reproductive use, except in extreme circumstances. (Android fat, stored in the trunk and abdomen, is readily drawn upon to support survival function when energy demands exceed calorie intake.) Steroid hormones affect fat deposition and estrogen enhances fat storage in typical female regions—the breasts, buttocks, hips, and thighs. The ratio of estrogen to testosterone predicts the ratio of gynoid to android fat in women, and this in turn predicts fertility (Singh, 2002).

Of course, breasts are attractive to men but their preference is not so much for size as for shape. Men like firm upright breasts with subtle nipple pigmentation; characteristics of young women who have not yet given birth (Schaefer et al., 2006). Women with symmetrical breasts are rated as more attractive (Singh, 1995b) and, however whimsical this male preference may seem, it turns out that asymmetric breasts are associated with lower fecundity (Manning et al., 1997; Moller, Soler, & Thornhill, 1995). Breasts contain both android and gynoid fat stores, but breasts with less of the former and more of the latter are considered most attractive (Grammer, Fink, Moller, & Manning, 2005). Breast size is correlated with estrogen and progesterone levels (Jasienska, Ziomkiewicz, Ellison, Lipson, & Thune, 2004).

The storage of fat on women's breasts and hips creates the hour-glass silhouette that almost defines womanliness. Evolutionary psychologists have been particularly interested in the waist–hip ratio (WHR). Men's favorite body shape is a smaller waist in relation to the size of the hips—a WHR of 0.7 (Singh, 1993). Although men's preference for fatness or thinness varies over cultures, this particular ratio remains constant. At puberty, a girl's body is transformed from its straight-up-and-down androgyny to this curvier shape and, during their fertile years, women continue to store gynoid fat on their hips and buttocks. Singh believes that this gynoid distribution of fat is necessary for the hormonal changes associated with female fertility (anorexic girls lack the gynoid fat necessary for menstruation). As fertility declines and disappears in middle age, a woman's waist begins to thicken. Between menarche and menopause, a low WHR is also a casualty of pregnancy. To a man, a low WHR signals that a woman is neither too young not too old for reproduction, and is not already pregnant by someone else. But beyond meeting these basic requirements, Singh (1993) believes that small-waisted women are more likely to be fertile and there is evidence that differences in WHR can be revealing about differences in a woman's reproductive potential. Women with high levels of estrogen and low levels of testosterone have smaller WHRs. A small WHR is associated with higher fertility and higher neonatal birth weight, a strong predictor of infant survival. So men would do well to pay attention to WHR. But that does not mean that it evolved simply to advertise women's fertility to men. There are benefits to women and their offspring also.

WHR is a useful proxy for the ratio of upper body to lower body fat. Lower body (gluteofemoral) fat enhances the supply of long-chain polyunsaturated fatty acids (especially DHA, omega-3 docosahexaenoic acid) that are needed for neural development in the growing fetus. These fatty acids make up 20 percent of the dry weight of the human brain and a child's IQ increases by an average 0.13 points with every 100-milligram increase in daily maternal intake of DHA during pregnancy (Cohen, Bellinger, Connor, & Shaywitz, 2005). In a national United States sample, Lassek and Gaulin (2008) found that teenage mothers with lower WHR (and hence greater reserves of gluteofemoral fat) and their children had higher scores on cognitive tests. Both the infants and their still-growing mothers were protected from the cognitive decrements usually associated with teenage births. It seems that WHR reflects the availability of resources needed for neurodevelopment in the mother and her child. This natural selection advantage of low WHR to women may well have preceded men's preference for it.

Despite men's greater emphasis upon youth, looks, and fidelity, it is important to bear in mind that men and women are perhaps more similar than different in what they seeking a long-term partner. In comparing the minimum acceptable standards in a marital partner between men and women, there were no sex differences for a number of qualities including intelligence, aggressiveness, sexiness, exciting personality, creativity, friendliness, sense of humor, easy going, healthy, religiosity, desire for children, kindness, and understanding (Kenrick et al., 1990). Both sexes in all of the 37 cultures surveyed by Buss (1989a) ranked kind, understanding, and intelligent higher than earning power and physical attractiveness. Both men and women seek mates who are easy to live with. Despite the conflicting reproductive interests of men and women, they are nonetheless locked together under monogamy and biparental care: both sexes seek qualities that will contribute to the day-to-day cooperation and compromise that such an arrangement requires.

Under monogamy then, both sexes become selective about their partners but there is a consensus in each sex about the attributes they most prefer in an opposite-sex partner. Inevitably some are bound to be disappointed. What you receive is connected with what you can offer. In the mating market-place, buyers and sellers find their own level. Women with youth and good looks on their side can select the males with the highest resources, just as rich men have their pick of attractive female partners. The less blessed must eventually settle for the best that they can get. This is the phenomenon of assortative mating.

Flexible mating strategies

Recall the familiar mantra of evolutionary theory: the reproductive success of men depends upon the number of partners that they can inseminate and the reproductive success of women depends upon their ability to secure the resources that they need to ensure the survival of their children. Under monogamy and biparental care, this predicts that women should generally favor long-term relationships and men should always be tempted by short-term arrangements. There is much data that supports this general viewpoint. Men's increased sex drive, their preference for a larger number of sexual partners, and their willingness to drop their standards in order to procure short-term mates all testify to men's polygynous (if repressed) urges. Mothers fare better when they receive assistance in childrearing. This assistance is chiefly economic with men being far less involved in hands-on care of children. In the environment of evolutionary adaptation, men provided meat which augmented the calories that women themselves were able to provide by foraging. In more extreme northern environments, men's fishing may have been the chief means of sustenance and one which precluded participation by lactating women or mothers of young children (Miller, 1994). In our own society, the inflexible labor arrangements imposed by agriculture, industry, and service economies make it difficult for a woman to simultaneously rear children and work full time. So, it is argued, women seek resources by attracting a male who is able and willing to provide long-term investment. Studies show that women are choosier in their selection of partners than men, preferring to wait longer before sex and placing more value on resource provision and parenting qualities.

But there are some problems. One is logical: if women engage only in long-term relationships, where are promiscuous men finding their mates? Another is a problem thrown up by the evidence of our everyday experience: why do women ever acquiesce to short-term relationships which do not carry the benefits of resource provision and why do so many men marry and remain faithful? In recent years, evolutionary theory has begun to grapple with the problem of intra-sexual variability. Women differ amongst themselves (and at different points in their own lifetime) in the sexual strategies that they favor. The same is true for males.

The solutions that have been offered depend in the concept of conditional strategies. A conditional strategy has a number of properties (Gross, 1996). First, there are a number of behavioral tactics available apart from the one that is chosen. Second, the choice that is made is responsive to specific cues in the environment. Third, all individuals are genetically monomorphic—they are all genetically able to enact the full range of strategies. Fourth, when these tactics evolved, they were not equal in their average adaptive value. Fifth, the selected tactic tended to have a higher fitness value for the individual, given the current environmental conditions, than other tactics. So human beings are equipped with multiple strategies from which they choose during their lives. Some may favor a single tactic throughout and genetic factors may influence this behavioral preference. But a consistent preference and strategic variability may also reflect environmental cues or life-history variables which are either stable (in the case of consistency) or shifting (in the case of flexibility). Three theories have been proposed to explain variable mating strategies.

In the strategic pluralism argument, a woman's key choice is between good genes and good paternal investment (Gangestad & Simpson, 2000). Women who opt for short-term relationships can garner the best genes at the cost of paternal care; women who opt for long-term relationships may have to sacrifice some genetic quality in order to secure resources and commitment. "Unrestricted" women who pursue short-term relationships find symmetrical men more attractive and care more about a man's appearance. When forced to choose between dating an attractive man who is not very loyal versus a loyal man who is averagely attractive, unrestricted women choose the former while restricted women choose the latter (Simpson & Gangestad, 1992). But sexual strategies are variable—today's unrestricted woman may be tomorrow's long-term strategist. What factors might affect a woman's decision about her best current strategy? Gangestad and Simpson (2000) believe the answer lies in the survival threats that the environment presents. Where the environment is harsh, unpredictable, and dangerous, a woman does best to find a long-term mate. A stable male partner can provide assistance with food during times of shortage, and can offer protection against human raiders and animal predators. But where the chief danger to children comes from environmental parasites and pathogens, a woman would do better to seek evidence of genetic quality in the father. The best things she can offer her children are good genes and a strong immune system. A resident male partner can do nothing to cure malaria. To put it more formally, there is decreased marginal value in paternal investment when child mortality rates are high. Over 29 countries, men and women in regions containing more pathogens rated the importance of physical attractiveness higher than in low-pathogen regions. The greater the pathogen prevalence the less importance was placed upon mate dependability, character, disposition, emotional stability, and desire for home and children (Gangestad & Buss, 1993). The proposal turns on women's choices because these determine which men will be chosen to father the next generation, and these choices are affected by changing ecological circumstances. At times and places where parasite infestation is a problem, attractive men are selected to procreate and their genes do well. When resources are scarce, less attractive but faithful men reproduce their genes more prolifically. So the advantages of both strategies are maintained over evolutionary time as the threats to infant survival shift back and forth. This is an example of balancing selection—alleles for both types of female strategy and both types of men are maintained in the population.

The chief problem is that this model assumes that pathogens and environmental harshness rise and fall independent of one another. Even speculating on ancestral evolutionary environments, such a supposition seems doubtful. In the harsh sub-zero climate of the Arctic, pathogen prevalence is likely to have been low but at the same time food resources would have been scarce. In hotter climates, food would have been more abundant but so also would have been parasites. And in contemporary environments, poverty is associated both with resource scarcity *and* poor health. According to this model, the rise in female-headed households in the West over the last 40 years would be the result of increased pathogen load. But this seems unlikely given that this was the very time when immunization became common, prenatal care improved, and health care was more widely available.

Another account of conditional mating strategy does a better job of addressing women's shift to lone parenting. This argument depends upon the proportion of men and women in the population because this has an effect upon which sex achieves their preferred reproductive modus operandi (Guttentag & Secord, 1983; Pedersen, 1991). Imagine a community of men and women of reproductive age. Now suppose that an imbalance begins so that there are too many women relative to men—a skewed operational sex ratio. This can occur when the birth rate rises. Because women want to marry men who are older than they are, when they reach marriageable age they will find too few eligible men to go around. But men have no such problem since they are seeking their mates from the expanding pool of younger women. Operational sex ratio imbalances can also result from a high proportion of males who are drug addicts, alcoholics, unemployed, and long-term sick. Though available, they are unlikely to chosen as long-term partners since they represent a drain on the women's assets rather than an economic advantage.

Too many women means that men are in a good market position to enforce their preferred reproductive strategy and that strategy is likely to be one that minimizes paternal investment in favor of maternal investment (Guttentag & Secord, 1983). Just such a shift in the sex ratio occurred in the United States between 1965 and the 1970s and, as predicted, divorce rates, illegitimate births, and single-parent families increased, more permissive sexual attitudes predominated, and the number of women in the workplace rose. When there is an oversupply of men, there is reversal in these trends with an increased commitment of men to marriage and lower divorce rates. In this scenario, women's preference for a long-term partner is taken as given (it halves the cost of childrearing) as is men's preference for a polygynous strategy (which maximizes reproductive success at zero cost in child care). Women are forced into an unrestricted strategy by the sheer paucity of males.

Both the strategic pluralism and the operational sex ratio arguments suggest that women track the environment to ascertain parasite load, ecological difficulties, or the number of marriageable males. By highlighting the facultative and flexible nature of women's choices, these theories pay little attention to the possibility that environmental factors can also produce consistency in a woman's choice of mating strategies. Draper and Harpending (1982) have offered an explanation of how such a preference might be set up early in their development and how this preference might be influenced by indirect cues to the availability of investing males. They argued that the absence of a stable provisioning father in the home signals to the growing girl that paternal investment is rare and pair-bonds are unstable. In these circumstances, her best strategy might be to seek a series of short-term mates and to undertake child-rearing alone; "a young woman who waits for the right man to help rear her children may lose valuable reproductive opportunities at a time when her health and physical capability are at their peak" (Belsky, Steinberg, & Draper, 1991, p. 653).

There are a series of steps in the developmental sequence that lead to a short-term mating strategy. The girl's home is marked by father-absence, marital discord, or inadequate resources which creates a climate of stress. This stress manifests itself in harsh, rejecting, or inconsistent parenting practices which results in the child forming an insecure attachment to the parent and developing an internal working model of relationships characterized by mistrust. In girls, this is manifested in anxiety and depression (internalizing symptoms) while in boys it is more frequently externalized as aggression and non-compliance. In both sexes, these psychological states induce early physical sexual maturity. Subsequently sexual relationships tend to be opportunistic, short-term, and lacking in emotional commitment.

This model has much data to support it. Resource shortage and stress have both been linked to poor parenting practices (Belsky, 1984; McLoyd, 1990; Patterson, 1986), as has marital discord (Jouriles, Pfiffner, & O'Leary, 1988). Maltreated children are at high risk of developing insecure attachments not only to their parents but also to peers (Howes & Eldredge, 1985; Lyons-Ruth, Connell, Zoll, & Stahl, 1987). Although pubertal timing is associated with a range of variables including genes, socioeconomic status, diet, and body weight, many prospective and retrospective studies have found that early menarche in girls is associated with family conflict and father absence (see Belsky, Houts, & Fearon, 2010; Belsky et al., 2007; Ellis, 2004). Boys and girls who mature early initiate intercourse at an earlier age than their peers (Smith, Udry, & Morris, 1985). Furthermore, girls from never-married or divorced mothers are also more likely to be sexually active at an earlier age (Jessor, Costa, Jessor, & Donovan, 1983; Newcomer & Udry, 1984). Compared to girls from intact families they have more sexual partners, although girls who lose a father through death do not (Demo & Acock, 1988; Hetherington, 1972). Early dating, sexual activity, and marital stability are all associated with exposure to divorce in childhood and children of divorced parents are themselves at greater risk for divorce (Keith & Finlay, 1988). Nonetheless we cannot rule out a simpler genetic effect—mothers who engage in short-term relationships may give their genes to daughters creating a similar preference.

When we compare these models of variability in women's strategies, we see that in most of them selection of a short-term sexual strategy by a woman is a less preferred option resulting from some curtailment of her choice. Women select short-term sexual relationships when men cannot improve their children's survival, when there are too few men, or when their upbringing has signaled that men are unreliable investors in their progeny. Short-term relationships for women often amount to serial monogamy in response to a population of males, none of whom can or will provide sustained economic and emotional commitment. And if she can maintain her attractiveness in the face of her increasing age, decreasing looks, and the handicap (from a prospective partner's viewpoint) of already born children, she can also gain the advantage of genetic diversity and perhaps better genetic quality in her children. But the most secure and stable route is to attract a male who will commit, providing the long-term assistance and resources that she needs to raise multiple offspring simultaneously. Unfortunately that idea has occurred to other women also and she is in a competitive market-place. The currency of the marketplace is what men want in a female partner. To trade successfully, she must advertise her assets by showing that she has more desirable qualities than her female rivals.

Tacit competition: Looking good

Though systematic studies of men's mate preferences may be relatively recent, it seems that women knew all along what men liked. A youthful body and face are exactly what women compete with each other to achieve. In the United States, 88 percent of American women aged over 18 wear make-up, and twice as much is spent on personal grooming products as on books. Women's fascination with enhancing their appearance is far from new as Nancy Etcoff (1999, p. 101) describes:

> Women conceal, bleach and blush. They have applied poisonous lead and mercury to their skin mixed in with egg whites, lemon juice, milk and vinegar. They have attached leeches to themselves and swallowed arsenic wafers. To mimic skin translucency, the Greeks and Romans and later Queen Elizabeth I painted the veins on their breasts and their forehead blue. For two thousand years European face makeup was made from white lead, which was combined with chalk or used in a paste with vinegar and egg whites and applied thickly to completely mask the skin's surface and colour . . . Over this pale canvas, women apply exclamation points of red to their lips and their cheeks. Red, the colour of blood, of blushes and flushes, of nipples, lips and genitals awash with sexual excitement, is visible from afar and emotionally arousing.

Make-up is in short designed to mimic youth, correct asymmetries, and signal sexuality. And it is used almost exclusively by women, not men. If ever there was a prima facie case for the idea of two-way sexual selection, here it is. The cost, time, and energy women devote to enhancing precisely those facial features that attract men makes it abundantly clear that women are far from passive in the mating game. Though cosmetics can help to conceal the ravages of ageing, they are fighting a powerful enemy. In youth, skin cells are replaced every two weeks but, as we age, the cycle slows down. The cells on the surface of the skin remain there longer and begin to look dull and tired. Natural oil production decelerates and collagen and elastin, which give the skin elasticity, break down, especially after menopause. Pockets of fat beneath the skin's surface become thinner. The overall effect is a face that is wrinkled, sagging, and boney.

Some turn to a more radical approach—surgery. Ninety percent of cosmetic surgical procedures in the United States, such as face lifts and eyelid surgery, are performed on women. Surgery is also used to make women's bodies conform to male preferences. Every year in the United States approximately 340,000 women have breast implants and 300,000 have liposuction. Comparing women who married upward in the class structure with women who stayed demographically where they started, researchers have found a significant difference in weight: hypergamously married women are thinner. Given a choice, men prefer slim women but they do not favor the skinny (Singh, 1993).

Attractiveness appears as the currency of female competition even when no mention is made of what the competition is about. Using diaries to examine the everyday experience of competition, in which subjects were asked to record their thoughts and actions, Cashdan (1998) found that while men competed with other men chiefly in the domain of sports, women competed with one another in terms of looking attractive. Women, far more than men, deceive the opposite sex by alterations to their appearance such as wearing make-up, painting their nails, getting fake tans, and wearing tight clothing (Tooke & Camire, 1991; Walters & Crawford, 1994). David Buss (1988a) compared men and women in how effective they judged various acts to be in attracting the opposite sex. For women, wearing sexy and stylish clothing and using cosmetics were judged particularly effective, whereas displaying resources was judged as a more effective tactic for men. Having found a mate, Buss (1988b) went on to investigate the ways that men and women attempt to retain them. Both sexes were most likely to report positive behavior and inducements to keep a mate's interest such as being kind, helpful, and supportive. They also used "tie signs" such as putting their arms around their partner to advertise their relationship to others. They were least likely to admit to the use of negative tactics such as violence against same-sex rivals but nonetheless there was a significant sex difference. Men were much more likely to physically threaten and pick a fight with rivals. For women these directly aggressive acts were the least frequently used and judged to be the least effective. However, short of actual physical attack, there are other ways of dealing with same-sex competition. One is to derogate or devalue potential rivals. And here again we see a predictable sex difference. While men tend to derogate other men's financial resources, goals, and achievements, women criticize other women's appearance (Buss & Dedden, 1990).

A woman's most likely rival is a close friend: after all, friends choose each other precisely because of their similarity and hence whatever attracted a man to one member of the pair may also attract him to her best friend. Friends also spend time together and hence are likely to be exposed to the same pool of potential mates where their tastes are likely to overlap. A woman's relative attractiveness affects her view of the friendship. Studying pairs of female best friends, Bleske-Rechek & Lighthall (2010) found that the less attractive member of the two (as determined by outside judges as well as by the pair's own ratings) perceived more mating rivalry than her more attractive friend. They were more likely to agree with statements such as "She flirts with guys I am interested in," "It is harder to meet guys when she is around," and "I feel in competition with her for attention from members of the opposite sex." Both sexes experience more distress when their rival is a close friend rather than a stranger, but both sexes also admit to deceiving their best friends about how often they have attempted to poach their friend's partner (Bleske & Shackelford, 2001). Women especially resent it when a friend tries to steal their mate by improving her appearance and advertising her sexual availability.

Lurking in young women's friendships there is the cloaked specter of rivalry (a rivalry that predictably and happily decreases around the time of menopause, Vukovic et al., 2009.) It simmers beneath the surface and, if it becomes visible, it is dealt with by stealth. A woman's first line of defense against mate poaching is to strengthen her bonds with her male partner by lavishing care and attention on him, and by making herself more attractive. If that fails, she may resort to derogating her rival's appearance and desirability. But many of the studies I have described used relatively privileged undergraduate students as informants. Playing nice is nice—if you can afford it. We turn now to more extreme tactics that women may be forced to use when times are hard and good men are scarce.

When push comes to shove

Women come to blows far less often than men because the risks are usually too great. Instead women prefer to restrict their competition to less direct contests for sexier faces, clothes, and figures. But the confluence of some important factors can create a recipe for female–female assault. Let us examine the ingredients.

First, age. Young women fight more than older ones. And if my thesis—that much female aggression is about mate competition—is correct, it is a tribute to the strength of their inhibitory control that women are not much more violent than they are. Here's why. Everywhere, young men between the ages of about 20 and 24 fight much more often than more mature men (Gottfredson & Hirschi, 1990; Kruttschnitt, 1994). Daly and Wilson (1988) have offered a persuasive reason why this should be. At this age men are seeking mates and for those who lack material resources to signal status, physical dominance is an important attribute. It causes other men to back off and their fearful respect provides evidence to women of a man's dominance. This adolescent bellicosity testifies to the importance of mate choice at this critical age when young men enter the sexual arena. Traditional theories of mate selection followed the axiom that males compete and females choose (Andersson, 1994; Bateman, 1948; Trivers, 1972) and this one-way form of selection may be adequate to describe the behavior of species where males invest little more than sperm. But if we look at human data we find something that such a position would not predict. Plotting age against assault rate we find a remarkably similar age-assault curve for both sexes. In fact the correlation between them is 0.89 for US data and 0.98 for British data (Campbell, Muncer, & Bibel, 2001). The female rate is only a fraction of that of males—women commit about 15 percent of criminally violent acts—but nonetheless there is a clear correspondence between the age at which violence is most likely in the two sexes. The obvious explanation for this astonishingly high correlation is that sexual selection (and the aggression that goes with it) is a two-way street, although men engage in such risky strategies far more frequently than women.

Yet if we take the idea of two-way selection seriously, what is surprising is the astonishingly low rate shown by women. Men are fighting, though not consciously, for the status that can buy them reproductive opportunities. Yet recall that men become increasingly attractive to women as they gain more resources and this is likely to be a function of increasing age. Consider too that women are far less choosy about their partner's physical appearance (which declines with age) than men are. Also bear in mind that a man's ability to father children extends throughout his adult life span because, unlike a woman, his career is not cut short by menopause. (Novelist Saul Below fathered a child at the age of 84.) Taken together, age should have less impact on a man's mating opportunities than on a woman's and it should take some of the urgency out of his sexual competition.

But for women, age is of the essence. Between the ages of 15 and 25 a woman reaches her maximum attractiveness. Never again will she have such a good chance to acquire the best of the available men. Men's preference for youth places serious constraints on the mate opportunities that are open to her after her "best" years—a younger, more attractive cohort of women is already snapping at her heels. And from a purely biological viewpoint, a woman of 20 is looking at a maximum of 30 years of reproductive possibility compared to about 50 years in a comparably aged man. Age matters—but more so to women than to men. Hence it is all the more surprising that female competition, however extreme it may be in the area of achieving physical perfection, rarely reaches the boiling point of violent confrontation. But if a woman is ever to attack another woman it is more likely to happen in her teens than at any other age.

Girls mature earlier than boys and menarche occurs relatively late in the sequence of developmental changes—approximately 18 months after the growth peak has reached its peak. Menstrual periods occur without ovulation for as long as two years. Thus from the time that a girl begins to show signs of sexual development, she has a period of over three years during which time she is unlikely to conceive. This provides her with a safe period of sexual experimentation as she trawls the market for a long-term mate. It also means that we would expect girls to show an earlier interest in establishing relations with the opposite sex (they do) and also a slightly earlier involvement in competitive aggression. Just as we would expect, girls' involvement in assault peaks about two years earlier than boys' whether we use official criminal statistics (Kruttschnitt, 1994; Piper, 1983) or self-reported involvement in aggression (Elliott, Huizinga, & Morse, 1983).

The next ingredient is the intensity of competition that a woman faces. In societies where the number of women exceeds that of men, female competition escalates. Of particular importance is the local sex ratio since we know that a woman is likely to marry a man from her own geographical area who matches her in social class, ethnicity, education, and intelligence (Hill, Rubin, & Peplau, 1976; Tharp, 1963). This is the pool of available men for which woman must compete. In poverty-level, inner-city areas, male mortality is high and this decreases the available pool of males. To make matters worse, those men that are available may not constitute acceptable partners. Incarceration, drug addiction, alcoholism, mental illness, homelessness, and unemployment effectively remove a proportion of males from the realistic marriage market. Though available, such men are likely to constitute a drain on the woman's own meager resources rather than providing any additional ones. In these areas, there is marked variation in men's ability to support a wife and children. With the exodus of upwardly mobile and well-educated men from these areas, those that remain are often forced to take irregular, menial, or low-paid work. The few wealthy men often make their money from illegal enterprises, but nonetheless such men are highly valued by women. Carl Taylor's (1993, p. 130) interviews with young black women makes clear that the source of a man's income is less important than its size and his willingness to share it:

> Dope guys is straight if they think you ain't dissing them. They got coin and they will spend on you, and that's better than getting messed over for nothing. At least dope guys will buy you dinner at some place besides Mickey Dee's . . . I date whoever is treating your girl the right way. Me, if a guy got some paper well, it's okay with me. I like fellas that's rolling, least they making it.

The marked variation between high rollers and losers (compared to the smaller variation among middle-class males) also increases competition between women. The difference between marrying a doctor or an accountant is less extreme (and much less worth risking violence for) than the difference between a successful drug dealer and a drug addict (Campbell, 2011). As the disparities in male wealth increase, so does the tension between women.

Added to this is a further dynamic that feeds off the paucity of good men. As we have noted, the fewer of them there are, the stronger is their ability to pursue their preferred mating strategy. Men's greater interest in uncommitted sex and short-term relationships can flourish since women have little leverage against it. "If you won't give it to me, someone else will" is a form of sexual coercion that is all too true and that drives women to accept temporary sexual relationships that, from their point of view, are far from ideal. In underclass communities men are able to get their way. Women compete not only for a faithful and committed man, but even for a temporary liaison with a man who can provide material resources in the short term. These women understand the equation of sex for money, the rarity of long-term relationships and the dynamic that drives male choice.

> I know why some girls ration out the sex, that's all you got and the dogs be sniffing and you got to let them smell it (laughing); they want them boots and you got to keep 'em as long as you can. When men get what they want then you never get what you want if you didn't play it right . . . I tell her take all his paper, all of it, 'cause it's just a matter of time and he's gonna do some rotten dog shit on her . . . Got to get it when you can. You never know when it's gonna stop and you better get much as you can while you can . . . When fellas get tired of your pussy, it's good-bye girl, naw, it's get the fuck out of my life bitch! Next bitch! (Taylor, 1993, pp. 97, 131)

A woman's attractiveness is another part of the violence equation and it is a two-edged sword. While pretty girls do not need to fight to secure the attention of men, they are also likely to be the target of other girls' jealousy. Physical attractiveness increases a girl's chances of being the victim of indirect aggression by 35 percent, but decreases a boy's chance by 25 percent (Leenaars, Dane, & Marini, 2008). In Philadelphia, United States, attractive girls are accused of "thinking they're special" and this can constitute grounds for assault: "It's like, if another girl gets attention, she's taking it away from you. It's as if she's saying she's better than you. So you gonna knock her down a notch" (Ness, 2004, p. 40). A British girl describes the dangerous effects of her friend's attractiveness:

> They were jealous of Beverley because she could get quite a few boyfriends and half of them [other girls] were too fat or too skinny. They were following us and we got up and started walking off and they was calling out names and I turned round and said "Just because you are too fucking fat, Smith." They come over from the pub and I was walking ahead of Bev and next minute I heard one of them slap Bev round the face. There was a whole gang of them onto her. (Marsh & Paton, 1984)

Precocious sexual maturity can also make a girl the target of other girls' resentment. Girls who reach menarche early are popular with boys yet rejected by other girls, making them more vulnerable to depression and anxiety (Copeland, Shanahan, Miller, Costello, & Angold, 2010; Faust, 1960). A number of explanations have been offered including feelings of awkwardness among teenage girls who prize conformity and hate being different (Jones & Mussen, 1958) and the association of early menarche with shortness and chubbiness which are devalued as body types (Tobin-Richards, Boxer, & Peterson, 1983). Perhaps there is a more direct explanation that encompasses both boys' attraction and girls' hostility: early-maturing girls have a distinct advantage in terms of mate selection. Early maturing girls begin dating and having intercourse before their peers (Phinney, Jenson, Olsen, & Cundick, 1990) and they have a larger number of sexual partners (Copeland et al., 2010). Recent sexual experience with a larger number of partners increases a girl's risk for indirect aggression (Leenaars et al., 2008). Early maturing girls garner a disproportionate amount of male interest and by entering the mate market earlier, have a wider choice of prospective men. Not only that but, by starting early, they can look forward to a longer reproductive career than their developmentally more leisurely peers.

Aggression, like any other strategy, comes more easily to some than to others simply because they are familiar at it. And aggression in girls, as in boys, shows considerable stability over time (Cairns & Cairns, 1984; Cairns, Cairns, Neckerman, Ferguson, & Gariepy, 1989; Pitkanen-Pulkkinen, 1981; Pulkkinen, 1987). A tendency to aggression has a strong component of heritability (Rushton, Fulker, Neale, Nias, & Eysenck, 1986) but its expression depends upon circumstances. The backgrounds of violent offenders, both male and female, show a consistent thread (see Moffitt, 1993). They come from families which are turbulent and unstable. The parents as well as the children use aggression as a coping strategy. When conflict erupts, abuse and slaps displace reasoning and debate. Children's early years set the parameters of what they can expect from the environment around them and what they learn is that the pre-emptive strike wins out over withdrawal or tolerance. The world is a competitive place in which access to money, food, and clothes depends upon a willingness to shout louder or hit harder. Children from such homes begin to show higher levels of aggression even before they are school aged. Expecting others to be hostile, such children generate conflicts in response to the slightest perceived threat. What is to be feared—more than injury—is becoming a victim. These girls achieve reputations as bullies: they are deferred to and feared by classmates, as well as co-opted as allies by those who wish to settle a score with others. The more they fight, the more adept they become at controlling their fear and vanquishing opponents (Campbell, 1984). By their teens, they are seasoned veterans with a 'tough' reputation to defend and an armory of combative techniques. For these girls, fighting has become, if not routine, then at least a strategic option.

These ingredients of aggression do not travel independently but together. The same impoverished neighborhoods that have more than their fair share of male unemployment and single mothers also have daughters who reach menarche early, begin their sexual careers sooner, and have greater experience of fighting for what they need. Each ingredient depends upon the others. The absence of supporting men drives women's short-term sexual strategies which result in female poverty and a hand-to-mouth existence. These in turn set the strategies for their children who learn to fight for what they want. Daughters in father-absent families become sexually mature at an earlier age and pursue their own search for short-term mates with the aggression that has been honed in an environment where forbearance and patience produce few rewards.

We know precious little of the "who" and "why" of female fights. Female victims report that their attacker was another woman in 20% of all reported incidents of contact crime in Britain (Home Office Research and Planning Unit, 1993; Home Office Statistical Bulletin, 1996). Women are attacked by other women in 22 percent of stranger assaults, 39 percent of acquaintance assaults, 33 percent of home-based assaults not involving partners, 35 percent of street assaults, 22 percent of work-related violence, and 56 percent of assaults in pubs and clubs. George (1999) obtained data from a random sample of 1,455 British male and female respondents concerning incidents of attacks by women during the preceding five years. Seven percent of women reported an actual assault by another woman and a further 4 percent reported a threat of assault. Female assaults were most commonly directed at and committed by 15- to 24-year-olds; they occurred predominantly between friends and acquaintances and the most frequent forms of attack were pushing, shoving, grabbing, tripping, slapping, kicking and punching (George, personal communication). I conducted a questionnaire study of 251 16-year-old girls from cities in Britain that attempted to gather information not just from victims but from the attackers themselves (Campbell, 1986). All of the girls had witnessed a fight, 89 percent had been involved in at least one, and 43 percent had fought during the preceding year. The majority of fights (73 percent) were against another girl (see also Campbell, Muncer, & Bibel, 1998) and the same figure has been reported in the United States (Greenfeld & Snell, 1999). They most often occurred in the street (47 percent) or at school (29 percent). Only 10 percent of the fights involved weapons and the most common tactics were punching (80 percent), kicking (79 percent), and slapping (57 percent). One-quarter of the girls reported no injuries from the fight while others had bruises (41 percent), scratches (22 percent), and cuts (11 percent). In the United States also, young women's fights are less dangerous than those of their male counterparts, rarely employing weapons (Ness, 2004). Three-quarters of their violent offences are limited to simple rather than aggravated assaults (Greenfeld & Snell, 1999). Taken together these studies suggest that female–female attacks often occur between young and similarly-aged acquaintances in drinking establishments or in the streets and involve non-weapon, hand-to-hand tactics.

But what are they fighting about? I posed this question to the girls who answered my questionnaire. The most common category which accounted for 46 percent of fights was an attack on the girl's personal integrity which included instances where there had been allegations about the girl's promiscuity, false accusations, or pejorative gossip behind her back. The next most common category was loyalty where the girl fought to defend the good name of a friend or relative who had been the butt of an integrity attack. The third most common category was jealousy about a romantic partner (12 percent). (As part of this study, I also gave the same questionnaires to girls aged 16 to 20 in a juvenile prison and to adult imprisoned women. In these two older samples, the category of jealousy accounted for 25 and 42 percent respectively of the responses). The importance of sexual reputation was underlined when I asked girls about the last remark that was made before the first blow was struck. Equal proportions of responses (31 percent) cited accusations of promiscuity ("slut," "whore") and dispute-related responses to such epithets ("Come on then and get some, slag," "Takes one to know one").

This suggests that female fights are indeed about mating issues—an attempt to retrieve a sexual reputation that has been verbally impugned or about jealousy over a boy. Marsh and Paton (1986, p. 62) found a similar pattern in their ethnographic study of British girls' reasons for fighting: "Highest on the list, however, was "rumour spreading" or sexual insult. It was agreed that it was wholly justifiable to use physical violence in the defence of one's sexual reputation: 'If anyone slags you off—calls you a tart or something you've got to be able to do something about it.'" Their interview transcripts clearly support this interpretation (Marsh & Paton, 1984):

> If a girl's going out with a boy and he's two-timing her, they tend to take it out on the other girl. Well, it takes two doesn't it?
> (Interviewer) Are the fights generally over boyfriends?
> Mainly.
> The thing you said earlier about girls being accused of being sluts, they fight for their reputation. . . .
> (Interviewer) What do you reckon is the reason girls fight?
> Jealousy.
> Yeah.
> (Interviewer) What over?
> Boys usually.
> Like a lot of girls say they fight to protect their reputation.
> Yeah . . .
> (Interviewer) Why do girls fight?
> Over boys—yeah, there ain't really any other main reason is there?

A similar theme emerged in interviews that I conducted with girls from several British cities (Campbell, 1982):

> (Interviewer) What do girls fight about?
> Boys.

> Ripping up one another's clothes and calling each other names.
> Jealousy.
> (Interviewer) So do girls and boys fight about the same things or not?
> Boils down to the same thing really 'cos girls fight over boys, boys fight over girls. Fight for their pride, things like that and boys fight about the same thing.

The same conclusions about girls' fights come from teachers (Davies, 1984) and from male peers (Duncan, 1999, p. 94):

> ND (interviewer): What do you think girls fight about?
> CIARAN: Calling names.
> BILLY: Well if one girl is nicer looking than another girl, then that girl will call the nice looking one slut or slag or something.
> CIARAN: Whore.
> ARTHUR: Or if one girl knows that a girl fancies a boy and she has gone out of her way to ask this boy out and the girl fancies him as well, well that might cause friction.
> ND (Interviewer): So jealousy of boyfriends, stuff like that?
> ARTHUR: Yeah.

Cindy Ness (2004, p. 41) also found that boys loomed large in her investigation of girls' fighting in inner city Philadelphia:

> Even in the early stages of "talking" to a boy, a girl does not take kindly to another girl's getting too close. Although there is a shared understanding among girls that "messing with someone's man" is off limits, in practice, girls (and boys) move in on each other's romantic interests all the time. Whether the violation is real or imagined, the disrespect that a girl often perceives and then dishes out is enough to start two girls down a path to a physical confrontation.

Clearly mate selection plays a major role in female aggression. But we can be a bit more specific and identify three motives that should be especially likely to ignite violence: the management of a woman's *sexual reputation*, the degree of *competition* for desirable partners, and the expression of *jealousy* in response to another woman's attempt to "steal" a man whose resources are already committed.

Fighting and sexual reputation

A woman's chance of securing a desirable long-term mate depends in large part upon his evaluation of her future fidelity, which will guarantee certainty of paternity and encourage his paternal investment. The best way to predict her future is to look at her past but, although this may be hidden from a prospective suitor, other women may be keen to fill in the missing information. Derogating a rival's sexual reputation is a tactic more often used by young women than men (Buss & Dedden, 1990). Terms such as "slag," "tart," or "whore" are powerful triggers to aggressive incidents (Campbell, 1982; Duncan, 1999; Lees, 1993;

Marsh & Paton, 1986). Despite the achievements of the women's movement and the manifest inequity of the sexual double standard, women respond angrily to accusations of "loose" sexual standards in a way that men do not.

> ND (Interviewer): What do girls get called if they go out with lots of lads?
> SPIRO, GARAHAM, FAZAL, NASUR: A slag! (Laughter)
> FAZAL: A slut. They hate it an' all, the girls do.
> ND: Is that (being called a slag) a bad thing?
> PSIRO, GARAHAM, FAZAL, NASUR: Yeah.
> NASUR: You don't know where they've been, do you? (Duncan, 1999, p. 53)

Back in 1978, Wilson noted the "repressive triangle" of love, sex, and marriage in the lives of working class girls. Girls took love to be a prerequisite for sex and this in turn was a precursor to marriage. Sex without at least lip service to marriage placed the girl in danger of developing a sexual reputation. It was the girls themselves who were most vocal in enforcing this code. "The girls regulated their contact with other girls who were known as 'lays' in order to preserve their own reputations. In fact they openly ridiculed the girls referring to them as 'whores'" (Wilson, 1978, p. 70). Fifteen years later, teenagers were still alert to the distinction between nice girls and tarts. "If you don't want to get married and want to live a free life . . . everyone will call you a tart, like you've got to go out with a bloke for a really long time and then marry him" (Lees, 1993, p. 105). And boys continued to make the same distinction between prospective wives ("Attractive, clever, nice personality, trustworthy, older, not someone that everyone knows. Not someone who's been out with people I know." Lees, 1993, p. 139) and slags ("You wouldn't go out with her, you would just knock her off. She is just easy, she is just easier to get off with . . . So you would use her . . . Yeah, skank her." Duncan, 1999, p. 54). In response, girls continued to avoid friendships with sexually available girls for fear of reputation-by-association. Indeed girls themselves actively colluded in enforcing the double standard through gossip, rumor spreading, and ostracism, as Sue Lees notes:

> The most risky confidences centre around sexual behaviour and feelings. One reason why so few girls even talk to their closest friends about sexual desire or actual sexual behaviour is through fear that their friends might betray them and gossip—spread the rumour that they are a slag. There is no parallel for boys to the risk of betrayal which can destroy a girl's whole social standing. (Lees, 1993, p. 80).

Lees goes on to analyze a fairly typical response by one of her female informants to being called a slag (in this case by a male):

> "I've been walking down the street and someone's said to me, across the road, being rude, and says 'You slag,' and I think, 'How do you know? You've got no evidence.' That makes me angry, 'cos, like, you see someone and you're meant to know whether they sleep around or not." Here Kate is angry that the boy calls her a slag without

having any evidence. Even when the boy does not know her, a girl reacts by denying the accusation rather than by objecting to the use of the category. For them what is important is to prove that you are not a slag: what they unquestioningly accept is the legitimacy of the category of slag. In other words, the category has uncontested status. (Lees, 1993, p. 267)

In this day and age, with the inequity of the double standard publically acknowledged, "slut" should have lost its power long ago. Yet in a national sample of 10,000 respondents aged between 12 and 20, Kaeager & Staff (2009) found evidence that it lives on. They examined data on peer acceptance (the number of nominations an individual received from classmates, each of whom were asked to indicate their five best male and female friends). Girls who had had more than eight sexual partners in their lifetime were significantly less likely to be nominated as a friend by their classmates, whereas the reverse was true for boys. These sexually experienced boys gained their popularity advantage chiefly from nominations by girls and it was girls again that explained sexually experienced girls' relative lack of popularity. As the authors note, "These results suggest that female reactions to sexual behavior simultaneously escalate the status of permissive boys and decrease the status of permissive girls" (Kaeager & Staff, 2009, p. 156).

There is ample evidence that it is women who suppress women's sexuality more than men do (Baumeister & Twenge, 2002). Despite feminist arguments about male patriarchal control, a range of psychological, sociological, and anthropological studies suggest quite the opposite. It is not fathers, but mothers who deliver warnings to their daughters about the dangers of promiscuity. Girls are much more strongly influenced by their female (rather than male) friends' attitudes to casual sex and girls typically go as far their friends in terms of sexual intimacy. Female friendships operate to extricate girls from casual sexual encounters, while male friendships encourage them. A potential source of male control might be boyfriends but here the data point to exactly the opposite direction of influence: boyfriends pressure girls to engage in intercourse. As for the double standard itself, 46 percent of university women believe that it is women who make the harshest judgments of women who have multiple sexual partners; only 12 percent thought it was men. Highly sexual women report more difficulties in same-sex than opposite-sex friendships, with other women putting pressure on them to curtail their sexual activity. In Africa and the Middle East, genital mutilation (excision of the clitoris) and infibulations (partial suturing of the vagina), designed to reduce sexual desire and ensure virginity, are practiced by women, despite the fact that husbands prefer wives without surgery. In the West, it is women more than men that disapprove of pornography and prostitution. The sexual revolution of the 1960s to 1980s changed women's sexual behavior more than men's yet it is women not men who report regrets and doubts about the increased permissiveness it brought. Why should women be so keen to curtail the sexual behavior of other women? Baumeister and Twenge conclude that we need to look at the sexual market place:

> The female control theory is based on social exchange theory. It rests on the assumption that sex is a resource that men want but that is under female control. To the extent that women want to obtain other resources in return for sex, they want the price of sex to be high, and thus they seek to suppress female sexual activity generally so as to maintain a chronic shortage (and hence high prices). Women together act to restrain female sexuality, for the sake of benefiting all women. Whereas the male control theory emphasized stifling the sexuality of wives and mates in ongoing relationships, the female control theory emphasizes stifling the sexuality of single women who are seeking mates and negotiating the terms of exchange for beginning a sexual relationship. (Baumeister & Twenge, 2002, pp. 172–173)

This viewpoint meshes well with an evolutionary perspective. Women's higher parental investment means that they represent a limiting resource for men and it is for this reason that men's interest in having sex frequently and with many partners is higher than that of women (Baumeister, Catanese, & Vohs, 2001). In terms of maximizing reproductive success, women prioritize successful reproduction and care of offspring, rather than copulation number. An assisting male partner enhances this by enabling her to raise more than one child at a time. A woman who provides sexual access without expecting continued support is likely to be popular with men (at least in the short term) but extremely unpopular with women because she reduces the going rate for sex. Of course, this type of reasoning does not occur consciously to either sex. But it provides a way of understanding why in all parts of the world, cultural values about appropriate sexual behavior seek to control women, and why it is women who enforce these beliefs. The sexual marketplace approach also explains why women should be particularly keen to protect their own sexual reputation.

> . . . a woman has two resources to consider. Actual sexual activity is a fully renewable resource, insofar as her ability to engage in sex is not heavily dependent on what she has done previously. In contrast, her reputation is a nonrenewable resource. A fully rational approach to social exchange would therefore cause the woman to care less about what she actually does than about what she is perceived by the community as doing. Whenever she engages in sex, she should seek to keep it somewhat secret and deniable, so that her reputation is that of someone whose sexual favors are highly exclusive and therefore of high value. (Baumeister & Vohs, 2004, p. 345)

On the streets, community perception of a girl's sexual activity can be manifested in stigmatization and name calling. Whether they are true or not, accusations of promiscuity are provocative. As one girl remarked to me, "A girl that's been called a slag is the same as a boy that's been called a chicken" (Campbell, 1982, p. 142) and indeed, from the point of view of threat to their future mating opportunities, they are equivalent. But while a boy can demonstrate he is not a chicken by fighting anyone who so impugns him, a girl is unable to demonstrate in any public way that the accusation is false. This places her in a difficult, if not impossible, situation. A girl can attempt to prove her innocence by confronting the boy with whom she is alleged to have had sex. But it is his word against hers, he has every reason to lie and in general his word prevails. If she fails to respond to the accusation, her silence may be seen as a tacit admission of its truth. By ignoring gossip, she runs the risk of developing a reputation for non-conformity that may fuel her image as an outsider:

> Ignoring insults can be an effective way of counteracting the abuse. If girls can recognise the double standard, then they will not be so shaken by it. Yet being independent in thought or deed carries risks. Being free and independent can signal promiscuity. The freedom of women can be equated with prostitution. What is lacking is a language through which the legitimacy of slag as a way of censoring girls can be contested. (Lees, 1993, pp. 275–276)

The best she can do is to forcefully repel anyone who labels her as a tart and so minimize the likelihood of such a reputation attack being repeated. A major factor that fuels girls' fights is the spreading of rumors which triggers a violent reaction from the target of the gossip:

> She started spreading rumours about me saying that I used to sneak out in the middle of the night in my night-dress and meet ten boys or something really stupid . . . Well, we were arguing with each other about the rumour mainly and she was saying she didn't say it . . . and then she started calling me names like that and then she started to walk off across the road and she said "I'll get you sometime, you fucking bitch." And that made me mad because if she was going to get me, she was going to get me there and then. I mean there was no point in getting me later and so I kicked her in the back and she fell flat on her face and I said "If you are going to get me, get me now" and we started fighting. (Marsh & Paton, 1984)
>
> I was walking round to your house and you know one of the girls we used to walk to school with said "Oh my God. You look a right slut. Look at all that make-up you've got on". Now I never batted an eyelid. I just told her to shut her mouth—there was three of them. I said "Oh, shut your mouth". Yet that was on my mind all night and we got up to Scamps (night-club), didn't we? And she was there and I just went over to her and hit her round the face. "Now say it" I said and she poked me in the eye. (Marsh & Paton, 1984)

But even today, young women cannot afford to shrug off a reputation for promiscuity and attempts to turn the double standard on men simply provokes laughter (Duncan, 1999). Sexual conquests enhance rather than detract from a young man's reputation—his past desirability to women increases his

future success with others. When we learn that an unattractive man has bed-
ded a hundred women, we suppose that he must have hidden qualities that
have escaped us. But when we learn the same about a woman, we guess she is
desperate. The most desirable women can pick and choose—they don't need to
resort to the "cheap trick" of sex. A woman who is discriminating in her choice
of partners signals that she believes she is worth waiting for.

And it is men's choosiness about who they will accept as a long-term partner
that drives the dynamic. Paternal investment is costly and it closes down a man's
opportunities for short-term and cost-free alliances. Most importantly, if he
selects an unfaithful partner he runs the risk of a lifetime investment in another
man's child. Men, under monogamy, are as choosy as women and high on their
list of desirable qualities comes fidelity—which he can only estimate by the ease
with which other men have gained sexual access in the past. So men, as the saying goes, may want a wife who is "a whore in the bedroom"—as long as she is
their whore and nobody else's.

Fighting and male resources

Competition among women for men has been documented cross-culturally.
Glazer (1992) argues that female economic dependence on male resources
drives competition to extreme levels. "The more subordinate women are to
men and the more dependent they are on patriarchal social structures, the more
injury they inflict upon one another" (Glazer, 1992, p. 164). To illustrate her
point, she compared levels of female–female aggression at two time periods
in Zambia. In pre-colonial times, communities were matrilocal—women inherited farming rights and had major responsibility for food production and
distribution. Their closest cross-sex relationships were with their brothers who
had every genetic interest in encouraging their sister to produce children (for
whom they were jointly responsible) without the attendant male proprietal jealousy of a marriage. Women's sexuality was encouraged and divorce was easy
and frequent. During this period, when women were not economically dependent upon men, rates of intra-female aggression were low (Schuster, 1983).
Similar findings have been reported in other matrilineal societies including the
Mundurucu of Brazil and the Hopi North American Indians (Benedict, 1934;
Murphy & Murphy, 1974). With colonial rule, female economic dependence
on men increased while at the same time men were unreliable and uncommitted fathers. Female–female aggression rose as women competed for men
with urban jobs and steady incomes. The intensity of competition was inversely
related to the financial independence of the woman and was also moderated by
social class. Elite women could not "marry up" and so were forced to search for

mates among men of their own class. Ambitious sub-elite women, in their striving for hypergamy, represented a direct threat to them. Other sub-elite women
were willing to accept the best and most ambitious of the class below them, but
this brought them into conflict with lower-class women who found that the
cream of their potential mates were being lured away from them.

In a similar argument, Burbank (1987) examined episodes of female-initiated
aggression across 137 societies in the Human Relations Area File, which collects and collates cross-cultural anthropological observations. She concluded
that women's aggression is largely directed against other women (over 90
percent of attacks) and often appears to be a means of competing for men or
subsistence products. Out of a total of 297 female–female fights in which reasons were recorded, 121 were about men and 67 about subsistence concerns,
including food, crops, essential domestic goods, money, tools, and implements.
Schuster and Burbank both argue that it is chiefly when women cannot provide
for themselves that they are forced into competition for men who have the necessary resources.

In support of this, Campbell, Muncer, and Bibel (1998) found that female
same-sex assault in the United States was closely related to female resource
shortage as indexed by rates of female unemployment and AFDC receipt.
Among the American underclass, as I have noted, well-resourced males are in
short supply. Carl Taylor's interviews with young women in Detroit shows that
they make a clear differentiation between drug users ("the living dead") and
drug dealers who are in a position to furnish abundant, albeit temporary, resources. As Taylor describes their viewpoint:

> They can see the power of the gang, the celebrity status. This is real, it can happen to
> people just like them. These women remember seeing "that girl" at school, in the shop-
> ping malls, driving a new Mercedes, BMW, Corvette, sporting Gucci, Louis Vuitton,
> Fendi and smelling of expensive perfume, going to Auburn Palace to see the Pistons,
> meeting John Salley at parties. (Taylor, 1993, p. 198)

The desirability of access to such material resources means that, even among
college girls, drug dealers are considered desirable partners worth fighting for.
As one girl explained:

> It's hard to get a good man and girls grab any fella that treat you special . . . It's just tight
> out here, the campus is fucked up 'cause we ain't got nothing but girls, girls, girls and
> the guys got their pick. We just start fighting each other over the same guys. (Taylor,
> 1993, p. 129)

Men's preference for novelty is not lost on these girls. Girls who are involved in
mixed-sex groups or gangs are acutely sensitive to incursions by strange females
who—by virtue of their novelty—have an in-built advantage over the "home

girls." Fights can occur when new girls seek to enter the group or to establish relations with males who are already spoken for. As British girls describe it:

> If you get some girls what come in the Oranges (pub), they have been in there once and they come in. They really start slagging themselves around. They ain't been in there for about two years kind of thing and they just start hanging around the boys and showing off.
>
> I cannot stand that.
>
> And that attracts the blokes more than anything. (Marsh & Paton, 1984)
>
> Well, most of the fights are in the Oranges and Lemons (pub) between the girls. Get a bird in the bog (toilets) and beat her up. You've done it. Rosie has done it. We are really possessive. If there is a bloke, we like think "Oh, he's eyeing her up" so I follow her into the toilet. (Marsh & Paton, 1984)
>
> There was a fair and there was all these girls up there and there is this girl called Della— she is supposed to be a right old scrubber and she went up to her, in front of her and that, and then she pushed her so Jackie had a fight with her. (Marsh & Paton, 1984)

A virtually identical scenario was described by a member of a New York City mixed-sex gang called the Sex Girls:

> I had a fight with this girl, her name was Sugar, right? So she was new on the block . . . She just came on the block, right, and you know how the guys are. I used to be going out with Chico? And the guys, they see a new girl? This guy—our guys when they see a new girl, they be checking her out you know. We don't like that. So she came to the block but she didn't come to make friends with us, she just came to make friends with the guys, you know? . . . So then one day, she was on the corner and Big L. was in the corner with her and she was over there, you know, real flashy and everything, like nothing happened. And I had that in my mind and then I was in the corner and Booby was in the corner and Booby's talking and we was laughing. And I see *her* laughing and I tell Booby, "I bet you I'll go over there and slap her in the face". I tell Booby and Booby tell me "Go ahead, Weeza." I went over there and I almost going to hit her and Big L get in my way. He goes "Hey, Weeza, you hit her? I'm going to hit you," and I say "Go ahead, Big L, hit me. If you're going to hit me, hit me now." And he didn't do nothing and then he took her to his house like always . . . Then she came with a sweat shirt, her hair was all grease like she was ready to fight me. So I don't know what happened. Big L said "OK, Weeza, she's ready for you." And I tell her, "Oh yeah? She's ready for me?" And I took my shoes off and I rolled my pants up and I said "Oh yeah? Come on. You ready for me?" I just hit her once. The fight only last three minutes. That's it. I just hit her and I bit her over here. . . . When I spit, I spit only blood. That's it. They got to take her to the hospital. She used to go with them all. That was finished. (Campbell, 1984, pp. 147–148)

The Turban Queens of Brooklyn told a similar story:

> They (the boys) go to where they think we ain't gonna find out. No matter how far they do it, there's always somebody so scared of us that they'll come running to tell us. We'll still find out. We'll always find out. They'll swear on their mother, their father their sister, their brother, "I didn't do it, I wouldn't do it with that bitch. I wouldn't make good with that bitch." Then they try to soup. But I already know the deal with them. "Alright,

yeah, yeah, yeah." And that's when I go. I go up to the girl. And they won't even bother hitting us 'cos they know they're gonna get worse. I would just go up, "Hey, I hear you made it with my old man." This and that. And blat, that's it. The whole thing is over 'cos they don't even raise their hands. They put their head down and they cut out fast.

Aggressive female competition of a less serious nature has been documented in a variety of cultures. In Buenos Aires, Argentina, the principal reason for female fights is over a man:

> While both men and women in Argentina are competitive, a recurring theme through-out the ethnographic interviews is that women in Buenos Aires are *very* competitive, envious and jealous of each other. For example, female competition is expressed through invidious comparisons regarding clothing and appearance. Women are very concerned with remaining thin and attractive. They place great emphasis upon dressing fashionably, often in clothes that accentuate their figures. Both female and male informants concurred that competition among women is generally over men, either a particular man, or else for the attention of men in general. Fighting among women results according to one man from "competition for a man for sexual reasons." (Hines & Fry, 1994, p. 228)

Among the Zapotec of Mexico, women attack other women more often than they attack men and these episodes are predominantly disputes over men, triggered by malicious rumors about sexual rivals (Fry, 1992). Bellonese women from the Solomon Islands live in a society of extreme male domination and have specific fighting techniques that are only used against other women:

> The attacker grabbed the other person's hair and hanked it back and forth, trying to pull her antagonist to the ground. Once the opponent was grounded the victor raked her long fingernails down the loser's face, neck or chest. Such a treatment was felt as a serious humiliation and could only be used by a woman toward another woman. (Kuschel, 1992, p. 180)

Across the world, when economic survival can only be secured through men, women will fight to gain and hold control of them.

Fighting and jealousy

But attracting a man is not the end of the story. Women also strive to maintain "ownership" of males against incursions by other females. This has been noted most forcibly by anthropologists in the resistance expressed by first wives to the introduction of prospective co-wives and the female conflict that is associated with polygamy (Collier, 1974). Burbank (1994) points out that the co-wife relationship is so implicitly filled with venom that it is reflected in the very vocabulary of aggression. In East Africa the Gusii word "engareka" means "hatred between co-wives," in Luo co-wives call each other "nyieka" which means "partner in jealousy," and in Surinam the word for fight is literally translated as "act like a co-wife." They compete for food, for money, for their own children's inheritance, and ultimately for sex as a route to all of these, as Holmberg (1969, p. 46) explains among the Siriono of Bolivia:

> Since food and sex go hand in hand in Siriono society—and there is a scarcity of the former—the wives with whom the husband most frequently has sex relations are also the wives who generally get the most to eat. Consequently co-wives frequently vie with each other for the sexual favours of their husband. This sometimes leads to bitter fights and quarrels.

Burbank's finding that 90 percent of recorded instances of female aggression worldwide are against other women is perhaps more surprising than the fact that co-wives, sexual rivals, and "the other woman" are the most frequent victims. Among co-wives, the three principal reasons for fights are jealousy, the husband's distribution of favors, and the acquisition of an additional wife. As Burbank notes:

> Where co-wives are competitors, a man's acquisition of an additional wife presents one of the most immediate threats to the women of the household and thus creates a reason and a target for female aggression. To find this reason accounting for a proportionately greater amount of the reasons for physical aggression between co-wives is therefore not surprising. (Burbank, 1987, p. 94)

She found that even in societies with sororal polygyny at least 20 percent of co-wife aggression was between sisters. Even a close genetic relationship may be insufficient to contain the explosive jealousy between women who share the same man.

Tension between women resulting from their mutual economic and social dependence on a man can be seen inter-generationally between women who are not even sexual rivals. Collier (1974) and Lamphere (1974) have shown how patrilocal extended families, where the power and authority reside with men, can give rise to intense competition between women to gain preferential access to and influence over the man. The archetypal example is the tension that exists, in all societies, between the husband's mother and her daughter-in-law. Glazer (1992) describes traditional Chinese family structure as one almost guaranteed to produce conflict between women. From about 1000 BC women lived a cloistered existence in patrilocal, patrilineal and patriarchal households with little opportunity to travel, work, or socialize beyond the home. A superfluous daughter was often sold into slavery or prostitution and, in her place, the family adopted a new girl whose labor they could exploit as a child and who later might become their son's bride. Adopted and biological daughters were natural enemies. Sisters-in-law were also at loggerheads since a wife was deprived of her husband's earnings if his younger sister needed to be married off. Wealthy husbands might also take a concubine, adding further competitors to the struggle to control the man's resources. Within these households, beatings by the mother of daughters-in-law, daughters, and adopted daughters were common: mutual dependence on the economic support a single man drove division through the whole female household.

Burbank (1994) has provided a detailed ethnography of Aboriginal women and their involvement in and attitude to fighting. She uncovered 147 episodes of female–female violence and was able to ascertain reasons for 50 of them. Again, men occupied a prominent place:

> When it comes to "men" as a reason for aggression however women's attacks on each other are much more frequent. Thirty cases of aggression between women were attributed to jealousy or conflict between unmarried women over men, a husband's real or suspected adultery or a husband's attempt to bring another wife into the household—all situations in which women are pitted against one another in competition for men's favours, if not their resources . . . what we would call "sexual jealousy" and the knowledge or suspicion that a husband is having an adulterous affair are the most common. It should also be noted that twenty one of the thirty cases of aggression between women for these reasons involve fights. . . . "Jealousy" of both married and unmarried women is clearly the cause associated with the most amount of injury. (Burbank, 1994, pp. 104–105)

In Western society too, women strive to hold on to their men. Indeed, among adolescent girls, a sense of ownership may not require the bonds of marriage, cohabitation, engagement, or even an ongoing courtship (Marsh & Paton, 1986). The most serious disputes arise in the course of steady dating relationships which girls feel they have a right to protect against blatant take-over attempts.

> This mate of mine, her boyfriend was sat talking to another girl. And my mate she was really drunk and she's the type of person—she's really possessive over her boyfriend. I mean I can put up with it to a certain extent but anybody will lash out. And she followed this girl into the toilets and I was sat in there and she threatened her with a bottle and this girl started pulling her hair and Karen was slapping her and it just amazed me. The bouncer come in and tried to split it up. (Marsh & Paton, 1984)
> Say she was leading him on, I would tell her to shut her mouth or something like that. She would either lay off or if she carries on, she gets the worst doesn't she? It just goes into an argument and then it could end up in a fight . . . Well, I was going out with this boy called Steven. This was on holiday, because I met him on holiday, and this girl I was going about with—her name was Mary—she was flirting round with him and that, and I didn't like it and one night I saw her just about to kiss him so I went up and hit her. (Marsh & Paton, 1984)

And a girl can feel a sense of proprietary rights both before a boy is aware that they have a relationship at all and long after he believes it has ended (Ness, 2004). At one extreme of this ownership "spill-over," girls believe that merely being attracted to a boy should deter any other girl from approaching him, as Duncan (1999, p. 97) found in his study of secondary school girls:

> Prospective paramours were sometimes told that they should not go out with a certain boy because another girl had claims on him. Even if the boy did not agree, the clique would maintain that he was doing one of their friends an injustice and any girl who broke the embargo would suffer accordingly.

At the opposite end of the relationship spectrum, girls may continue to fight for a romance that has officially ended.

> Me and my boyfriend finished for a while. I went to London. Then I came back and if I see him with any bird I just went mad and then seeing him with her as well . . . I walked up to her and I says "You fucking leave him alone or else you've had it." I really went mad at her. (Marsh & Paton, 1984)
> This girl (Suzie) has been going out with his boy for a year and she packed him up and her friend (Linda) goes out with him so Suzie keeps calling the girl a slut all the time but the girl won't say nothing.
> Well. It's only because Linda can't have her (beat her up) though, isn't it?
> Because she knows that she would probably get beaten up. (Marsh & Paton, 1984)

It is perplexing that young women direct their attacks to their own sex rather than to the errant boyfriend or husband who would appear to be just as guilty as the "other woman." Burbank suggests that women may be fearful of a man's retaliation, or believe that a man's love cannot be physically compelled. Among gang girls, the reason for their choice of target was quite clear. Men, they reason, cannot be expected to turn down an offer of sex from a woman. It is in a man's nature to take sex wherever he can find it and indeed failure to take advantage of an unsolicited offer would cast serious doubt on his manhood (Campbell, 1984). Men, in this regard and despite their macho posturing, are viewed as weak. It is women who are the controlling players in mate retention because of men's priapic lack of discrimination when it comes to one-night stands. Women know all too well what men want. And when other women take advantage of men's weakness, they know too how to protect their own interests.

Our understanding of mate selection has come a long way since Darwin first proposed that males are eager and females coy. It is true that where females undertake virtually all of the parental care and constitute a limiting reproductive resource, men should be eager and women should be, if not coy, at least highly selective in their choice of mate. But when men and women not only cooperate in rearing offspring but face an extended future together because of the long period of infant dependency, the dynamics change. Men also become choosy because commitment to a single woman is a choice of quality over quantity. And, where committed and well-resourced men are in short supply, this can engender competition between women. Rivalry can escalate from appearance enhancement, to indirect attacks and, in extreme circumstances, to outright violence. Even when circumstances militate against acquiring a permanently faithful and committed "good man," it is a dream that never goes away. Girls in street gangs, when asked to describe their perfect future, come back to the traditional desire for a man who will provide resources, security, and unconditional love. Short-term partners are a default option, not an ambition. Even girls who will freely admit to theft, robbery, and assault, bridle at the suggestion of cheapness or prostitution (Campbell, 1984). Shakespeare as usual put it best:

> Who steals my purse steals trash; 'tis something, nothing;
> 'Twas mine, 'tis his, and has been slave to thousands;
> But he that filches from me my good name
> Robs me of that which not enriches him,
> And makes me poor indeed.
>   (Othello, Act III, Scene III)

Chapter 7

A coincidence of interests: Women and monogamy

We see marriage and long-term cohabitation as a partnership, a pooling of our resources, a striving for mutual happiness. Two become one. From an evolutionary and genetic perspective, this is a rather rose-tinted view. The reproductive goals and strategies of men and women are different. Marriage is the triumph of compromise over individual satisfaction. In this chapter, I want to take an evolutionary view of the obstacles that stand in the way of sustaining successful long-term partnerships and, more optimistically, to consider some of the mechanisms that make it possible. As with other aspects of evolutionary biology, the focus to date has been very much on men—their goals, their strategies, and their successes. Despite Darwin's emphasis on female choice, women have been sidelined in the consideration of the benefits and costs of monogamy. But it takes two to reproduce and here I want to look at long-term bonds from women's perspective.

Genetic conflict

In high school biology, we all learned about arms races between species. Slower prey are caught by faster predators, leading to natural selection for faster running speed in the prey species. This in turn means that the predator comes under selection for even greater speed to ensure she gets enough meals. Stealthy predators select for greater visual and auditory acuity in their prey, which means that the predator must become less detectable by developing better camouflage or a more silent approach. Sharper teeth in the predator can select for thicker skin in the prey, and so on.

And so it is with males and females. The optimal reproductive strategies of the two sexes are different and each tries to work the mating system to their own advantage. Males benefit from frequent copulations with multiple partners. For females, multiple matings have costs: of course females need to reproduce but one fertilization is all that is technically required in a single cycle. Extra copulations are risky in terms of exposure to predators during mating, aggression from males, sexually transmitted diseases, and the toxins that semen deposits into their bloodstream. (More on that later.)

Sometimes this arms race is relatively benign and males seek to charm females into mating with them. Consider poeciliid fish which come in two varieties. One called *Xiphophorus* have long swords, while *Priapella* do not. The longer the sword, the more attractive the male is to *Xiphophorus* females. It operates as a persuasive seduction device; it encourages females to mate more than they would usually do. Indeed it is so effective that *Priapella* females also find it attractive when experimenters attach artificial swords to the normally swordless males of their own species. But if excessive mating (while good for the male) is bad for the female then we would expect that over time females would develop a resistance to its attractiveness. Sure enough, the *Xiphophorus* females have begun to resist its charms, evidenced in the fact that they are attracted significantly less to the sword than their sister *Priapella* who have not had the opportunity to develop an adaptive resistance. It may be that frivolous seductive ornaments have a limited evolutionary shelf life. Gimmicky male tricks will not work forever. Like fashion, what seemed stylish today looks ridiculous tomorrow.

Sometimes, however, the contest turns nastier. It steps up from seduction to coercion. In the mating season, male robber flies fly about searching for females. A female makes a rapid U-turn when she sees a male approaching. She is wary and rightly so. If the male catches her, he grapples with her aggressively to prevent her escape. But in some species, females have evolved a counter-strategy. When grasped by the male, they become completely inert. Playing dead seems to be effective: the male no longer views her as a possible sexual partner so he releases her. She falls to the ground and lives to mate another day. The female dung fly faces an equally unhappy courtship experience. She is often the object of prolonged struggles between her male mate and other ardent suitors who launch mid-copulation takeover bids (Parker, 1970b). In the general melee the female can be severely injured, sometimes drowning in the pile of liquid dung on which she has chosen to lay her eggs. Females have co-evolved a preference for mating with larger males who are best able to minimize these lethal fights in which the hapless female is just collateral damage.

These Red Queen arms races between male and female happen at a genetic as well as a behavioral level. Groundbreaking studies by William Rice (1992, 1996) show just how dangerous it can be for females to pause for breath in the co-evolutionary race. His work is on interlocus genetic conflict which occurs when the optimal outcome of a male–female interaction is different for the two sexes. This has been examined in conflicts over mating frequency, fertilization, relative parental effort, female re-mating, and female reproductive rate

(Arnqvist & Rowe, 2005; Chapman, Arnqvist, Bangham, & Rowe, 2003). Rice was able to show the evolutionary process happening in real time by working with houseflies whose generation length is short enough for us to observe the effects of selection over several generations. The male's seminal fluid is mildly toxic to females but because females co-evolve with males, they develop tricks to counter its effects. But what would happen if females were removed from the Red Queen contest and males could pursue their own interests unhindered? Rice (1992, 1996) decided to find out. He separated an initial population of house flies into males and females. The female flies were housed with a new set of males and evolution was allowed to proceed normally over the generations. The males had a different experience. At each generation, they were given a fresh batch of females to mate with. This meant that males were free to evolve male-benefitting tactics to their heart's content because the females were denied the possibility of co-evolving opposing strategies. After three dozen or so generations, the males had the uncontested upper hand. When the descendants of the initial population of females were returned to them, the females began to die from the effects of sex. The males' sperm, unopposed by female counter-adaptation, had become more and more toxic. To make matters worse, these males had evolved the ability to make females re-mate with them (against the females' own interests) and even to deny subsequent matings to safer male competitors who might have displaced the lethal sperm. Females need to hold their own in the battle of the sexes just to stay alive.

Once our species switched to a genetic method of sex determination (instead of relying, for example, on the temperature surrounding the egg as some reptiles do), it opened the door for sexually antagonist genes. A genetic battle between the sexes could now begin. Genetic conflict between the sexes takes place on the sex chromosomes (X and Y) or on sex-limited genes (genes which are present in both sexes but expressed only in one sex). Recall that the sex chromosomes are the only pair that do not exchange genetic material during meiosis (except for a tiny pseudoautosomal region). Recall also that the Y chromosome carries the master sex-determining gene and genes on the Y chromosome are present only in males which make them a perfect spot for male-benefitting genes to accumulate. During male meiosis when sperm are created, X- and Y-linked genes co-segregate. This means that different genes on the same sex chromosome can work together to code for complex phenotypes (rather than relying on pleiotropy of a single gene). Because Y chromosomes only ever inhabit male bodies, they can carry traits that are good for males—no matter how bad they are for females. As long as it was located on the Y chromosome, a hypothetical gene for killing females would only ever result in male-on-female homicide.

What about the X chromosome? Recent studies suggest that the majority of sexually antagonistic variation in the genome is located on the X chromosome. But here the conflict is an intralocus (rather than an interlocus) one: the X is carried in the cells and gametes of both sexes and so can carry genes favoring males as well as females. Sometimes an X-linked gene can give an advantage to males. To see why we have to compare the situation with a gene carried on a normal autosome. Imagine a newly-arisen autosomal gene that is quite good for males (+1) and very bad for females (−3). This gene will not increase in the population because, given an equal number of males and females, its net effect is negative (−2). But if that mutant gene is on the X chromosome and recessive, it can increase in frequency even though it is very bad for the female half of the population. This is because it will rarely be expressed phenotypically in females because they have two X chromosomes and the mutation will be masked by the healthy X partner. But all males who carry it will express the new beneficial gene. So this gene can spread rapidly in a population—even when the cost to females is 50 times greater than the benefit to males (Rice, 1984). Now imagine that another X-linked mutant gene appears that is dominant and this time it benefits females. This gene would be expressed equally in the two sexes, but because an X spends twice its time in female rather than male bodies, the effect of selection would be stronger on females. This means that such a dominant X-linked gene would be selected twice as often when it benefits females rather than males.

It seems that the evolution of sexually antagonistic alleles was responsible for the loss of recombination (the exchange of genetic material) between X and Y chromosomes during meiosis. It was this segregation that allowed Y genes to begin their exploitation of the opposite sex. But once that had happened, males had to pay a price. The Y chromosome began to shrink. X chromosomes continued to line up in pairs to exchange genetic information, and they were also able to repair mutation errors. An error on one X could be detected and corrected by reference to its partner. But the Y chromosome had no partner for proof reading and mutations accumulated over time: a phenomenon known as Muller's ratchet. In addition, Y is passed to sons via sperm which undergo multiple cell divisions during their production. Each mitosis event is a chance for more copying errors to creep in. To make matters worse, sperm are stored in a highly oxidative environment—the testes. Y degeneration can also be the result of genetic "hitchhiking." Because the Y chromosome is passed on to sons all of a piece, individual alleles are not exposed to the forces of selection. This means that deleterious genes can be passed on as long as they are associated with other beneficial genes. As a consequence of all this, the Y chromosome mutation rate is nearly five times higher than the rest of the genome. The Human Genome Project revealed that the Y chromosome now carries only 86 genes compared to about 2,000 on the X chromosome. These facts led some commentators to suggest that the Y chromosome will eventually die out. And if males disappear, females will not be long behind them. But it seems that things are not so bleak. Some parts of the Y chromosome have found a way to avoid the problem of non-recombination with the X. The genes are written in palindrome sequences and a faulty gene sequence can correct itself by examining its adjacent mirror image (Rozen et al., 2003).

And happily, the Y chromosome may be small but it is fast. Comparing humans with chimpanzees, from whom we diverged about five million years ago, researchers have concluded that it is the most rapidly evolving part of the genome (Hughes et al., 2010). Ironically this may be the beneficial side of the genetic hitchhiking coin: when one Y-linked trait is favored by selection, the whole chromosome is selected, allowing very quick overall change in response to new and adaptive mutations. But perhaps the most compelling reason for its speedy evolution is this: the Y chromosome is responsible for sperm production and under polygyny a female may have sperm from multiple males in her reproductive tract. This gives rise to sperm competition and only the genetic information from the sperm with the most successful Y chromosome will be passed on to her sons. This is a very strong selection pressure and strong selection creates fast evolution.

The Y chromosome carries an all-important gene: the *SRY* gene (which stands for sex-determining region of Y). It codes for a protein called the testes determining factor, which begins the process of male anatomical differentiation. *SRY* is one of the fastest evolving genes. Comparing humans to other primates, there is 10 times more variation on this gene than on other genes. Vacquier, Swanson, and Hellberg (1995) have tried to understand why this should be by studying the abalone, a marine snail in which the female lays her eggs in water to be subsequently fertilized by a male. The male's sperm carries a protein called lysin which is released from the front of the sperm when it encounters an egg. Lysin's job is to bore a hole though the matrix that surrounds the egg so that the sperm can enter, fuse, and fertilize. Lysin is an asset to males. But it is a problem for females—it creates a channel that permits too many sperm to enter and it is also an open door for pathogens. These are twin threats to zygote survival. The very rapid evolution of lysin seems to be a function of an escalating arms race between what males want and what females want. Lysin causes faster sperm entry and the female counters by changing the egg matrix which slows the sperm down. The male then evolves a new faster form of sperm entry that the female resists by changing the glycoprotein matrix to protect her egg from multiple fertilization. The arms race drives evolution at a faster and faster pace as the male and female attempt to out-maneuver one another. These conflicts move even faster in animals with internal fertilization resulting in a very rapid evolution of the male and female reproductive tracts and genitalia (Eberhard, 1996).

Males are unmoved by the injury they might inflict on females and, after they have gifted her with their semen, many of their strategies are aimed at deterring a female from mating with another male. Male bed bugs copulate using "traumatic insemination" in which the male repeatedly injects his semen directly into the female's body cavity by piercing her abdominal wall with his genitalia. Females seem unable to effectively resist even though it reduces their lifespan (Hosken & Stockley, 2004). In domestic cats, the male's barbed penis causes pain and tears the female vagina when he withdraws: the barbs may deter her from re-mating, remove the semen of his rivals, and stimulate ovulation. The males of one species of South American butterfly introduce an anti-aphrodisiac into the female which repels other males for weeks at a time (Gilbert, 1976). And if you ever believed that sperm was a benign gift to females, Rice's work certainly makes you think twice. The male housefly's seminal fluid proteins not only enter the reproductive tract but they enter the female's bloodstream and bind to receptors in the brain altering her behavior. They trigger a series of responses that are clearly beneficial to males; they decrease her sexual appetite (making her less likely to re-mate with a rival), they increase her ovulation rate, and they control sperm competition with alien sperm in her reproductive tract. As we have noted, they also slowly poison her so that the more she copulates, the sooner she dies. What is happening is literally a conflict of life and death. From the female's perspective, her best bet is to mate wisely (select a mate with motile sperm and good genes) but not too frequently. The male, however, benefits from ensuring she does not re-mate but invests heavily in his current zygote. If a second male that now appears on the scene, he will have his own agenda. He aims to entice the female to mate again (she must trade off the quality of the new male's genes against the toxicity of a double sperm dosage) and to displace or immobilize the previous male's sperm. This tri-partite conflict of interest generates gene warfare between all the parties.

Genomic imprinting

The battle between the sexes is also played out in the offspring that they jointly create and it can happen on any of the chromosomes, not just the X and Y. At bottom, the conflict stems from males' ancient wanderlust and deep attachment to promiscuity. Because a man comes and goes (so to speak), there is a good chance that the embryo created in a single act of intercourse may be the only one that he ever shares with this particular woman. This means that her long-term reproductive health is of only minor interest to him. Provided that she carries, bears, and raises his child, why should the father care if she endures a difficult pregnancy or never conceives again? Polygyny is a heartless strategy from a female's point of view. So when females undertake virtually all of the paternal investment, they must have an eye to the future—a woman must consider all the future children that she will bear. Each one will be unambiguously a bearer of her genes despite uncertainty about who the father might be. She must look out for her long-term reproductive interests for it is very clear that her current mate will not. The male's genes exploit the female's body in the interests of his offspring, the female's genes counter them in any way that they can.

This principle has been demonstrated by the creation of individuals (mice, in fact) who have a single parent, either male or female. How can this be done? Both sperm and egg carry their genes in their nucleus. When a sperm first penetrates an egg, the two pronuclei are briefly separate before they fuse together. This moment is the brief opportunity for human intervention. If the sperm nucleus is removed and replaced with a second egg nucleus, a zygote with no father is created. Similarly, the removal of the egg nucleus and the replacement with a second sperm nucleus results in a motherless zygote. But the effect on development is very different in each case. A zygote composed of maternal genes looks fairly normal but the placenta and yolk sac are grossly undersized. Father-only genes create a healthy placenta but instead of an embryo there is a disorganized aggregation of cells. Male genes build the placenta while female genes build the embryo's body and especially its head. It was David Haig (Haig & Westoby, 1989) who suggested the reason: the placenta favors the fetus even at the expense of the mother—it parasitizes the mother's body. Of course, the mother has her own reasons for accommodating the infant with a blood supply but she must also watch out for herself and her own survival. After this pregnancy, there will be others. She favors a placenta large enough to support the current fetus, but not so large as to place excess demands on her body. Faced with this lack of female cooperation, the father ensures his own genetic interests over those of the mother by constructing the placenta himself. (It has also been suggested that the growth of the placenta may serve to sequester and deny resources to any unrelated siblings rather than to enhance fetal growth, Hurst & McVean, 1997). As Ridley (1999, p. 209) succinctly describes it, " . . . the father's genes do not trust the mother to make a sufficiently invasive placentas; so they do the job themselves." The male is less concerned with the long-term welfare of the mother than with exploiting her as an accommodating vehicle for his offspring. (Oddly the fetus should be more concerned about the mother than the father is. This child will be 50 percent related to any further children she produces and therefore his inclusive fitness is related to hers.)

The mechanism behind these exploitative genes is a phenomenon called genomic imprinting. Until recently it was believed that genes from the mother and father had equal chances of being expressed in the offspring. Every generation, genes are shuffled in the process of meiosis and crossing over so that the 23 chromosomes that a woman or a man contributes to the total of 46 needed to build a baby are a random set taken equally from each partner. But we know now that some genes are "tagged" with the sex of the parent who donated them and that tag determines whether or not they expressed. The "imprinted" gene is silenced while its opposite number is switched on and this imprinting can occur on both the mother's and the father's genes. Many of the phenotypic effects we see occur via the impact of imprinting on other genes that regulate cell behavior. It is paternally-active genes that build big placentas and maternally-active genes that build the body and brain. The conflict between what suits men and what suits women must reach far back in our history and must have been a sufficiently powerful dynamic to drive genomic imprinting—the tug-of-war between maternal genes devoted to embryonic growth and paternal genes devoted to uterus exploitation.

In an optimistic frame of mind, we might be tempted to think that the genes are not in conflict at all but rather are cooperating in the production of a viable placenta and a viable embryo. But if this were so, then why not have both parents contribute equally and at half dosage to both? What we see is the end point of a Red Queen struggle in which reproductively successful men have shown a casual genetic disregard for the mother's long-term survival and women have developed counter-ploys of their own.

One such counter-ploy is genomic imprinting of a protein called insulin-like growth factor (IGF2). IGF2 is a protein essential to fetal growth. It promotes the transition of metabolites across the placenta and so is vital to acquiring resources from the mother. The paternal *IGF2* gene is expressed while the mother's version is silenced. But the mother has not allowed this potential exploitation to go unchallenged. IGF2R is a receptor whose purpose seems to be to mop up IGF2 protein and so turn down the delivery of resources across the placenta. The maternal gene coding for this receptor is expressed. And the necessity of this female counter-ploy is evident in individuals who lack the maternal receptor gene—they are 16 percent larger than normal (Haig & Graham, 1991). In cases where an individual inherits two copies of the paternal *IGF2* gene, they develop enlarged hearts and livers and are prone to embryonic tumors. Like two wrestlers straining against one another, the opposing maternal and paternal effects keep everything upright. When one lets go, the imbalance is disastrous.

But mothers and fathers also have conflicts about which parts of the embryo are most important. To study this, Keverne and his colleagues (Keverne,

Fundele, Narasimha, Braton, & Surani, 1996; Keverne, Martel, & Nevison, 1996) created chimeric mice. To do this, they took advantage of the technique of egg and sperm pronuclei replacement that we have already described. But such manipulations are not viable—they rarely survive the 11th day of gestation. To build a chimerical baby that could actually survive, they fused a normal embryo with an embryo made from two egg pronuclei. The result was a mouse with a very large head. But when they fused the normal embryo with one derived from an embryo made from two sperm pronuclei, they grew a mouse with a big body and small head. Indeed the body of the paternal chimeras grew so large that they had to be delivered by Caesarean section. So fathers contribute more to bodies and muscle while mothers specialize in brains.

But not just brains—particular parts of them. By biochemically marking the maternal and paternal cells, the researchers were able to see where they ended up (Keverne, Martel, & Nevison, 1996). The input of the paternal cells to brain construction was to the hypothalamus, amygdala, and preoptic area—the areas that control emotion and evolutionarily-critical "automatic" behaviors such as sex, reproductive behavior, aggression, and fear. The mother's cells migrated and proliferated in the cortex, striatum, and hippocampus—areas implicated in reasoning, memory, and behavioral inhibition. (If you are now blaming your father for inheriting his emotional tempo remember that half the hypothalamus-building genes that he bequeathed to you came from his mother. They may not have been expressed in him but they were inherited from his mother, re-tagged in him as paternal instead of maternal, and then passed on to you.) Why should females be so committed to constructing the cortex? What is in it for them? We don't yet know but there are several fascinating suggestions.

Badcock (1994) took the most daring and speculative viewpoint to date when he suggested that the conflict between the male-constructed limbic system and the female-constructed cortex parallels the psychoanalytic tension between the id and the ego. The paternally-built id makes egocentric, infantile, and constant demands upon the mother, while the maternally controlled cortex represses them. In this view, the cortex is essential for children's growing autonomy and hence the mother's ability to reinvest in new offspring. Badcock saw the genomically imprinted two-part brain as biological support for Freud's psychoanalytic model. (Since then, however, he has become far more skeptical of Freudian theory, Badcock, 2009.)

According to Haig's theory, one of the chief functions of the hypothalamus is growth promotion and so it makes sense that, just as the father's genes try to maximize fetal resources, they also try to maximize growth beyond the womb. Lactation requires a high calorie intake and, faced with a hungrier infant, the pressure on the mother to find and consume resources is even greater. Why should the father care about this extra female effort? He will be long gone by then and his farewell gift is a fast-growing, highly demanding infant that will push the mother's foraging ability to its limit.

Another way of looking at this is as a special case of Red Queen contest. Rice has shown that one result of interlocus conflict is very fast evolutionary pace. The enemy of male adaptation is always snapping at a woman's heels and she must run fast to outpace him. The frontal cortex, with its ability to promote planning and foresight, is in a unique position to over-ride the emotional tyranny of the limbic system. As males' built bigger limbic systems, females fought back by building an ever-larger cortex and the result is the massive expansion of the human brain (Keverne, Martel, & Nevison, 1996) that seems to be constrained only by the sheer impossibility of getting an infant with a bigger brain through the female pelvis. If the male–female contest gave us bigger brains, it was the female contribution that steadily increased our powers of reason and rationality. And over evolutionary time, the cortex has expanded in size much more than the lower brain suggesting that women have been winning this particular race.

From my viewpoint, it is hard to resist the speculation that females have always had more to gain than males by emotional and behavioral inhibition and this is controlled by the frontal cortex (see Chapter 3). An impulsive approach to aggression and sex may be advantageous to males in their short-term, all-out competition to vanquish other males and inseminate females, but the benefits to females are less evident. Males try to build offspring with plenty of derring-do motivation (and let the females take the consequences) while females counter by trying to slow the offspring down with longer-term reasoning (and extend their life expectancy). Fathers, it seems, wanted a little more "gut feeling" in their children while females opted for more planning and restraint.

The battle of the sexes occurring at this genetic level derives from the tension between the different strategies that are optimal for males and females. The genetic arms race suggests that men want the drama of fast-track sex without personal consequences and that women take a longer view incorporating protracted parental commitment. We now turn to a crucial question that evolutionary psychology frequently glosses over: If polygyny is so adaptive for men, why are the vast majority of them monogamously married? To put it in a way more congenial to my focus on women: Why do women want men around?

Strategic conflict

Evolutionary theory tells us that a gene supporting a behavioral strategy which increases an individual's survival and reproductive success will tend to be selected. Men should have been selected to pursue a monogamous strategy if it increases their reproductive success above what they could achieve by pursuing polygyny. A man has a strategic "choice": he can make a lifelong commitment to just one woman, or spend his life inseminating and abandoning a series of them. If the help he gives to his monogamous partner guarantees the survival of the four children they jointly produce, whereas his lack of assistance to the eight women he causally inseminates means that five of the eight children die, then monogamy is a superior male strategy. Early explanations of monogamy rested heavily on this premise. Because the extended period of infant dependency and the short inter-birth interval in humans took a heavy toll on women, men could increase their reproductive success by offering assistance (Lancaster & Lancaster, 1983).

But there is increasing evidence of a hugely important and under-appreciated fact: the presence of a father does very little to increase the probability of offspring survival. Sear and Mace (2008) reviewed studies of child survival in natural fertility populations. In the 15 studies that included appropriate controls for possible confounding factors, 53 percent show no association between the death of a father and the death of his child. This rises to 68 percent if all available studies are included. Differences between societies in their degree of paternal involvement do not appear to explain this effect. Among the Ache, where fathers are little involved with their children, the death of a father has a negative effect on child survival while among the Hiwi, where fathers are much more closely involved in child rearing, there is no effect of a father's death. It may be that the chief threats to children are disease and famine and that the presence of a father can do nothing to prevent these tragedies. Fathers do indeed reduce their parental effort as local pathogen stress increases (Quinlan, 2007) suggesting that effort expended here is not effective in preventing infection and death in their children. But this fact only makes the question of why fathers stay even more opaque.

Another way to approach the value of paternal investment is to examine whether it improves not the survival but the reproductive success of their children. This was tested among the Tsimane of Bolivia who show high levels of paternal provisioning and low divorce rates (Winking, Gurven, & Kaplan, 2011). The early death of a father had no impact on their children's age of first reproduction, completed fertility, or number of surviving offspring. Overall, a father's death had virtually no impact on their children's reproductive success.

I want to approach the enigma of men's willingness to abandon the advantages of polygyny by focusing on women. After all, a truism of reproductive strategies is that females are a limiting resource and this gives them considerable power in the marketplace. Their behavior dictates the possible strategies that males can adopt. In other primates, the spatial distribution of females modulates male strategies. A single-male polygynous strategy can work when females congregate together so that they (and the food resources they need) can be easily monopolized by a single male. If it takes more than one male to manage this, then multimale–multifemale groups emerge. If females are widely dispersed over a territory so that they cannot be controlled by a single male, a monogamous mating system can develop. The important point is that, because males need access to females, females gain a considerable amount of leverage over male reproductive strategies. If women wanted men to be monogamous, what were their reasons? We know that it cannot be because a male presence increased her children's chances of survival—the evidence we have just reviewed shows that this is far from always true. What other advantages could a man offer?

The bodyguard hypothesis

One possibility is that women want a committed man to protect them from the aggression of other men. Males can be brutal when sex is at stake and the price that copulation exacts on the female is not in the forefront of their mind. (Remember the toxic semen of the humble housefly and the traumatic insemination of the lowly bed bug.) An extreme example of the sheer brutality of sex is provided by the Northern elephant seal because there is such a huge difference in the size and weight of males and females. Males are typically four times bigger but can be up to 11 times larger. When a male lets his body weight fall on her during intromission, she can be crushed—to say nothing of his less-than-affectionate biting during copulation. But if injury from a partner is a hazard, things get worse when a female attempts to leave the colony and return to the sea. She must run the gauntlet of dozens of sub-dominant males who attempt to intercept and mate with her. During the 30 minutes it takes her to get to the safety of the water, she receives on average 20 times more blows, mounts, and copulations than when she was in the harem (Mesnick, 1997). Among primates too, females receive more threats, attacks, and wounds when they are in estrous than at any other time. During estrous, rhesus macaque females who approach low-ranking males are punished by the dominant males resulting in between three and six attacks every day. In chimpanzees, males try to persuade females to join them in consortships—mating trips away from the main body of the group that can last for hours or days. Sometimes the female is willing but, if she is not, the male performs aggressive displays to intimidate her and if that fails, he simply attacks her. What can a female do to protect herself?

Where the aggression is sexual, one avenue is to simply give way in order to protect her own life—a depressing capitulation called "convenience polyandry." Chimpanzee females do it. So do the poor elephant seals as they desperately try to reach the freedom of the sea (Mesnick, 1997). Eighty-eight percent are mounted by at least one male and 60 percent of the females lay quietly, even speeding up the unwanted copulation by spreading their hindflippers. Those who do this decrease the number of blows they receive by eight percent. And it seems their strategy has another pay-off. After the copulation, 78 percent of the male rapists escort the female to the sea and aggressively drive away other males (doubtless to protect their own seminal investment rather than out of any gallantry). On the face of it, protection from male aggression appears a reasonable candidate for explaining a female preference for monogamy. However, a systematic study of 26 primate species failed to find evidence supporting the protection proposal (Fuentes, 2002).

But do males in our own species engage in such brutal sexual attacks sufficiently often for females to seek a mate for protection? In contemporary Western samples, rape may be experienced by as many as 13 percent of women. The costs of rape are substantial: not only the trauma and pain of the attack itself, but also the deprivation of a woman's reproductive choice which in evolutionary terms constitutes a severe fitness cost. Wilson and Mesnick (1997) argued that the ubiquity and cost of rape to women resulted in their need for a long-term male protector. There is evidence that partnered women are significantly less likely to have experienced sexual aggression during the last year than are women who are single, separated, divorced, or widowed (Wilson & Mesnick, 1997). However, it may be the lifestyle of married women, rather than their resident bodyguard, that offers protection from rape. In a study of rape avoidance strategies, McKibbin et al. (2009) reported four tactics of rape avoidance used by women: avoid strange men (e.g., men who appear drunk or overly-familiar), avoid appearing sexually receptive (e.g., provocative clothing or sexual contact with recently-met men), avoid being alone (e.g., go out in a crowd), and be defensively prepared (e.g., be aware of surroundings, carry a weapon). Perhaps partnered women are less likely to find themselves in clubs and streets after dark where such strategies would be necessary. In short, they may be less situationally vulnerable to rape with or without the physical presence of a husband. The bodyguard hypothesis predicts that unattached women that should be most fearful of rape and most likely to take measures to avoid it. Yet married women reported more frequent use of rape avoidance behaviors than single women. Interestingly, the authors interpret married women's greater use of precautionary tactics as showing that mated women bear additional costs of rape because, after a sexual attack, their partners may suspect that the sex was consensual and abandon them. This is also supported by Thornhill and Thornhill's (1990) finding that, among married women, the use of physical force during a rape decreased their subsequent psychological pain—presumably because evidence of physical injury decreased their partner's suspicion that the act had been consensual. Neither of these two findings supports the value of husband-as-body guard. Indeed they suggest that male partners simply add an additional psychological burden (threat of blame and abandonment) on top of the rape trauma itself.

But perhaps the major difficulty for the bodyguard hypothesis is the fact that stranger rape is less common than date rape, or rape by a current or ex-spouse (Greenfeld, 1997). Seventy-seven percent of completed rapes are by non-strangers and recent reviews suggest that between 10 and 26 percent of women experience rape by a husband or intimate partner (Kaighobadi, Shackelford, & Goetz, 2009; Martin, Taft, & Resick, 2007). How can we unite the twin facts of a man's anger when a stranger rapes his wife with some men's willingness to use rape as a marital weapon? Men's feelings of sexual ownership about their wives may be an artifact of men's monogamous strategy, rather than a reason why women opted for it. Once attached exclusively to a woman, fear of cuckoldry made men particularly sensitive to her rape. This would result both in the additional costs to married women of stranger rape and husbands' use of rape within marriage—especially when a husband suspects infidelity (Buss & Duntley, 2011). Marital rape may be a form of punishment, a reassertion of ownership, and an unconscious means of displacing alien sperm.

Such an argument was made by Barbara Smuts (1992) who suggested that a key shift in human evolution was the need for increased male alliances and it was this that paved the way for monogamy and male control over women. Male alliances were essential for intergroup warfare and hunting. Such alliances were enhanced by practices that reduced intra-group male competition and made men's relationships more egalitarian. One such practice was monogamy—an exclusive relationship between a man and a woman. As Smuts (1992, p. 11) explains it: " . . . human pair bonds, and therefore human marriage, can be considered a means by which cooperating males agree about mating rights, respect (at least in principle) one another's 'possession' of particular females, protect their mates and their mate's children from aggression by other men, and gain rights to coerce their own females with reduced interference by other men." Women's victimization by an intimate partner seems a very high price to pay for a live-in bodyguard. But perhaps women sought protection not for themselves but for their offspring?

The infanticide hypothesis

Among primate species, infanticide by immigrant males is a real and lethal threat accounting for more than a third of infant deaths (Smuts, 1992). When new males take over a group, infanticide not only dispatches the genes of the deposed leaders but brings the female back into estrous, ready to be inseminated by the new arrivals. In baboons, it has been suggested that what monogamy offers females is male protection against infanticide. Van Schaik and Dunbar (1990) dismissed the commonly held belief that monogamy was a masculine default option—the result of a male's inability to monopolize sexual access to more than one female. They argued that the advantages of monogamy must lie in the fact that monogamous males could produce surviving children at a rate which exceeded the number of females whose insemination they had to forego. Close scrutiny of the baboons' behavior showed that the appeal of monogamy did not lie in the reduced risk of predation conferred by male bodyguards, or in the males' ability to defend a foraging area for the female. What made monogamy successful was the dramatic decrease in infanticide among monogamously fathered infants. If a male is to risk his life to defend an infant against such a vicious attack, it pays him to make very sure that it his own—hence the co-occurrence of monogamy and male protection of infants. Fuentes (2002) tested a series of hypotheses that flow from the idea that primate pair bonds evolved in response to the threat of infanticide. Most strikingly, he reported that in only two of the 26 primate species studied was infanticide ever observed. He hypothesized that the females in pair-bonded species, reliant on their male partner's assistance, would be unable to defend their young from male attack by themselves. He found no evidence for this. He hypothesized that the high value of the pair bond to females meant that they would be chiefly responsible for maintaining it. Again, he found no evidence. He hypothesized that both sexes would show extreme wariness of extra-group males (but not females) and there would be a male-skewed sex ratio (creating an excess of dangerous unmated males). Again, the data showed no such effects. His conclusion—that pair bonding could not be adequately explained by infanticide prevention—reinforced those of others (e.g., Palombit, 1999; Sussman, 1999).

But a quite different spin has been put on the relationship between infanticide and mating patterns in primates by Sarah Hrdy (1979). Not only was she the first primatologist to document the use of infanticide by strange males but she also noticed that langur males never attacked an infant born to a female with whom they had mated. They seemed to err on the conservative side of paternity certainty showing reluctance to risk killing their own possible children. She reasoned that, this being so, a useful female strategy would be to copulate with as many males as possible in the hope that each one would have reason to believe any subsequent child was his own. Perhaps that is why females show a preference for sub-adult males on their way to the top and for strange males who are not yet part of the group. In a promiscuous mating system, Hrdy argues, males should avoid infanticide because of the uncertainty that surrounds paternity. Although there has been considerable support for this view in promiscuous species (Pradham & van Schaik, 2008; van Schaik, Pradhan, & van Noordwijk, 2004), it does not easily sit with the predominantly monogamous mating patterns of humans.

Could it be that the threat of infanticide promoted monogamy in our own species? One strong argument against it is patrilocal residence. Male killing of infants would include the killing of kin which does not amount to an adaptive strategy. Quinlan and Quinlan (2007) reasoned that, under the infanticide hypothesis, pair bonds would be most stable in those societies where levels of male aggression are high. In fact they found the reverse: divorce was most common in societies where men were more aggressive. And if women chose husbands to be their children's bodyguards, there is little evidence that they were good at: as we have seen, the presence of a father makes precious little difference to the survival of his children.

The direct care hypothesis

Raising a helpless infant is tiring. Raising several children at the same time is exhausting. Perhaps women wanted a man around to help with the feeding, holding, soothing, and monitoring. It seems eminently reasonable yet there is little evidence that fathers and mothers share childcare equitably, even in today's liberal societies. Cross cultural observational studies show that mothers spend a disproportionate amount of time with their children. During the first three years of life, fathers in Liberia, Kenya, India, Guatemala, and Peru are rarely or never engaged in infant care (Whiting & Edwards, 1988). Between the ages of three and six, children are in the presence of their mothers between three and 12 times more often than their father in societies as disparate as Kenya, Mexico, India, Japan, the Philippines, and the United States (Whiting & Whiting, 1975). By the age of between four and 10 years of age, children were between two and four times more often with their mother than their father in Africa, South Asia, and in South, Central, and North America (Whiting & Edwards, 1988). Perhaps, fathers are simply less available than mothers because they are occupied elsewhere. This may be a partial explanation (as we shall see) but even in contemporary Western societies during periods when both parents are present in the home, routine care is given between two and four times more often by the mother, and mothers engage in spontaneous interaction with their children about twice as often as fathers (Beitel & Parke, 1998; Cooke, 2004, 2007; Lamb, Frodi, Hwang, & Frodi, 1982a).

But what about smaller-scale societies similar to those in which humans evolved? Studies of the Ache, Kung San, Hadza, Efe, and Aka all concur that mothers spend far more time with children than fathers (Konner, 2010).

Among the Kung San, fathers provide less than 7 percent of infant care and even among the Aka, who are notable for fathers' high level of involvement with their children, fathers hold their infants for 70 minutes compared with the mother's 490 in a typical day (Hewlett, 1988). In a study of the Tsimane of Bolivia, mothers provide nearly 83 percent of care during daylight hours during the first six months (Winking, Gurven, Kaplan, & Stieglitz, 2009). They provide 69 percent of care during the first six years, compared to the father's 7 percent. But when fathers help, it is clearly directed at relieving the load on the mother because paternal help is most likely when the mother is absent or occupied with other tasks. They are also more likely to take over parental supervision with older rather than younger children. Fathers help out, but perhaps the main source of that help is indirect rather than direct.

The indirect help hypothesis

To survive and reproduce humans need food. This is particularly true for women whose bodies must sustain the additional energetic costs of pregnancy and lactation. For many years, anthropologists studying hunter-gatherer and subsistence societies believed that women's gathering provided the majority of calories consumed. This was generalized from a pioneering study of the Kung San by Richard Lee (1979). A synthesis of data from 10 intensive studies of gatherer societies (Kaplan, Hill, Lancaster, & Hurtado, 2000) suggests that this finding was anomalous and may have been an artifact of observation method. Lee's observations were taken during a single month in a season when mongongo nuts, which women collect, were abundant. On two of the observation days, he took the women out to forage in his vehicle which may also have inflated the amount collected. However, other researchers have reported that Kung women do contribute substantially more calories than women in other societies, perhaps because they inhabit warm climates where berries and tubers are abundant (Marlowe, 2003). Nonetheless, when results from several studies across different ecological niches are examined, it is clear that men provide the majority of calories consumed by children and reproductively-aged women. Between 60 percent (among the Nukak) and 84 percent (among the Ache) of the calories consumed are contributed by men. A nutritional breakdown reveals that more than half of consumed calories come from meat, hunted almost exclusively by men. An average of 15 percent comes from roots, foraged almost exclusively by women. Among the Ache, over the course of a lifetime (from aged 18 to death) it is estimated that net calorie production (calories produced minus calories consumed) is + 121,638,000 for men and −924,000 for women (Kaplan et al., 2000). In short, women benefit considerably from men's hunting provision.

During pregnancy and lactation women need extra calories—the suggested intake is about 2,500 per day. This calorie-loading happens through increased energy intake and reduced energy expenditure, rather than by fat mobilization. Kaplan et al. (2000), armed with impressive anthropological evidence, argue that it was the meat provided by men that increased women's rate of reproduction relative to other primates. By relieving women of the burden of provisioning themselves, women were better able to sustain pregnancy and lactation, and to feed their dependent children. They could also speed up their rate of reproduction by decreasing the inter-birth interval. In hunter-gatherer societies, birth spacing is approximately 41 months. Compare this with 65 months among chimpanzees whose offspring mature and become independent considerably faster than human children. This help may be most critical during breastfeeding. Better nutrition and reduced workloads during lactation bring women back into normal cycling more quickly, speeding the occurrence of the next pregnancy (Worthman, Jenkins, Stallings, & Daina, 1993). When a Hadza woman is lactating, her decreased calorie provision is compensated for by her husband (Marlowe, 2003). Across 58 traditional societies, women who divorce and hence lose paternal provisioning wean their infants on average three to four months earlier than women who remain married (Quinlan & Quinlan, 2008). The biological costs of reproduction on women can be easily forgotten in our smaller contemporary families. Without contraception (and that is how we evolved) women spend a substantial portion of their reproductive lives either pregnant or lactating. In foraging societies, the average age of first birth is 19 and the last birth occurs at 39 (Kaplan et al., 2000). Women typically wean their infants at about two and a half years old (Kennedy, 2005). Each child "costs" a mother 39 months of her reproductive life (nine months pregnant plus 30 months lactating) so that a fertile woman spends about 95 percent of her life either pregnant or lactating.

None of this should be taken to endorse the caricature of women sitting at the camp fireside while men roam the savannah hunting for meat. Women can and do contribute to subsistence by foraging for fruit, tubers, and nuts. These are vital during times when men's hunting brings low returns. Beyond that, women prepare food, cook, launder, and care for one or more dependent children. These activities can be undertaken in and around the camp, where childcare can be integrated with other tasks. Men are thus able to leave the camp and hunt. It is this complementarity between the sexes that has resulted in human's short inter-birth interval and has sustained the long period of infant dependency and learning that has led to our success as a species.

So it is probable that women's preference for monogamy was not to save their children's life or their own, nor was it to hire a live-in nanny. What women wanted was time and energy to produce and raise multiple dependent off-spring—time that could be bought by finding a mate to shoulder some of the necessary costs of subsistence. Other women might assist through allomothering but they have children and obligations of their own. And what a woman wants is not someone to take over her mothering role, but someone to support her while she does it. A mate whose genes are carried in the bodies of those children has strong motivation to provide for her and their joint progeny.

Male mating effort hypothesis

If ancestral women wanted a permanent male to augment their much-needed calorie intake and free up time to raise their children, why should men comply? Isn't it a man's best interests to inseminate as many women as he can, rather than tie his reproductive output to a single woman? The answer lies in numbers, specifically the operational sex ratio. This is the number of reproductively available females relative to males. Because women spend a substantial part of their lives either pregnant or lactating, they are not sexually available and this skews the sex ratio so that there are more men seeking mating partners than there are available women. A few top men gain access to numerous women while at the bottom of the ladder some men achieved no mating success at all. Market forces put females in a strong position to demand monogamy. For those men without the physique or charisma to attract multiple mates, the next best thing is to commit to a single woman and thereby gain at least a modicum of mating success. The power of the mating market can be seen in unusual times and places where the sex ratio swings in the direction of a paucity of women. Here women have the edge and there is a shift toward monogamy and biparental care, and away from single motherhood and divorce (Barber, 2003; Schmitt, 2005). For most men, most of the time, monogamy is a safe compromise between the wild bonanza of polygyny (achievable only by an elite few) and the reproductive death of complete mating failure.

In societies that allow polygyny, the disparity between men can become extreme because men must provide for and often "buy" their wives (either by bride price or by providing unpaid labor for her family). This makes polygyny the preserve of the richest and most powerful men. No surprise then that polygynous societies are the most non-egalitarian with strong hierarchies, and marked power and wealth differentials (Betzig, 1982). Polygyny ensures an excessive number of children to any man who can afford it. But while he may benefit, most others do not. Anthropologists tell us that 84 percent of world societies condone polygyny. (The implicit or explicit contrast is with the tiny prevalence of polyandry (0.5%) which is often used to document the greater sexual appetite and sexual proprietariness of males compared with females.)

But counting societies is not the same as counting people. The vast majority of the world's population inhabit societies that prohibit polygamy and, even where it is legal, only about 10 percent of men take multiple wives. Even if polygyny is limited to only two wives it creates a very marked shortage of available women (Quinlan, 2008). And this means that women are in a strong position to demand commitment and assistance in return for giving these supernumerary men at least a modicum of reproductive success. Yet, these men still see their glass as half empty: They view monogamy as a sacrifice compared to women (Schmookler & Bursik, 2007).

And there is evidence that polygyny was not a strategy that appealed to women, despite some theoretical arguments to the contrary. These theoretical arguments are based on the notion of the "polygyny threshold," developed from the study of bird species where a male's territory is crucial to attracting mates. Sometimes, it is to a female's advantage to select an already-mated male with an impressive territory rather than an unmated male with only a poor site—a strategy called resource defense polygyny. This idea was applied to women too by anthropologists who suggested that women may find it in their own interests to become the second or third wife of a rich man, rather than the sole wife of a poor man (Borgerhoff Mulder, 1990).

Robert Wright (1994) argued that polygyny is a positive benefit to the majority of women and gave a simple demonstration of why. Imagine a group of 100 women and 100 men each ranked according to how desirable they are on the marriage market. Under monogamy each woman will end up with a man who shares her ranking. (This is assortative mating. Though men and women both would both prefer to have a mate who ranks higher than them, simple market forces make gross disparities between mates unlikely.) But now imagine we legalize polygyny. The first woman to take advantage of it rises from rank 80 to rank 20 (admittedly sharing the wealth with her co-wife). But the effect on every other woman is to move them up one place so that they each marry a man who is one rank higher than their last partner. Polygyny, Wright argues, redistributes male wealth in a much more egalitarian way between women. So, even if a given woman refuses to share a husband, she is still better off under polygyny because the fact that some other women opt for it, benefits her by freeing up males who rank higher than her current mate. The losers are top ranking women (who have nowhere to advance to and now have to share what they previously had to themselves) and the "bottom ranked men" (who miss out on marriage altogether).

But polygyny carries numerous costs to women that affect not just the cream of the crop. Second and later wives have lower fertility than monogamous women (Daly & Wilson, 1983; Josephson, 2002; Sichona, 1993) and their children are less likely to survive (Dorjahn, 1958; Strassmann, 1997). Most importantly, women just do not seem happy in polygamous marriages: as we saw in Chapter 6, the co-wife relationship is the epitome of resentment, unhappiness, and conflict. In an analysis of 69 polygynous societies, 90 percent of the disputes between co-wives centered on sexual and emotional jealousy (Jankowiak, Sudakov, & Wilreker, 2002). These tensions erupted into physical fights, name-calling, attempts to devalue co-wives' sexual attractiveness to their husbands, and black magic. As the authors concluded:

> Our data suggest that the majority of young women react to the arrival of a new co-wife with feelings of fear, anger, sadness, and loss. This sentiment is expressed through a variety of culturally acknowledged and measurable behaviors; for example, witchcraft accusations, statements of concern for the welfare of children, accusations of favoritism, demands of greater access to the husband, complaints of being sexually ignored, outbreaks of physical or verbal abuse, and expressing an intention to divorce or actually doing so. (Jankowiak et al., 2002, p. 90)

The brutal emotional impact of husband-sharing strongly suggests that women have evolved no psychological adaptation to it. And that indicates that polygyny has not been a successful strategy for women.

Sexual conflict: Women, men, and monogamy

There is plenty of evidence that women are keen on monogamy. To support it, they have found ways both to deter rogue women from pursuing alternative strategies and to make the monogamy proposition appealing to men.

As we saw in Chapter 6, the marketplace approach has been useful in thinking about how women can gain an edge in sexual bargaining with men (Baumeister & Vohs, 2004). Because sex is valued more highly by men and their access depends on women's willingness to supply it, sex can be seen as a valued good in which women act as "sellers" and men as "buyers." The more difficult the product is to come by, the higher the price. Thus if women dispense sex too freely, its price drops and women lose their bargaining position with regard to exacting monogamy from men. It is for this reason that women are keen to control one another's sexuality. A woman who gives sex away cheaply threatens the implicit exchange inherent in monogamy. Women are particularly censorious of such women, branding them as "cheap" in an attempt to devalue their sexual worth to men. A woman who provides sex outside the bonds of monogamy, may gain a short-term advantage since her price undercuts her more conservative rivals but she is also likely to incur their wrath. In the long term, she benefits from maintaining the higher market price that is enforced by other women, not least because her reputation for sexual availability and increasing age will lower still further the price that she can hope to exact from men. Pornography and prostitution provide further outlets for male sexuality beyond monogamy and predictably women are more opposed to their availability than men (Baumeister & Twenge, 2002) but they reserve particularly condemnation for the "other woman." Women's magazines carry cautionary stories of the sad fate of these women, sending a clear and aggressive warning from the female majority that, whatever promises he may make to a mistress, a man will rarely leave his wife. There are no statistics to my knowledge confirming whether this is correct or simply a warning shot fired by monogamous women at their rivals.

Warning off "other" women reduced a man's options, but men's attraction to sexual variety remained a problem for women's promotion of monogamy. What could women offer men to increase the attraction of monogamy? The answer was sex, or more precisely continuous female sexual receptivity. Women are unusual in not advertising the time at which they are capable of becoming pregnant, as we saw in Chapter 2. Instead they are willing to engage in sex throughout the menstrual cycle—unlike their primate sisters most of whom are indifferent to sex except when they are in estrous. Men want sex more often than women do (Baumeister, Catanese, & Vohs, 2001). Ideally, they would like sex with many partners. But failing that (and this is the case for most men), a good second best is frequent sex with the same partner. Women are willing and often happy to provide it. (In some cases, their willingness may be strategic: as one woman in a polygynous explained, "I will continue with sex till death in order to prevent my husband from taking another wife," Madhavan, 2002, p. 78.) It is women who act as the gatekeeper in terms of the frequency of sex. For example, it is women, not men, who decide at what point in a relationship sexual intercourse will take place and that point is later than men typically want (Cohen & Shotland, 1996). Since ovulation is concealed from women as well as men, women have evolved to maximize the chance of pregnancy by engaging in sex throughout their cycle and this has the added benefit of pleasing their mates. Evolution may ultimately act on the deeper level of genes but proximally it acts on behaviors (that are in part controlled by genes). Hence men's evolved phenotypic eagerness for sex can be "fooled" by a woman who provides it on a continuous basis. And women's willingness to provide it is partly motivated by the pleasure of orgasm. Female orgasm remains something of an evolutionary conundrum with some believing that it is no more than a by-product of the fact that the clitoris and penis develop form the same underlying structure (Gould, 1992; Lloyd, 2005; Symons, 1979). However it came into being, it certainly means that women do not merely tolerate sex for the purpose of keeping a male partner around, but actively enjoy it. Concealed ovulation also helps to keep her mate at home in another way. A man's best bet for producing offspring is to mate during a woman's fertile phase but if neither he nor she knows when this is, the man has little choice but to stay with her, guard her well, and copulate often (Alexander & Noonan, 1979).

Some have argued that concealed ovulation also opens the door to women's extramarital affairs (or as biologists would have it, extra-pair copulations). In many primates, when estrous is advertised, the female becomes the target of a great deal of (albeit transitory) male interest since all the males know that she is fertile. Swollen, scarlet genitalia may not do much for the human primate but imagine a human version of estrous that magically and temporarily bestowed large breasts, a tiny waist, shiny hair, pouting lips, and a Marilyn Monroe walk. Every man in the vicinity would take note and heads would turn. A man would know exactly when he had to watch his partner most carefully. The woman would face double trouble—too many overt, competitive suitors and a too watchful husband. By concealing her fertile time, a woman would dilute her husband's watchfulness by distributing more evenly across the menstrual cycle and increase the possibility of undetected infidelity. In an optimal-for-women world, the woman alone would know the timing of her most fertile days. Though a few women claim to experience a brief pain at "mittelschmerz," when the egg bursts out of the ovary, most women are not consciously aware (in the absence of a diary) when they are ovulating. But some studies suggest that, though women protest ignorance, their bodies know. As we saw in Chapter 2, there is some evidence that women in the most fertile phase of their cycle are preferentially attracted to men other than their partner who show signs of "good" genes (Thornhill & Gangestad, 2008). This estrous preference shift is more marked in partnered rather than single women, is associated with temporarily lowered commitment to their partner, and is most evident in women who are married to less symmetrical (less genetically desirable) men.

Infidelity is not confined to human females. Over ninety per cent of bird species were assumed to be pair bonded and sexually monogamous because two parents are obligatory in order to simultaneously protect the nest and collect food. Yet even in these "monogamous" species an average of at least 11 percent of offspring are the result of extra-pair paternity (Griffith, Owens, & Thuman, 2002). By exercising free choice outside of the partnership, a woman can garner all the advantages of being a free agent without sacrificing the benefits of a supporting male. She can have the best genes (desirable males will be happy to oblige her if there is no price in terms of paternal investment). She can solve potential infertility problems—approximately 10–20 percent of infertile couples are genetically incompatible. She can increase the genetic diversity of her children—with different fathers each will have slightly different traits fitting them to survive in a range of unknowable future ecologies. She can select mates who have a different major histocompatibility complex (MHC) than her own. These are a set of genes that code for glycoproteins in the T cells of the immune system and genetic heterozygosity in the offspring is an advantage, conferring wider immunity to disease. Women prefer the scent of men with MHC different to their own and find them attractive as extra-pair partners (Garver-Apgar, Gangestad, Thornhill, Miller, & Olp, 2006; Wedekind, Seebeck, Bettens, & Paepke, 1995). There is some evidence that women spontaneously abort pregnancies where MHC genes are homozygotic. Multiple mates during a single cycle also allow for sperm competition and for cryptic female choice which favor the best male genetic quality.

In the battle between the sexes, women seem to have made some shrewd moves to promote monogamy and so ease their workload: They deter other women from undercutting the system and lowering male commitment. They offer their partner sex *ad libitum* to keep him around. Through concealed ovulation, they reserve the possibility of extra-pair sex with their unwitting male partner taking on the full burden of misattributed paternity.

Monogamy reduces the exploitation of one sex by the other by creating equality between a man and a woman in their reproductive output. This was elegantly demonstrated in the humble house fly by Holland and Rice (1999). Normally promiscuous, some of these flies were randomly selected to have monogamy forced upon them. The experimenters acted as marriage brokers, teaming up and housing together individual males and females over 32 generations. Monogamy means not only that the reproductive success of males and females is identical but also that their reproductive interests should converge. While polygyny allows males to exploit females quite ruthlessly without suffering themselves, monogamy means that anything that hurts a female (prevents her from achieving her reproductive potential) hurts her male partner just as much. After several generations of monogamy, Holland and Rice performed the key tests. First, they introduced non-experimental, traditional females to mate with the monogamous "new males." They found that monogamy had led to a decrease in the toxicity of the male's seminal fluid and also to a reduction in male courtship—an activity that is harmful to females. Then they looked at the effect of monogamy on the experimental females. During monogamy, these females' male partners had behaved in a less exploitative way toward them and so the monogamous females did not need to evolve counter-strategies of resistance. As expected, when these monogamous females mated with normal males, a larger proportion died than among those females who had been allowed to co-evolve with male polygyny.

Take another example; the seed beetle (Cayetano, Maklakov, Brooks, & Bonduriansky, 2011). The tip of the male's intromittent organ is densely covered with spines. These seem to act as an anchor, enhancing the male's ability to cling to the female and improving his performance in sperm competition with other males. But these spines cause scarring in females, as well as reducing her longevity and lifetime fertility. In species where the males have longer spines, the females have co-evolved by building a thicker wall in the copulatory tract and developing their own blade-like spines at the entrance to the reproductive tract. As Rice had done with flies, the experimenters imposed monogamy over 18 generations on some samples, while allowing control beetles to continue with their usual polygamy. Under monogamy, the males' spines shrank in length. As predicted, no change was seen in the female spines because they evolved as a defensive response to male damage and hence are only likely to reduce in size after several more generations—when the natural selection "realizes" that the male threat has diminished and that the resources she expended in growing them can be better used elsewhere.

In both flies and beetles, the monogamous insects also produced more offspring having been freed from the extra "load" of sexual selection (developing ploys and counter-ploys takes time and energy as well as being potentially fatal). Non-monogamous arrangements may have advantages for females (such as getting the best genes) but they also have costs (males evolving to "dupe" females into behavior that is counter to their own best interests). Freed from this antagonistic tussle, males become more benign and females produce more offspring and suffer lower mortality.

In the end, monogamy is a compromise between all parties—and one with definite pay-offs. The two chief beneficiaries are women and the majority of men without the resources to support successful polygyny. But never forget that official monogamy does not rule out temporary episodes of infidelity. To describe infidelity as "cheating" is entirely accurate: one party gains a reproductive advantage at the expense of their partner. Small wonder then that both sexes have evolved a sharp sensitivity to it and a strong emotional response.

Marital troubles

Given the inherent conflict in the reproductive strategies of men and women, we should expect to see disputes as each party tries to promote their own strategy and prevent exploitation by their partner. We would also expect marriage to be a relatively fragile institution, vulnerable to collapse when the cost–benefit equation for either the man or the woman becomes too imbalanced. One way to examine the kinds of costs that trigger marital strife is to look at the causes of divorce. Divorce has become increasingly easy and, in the United States and Europe, between 30 and 50 percent of first marriages end in divorce (Hatfield & Rapson, 1996). Of these divorcees, about 75 percent will marry again and about half of these second marriages will also fail. The number of divorces in a society is, of course, a function of how easy divorce is to obtain but the reasons that drive people to dissolve their unions are likely to be the same sources of dissatisfaction that, in less liberal eras, couples simply had to endure. Marriages fail because of a clash of personalities—at least that is how the parties involved often explain it. They made the wrong choice—over the years it became clear that they just did not approach life in the same way, share the same values, or "gel" as a functioning partnership. But behind these kinds of general statements, we can look for the specific areas of disagreement that seem to give rise to couples' realization that they were not "meant for each other."

Betzig (1989) used ethnographic data on causes of divorce from 160 cultures. She was able to identify the leading causes on a worldwide basis by simply tabulating the percentage of societies that recognized divorce as a reasonable response to each of a number of possible "wrongdoings." The most common cause was wifely infidelity; "If marriage qualifies as near universal, so must the double standard. Almost every one of the causes of conjugal dissolution that might be related to infidelity is ascribed significantly more often to one sex than to the other" (Betzig, 1989, p. 658). Another common reason was failure of economic support and here we see a reversal of the double standard—in all but one case it is failure of provision by the husband that is grounds for divorce.

One of the most comprehensive studies of the reasons for divorce in contemporary Western society was undertaken by Kitson (1992) who interviewed men and women divorcees in Cleveland, Ohio, United States. Men were more likely to be unsure about what had caused the divorce and blamed external events such as over-commitment to their job, a death in the family, or interference by in-laws. Women were significantly more likely to mention their husband's involvement in extramarital sex, his untrustworthy nature, too much time spent "out with the boys," excessive drinking, and money problems. Men seem out of touch with the social and emotional troubles that have beset their marriage whereas women focus clearly on the two of the worldwide leading causes of breakdown: infidelity and failure of a man's economic contribution to the marriage.

But the problem with the majority of studies of divorce is that they collect their data retrospectively. Perceptions of the reasons for the divorce not only vary between husband and wife but they also change over time. After-the-fact accounts can involve redefining what had previously been acceptable behavior in order to rationalize and justify the divorce (Rasmussen & Ferraro, 1979). Amato and Rogers (1997) avoided this problem by undertaking a prospective study of divorce. In 1980, they contacted a random sample of 2,033 married persons and asked about sources of conflict in their marriage and whether the problem was caused chiefly by the husband or the wife. They managed to re-contact 78 percent of their sample again three years later, 71 percent eight years later, and 61 percent after 12 years. They could then examine the problems that had preceded the divorce in real time. Their results confirmed the findings of Betzig and many other researchers (Kitson, Babri, & Roach, 1985) that the chief source of divorce is infidelity or suspected infidelity. Husbands who reported that their wife was unfaithful showed a 363 percent increase in the likelihood of divorce while wives who believed their partner was unfaithful increased their chances of divorce by 299 percent. Behind this, came a cluster of reasons that all seem to reflect Betzig's category of failure to economically support the partner—spending money foolishly. Men's profligacy (as viewed by their wives) increased the odds of divorce by 187 percent while women's foolish use of money increased divorce odds to a much lesser extent (77 percent) again suggesting that men's lack of economic responsibility matters more than women's. Let us take a closer look at the two chief threats to marital stability—infidelity and money problems.

Fidelity—who cares?

In countries around the world until the nineteenth century, the notion that a wife was a man's possession was encoded in laws which were made by men and reflected male interests. A wife who had intercourse with a man other than her husband was guilty of a crime (Daly & Wilson, 1988). From an evolutionary viewpoint there is no real mystery as to the peculiar importance that men attach to wifely fidelity—a woman who has sex outside marriage places her husband in danger of raising and investing in another man's child. Daly and Wilson (1988) undertook a comprehensive study of homicides committed in Detroit in 1972 where the offender and victim were legal or common law spouses. They focused on 16 cases in which the husband committed murder and concluded that men's spousal homicides result from strong proprietary feelings about their wives. The wife is his property and he owns her. Hence if she threatens to leave him (and may start a new relationship with another man) some men believe that she must be killed. A distinct male pattern involves the offender not only killing his wife (and sometimes the children too) but taking his own life also. As Daly and Wilson (1988, p. 215) succinctly put it: "The prospect of losing his family through death apparently strikes the desperate familicidal father as no more disastrous than the prospect of losing them through desertion! Central to male killing patterns is his determination that 'If I can't have her no-one can.'" Separated and divorced women are between five and seven times as likely to be killed by their partner than those who are still residing with him (Wilson, Daly, & Wright, 1993) and over 90 percent of these killings occur in the first year of separation. This pattern has also been found in Australia, Chicago (United States), and Canada (Wilson & Daly, 1993).

Wilson and Daly (1993) describe male sexual jealousy as an evolved psychological module. A man who was a conscientious mate-guarder, alert to the possibility of cuckoldry, left a greater proportion of his genes in the subsequent generation's gene pool than one who took a laissez-faire attitude to his wife's desire for sexual novelty. But mate-guarding can become paranoid and extreme; the wife finds that she is prevented from leaving the house unescorted, punishment ensues for tardiness, she is barred from seeing relatives or female friends, she is subject to phone calls throughout the day to check on her whereabouts. This pattern of obsessive concern can erupt into violent acts aimed at deterring her from pursuing not just affairs, but even a normal degree of autonomy. The majority of women who seek refuge in shelters report these patterns of excessive control which, at the start of the relationship, the woman often interpreted as evidence of his devotion to her.

And there may be an element of truth in these women's belief. Extremes of male mate-guarding cause appalling suffering and even physical injury, but David Buss (2000) has argued that a husband who shows no concern about his partner's interest in other men, is a man who may be less than fully committed to her. He calls this the "jealousy paradox." A degree of jealousy is an inevitable part of love. For better or worse, human pair bonding depends upon a sense of exclusivity. We feel that our chosen partner is uniquely suited to us, he is the "other half" of ourselves. Like a lock in a key, we feel ourselves predestined to come together. And that sense of the partner as "specially designed" for us is utterly crushed by romantic and sexual betrayal. We realize that we are just one of many potential partners. Worse still, we have been chosen and then found wanting. Such rejection prompts not only depression but anger too. A degree of jealousy may be an index of the intensity of love. A study that followed dating couples found that those pairs who expressed greater jealousy about their partner were more likely to marry them subsequently (Mathes, 1986). Jealousy reveals how highly a person values their mate. The probability of infidelity in men and women is associated with their attractiveness relative to their spouse. Individuals who rate themselves (and are rated by others) as the more attractive of the pair are more likely to have affairs and to have them earlier in the marriage (Berscheid, Hatfield, & Bohrnstedt, 1973; Buss & Shackelford, 1997; Prins, Buunk, & VanYperen, 1993). So attractive and desirable people have to be guarded more carefully. On a darker note, spousal homicides confirm that women who are younger and hence more attractive to rival men are more likely to be killed by their husbands (Daly & Wilson, 1988; Willbanks, 1984).

The path of jealousy that leads to divorce has an evolutionary logic (Buss, 2000). To detect infidelity, a person must become highly attuned to even subtle variations in their partner's behavior—the credit card statement that goes missing, the new dress that seems an unusually fashionable choice, the race to answer the phone which often turns out to be a wrong number. Once a sign has been picked up, the husband lowers his threshold for detecting further signs. A wife who senses her husband's suspicion must in turn raise her level of deception. A self-reinforcing spiral develops where one person's ability to see through deception results in their partner becoming increasingly skilled at concealment. This process, spread out over evolutionary time rather than the microscopic time scale of a human marriage, may have made all of us more proficient at both deceiving and detecting deceit. Jealousy seems to be the result of selection for strong sensitivity to signals of sexual infidelity. And such sensitivity can develop when the costs of failing to detect a true signal are greater than the costs of a false alarm. Such a finely-tuned detection system can lead to unfounded and abnormal jealousy. And persistent jealousy, as well as occasional infidelity, can ruin marriages (Amato & Rogers, 1997). From the outside, it is sometimes impossible to know whether a spouse's jealousy is pathological or a legitimate response to real betrayal.

But does evolutionary theory propose that women experience jealousy less intensely as men? Not at all. A number of studies have asked men and women to report how distressed they would feel in jealousy-eliciting situations such as watching their partner flirting, dancing, hugging, kissing, or having sex with somebody else. One of the most extensive studies investigated jealousy in over two thousand people in seven countries and found no sex differences (Buunk & Hupka, 1987). Many other studies confirm this finding as David Buss (2000, p. 51) concludes in a wide-ranging review: "The conclusion is clear: women and men alike can be plagued by jealousy, both in its everyday manifestations and in its most florid clinical expressions."

But what are women so jealous about? A man's infidelity carries no parallel threat of maternal uncertainty: a woman can never be duped into unwittingly raising another woman's child. Rather, in a biparental species such as our own, women's jealousy should center upon the possible loss of a supporting male. Abandonment is more likely if her partner forms a strong attachment to another woman. (Men's casual sexual liaisons pose less of a threat. When asked "Have you ever continued to have sex on a regular basis with someone you did not want to get emotionally involved with?," 76 percent of men (but only 37 percent of women) answered "Yes," Townsend, 1995.) Since desertion is more likely if a man falls in love, women should be especially sensitized to signs of attachment (not mere attraction) to another woman.

David Buss and his co-workers made a clear evolutionary prediction about sex differences in the focus of jealousy (Buss, Larsen, Westen, & Semmelroth,

1992). Males should be most upset by the prospect of a partner's sexual infidelity and women by emotional betrayal. To test this, studies have asked men and women to imagine these two situations and to say which one made them more distressed and jealous. The prediction that males would opt for sex and women for emotion was borne out (Bailey, Gaulin, Agyei, & Gladue, 1994; Buss et al., 1992; Buunk, Angleitner, Oubaid, & Buss, 1996; DeSteno & Salovey, 1996; Geary, Rumsey, Bow-Thomas, & Hoard, 1995; Harris & Christenfeld, 1996; Shackelford & Buss, 1996; Tiesmann & Mosher, 1978; Wiederman & Kendall, 1999). Typically slightly over a half of male subjects selected sexual infidelity as most upsetting. The sex difference was largely driven by women's greater selection of emotional betrayal.

Some have objected that these hypothetical scenarios are logically flawed (DeSteno & Salovey, 1996). Suppose that most women, quite reasonably, believe that men are eminently capable of sex with a variety of women without emotional involvement but that sometimes a man may begin to form a strong attachment to one of those women. If a woman is told to imagine that her partner is emotionally involved with another woman, she naturally assumes that he has already had sex with her. Hence the women tend to choose this scenario as the most upsetting because it represents a "double shot" of jealousy. Men, however, believe that women only have sex with men that they are already emotionally involved with—hence sexual infidelity implies the existence of prior emotional infidelity—the male "double shot." Buss and his co-workers (Buss et al., 1999) addressed this issue by varying the instructions in their next studies. This time, participants were asked which would upset them more and the two choices were "Imagining your partner forming a deep emotional (but not sexual) relationship with another person" or "Imagining your partner enjoying a sexual (but not emotional) relationship with that person." The results were the same as the original study—men tended to opted for sex (even without emotional attachment) more than women did. In a further study, they asked men and women to imagine that their partner was both emotionally and sexually involved with another person and they had to indicate which component of the relationship troubled them more. Once again, the original predictions held.

However, in all these studies subjects are forced to make a choice between two options. When men and women were offered a third option—that both forms of infidelity are equally distressing—the majority of both sexes endorsed it (Lisher, Nguyen, Stocks, & Zillmer, 2008). And when men and women were presented with both scenarios and asked to rate each one independently in terms of how upsetting it would be, no sex differences appeared (DeSteno, Bartlett, Braverman, & Salovey, 2002). Both sexes score between six and seven on a seven-point scale for each scenario (Buss, 1989c). In the real world, and in the world of our imagination, sexual betrayal and emotional betrayal are so tightly interwoven as to be effectively equal in their impact. Neither sex is happy about infidelity of either kind.

Other researchers have relied heavily on homicide data to make the argument that men are more prone to jealousy than women (Daly & Wilson, 1988). Could the difference in jealousy-motivated homicides stem from a difference in how easily jealousy evokes anger in the two sexes? To examine this we have to narrow our focus to studies that explicitly asked about *anger* in reaction to infidelity. Most studies find that women report as much anger as men (Hansen, 1982; McIntosh, 1989; Paul, Foss, & Baenninger, 1996; Pines & Aronson, 1983; Pines & Friedman, 1998; White, 1981; Wiederman & Allgeier, 1993; Yarab, Allgeier, & Sensibaugh, 1999). Some studies even find women to be angrier (Bryson, 1991; Buss, 1989c; Buunk, 1981, 1982; De Weerth & Kalma, 1993; Geary et al., 1995 (US sample only); Hansen, 1985; Paul, Foss, & Galloway, 1993). When asked their likely response to infidelity, women were more likely than men to physically and verbally abuse their partner (De Weerth & Kalma, 1993). These studies, like many others, confirm that it is not the emotional drive to aggression that differs between the sexes.

The apparent disjunction between the similarity of men and women's emotional response (anger) and the sex difference in behavior (murder) lies with a simple error in interpreting homicide statistics. Daly, Wilson, and Weghorst (1982) gathered data on all the jealousy-motive homicides they could track down and then calculated the percentage committed by men and women. But men commit more homicides in general than women do: In the United States they are responsible for over 90 percent of them. If men kill more than women across all categories of motives, then it is not surprising that they also kill more from jealousy. If we want to know whether men are specifically more likely than women to kill out of jealous, the correct analysis is to take the total number of homicides committed by each sex and calculate the proportion that is motivated by jealousy. Harris (2003) did just this. Across 20 studies, she found that women were slightly (but not significantly) more likely than men to kill out of jealousy. So there is no difference in the proportion of men and women killers who kill for this motive. If this seems surprising, there are more surprises that I will discuss later. For example, although women are more often killed by their spouses than men are, this is due to men's higher rate of killing in general. When women do kill, they are more likely than men to victimize their partner (Fernando Rodriguez & Henderson, 1995; Greenfeld & Snell, 1999).

With all my worldly goods

Monogamy offered ancestral women male assistance with provisioning especially during the years when her children were young and demanding of her time and energy. Note the word "assistance." There is a real danger of imagining a primeval scenario in which the woman sits in her hut singing lullabies to her children, waiting patiently for her mate to return with food for them all. This picture corresponds quite closely to a particularly unusual time and place for the division of labor—the Western world in the immediate post-war era. So short is our historical perspective that sociologists are tempted to see women's entry into the labor force in the late twentieth century as something of a novelty. But this is a serious misunderstanding.

If contemporary hunter-gatherers are a useful proxy for the lifestyle that we enjoyed about 100,000 years ago, then women played a very active role in provisioning the family. Two or three times a week a woman would set off carrying her youngest child (perhaps with an older child in tow) into the surrounding territory to search for food—wild onions, mongongo nuts, plums, baobab fruit, birds' eggs, tortoises, and honey. Men might hunt several days a week but on average they made a kill on every fourth attempt—a woman who depended solely on men would have been hungry. The shift away from nomadic hunting and gathering life came with the swidden farmers—sometimes called "slash and burn" agriculturists (Jolly, 1999). In the Amazon forest, they cleared trees, created fields, and grew plants before moving on to begin the cycle anew in a different spot. Eventually they would return after sufficient time had passed for the land to become enriched again during its fallow period. The forest was renewed by carbon and minerals from the burned trees, new tree shoots turned the soil over, weeds died out as the trees grew above them, and the crop pests were forced out. Population density meant that this pattern of continuous relocation could not go on forever. As the number of people increased, the fallow time shortened. Eventually movement to new spots became impossible and the only way to sow seed was to plow. Helen Fisher (1993) believes that the plow has much to answer for. Plowing is a task too heavy and time-consuming to be taken on by a woman with children. And a man needed a woman to sow, weed, pick, prepare, and store the vegetables and crops he produced. Men and women became more dependent on each other. Agriculture also meant that there was a joint investment in the family's parcel of land. If one partner wanted to move away, they would lose half of their lifetime's work and have no capital to buy another. As Fisher (1993, p. 106) puts it: "Farming women and men were tied to the soil, to each other, and to an elaborate network of stationary kin. Under these ecological circumstances, divorce was not a practical alternative." The greater the economic dependence, the greater the expressed commitment to (though not necessarily happiness with) the marriage (Nock, 1995). The lowest rates of divorce are found in pre-industrial Europe and in India and China—all cultures where plowing and agriculture are the chief means of subsistence.

Then came the industrial revolution. Men and women left the land to exchange their labor directly for money. Money is paid to an individual, not to a couple. Even mutual wealth can be divided and carried away. The divorce rate began to climb in the early twentieth century as women began to earn their own wages. In the post-war years there was a drastic but temporary interruption of this pattern as men returned from the war and women vacated their jobs to make way for them. Women were warned of the dangers of "failing their children" by working and a full-time wife at home became a status badge for men. But women were not content to be relegated to the kitchen permanently. With the arrival of the women's movement, women entered the waged economy in increasing numbers and the divorce rate began to soar, doubling between 1966 and 1976 (Cherlin, 1981). The moral of the story seems straightforward, if unromantic. Men and women are more likely to remain married when their fates are economically inter-linked.

But waged work in contemporary Western society presents mothers with problems that they simply did not have to face in pre-industrial society. How can a woman be in two places at the same time? How can she earn some financial autonomy and simultaneously earn her child's love? It is a new and cruel bind. Farm work allows childcare to take place alongside milking or weeding. Foraging can be done with children, as well as alone. But work in the industrial or service economy takes place at regulated times and places at which infants are not welcomed. To make matters worse, the increasing mobility of the labor force means that there is a good chance that she is far away from supportive and babysitting kin. She may not even remain in one place long enough to establish strong bonds with neighbors. If she elects to work, she must place the safety and happiness of her child (as well as the lion's share of her pay packet) in the hands of a stranger. To buy this right to work, working women must often rely on a second income from their spouse (Herzog, Bachman, & Johnston, 1983). Perhaps then it should come as no surprise that, not just among societies living on the edge of starvation but in "liberated" ones also, a leading cause of divorce is a man's failure to provide for his family. If marriage is an agreement in which the woman is responsible for childrearing (even if she also holds a waged job) and the man provides economic support, it seems reasonable that failure to hold up his end of the bargain might well lead to trouble. From this we can make predictions. Marriage should be less frequent and divorce more common under two particular conditions. First, when men's economic situation makes them poor providers. Second, when women are able to earn sufficient resources to lessen the need for male assistance.

In the United States, the trend in births to single mothers shows a steep rise from 5 percent in 1960 to nearly 37 percent in 2005. This was especially marked in the black community where 70 percent of births are now to single women. With economically supportive males thin on the ground, young black women are likely to seek support from female kin and this arrangement has knock-on effects on their fertility patterns (Weinraub & Gringlas, 1995). Black women die earlier than their white counterparts and are more prone to illnesses that make child care difficult or impossible. In black urban communities, a teenager who bears a child has a 75 percent probability that her mother will still be alive and able to assist in child rearing when her child is five years old. A woman who waits to the age of 20 has only a 40 percent chance of maternal assistance (Low, 2000). When men cannot provide resources, women adapt and adjust their reproductive strategy.

A husband who fails to contribute is not merely economically neutral. The wife is effectively paying for the privilege of having him around and, given the still modest contribution of men to household duties, she is likely to receive little in return. Ethnographic studies of black "cultures of poverty" in the United States have documented again and again the male response to such situations. Unable to effectively contribute in the home and viewing it as a female preserve, the men head for the streets to pass their days talking, drinking, and attempting to salvage some pride—if only in their ability to attract women despite their conspicuous absence of resources (Liebow, 1967). Divorce rates among black Americans are higher than among other ethnic groups (Norton & Glick, 1979). In a recent study that followed couples over 25 years, 63 percent of black marriages had dissolved, compared to 47 percent of white marriages (Teachman, 2010). However, when the effects of income, differences in family size, and home ownership were controlled, black families were *less* likely to separate than whites (Hampton, 1975). This underlines the central importance of economic rather than cultural factors in divorce. Black men earn less, are unemployed more often, and occupy low status positions—all of which make them economically dispensable (Becker, 1981).

Across all ethnic groups there is a clear relationship between socioeconomic status and divorce (Kitson et al., 1985). Divorce is higher among the less educated and those with the most restricted access to high earnings. A husband's level of education remains a protective factor for divorce even controlling for his income: women who are married to men with the educational potential for high earnings are less likely to divorce. Divorce rates rise as the husband's job status and income decline and as male unemployment and income instability increase (Cherlin, 1979; Hoffman & Duncan, 1995). Women married to richer men are more likely to stay married to them.

Our second prediction is that increasing economic success of women will also make marriage less appealing. The increase in cohabitation without marriage began to soar in the 1970s at the same time that women began to gain financial autonomy and had less financial need to tie themselves to one man (Fisher, 1993). This pattern of female independence was visible in other statistics too. Although less than 10 percent of births are to college-educated single women, the numbers are rising. They climbed by 145 percent between 1980 and 2005, compared to a 60 percent increase in the birth rate for non-college-educated unmarried women. These women tend to be older than the typical single mother with 40 percent of them giving birth for the first time after the age of 30, as compared to 8 percent among all single mothers. There is a fairly typical pattern that emerges: these women had expected to marry, but when they had failed to find a suitable partner after reaching their thirties, they decided to go it alone.

As for divorce, the anthropological record attests to the fact that in societies where women have more economic power, the divorce rate is higher. In the Mayan peninsula, the Caribbean, New Guinea, southern Africa, Polynesia, Alaska, Brazil, and among North American native people, there is a consistently positive relationship between female autonomy and divorce (Fisher, 1993). Among the Yoruba of western Africa, women take principal responsibility for growing crops and selling them at an all-female market. The women have their own income and nearly half of marriages end in divorce.

The effect of a wife's income on her marriage depends on how much she earns. A study by Ono (1998) showed that divorce was more likely when the wife had no earnings than when she earned a small or moderate amount (up to $18,000). The extra money she contributes seems to stabilize the marriage. Her salary is not enough to live on independently, but may be enough to remove some of the economic stress that contributes to marital disruption. However when her earnings rise above $18,000 the odds of divorce increase significantly—in line with her ability to support herself independently. Here we see the "independence effect"— the probability of divorce rises as a woman's income matches and then exceeds that of her husband (Kalmijn, Loeve, & Manting, 2007; Sayer & Bianchi, 2000).

But is the independence effect really what it seems? Many studies of working wives do not distinguish between the effects of a woman's income and the time that she spends in the labor market. This time outside the home might work in two opposite ways. It might increase the likelihood of divorce either by decreasing the "quality" time that she might have invested in the marital relationship or by exposing her to the possibility of extramarital relationships. On the other hand, in this day and age both members of a couple expect the woman to contribute to the common pool of their resources (Buss, Shackelford, Kirkpatrick, & Larsen, 2001) so time spent working outside the home might decrease the likelihood of divorce.

To answer this, Jay Teachman (2010) used data from a national longitudinal survey to track women's marriages over a 25-year period. He examined a woman's income and the number of years she spent in paid employment. A wife who consistently earns more than her husband is significantly more likely to divorce than a woman who earns the same or less than her spouse, in line with the independence effect. And the cumulative time that a woman spends in the labor force, far from disrupting the marriage, seems to scaffold it. A wife's employment conforms to modern norms about parity between the sexes as well as providing fulfillment and a sense of self-worth for women.

Around the world, complementarity between husband and wife predicts marital stability. Marriage bonds are most stable when husband and wife jointly and equally contribute to supplying the family's needs (Quinlan & Quinlan, 2007). Where the man provides all or none of the subsistence, divorce becomes increasingly likely. There are two ways of looking at this. In a positive frame of mind we might view a happy marriage as the triumph of a man and a woman's cooperation and reciprocity. Less optimistically we might conclude that money buys independence. Perhaps people stay married when they have to—when the only way to get by is with the joint contribution of two partners. But achieving economic survival does not guarantee happiness.

The fight for control

Marriage and cohabitation demand compromise from both parties. Each partner has good reason to want the other to contribute a little more so they can contribute a little less. And each partner, now and again, has to lay down a marker for just how far they are willing to be exploited by the other. From time to time, matters come to a boil, abused is shouted, threats are made, and sometimes blows are struck.

Most accounts of aggression between intimate partners have focused on male perpetration and female victimization. For a long time it was widely held by feminists that society's patriarchal nature positively fostered a culture of "wife-beating": unilateral violence suffered by women at the hands of men (Dobash & Dobash, 1979). Evolutionary accounts of partner aggression used this contention as their starting point and therefore focused almost exclusively on explaining male violence towards female partners (Dobash, Dobash, Wilson, & Daly, 1992). As we have seen, this evolutionary argument was based heavily on the role of male sexual jealousy. Partner aggression, it was proposed, is a tactic for ensuring paternity (Daly, Wilson, & Weghorst, 1982; Wilson & Daly, 1996). Patriarchal societies condone male aggression, upholding the belief that a man has the right to control his own home. This leads to police and judicial reluctance to intervene in "domestic" disputes and allows male abuse of partners to go unchecked. In this view, women's aggression towards male partners is rare and, in cases where it does occur, is "almost always . . . in response to cues of imminent assault" (Dobash et al., 1992, p. 80).

It is certainly true that the majority of people who are killed or injured at the hands of an intimate partner are women (Archer, 2000; Daly & Wilson, 1988; Whitaker, Haileyesus, Swahn, & Saltzman, 2007) and that the majority of cases of intimate partner violence that reach a criminal court involve a female victim and a male defendant (Smith & Farole, 2009). Women sustain serious injuries as a result of the markedly greater size and strength of men and male-on-female violence represents a major public health concern. But is it true that societal norms encourage (or at least tolerate) men's aggression towards female partners? Is intimate partner aggression chiefly a male-perpetrated form of aggression?

There is little evidence that social norms support men's right to hit their wives. In the West at least, men's aggression towards a woman is seen as more reprehensible than aggression towards a man (Davidovic, Bell, Ferguson, Gorski, & Campbell, 2011; Felson & Feld, 2009). Third parties are more likely to call the police if they witness a man assaulting a woman than if a man is assaulting another man (Felson, Messner, & Hoskin, 1999). Within intimate partnerships, men's aggression towards a female partner is deemed more serious and more deserving of police intervention than women's aggression towards their male partner (Felson & Feld, 2009; Sorenson & Taylor, 2005). Men who assault their partners are more likely than their female counterparts to be convicted (Felson, 2008) and incarcerated (Smith & Farole, 2009). Women who assault male partners are disproportionately likely to avoid arrest (Felson & Pare, 2007) or criminal charges (Brown, 2004). Such findings strongly refute the argument that male aggression towards female partners is condoned, tolerated, and even encouraged by a patriarchal society (Felson, 2002). Indeed some have argued that, because women feel safe in the knowledge that men will not risk breaching social norms by retaliating, they are more likely to initiate assaults on their male partners (Fiebert & Gonzalez, 1997).

Is intimate partner violence a one-way street with women as the only victims? Research on controlling behavior in relationships reveals that men and women use controlling behaviors with equal frequency (Graham-Kevan & Archer, 2009), although the forms of control may differ (Felson & Outlaw, 2007). Furthermore, controlling behavior predicts partner-directed aggression equally well for both sexes (Graham-Kevan & Archer, 2009). The evidence therefore suggests that both sexes are motivated to control the behavior of a partner and aggression is a tactic used by both sexes.

The fact that women are more frequently injured than men might seem to suggest that aggressive acts are predominantly perpetrated by men. However, this conclusion equates acts with outcomes. Acts and outcomes are distinct concepts, although there is considerable disagreement on how desirable it is to measure one or the other (Archer, 2000; Dobash et al., 1992). Researchers interested in the impact of partner aggression focus more on outcomes than on acts: the same act (such as a punch) will have a different outcome depending on whether the perpetrator is male and the recipient female, or vice versa. However, researchers interested in the dynamics that precipitate aggression focus more on acts than on outcomes: if we ignore women's aggressive acts because they are less likely to cause serious injury than the same acts committed by a man, we will have a major omission in our understanding of intimate partner aggression.

The fact that women are more frequently injured by intimate partners than men therefore begs the question: Is it true that men use more aggressive acts towards partners than women do? In the West, the answer appears to be no. Self- and partner-report studies conducted in community samples show that women commit aggressive acts towards partners as often as men do, if not more often. A large-scale meta-analysis of act-based measures of partner aggression (Archer, 2000) found an effect of $d = -0.05$, a very small but statistically significant effect in the female direction. To examine if this might be a function of inflated self-reports by women or under-reporting by men, partners' reports were also examined. Although the sex difference favoring women on self-reports became non-significant when partner reports were used, it did not reverse in favor of men. More recent studies have also found either gender symmetry in aggression (Robertson & Murachver, 2007; Straus & Ramirez, 2007) or greater use of aggression by women (Thornton, Graham-Kevan, & Archer, 2010). The most common pattern of aggression between partners is one of mutuality and in at least half of cases of intimate partner violence where only one partner is aggressive, it is the woman (Langhinrichsen-Rohling, Neidig, & Thorn, 1995; Straus & Ramirez, 2007; Whitaker et al., 2007).

The argument that women's aggression is "almost always" motivated by self-defense (Dobash et al., 1992, p. 80) is not borne out by the data. In studies in which both partners are asked who initiated the attack, it is either more frequently the woman or there is no sex difference (Archer, 2002). Furthermore, Hettrich and O'Leary (2007) found that self-defense was one of the reasons most frequently cited by women as "*not* a cause" of their own aggression. Studies of college students have found no sex differences in the reporting of self-defense as a reason for aggression, although absolute rates vary widely between studies (Follingstad, Wright, Lloyd, & Sebastian, 1991; Harned, 2001).

The argument that women's aggression towards their partners is confined to "minor" acts while men dominate in more severe acts was also found to be false in a second meta-analysis by Archer (2002): there was no sex difference in the use of guns or knives to threaten or to attack a partner. Furthermore, although men were more likely than women to report choking, strangling, and beating up their partner, a substantial minority of those who committed these acts were women. And women were slightly more likely than men to report punching, biting, kicking, and slapping a partner. The sex differences in injury, therefore, are mainly attributable to physical differences between the sexes such as men's greater upper-body strength, rather than a sex difference in frequency or type of aggressive act (Archer, 2009). There are deplorable physical and psychological consequences of men's aggression to women (e.g., Felson & Pare, 2007). But for researchers trying to gain a fuller understanding of female aggression, or indeed intimate partner aggression as a whole, women's equality with their male partners in the frequency of intimate aggression presents a real explanatory challenge. How can we explain the disjunction between the very marked sex difference in same-sex aggression and its absence (or even reversal) in intimate partner violence?

Do men lower their aggression in the context of an intimate partnership, or do women raise theirs? Both of these shifts occur (Cross & Campbell, 2010; Cross, Tee, & Campbell, 2011). Given the same provocation, men report being less likely to aggress towards a partner than towards a friend of the same sex. However, this effect is not specific to intimate partners: men are unlikely to report using direct aggression towards a female target irrespective of whether she is a partner. This conclusion was confirmed in a further study which showed that men report stronger inhibitory control and weaker impulsion to violence against women (whether partners or friends) than against men (Davidovic et al., 2011). In laboratory settings also, men also inhibit their aggression to female targets relative to male targets (Taylor & Epstein, 1967), and in society at large men are more likely than women to be the victims of male criminals (Hall & Innes, 2010). Men appear to lower their aggression in the context of an intimate partnership, not because they are interacting with a partner, but because they are interacting with a *woman*.

Women, on the other hand, raise their aggression in the context of an intimate relationship (Cross et al., 2011). This poses a serious challenge to my explanation of sex differences in aggression which is predicated on women's lower threshold for experiencing fear. If women are adapted to place a premium on their own safety, why do they take the risk of attacking a male partner? Given male superiority in size and strength, such an attack is even more dangerous than attacking a woman—and women rarely attack other women.

If it is true that fear typically restrains women's aggression, then women's characteristic fear of men must be reduced somehow in the context of an intimate relationship. But why should this be? Fiebert and Gonzalez (1997) argue that women who strike their partners believe that they are not in danger of being struck in retaliation. In the United States, social norms proscribe male aggression towards women even in response to attack (Feld & Felson, 2008). But this would predict that women should raise their aggression levels towards *men in general* because norms proscribing male aggression towards women apply to all women—not just intimate partners. Yet women's aggression towards male acquaintances is lower than their aggression towards other women, as we would expect based upon women's fear of injury (Cross et al., 2011). There is something about women's intimate relationships specifically that makes their partners more likely to be the target of aggression. I believe that the emotional bond between intimate partners causes a reduction in women's fear that is specific to their partner, and that this fear reduction might be mediated by the hormone oxytocin.

As we have seen, oxytocin is a peptide hormone involved in giving birth and lactation. It also plays a role in sex and in the formation of pair bonds (Young & Wang, 2004). Mating is considerably more risky and costly for women than for men. In most species, the optimal mating rate for females is lower than that of males and "supernumerary" copulations increase a female's vulnerability to predation, injury, and disease transmission, as well as reducing her life expectancy (Chapman, Arnqvist, Bangham, & Rowe, 2003). We have seen that studies of sexually antagonistic co-evolution show that males in many species have evolved tactics, detrimental to female interests, which function to overcome female reluctance to copulate. In human females also, mating brings risks of coercive male violence, unwanted pregnancy, and infection (sexually transmitted diseases pass more easily from male to female than the reverse, Devincenzi et al., 1992). One in six women is raped during her lifetime in the United States. The more partners a woman has, the greater are the chances that one of them will turn out to be sexually aggressive (Franklin, 2010; McKibbin, Shackelford, Goetz, & Starratt, 2008). Women are sensitive to this threat: over half of women said they would fear being harmed if they were left alone in a bar with an opposite sex stranger, compared to fewer than 10 percent of men (Herold & Mewhinney, 1993). Furthermore, women experience greater disgust than men at the thought of "potentially fitness-reducing" sexual behaviors such as having sex with a stranger (Tybur, Lieberman, & Griskevicius, 2009). This suggests that, in order for a woman to enter a sexual relationship, a certain degree of fear or trepidation must be overcome.

Establishing an intimate relationship entails a partner-specific reduction in a woman's fearfulness (Campbell, 2008, 2010; Cross et al., 2011). Oxytocin reduces fear (Baumgartner, Heinrichs, Volanthen, Fischbacher, & Fehr, 2008). By reducing the normal apprehension associated with stranger interactions, it also enhances trusting behavior. This has been shown in studies of willingness to transfer money without a guarantee of return (Kosfeld, Heinrichs, Zak, Fischbacher, & Fehr, 2005) and in the sharing of confidential information (Mikolajczak, Pinon, Lane, de Timary, & Luminet, 2010). This decrease in fear and establishment of trust in a prospective male partner may set the stage for sexual intercourse which, as with parturition in which oxytocin is also implicated, constitutes an intimate and potentially painful breach of a woman's bodily integrity. In rodents, for example, estrous females are typically wary of a strange male and the release of oxytocin facilitates lordosis—the back-arching that permits intromission (Debiec, 2007; Pedersen & Boccia, 2006). In humans, oxytocin is also released during intercourse (Carmichael et al., 1987) and is associated with pair bonding and attachment (Edwards & Self, 2006). So the oxytocin-mediated reduction in fear that is responsible for trust and intimacy toward their partners, paradoxically increases women's readiness to express aggression toward them. A study by Ditzen and colleagues (2009) showed that administering a dose of oxytocin to couples, prior to a discussion about a topic that had caused conflict in the past, reduced their levels of the hormone cortisol associated with the body's stress response. This effect was slightly more pronounced in women than in men. Given that stress responses are negatively correlated with aggression in women (Verona & Kilmer, 2007), this suggests that oxytocin might facilitate women's aggression towards their partners. If fear usually holds women back from risky behavior, then ironically the reduction in fear that women need to enjoy sexual intimacy brings with it a greater readiness to strike out at their lovers.

All you need is love?

All this talk of marketplaces, bargaining, conflict, exploitation, and aggression may seem a rather cold-hearted approach to marriage. Given all the potential for disruption in relationships, what is the glue that holds a man and a woman together? The answer of course is love—a human universal (Jankowiak & Fischer, 1992). But for psychologists, this answer simply raises another question: What is love and where did it come from?

Current thinking in neuroendocrinology points us back toward oxytocin (Campbell, 2008, 2010). Researchers began to wonder if the same mechanisms that governed maternal love might also be involved in partner-preference. In mammalian species, the primary bond is between mother and offspring. This primitive and vital attachment is seen even in promiscuous species where little love is lost between adult males and females. It seemed reasonable to suppose that in some species pair bonding might have piggybacked on the same mechanism: it might have been "exapted" the basic system that governed mother–infant bonding—oxytocin.

Two closely related species provided a convenient natural experiment (see Young, Gobrogge, Liu, & Wang, 2011). The prairie vole shows a strong partner preference and biparental care in contrast to the promiscuous montane vole. Prairie voles are sociable and deeply monogamous creatures. Together they support one another and cooperate in raising their young. The male not only defends his mate against rival male intruders but prefers her over any other available female. If their mate is removed, 80 percent of them refuse to re-mate and spend their rest of their life alone. The bond is normally established at the time of mating and seems to involve two peptides that are especially relevant to females and males respectively: oxytocin and vasopressin. These peptides are remarkably similar in structure differing only in the position of two amino acids. The distribution of their receptors varies markedly across even closely related species but, wherever species share a marked behavioral characteristic such as monogamy, they have a very similar pattern of receptor distribution in the brain. Both peptides are manufactured in the limbic system and there is one important site that contains a high density of oxytocin receptors, the nucleus accumbens. The nucleus accumbens is part of the brain's pleasure circuit sensitive to the neurotransmitter dopamine and closely involved in wanting (motivation) and liking (reward).

Partner preference has been linked to increases in the release of dopamine in this same part of the brain where oxytocin is active. The co-action of oxytocin and dopamine appears to be critical for partner preference (Edwards & Self, 2006; Liu & Wang, 2003; Young & Wang, 2004). In the wild, a female vole copulates between 15 and 30 times in a 24-hour estrous period and the vaginal stimulation triggers the release of oxytocin. It seems likely that it is the presence of oxytocin together with the neurotransmitter dopamine that generates the pair bond (Gingrich, Liu, Cascio, Wang, & Insel, 2000). In monogamous species, blocking the uptake of dopamine after mating eradicates the female's partner preference and, by using chemicals which enhance dopamine's effects, experimenters can generate a preference for a male even without copulation. Conversely, oxytocin facilitates her preference for a familiar partner even without mating and an oxytocin antagonist, given before she mates, blocks the formation of a partner preference (Insel, Winslow, Wang, & Young, 1998). The promiscuous montane vole has very few oxytocin receptors in the nucleus accumbens and perhaps this is why they form no association between sexual pleasure (dopamine release) and their partner. For them, the two vital systems of pair bonding—pleasure and attachment—are uncoupled.

In the male prairie vole, our monogamous hero, administration of vasopressin, but not oxytocin, directly into the brain also induces pair bonding and male parental care without mating. The administration of an antagonist (that blocks the binding of the peptide) leads to a decrease in these behaviors even among males who have mated repeatedly with the female. In short, by artificially administering vasopressin it is possible to cause males to bond without sex and by blocking its action, to have sex without longer-term commitment. Scientists have discovered a long DNA sequence in the promoter region of the vasopressin receptor gene that seems to be important in determining when and where the gene is activated. Scientists created transgenic mice by inserting the genetic sequence that codes for the vasopressin receptor gene from a monogamous prairie vole into a polygynous and unsociable mouse (Young, Nilsen, Waymire, MacGregor, & Insel, 1999). The "monogamice," as they were christened, showed the same pattern of receptors in the brain as intact prairie voles and although they did not become magically monogamous, when given vasopressin, they did show a significant and atypical increase in interest and contact with the female.

Prairie voles are one thing, but does oxytocin work for humans too? Oxytocin levels have been reported to rise during genital stimulation, copulation, and orgasm (Carmichael et al., 1987; Uvnäs-Moberg, 1998). Viewing pictures of a romantic partner activates dopamine pathways that are also rich in oxytocin receptors (Bartels & Zeki, 2004; Fisher, Aron & Brown, 2006). Affectionate touch by a partner seems to increase oxytocin levels (Ditzen et al., 2007; Grewen, Girdler, Amico, & Light, 2005; Holt-Lunstad, Birmingham, & Light, 2008; Light, Grewen, & Amico, 2005; Shermer, 2004) but being massaged by a stranger does not (Turner, Altemus, Enos, Cooper, & McGuiness, 1999; Wilkstrom, Gunnarsson, & Nordin, 2003). During social interactions with a partner, oxytocin is higher during positive social behaviors such as acceptance of the other person, self-disclosure, and humor (Gouin et al., 2010). Some studies have examined short-term changes in oxytocin levels when people recall positive and negative experiences of romance. One study found a tendency for negative recollections to be associated with oxytocin reduction, although there was no effect for positive emotions (Turner et al., 1999). However, a later study by the same team (Turner et al., 2002, p. 269) concluded that oxytocin levels were not reliably altered by either positive or negative relationship memories and were probably "not functionally significant"—but then, thinking about someone is a very far cry from being lovingly caressed by them.

Other studies have taken a wide-angle view and examined the association between oxytocin and the quality of the long-term pair bond itself. And here there are diametrically opposed results. Based on animal findings, scientists expected that oxytocin levels would be high in individuals currently experiencing warm and satisfactory romantic partnerships. And indeed, Grewen et al. (2005)

found that individuals who reported a more supportive relationship with their partner had higher oxytocin levels throughout a series of three blood draws taken before, during, and after warm partner contact. Light et al. (2005) found that oxytocin was positively associated with reported frequency of partner hugs and massages.

But findings from other studies ran exactly counter to the hypothesis. Turner et al. (1999) found that higher basal levels of oxytocin were associated with greater self-reported interpersonal distress. In a study of postmenopausal women, there were consistently negative correlations between oxytocin levels and physically affectionate partner contact and relationship quality—the extent to which they could open up to their partners and were understood and appreciated by them (Taylor et al., 2006). Oxytocin was also negatively associated with the quality of other relationships and the frequency of social contacts generally. Another study confirmed this finding: women who reported poor relationships—who felt unsupported by their partners, were criticized by them, and felt under-appreciated—showed higher oxytocin levels (Taylor, Saphire-Bernstein, & Seeman, 2010). (Interestingly, among men, it was vasopressin that showed an association with relationship distress.)

Findings like these prompted Shelley Taylor (2006) to propose that elevated oxytocin levels act as a marker for gaps in relationships and trigger a search for affiliative contact. But it seems peculiar that high oxytocin could be associated on one hand with distress and isolation and on the other with affection and trust. Experientially, the two seem like polar opposites. Perhaps endogenous oxytocin is a marker of an individual's social motivation and sensitivity to positive social cues. (After all, oxytocin levels are often low in individuals suffering from autism, whose condition is associated with social withdrawal.) If so, individuals who are characteristically high in oxytocin (and therefore high in social motivation) should do fine when their social needs are met. But when relationships go badly, they may be especially distressed by it (Bartz, Zaki, Bolger, & Ochsner, 2011).

But it may be that the discordant results stem from the nature of oxytocin and how it is studied (Campbell, 2010). Oxytocin is manufactured in the hypothalamus of the brain but it then takes two distinct routes to affect emotion and behavior. The first is through the bloodstream where, like other hormones, it travels to remote sites in the body. When researchers take plasma samples, this is the oxytocin level they detect. But oxytocin also has effects within the brain itself. The only way to estimate these levels is by sampling cerebrospinal fluid and that means using lumbar puncture—not a comfortable experience at the best of times and few experimental participants would agree to it merely for the sake of research. To make matters worse, the two systems do not seem to be closely coordinated so measuring one tells us very little about the other. We can investigate these central "brain" effects—the effects psychologists are most interested in—by administering synthetic oxytocin and this has been done in the many studies which have shown increased trust, decreased fear, and a host of other prosocial effects. But such studies can only tell us which behaviors and emotions are altered by artificially increasing central oxytocin: they do not tell us what events cause central oxytocin to rise or fall. Microdialysis—the insertion of a catheter into the brain to record minute-to-minute changes in oxytocin levels—could reveal exactly what we want to know but I suspect that human volunteers would be hard to find. The conundrum of oxytocin's association with positive satisfying relationships (usually derived from experimental administration of central oxytocin) and with negative dissatisfying ones (usually derived from plasma studies) may be a result of relying on different circulatory systems. The coming years will tell us because research in oxytocin is burgeoning.

Is that all there is to love? Is it just a couple of interacting neurochemicals? Certainly not. Sex and love may go together like dopamine and oxytocin, but they are also dissociable. We can have enjoyable sex without love. We can feel unrequited love for someone whom we have never touched. Even when we finally track down all the chemical changes and neural circuits that underpin the experience of love, we will still face the great brain-mind problem: How can we reconcile the experience with the biological basis? How can exhilaration, obsessive thinking, self-sacrifice, adoration, and empathy arise from electric impulses, axon terminals, and neurotransmitters? Perhaps this is the biggest question and one that we will never fully answer.

But there is another question too. Why him? Why her? In a lifetime, a woman may have sex with several men but only one or two may have that indefinable quality that makes her fall hopelessly in love. Or she may carry a secret passion for a man who barely notices that she exists. What makes a man attractive to you, but not to me (and vice versa)? How can we explain differences between women in what they want in a man? Or the differences in the kind of men they attract? Women may have their species and sex in common, but each one is unique. How can evolution, with its emphasis on the universality of human nature, cope with the evident fact of our individuality? It is to this challenge that we now turn.

Chapter 8

Individual differences: The unique woman

Women are everywhere the same and yet everywhere different. How can we reconcile the idea that natural selection winnows down variability and hones in on an improved female phenotype (but never perfect—environments change, arms races are eternal) with the manifest evidence that each woman is unique? How can there be a universal female nature when every baby who is born carries her uniqueness not only in her finger prints but in her shyness, determination, or musical ability?

There can be few areas of evolutionary psychology that raise critics' hackles more than its apparent failure to acknowledge the manifest differences between people. And it has taken time for evolutionary psychologists to seriously address this issue. Their principal quest has been to describe the universal aspects of human behavior, to find the fundamental commonalities that typify our species. This task has been driven by the desire to challenge wholly environmental theories which argue that the human mind contains only the capacity for learning and little else. The tactical emphasis that has been placed upon a species-typical psychology has obscured consideration of individual as well as cultural differences. At a more pragmatic level, the emphasis upon human universals has also provided a bulwark against those who would use evolutionary premises to argue for innate racial differences. The greatest enemy of evolutionary psychologists is the ghost of social Darwinism. Some believe that opening the door to individual differences might also open it to group differences and to the exploitation of Darwinian theory for racist politics. Increasingly, however, evolutionary psychology is creating a broader sociobiological framework in which individual differences can be understood. The task has only just begun and, as we shall see, there are opposing positions and, to date, more theoretical speculation than corroborating data.

The principle from which all theorists start is that there is a single fundamental human design. The basic components of mind—memory, language acquisition, the ability to recover depth from a two-dimensional retinal image, the use of electrical and chemical signals to pass information along and between nerve cells—have the same fundamental architecture in each of us. When we speak of individual differences we speak of modifications to this blueprint, rather than differences in kind. Individuals may vary in their threshold of response to certain stimuli or in their sensitivity to certain neurotransmitters, but the modules of the brain are built and organized in much the same way for everyone. The difference between an extravert and an introvert does not depend upon them being born with a different kind of mind—though it may depend upon their being born with a different rate of synthesis or uptake of certain neurotransmitters. Brains have been built by millions of years of evolution and nobody supposes that natural selection operated on two distinct ancestral species—extraverts and introverts—converging by sheer chance to produce two brains that were indistinguishable except for a difference in their sociability.

The emergence of a unique never-to-be-replicated person is a result of genes and environments and their interaction with one another. To find our way through the tangled origins of individual differences in personality, let us begin with the most baffling question of all—why natural selection should have retained genetic differences in personality between different members of our species.

Explaining genetic variance in personality

There is no longer room for doubt that personality differences between people have a strong genetic basis. This has been clearly established by behavior geneticists over the last 30 years.

The two main methods they use are twin and adoption studies. In twin studies a trait, such as risk taking, is measured in both members of monozygotic (MZ) and dizygotic (DZ) twin pairs. Because identical twins share all their genes while non-identical pairs share only half, we would expect that, if genes have an effect on risk taking, monozygotes should be more similar than dizygotes. We have to qualify this prediction in two ways. First, because MZ twins are genetically identical they also share the same patterns of dominance (for each heterozygous allele) and epistasis (the interaction between genes at different loci). This is what geneticists mean when they say that they are matched for broad, as well as narrow sense, heritability. This means that, if risk taking depends on these non-additive sources of variance, they would be slightly more than twice as similar as dizygotes. The second critical assumption is that both types of twin share an equally similar environment. In other words, MZ twins are not treated more similarly than DZ twins. This has been the assumption that has been most strongly questioned by critics. Yet studies which have included measures of parental treatment find that similarly-treated MZ twins are no more alike in personality than are MZ twins whose parents make conscious efforts to raise them as distinctive individuals (Plomin, Asbury, & Dunn, 2001). Parents who mistakenly believe that their twins are MZ produce children who are no more similar than other DZ twins. MZ twins who are so physically similar that they are frequently mistaken for each other are not more psychologically similar than MZ twins who look less alike (Loehlin & Nichols, 1976). Perhaps most importantly, the similarity in personality traits between identical twins who have been reared apart is comparable to the degree of similarity found for MZ twins who have been raised in the same household. Raised as individuals (not as twins) by different sets of parents, their similar personalities cannot be the result of parents treating them more similarly because of their physical resemblance.

The second kind of study looks at early-adopted children. Here, for any given trait, the resemblance between a child and its biological mother can only be genetic. Any resemblance to the adoptive mother can only be environmental. This follows if we can be sure that there is no important effect of selective placement (Rowe, 1994). If a child were placed with an adoptive mother who was genetically similar to the biological mother, the child's phenotypic similarity to the adoptive mother would come not just from their shared environment but also from shared (but not commonly inherited) genes. Behavior geneticists can establish the extent of selective placement by computing the correlation between the biological and adoptive mother on the trait that they are examining in the child. This effect can then be statistically removed from their estimates. In practice, correlations that are found tend to be for social class and IQ—they do not present a serious threat to studies of personality traits since most traits do not vary along class lines. Convergence of results from different adoption studies with varying degrees of selective placement also increase confidence in the conclusions. (It is ironic that the "selective placement" objection to the findings of behavior genetic studies is often made by strong environmentalists who dispute the idea of a biological basis to personality. The fact that some agencies attempt a degree of selective placement is precisely because they implicitly accept the idea of a biological basis to the child's character.)

The most powerful quasi-experimental design blends these two methods by comparing identical and non-identical twins, some of whom have been raised together and some of whom have been separated and adopted at birth (Bouchard, Lykken, McGue, Segal, & Tellegen, 1990). Here the effects are unambiguous—if MZ twins are just as similar when raised apart as when raised together then there is clearly a powerful impact of genetics on the trait in question. For 18 scales measuring different facets of personality from an instrument called the California Personality Inventory, the average correlation between identical twins reared together is 0.49. The correlation between identical twins who have lived in different homes with different parents is 0.48.

The results from these different methods converge on the same general pattern. For traits such as extraversion and other personality factors, heritability accounts for approximately 50 percent of the phenotypic variance. Significant heritability has been found even for characteristics that have been assumed to be the indisputable products of rearing, such as social attitudes (Tesser, 1993), time spent watching television (Plomin et al., 1990), and divorce (McGue & Lykken, 1992).

Heritability is a measure of the amount of variance in the distribution of a trait that is explicable by genetic factors. Heritability is a *ratio* of the genetic variance to total phenotypic variance. It is not an absolute measure that holds true for all people at all times. Because genetic and environmental factors must always sum to 1.00, the ratio can fluctuate depending upon how much variability there is in the genes and in the environment. As environments become more similar for all members of a population, the environmental variance decreases and consequently the heritability estimate must increase. For example, as opportunities for success become more widely spread through a society, the heritability of "social success" will become larger. By the same logic, when individuals differ very little in the relevant genes governing a trait, the environmental component tends to increase.

The fact that personality traits show genetic variation is problematic for evolutionary psychology because, when a trait is essential for survival, it is under strong selection and goes to fixation. That is why most human morphological structures are universal. People who lacked the genes to build hearts, brains, or two legs simply did not survive to reproduce. It is impossible to perform a meaningful analysis of the genetic contribution to "leg building" precisely because there is virtually no variance that can be partitioned into genetic or environmental origin. Counter-intuitive though it seems, if such an analysis was attempted, it would show a heritability of near zero. People who have only one leg have overwhelmingly lost one through trauma rather than being born with only one. Those characteristics that are indispensable to a species, such as the ability to construct two legs, would appear to have no heritability. Yet nobody in their right mind would say that legs are not built by genetic instruction. To keep matters clear, it is helpful to make a distinction between "inherited" (genetically instructed species-typical attributes) and "heritable" (characteristics that vary between people where that variability is genetic in origin).

The issue that has sparked much debate among evolutionary psychologists is the explanation of such genetic heritability. If a particular value of a personality trait was optimal for survival and reproduction, then why is there not uniformity among all members of the species? Brain size and intelligence have grown dramatically during our evolutionary past so that, as a species, *Homo sapiens* is smarter than *Australopithecus*. (We may also be more or less extraverted as well—although we will probably never know how outgoing our foremothers were.) But the point is that we show genetic variability in intelligence today and always have. Why are we not identical in our intelligence, our willingness to take risks or in our levels of anxiety or aggression? There seem to be two possible answers. One is that individual differences are largely irrelevant to our reproductive success and survival. The other is that evolution actively selected for diversity because it was advantageous.

Inherited personality differences: Invisible to evolution?

However large individual differences may seem to our eyes when we interact with one another, they are quite minor in the grand scheme of things. They are reserved for small variations in sensitivity and preferences that lie at the margins of our fundamental human design. Individuals who differ too much in the basic blueprint of our species (such as lacking a liver or having a seriously deformed heart) would have rarely survived in our evolutionary past. The human mind has been compared to a car (Tooby & Cosmides, 1990b). Both are complex machines that are composed of many subparts that have to interact and function together as whole. Because all the parts have to coordinate with one another to work effectively, cars and brains have a "monomorphism of integrated functional design" (p. 27). Changing one component (e.g., fitting a radiator from a Jaguar into a Toyota) will cause the car to fail, but changing the color of the radiator from silver to black will have no important effect on the functioning. In the same way, the human brain cannot tolerate genetic mutations that radically alter one of its components (e.g., a short-term memory system that generates products that cannot be stored in long-term memory) but can function quite well if the genetic variation is so superficial that it does not affect the inter-dependence of the parts (a preference for opera rather than rock music). Tooby and Cosmides decompose the kinds of evolutionary and genetic changes that can occur into four types. The first is superficial variation (such as radiator color) which is analogous, as they see it, to personality differences. At a slightly more radical level comes limited functional variation: these are small incremental changes in a single part that either improves or degrades the overall performance. These are the kinds of small random mutations which provide the basic fodder of natural selection: improvements, by definition, increase the reproductive success of the individual and are retained but detrimental mutations tend to be selected out. (We shall return to the question of whether this kind of variation can adequately explain personality differences.) Third, there is disruptive variation: critical mutational change that causes the car to malfunction. Mutations that affect the synthesis of some proteins can be devastating. For example, PKU (phenylketonuria) results from an error in the production of an amino acid so that the affected individual cannot convert phenylalanine into tyrosine. Without intervention, this results in mental retardation. Finally, there is the (hypothetical) possibility of radical but coordinated functional variation. In this case, simultaneous major inter-related changes produce a whole new variety of functioning car. Often referred to as "hopeful monsters," these unlikely creatures have rarely been taken seriously even by Stephen Jay Gould who controversially questioned the gradualist view of evolution. Probability theory suggests the vanishingly small likelihood that a set of gene mutations, by chance, will be perfectly coordinated to produce an integrated design. It would be analogous to randomly selecting hundreds of car parts from a junk heap of different vehicles, putting them together and finding that the car actually worked.

In this "irrelevance" view of personality, extraverts and introverts do not differ in critical mental modules—they both acquire language using the same device and share a common sexual jealousy mechanism. Just as all humans have one stomach, one heart, and two lungs, so we all share the same basic architecture of the mind. However, no two stomachs are exactly the same size, nor do they produce identical amounts of acid. But this is mere superficial variation and as such it is simply too small a target for selection to hit. Selection can only act on organisms who vary in their survival and reproductive success— if being one standard deviation above or below the mean on extraversion has no discernible effect on either of these two outcomes then selection will not weed it out. So, just as having a larger-than-average stomach has no significant effect on survival, neither do minor fluctuations in personality. According to this theory, extraverts have not had more children than introverts in our evolutionary past and therefore the distinction between them is evolutionarily irrelevant. Charles Darwin himself subscribed to the idea that variability (polymorphism) indicated the irrelevance of a trait to natural selection: "The preservation of favorable variations and the rejection of injurious variations I call natural selection. Variations neither useful nor injurious would not be affected by natural selection and would be left a fluctuating element, as perhaps we see in the species we call polymorphic" (quoted in Majerus et al., 1996, p. 82).

Evolution is composed of two processes—selection and random genetic drift. We have spoken mainly of the former because this is the process that drives directional selection over time. But gene frequencies can also vary as a result of chance. When an individual dies before reproduction, they take their genes with them and this is as true when they die as a result of a chance effect (being struck by lightning) as when there is a genetic vulnerability (they are not resistant to flu). Chance deaths can cause fluctuations in allele frequency. Imagine a bag holding six white balls and six black balls (corresponding to two different alleles at a genetic locus). Put in your hand and randomly select six balls to go into the next generation of the game. You pull out four white and two black. The population is now reset at a new value for allelic diversity. Next time around, you select three white and three black; the population drifts back to equilibrium. (There is a chance that on second round you might have pulled out nothing but white balls—the white allele would have gone to fixation but as a result of chance not selection). The process is random and provides a continuous backdrop of genetic noise fluctuating up and down behind the directional force of natural selection. Random genetic drift is usually associated with characteristics that do not affect fitness. Levels of such neutral genetic variability—traits that neither increase nor decrease fitness—are larger in bigger populations. In a small population, mutations will not occur very often but when they do they will quickly go to fixation (all members of the population will inherit them) or be eliminated. In a bigger population, mutations will be more frequent but, because of the population size, it will take much longer for a new mutation to either spread through the whole population and become species-typical, or be eliminated completely (Majerus et al., 1996). This means that in large populations, such as human beings, many mutations are drifting toward either elimination or fixation at any one time. This might result in genetic variance in fitness-irrelevant traits.

Tooby and Cosmides (1990b) have offered their own explanation for the origin of these superficial individual differences. They believe that they are a side effect of selection for something quite different—disease immunity. They argue that it is only at the level of specific enzymatic pathways that qualitative differences between people appear. They believe that at this microbiological level of analysis, there are compelling advantages to genetic variability which hinge on the link between sexual reproduction and genetic polymorphism (Tooby, 1982). Why have sex? Many animals reproduce asexually and thrive. Sex has significant costs—a major one being that sex dilutes by half an organism's contribution to the next generation. But this latter factor becomes a positive virtue in Tooby and Cosmides' argument. Increasingly, biologists are finding that sexual reproduction has a significant although non-obvious benefit. The greatest threat to our species is disease. Disease-carrying micro-organisms survive as parasites on larger animals including humans and the two of us are in an antagonistic arms race. To survive, humans must evolve defenses against micro-organisms and in turn, microorganisms must counter-evolve ways around our defenses. But they have a very significant advantage over us—their generation time is short. This means that they can evolve at a far faster rate than we can. During a human lifetime, a pathogen has one million generations in which to find a way round our immune system (Tooby, 1982). Imagine a genetically identical human population from a pathogen's viewpoint. Once it has overcome one individual's defense, it has overcome everybody's. But sexual reproduction mixes genes from two genomes creating a unique individual which is a unique challenge to pathogens. Genes code for proteins—the environmental niche of the pathogen. The more alternative alleles that exist at different loci on the genome, the more unique is each individual and the harder is the pathogen's job. In this way, genetic variability is actively favored not because it is good for us (in any social sense) but because it is bad for pathogens. Enzymatic variability, coded in our genes, foils our smallest (and yet biggest) enemy.

For many years, a group of biologist called neutralists argued that this kind of variability was selectively neutral because, although the proteins look different structurally, many are actually functionally equivalent and therefore their variability is irrelevant. But this combination of functional equivalence and structural difference is precisely the most advantageous combination from a host's point of view. The proteins do the same job in our bodies and brains but are chemically distinct. Pathogens choose their micro-environments not according to their function, but according to their chemistry. Enzymatic variability gives us the twin advantages of disrupting the pathogen, while not disrupting the functioning of the body part that the enzymes control. As Tooby and Cosmides (1990b, p. 34) put it " . . . the resolution of this conflict is to produce variation which is significant from the point of view of the pathogen's life cycle, but superficial from the point of view of the ultimate functional design of the organ system." This analysis also throws light on the distribution of human genetic diversity. Eighty-five percent of human genetic variation occurs within groups, 8 percent occurs between nations, and 7 percent occurs between races. This is exactly what we would expect if the function of allelic diversity was protection from disease. We catch diseases from those with whom we come into daily contact and any protective device has to be geared to them—not to distant groups that we will never meet.

But what does this genetically based diversity of proteins have to do with personality? Tooby and Cosmides (1990b, p. 49) explain:

> Pathogens select for protein diversity introducing the maximum tolerable quantitative variation and noise into the human system . . . Given the intricate design complexity of the nervous system (as well as other organ systems), this protein variation gives rise to a wealth of quantitative variation in nearly every manifest feature of the psyche: Tastes, reflexes, perceptual abilities, talents, deficits, thresholds of activation, motor skills, verbal skills, activity level, abilities to remember different kinds of things, and so on—all vary from individual to individual in a quantitative way.

And just as there are differences in reflex speed, there are differences in anxiety, aggression, and risk taking. Personality is not disembodied and mystical.

It is genes that, via proteins, create receptors and neurotransmitter sensitivity. The production, uptake, and clearance in the synaptic cleft of neurotransmitters can result in different gradients of excitement seeking, fear, or contentment. Hormone production and target sensitivity can also affect our mental state—transiently and throughout our lives. But if the pathogen-resistance theory is right, these are by-products that carry no real significance in themselves. However pleasing we may find human diversity, whatever richness it brings to our social and emotional life, these are just bonuses that natural selection neither saw nor chose.

Inherited personality differences: Adaptive?

When natural selection selects for higher (or lower) values of a trait over generations so that whole populations become more intelligent or less selfish, we call it directional selection. It has been demonstrated in real time by observing finches on the Galapagos Islands (Grant, 1986). In 1977, the islands suffered a severe drought and the seeds, on which the finches depended for food, were scarce. The small soft seeds that the finches preferred were soon exhausted, and only the large tough seeds remained. To open these hard seeds, a deep strong beak was needed and those birds who, by chance, had these kind of beaks survived better than their shallow-beaked peers. The survivors passed the genetic trait of deep beaks to their offspring and, sure enough, the next generation showed an average beak depth that was significantly larger than in previous years.

But in addition to this kind of directional selection, there can be *balancing selection*. This occurs when both high and low values of a trait are favored at different times or places. Ultimately, the positive effects of the high and low values balance one another out across times and places, and the genes supporting both versions of the trait remain in the population. This too was shown in the Galapagos finches: in 1984, several years after the drought, there was unusually heavy rainfall which had exactly the reverse effect on available seeds. There were fewer hard seeds and many more small soft ones. Now the feeding circumstances favored the birds with shallower beaks and sure enough, they survived and reproduced more successfully than the deep-beaked birds. The population had re-balanced itself back to a new average beak depth.

In this example, the key variable driving the relative frequencies of the two types of beak was time (or at least micro-climate changes associated with different years). Environmental heterogeneity encompasses variations across place as well as time, and both have been argued to impact upon the genetic variation in human personality. Humans have been forced to adapt to rapidly changing ecological conditions. In Europe, there were unpredictable climate shifts: within a decade the temperature could fluctuate from glacial to warm and back again.

Equally unpredictable were the activities of volcanoes and earthquakes. Humans lived in environments ranging from warm forests to cold steppes. When times were harsh and food scarce, only the ingenuous and daring survived: in such a situation a risk-taking and adventurous personality might have been adaptive. At another time or place, the single biggest killer may have been disease. Here those who associated least with other people might have escaped contamination and fared better, resulting in selection for introversion. Individuals with a genotype that had greater ability to store fat may have had an advantage in times of famine but risked obesity in times of plenty (Bailey, 1998). Given thousands of such variable environments across evolutionary space and time, the optimal level of different traits has probably been at every conceivable value. The variability we see in the population today may be the result of these thousands of instances of varying selection pressure.

Other forces can have the same effect of retaining different levels of a trait (and the alleles that underlie them) in the gene pool. One of these is heterozygotic advantage. Suppose that there are two alleles (variants) of a given gene (let's call them A^1 and A^2). Neither one will go to fixation at the expense of the other if the best possible combination that an individual can inherit is one of each. So the frequencies at which the two alleles finally arrive depend upon the relative advantage that the heterozygote (A^1A^2) has over the homozygotes (A^1A^1 and A^2A^2). The classic example of balanced polymorphism in humans is sickle cell anemia. Most Europeans carry the two identical alleles for the normal oxygen-carrying hemoglobin gene. Their blood oxygen levels are healthy, but one negative side effect is that they are prone to malaria. Other individuals are also homozygous but for a mutant form of this gene—the sickle allele—that produce abnormal sickle-shaped red blood cells which are poor oxygen carriers and result in anemia. But for them, there is a positive side effect—their red blood cells are strongly resistant to malaria. In regions where malaria is common, the best possible combination is one each of the two alleles. Although it creates mild anemia, it protects the individual from malaria. When the heterozygote does better than either of the homozygotes (a situation called heterozygote advantage), the population remains polymorphic—it retains more than one form in the gene pool. Such polymorphisms would change only very slowly, reflecting the net balance of advantages and disadvantages. When the different forms are perfectly balanced in fitness, variability can be long-lasting and geographically widespread.

Another possible source of genetic differences is *negative frequency-dependent selection*. In this process, the fitness of a genotype is related to the proportion of others in the population who also carry it. The most often cited example is the case of Batesian mimicry. Some animals, notably butterflies, depend for their survival on mimicking related species that are toxic to predators. The success of the mimic strategy depends upon the relative frequencies of mimics and the "real things." When there are few mimics, predators are likely to meet the real thing on their first encounter with the prey and will henceforth avoid it—and of course the mimic who is indistinguishable from it. But as more and more mimics enter the population, the chances increase that the prey's first experience will be with a mimic who, lacking toxicity, will provide a tasty meal. The success of mimicry depends on a low ratio of mimics to models.

The same kind of dynamic can be responsible for the generation of new genotypes. Many birds form a search image of their prey (see Majerus et al., 1996). If the bird lives in an area where yellow snails are common, this will be incorporated into the search image and the bird will be on the lookout for yellow targets. If a mutation arises that makes a snail pink, it will be ignored by predatory birds and so the pink mutation will increase in frequency. But there is such a thing as too much success. Soon pink snails will be in the majority and yellow snails will be hard for the bird to find. At this point, the bird will alter its search image to pink, eventually removing the threat to yellow snails and allowing them to become more numerous. This process need not stop at only two varieties. As Majerus et al. (1996, p. 65) explain: "The simple balance between being common and eaten, or rare and ignored, will always favour new forms." The amount of variability around equilibrium depends upon how quickly the bird changes its search image. If the image is changed swiftly in response to even slight changes in yellow-pink frequency, there will be very little slack in the system, but if there is a longer latency to change, the balance of yellow and pink may be quite extreme at times. Although the swiftness of the correction factor may vary, frequency-dependent selection can maintain allelic diversity indefinitely.

Frequency-dependent selection may operate in our own species too. Left-handedness has been explained in this way. In combat, the right-handed majority automatically expect opponents also to attack with their right hand—they may be caught lethally off-guard by a left-handed attacker. So left-handers (and the genes for left-handedness) stay in the gene pool but never become the majority because, as they increase in numbers, they lose their advantage. Mealey (1995) provided another example in her analysis of primary psychopathy. This clinical label describes a syndrome including a deficit in the ability to experience empathy, a lack of guilt, a willingness to use others for their own ends, superficial charm, and low levels of fear. These individuals make their way through life, exploiting the goodwill of others—they con others into providing material goods, loyalty, and affection without feeling any need to reciprocate. They are social cheaters who take but fail to repay. This strategy can be extremely successful—they receive sex without commitment, money without work, shelter without rent, and friendship without emotional engagement. Before the victim realizes they have been conned, the psychopath is off in search of his next target. As a strategy, psychopathy can only work if it is used by a minority of the population. The proportion of psychopaths in a population reaches a stable level when their reproductive success matches those of the non-psychopaths. Suppose that 4 percent of the population is psychopathic (which is approximately correct) and they typically leave 4.8 children behind. As a subgroup of the population, their reproductive success is $0.4 \times 4.8 = 1.92$. Non-psychopaths represent 96 percent of the population and they typically have two children each ($0.96 \times 2 = 1.92$). The strategies are now in equilibrium because, all else being equal, each population subgroup leaves the same number of children. But such stability may not last. Too many psychopaths and the rest of the population start to alter its response to strangers. They become more wary, they hold back from generosity, they wait to see if this person can be trusted. The more wary they become, the lower the success of the cheater. If the number of children left behind by a psychopath drops from 4.8 to 2 (in line with the responsible non-exploitative citizenry), their reproductive success is only 0.8 and psychopathy becomes a less successful strategy than behaving responsibly. Psychopaths can only thrive in large populations where their anonymity and speedy exit can be guaranteed. It is hard to use this strategy successfully in a small, remote village because the first con trick will quickly result in a reputation that alerts others and there is nowhere to find a fresh stock of victims. And primary psychopathy does seem to have a strong biological component. Deficits have been identified in the functioning of the amygdala, the orbitofrontal cortex and the autonomic nervous system which makes them relatively fearless and poor at controlling impulses (Blair, Jones, Clark, & Smith, 1997; Raine, Lencz, Bihrle, LaCasse, & Colletti, 2000).

Female short- and long-term mating strategies (Gangestad & Simpson, 1990) may be another candidate for this kind of frequency-dependent selection (Buss & Greiling, 1999). Some women adopt a restricted sexual practice which enables them to evaluate the likelihood that the male will commit to long-term investment as a partner and parent. Others, who look for gene quality in their male partners rather than investment, will be prepared to have intercourse after only a short delay with attractive men. The dynamic that holds the strategies in equilibrium is their relative frequencies. As the number of unrestricted women rises so do the number of "sexy sons" that they produce and hence the value of selecting for good genes diminishes. But as the number of restricted women begins to rise in response, the competition amongst them increases and advantages begin to accrue to women who do not waste time and effort searching for providing fathers.

So far we have spoken of a finite number of competing and distinctive "strategies" such as mimicking a toxic species, being left- rather than right-handed, or being a psychopathic cheater rather than a reciprocal altruist. But everything we know about human personality tells us that it is not chunked into "categories" or "types" corresponding to discrete strategies. Personality is distributed along a continuum which we can vividly see in the ubiquitous normal curve. This is a problem because the strategy view of individual differences suggests that there is no adaptive value in looking a "bit" like a toxic prey or being "somewhat" left-handed. Could a continuously distributed trait such as extraversion or anxiety or conscientiousness really represent a distinct and adaptive strategy?

Before we consider this, bear in mind that the majority of our genes are homozygous—both parents supply the same alleles or gene version to the offspring. You and I share 99.9 percent of our genes (the same amount we also share with the "reference sequence" of the Human Genome Project). The 0.1 percent that makes us different from one another amounts to 3 million variants in the 3.2 billion base pairs that compose the genome (Wellcome Trust, 2001). For features or traits that are common to us all, both parents provide the same instructions at each genetic loci. But if extraversion and introversion were indeed two discrete strategies, they would require different alleles and would be polygenic—coded at many genetic loci. And sexual recombination creates a problem for maintaining the coordination of these multiple-allele complexes that need to travel together to create the two personality types. To get an extraverted individual, the whole suite of alleles and their activation must be passed intact to the offspring. When two different individuals mate (especially if one is an introvert and the other an extravert) the combinations will be broken apart, resulting in a mix of both types. This is likely what gives rise to the normal distribution that we associate with personality traits. If genes at each of 10 loci make an independent "choice" of activating or not, then the probability is that few individuals will switch on all 10 (extravert strategy) and equally few will switch on none (introvert strategy). A coin flipped 10 times will usually give about five heads and five tails creating a roughly normal distribution. This is in stark contrast to what we would expect to see if personality differences correspond to different strategic approaches: we should see a bimodal distribution with introverts and extraverts as two distinct types, clumped at the two ends of the personality continuum. There should be rather few individuals in the middle of the distribution (since there is no selective advantage in falling between two strategic stools). What we see is just the reverse. The normal distribution does seem remarkably ubiquitous—it is as true for personality as it is for height or weight. And it is clearly suggestive of additive genetic variance—a dosage effect of increasing numbers of relevant genes. Humans cannot be easily classified into a finite number of discrete types representing different strategies—rather we vary quantitatively and, to make matters worse, we do this on a whole range of personality dimensions simultaneously.

But there are mechanisms that could link the fate of multiple genes so that they are carried through generations together without being broken apart. This would create coordination between different behaviors that might look phenotypically like a trait. One is called linkage disequilibrium. It happens most often when particular combinations of alleles are especially advantageous. Imagine two genetic loci (A and B) each one segregating for two alleles. At each of these loci there are four possible allelic combinations that can be inherited: A_1B_1, A_1B_2, A_2B_1 and A_2B_2. If A_1B_1 and A_2B_2 (which, if real-world genetics were simpler, might be introversion and extraversion) are the fittest then there will be a selective advantage to these pairings that will keep their frequencies higher than the other alternatives. Linkage between genes depends on their physical location—linkage is more likely when the critical loci are close to one another on the same chromosome. This is because recombination is less likely to split them apart. Linkage disequilibrium has been shown in the butterfly *Papilio memnon*: it survives by mimicry and it can mimic one of two different species. To succeed it must resemble one of the two models in a variety of traits including color, morphology, and pattern. All the different genes that control similarity to one or other of the two species have to be passed on together because there is little to be gained by half mimicking one species and half mimicking another. In *P. memnon*, scientists have found a tightly-linked super-gene composed of six loci responsible for passing on intact the two alternative forms (Clarke & Sheppard, 1971).

Although the sheer number of genes that would have to be in linkage disequilibrium to generate the complexities of a human personality dimension are thought by some to be simply too great to withstand the forces of recombination (Tooby & Cosmides, 1990b), it might be the case that alteration to a single *switch gene* is all that is needed for us to see a whole suite of changes. Recall that the *SRY* gene on the Y chromosome switches on a series of biological events that cause production of high levels of testosterone and consequent masculinization. This hormonal change is manifested both morphologically (muscle strength, height) and psychologically (visuospatial ability, sex drive). Here a single gene has considerable power to alter the many components of the final phenotype. However, this is a rare example of a purely genetically controlled switch mechanism and, as we shall see later, a personality or strategy "switch" is more likely to be tripped by environmental and constitutional factors (Ellis, 2010). So with a personality trait such as extraversion, it is theoretically possible that a single gene controls the whole suite of its subsystems including sociability, impulsivity, and sensation seeking. In this case, individual differences in extraversion would arise because different experiences and circumstances trigger the switch point at different thresholds.

A related genetic mechanism that could potentially coordinate a range of related traits is *pleiotropy*—this is when a single gene has multiple phenotypic effects. When a selective breeding program was used to increase the tameness of a population of silver foxes, the researchers found that not only did the foxes become tamer across the generations but there were other unexpected changes in tail wagging, barking, and ovulation patterns in the females (Belyaev, 1979). It might have been the case that these different components of behavior were in linkage disequilibrium and all of them altered independently and simultaneously. However it seems that all the changes arose as a result of one thing: a reduction in adrenaline production. Foxes that were tamer (and hence were used in the breeding program) had lower levels of adrenaline, and adrenaline underpins a range of phenotypic traits associated with thresholds for fear and threat detection. Analogously in humans, research has found individual differences in a gene that is responsible for regulating serotonin levels. The *5-HTTLPR* gene codes for the serotonin transporter—this is a protein that clears serotonin from the synaptic cleft after transmission. There are at least two (and probably more) alleles of this gene: a short version and a long version. Serotonin controls emotional responses in the amygdala and the efficiency with which these are regulated by the prefrontal cortex, and individuals with the short allele show a stronger amygdala response to emotional faces than their long-gene peers (Munafo, Brown, & Hariri, 2008). But the effects can extend to seemingly disparate behaviors. Paradoxically, low serotonin function is associated with both aggression and depression. In the former case, individuals cannot exert sufficient prefrontal control over their angry approach behavior and, in the second, they cannot exert cortical control over their social disengagement (Carver, Johnson, & Joormann, 2008). Drugs such as Prozac® are serotonin reuptake inhibitors which make more serotonin available in the synaptic cleft. These drugs can be effective in treating the seemingly opposite emotional and behavioral syndromes of aggression and depression. If the root source of the problem lies with allelic variation in the *5-HTTLPR* gene, this is a nice example of downstream pleiotropic effects.

Explaining genetic differences in intelligence

I want to consider intelligence separately from personality for two reasons. Whether we believe that individual differences in personality are evolution-irrelevant noise or the result of their adaptive utility at different times and places, both viewpoints agree that the reproductive success of different personality constellations have *on average* been equal over the long evolutionary haul. Over hundreds of thousands of years, extraverts and introverts have not differed in their average reproductive output (although they might have differed at any one time or place in our evolutionary history). We can conclude that, while there are personality differences, there is no one "personality" that is inherently more adaptively successful than any other. But this is not true of intelligence and that makes it a very different proposition. As a species, being more intelligent carries an evolutionary advantage and so we have become cleverer over time. This means we need a different explanation of why individual differences in intelligence continue to persist. The second reason I want to consider intelligence separately is because I want to use it to challenge the massive modularity thesis described in the first chapter—the idea that minds are composed exclusively of a number of highly specialized problem-solving devices such as cheat detection and mate evaluation.

For clarity and simplicity, I will take "intelligence" to mean the capacity to generate effective (correct) solutions to never-before-encountered problems. Intelligence is related to, but separate from, the ability to learn from others (I will discuss this kind of social or cultural learning in Chapter 9). Humans are remarkably good at this kind of problem-solving intelligence and there is every reason to believe that it is part of our evolved architecture. The evolutionary ladder of ascent that brought us to this heady position has been called the Baldwin effect. On the bottom rung are the simplest organisms whose responses to environmental events are genetically programmed and inflexible. For example, sea anemones react to attempted predation by retracting their tentacles and then detaching from their underwater perch. For these hard-wired Darwinian creatures, a mistake (for example, a mutation that disrupts this "normal" response) means predation and death. When the earth was largely populated by such simple creatures, it created an evolutionary advantage for any creature that was capable of even a small degree of behavioral plasticity. This early plasticity was under the control of contingent rewards and punishers. For these Skinnerian creatures, actions that result in punishment are quickly extinguished and those that result in reward become more common. At the next level of the ladder are organisms with mental representational ability. They could imagine the future and by thinking off-line they did not have to enact a contemplated behavior to see its results. They could guess with high accuracy what would happen if they fell from a tall tree. Dennett (1995) called them Popperian creatures after Karl Popper who pointed out that this ability allows our hypotheses to die instead of us. This "new" form of organism, even with only the rudiments of an evolving representational system, held an evolutionary advantage over its peers and the chief advantage was increased behavioral flexibility. Building brains is costly and selection favors a net profit, so the advantages of representational thought for adaptive plasticity must have been great indeed. Human brains are three times bigger than those of *Australopithecus*, after adjusting for body size.

What caused this massive increase in cranial capacity? There are three main classes of theory. According to the first of these—the climatic argument—as *Homo* moved south and north away from the equator, they encountered increased seasonal variation which presented greater challenges in finding food sources throughout the year. At the same time, the climate was cooler which meant fewer parasites and so a decreased load on the immune system, releasing energy for brain expansion. Second, the ecological position argues that hunting (and some forms of foraging such as nut extraction) required intelligence in order to make and use tools. This enabled a high-protein meat diet that fuelled further brain growth in a positive feedback loop. Third, the social brain hypothesis argues that after humans had solved the basic problems of survival such as tool use for hunting, fire for cooking, and construction for shelter making, the primary source of selective pressure came from other humans. Because we became so successful at survival, there were more and more of us competing for resources. At the same time, war against rival groups supported within-group cooperation. There were advantages to a mind that could balance competition and cooperation in the social group. A mind that was capable of being both selfish and selfless—that could look after number one, yet still feel empathy and attachment to others.

A recent study pitted these explanations against one another (Bailey & Geary, 2009). Data were collected on 175 hominid crania dating from 1.9 million to 10,000 years ago and these were then correlated with measures designed to assess the three explanations. The climatic and ecological hypotheses suggest that the strongest predictors of variation in cranial capacity should be latitude, temperature, and parasite number. The social competition hypothesis suggests that population density should be the strongest predictor of increased brain size. The results showed that variations in temperature and climate did indeed explain much of the variation in brain size, but the major part of brain expansion was associated with population density suggesting that social competition was the main driver. However, the debate over the origins of the intelligence housed in our large crania is likely to continue (see Dunbar, 1992; Miller, 2000a; Mithen, 1996; Wills, 1995).

If greater intelligence meant that we were more effective at surviving and reproducing, there would have been a consistent directional selection for more of it. This is evident in the increase in brain size in hominins compared to apes. But if intelligence is so vital for our species, why do we not all have the same amount? Intelligence shows even more genetic heritability than personality traits. When measured at age 18, the proportion of variance attributable to genetic factors is 0.82 (Bouchard, 2004). Why do we continue to see genetic variation in intelligence? Why has it not gone to fixation at the highest possible value?

When we think of personality, it is easy to imagine that extraversion might be an advantage in some environments and a disadvantage in others. Similarly, it is easy to imagine that extraverts and introverts might on average survive and reproduce equally well and thus be invisible to selection. But intelligence appears to be the paradigm case of "more is better." It is almost impossible to think of a time or place where being more intelligent would be a handicap. Being smarter surely means that we are better at envisaging the future and avoiding dangers, solving survival problems and keeping our children safe. Even today with all our medical and social advances, every additional one-point increase in IQ is linked to a 1 percent reduction in the likelihood of death (Gottfredson, 2007). A one standard deviation advantage in IQ is associated with a 32 percent reduction in mortality (Batty et al., 2009). Selective neutrality and balancing selection, which seemed plausible explanations for individual differences in personality, do not look like good candidates for explaining differences in intelligence.

But Penke, Dennison, and Miller (2007) have made an intriguing and very plausible suggestion: mutation–selection balance. Despite much debate about the number of different kinds of intelligence, most researchers acknowledge the existence of the g factor. When individuals are given a large battery of tests assessing different kinds of intelligence, there is a strong first factor (sometimes called the positive manifold) which results from the positive correlation between all the different kinds of tests. This g factor is polygenic (the product of many genetic loci) and the more loci that are involved, the more easily the system is disrupted by mutations. A useful way to think about how mutation–selection balance might compromise intelligence is the watershed model. Imagine small creeks up in a hillside joining together as they run downhill to create streams, and imagine these streams joining to create rivers that flow into deltas and ultimately the sea. The sea is the phenotype—the end point of intelligence that we see in g and can detect as we interact with people. The tiny creeks at the top of the hillside might correspond to micro-level processes necessary for intelligence, such as neurotransmitter efficiency in the frontal cortex. Their efficiency feeds down into streams that enable good working memory capacity. (This is the ability to hold several facts in mind simultaneously when solving a problem. Try this for example: Is it true that "All Greeks are mortal" if we know it is true that "All men are mortal" and "All Greeks are men"?) This stream of working memory capacity flows into rivers of executive cognitive processes such as attention switching and focusing which we recognize as the chief components of intelligence. Now imagine that mutations arise in the system—and they do. Conservatively, each of us carries about 500 harmful mutations, some of which we inherited from our parents and some of which are ours alone. Mutations occur randomly throughout the genome and the more genetic loci that are involved in a trait, the more vulnerable it is to disruption. An upstream mutation in a small neurotransmitter "creek" will have downstream phenotypic effects on overall cognitive ability. In any population, deleterious mutations are eventually winnowed out by selection. But selection cannot act sufficiently fast to balance out the arrival of new mutations and this is especially true for complex polygenic traits such as intelligence. Selection cannot keep up. So at any given time, humans are subject to a mutation load that has not yet been eliminated.

If this is so, then intelligence is a fitness indicator: it tells us that the brain systems that govern it are relatively free of mutations. This means that it could be a signal of quality that we detect in prospective mates. And indeed intelligence is a trait that is reliably sought in prospective mates, although there is no such consistent preference for personality traits (Figueredo, Sefcek, & Jones, 2006; Miller, 2000b). Because intelligence is so highly valued, clever people are in a strong position to choose the best mates and they tend to choose other intelligent people like themselves resulting in assortative mating for intelligence. This is less true for personality. Intelligence is special.

Intelligence and modularity: Dual-process theory

If intelligence is the capacity to solve never-before encountered problems, humans are remarkably good at it. But, for evolutionary psychologists, where does this intelligence reside? Recall the original tenet of evolutionary psychology laid down in Chapter 1: the mind is a collection of domain-specific modules each of which has been shaped by natural selection to solve a specific problem such as mate retention, mind reading, or communication. The rationale for modularity was straightforward and persuasive: a general-purpose computational device is *too* general. A domain-specific module can respond immediately and automatically to dedicated inputs. Face recognition, jealousy, depth perception, theory of mind are all triggered by specific perceptions and can quickly orchestrate behavior in the correct direction. But a general device has no means of solving the "frame" problem: it has no heuristic to help it locate the relevant factors that might provide a solution to the novel problem. As Tooby and Cosmides (1992, p. 104) explain it, "At the limit of perfect generality, a problem-solving system can know nothing except that which is always true of every situation in any conceivable universe and, therefore, can apply no techniques except those that are applicable to all imaginable situations. In short, it has abandoned virtually anything that could lead to a solution." Imagine that a furious man is running toward you brandishing a weapon. What factors might be relevant in deciding what to do next? Is the weather important? Does his clothing make a difference? Is this a good time to investigate his mate potential? By the time a general problem-solving brain had answered these questions, you would probably be injured or dead. Efficiency was the chief argument for modularity.

But how can a collection of specific modules explain our intelligence? Some evolutionary psychologists maintain that the mind is nothing more than a collection of specialized modules that are capable of interacting with one another (e.g., Sperber, 2002). The nature of this interaction remains elusive, although Pinker (2010) has suggested that metaphorical abstraction can create linkages between domains (for example, a barber not cutting a man's hair short enough might remind him of his wife not cooking his steak long enough). But this leaves unanswered the question of which part of our mind "sees" the metaphorical connection. And sustaining the massive modularity argument often requires softening the concept of modularity to the point that it can seem almost meaningless (Kurzban & Clark Barrett, 2006). In fact, in their original manifesto for evolutionary psychology, Tooby and Cosmides (1992) did not completely dismiss a role for a general-purpose mechanism and, despite their predilection for domain-specific modules, they continue to do so ("There seems little doubt that the evolved architecture of the mind contains some inferential systems that are (relatively) content-free and domain-general," Ermer, Guerin, Cosmides, Tooby, & Miller, 2006, p. 197).

Enter dual-process theory (Evans, 2008; Lieberman, 2003; Stanovich, 2004). This theory emerged almost simultaneously from a range of psychology subdisciplines and it views the mind as having two communicating systems. The first lower-level system (System 1) is composed of specialized modules that deal automatically and unconsciously with stimuli that have been present throughout evolutionary time and for which natural selection has crafted a dedicated set of neural pathways. These include capabilities that are universal and develop naturally in response to a normal environment. Children develop language with a speed and efficiency that strongly suggests a dedicated module and, as adults, the production of language appears effortless. When we start a sentence we often have no idea of the exact words that will end it, but nonetheless we create correctly formed grammatical sentences. When we speak, we do not think about the act of speaking—the sentence formulation happens automatically as we focus on the meaning of what we want to convey. Another example is mind reading. By the age of four, typically-developing children everywhere have developed this ability: they know that the behavior of another person is dependent on what that person believes and wants, and they know that these beliefs and desires can be different from their own. It is this ability that allows children to engage in pretend play which requires simulating another's mental state in order to predict their likely behavior. These System 1 processes are encapsulated in that they are protected from penetration by other parts of the mind. For example, we see the world in three dimensions whether we choose to or not—we cannot "decide" to stop seeing it that way. We cannot "switch off" understanding what another person is saying when we hear them speak (as long as they are speaking our language). System 1 processes are not accessible to consciousness which means we cannot introspect or interrogate them about how they work. When I ask what your mother's maiden name is, the name simply pops into your consciousness but you cannot describe the process by which it arrived there. We have access to the products of the System 1, but not to its processes. This lower-level system contains modules that have naturally evolved to respond automatically to recurrent evolutionary challenges such as attraction to prospective mates, interpersonal communication, and threat. Often the product that is generated is emotional or affective; a feeling of hate or attraction or disgust or empathy. These involve ancient brain structures that we share with other animals including the amygdala, basal ganglia, and lateral temporal cortex. It also contains over-learned and automated knowledge acquired in a person's own lifetime. That is why we are able to walk, talk, drive a car, or type our name seemingly without even engaging our brain. Here ancient brain structures controlling automatic motor behavior are involved, such as the cerebellum, cingulate motor area, and putamen.

System 2 sits atop the lower level system and deals with the products of System 1. System 2 processes are effortful, conscious, slower, and sequential because the system has limited capacity. When we are asked to solve a problem ("What is the fastest route from here to the nearest garage?") we make use of memories and spatial representations which are outputs from System 1, but it is System 2 that manipulates the information, compares different solutions, and decides on the answer. When System 2 is operating, we are conscious that we are "thinking" such as when we are doing a crossword or solving an algebra problem. We are often conscious also of the limited capacity of the system and sometimes we try to circumvent it by writing down the steps of our thinking or "remembering" them on our fingers. Our attention is focused and we try to increase the system's capacity by ignoring extraneous information that could distract us. These processes are managed by the prefrontal cortex, anterior cingulate cortex, and medial temporal lobes which are involved in explicit learning and executive control.

To contrast the two systems, consider how humans catch a ball (Gigerenzer & Brighton, 2009). It might seem that a sophisticated mathematical calculation is taking place with System 2 attempting to predict the ball's trajectory by estimating and weighting its initial distance, velocity, angle, and air resistance. (Perhaps some physicists do this in their spare time as a form of intellectual amusement for System 2.) In fact, System 1 knows that such arcane calculations can be ignored as long as we fix our eye on the ball when it is high in the air and adjust our running speed so that the angle of gaze remains constant. This simple heuristic is used by predators for catching prey and by dogs catching a frisbee. For much of the time, we do not need to employ the full logical panoply of System 2. We need to make "good-enough" decisions rather than perfectly-analyzed ones. There is a tendency to caricature System 2 as the "clever" one but this may not always be correct. True, it is System 2 that inhibits us from eating that extra chocolate bar that our System 1 wants us to consume. But sometimes System 2 can become too bossy: an anorexic girl listens too much to System 2 ("Control yourself, resist your desire to eat, ignore that hunger") when it is System 1 that is righteously struggling to keep her on the path of survival.

Dual-process theories propose that System 1 is universal: all normally-developing humans develop these competencies. Even individuals with very low IQ acquire language and experience context-appropriate emotions. It takes a pathology, such as autism, to selectively disrupt System 1's ability to understand the beliefs and emotions of others. While System 1 can be thought of as species-typical, System 2 has a strong genetic component and shows heritable individual differences. There is much evidence that intelligence is strongly linked to working memory capacity that forms the platform for executive function—the ability to control and direct thinking in the service of problem solving (Colom, Rebello, Palacios, Juan-Espinosa, & Kyllonen, 2004). Indeed, some argue that intelligence *is* working memory capacity. Working memory allows us to hold many different pieces of information in our mind so that we can manipulate them in different ways and compare different potential solutions. Bigger working memory capacity means we have more information to play with. (If you want to engage your working memory and executive function, solve this problem. I pay $1.10 for a bat and a ball. The bat costs $1 more than the ball. How much was the ball? The answer is 5 cents but most of us try and then reject the incorrect solution of 10 cents. During this time, your working memory is holding the initial parameters of the problem, while your executive function is generating solutions and then deciding between them. If you found that problem too easy, you would find it much harder if you had to count back from one hundred in 3s while you were doing it. That is because you working memory capacity is limited.)

Dual-process theory and facultative adaptation

In response to novel problems, System 2 allows the human brain to generate and choose between solutions. Humans are extraordinarily ingenious strategists as a study by David Buss (1988a) shows. He was curious to know what tactics people employ to retain their partners and to prevent them from seeking new relationships with others. He decided the obvious first step was to ask them. He distributed questionnaires to 105 undergraduate students asking them to list up to five specific behaviors that men and women could use to retain their partners. After eliminating duplicated answers, he was still left with 104 different tactics that he classified as acts either directed toward one's mate or toward one's prospective rival. The first group were further subdivided into direct guarding (e.g., concealing mates from friends, monopolizing their time), negative inducements (e.g., threatening one's own infidelity or punishing their partner's, derogating competitors), and positive inducements (e.g., enhancing one's appearance, displaying resources). Tactics directed at rivals were broken down into public signals of ownership (e.g., possessive ornamentation, verbal signals of possession) and negative inducements (e.g., derogation of mate to rivals, threats of violence).

What is remarkable is the sheer variety of tactics used. When we look at the range of alternative strategies used by other animal species, we often find only two or three. For example, among one species of sunfish, males come in three types; "parentals" (large males who spend time courting the female and defending the nest), "sneakers" (who are smaller), and "mimics" (who resemble the female). The latter two stealthily fertilize the females' eggs while the parental males are spawning (Wilson, 1994). The strategy adopted probably relates to the environment the sunfish experienced during early development and, once set on a particular life history strategy, they remain on it. But among Buss' undergraduates there were in excess of a hundred different alternative strategies for mate guarding. These undergraduates were able to produce these various conditional tactics without undergoing any of the physiological change associated with actual jealousy. Evolutionary psychologists write much about "facultative strategies" and "behavioral flexibility" but we need to take a closer look at what they mean by these terms.

When used to describe animal behavior, conditional strategies are often described as a set of "If . . . then" rules. Question: Should I fight or flee? Answer: If the antagonist is large, then withdraw. If the antagonist has already been beaten by you (or another animal that you have beaten), fight. This algorithm does not explicitly address the origins of these rules because the implication is that they have been placed there by the process of natural selection. This kind of analysis does a reasonable job of explaining simple reflex phenomenon like why gulls will peck at a beak-like shape with a red dot on it but not at a beak lacking such a dot.

Sometimes the presumption that conditional rules are automatically available (i.e., hard-wired) is applied to humans also. In a famous analogy, Tooby and Cosmides (1992) describe a jukebox armed with navigational equipment that is programmed to play certain records as a function of its location, time, and date. Although each jukebox in the world might be playing a different tune, there is a fundamental lawfulness that determines which one it is. Here we have human strategy choice conceived of as a set of universal rules that are both situational-sensitive and "given." For Tooby and Cosmides, the tricky issue is how humans actually read the navigation device: in other words, how humans recognize a different situation as equivalent (and deploy the same strategy) or as distinct (requiring a different strategy). The strategy needed to find a mate is obviously different from the one needed to find food. Tooby and Cosmides argue that current psychological theories will "have to be replaced with theories positing a far more elaborate motivational architecture, equipped with an extensive set of evolved information-processing algorithms that are contingently sensitive to a *long list of situational contents and contexts*" (Tooby & Cosmides, 1992, p. 99). This seems to be an unwieldy solution and one that grossly underestimates human flexibility and intelligence.

Dual-process theory offers a plausible and economic alternative, and one that can explain commonalities and differences between individuals. First let us look at System 1. The brain needs a guidance system that detects a problem and knows when a correct solution has been reached. In humans, the automatic emotions housed in System 1 alert us to a problem situation. Jealousy indicates potential mate loss, anger indicates competition, lust indicates the need for sexual activity. System 1 also tells us when a solution has been found. Food satisfies and removes hunger, sex satisfies and removes lust, aggression ends anger and removes competition. The organism needs to define an adaptive target and it needs a "guidance system" that recognizes when the target has been met. It is this guidance system that has been constructed by evolution:

> In order to perform tasks successfully more often than chance, the architecture must be able to discriminate successful performance from unsuccessful performance. Because a domain general architecture by definition has no built in content specific rules for judging what counts as error or success on different tasks, it must have a general rule . . . The only unifying element in discriminating success from failure is whether an act promotes

fitness (design-propagation). But the relative fitness contribution of a given decision cannot be used a criterion for learning and making choices because it is inherently un-observable by the individual . . . Consequently our evolved psychological architecture needs substantial built-in content-specific structure to discriminate adaptive success from failure. (Tooby & Cosmides, 1992, pp. 102, 111)

Evolution has provided us with a cue that a problem needs to be solved and mechanisms for knowing when that end point has been achieved. These are System 1 processes and they are universal.

But System 2 offers a much more elegant description of human inventiveness in linking problems to solutions than does massive modularity. It explains how a sample of young Americans can generate 104 different ways to retain their mate. Humans can run thought experiments. Systems 2's intelligence allows us to manipulate representations of the external world inside our heads so that we can compare and evaluate the likely outcomes of different solutions. With sufficient working memory, we can project forward into several multi-move futures ("If I say X, he will say Y, but then I will tell him Z . . . ") and choose between them. More intelligence means more solutions and more cognitive space to evaluate them. It may also mean a weaker reliance on automatic responses. As an example, imagine a quarrel with a partner. As they provoke us more and more, we feel anger (an emotional product from System 1). System 1 also contains evolutionarily ancient, over-learned, and automatic behaviors such as lashing out at them. System 2 in the frontal cortex has inhibitory ability to suppress these prepotent responses, as well as to generate alternative solutions. System 2 output tells us to remain silent and look dejected. Our partner stops ranting and apologizes for upsetting us. System 1 is satisfied (the opponent has backed down) and emotionally signals this via decreased anger. We may be creatures of emotion but we are also creatures of creative intelligence. The solutions we find to problems are as varied as our imaginative intelligence. Emotions are a compass but intelligence creates the paths. As Symons (1992, pp. 138–139) puts it: "Human behavior is flexible, of course, but this flexibility is of means, not ends, and the basic experiential goals that motivate humans are both inflexible and specific . . . these (psychological) mechanisms merely make possible novel behavioural means to the same old specific ends."

This viewpoint allows for a rapprochement between evolutionary psychologists and behavioral ecologists (see Chapter 1). Behavioral ecologists study hunter-gatherer societies in terms of how their everyday practices solve problems presented by their ecological niche. Although ecologists remain silent on the psychological mechanisms by which they achieve this, the implication is clearly that some general problem-solving capacity is involved. Evolutionary psychologists who accept the massive modularity thesis disagree but they have failed to offer any satisfactory account of how humans have adapted swiftly and successfully to such a range of ecological niches. A System 2 problem-solver under the guidance of a System 1 problem-detector and solution-acceptor creates a common territory for debate.

But there remains yet another area of dispute: whether the goal of fitness maximization is built in to the human mind. Behavioral ecologists attribute to humans the ability to devise strategies that result in increased inclusive fitness. Many of their studies are aimed at showing that a particular strategy (polyandry, cannibalism) is adaptive in the sense of increasing the number of descendants of those that practice it. The question is whether this outcome was foreseen by the individuals who chose the strategy. For evolutionary psychologists the answer is no. Whether a behavior is adaptive can only be inferred retrospectively after many generations. Natural and sexual selection decide this in the currency of reproductive success. For evolutionary psychologists, evolution does not create a human ability to prospectively maximize fitness. (If it did, why is contraception so widely used?) Rather it selects for proximate psychological mechanisms that underlie problem-solving behavior. Systems 1 and 2 working together over evolutionary time might create such a mechanism. A solution that satisfies System 1 does so by evoking emotional and neural reactions that have become associated, via evolutionary processes, with adaptive choices: satiety after hunger or safety after danger. These experiences feel good because natural selection has made sure they do, not because we consciously seek to be a reproductively successful organism.

Genes and their environment

We all accept the truism that the nature-or-nurture debate is misguided, and that genes and environment "interact" to produce behavior. Yet the idea of a two-way street between genes and environments has a way of appearing mystical (or at least grossly underspecified) until we understand a little about how such mutual effects might be physically realized.

Genes have two major functions. The first is self-duplication, through meiosis and mitosis. The second function of DNA is the transcription of the genetic code. This code, held in the 23 chromosomes of each cell of our bodies, is translated into messenger RNA which moves from the cell nucleus to the cell body, where it is translated by ribosomes into amino acid sequences that are the building blocks of proteins and enzymes. These are called structural genes and their activity is largely unaffected by the environment. These are the genes that we most easily come to mind—the Mendelian structures that give us blue eyes or long legs.

But most genes are of another type: they are regulator genes that code for products that can bind with DNA and so control the action of other genes. Regulator genes are able to interface with the environment. An early description of how such an effect could occur won the Nobel Prize (see Plomin, 1994). The single-celled bacterium *Escherichia coli* depends upon lactose for nutrition and so it needs to be able to digest it. Next to the structural gene that codes for the enzyme that the bacterium needs to metabolize lactose is an operon which switches the gene off and on. But how does the operon "know" when the lactose-metabolizing gene should be activated? Far away on the genome, there is a regulator gene that produces an amino acid product—a repressor—that is able to bind both to the operon and to lactose. When there is no lactose available to consume, the repressor binds to the operon and, in doing so, switches it off. When lactose is present, the repressor binds to the lactose instead and this turns the operon on. In this way, the gene which enables lactose metabolism is only activated when lactose is present. Here, the internal environment controls gene expression.

In the human brain, genes are responsive to the external as well as the internal environment. Communication in the brain occurs chiefly between neurons but neuronal activity itself depends upon information obtained from the outside world (via the retina, for example) which is coded into the internal language of the brain. Neuronal cells carry incoming information electrically from their dendrites (which pick up as many as 150,000 inputs from adjoining cells) to the cell body which synthesizes their output and sends further electrical signals along the axon to form part of the incoming information to their neighboring cell. Between adjacent cells, chemical messengers—neurotransmitters—convey the information across the synaptic cleft. And these neurotransmitters can communicate with the very nucleus of the cell, the home of the genes. The neurotransmitter locks on to a receptor on the cell membrane and this alerts second messengers within the cell which communicate with intermediate switching proteins that are able to penetrate the cell nucleus. Inside the nucleus, they communicate with transcription factors that control the expression of regulator genes. These regulator genes are responsible for managing the sensitivity of receptors and the production of enzymes which create neurotransmitters (Comb, Hyman, & Goodman, 1987). Hormones have an even simpler route because they themselves are transcription factors that can operate directly on the genes.

Earlier we noted that males and females differ because the Y chromosome carries a genetic switch that shunts development down a male pathway. In the absence of the Y chromosome or if the *SRY* gene is not activated, the fetus develops as a female. In this case, the switch is a gene donated in the father's sperm to the offspring. But in other animals, the switch that canalizes sexual development can be the ambient external temperature or the prevailing sex ratio—variables that exist unambiguously beyond the organism. All an animal needs is the ability to "read" the correct external signals that activate the switch. As a species, we do not determine our sex this way but that does not preclude the possibility that sources of variability between individuals may work just like this (Wilson, 1994). The activation or deactivation of a variety of genes as a result of experience could create differences between people who began life with exactly the same genome.

Take post-traumatic stress disorder (PTSD), a condition that has been studied extensively in war veterans. For all of us, fear-provoking situations cause increases in norepinephrine (noradrenaline) implicated in processing threatening stimuli and linked to the activation of the "fight-or-flight" response of the sympathetic nervous system. Under stress, neurons in the norepinephrinergic pathways of the brain fire up to 10 times faster than their resting rate resulting in a massive increase in norepinephrine—synthesis of the transmitter is increased and enzymes that break it down work harder to free the synapse from the excess. And the effect is also felt by the genes contained in the nucleus of the brain cells. The c-Fos gene is switched on, coding for DNA transcription factors whose job it is to regulate the future behavior of receptors, enzymes, and proteins. In PTSD, persistent and repeated exposure to highly stressful events causes sensitization of the stress response system via the c-Fos gene. Hormones that synthesize norepinephrine are increased, resulting in a greater availability of the neurotransmitter. Baseline firing rates are ratcheted up to a new higher level, while post-synaptic receptors reduce their numbers in an attempt to keep a lid on the system. Threats that would previously have been tolerated now trigger a massive over-response in the fight-or-flight system (Niehoff, 1999; Post, 1992). Examples like this show how experience can dramatically affect the expression or suppression of gene products. We are, among other things, highly responsive biological machines.

Gene–environment interactions

Individual differences are as ubiquitous and enigmatic in the field of health as they are in personality. Admonished about the cardiovascular dangers of tobacco, smokers will point to an apocryphal relative who smoked 60 a day throughout their adult life and died peacefully in their sleep. Despite a pragmatic tendency to exaggeration, these stories are sometimes true. Recent studies have shown that smokers develop coronary heart disease (or not) depending on their genotype with respect to lipoprotein lipase. Those who carry the "high-risk" allele have a 10-fold increased chance of contracting coronary disease—but only if they smoke (Talmud, 2004). Similarly the likelihood of developing psychotic symptoms following youthful cannabis use depends upon having a particular variant of a polymorphic gene (*AKT1*, Di Forte et al., 2012).

This is the territory of gene–environment interactions: the effects of the environment on an outcome depend upon a person's genotype. Some of us are more susceptible to psychological damage from environmental perturbations than others. One way to examine this uses the logic of adoptive twin studies. This was done in the case of depression. The highest purely genetic risk is for MZ twins in which both have the disorder. The lowest genetic risk is for a healthy MZ twin whose co-twin has had depression because, despite shared genes, they have escaped the disorder. In between these extremes are DZ twins. Comparisons showed that in response to a negative life event, the probability of having a depressive response was greatest for those with the highest genetic liability. At least part of the vulnerability to depression following traumatic life events is genetic (Kendler, 1998). Using this method, the same results have been found for the likelihood of becoming seriously antisocial following childhood maltreatment (Jaffee et al., 2005).

But this finding was augmented by a remarkable molecular analysis. Avshalom Caspi's research team found that whether or not childhood maltreatment resulted in later antisocial behavior depended on which version of a particular gene the individual carried (Caspi et al., 2002). The scientists believed that the relevant gene might be in the regulator (promoter) region of an X chromosome gene that codes for the enzyme monoamine oxidase A (MAO-A). This enzyme is necessary for metabolizing a number of neurotransmitters including dopamine, serotonin and norepinephrine. Individuals who produce low levels of MAO-A enzyme—if they are subjected to childhood maltreatment—are indeed more likely to develop antisocial personalities and become criminally active. In another study, researchers found that individuals who received two copies of the short-allele version of a serotonin transporter gene (compared to those who received two copies of the long version) were more likely to become depressed in response to both stressful life events and childhood maltreatment (Caspi et al., 2003). In the absence of an environmental hazard, such as maltreatment or stress, there was no manifest difference between individuals with different versions of the gene. The effects were also very specific: the *MAO-A* gene had no effect on depression in response to early maltreatment, and the serotonin gene had no effect on antisocial behavior. Despite the genetic overlap between anxiety and depression, the serotonin promoter gene polymorphism did not increase anxiety in response to negative life events. Only depression was affected. If we imagine such specific and elegant gene–environment interactions multiplied

1000-fold (over many genetic loci), we can begin to appreciate the uniqueness of every individual that has ever lived. But interactions are only part of the story.

Gene–environment correlations

Negative parenting behaviors, such as rejection and conflict, are correlated with a child's antisocial behavior. Many previous studies have shown this using the standard design of comparing children raised in different households. With access to twins, full sibs, half sibs, and unrelated sibs, Robert Plomin and his co-workers have examined whether genes or environment are responsible for this association (Plomin et al., 2001). Recall that in most behavior genetic studies, variance in a single variable (such as child misbehavior) is decomposed into genetic and environmental sources. Statistical techniques can also partition the covariance between two variables, such as between child misbehavior and parental treatment. This analysis asks whether the association between the two variables is driven by a genetic or an environmental effect. To do this, a cross-correlation is computed (the correlation between parental negativity experienced by twin A and antisocial behavior by twin B). A genetic effect is implicated to the extent that correlations are higher for more genetically related individuals. The results showed that most of the associations were indeed mediated by genetic effects: the different ways in which the two siblings are treated by their parents are driven by genetic differences between them. This is a classic example of a gene–environment (GE) correlation in which the environment that children experience (negative parental treatment) is correlated with their own genotype (high levels of misbehavior). In GE correlations, both genes and environments conspire to jointly push the child toward a particular outcome.

This particular GE correlation uncovered by Plomin and his co-workers is one of three possible types (Scarr & MacCartney, 1983). Plomin's work suggests a *reactive* GE correlation—this is where the environment responds to the child in such a way as to augment a particular genetic predisposition. But the reactive environment need not be confined to the family. Studies of highly aggressive boys suggest that their peers respond to them by social exclusion which in turn sensitizes the boys to rejection. They start to interpret even neutral social events (an accidental ball to the back of his head) as hostile and intentional, which triggers further aggression in a vicious cycle (Dodge & Coie, 1987). At the other extreme are temperamentally happy children who are "easier" for parents to bond with: the sense of security that this parental love fosters in the child contributes further to their benign, easy-going nature. Nothing succeeds like success, and life is very far from fair.

Earlier in life, *passive* GE correlations are more likely to be at work. Here parents provide the child with genes and also with a home environment that is correlated with those genes. Literary parents not only supply "literary genes," but also shelves groaning with books. Athletic parents not only give their child athletic genes, but take their child with them to sports events. Extraverted parents are likely to produce genetically extraverted children, but they also provide an extraverted environment in the large circle of friends around the house during the child's early years. Correlated genes and environment work together to canalize the child's personality along a particular trajectory: we call the effect "passive" because the environmental component is given to the child without regard to their genotype. This type of effect is thought to be most prominent in infancy. Passive GE correlations seem to be the easiest to locate. For example, parents who produce easy-going infants are also parents who create a family environment high in expressiveness and cohesiveness (Plomin & DeFries, 1985). Twelve other matching correlations between parental behavior and infant development were significantly higher in biological than in adoptive families. This suggests that many links between the parents' behavior and infant outcomes are due to passive GE correlations. However, most work so far has been conducted on young children and we would expect another form of GE correlation to become stronger as the child grows up.

Active GE correlations are more marked in adolescence and adulthood: they result from the individual selecting those social niches that are congenial to her own genotype. Introverts are more likely to be librarians than actresses. People with good visuospatial skills are more likely to study sciences at university, while excellent verbal skills make for better linguists. Troublesome children seek out others who are equally alienated. This kind of "niche picking" may also explain an unexpected finding from genetic studies of IQ (Loehlin, Horn, & Willerman, 1989). In childhood, adopted children show some degree of similarity with their adoptive (biologically unrelated) siblings. Their IQ correlates about 0.26—but by the age of 18, that correlation has disappeared. Similarly, programs that offer young children enriched environments raise their IQ during the time the child is attending them—but the effects evaporate a few years later. It seems that you can lead a child to literacy but you can't necessarily make her enjoy books. All this suggests that with increasing age, active niche picking (which is driven by genetic differences in personality and intelligence) becomes more and more powerful. As children acquire independence from their parents, they are free to select their own hobbies, friends, and vocational interests. They gravitate to those that are most compatible with their genotype. By adolescence, measures of peer characteristics show even higher heritability than measures of parenting—the child's genotype is more predictive of the type of friends she chooses than of her parents' style of interaction with her (Plomin, 1994). Active GE correlation is why MZ twins show greater and greater similarity in personality and

IQ as the years pass. The relaxation of the early environmental constraints to which all children are subject (home and school life) evaporate with age, creating space for genetic predispositions to make themselves felt in the life choices that they make.

Far from the old idea that the work of the genes is done when they have constructed the body and brain of the developing embryo, we now know that genes are active in orchestrating behavior throughout life. Their threshold for activation can be altered by environmental events. They can be responsive under some environmental conditions, but not others. Environments can enhance genetic effects and suppress them. But environments have effects of their own too, which we look at next.

Environmental effects on individual differences

Imagine a population of individuals who do not differ genetically in any way from one another. They are effectively genetic clones—identical twins on a massive scale. Under such circumstances, we would still expect to see differences in their behavior as a result of the interaction between identical genes and different environments.

Before we continue with this thought experiment bear in mind that when we speak of environmental effects we are not saying that genes do not matter. Holding genes constant is not the same as removing their effect. It is our genes that allow the environment to act upon us and even then only in certain ways, as Tooby and Cosmides (1990b, p. 21) explain:

> The environment, per se is powerless to act on the psyche of an animal except in ways specified by the developmental programs and psychological mechanisms that already happen to exist in the animal at a given time. These procedures take environmental information as input and generate behaviour or psychological change as output. The actual relationship between environment and behavior is created solely by and entirely by the nature of the information-processing mechanisms that happen to exist in the animal.... The smell of excrement may be repulsive to us but it is attractive to dung flies.

In our population of clones, differences would arise as a result of whether or not a mental module was activated at all. Sexual jealousy is a good example—a mental module designed by selection to ensure mate fidelity. There are conceivably people who have never experienced this psychological state. In past times, when the media was not available to create widespread familiarity with this emotion, religious celibates may have gone to their graves quite unaware that such an emotion existed. Though the module is present in everyone, it is not necessarily activated in everyone—that depends upon environmental factors such as attraction to a desirable partner, forming an attachment to them, and becoming sensitized to cues that threaten the relationship.

But the environment can also contribute not just to the temporary state of being jealous but to the enduring trait of jealousy also (Buss, 1991). Lifelong vulnerability to jealousy might turn out to have a genetic component but that is not the only possibility. A state can become a trait if the situation that generated it in the first place persists over time. A woman may continue to experience jealousy over several years if her husband continues with his infidelity for that long. Or the environment might recalibrate her threshold of jealousy to a lower value. The wife may become aware that her value on the marriage market is lower than her husband's. A chance remark that she "made a good catch" or "got lucky" is enough to plant such an idea. From then on, even a relatively innocuous event (a glance held too long, an enthusiastic kiss in greeting another woman) can trigger apparently excessive bouts of jealousy despite continued reassurance from her husband.

Chance events that alter her attractiveness may manifest themselves as an enduring change in her level of jealousy. A facially disfiguring scar or a successful diet can lower or raise her assessment of her own attractiveness and lead to a lifelong change in her level of jealousy. As another example, long-term changes in a man's financial situation can alter his attractiveness to women and hence his ability to pursue a strategy of short-term relationships. If a man of only average good looks accumulates wealth over the course of his career, he may be able to jettison his long-standing wife in favor of a series of younger women (as long as the money lasts). Chance events such as a lottery win or a successful stock market investment can have the same effect. Temporary or local changes in the sex ratio can create market forces that allow one sex to cash in their preferred mating strategy, causing what we might conclude was a change in their personality. The arrival of US army personnel in Britain during World War II was greeted with delight by the many women whose menfolk were stationed abroad. The increase in fatherless Anglo-American children during the 1950s was perhaps a predictable result of a sex ratio imbalance combined with the influx of chocolate-laden, stocking-rich men. The change in American men's behavior when they reached British shores might have looked like a personality change but it was a response to a favorably changed sex ratio.

In childhood, the environment provides important cues about the social world to which the child must adapt their behavior. Early experience can alter personality over the long term in one of two ways. It can recalibrate a mental organ or trigger a distinct switch in life history strategy. Physically abused children are at greater risk than others of growing into aggressive adults—a puzzle that has exercised psychologists for years. Surely the dreadful experience of this kind of maltreatment would be expected to cause feelings of repugnance for violence? But violence experienced and witnessed as at early age delivers useful (though painful) information to the child about the degree of competitive hostility in her locality. This can cause her threshold for violence to be re-set to a lower level in order to increase her chance of survival in a hostile environment. The longitudinal stability of aggressiveness from an early age suggests that just such a mechanism is operating.

But in recent years a more radical proposal has been made about the effects of early experience on long-term outcomes: life history theory. Psychologists have taken this idea from reproductive biology (Promislow & Harvey, 1990). Every organism has a finite amount of time and energy which means that decisions must be made about how to allocate these resources most effectively. "Decisions" (unconscious, of course) involve trade-offs. How much time should an organism devote to growing before beginning to reproduce? Is it a better strategy to have many offspring and invest little in any one of them, or to produce fewer offspring but devote resources to ensuring their survival? Zoologists observed that species differ radically along these dimensions. Some species live fast, reproduce copiously and die young—this is known as a fast or "r" strategy. Others develop slowly, produce relatively few offspring in which they invest heavily and live longer. This is a slow or "K" strategy.

As a species, humans are remarkably slow in their life history tempo but evolutionary psychologists have suggested that there is variation among us in our tendency to live relatively faster or slower. The theory proposes that these two strategies are suited to different ecological niches. For example, when pathogens are abundant and the risk of death is high, it is advantageous to start reproduction early and to lower investment in offspring because parental effort will have little effect on shielding the child from illness and death. Where the major environmental risk is resource scarcity, it is a better strategy to mature more slowly, delay reproduction, and increase investment because parental effort can to some extent mitigate the effects of food scarcity by sharing it between a smaller number of offspring.

In women, a particular twofold pathway has been uncovered that unites a set of reproductive events. Some young women are fast developers: they reach menarche early, have sex younger, and reproduce at a younger age. The core milestone is pubertal timing. Younger age of menarche is associated with earlier age of dating, kissing, genital petting, and first intercourse; with higher rates of adolescent pregnancy; and, in natural fertility populations, with earlier age of first birth. The children of these younger mothers tend to have worse cognitive, behavioral, and social outcomes than their peers (see Ellis, 2004). Other young women show the opposite pattern with slower rates of sexual and reproductive development. Evolutionary psychologists have offered a variety of explanations of this syndrome but all agree earlier sexual maturity is a response to stress.

This stress may take the form of conflicted and coercive family relationships that fail to provide support for the child (Belsky, Steinberg, & Draper, 1991). Others have identified the father as a key player—early menarche is associated with father absence and the presence of a step-father (Draper & Harpending, 1988). Some have argued that family stress is a proximal indicator of intensified competition and high mortality rates in the local ecology (Chisholm, 1993). In all cases, the propulsion into early maturity is seen as functional. True, a longer period spent in childhood offers advantages in allowing a more extended period of learning and socialization prior to entering the adult world. But if the home is chaotic and dangerous, the benefits of remaining in it may be so low that a girl would do better to enter the reproductive arena early even though she is less than psychologically adult (Ellis, 2004). The presence of a step-father (even more than the loss of a father) provides an impetus to early maturity and flight from the parental home (Ellis & Garber, 2000). This may be because her mother's acceptance of a new partner signals the transient nature of adult relationships. Or the presence of a genetically unrelated male may accelerate sexual maturity, as has been found in other mammalian species. But whether it results from resource scarcity, family conflict, father absence, or step-father presence, stress is the common denominator. It signals to the growing girl that relationships are unstable, resources are scarce, and men are undependable. In this environment, her best strategy may be to mature early and begin her reproductive career.

Life history theory predicts not only earlier reproductive timing, but a preference for an unrestricted (more promiscuous) sexual strategy. Yet studies that have examined age of menarche in relation to number of lifetime sexual partners have failed to find a convincing linkage (Ellis, 2004). Although sexual strategy does not appear to be mediated by early menarche, a preference for short-term sexual relationships is nonetheless associated with many of the same negative childhood experiences. In infancy and childhood, attachment between mother and child creates a close bond that is represented emotionally by a secure internal working model of relationships. A secure child trusts her mother to be available when needed and this provides a base from which she can explore her environment, including other people. A safe and trusting early bond predisposes individuals to treat others as reliable and benign in later life. Children who are securely attached tend to have more stable and successful long-term relationships as adults. The converse is also true. Disruption of these early bonds and perhaps especially those with the father (whose parental investment is far more discretionary than that of the mother) signal a hostile and unsupportive reproductive environment which favors early reproduction. Early attachment failure can result in one of two personality profiles. An "avoidant" attachment pattern is seen in individuals who shun close emotional connection with others and have problems with intimacy. Because of this, such individuals are often promiscuous, preferring short-term relationships to long-term bonds (Del Giudice & Belsky, 2010). But the more typical attachment disturbance in women is "anxious" attachment. These women are mistrustful of relationships but extremely needy of them, resulting in jealousy and clinginess. In women this form of attachment disturbance is associated with earlier sexual inter-course, impulsive partner choice, and infidelity (Del Giudice, 2009). For life history theory, these individual differences in attachment and sexual strategy are not pathologies, but a suite of traits that are finely tuned to the local environ-ment and hence adaptive. All individuals are seen as having the potential for all three strategies but the one that is activated depends upon early environmental input. The developmental program is triggered by an "if . . . then" switching device. And a given strategy is not simply the result of selecting one behavior rather than another (e.g., have sex now not later) but entails the activation of a whole suite of changes—psychological and biological—that together constitute a coherent reproductive alternative. If the environment is unpredictable and re-sources scant, then invest in mating and hope that some of your many offspring survive. If the environment is more predictable and benign, invest in parenting and forego quantity of offspring in favor of quality of rearing.

Life history theory is not without interpretative problems. One is that the link between parental and child behavior may be genetic, rather than environmen-tal. Age of menarche is positively correlated in mothers and daughters, with a heritability estimate of over 50 percent. If mothers can transmit their develop-mental timing to their daughter, it is likely that they can also transmit their un-stable temperament which interferes with bonding and disrupts partnerships. However, studies which have statistically controlled for the mother's age at me-narche (to remove common genetic effects) still find significant associations between family predictors such as conflict, the presence of a step-father, and the daughter's age at menarche.

Nevertheless the correlations between a stressful childhood, early maturity, and sexual activity are never perfect. It may be that responsiveness to the envi-ronment is itself an individual difference variable: children may differ in how much the environment impacts upon their development (Belsky, Bakermans-Kranenburg, & van IJzendoorn, 2007). Some of us may be "fixed" strategists who pursue one strategy regardless of environmental input, while others are "plastic" strategists whose future is decided by early life experiences. As we saw earlier, some individuals exposed to childhood maltreatment later become in-volved in crime but whether this occurs depends on their specific genotype. This kind of gene–environment interaction may be at work here too. Some children are highly sensitized to early experiences and this sensitivity serves to adjust their reproductive strategy to the constraints of their ecological niche (Boyce & Ellis, 2005). Others may have stronger genetic propensity to one strategy or the other. It is likely that over vast stretches of evolutionary time, fast and slow strategies have both been adaptive depending on the environment and hence both gene versions have stayed in the gene pool. Parents hedge their bets by producing "fixed" and "plastic" offspring in the hope that some at least will prosper in the reproductive sweepstakes.

****

Throughout this book we have seen that sex differences are at the heart of evolutionary psychology. We are one species with two morphs, each sex's mind orchestrated to reflect the role they play in reproduction. But a more challenging question is why we see such marked variation within each sex. Speculations abound with some arguing for the irrelevance of this variability in the big evolutionary picture and others convinced that individual differences results predictably and functionally from the evolutionary process. There is at least agreement that genes, environment, and their interaction are involved. Although environments can directly mold personality, they often exert their effects through genes by altering their expression, or enhancing their effects. We have seen also that higher cognitive functions can modify individual differences in lower-level emotional reactions to the environment. But we are not only "clever" as individuals, we are clever as a species. Human intelligence allows us both to invent our own solutions to novel problems and to learn solutions from others. This eternal feedback loop between discovery and learning is what we know as culture. It allows us to stand on the shoulders of giants and see further into the future than any other species. We now look closer at this process of cultural evolution and the implications it has had for women.

Chapter 9

The flexible phenotype: Women and culture

An important early aim of evolutionary psychology was to question the traditional notion that the entire content of our mental life is put there by the social world around us. In this blank slate view of human behavior, each baby is born an empty vessel, equipped only with the power to acquire information. Children are socialized or "enculturated" into the values and beliefs of their local community. Culture became a one-size-fits-all explanation of all human behavior—and evolutionary psychologists railed against it:

> The invocation of culture became the universal glue and explanatory variable that held social science explanations together. Why do parents care for their children? It is part of the social role that culture assigns to them. Why are Syrian husbands jealous? Their culture ties their status to their wives' honor. Why are people sometimes aggressive? They learn to be because their culture socialises them to be violent. Why are there more murders in America than in Switzerland? Americans have a more individualistic culture. Why do women want to look younger? Youthful appearance is valued in our culture. And so on. (Tooby & Cosmides, 1992, p. 41)

This tendency to use enculturation as the explanation-of-everything ducked the most obvious questions. What exactly is culture? Where did culture come from? Do other species have it? How do people acquire it? Is culture subject to the same processes of evolution as genetic inheritance? These were the questions that evolutionary psychologists posed when they turned their attention to understanding culture. In this chapter I will look at some of the answers that have been found to date, before examining three areas of culture that have had a tremendous impact on the way that women live today.

Culture has been defined in over 150 ways by anthropologists whose stock-in-trade is its study (Kroeber & Kluckhohn, 1952). Evolutionary psychologists quickly cut through this futile semantic debate by agreeing that, for the purposes of their research, culture simply means socially transmitted knowledge—knowledge that has not been individually discovered but has been acquired by observation of or interaction with other people. There are great swathes of everyday activities that are neither innate nor individually discovered. Cooking pasta, driving a car, solving an algebra problem are all things that we learn from other people.

The idea that culture was something that evolutionists ought to take seriously was suggested by Richard Dawkins in his influential book *The Selfish Gene* (1989). He wondered if the evolutionary dynamics that had so successfully explained genetic change could also be applied elsewhere. Years earlier, Campbell (1960) had pointed out that the bare bones of the evolution process could be reduced to just five words: blind variation and selective retention. What if this same process was also happening with human inventions, ideas, and practices? Dawkins (1989) coined the term "meme" to describe a unit of cultural transmission analogous to a gene. A meme is a concept or an idea. Rather flippantly, Dawkins' example was wearing a baseball cap backwards but it could refer to much bigger conceptual ideas (democracy, string theory) or smaller practical ones (how to manufacture a needle for sewing skins to make clothing). Above all, a meme is a replicator that, unlike a gene which passes from body to body down generations, travels from brain to brain both horizontally and vertically and can replicate at much higher speeds. As with genes, the success of a meme depends upon longevity (staying alive in the human brain long enough to be "reproduced" or passed on to others), fecundity (how successfully it is copied into many different brains—its "catchiness" or popularity), and copying fidelity (its capacity to maintain its integrity when transmitted, despite some degree of personalization). Dawkins' idea has been taken up and expanded by many academics, generating a new sub-discipline known as memetics (Aunger, 2002; Blackmore, 1999; Dennett, 1995). Dawkins' thinking (and that of his followers) concentrated upon the memes themselves and much less upon their human vehicles. He pictured memes as parasites or viruses actively striving for replication in the human brain and evolving ways to make their spread more successful. One way they can do this is through co-adapted meme complexes. These are individual memes that have coalesced into coherent higher-order concepts that in turn influence the uptake of new memes. Religion, of course, is Dawkins' favorite example. But the same argument might be applied to political ideology—a philosophy that endorses the primacy of the individual over the state can more easily accommodate memes for unfettered capitalism, low taxes, severe criminal penalties for expropriative crime, and private health care. Dawkins' ideas proved politically controversial but evolutionary psychologists saw the power of the raw concept.

If memes could be passed through generations, then each new generation was standing on the cultural shoulders of the previous one. This meant that culture was selective, cumulative, and ratchet-like. It explained how humans, over generations, had created and spread useful inventions unknown to other species.

One human lifetime is too short to discover the workings of gravity or the immune system, but if each generation is given a head start by the previous one, superhuman ideas become possible. But what about the nuts and bolts? Where do conceptual and practical innovations come from? How do they spread from one person to another? What kind of cultural mind do humans have?

Cultural invention and transmission

Cultural change is a simple process in principle. Someone makes an independent discovery which is copied by someone else who tinkers and improves it. Their discovery is copied by someone else . . . and so on and so on. An obvious question concerns which came first in phylogeny: the ability to make insightful discoveries (invention) or the ability to copy others (social learning)? But this turns out to be a chicken-and-egg question. It seems that they developed together. This was demonstrated in an ingenuous cross-species study. Reader, Hager, and Laland (2011) gathered together data that had been collected on 62 different species of primate. For each species, they looked at the evidence for five cognitive abilities: innovation (individual discovery of novel solutions to environmental or social problems), social learning (learning skills and acquiring information from others), tool use, extractive foraging (the ability to extract concealed or embedded food), and tactical deception (misleading others to one's own advantage). They used factor analysis to examine the correlation between these different abilities. In humans, as we have seen, factor analysis consistently reveals one key factor—called "g" or general intelligence—that unites a range of cognitive abilities. Would the same thing be found for primates? Or would they find two factors; one connected to independent discovery and another connected to social learning? If this was found, then the researchers could map different species' scores to the phylogenetic tree to see when and in what order the two abilities appeared. They discovered that non-human primates have a "g" factor just like us. This general intelligence reflects abilities associated with cultural transmission (learning by imitation) and also individual problem-solving in domains that are social (tactical deception), technical (tool use, innovation), and ecological (extractive foraging). Across species, brain size (the ratio of the size of the neocortex to the rest of the brain) is correlated with this g factor. Phylogenetic analysis revealed that "g" evolved independently at least four times (in capuchin, baboon, macaque, and ape lineages). Performance in social learning and independent problem-solving both improve as we move up the phylogenetic tree from prosimians, to monkeys, to apes, and finally to humans (van Schaik & Burkart, 2011). General intelligence and social learning go together, each reinforcing the other. This suggests that in species where there is more opportunity to learn from others, we should see higher intelligence. These opportunities for social learning are greater where the social system is tolerant and gregarious (adults are willing to spend time with young learners), the rate of development is slow (the young have plenty of time to acquire skills from adults), and the rate of unavoidable mortality is low (the young are likely to live long enough to benefit from what they have learned and can use their knowledge to avert avoidable death). The species that fit this description are the ones in which we see clear evidence of intelligence and social learning: the great apes, capuchin monkeys, dolphins, toothed whales, and elephants (van Schaik & Burkart, 2011).

Not only did individual learning and imitation appear at roughly the same phylogenetic point in evolution, but their co-occurrence confers a distinct advantage over either strategy alone. This conclusion is not as obvious as it seems: many evolutionary psychologists assumed that imitation is a cheaper, safer, and faster way to learn than by individual discovery. It took a mathematical model to demonstrate otherwise.

Rogers (1988) showed that if two populations of individuals—one of which learns and one of which imitates—are allowed to co-evolve, neither one ultimately takes over. The result is a population that uses both strategies. Rogers began his computer simulation with two hypothetical environments (wet and dry) for which there are two optimal behavioral strategies, one which is suited to the wet environment and one to the dry environment. The environment switches randomly between wet and dry, spending about half of the time in each state. During periods in which the environment switches often, information from the previous generation about the best behavioral strategy is not helpful because it is out of date. When it remains fairly stable, the knowledge of previous generations is useful. Now imagine that there are two types of individuals: "learners" who figure out the best strategy for themselves through trial and error, and "imitators" who pick a random individual and copy what they are doing. Rogers modeled the consequences over several generations by assigning mathematical rewards and costs to the possible outcomes and allowing those with a positive net utility to breed into the next generation proportionate to their success.

Learners pay a cost for their learning in terms of time and energy but they have a benefit too: when the environment changes, they alter their behavior to suit it. Their behavior is adaptive so they increase in frequency. But now that a greater proportion of the population are learners, the advantages of imitation increase: imitators are likely to pick someone who has road tested the new behavior (learners), added to which imitators do not pay the costs of trial-and-error learning. So imitators start to increase in number. But when there are too many imitators, the random person they choose to imitate is likely to be another imitator like themselves, rather than someone who has personally discovered the optimal fit between current environment and behavior. The imitator they are copying probably acquired her behavior from yet another imitator so by now it is out of date—it hasn't kept pace with the change in the environment. The population swings back and forth for a while. Ultimately it settles down to a stable mix of learners and imitators when the cost of individual learning is equal to the cost of maladaptive imitation when the environment changes. In other words, it settles at a point where imitators have no advantage over learners. So what is the point in evolving an "imitation" adaptation at all?

Rogers' model assumes that people are *either* learners *or* imitators. But imitation may be adaptive if the two strategies are both available to all people at all times and, as we have seen, the two are indeed highly correlated. The question becomes when should we use each of them? When individual learning is cheap, then it is likely to give the best outcomes. We can cheaply learn that cooking fusilli in boiling water is effective if we already know that this works for spaghetti. But sometimes individual discovery is expensive, time-consuming, or very difficult for the average mortal (e.g., developing the concept of algebra). In some cases, individual discovery is downright impossible because the effects of our actions are so probabilistic or so far removed in time that we cannot know if our action really caused them. (It was not until the nineteenth century that physicians accepted a causal connection between hand washing and disease prevention.) Then it pays to learn from others. The trick is to know what we should imitate and who we should copy. Richerson and Boyd (2005) suggest that evolution has equipped us with three useful built-in mental heuristics to help us solve this problem.

The what-to-imitate problem is solved by *content bias*. When there are a number of different cultural variants, we tend to select those that are immediately attractive, or easier to learn, or that accomplish the goal most efficiently. Some forms of information about the world seem to have a natural priority, grabbing our attention and installing themselves in our minds. Many urban legends seem to owe their spread and popularity to their ability to elicit the evolutionarily useful emotion of disgust. People are more likely to pass such stories on. In one study, urban legends were manipulated to increase or decrease the level of disgust they elicited (Heath, Bell, & Sternberg, 2001). For example, a story about a rat found in a soft drink bottle was given in three different versions (the unfortunate consumer either saw the rat before he took a drink, while he was drinking, or after he had partially swallowed it). The more repellent the story, the more likely people were to repeat it to others. We are also more likely to favor cultural variants that are easier to remember. Our minds seem to have pre-existing cognitive biases that act as "attractors" by simplifying more complex information into forms that our brain finds easy to store and recall. As information passes along chains of people, it converges to simpler and more memorable forms. For example, we find the idea of a linear relationship between two variables easier to understand than other forms of association and single-dimension categories are easier to recall than multi-dimensional ones. We also choose cultural variants based on our capability and the best use of our time. For example, there are many ways to tie a knot which vary in their advantages but also in their difficulty. For some activities, complex knots that have particular attributes are needed. We may need a knot that is quick to untie or one that holds fast in wet or dry conditions. The uses to which we plan to put the knot determine whether or not it is worth investing the extra practice required to master more complex forms.

We become more discriminating imitators with increasing age and experience. Indeed children are remarkable for the slavishness of their imitation. They copy precisely the sequence of movements that they see an adult perform and only if an action is clearly unintentional (for example, if the adult model drops a tool by mistake when performing the action) do children omit that part of the sequence. This is where children differ from chimpanzees. Imagine a puzzle box that is opened successfully by an adult who also uses a series of quite irrelevant actions, such as straightening some rods that play no part in the actual opening of the box. Chimps seem remarkably efficient, editing out superfluous actions. But children copy everything they see the adult do. Researchers disagree about the rationale for the apparent inefficiency of children's copying. Perhaps it is to do with cementing social relationships ("I want to be like you") or perhaps it is because the long period of childhood affords plenty of time to edit out irrelevant actions after many different models have been observed and compared. Or perhaps such slavish imitation is necessary for successful cultural transmission: if different imitators alter the action sequence (some increasing and some decreasing the effectiveness of the outcome), it would corrupt the high-fidelity reproduction necessary for successful transmission. We know that by adulthood we have become more selective decision-makers, choosing to copy the easiest-to-acquire versions of actions or those that are most relevant to our goals. For example, most of us slice a radish the simple way. But five star chefs take the extra time to practice the specialized skills that turn radishes into rosebuds.

The who-to-imitate problem is resolved by two forms of biased transmission. The first of these—*frequency-dependent bias*—is what social psychologists have traditionally studied under the name of conformity. If the cost of finding out for yourself is high (either because the outcome of the choice—whether good or ill—is far in the future, or because of the inherent difficulties of the problem itself) then it is a good bet that the solutions that have been selected by the majority of people are likely to be successful. Is it a better idea to invest time and energy in sowing seeds (agriculture) or would it be just as successful to collect whatever nature provides (forage)? Looking at the choices made by others can be a guide, especially if they have experienced this habitat for a long time and the habitat is stable. But conformist transmission is more than just a tendency to copy the majority—it is about giving disproportionate weight to the majority. Imagine a group of 10 people whom you might copy. Six people select behavior option A and four select option B. If you copied at random, you would select option A with a probability of 0.6 and option B with a probability of 0.4. But conformist bias means that you are disproportionately likely to copy option A (with a probability greater than 0.6). Over the long haul, these two forms of imitation lead to different population effects. Choosing models at random does not result in a net increase in option A. But weighting the majority choice above its prevalence level does: eventually, option A will go to fixation. It will characterize the whole population. The effect is to decrease within-group variability in behavior and increase between-group variability. If one group transmits values that strongly enhance cooperation and reciprocity, conformist bias will enhance this group-level trait giving that group a distinct advantage over a group that values selfishness. Genetic selection works against such group-level prosocial effects (at least between non-kin) because, as Darwin himself noticed, any tendency to sacrifice one's own interests will lower an individual's reproductive success and be removed from the gene pool. Yet with cultural selection, underpinned by conformist bias, such traits could be passed down generations increasing the efficiency of the group and providing an advantage over competing groups who lacked this tendency to in-group cooperation.

A second inherent rule of thumb for choosing models is *prestige bias*: a tendency to copy the most successful or admired people in society. The rationale is simple and intuitive: people become successful because they have made adaptive choices, hence copying their choices will probably guide you to the right outcomes. The closer the correspondence between the measure of visible success that stimulates copying and the trait that is copied, the more successful such as bias will be. If wealth (the prestige cue) and hard work (the trait to be copied) are closely linked, then a bias to imitate hard work will prove successful. However, sometimes the linkage can break apart and our tendency to copy celebrities leads us down irrelevant and unproductive paths. Companies often employ star names to endorse their products. They are betting that our natural tendency to copy successful people will win out over our more rational judgment that David Beckham's choice of aftershave was not crucial to his becoming a world-renowned footballer (Mesoudi, 2009). Prestige bias can also generate cultural runway effects in much the same way as genetic runaway selection.

Recall the peahens' preference for longer tails in their prospective peacock mates. This causes tails to become longer and longer over generations because the long tail and the female preference for it are passed to male and female offspring respectively. If owning a large house is taken as an indicator trait for imitation, then people with a prestige bias will copy the attitudes of people with large houses—including their belief that bigger houses are better. Large houses and the belief that they are good will mutually reinforce one another over time in a positive feedback loop until people are demanding extravagant mansions that are far bigger than anything a normal-sized family actually requires.

This example illustrates how culture can have maladaptive effects. Yet for many years, it was argued that culture must ultimately serve our best genetic interests. E.O. Wilson (1978), an early and influential sociobiologist, concluded: "The genes hold culture on a leash. The leash is very long, but inevitably values will be constrained in accordance with their effects on the human gene pool." He reasoned that the cost of building a brain of sufficient complexity to generate and transmit cultural information could only be economical if such a brain made wise cultural choices. Certainly, a brain that was inclined to accept and act on evidently self-destructive ideas would remove itself fairly swiftly from the gene pool. (Events such as the mass suicide that took place in Guyana under orders from the religious sect leader Jim Jones are vanishingly rare. They attract attention precisely because to obey such an order is beyond the conception of most ordinary people, see Chidester, 2003). But, on a more mundane level people act in self-destructive (albeit less dramatic) ways quite often. Our consumption of fats and sugar; our abuse of alcohol, drugs, and tobacco; our destruction of the ozone layer; and our sedentary lifestyles all attest to the fact that we are capable of making choices that are more likely to harm than help our genetic fitness. There is plenty of evidence that E.O. Wilson may have been over-optimistic in his conclusions. Of course, genes underlie our ability to solve problems and transmit social information and, in that sense, they constrain culture. But that is a far cry from saying that genes will prevent us from pursuing maladaptive pathways. Genes may supply the cerebral machinery necessary for culture but, once that process of cultural transmission has begun, it can take on a life of its own. Cultural information is passed nearly instantaneously in this Internet age, far too fast for its behavioral effects on survival and reproduction to be tracked by natural selection.

Culture can lead us astray in many ways. Content bias is a mechanism that should, in principle, guide us to select the cultural variants that appear to be the most useful and economical. But as humans enter into worlds of knowledge and technology that are new to us, we may lack the criterion against which to make such judgments. In my generation at least, many of us lack sufficient knowledge of computer science to evaluate the relative benefits of different types of personal computer. Instead, we must rely on prestige bias or conformity to guide our choice. Even in a technologically less sophisticated society, consider the complexities of designing a kayak (Richerson & Boyd, 2005). Unless one has spent a good part of one's life exposed to different models, as Inuits are, the combinatorial complexity created by all the potential permutations of different frames, keels, and construction materials makes it impossible to anticipate which design will perform best. The capacity of content bias to guide our choices of cultural variants is also reduced by the time lag between making a choice and being in a position to evaluating whether it was the right one. The success of seed planting rather than foraging will not be known for a year, so at any one time a good proportion of the population may be wasting their time and effort. (To say nothing of their numbers being swelled by imitators.) In many cases, it can take longer than a human lifetime to evaluate the success of a strategy. Sometimes the outcomes of a choice are hard to discern because the cause–effect relationship is opaque—the "trialability" of the behavior is low. Suppose we want to avoid dying from malaria, we have to consider what might cause this illness. If we entertain two hypotheses (it could be caused by standing water or by insects) it may be well-nigh impossible to choose between them in a single lifetime since the two causal agents co-occur most of the time. At other times, we can be misled by our human tendency to seek confirmation for our hypotheses, rather than to disprove them. Does an unseen deity answer prayers? Is that woman a witch? If we look carefully, we will nearly always find evidence that we are right. Another human tendency militates against adaptive cultural choices. Much of our cultural information is transmitted horizontally within age cohorts. Teenagers are more concerned about the preferences of their peers than their parents. Behavior genetic studies affirm that a strong influence on behavior is the unshared environment—those influences that differ between siblings who share the same parents and the same home life. The age-graded and sex-segregated nature of youthful social interactions means that this is usually their peer group. It makes good adaptive sense for teenagers to prioritize attention toward their age mates because these are their rivals, allies, and future mates. But horizontal transmission means that untested, maladaptive memes can be passed easily and the teenage years seem to be ones where the power of conformity is most marked. Websites that encourage anorexia not only pass on peer approval for it, but practical tips on how to evade parental monitoring and medical intervention.

Rather than genes constraining cultural choices as Wilson suggested, the direction of causality more often flows in the opposite direction: we now live in an age in which human cultural inventions modify natural selection. We know that evolution acts on the fit between an organism and its immediate environ-ment: so what happens when humans begin to create their own environments? This is the territory of niche construction. Some cultural discoveries increase selection pressures and so decrease the frequency of certain genes in the next generation. Other inventions relax selection pressures allowing genes to pass through which, at another point in history, would have killed off their bearers.

Consider our ability to digest milk. Babies all over the world can do this, dependent as they are on their mother's milk. But by adulthood, most of the world's population have lost this ability: milk causes them abdominal pain, di-arrhea, and flatulence. The enzyme lactase, present in the villi of the small intes-tine, is necessary to digest milk products. In most humans, this gene switches off at some point during the first four years of life. However, in some popula-tions a mutation in the gene controlling the "off" switch has become common allowing them to consume lactose-containing milk products throughout life. It transpires that this ability is common among populations that have a cultural history of dairying. Lactose tolerance is common among Europeans and pasto-ralist populations in Africa and the Middle East. But in China, where milk con-sumption is rare, only about 1 percent of the population carry the mutated gene that preserves lactase production after infancy. In regions where fermented dairy products such as cheese and yogurt (which have lower levels of lactose) are consumed, rates of lactose tolerance fall between these extremes. The lactase gene mutation was not present in the DNA of early Neolithic Europeans sug-gesting that it was absent (or very infrequent) even 7,000 years ago. It seems that the domestication of cattle and the invention of dairying exerted strong selec-tion pressure on the ability to digest milk so that lactose intolerant individu-als were at a marked disadvantage in terms of survival and reproduction. Data from a range of sources now confirm that it was dairying that led to increased prevalence of lactose tolerance and not the reverse (Laland, Odling-Smee, & Myles, 2010). In other populations, a similar effect has been found for the sali-vary amylase gene (Perry et al., 2007). This enzyme helps to digest starch and high copy numbers of this mutated gene are found in peoples with a tradition-ally high-starch diet such as agriculturalists. The higher the copy number, the easier the digestion process is and the stronger the resistance to intestinal dis-ease. The rise of theses adaptive genetic mutations has been recent, strong, and a direct result of human cultural practices.

In West Africa, the Kwa-speaking people are agriculturalists. They clear areas of the forest floor and plant crops, usually yams. But while this practice improves their supply of food, it has another less fortunate and sometimes lethal effect. Where trees are felled for yam plantation, rainfall collects in swampy pools. This attracts malaria-carrying mosquitoes creating increased selection pressure for malarial resistance. The hemoglobin S allele, a recessive gene, causes sickle cell anemia when an individual receives two copies. But when inherited in heterozygous form it protects against malaria because the disease-causing malaria pathogen spends part of its life cycle in red blood cells where the sickle-shaped cells imprison it until it can be destroyed by the immune system. The S allele is common among yam horticulturalists because of its malaria-protective properties, despite the danger if two homozygous copies are received. The culturally-triggered selection pressure is shown by the fact that nearby populations with different agricultural practices do not show the same increased prevalence of the S allele (Durham, 1991).

The evolution of the human brain may also owe much to niche construction. It is a costly organ: the metabolic rate of the human brain, pound for pound, is nine times higher than for the rest of the body—and that has to be paid for. Somewhere energetic savings had to be found to fuel humans' enormous increase in cerebral capacity and the suggestion is that the gut economized on its activities to free up the needed energy investment. When early humans began hunting, about two million years ago, they began to consume compact portions of protein that would previously have been extracted from digesting large quantities of plant matter (Aiello & Wheeler, 1995). With the arrival of *Homo sapiens*, fire was used for cooking and this further reduced the load on the gut (Wrangham, Jones, Laden, Pilbeam, & Conklin-Brittain, 1999). The act of cooking food partially predigests it so that a smaller gut is needed and energy savings can be spent on running a larger brain.

But cultural evolution can not only alter our genotype (and phenotype), it can relax the selection pressures that would previously have removed some genotypes entirely. Here the most obvious cultural inventions are in public health and medicine. Sanitation and a clean water supply have reduced cholera and gastrointestinal disease in many parts of the world. Preventative immunization has reduced many childhood diseases that once were fatal. Advances in the care of premature babies have meant that thousands of infants have survived against the odds. On a regular basis, surgical intervention saves us from the fatal consequences of diseases ranging from appendicitis to heart failure. Antibiotics provide a good example of a drug that not only has saved millions but is also a reminder of the perpetual arms race between man and microbe. As antibiotics have become more widely used, they have become increasingly ineffective. Every time you stop taking an antibiotic before it has finished its work, your body is a selecting environment for the survival of the most antibiotic-resistant bacteria. These steely individuals are passed on to others, in an arms race between these speedily-reproducing organisms and our slowly-reproducing selves.

Through cultural transmission we have created a world that is, in many respects, different from the one in which we evolved. I want to turn my attention now to two related questions: What impact has culture had on the lives of contemporary women? How much has culture altered women's evolved nature? In this brief survey I will look at women's recent preference for having fewer children, the trend toward valuing extreme female thinness, and the impact of the "sexual revolution."

How many children?

A fundamental tenet of evolutionary biology is the expectation that organisms will evolve to maximize their reproductive success by producing the optimal number of offspring. For a society, the optimal number depends on the harshness or benevolence of the environment and, for an individual, on their access to resources. Individuals who achieve status and dominance in the group have sufficient resources to support more offspring. So in humans, as in other primates, dominant males tended to out-reproduce subordinates. Often this imbalance has gone to outlandish extremes: despots in India, China, Mexico, and Peru had between 4,000 and 16,000 women in their harems (Betzig, 2008). Rameses the Great's 200 children pale into insignificance against the 888 produced by Moulay Ismail, the Moroccan Emperor. But since the eighteenth century, starting in Europe and spreading around the world, a trend began for the rich to have no more children than the poor (and in many cases, fewer). This has become known as the demographic transition. For the population level to remain stable, couples should on average produce just over two children; yet currently half the population of the world inhabit countries where fertility rates have fallen below this replacement level. For an evolutionary psychologist, this is a real conundrum and there has been a flurry of explanations offered for this apparent fitness anomaly. The answers can broadly be divided into two camps: strategic approaches and cultural transmission approaches. However, what is remarkable is the virtual absence of explicit attention to women in these explanations. The units of analysis are "social strata," or "families," or "cultures"; rarely are women considered specifically in terms of their role in this transition or the effects that it has had on their lives.

Strategic approaches argue that the reduction in the average family size is a sensible and adaptive decision. These days, large families mean large costs. In pre-industrial societies children are an economic investment: children work for their parents and even support them economically in old age. Of course, parents make an initial and protracted investment in bearing and raising their children because it is many years before children begin to pay for themselves by contributing more calories to the family than they receive (Kaplan, 1994). Even if parents don't break even overall, at least there is a later return for their efforts in the form of a more secure middle and old age. But in modern industrial and service economies, this is no longer true: the majority of wealth flows exclusively downwards from parents to children. A greater number of children stretches the household budget: parents sacrifice to feed, clothe, and house their children, across all levels of income, education, and ethnicity (Lawson & Mace, 2010). The erosion of financial capital combined with a large family size mean that these children have a reduced chance of receiving an inheritance (Keister, 2003) and face a less financially secure future (Kaplan, Lancaster, Bock, & Johnson, 1995). There are psychological costs too. Regardless of income or parental age, family size reduces the amount of time parents spent on child care during the early years of a child's life (Lawson & Mace, 2009). Perhaps related to this, children from large families perform worse in their school work and score lower in intelligence tests (Steelman, Powell, Werum, & Carter, 2002). Limiting the number of children may have short-term benefits (including increased resources and time, and reduced stress) as well as long-term benefits—children become competent and wealthy adults capable of attracting high-quality mates.

Parents face a trade-off between quality and quantity: more children mean that finite parental resources have to be divided by a larger denominator resulting in less money, time, and attention for each of them. It would be reasonable to suppose that wealth acts as a buffer permitting the more affluent to afford to have more children without feeling the additional strain and this seems to be the case in traditional societies (Borgerhoff Mulder, 2000). Yet studies in Western society have pointed to an unexpected conclusion: additional children, beyond the normative two or three, exact a greater cost in terms of parental investment from richer parents rather than poorer ones. Data from a British longitudinal study were used to discover the best predictors of parental investment which was measured as the frequency of direct interactions with a given child in the family (Lawson & Mace, 2009). The outright winner was family size—the more children, the less time spent with any one of them. But the effect of socioeconomic status was not as expected. When a couple has their second child, the richer parents feel the additional burden less: there is little reduction in the time they spend with the new child. With the birth of the third child, richer and poorer parents show an equal reduction in contact time with the new baby. But when we reach large family size—the arrival of the fourth child—it is the richer parents that experience the most change. The fourth child makes no difference for low-income families who have "bottomed out" in terms of contact time after the third child. But the fourth child of middle- and high-income parents experiences a marked reduction in the amount of time that the parents spend with it.

So the relationship between larger family size and more negative child outcomes seems to work through reduced parental time investment. And that reduction in time spent with later-born children in large families is particularly evident among middle- and higher-wage earners. The older children benefit from being taken to sports events, helped with their homework, and having conversational time with parents but these advantages peter out more markedly for the later-born children of richer parents. Similar findings have been reported in the United States (Keister, 2004). This increased trade-off between quality and quantity may help to explain why the more affluent limit their family size.

If we extrapolate beyond parental time investment, we can glimpse the possible reasons for the apparent anomaly of richer parents experiencing higher costs (Downey, 2001). In the West, even the poorest families are able to provide "base" investment in their children. The state ensures that survival needs are met through nationalized health care, free education, and welfare benefits. Additional children do not limit access to these core provisions. Richer families can provide additional "surplus" investment (tutors, private schooling) and it is these optional but advantageous investments that are jeopardized by additional children. On the other hand, it may be that parents simply err by overestimating the costs and the benefits of investing in children (Kaplan, 1996). As for the costs, parents want their children to do as well or better than they have themselves and, for the rich, this is perceived as requiring a very large investment indeed: private schools, music lessons, personal tutors, sports trainers, international travel, and acquiring the right cultural capital. As for the benefits, the relationship between parental investment and offspring income is not linear. It curves upward initially before leveling off. In hunter-gatherer societies, parents' investment is moderate: at this lower end of the investment curve their efforts reap rewards because their children are more likely to be well nourished, protected from survival threats, and to achieve reproductive adulthood. But there is a ceiling to the effects of parental investment beyond which additional levels have little further effect. This law of diminishing returns means that the extreme parental investment associated with smaller family size is essentially wasted effort and resources. Crucially, there is little evidence that restricting offspring number and increasing parental investment translate into gains in the real currency of reproductive success—grandchildren (Lawson & Mace, 2011).

Where do women stand in this strategic approach to explaining the demographic transition? Although these approaches focus on the costs and benefits of children to the parents as a couple, there is much evidence that men and women may have different reproductive optima. Men opt for quantity and women for quality. Now it might seem that the best strategy for both sexes is to go for numbers: surely more offspring born must mean a greater number will survive to adulthood, all else being equal. But we know from early studies of birds that this is not true: more eggs laid do not translate into more chicks fledged (Lack, 1954). If this is true for birds, it is even truer for humans. For women, children are an expensive commodity because they invest far more in each of them than men do. Women's reproductive ceiling is lower than men's because each child is costly in terms of time: nine months of gestation, typically followed by two or three years of nursing during which time a woman is unlikely to become pregnant again. This inter-birth interval is quite short in comparison to other primates yet it is vital. Each pregnancy depletes the mother's resources and can result in anemia, bone softening, and inadequate weight gain during the next pregnancy. Shorter inter-birth intervals shorten a woman's lifespan: the overall number of children she produces is associated with higher mortality rates within five years of the birth of the last child (Penn & Smith, 2007). Although more children reduce paternal survivorship also, the effect is significantly higher for mothers. High parental fertility also affects offspring: the more siblings a child has, the lower the probability of surviving to reproductive age. And this effect is significantly stronger for later-born children. Women must invest judiciously in children. Compared to men they have a shorter reproductively life that is abbreviated by menopause and each child lost exacts a much higher price in terms of replacement costs.

The outcome of this sex difference is that men typically want to have more children than women do, especially in developing countries (Bankole & Singh, 1998; Mason & Taj, 1987). This sets the stage of sexual conflict and it seems that women are winning this contemporary battle for child quality over quantity. Why have women's preferences triumphed? One piece of this puzzle may be monogamy, an institution that tends to equalize power between the sexes (Henrich, Boyd, & Richerson, 2012). Under polygyny, the supply–demand equation for women becomes distorted. Because some men acquire many wives, there is a shortage of marriageable women. Men are driven to seek younger and younger women as wives, and these child brides have virtually no voice in their reproductive decisions. Male–male competition is intensified, and not just in terms of securing a bride and driving rival males away. Because women are valuable commodities, men can barter and trade them. Fathers and brothers "protect" a young woman's virginity to keep her price high and monitor any attempts at independence. In short, polygyny is bad for gender equality: women have little power in the domestic arena and, as a result, polygynous countries have higher fertility rates.

The institution of monogamous marriage equalizes power between the sexes. In monogamous societies, a man's reproductive output is constrained by his wife's ability or willingness to produce children. Men want sex more frequently than women (Baumeister, Catanese, & Vohs, 2001; Smith et al., 2011) and, for many years, contraception was in their hands too. The use of condoms and coitus interruptus was decided by the husband (Fisher, 2000). Male control was also visible at the level of technological dissemination: in Japan, regulatory agencies took 40 years to approve oral contraceptives for women and six months to approve Viagra˚ for men (Campbell & Bedford, 2009). When female methods of contraception became widespread, power began to shift in a female direction. In less developed nations today, even where women have access to contraception, they sometimes accommodate their husband's desire not to use it (Borgerhoff Mulder, 2009; Campbell & Bedford, 2009). Husbands' objections may be based more upon concern with wifely infidelity than with a desire to limit family size (Bawah, Akweongo, Simmons, & Phillips, 1999; Speizer, 1999). Nonetheless, in developed countries there is increasing convergence between men and women in their preference for a small family size. Women's ability to influence fertility decisions is strongly tied to increasing gender equality. This is true at the national and regional level (Kritz, Makinwa-Adebusoye, & Gurak, 2000; Mason & Smith, 2000) but also within the family (Larsen & Hollos, 2003). It would take a book to do justice to tracing the historical empowerment of women that has taken place in the West over the last hundred years. But at a cultural level, its ramifications for both sexes have been powerful, wide ranging, and rapid. Women, once considered as breeding machines, have taken center stage in deciding their own fertility and, in line with their evolved preference for quality over quantity, they have made their choice clear. And with good reason. In a recent longitudinal study, mothers invested more time in childcare than fathers at every child age studied (Lawson & Mace, 2009). At 18 months, 86 percent of mothers (compared to 50 percent of fathers) play with their child every day. At four years of age, 80 percent of mothers compared to 46 percent of fathers often read to their child. At five, 84 percent of mothers and 47 percent of fathers put their child to bed. At seven years, 75 percent of mothers and 12 percent of fathers prepare things for their child to take to school. Given the disparity in invested time, no wonder mothers are keen to limit the size of their families.

The importance of the female sex in explaining the decline in family size can be seen in the fact that, even in contemporary Western societies, the association between a man's wealth and family size has remained slightly positive (Nettle & Pollet, 2008; Weeden, Abrams, Green, & Sabini, 2006). But it has been massively outweighed by the negative association between women's income and family size (Huber, Bookstein, & Fieder, 2010). Women's workforce participation decreases the time available for investing in children. And this "working woman effect" forms part of a package. The more she currently earns, the longer she and her husband have spent in further education and the later they began having children. So her residual reproductive life is shortened and the time commitment she invests in work decreases her ability to cope with more children. In hunter-gatherer societies there is no real conflict between mothering and "working": they are a seamless whole. A woman may be pounding maize, weaving baskets, or foraging for tubers but she can monitor her children or carry them with her. Add to this the fact that Western women often reside many miles away from their relatives and cannot count on them for day-to-day help, support, and child care advice. In our society, women face an emotional choice between the home and the workplace—witness the distress that women feel as they hand over their baby for the first time to the care of paid strangers. It is this choice that has galvanized so much hostility between women as they seek to morally justify the different priorities they have given to work and children.

But when women gain further education, move into the labor market, and relocate to find work, there are other effects that go beyond strategic allocation of their time and energy. They are exposed to a wider group of people with values and attitudes different from their own. They are less influenced by their immediate family or the community in which they were raised. They have entered a whole new cultural milieu. And some have argued that it is this *cultural* shift that has caused the demographic shift.

Traditional societies are small by Western standards: most interactions occur between people who are kin or have known one another for many years. Fertility is highly valued. Among the Ashanti of Ghana: "Childlessness is felt by both men and women as the greatest of all personal tragedies and humiliations. Prolific childbearing is honored. A mother of ten boasts of her achievement and is given a public ceremony of congratulation" (Fortes, 1950, quoted in Newson, Postmes, Lea, & Webley, 2005). More children increase the sustainability and power of the group and they are the young genetic kin of many of its members. The arrival and acceptance of new ideas, such as contraception, depends on contacts with the world outside. And studies suggest that contraceptive use is higher where women extend their social horizons by traveling to market, belonging to social organizations, living near bus stops, or watching movies (see Newson et al., 2005). This widening of social networks is associated in real time with fertility decline: prior to the shift to smaller families, villages in Europe showed very little variance in family size (Watkins, 1990). It appeared that people were conforming to the norms of their own local community. When modernization began, population migration and economic opportunities brought together people from different villages and backgrounds. Fertility declined and average family size moved toward regional and national levels.

Prestige bias offers one account of the cultural dynamics involved. Within a local village, if power or status is correlated with producing more children, this enhances the tendency of villagers to imitate this prestige cue, keeping family sizes high. But the attainment of prestige in a more developed society requires undergoing years of education and working many hours outside the home, so prestigious individuals tend to have fewer children. They become models to those people who use prestige cues to decide who to emulate. Once this runaway dynamic begins, the majority of people choose to have fewer children and a second transmission bias—conformity—comes into play. The emergence of low-fertility norms in modern society is visible in the fact that having a large number of children is now considered "deviant"; something that requires explanation. Television documentaries about women with children in double figures depend on public fascination, driven less by admiration than by prurient disapproval (Villarreal, 2009).

Women, as I have noted, seem to be the drivers of family size and as women's fertility has been truncated by the years devoted to education and employment, they have become figures for emulation by the next generation. Many of these are high-achieving women—company directors, lawyers, and political figures. But in recent years, young women have been as much (if not more) influenced by celebrity culture. In an age where global fame can be virtually instantaneous, we see a paradoxical effect of the first-wave women's liberation movement. Their goal of de-emphasizing women's sexuality so that they (like men) would be judged by their character and ability has strangely backfired. Young women have learned from movie and rock stars that sexiness is a highly marketable commodity. The trading of sexuality for celebrity means babies take a back seat (or as Lily Allen put it, "Life's about film stars and less about mothers"). Fame entails a lifestyle of late nights, exclusive clubs, expensive drugs, and a stream of accompanying men. Young women who dream of such heady lifestyles learn from their idols to prioritize the sexiness (not the fecundity) of their bodies.

But the cultural argument has been taken one step further by Newson et al. (2005). They argue that it is not just emulation of nulliparous icons that reduces fertility, but exposure to non-kin individuals. Increasingly, women live far from their natal families and spend far more time with friends and acquaintances. School, college, and work introduce us to a wider circle of our contemporaries who act as cultural transmission channels. This diffusion of culture happens through the simple medium of conversation from which we learn about other people's values and attitudes. There have been changes in many aspects of reproductive life: the age at which we think it normal to marry, the increasing importance of mutual love and sexual attraction as a basis for marriage, men's decreasing concern with domestic capability in a prospective wife . . . and the number of children that we typically expect to produce. These values are rarely transmitted overtly but they lurk in many conversational topics: women's discussions of the pressures of combining childrearing and work, the rising cost of a university education, the material demands of teenage children trying to keep up with their friends, the holiday abroad forgone in order to finance a daughter's wedding. The message is clear—too many children tie you down and stress you out. There is no malice here: friends are not malignly trying to subvert their competitors' reproductive output. But on the other hand, they have no reason to support it either. This is what makes genetic kin different. They have an interest in encouraging the replication of their genes via their relatives. Desire for grandchildren is effective in encouraging children to produce them (Barber, 2000; Barber & Axinn, 1998). Daughters who maintain more contact with their genetic kin give birth earlier and have more children for their age than women with low contact and this is not because of the practical support kin offer (see Newson et al., 2005).

But if current norms are leading us away from childbearing, could culture push us to the population precipice? Could we reach a stage where fertility dwindles far below replacement level and we face extinction? Foster (2000) believes not and argues that current fertility levels—the population of countries now below replacement level is 2.6 billion—represent the nadir of population decline. The only way is up. The modern invention of contraception is an evolutionary novelty that has driven a wedge between sex and reproduction. For thousands of years, the pleasures of sex would naturally lead to children. Many evolutionists have argued, on the basis that nature is a miser, that there was no need to evolve a separate "broody" desire for children. Like other species, we can manage with a simple lust for sex backed up by a cocktail of hormones (including oxytocin) that kick in to guide women through pregnancy, delivery, and caretaking. Certainly these biological events have biochemical correlates but, as adoptive mothers show us, childbirth is not necessary for maternal caretaking. The availability of contraception means that women face a future in which every baby that is born is a wanted one. And that means that over the next hundred thousand years, for the first time, there will be selection for women and men who want children, not just men and women who like sex. This is even truer with the advent of medical technologies such as ovulation induction, IVF, intra-cytoplasmic sperm injection, gamete intra-fallopian transfer and surrogacy. The desire to nurture begins early in childhood but shows a consistent sex difference. More girls than boys play with dolls, exhibit spontaneous nurturing behavior toward infants, and are attracted to the "cute" neonatal features of infants. Particularly revealing are studies of girls with congenital adrenal hyperplasia who suffer from excessive exposure to androgens during fetal development. These girls play less with dolls, express a preference for a career over mothering, score lower on tests of nurturance, and show significantly less behavioral interest in infants (Leveroni & Berenbaum, 1998). But nurturance also depends heavily upon early experience and in humans, as in other species, females who themselves experienced high-quality mothering make the best mothers (Barrett & Fleming, 2011). So there is a continuum of nurturance, probably approximating a normal distribution, which runs from women with no interest in children to women whose lives are dedicated to them. The threshold on this continuum that separates those who choose motherhood from those who do not probably varies as a function of many interacting factors such as their opportunity for fulfilling or lucrative careers, countervailing pressures from family or peers, economic considerations, and the preferences of their partners.

At present, in the United States, 18 percent of women aged 40–44 are childless. The majority of these women are highly educated professionals and the trajectory that they follow is a predictable one. They (and their natal families) have invested heavily in their education and they delay reproduction until they begin to see some economic return on that investment. Combined with this, their impressive economic capital translates into a social expectation that they will find a mate of at least equal worth. High-earning women seek mates who are older than themselves and, while some studies suggest they want mates with higher earnings than their own (Buss, 1989), others suggest that this preference is replaced by a desire for physical attractiveness (Eagly & Wood, 1999). In either case, such women have high standards in their mate choice. Setting such a high bar results in a later age of marriage or no marriage at all. A glance at women's magazines reveals the consistent advice to would-be mothers not to leave it too late. Increasingly women are choosing to have children alone rather than miss out entirely. The nurturing instinct is a strong one in many women— strong enough to overcome the obstacles of single parenthood.

Who is the thinnest of them all?

Here is a fact that offers a challenge to evolutionary psychology: women aim to be thinner than men want them to be (Furnham & Radley, 1989). If men place a strong value on physical attractiveness, surely women should be acutely alert to what men want? How can some women diet their way to a size 0 (British size 4), when most men find such a figure repellently skinny? We have seen that men generally appreciate a waist-hip ratio of 0.7 (Chapter 6). But a ratio is just a ratio—it does not stipulate the exact measurements of waist or hips. What is at issue here is absolute body mass. Men prefer the body size of normal women to the smaller size of Playboy centerfolds, models, and escorts (Donohoe, van Hippel, & Brooks, 2009).

For evolutionary psychologists, body shape is an important arena of female competition. Women compete to be attractive to men and the currency of that competition is bodies (as well as faces). Studies have shown that women over-estimate the attractiveness of same-sex rivals (Hill, 2007), dislike being in their company, and derogate them by drawing male attention to their physical imperfections (Buss & Dedden, 1990). In one study, women and men were asked how upset they would be if a rival exceeded them on a range of characteristics. In Holland, Korea, and the United States one of the largest sex differences on which women exceeded men was a rival having an "attractive body"—the effect was even larger than for "attractive face" (Buss, Shackelford, Choe, Buunk, & Dijkstra, 2000). The sex-specific impact of this competition was shown in an experiment in which men and women viewed photographs of averagely attractive members of their own sex (Li, Smith, Griskevicius, Cason, & Bryan, 2010). The images were accompanied by a short piece of text describing the person and these descriptions were varied to reflect either high or low competitiveness. (Importantly, no reference was made to physical appearance.) After this, participants were asked to complete a series of questions about their eating habits, including how satisfied they were with their own physical appearance. Exposure to competitive same-sex peers had an impact only on women: they rated themselves as more restrictive in their diet and more eating-averse than the other three groups. Even if no mention is made of physical appearance, cueing same-sex competition triggers more attention to food intake in women than men. Of course, women's concern with bodily attractiveness derives from the priority that men place on it—and this priority is also evident in homosexual men's partner preferences. Gay men, unlike lesbian women, place a high value on physical attractiveness in a partner. While gay men are more likely to experience body dissatisfaction and eating disorders than their heterosexual counterparts, the reverse is true for lesbian women (Beren, Hayden, Wilfley, & Grilo, 1996; Stiegel-Moore, Tucker, & Hsu, 1990). This provided researchers with a platform for another experiment to demonstrate that eating patterns are associated with mate competition. They repeated the experiment using the averagely attractive same-sex photos and descriptions of competitiveness, but this time they used heterosexual and homosexual participants of both sexes. The body satisfaction of two groups was completely unaffected by the exposure to competitive peers: heterosexual men and lesbian women. However, heterosexual women and gay men both showed greater body dissatisfaction and a rise in disordered eating attitudes after viewing the highly-competitive potential rivals.

It comes as no surprise that women compete and probably always have—at least since the onset of monogamy and two-way sexual selection. What needs explanation is why, in this era of Western history, they should have chosen to do so by emphasizing thinness. When we look back at sixteenth-century paintings by Rubens and Goya, we see women of much larger size (although they maintain the hour-glass figure of small waist relative to hips). The culprit that springs to most people's lips is "the media." Magazine models and red-carpet celebrities unite to place a premium on thinness. Only a few academics have questioned why such a media conspiracy might have occurred. Mealey (2000b) has suggested, along evolutionary lines, that this conspiracy against younger women (who are the most vulnerable to eating disorders such as anorexia) has been masterminded by an elite group of older, dominant women. The biological background to this ploy is that, in response to signals of nutritional scarcity, the body defers reproduction. Anorexia can cause anovulatory menstrual cycles and amenorrhea when the body detects reduced body fat, energy imbalance, and high aerobic activity. In this view, older women (who are past their peak reproductive years) encourage malnourished body images in order to reduce the reproductive success of their younger competitors. However, while it is true that fashion editors are often older women, they are often remarkably thin themselves which suggests that they are as much the victims as the younger generation. Another suggestion has been that thinness signals reproductive health. It seems that the most desirable body shape depends on local ecological factors. Cross-cultural studies show that in societies where food supplies are scarce and unreliable, a larger female body shape is more attractive, perhaps because fat stores suggest a greater likelihood of fecundity and successful pregnancy (Anderson, Crawford, Nadeau, & Lindberg, 1992; Swami et al., 2010). By contrast, in the West where food is abundant, obesity is a greater health threat and thinness indicates a healthier lifestyle. Obesity, especially among women, is more prevalent in lower social classes suggesting that thinness may also act as a signal of wealth (National Health Service, 2010).

Despite evolutionists' attempts to provide a rational explanation for cultural trends in female body shape, I suspect it may be a lost cause. There is a built-in randomness to fashion. The media, as cultural trend setters, are in the business of promoting change not stasis. Newness and originality catch the eye. Fashion is about whimsy and *female* whimsy at that—designers target their creations at women, not men. Body shape is a key component of fashion and as the trend for thinness took off, whether serendipitously or as an expression of marketable "newness," the rest of the media followed suit. As the runaway bandwagon headed downhill, the 1990s saw a brief period of "heroin chic" and models of anorexic size. It was only when the trend was criticized as a health risk that magazine editors thought it prudent to back off. Images in women's magazines do not represent what *men* want: they are run by people (mostly women) who sell their product to readers (mostly women) by emphasizing change and the need to stay up to date.

In 2010, the American Psychological Association held the media to blame for their role in the high rate of body dissatisfaction among young women and girls (American Psychological Association Task Force on the Sexualization of Girls, 2010). But the media cannot be the whole story. All women in the West are exposed to similar images through movies, magazines, and television but not all women become obsessed with their body size. A meta-analyses of empirical studies suggest that the effect of the media is not as large as expected (see Ferguson, Winegard, & Winegard, 2011). The correlation between media exposure and body dissatisfaction comes out at between $r = 0.09$ and $r = 0.17$, which translates to the media explaining only about 3 percent of women's body dissatisfaction. The media may exert a distal influence but many psychologists believe that the real work is done much closer to home.

Peer groups exert powerful effects on their members' behavior, especially during the adolescent years (Jones, Vigfusdottir, & Lee, 2004). They channel the values promulgated by the media directly into the daily life of teenagers (Clark & Tiggemann, 2008). One way that peers can affect body image is through direct visual comparison. One naturalistic study surreptitiously organized gym sessions so that the participant exercised near a fit or an unfit confederate (Wasilenko, Kulik, & Wanic, 2007). Other researchers set up experiments in which a participant interacted with an attractive or less attractive female stranger (Krones, Stice, Batres, & Orjada, 2005). In both cases, exposure to attractive peers diminished girls' body satisfaction. Perhaps it should come as no surprise that we compare ourselves more intensely with those in our own social circle more than with distant media figures (Wheeler & Miyake, 1992). After all, it is within our immediate age-graded cohort of acquaintances that we compete for mates. A girl does not have to be the more attractive than a film star, only more attractive than those girls who are vying for the same boys as she is.

But friends can also play active roles in calibrating a girl's sense of attractiveness. Gossip is a mainstay of young women's conversations and a great deal of it is about same-sex peers and potential love rivals (McAndrew, Bell, & Garcia, 2007; McAndrew & Milenkovic, 2002), especially their physical appearance (Massar, Buunk, & Rempt, 2012; Owens, Shute, & Slee, 2000). Gossip serves a dual function: it allows us to calibrate our appearance or behavior against those of others ("Am I thinner than her?" "Am I eating too much at lunchtime?" Wert & Salovey, 2004) and it teaches us about local social norms of appearance ("How thin is considered attractive in our group?" Baumeister, Zhang, & Vohs, 2004).

Gossip, which by definition is about a third person who is not present, allows for a degree of forthrightness that would never be expressed in that person's presence. The judgments are honest and occasionally brutal. ("She's gained so much weight!" "Did you see the size of her stomach in those jeans?") Through these vicarious judgments, powerful lessons are learned about the importance and acceptable parameters of appearance. And for any girl, the prospect of becoming the object of such third-party criticism is a strong incentive to stay thin.

In face-to-face conversations, teasing can be used as a way to hint at overweight and the recipient gets the message only too clearly (Menzel et al., 2010). But in the main, messages about weight are conveyed much less overtly, if at all. Reflecting women's typical "one-down-womanship" conversational style, when pejorative remarks are made they are usually self-directed. In fact, it seems there are only two appropriate targets for criticism: a third person who is out of earshot and the speaker herself. Women's "fat talk" conversations are an opportunity for women to commiserate with one another about their deficiencies and to complain about their shared struggle with dieting. These sessions have the familiar quality of depressive co-rumination, in which each party actively contributes to the female pastime of putting herself down while her partner lifts her back up (O'Dougherty, Schmitz, Hearst, Covelli, & Kurzer, 2011):

> ... if I complain about my body, that's kind of an open invitation for her to complain about her body, so it's like a contest and we keep complaining. It's not good!
> When she and I talk about our appearances, what we usually do is like share all of our insecurities and what we think are our worst flaws, and try to comfort each other with, like, "That's not so bad. Listen to this." [laughter]

Expressing satisfaction with one's size, as with expressing satisfaction in many areas of achievement, runs the risk of appearing smug or superior. So women denigrate their body to emphasize their common experience with other women. But it serves another function too: the pre-emptive strike. Women criticize themselves to ward off others' anticipated criticisms (Nichter, 2000). These interchanges have clear ground rules. One woman will complain about her weight and in response her conversation partner will challenge the validity of her statement ("But you don't look big") or mitigate its importance ("It's just baby weight—that's normal"). Sometimes the response is an exaggerated contradiction, describing the other woman as "emaciated" or "tiny." Failing to respond in such a way to another woman's complaint about her size can be dangerous—silence can be seen as tacitly endorsing the truth of her negative self-assessment (O'Dougherty et al., 2011).

Women are not insensitive to the way in which the media manipulates their anxieties and they often question or reject these externally imposed standards.

Yet regardless of whether they accept or contest them, the sheer frequency of "fat conversations" maintains and underlines the acute relevance that weight has for women's lives (Ousley, Cordero, & White, 2008). Even strongly feminist women who publically celebrate "bodily diversity" find that they cannot avoid wanting to achieve the "ideal" body shape (Rubin, Nemeroff, & Russo, 2004). So the distal media call for slimness is amplified by the peer group and a young woman's hearing is made more acute by her need for their approval and acceptance. But beneath the apparent friendship and sympathy, a competitive element remains. Although girls understand the need to avoid bragging about their superior slimness, they equally understand the need to avoid being the "fat one" who excites sympathy or—worse—teasing and gossip.

The remarkable thing is that body shape, as an avenue of female competition, has taken on a life of its own. It has escaped from its roots in men's actual mate preferences. Despite this, many feminist writers have identified men as the chief culprits responsible for alienating women from their own bodies. Objectification theory finds its roots in the writing of psychoanalyst Karen Horney who defined it as "the socially sanctioned right of all males to sexualize all females, regardless of age or status" (Fredrickson & Roberts, 1997). This is manifested in the male "objectifying gaze" which causes women to view their own bodies as sexual objects. Patriarchy, these feminists argue, is the institution that objectifies women and hence it is men who are responsible for women's over-concern with their appearance. In this psychoanalytic view, women's preoccupation with their body shape mirrors men's preoccupation with it. While evolutionary theorists might well agree that men are attuned to female body shape, this feminist account leaves out the marked element of intra-sexual competition among women. That competition is revealed in the fact that women themselves collude in the body shape obsession. It is women's media which promote the need to strive for the slim ideal and which castigate female celebrities who have gained (or lost) too much weight. Far from being a male conspiracy to oppress women, magazines and programs directed at women (and usually overseen by women) respond to women's interest. Their very existence depends on audience numbers and sales figures: if articles about body shape did not interest women, they would quickly disappear.

Just as women dress for other women and not for men, the criterion for success in this all-female body shape competition is determined by women not men. At its most extreme, this competition becomes pathological (Abed, 1998). As young women become slimmer, competitors need to push the upper limit of thinness higher. Eating disorders such as anorexia nervosa and bulimia are the final and deadly frontier of this culturally-initiated competition. The body has become dislocated not only from men's preferences but even from the feminine cultural ideal: there is a point at which slimness becomes grotesque and ano-rexic sufferers have lost touch with the ultimate goal of their self-denial. Not eat-ing becomes an end in itself and a way of life that is painfully hard to abandon. In the United States, one in 60 (1.7 percent) of 13–18-year-olds have anorexia. The mortality rate is 12 times higher than for any other cause of death among young women aged 15–24. Among survivors, about 30 percent will have the illness long term. Clinicians continue to struggle to understand the causes and cures of anorexia, increasingly pursuing genetic and neuroscience approaches (Kaye, Fudge, & Paulus, 2009). However, we do know that some personality traits can increase girls' vulnerability or exacerbate their recovery (Lilenfeld, Wonderlich, Riso, Crosby, & Mitchell, 2006; Stice, 2002). The key parts played by neuroticism, obsessive–compulsive traits, and perfectionism all suggest that competitive stress is involved. Anorexic women experience high levels of anxi-ety and are consumed by concern about calorie intake and their appearance. As perfectionists, they hold themselves to extreme, even unrealistic, standards and feel compelled to meet them at whatever cost (Egan, Wade, & Shafran, 2011).

If runaway effects are at work, then we would expect that anorexia and perfec-tionism would be associated with female competition per se and not just with intra-sexual competition for mates. This was supported by a study in which young women completed a set of questionnaires about their eating patterns, personality traits, and two specific types of competition: competition for female status (e.g., "I feel powerful when I am thinner than other women") and com-petition for mates (e.g., "The skinnier I am, the more attractive I am to men") (Faer, Hendriks, Abed, & Figueredo, 2005). As we would expect, there was a very high correlation (r = 0.80) between status competition and mate competi-tion. This essentially confirms that mate competition is an important arena of status in young women. Both forms of competition had an effect on anorexic eating patterns but they did so by different routes and with different strengths. Competition for mates increased women's drive for thinness and, given that this is a measure of motivation to lose weight, it is no real surprise that it was associated with anorexic eating patterns. By contrast, female status competition had its effect on eating disorders through its association with perfectionism. Interestingly, perfectionism was *negatively* correlated with mate competition. In other words, the proximate personality variable associated with anorexia—perfectionism—was driven by same-sex status competition while mate compe-tition paradoxically tended to diminish it.

So there are layers of explanation for anorexia that begin with the distal mes-sage of the media that is then relayed interpersonally through the peer group. While providing a forum for co-rumination, friends also underline the im-portance of body shape, identify the weight parameters of acceptability, and encourage social comparison. For highly competitive and perfectionist girls, the end result can be pathological. Earlier, I described the potential runaway effects that can be caused by prestige bias in imitation. In body shape obsession, we see it vividly played out. Young women who have a prestige imitation bias will pay particular attention to high-status individuals and imitate them. When fame and celebrity become associated with being thin, these women will copy both their behavior and the thin-glorifying attitudes they hold. (Recall Kate Moss's famous edict that "Nothing tastes as good as skinny feels" or the Duchess of Windsor: "A woman can never be too rich or too thin.") Over time the attitudes and behavior reinforce one another in an upward spiral, driving thinness to extremes. For most of us there is a limit to that extremity. We jump the diet ship when the depressing reality of the super-thin lifestyle becomes too much: the nagging hunger, the permanent calorie counting, the forward planning, the loss of spontaneity, and the asocial egocentricity that is the hallmark of obsessive–compulsive behaviors. These grate against our normal human instincts which steer us unconsciously to eat when we are hungry, to salivate to the sight and smell of tasty food, and to socialize with others. This is what cultural theorists call content bias—the inherent (un)attractiveness of some cultural variants. In genetic runaway selection, we say how the length of a peacock's tail lengthens in response to female preference. But that process is counteracted by natural selection when the tail becomes long enough to threaten the male's survival. So it seems with cultural selection: for most of us, content bias sets a limit to how far away from our natural inclinations culture can take us.

Women and the sexual revolution

The sexual revolution represents little more than a historical event for contemporary young women. As with all cultural shifts, it is hard to place a firm date on its arrival but most estimates place it between 1965 and 1975 (Robinson, Ziss, Ganza, & Katz, 1991). A cover story on *Time* magazine proclaimed its genesis in 1965 and by 1985 a second cover story proclaimed that the "revolution is over" (Smith, 1994). Until the 1960s, the double standard of morality was broadly accepted: for men, sex before marriage was acceptable (even desirable) but not for women. The same behavior that attracted the accolade of "stud" to men, evoked epithets like "whore" or "slut" to women. As premarital sex became more widely accepted for both sexes, the double standard took on a new and broader meaning, referring to the cultural values according to which men and women are judged by different standards for aspects of sexuality such as casual sex and sex with a large number of partners (Robinson & Jedlicka, 1982). Women rose up in resentment that their sexuality was being suppressed by patriarchal and unjust value judgments.

Their vocal objections were prompted in part by the increasing availability of birth control, especially the contraceptive pill. But the removal of the threat of pregnancy cannot be the whole story since prior to the pill women had been free to engage in many sexual behaviors such as oral sex that carried no risk of pregnancy. The sexual revolution went hand in hand with other social changes. The entrance of women into the workforce, as well as giving women greater economic independence and social power, brought a wider realization of unequal pay and gender discrimination. Questions about why women received unequal treatment were raised in a range of spheres including education, the family, the workplace, the criminal justice system, and the bedroom. Women should be entitled to enjoy sex as much as men and to have as many partners as they chose without incurring discriminatory judgment by an old vanguard of Victorian moralists.

The link between women's increasing financial independence and their demand to be allowed the same sexual freedom as men has been explored by Roy Baumeister (Baumeister & Mendoza, 2011; Baumeister & Twenge, 2002; Baumiester & Vohs, 2004). He views sex as a marketplace that responds to normal market forces—especially the law of supply and demand. Men want sex more than women: they think and fantasize about it more, want a larger number of sexual partners, use masturbation as a substitute for intercourse more frequently, are less willing to abstain from sex, and rate their sex drive as stronger. Sex is a resource that men want and that women can supply. This puts women in a position of relative power. Men must cajole, flatter, and expend time and energy to obtain sex. The more women withhold sex (for example, by requiring long-term commitment before they will agree to it), the harder men must work to obtain it and the stronger the bargaining power of women becomes. Of course, to the extent that women also enjoy sex, women incur a cost for this strategy. But the cost, given their lower sex drive, can be compensated for by their improved bargaining position. (If you doubt this description of the seller–buyer dynamics in relation to sex drive, consider the real "monetary" sexual marketplace. Women can make a good living as prostitutes and phone sex workers while men who take up this career path are more likely to find themselves servicing gay men rather than heterosexual women.) It is when women have few other ways to obtain the resources they need that they are more likely to restrain their sexuality and trade it as a commodity. Across 37 countries, there is a significant positive correlation between gender empowerment for women and the prevalence of casual sex (Baumeister & Mendoza, 2011). Another study showed that across 34 cultures, there is a positive correlation between gender empowerment and women's (but not men's) endorsement of unrestrictive sexual attitudes and behaviors. The more empowered women are in a given culture, the smaller is the difference between men and women in sexual behavior (Petersen & Hyde, 2010; Schmitt, 2005). When women lack power and must depend on men for the necessities of survival, they keep the "price" of sex high by restricting its supply: female chastity is encouraged, female promiscuity is condemned, and sex is exchanged for marriage. The entry of women into the workplace that began in the 1960s afforded them the economic independence to free them from the need to use sex as a bargaining chip. As Baumeister and Vohs (2004, p. 358) rather laconically summarize the period: "If sex is a female resource, then the Sexual Revolution was a 'market correction' in which the exchange price of sex was significantly reduced."

Expressed in this way—as the loss of a strong bargaining position—the sexual revolution does not sound like an adulterated blessing for women. The bonuses were the opportunity to experience sex with as many partners as a woman wanted, to explore more avenues of sexual pleasure and the freedom to express her sexuality without stigma. But it seems that not all women thought that these outweighed the negatives. Surveys and studies have shown that women came to regard the revolution more negatively than men and experienced more regret about their behavior (Rubin, 1990; Smith, 1994). A British newspaper columnist reflected on her experiences like this:

. . . we'd been brought up to say "no" to sex, but the only reason for that was because we might get pregnant. And if we'd got pregnant then of course we might have been thrown out of our parents' home, or forced to give the baby up for adoption . . . But now, armed with the pill, and with every man knowing you were armed with the pill, pregnancy was no longer a reason to say "no" to sex. And men exploited this mercilessly. Now, for them, "no" always meant "yes". To be honest, I mainly remember the 60s as an endless round of miserable promiscuity, a time when often it seemed easier and, believe it or not, more polite, to sleep with a man than to chuck him out of your flat. I recall a complete stranger once slipping into bed beside me when I was staying in an all-male household in Oxford, and feeling so baffled about what the right thing was to do that I let him have sex with me; I remember being got drunk by a grossly fat tabloid newspaper journalist and taken back to a flat belonging to a friend of his to which he had a key, being subjected to what would now be described as rape, and still thinking it was my fault for accepting so much wine. I remember going out to dinner with a young lawyer who inveigled me back to his flat saying he'd got to pick something up before he could take me home, and then suggested we have sex. "Oh no," I said feebly, "I'm too tired." "Oh, go on," he replied. "It'll only take a couple of minutes." So I did . . . the result was that lots of us girls spent the entire 60s in tears, because however one tried to separate sex from love, we'd been brought up to associate the two; so every time we went to bed with someone, we'd hope it would lead to something more permanent and each time it never did . . . The other reason that sex was so grim was that now it was so easy, the art of seduction had flown out of the window . . . as for men considering women's feelings – why should they? They continued to satisfy their own needs and never for a moment considered whether the women they were having sex with found it pleasurable or satisfying. (Ironside, 2011)

(It is worth pausing to consider some of the comments that were posted in response to this journalist's recollection of her youthful misjudgment. "Most girls did not behave like tarts"; "Some of us still had morals and didn't leap into bed with any man who asked!"; "Sounds like the London scene was filled with a lot of slappers!" We will return soon to the question of whether the double standard has really disappeared.) As others have noted (Jeffreys, 1990), the downside of "free love" for many women was a pressure to engage in sex to avoid being labeled by men as frigid, prudish or a "tease." This pressure was ratcheted up by women's magazines which provided plenty of advice on sexual technique and contributed to readers' beliefs that failure to enjoy casual sex was tantamount to a betrayal of women's liberation. There was also the danger of sexual coercion and assault by men who no longer saw any valid reason for a woman to refuse sex. Women's sexual satisfaction was hardly enhanced by men's belief that, if women were as eager for sex as men, then foreplay could be dispensed with.

To take stock of the revolution, we need to ask three questions: Did women's sexual behavior really change? Did their attitudes to casual sex change also? What about their emotional reaction to these one-night stands? To help us, we have three meta-analyses that have addressed changes in the magnitude of the sex difference in a range of behaviors and attitudes (Oliver & Hyde, 1993; Peterson & Hyde, 2010; Wells & Twenge, 2005). Measures of sexual behavior have been extremely inclusive, encompassing everything from anal and oral sex to masturbation. For the purposes of considering the impact of the sexual revolution on women, we will focus chiefly on measures of age of initiation and number of sexual partners.

Since the 1940s, the percentage of young people who report being sexually active has risen markedly and the effect has been stronger in women. For example, in the 1950s only 13 percent of teenage girls were sexually active compared to 47 percent in the late 1990s. Before 1970, the average age at which women first had sex was 19 years (18 for men). By the 1990s, this had dropped to the age of 15 for both sexes. The sex difference is very small and became smaller still by 2007, suggesting that both sexes have been affected equally in terms of an earlier start to their sexual careers.

But once their sexual careers have begun, men have more partners than women and the size of that sex difference increased in the 14 years between 1993 and 2007. A recent study in the United States, whose participants had a mean age of 22, found that men reported an average of 4.43 sexual partners to women's 2.71 (Ostovich & Sabini, 2004). In the 20–34 age group, 36 percent of Canadian unattached men reported more than one sexual partner in the previous 12 months compared to 29 percent of women (Rotermann & McKay, 2009). Allied to this, men more often engage in casual sex (Petersen & Hyde, 2010). In a national British survey, 39 percent of men had their most recent sexual experience in a casual relationship, compared to 20 percent of women (Mercer et al., 2009). Sex within 24 hours of meeting a new partner took place for 23 percent of men and 11 percent of women. It seems that, young people of both sexes have sex earlier and the difference in their involvement in casual sex is beginning to diminish—especially when we bear in mind that women may be under-reporting the number of casual sexual partners (Brown & Sinclair, 1999).

Attitudes have also changed. The most remarkable of these occurred between the 1950s and 1980s during which acceptance of premarital sex rose from 12 percent to 73 percent in young women and from 40 percent to 79 percent in men. Attitudes to casual sex have changed too: men still approved of it significantly more than women but the magnitude of the sex difference is diminishing as women become more liberal. For example, on a scale of 1 to 5 (where 1 is the most favorable attitude), European-American men in the United States scored 3.1 compared to women's 3.9 (Ahrold & Meston, 2010).

Given the greater similarity between men and women in sexual attitudes and behaviors over the last 60 years, some academics have argued that the double standard has disappeared. Indeed when people are asked if the same sexual standards should apply to men and women, they believe they should (Milhausen & Herold, 1999). And when people read a description of a man and a woman with the same number of sexual partners, they do not judge one sex more harshly than the other (Marks & Fraley, 2005). But there are strong social desirability factors at work here: Westerners are now acutely aware of gender discrimination and are likely to monitor their answers to these kinds of sensitive questions carefully. In the world beyond the laboratory, things are not so liberal.

Women are still more stigmatized than men for having sex at too young an age, for having too many partners, for having sex outside of a committed relationship, and for initiating sexual contact (Crawford & Popp, 2003; Kreager & Staff, 2009; Robinson et al., 1991). Although college-educated women tend to be more liberal in their sexual attitudes and behavior (Stanik & Ellsworth, 2010), 40 percent of sexually active undergraduates conceal the extent of their previous sexual experiences from their male partners (Rubin, 1990). In middle school, observation and interviews reveal that girls can be labeled as sluts for a range of misdemeanors such as making a pass at a boy, or wearing make-up and clothing that is considered provocative (Eder, Evans, & Parker, 1995; Orenstein,

1994). The double standard is especially visible in language itself. Over 90 percent of slang synonyms for women had negative connotations (compared to only 46 percent for men) and many of these had sexual connotations such as, "slag," "tramp," "hooker," and "bait." The power of these terms is not to be underestimated: although girls object strenuously to these labels, they less often question the double standard on which they are predicated (Lees, 1993).

Women's greater willingness to engage in casual sex (also known as hookups or one-night stands) may in part stem from a misapprehension about other women's experiences. Women attribute to other women more positivity about casual sexual liaisons than they themselves feel (Reiber & Garcia, 2010). College students were asked to rate how comfortable they felt about engaging in a series of sexual acts during a hook-up and also to rate how comfortable they believed other members of their own sex and the opposite sex felt. Their responses were rated on a scale from very uncomfortable (−5) to very comfortable (+5). They rated their own comfort level in the negative zone at −2.23 for intercourse and −1.87 for giving oral sex. Yet they attributed significantly higher and positive rates of comfort to other women (+0.06 for intercourse and +0.54 for oral sex). (Not surprisingly they attributed the highest comfort levels to men—in fact significantly greater comfort than men actually reported feeling.) Women may be acting on the basis of pluralistic ignorance: each woman believes that she is unusual in not enjoying casual sexual activity as much as her female peers (see also Lambert, Kahn, & Apple, 2003). Statistics indicate that between 65 and 80 percent of American students experience at least one hook-up during their time at college. A woman's decision to engage in hook-ups might be fuelled by (misinformed) conformity pressure or by competition with other women.

Women's "comfort" with casual sex taps their emotional response to it and it is here that sex differences remain marked. When men and women were asked to endorse the applicability of positive and negative descriptors of their hookup experiences, the sex difference was clear (Owens, Rhoades, Stanley, & Fincham, 2010). Forty-nine percent of women endorsed only negative adjectives, compared to 26 percent among men. Fifty percent of men endorsed only positive adjectives compared to 26 percent among women. In one of my own studies, I asked respondents to describe their "morning after" experience by rating how well 12 statements (six positive and six negative) described their feelings (Campbell, 2008a). Men were significantly higher on all six positive statements, especially feelings of increased confidence and well-being, and hoping that their friends would hear about it. Women were higher on all but one of the six negative statements, especially feeling used and believing they had let themselves down. The one negative item on which men scored higher? Feeling that they had used another person.

Among sexually active college women, feelings of regret are stronger for those who have had sex with someone on one occasion only (especially with someone they had known for less than 24 hours) and for those who have had many sexual partners in the last year (Eshbaugh & Gute, 2008). For women, number of sexual partners during the last year is positively associated with worry and feelings of vulnerability although the reverse is true for men (Townsend & Wasserman, 2011). This sex-reversal is true for depressive symptoms also: having had more sexual partners is positively associated with depression and psychological distress in women but the opposite is true for men (Fielder & Carey, 2010; Grello, Welsh, & Harper, 2006). Regret and self-blame are high among women who engage in casual sex (Paul & Hayes, 2002).

What is causing this distress to women but not to men? One possibility is that women more than men expect that a casual sex liaison will blossom into a fully-fledged romantic relationship. But in terms of motivation for casual sex, men and women do not differ in their hope that it might be the beginning of a romantic relationship (Garcia & Reiber, 2008) and in my study I found this to be the weakest of all the sex differences found. The answer is more subtle than dashed expectations of romance. Despite the fact that women genuinely accept the short-term nature of the sexual encounter, they feel "used" more than "using," whereas the reverse is true for men. The spontaneous comments made by women about their feelings after a one night stand provide clues about the source of this imbalance (Campbell, 2008a):

"Upset because he hasn't talked to me after it happened."

"If they blank you the next time they see you rather than just say 'Hi' and smile or something, then they can shatter your confidence in an instant."

"I called him a few times after we had sex; then we did not speak for a long time after that. When we did meet again, he made it seem as though I had been stalking him. He reminded me that the night we spent together was just a one night stand. I found his arrogance annoying."

"He seemed more embarrassed the next day more than anything else, and the sex hadn't been that great."

"Even if I didn't want anything to do with them after a one-night stand I would like to know whether they liked me."

"Disappointment when not receiving a phone call the next day just to say 'thank you.' The call came eventually, but by then it was not the same."

What the women, but not the men, appeared to resent was the insufficiency of recognition following the event. Given men's generally higher sex drive and eagerness for casual sex, women typically act as a limiting factor or gating mechanism (Symons, 1979). When a woman agrees to sex after a short period of courtship, she expects a degree of appreciation since in the economics of sexual exchange she has lowered her usual market price for the interaction

(Baumeister & Vohs, 2004). A failure to express appropriate gratitude may be read as an implication that her price is habitually low. In addition, the fact that men typically drop their standards appreciably for short-term partners raises the possibility that her partner did not find her sufficiently attractive for a longer relationship. As the woman sees it, her male partner was willing to have a private sexual encounter but would not be willing to conduct a public relationship with her. (Being "blanked" subsequently tends to confirm her hypothesis even though the man may be merely trying to avoid embarrassing her.) Although women did not express excessive disappointment at the transient nature of the relationship and indeed might well have rejected the partner's invitation to continue it, they nonetheless felt the absence of such an invitation as a blow to their self-esteem. Echoing these findings, Townsend, Kline, and Wasserman (1995) found only a small sex difference among highly sexually active undergraduates in spontaneous concern about whether the relationship would last. However, women were much more likely to express concern about whether the partner wanted only sex and whether or not they would call them the next day (81% of women compared with 17% of men). This also hints at the subtle but critical distinction between a disappointed yearning for a long-term relationship and a damaged sense of self-worth at not being invited to consider (and possibly refuse) one.

Although women's post-hookup feelings have been described as "confused," "hurt," "upset," and "vulnerable," such emotions arise when men fail to treat women with an appropriate degree of appreciation and respect. In the sexual marketplace, the law of supply and demand give a woman the upper hand. Her behavior is magnanimous: her partner has obtained sexual pleasure without paying the traditional price of financial, emotional, and time investment. This is an act of generosity on her part to which the appropriate response is warmth and gratitude. When a man responds with embarrassment, avoidance, or indifference, it amounts to rudeness. Women are most likely to enjoy casual sex when they feel desirable, valued, and in control (Glenn & Marquardt, 2001; Paul & Hayes, 2002; Townsend, 1995). A little post-coital politeness is surely not too much to ask?

Culture has consequences. The sexual revolution "liberated" the behavior and attitudes of women more than men. The desire to be men's equals was expressed in a mimicking of their sexual behavior and attitudes. (Why did we not express this quest for equality by demanding that men behave more like us?) "Free love" became a pressure rather than an option for women. Driven by pluralistic ignorance, women conformed to what men wanted: they lowered their bodies' market value. Women successfully walked the walk and talked the talk of sexual liberation: They continue to do so. But to reach the evolutionary bedrock, we have to penetrate deeper than culturally prescribed attitudes and behavior: it lies in women's emotions. Emotions are ancient and useful devices, honed over time to nudge us in the right direction. In the experience of casual sex, men's and women's emotions can be very different based as they are on thousands of years of "gut" knowledge provided by sexual selection. Men have always had more to gain and less to lose from casual sex than women and it is reflected in our contemporary emotional reactions. For most women, sexual pleasure depends more strongly on an emotional attachment to their partner than it does in men (Paul & Hayes, 2002; Schmitt, 2005). But there are large individual differences. I have no moral axe to grind here. Sexual freedom means we make our own choices and live with the consequences both good and bad. But a word of advice, ladies: trust your instincts.

Women, culture, and evolution: A personal view

The last 20 years have seen huge advances in thinking about the evolution of mind but we are still many years away from seeing the full picture. Rashly premature though it may be, I would like to indulge my personal view of where women stand in relation to evolution and culture.

As an undergraduate I was mightily impressed by the linguist Noam Chomsky and particularly by his vision of a universal grammar that united the deep and surface structure of language. Although the surface structure of different languages appear quite disparate, lying beneath the variation are rules that transform a common and universal deep structure into what we hear in our local language community. This image has parallels in my view of evolved sex differences. Although we see surface variation in women's phenotypic behavior across history and culture, lying beneath is an ancestral commonality—a deep structure—that unites women over place and time. As I see it, there are layers of psychological processes of increasing sophistication beginning with affective responses at the deepest level (which we share with many species), through intelligence and decision-making (which we share with some primates), to transient and variable cultural behaviors (almost exclusively human) at the surface level. I believe that men and women differ most fundamentally at the deepest level—but it has important knock-on effects higher up. Let's start at the top and work our way down.

Cultural learning—the ability to acquire behavior from others in our community—is an ability that men and women share. An evolutionary stance toward sex differences always starts by asking whether or not a given ability is tied to sexual selection. Is there any reason to think that better imitative ability would be more valuable to one sex's reproductive success than to the other?

Here the answer seems obvious: no. The ability to efficiently acquire and use knowledge is just as relevant to hunting a prey as to weaning a child. In contemporary studies, there is certainly no consistent evidence that one sex imitates more accurately or frequently than the other.

Cultural transmission—ancestrally in our social group and more recently via access to global electronic communication—creates differences in lifestyles between women. From the point of view of women's lived experience, cultures differ in profound and more superficial ways. The most profound cultural effects come from social institutions (such as education, health care, and legal systems) and ideologies (such as democracy, gender equality, and religion) that directly affect women's lives. Forced marriages continue in societies where parents' rights supersede those of their daughters. Female infibulation and clitoridectomy, outlawed in more gender equal societies, are still practiced in some African and Middle Eastern nations. In Nepal and Saudi Arabia, women continue to be burned or beheaded for practicing witchcraft. Patriarchal states turn a blind eye to wife abuse. But education brings empowerment to women and democracy gives them a voice. Access to health care and contraception allows them greater control over family size. Enlightened legal systems can ensure equal rights and pay for women. These factors have dramatic effects on the quality of women's lives and the role they can play in society. Other historical and cultural differences are more superficial. In Pakistan, women have traditionally worn shalwar kameez, long before trousers were acceptable for women in the west. Fifty years ago, women's friendships were conducted over the garden fence rather than on the telephone or Internet. Girls have played with dolls of one kind or another since time immemorial although their shape and appearance have altered. In short, the expression of what it is to be a woman changes across time and place in ways that range from the fundamental to the merely fashionable. Culture can limit women or liberate them. It can constrict or release the outward manifestation of our nature.

At the next level up, we have the reflective processes that were described in Chapter 8. There are plenty of synonyms for this cognitive system that capture its essential quality: "higher order," "conscious," "explicit," "analytic," and "controlled" (Evans, 2008). Sometimes we just call it intelligence. Intelligence may seem like a slippery concept to the layperson but researchers are clear about what they mean by it:

> Intelligence is a very general capability that, among other things, involves the ability to reason, plan, solve problems, think abstractly, comprehend complex ideas, learn quickly and learn from experience. It is not merely book learning, a narrow academic skill, or test-taking smarts. Rather, it reflects a broader and deeper capability for comprehending our surroundings—"catching on," "making sense" of things, or "figuring

out" what to do. Intelligence, so defined, can be measured, and intelligence tests measure it well. (Gottfredson, 1997, p. 13)

Do men and women differ in their general intelligence? This question has generated considerably more heat than light. One controversial study claimed a three to five IQ point advantage for men (Irwing & Lynn, 2005) but doubts have been expressed about the selectivity of the statistical analysis (Blikhorn, 2005). Other studies have found a one point advantage for boys, or girls, or no sex difference at all (reviewed in Deary, 2012; Dykiert, Gale, & Deary, 2009). Despite this similarity in IQ, neuroimaging studies have shown sex differences in overall brain size as well as in the structures (axons versus cell bodies) and brain regions that best predict intelligence in women and men. The two sexes achieve a similar performance in IQ tests by using their differently structured brains in their own particular ways. With IQ tests, as with all assessments, the size of the sex difference depends on what questions are posed. Item selection can nudge results in favor of one sex or the other. But the tests that inter-correlate to make up the general intelligence factor come from five domains: reasoning, memory, processing speed, vocabulary, and spatial ability. Sex differences are found consistently only in these last two domains.

Spatial ability can be broken down further to reveal sex differences that go in opposite directions. To test three-dimensional rotation, people are shown a two-dimensional representation of a novel three-dimensional object and asked to compare it to another representation that has been mirrored or rotated. They have to decide if the two objects are identical. Men perform better than women and show less brain activation during the task. Men seem to represent the object geometrically in Euclidian space and "turn it round" in their mind, while women often use a language-based approach to solving it. However, women do better than men on another spatial task: remembering the location of objects. When briefly shown a pictorial array of objects, women are more successful at subsequently recalling the location of any single object. This sex difference is manifested in the way that men and women orient themselves as they move through their surroundings. When asked to create a map after exploring a new neighborhood, men create a geometric map based on cardinal "compass point" relationships between features ("We walked north-west from the starting point") while women rely more on landmarks and their relationship to one another ("We turned left at the traffic lights and the school was on our right"). Evolutionary hypotheses have been offered of these differences (Geary, 1995; Silverman & Eals, 1992). Ancestral men traveled far from home when hunting and defending territory. Often they were in unknown areas and depended on a good ability to abstractly encode their current location and orientation without recourse to familiar landmarks. Women spent their work time foraging and for them a key ability was to recall the exact position of plants, tubers, and honey-combs in the nearby vicinity.

Women outperform men in some (but certainly not all) verbal abilities (Halpern, 2000). They have an advantage in reading, and in language production and comprehension. For example, women produce longer and more grammatical utterances; they are faster and more efficient at articulating complex words; they retrieve words from long-term memory more rapidly; and when speaking they use filled pauses ("umm. . . . ") much less than men. This may be because women tend to employ both hemispheres for language processing, while men show a left-hemisphere bias. An area called the plenum temporale (situated close to Wernicke's area that specializes in processing written and spoken language) is larger in women. For men, the size of this area is proportionate to the size of the rest of their brain but in women it remains large regardless of overall brain size. Evolutionary psychologists have linked this ability to the ancestral importance of women maintaining vocal contact with dependent offspring and to the close intimate ties between women given the lengthy time spent together at camp (Mildner, 2008). So, although men and women excel in different aspects of intelligent thinking and sometimes capitalize on their special abilities to tackle the same task in different ways, there is little to choose between them in their ability to manage mundane problem solving. However, the problems that men and women enjoy solving often differ and this is a function of the next level down: the affective system.

Not so long ago, the study of emotion was the poor relation in psychology. The second half of the twentieth century was the epoch of the "cognitive revolution" (Miller, 2003). Brains were computational machines and psychology's task was to discover the algorithms and write the software programs that simulated human thought. The Turing test was the Holy Grail of the cognitive movement: if a naive subject could not tell whether she was interacting with a real person or a machine, the computer had successfully duplicated the working of the human mind. The implicit and sometimes explicit dichotomy was between reason and emotion, with academic kudos firmly attached to the former. But as neuroimaging technology developed, emotion became visible, measurable, and therefore scientific: anger or sadness "lit up" brain regions on magnetic resonance images. At the same time, an evolutionary focus on the "wet" brain as a biological organ (rather than a computer program) drove studies on brain biochemistry and structure. Above all, evolutionary theory invited comparisons with other species. They may lack the sophisticated cognitive machinery residing in humans' massively expanded neocortex, but we share with them many fundamental emotions and behaviors: aggression, lust, sex, jealousy, mothering, hunger, despair. These emotions stem from the more primitive centers of our brain (such as the amygdala, thalamus, hypothalamus, hippocampus, and anterior cingulate cortex) although they have bidirectional connections with higher cortical structures, especially the orbitofrontal cortex. They intertwine with motivational systems of approach (mediated by dopamine and opioids) and avoidance (mediated by serotonin) to create a "social brain." It is from this social brain that "whisperings within" emanate: preverbal feelings of anticipatory pleasure or dislike, engagement or avoidance, anger or fear. As we saw in Chapter 3, emotions—far from being antithetical to reason—are vitally important for decision-making. Decisions are not about the application of cold, calculated reason but are informed and guided by our gut feelings. The sex differences that we have reviewed throughout this book are the result of people's (often unconscious) decisions about what interests them or gives them pleasure. Contemporary outward manifestations—couples' nightly arguments about what to watch on television—derive from preferences and competencies shaped by thousands of years of evolution. Women disproportionately choose occupations that allow them to solve "people" problems such as teaching and counseling. They are less supportive than men of war and invasions, not because they disagree about their tactical utility but because they find violence more abhorrent. They are more sensitive to the negative consequences of risk taking. These affective bedrock processes, which we share with other species, are the sites at which evolution is most likely to work. When we see the same sex differences in chimps' as in humans' behavior—males' greater intergroup hostility and aggression, and females' nurturance and risk-aversion—there are good grounds for thinking that these common differences have been conserved for good reason. That reason is sex-specific reproductive advantage.

Intelligent problem solving and cultural learning are adaptations—but they are adaptations that fill a gap created by the very slowness of genetic adaptation. Between an environmental problem and an evolutionary solution falls the shadow of perhaps a thousand years and many deaths: the "generational lag" time. Our genes carry an ancient and implicit wisdom about how to react to the world, but it can be years out of date. Genetic knowledge cannot keep up with changing circumstances and novel problems. Learning is an open-ended facility to solve problems as they appear within the lifetime of a single organism. The very point of learning is flexibility. Hence it seems profoundly unlikely that any specific content is built into the learning adaptation. Its virtue is its content-free nature: once we have learned how to do subtraction, we can use the procedure to keep track of beans, bananas, or babies. Content is built-in at lower levels of brain processing for dealing with aspects of the world that are relatively unchanging. This built-in content obviates the need to learn: we "automatically" see the world in three dimensions, break speech at phonemic boundaries, experience hunger and cold, feel happiness when reunited with a loved one, and so on. It is down here at this level that sex differences, where they exist, are chiefly instantiated. Sex differences become harder to detect as we climb up from emotion to intelligence and cultural learning.

I imagine these three components of our mental life—cultural learning, intelligent problem solving, and emotion—as a tree. Deep in the soil are the roots, the oldest part of the tree and the source of its stability and nourishment. These are adaptations honed over millions of years. Many are exquisitely adjusted for men and women to maximize each sex's reproductive success. These roots are enigmatic, ineffable, and implicit. Rising from them come the tree's trunk and branches, corresponding to intelligence and problem solving. They depend on the nutrients sent from the roots but are directly exposed to the vicissitudes of the elements: drought, rain, and frost. Far out along the branches are the transient and colorful blossoms that are tugged this way and that by the wind, that grow and wither with the seasons, and that are shed and replaced each year. This is culture.

Culture matters because it intimately affects the way we live our lives. To be a European peasant in the Middle Ages is to experience a quite different existence from a nineteenth-century Japanese geisha or a contemporary business executive. Womanhood is expressed in a dazzling variety of ways, shaped by its unique temporal and spatial location. But beneath the roles in which we are cast, the freedoms we gain or lose, and the superficial fashions that dictate our appearance, are buried the roots that bind us together. The chain that links daughter to mother extends back thousands of years in time, each generation shaped by the evolutionary demand to survive and reproduce. We have all descended from the archetypal Eve and each carry her image in our minds, hearts, and bodies.

References

Abed, R.T. (1998). The sexual competition hypothesis for eating disorders. *British Journal of Medical Psychology, 71,* 525–47.

Abrams, D. (1989). Differential association: Social developments in gender identity and intergroup relations during adolescence. In S. Skevington & D. Baker (Eds.), *Social identity of women* (pp. 59–83). London: Sage.

Ackerman, J.M., Kenrick, D.T., & Schaller, M. (2007). Is friendship akin to kinship? *Evolution and Human Behavior, 28,* 365–74.

Adler, P.A., & Adler, P. (1998). *Peer power: Preadolescent culture and identity.* New Brunswick, NJ: Rutgers University Press.

Adolphs, R., & Spezio, M. (2006). Role of the amygdala in processing visual social stimuli. *Progress in Brain Research, 156,* 363–78.

Ahlgren, A. (1983). Sex differences in the correlates of co-operative and competitive school attitudes. *Developmental Psychology, 19,* 881–8.

Ahlgren, A., & Johnson, D.W. (1979). Sex differences in cooperative and comparative attitudes from the 2nd through the 12th grades. *Developmental Psychology, 15,* 45–9.

Ahrold, T.K., & Meston, C. (2010). Ethnic differences in sexual attitudes of U.S. college students: Gender, acculturation, and religiosity factors. *Archives of Sexual Behavior, 39,* 190–202.

American Psychological Association Task Force on the Sexualization of Girls. (2010). *Report of the APA Task Force on the Sexualization of Girls.* Washington, DC: American Psychological Association.

Amsterdam, B. (1972). Mirror self image reactions before age two. *Developmental Psychobiology, 5,* 297–305.

Aiello, L.C., & Wheeler, P. (1995). The expensive-tissue hypothesis. *Current Anthropology, 36,* 199–221.

Alema, G., Rosadini, G., & Rossi, G.F. (1961). Psychic reactions associated with intracarotid amytal injection and relation to brain damage. *Excerpta Medica, 37,* 154–5.

Alexander, R.D., & Noonan, K.M. (1979). Concealment of ovulation, parental care and human social evolution. In N. Chagnon & W. Irons (Eds.), *Evolutionary biology and human social behavior* (pp. 436–53). North Scituate, MA: Duxbury.

Altmann, S.A. (1962). A field study of the sociobiology of rhesus monkeys, Macaca mulatta. *Annals of the New York Academy of Sciences, 102,* 338–435.

Amato, P.R. (1998). More than money? Men's contributions to their children's lives. In A. Booth & A.C. Crouter (Eds.), *Men in families: When do they get involved? What difference does it make?* (pp. 241–78). Mahwah, NJ: Erlbaum.

Amato, P.R., & Rogers, S.J. (1997). A longitudinal study of marital problems and subsequent divorce. *Journal of Marriage and the Family, 59,* 612–24.

Amico, J.A., Johnston, J.M., & Vagnucci, A. (1994). Suckling induced attenuation of plasma cortisol concentrations in postpartum lactating women. *Endocrinology Research, 20,* 79–87.

Anderson, J.L., Crawford, C., Nadeau, J., & Lindberg, T. (1992). Was the Duchess of Windsor right? A cross-cultural review of the socioecology of ideals of female body shape. *Ethology and Sociobiology, 13*,197–227.

Anderson, M.J., Dixson, A.S., & Dixson, A.F. (2006). Mammalian sperm and oviducts are sexually selected: Evidence for co-evolution. *Journal of Zoology, 270*, 682–6.

Andersson, M. (1994). *Sexual selection.* Princeton, NJ: Princeton University Press.

Andrews, P.W., Gangestad, S.W., & Matthews, D. (2002). Adaptationism: How to carry out an exaptationist program. *Behavioral and Brain Sciences, 25*, 489–553.

Angier, A. (1999). *Woman; An intimate geography.* New York, NY: Houghton Mifflin.

Archer, J. (1984). Gender roles as developmental pathways. *British Journal of Social Psychology, 23*, 245–56.

Archer, J. (1992). Childhood gender roles: Social context and organisation. In H. McGurk (Ed.), *Childhood social development: Contemporary perspectives* (pp. 31–61). Hove: Erlbaum.

Archer, J. (2000). Sex differences in aggression between heterosexual partners: A meta-analysis. *Psychological Bulletin, 126*, 651–80.

Archer, J. (2002). Sex differences in physically aggressive acts between heterosexual partners: A meta-analytic review. *Aggression and Violent Behavior, 7*, 313–51.

Archer, J. (2004). Sex differences in aggression in real-world settings: A meta-analytic review. *Review of General Psychology, 8*, 291–322.

Archer, J. (2009). Does sexual selection explain human sex differences in aggression? *Behavioral and Brain Sciences, 32*, 249–66.

Archer, J., & Coyne, S. (2005). An integrated review of indirect, relational and social aggression. *Personality and Social Psychology Review, 9*, 212–30.

Aries, E. (1976). Interaction patterns and themes of male, female and mixed groups. *Small Group Behavior, 7*, 7–18.

Aries, E., & Johnson, F.L. (1983). Close friendships in adulthood: Conversational content between same-sex friends. *Sex Roles, 9*, 1183–96.

Arnqvist, G., & Rowe, L. (2005). *Sexual conflict.* Princeton, NJ: Princeton University Press.

Arrindell, W.A., Kolk, A.M., Pickersgill, M.J., & Hageman, W.J.J.M. (1993). Biological sex, sex-role orientation, masculine sex role stress, dissimulation and self-reported fears. *Advances in Behaviour Research and Therapy, 15*, 103–46.

Arrindell, W.A., Mulkens, S., Kok, J., & Vollenbroek, J. (1999). Disgust sensitivity and the sex difference in fears to common indigenous animals. *Behaviour Research and Therapy, 37*, 273–80.

Aunger, R. (2002). *The electric meme: A new theory of how we think.* New York, NY: Free Press.

Badcock, C. (1994). *PsychoDarwinism: The new synthesis of Darwin and Freud.* London: HarperCollins.

Badcock, C. (2009). *Product withdrawal notice: I was wrong about Freud.* Retrieved from http://www.psychologytoday.com/blog/the-imprinted-brain/200909/product-withdrawal-notice-i-was-wrong-about-freud-0

Bailey, D.H., & Geary, D.C. (2009). Hominid brain evolution: Testing climatic, ecological, and social competition models. *Human Nature, 20*, 67–79.

Bailey, J.M. (1998). Can behavior genetics contribute to evolutionary behavioral science? In C. Crawford, & D.L. Krebs (Eds.), *Handbook of evolutionary psychology* (pp. 211–33). Mahwah, NJ: Erlbaum.

Bailey, J.M., Gaulin, S., Agyei, Y., & Gladue, B.A. (1994). Effects of gender and sexual orientation on evolutionarily relevant aspects of human mating. *Journal of Personality and Social Psychology, 66*, 1081–93.

Bailey, J.M., & Zucker, K.J. (1995). Childhood sex-typed behavior and sexual orientation: A conceptual analysis and quantitative review. *Developmental Psychology, 31*, 43–55.

Baker, R. (1996). *Sperm wars*. London: Fourth Estate.

Baker, R.B., & Bellis, M.A. (1993). Human sperm competition: Ejaculate manipulation by females and a function for the female orgasm. *Animal Behaviour, 46*, 887–909.

Bankole, A., & Singh, S. (1998). Couples' fertility and contraceptive decision-making in developing countries: Hearing the man's voice. *International Family Planning Perspectives, 24*, 15–24.

Barash, D.P. (1981). *Whisperings within: Evolution and the origin of human nature*. London: Penguin.

Barash, D.P., & Lipton, J.E. (2009). *How women got their curves and other just-so stories*. New York, NY: Columbia University Press.

Barber, J.S. (2000). Intergenerational influences on the entry into parenthood: Mothers' preferences for family and nonfamily behavior. *Social Forces, 79*, 319–48.

Barber, J.S., & Axinn, W.G. (1998). The impact of parental pressure for grandchildren on young people's entry into cohabitation and marriage. *Population Studies—A Journal of Demography, 52*, 129–44.

Barber, N. (1995). The evolutionary psychology of physical attractiveness: Sexual selection and human morphology. *Ethology and Sociobiology, 16*, 395–424.

Barber N. (2003). Paternal investment prospects and cross-national differences in single parenthood. *Cross-Cultural Research, 37*, 163–77.

Bar-Haim, Y., Lamy, D., Pergamin, L., Bakermans-Kranenburg, M. J., & van IJzendoorn, M. H. (2007). Threat-related attentional bias in anxious and nonanxious individuals: A meta-analytic study. *Psychological Bulletin, 133*, 1–24.

Barkley, R.A. (1997). Behavioral inhibition, sustained attention, and executive functions: Constructing a unifying theory of ADHD. *Psychological Bulletin, 121*, 65–94.

Barkley, R.A., Ullman, G., Otto, L., & Brecht, M. (1977). The effects of sex-typing and sex-appropriateness of modeled behavior on children's imitation. *Child Development, 48*, 721–5.

Baron-Cohen, S. (1997). How to build a baby that can read minds: Cognitive mechanisms in mindreading. In S. Baron-Cohen (Ed.), *The maladapted mind: Classic readings in evolutionary psychopathology*. Hove: Psychology Press.

Baron-Cohen, S., & Hammer, J. (1997). Is autism an extreme form of the "male brain"? *Advances in Infancy Research, 11*, 193–217.

Baron-Cohen, S., Leslie, A.M., & Frith, U. (1985). Does the autistic child have a "theory of mind"? *Cognition, 21*, 37–46.

Baron-Cohen, S., & Wheelwright, S. (2004). The empathy quotient: an investigation of adults with Asperger syndrome or high functioning autism, and normal sex differences. *Journal of Autism and Developmental Disorders, 34*, 163–75.

Barrett, H.C., & Kurzban, R. (2006). Modularity in cognition: Framing the debate. *Psychological Review, 113*, 628–47.

Barrett, J., & Fleming, A.S. (2011). Annual research review: All mothers are not created equal: Neural and psychobiological perspectives on mothering and the importance of individual differences. *Journal of Child Psychology and Psychiatry, 52*, 368–97.

Bartels, A., & Zeki, S. (2004). The neural correlates of maternal and romantic love. *NeuroImage, 21*, 1155–66.

Bartz, J.A., Zaki, J., Bolger, N., & Ochsner, K.N. (2011). Social effects of oxytocin in humans: Context and person matter. *Trends in Cognitive Sciences, 15*, 301–9.

Bateman, A.J. (1948). Intra-sexual selection in Drosphila. *Heredity, 2*, 349–68.

Batty, G. D., Wennerstad, K.M., Smith, G.D., Gunnell, D., Deary, I.J. Tynelius, P., *et al.* (2009). IQ in late adolescence/early adulthood and mortality by middle age: Cohort study of one million Swedish men. *Epidemiology, 20*, 100–9.

Baumeister, R., & Mendoza, J.P. (2011). Cultural variations in the sexual marketplace: Gender equality correlates with more sexual activity. *The Journal of Social Psychology, 151*, 350–60.

Baumeister, R., Zhang, L.Q., & Vohs, K.D. (2004). Gossip as cultural learning. *Review of General Psychology, 8*, 111–21.

Baumeister, R.F. (1990). Suicide as escape from self. *Psychological Review, 97*, 90–113.

Baumeister, R.F., Catanese, K.R., & Vohs, K.D. (2001). Is there a gender difference in strength of sex drive? Theoretical views, conceptual distinctions, and a review of relevant evidence. *Personality and Social Psychology Review, 5*, 242–73.

Baumeister, R.F., & Sommer, K.L. (1997). What do men want? Comment on Cross and Madson (1997). *Psychological Bulletin, 122*, 38–44.

Baumeister, R.F., & Twenge, J.M. (2002). Cultural suppression of female sexuality. *Review of General Psychology, 6*, 166–203.

Baumeister, R.F., & Vohs, K.D. (2004). Sexual economics: Sex as a female resource for social exchange in heterosexual interactions. *Personality and Social Psychology Review, 8*, 339–63.

Baumgartner, T., Heinrichs, M., Volanthen, A., Fischbacher, U., & Fehr, E. (2008). Oxytocin shapes the neural circuitry of trust and trust adaptation in humans. *Neuron, 58*, 639–50.

Bawah, A.A., Akweongo, P., Simmons, R., & Phillips, J.F. (1999). Women's fears and men's anxieties: the impact of family planning on gender relations in northern Ghana. *Studies in Family Planning, 30*, 54–66.

Becker, G.S. (1981). *A treatise on the family.* Cambridge, MA: Harvard University Press.

Beer, J.S., Knight, R.T., & D'Esposito, M. (2006). Controlling the integration of emotion and cognition: The role of frontal cortex in distinguishing helpful from hurtful emotional information. *Psychological Science, 17*, 448–53.

Beitel, A.H., & Parke, R.D. (1998). Paternal involvement in infancy: The role of maternal and paternal attitudes. *Journal of Family Psychology, 12*, 268–88.

Belensky, M.F., Clinchy, B.M., Goldberger, N.R., & Tarule, J.M. (1986). *Women's ways of knowing.* New York, NY: Basic Books.

Bellis, M.A., & Baker, R.R. (1990). Do females promote sperm competition? Data for humans. *Animal Behaviour, 40*, 997–99.

Belsky, J. (1984). The determinants of parenting: A process model. *Child Development, 55*, 83–96.

Belsky, J., Bakermans-Kranenburg, M.J., & van IJzendoorn, M.H. (2007). For better and for worse: Differential susceptibility to environmental influences. *Current Directions in Psychological Science, 16*, 300–4.

Belsky, J., Gilstrap, B., & Rovine, M. (1984). The Pennsylvania infant and family development project. 1. Stability and change in mother-infant and father-infant interaction in a family setting at one, three and nine months. *Child Development, 55*, 692–705.

Belsky, J., Houts, R.M., & Fearon, R.M.P. (2010). Infant attachment security and the timing of pubertal development. *Psychological Science, 21*, 1195–201.

Belsky, J., Rovine, M., & Fish, M. (1989). The developing family system. In M.R. Gunnar and E. Thelen (Eds.), *Systems and development: The Minnesota symposium on child psychology, Volume 22* (pp. 119–66). Hillsdale, NJ: Erlbaum.

Belsky, J., Steinberg, L., & Draper, P. (1991). Childhood experience, interpersonal development, and reproductive strategy: An evolutionary theory of socialization. *Child Development, 62*, 647–70.

Belsky, J., Steinberg, L., Houts, R.M., & Halpern-Felsher, B.L. (2010). The development of reproductive strategy in females: Early maternal harshness → earlier menarche → increased sexual risk taking. *Developmental Psychology, 46*, 120–8.

Belsky, J., Steinberg, L.D., Houts, R.M., Friedman, S.L., DeHart, G., Cauffman, E., *et al.* (2007). Family antecedents of pubertal timing. *Child Development, 78*, 1302–21.

Belyaev, D.K. (1979). Destabilizing selection as a factor in domestication. *Journal of Heredity, 70*, 301–8.

Bem, D.J. (1996). Exotic becomes erotic: A developmental theory of sexual orientation. *Psychological Review, 103*, 320–35.

Bem, S.L. (1974). The measurement of psychological androgyny. *Journal of Consulting and Clinical Psychology, 42*, 155–62.

Bem, S.L. (1981). Gender schema theory: A cognitive account of sex-typing. *Psychological Review, 88*, 354–64.

Bem, S.L. (1993). *Lenses of gender: Transforming the debate on sexual inequality*. London: Yale University Press.

Benedict, R. (1934). *Patterns of culture*. New York, NY: Mentor.

Benenson, J.F., Apostoleris, N.H., & Parnass, J. (1997). Age and sex differences in dyadic and group interaction. *Developmental Psychology, 33*, 538–43.

Benenson, J.F., & Schinazi, J. (2004). Sex differences in reactions to outperforming same-sex friends. *British Journal of Developmental Psychology, 22*, 317–33.

Bereczkei, T., & Csanaky, A. (1996). Mate choice, marital success and reproduction in a modern society. *Ethology and Sociobiology, 17*, 17–35.

Beren, S.E., Hayden, H.A., Wilfley, D.E., & Grilo, C.M. (1996). The influence of sexual orientation on body dissatisfaction in adult men and women. *International Journal of Eating Disorders, 20*, 135–41.

Berenbaum, S.A. (1999). Effects of early androgens on sex-typed actuivities and unterests in adolescents with congenital adrenal hyperplasia. *Hormones and Behavior, 35*, 102–10.

Berenbaum, S.A. (2006). Psychological outcome in children with disorders of sex development: Implications for treatment and understanding typical development. *Annual Review of Sex Research, 17*, 1–38.

Berenbaum, S.A., & Beltz, A.M. (2011). Sexual differentiation of human behavior: Effects of prenatal and pubertal organizational hormones. *Frontiers in Neuroendocrinology, 32*, 183–200.

Bergstrom, M.L., & Fedigan, L.M. (2010). Dominance among female white-faced capuchin monkeys (*Cebus capucinus*): Hierarchical linearity, nepotism, strength and stability. *Behaviour, 147*, 899–931.

Berndt, R.M. (1964). Warfare in the New Guinea Highlands. *American Anthropologist, 66*, 183–203.

Berscheid, E., Hatfield, E., & Bohrnstedt, G. (1973). The body image report. *Psychology Today*, *7*, 119–31.

Besag, V. (2000). *A study of the changing friendship relations within a group of primary age girls and their use of insult, gossip, rumour and grassing in this process*. PhD dissertation, Durham University, United Kingdom.

Best, M., Williams, J.M., & Coccaro, E.F. (2002). Evidence for a dysfunctional prefrontal circuit in patients with an impulsive aggressive disorder. *Proceedings of the National Academy of Sciences of the United States of America*, *99*, 8448–53.

Best, R. (1983). *We've all got scars: What boys and girls learn in elementary school*. Bloomington, IN: Indiana University Press.

Bettencourt, B.A., & Miller, N. (1996). Gender differences in aggression as a function of provocation: A meta-analysis. *Psychological Bulletin*, *119*, 422–47.

Betzig, L. (1986). *Despotism and differential reproduction: A Darwinian view of history*. Hawthorne, NY: Aldine de Gruyter.

Betzig, L. (1989). Causes of conjugal dissolution: A cross-cultural study. *Current Anthropology*, *30*, 654–76.

Betzig, L. (1997a). People are animals. In L. Betzig (Ed.), *Human nature: A critical reader* (pp. 1–17). Oxford: Oxford University Press.

Betzig, L. (1997b). Roman polygyny. In L. Betzig (Ed.), *Human nature: A critical reader* (pp. 375–98). Oxford: Oxford University Press.

Betzig, L. (1998). Not whether to count babies, but which. In C. Crawford & D. Krebs (Eds.), *Handbook of evolutionary psychology* (pp. 265–73). New Jersey, NJ: Erlbaum.

Betzig, L. (2008). *Despotism, social evolution, and differential reproduction*. London: Aldine.

Betzig, L.L. (1982). Despotism and differential reproduction: A cross-cultural correlation of conflict asymmetry, hierarchy and degree of polygyny. *Ethology and Sociobiology*, *3*, 209–21.

Bhatt, R.S., & Rovee-Collier, C. (1996). Infants' forgetting of correlated attributes and object recognition. *Child Development*, *67*, 172–87.

Birkhead, T.R. (2010). How stupid not to have thought of that: Post-copulatory sexual selection. *Journal of Zoology*, *281*, 78–93.

Birkhead, T.R., Chaline, N., Biggins, J.D., Burke, T.A., & Pizzari, T. (2004). Nontransitivity of paternity in a bird. *Evolution*, *58*, 416–20.

Bischoping, K. (1993). Gender differences in conversation topics, 1922–1990. *Sex Roles*, *28*, 1–13.

Björkqvist, K., Lagerspetz, K., & Kaukiainen, A. (1992). Do girls manipulate and boys fight? Developmental trends in regard to direct and indirect aggression. *Aggressive Behavior*, *18*, 117–27.

Blackmore, S. (1999). *The meme machine*. Oxford: Oxford University Press.

Blair, R.J.R. (2004). The roles of orbital frontal cortex in the modulation of antisocial behavior. *Brain and Cognition*, *55*, 198–208.

Blair, R.J.R., Jones, L., Clark, F., & Smith, M. (1997). The psychopathic individual: A lack of responsiveness to stress cues? *Psychophysiology*, *34*, 192–8.

Blakemore, J., LaRue, A., & Olejnik, A. (1979). Sex-appropriate toy preference and the ability to conceptualise toys as sex role related. *Developmental Psychology*, *15*, 339–40.

Blanchard, C.D., Hynd, A.L., Minke, K.A., Minemoto, T., & Blanchard, R.J. (2001). Human defensive behaviors to threat scenarios show parallels to fear-and anxiety-related defense patterns of non-human mammals. *Neuroscience and Biobehavioral Reviews*, *25*, 761–70.

Bleier, R. (1984). *Science and gender: A critique of biology and its theories on women.* New York, NY: Pergamon.

Bleske, A.L., & Shackelford, T.K. (2001). Poaching, promiscuity and deceit: Combating mating rivalry in same-sex friendships. *Personal Relationships, 8,* 407–24.

Bleske-Rechek, A., & Lighthall, M. (2010). Attractiveness and rivalry in women's friendships with women. *Human Nature, 21,* 82–97.

Blickhorn, S. (2005). A gender bender. *Nature, 438,* 31–2.

Block, J. (1993). Studying personality the long way. In D.C. Funder, R.D. Parke, C. Tomlinson-Keasey, & K. Widaman (Eds.), *Studying lives through time: Personality and development* (pp. 9–41). Washington, DC: American Psychological Association.

Boehnke, K., Silbereisen, R., Eisenberg, N., Teykowski, J., & Palmonari, A. (1989). Developmental patterns of prosocial motivation: A cross-national study. *Journal of Cross-Cultural Psychology, 20,* 219–43.

Boesch, C., Kohou, G., Nene, H., & Vigilant, L. (2006). Male competition and paternity in wild chimpanzees of the Taï forest. *American Journal of Physical Anthropology, 130,* 103–15.

Borgerhoff Mulder, M. (1990). Kipsigis women's preference for wealthy men: Evidence for female choice in mammals? *Behavioral Ecology and Sociobiology, 27,* 255–64.

Borgerhoff Mulder, M. (2000). Optimizing offspring: The quantity–quality tradeoff in agropastoral Kipsigis. *Evolution and Human Behavior, 21,* 391–410.

Borgerhoff Mulder, M. (2009). Tradeoffs and sexual conflict over women's fertility preferences in Mpimbwe. *American Journal of Human Biology, 21,* 478–87.

Borgerhoff Mulder, M., & Rauch, K.L. (2009). Sexual conflict in humans: Variations and solutions. *Evolutionary Anthropology, 18,* 201–14.

Bouchard, T.J. (2004). Genetic influence on human psychological traits: A survey. *Current Directions in Psychological Science, 13,* 148–51.

Bouchard, T.J., Lykken, D.T., McGue, M., Segal, N.L., & Tellegen, A. (1990). Sources of human psychological differences: The Minnesota study of twins reared apart. *Science, 250,* 223–8.

Boulton, M. (1996). A comparison of 8- and 11-year-old girls' and boys' participation in specific types of rough-and-tumble play and aggressive fighting: Implications for functional hypotheses. *Aggressive Behavior, 22,* 271–87.

Bowker, L.H. (1984). Coping with wife abuse: Personal and social networks. In A.R. Roberts (Ed.), *Battered women and their families* (pp. 168–91). New York, NY: Springer.

Bowlby, J. (1969). *Attachment: Attachment and loss, Volume 1.* Middlesex: Penguin.

Boyce, M.S. (1990). The red queen visits sage grouse leks. *American Zoologist, 30,* 263–70.

Boyce, W.T., & Ellis, B.J. (2005). Biological sensitivity to context: I. An evolutionary-developmental theory of the origins and functions of stress reactivity. *Development and Psychopathology, 17,* 271–301.

Boyer, P., & Bergstrom, B. (2011). Threat-detection in child development: An evolutionary perspective. *Neuroscience and Biobehavioral Reviews, 35,* 1034–41.

Bradley, B.J., Robbins, M.M., Williamson, E.A., Steklis, H.D., Steklis, N.G., Eckhardt, N., et al. (2005). Mountain gorilla tug-of-war: Silverbacks have limited control over reproduction in multimale groups. *Proceedings of the National Academy of Sciences of the United States of America, 102,* 9418–23.

Bradley, M.M., Cuthbert, B.N., & Lang, P.N. (1999). Affect and the startle reflex. In M.E. Dawson, A.M. Schnell, & A.H. Bohmelt (Eds.), *Startle modification: Implications for neuroscience, cognitive science and clinical science* (pp. 157–83). New York, NY: Cambridge University Press.

Brebner, J. (2003). Gender and emotions. *Personality and Individual Differences, 34,* 387–94.

Broad, K.D., Curley, J.P., & Keverne, E.B. (2006). Mother–infant bonding and the evolution of mammalian social relationships. *Philosophical Transactions of the Royal Society of London, Series B, Biological Sciences, 361,* 2199–214.

Brody, L.R., & Hall, J.A. (1993). Gender and emotion. In M. Lewis & J.M. Haviland (Eds.), *Handbook of emotions* (pp. 447–60). New York NY: Guildford Press.

Brody, L.R., Lovas, G.S., & Hay, D.H. (1995). Gender differences in anger and fear as a function of situational context. *Sex Roles, 32,* 47–78.

Brooks, J., & Lewis, M. (1974). Attachment behavior in thirteen-month-old, opposite sex twins. *Child Development, 45,* 243–7.

Brown, D.E. (1991). *Human universals.* New York, NY: McGraw Hill.

Brown, G.A. (2004). Gender as a factor in the response of the law-enforcement system to violence against partners. *Sexuality and Culture, 8,* 3–139.

Brown, L.M. (1998). *Raising their voices: The politics of girls' anger.* London: Harvard University Press.

Brown, N.R., & Sinclair, R.C. (1999). Estimating number of lifetime sexual partners: Men and women do it differently. *Journal of Sex Research, 36,* 292–7.

Brown, S.L., & Brown, R.M. (2006). Selective investment theory: Recasting the functional significance of close relationships. *Psychological Inquiry, 17,* 1–29.

Browne, A. (1987). *When battered women kill.* New York, NY: Free Press.

Browne, K.R. (1995). Sex and temperament in modern society: A Darwinian view of the glass ceiling and the gender gap. *Arizona Law Review, 37,* 971–1106.

Browne, K.R. (2006). Evolved sex differences and occupational segregation. *Journal of Organizational Behavior, 27,* 143–62.

Bryson, J.B. (1991). Modes of response to jealousy-evoking situations. In P. Salovey (Ed.), *The psychology of jealousy and envy* (pp. 1–45). New York, NY: Guildford.

Buckle, L., Gallup, G.G., & Rodd, Z.A. (1996). Marriage as a reproductive contract: Patterns of marriage, divorce and remarriage. *Ethology and Sociobiology, 17,* 363–77.

Bugental, D.B., & Beaulieu, D.A. (2009). Sex differences in response to coalitional threat. *Evolution and Human Behavior, 30,* 238–43.

Bukowski, W.M., Gauze, C., Hoza, B., & Newcomb, A.F. (1993). Differences and consistency between same-sex and other-sex peer relationships during early adolescence. *Developmental Psychology, 29,* 255–63.

Burbank, V. (1987). Female aggression in cross-cultural perspective. *Behavioral Science Research, 21,* 70–100.

Burbank, V. (1994). *Fighting women: Anger and aggression in Aboriginal Australia.* Berkeley, CA: University of California Press.

Burley, N. (1979). The evolution of concealed ovulation. *American Naturalist, 114,* 835–58.

Burnham, T.C. (2007). High-testosterone men reject low ultimatum game offers. *Philosophical Transactions of the Royal Society of London, Series B, Biological Sciences, 274,* 2327–30.

Bushnell, I.W.R., Sai, F., & Mullin, J.T. (1989). Neonatal recognition of the mother's face. *British Journal of Developmental Psychology, 7,* 3–13.

Buss, D., & Duntley, J.D. (2011). The evolution of intimate partner violence. *Aggression and Violent Behavior*, *16*, 411–19.

Buss, D.M., Shackelford, T.K., Choe, J., Buunk, B.P., & Dijkstra, P. (2000). Distress about mating rivals. *Personal Relationships*, *7*, 235–43.

Buss, D.M. (1988a). The evolution of human intrasexual competition: Tactics of mate attraction. *Journal of Personality and Social Psychology*, *54*, 616–28.

Buss, D.M. (1988b). From vigilance to violence: Tactics of mate retention in American undergraduates. *Ethology and Sociobiology*, *9*, 291–317.

Buss, D.M. (1989a). Sex differences in human mate preferences: Evolutionary hypothesis tested in 37 cultures. *Behavioral and Brain Sciences*, *12*, 1–14.

Buss, D.M. (1989b). Toward an evolutionary psychology of human mating. *Behavioral and Brain Sciences*, *12*, 39–49.

Buss, D.M. (1989c). Conflict between the sexes: Strategic interference and the evocation of anger and upset. *Journal of Personality and Social Psychology*, *56*, 735–47.

Buss, D.M. (1991). Evolutionary personality psychology. *Annual Review of Psychology*, *42*, 459–91.

Buss, D.M. (2000). *The dangerous passion*. London: Bloomsbury.

Buss, D.M., & Dedden, L.A. (1990). Derogation of competitors. *Journal of Personal Relationships*, *7*, 395–422.

Buss, D.M., & Greiling, H. (1999). Adaptive individual differences. *Journal of Personality*, *67*, 209–43.

Buss, D.M., Haselton, M.G., Shackelford, T.K., Bleske, A.L., & Wakefield, J.C. (1998). Adaptations, exaptations and spandrels. *American Psychologist*, *53*, 533–48.

Buss, D.M., Larsen, R.J., Westen, D., & Semmelroth, J. (1992). Sex differences in jealousy: Evolution, physiology, and psychology. *Psychological Science*, *3*, 251–5.

Buss, D.M., & Schmitt, D.P. (1993). Sexual strategies theory: An evolutionary perspective on human mating. *Psychological Review*, *100*, 204–32.

Buss, D.M., & Shackelford, T.K. (1997). Susceptibility to infidelity in the first year of marriage. *Journal of Research in Personality*, *31*, 193–221.

Buss, D.M., Shackelford, T.K., Kirkpatrick, L.A., Choe, J., Hasegawa, M., Hasegawa, T., & Bennett, K. (1999). Jealousy and the nature of beliefs about infidelity: Tests of competing hypotheses about sex differences in the United States, Korea and Japan. *Personal Relationships*, *6*, 125–50.

Buss, D., Shackelford, T., Kirkpatrick, L., & Larsen, R. (2001). A half century of mate preferences: The cultural evolution of values. *Journal of Marriage and Family*, *63*, 491–503.

Buunk, B.P. (1981). Jealousy in sexually open marriages. *Alternative Lifestyles*, *4*, 357–72.

Buunk, B.P. (1982). Strategies of jealousy: Styles of coping with extra marital involvement of the spouse. *Family Relations*, *31*, 13–8.

Buunk, B., & Hupka, R.B. (1987). Cross-cultural differences in the elicitation of jealousy. *Journal of Sex Research*, *23*, 12–22.

Byrnes, J.P., Miller, D.C., & Schafer, W.D. (1999). Gender differences in risk taking: A meta-analysis. *Psychological Bulletin*, *125*, 367–83.

Cairns, R.B., & Cairns, B.D. (1984). Predicting aggressive patterns in girls and boys: A developmental study. *Aggressive Behavior*, *10*, 227–42.

Cairns, R.B., Cairns, B.D., Neckerman, H.J., Ferguson, L.L., & Gariepy, L.-L. (1989). Growth and aggression: 1. Childhood to early adolescence. *Developmental Psychology, 25,* 320–30.

Caldera, Y., Huston, A., & O'Brien, M. (1989). Social interactions and play patterns of parents and toddlers with feminine, masculine and neutral toys. *Child Development, 60,* 70–6.

Caldwell, M., & Peplau, L. (1982). Sex differences in same-sex friendships. *Sex Roles, 8,* 721–32.

Campbell, A. (1982). Female aggression. In P. Marsh & A. Campbell (Eds.), *Aggression and violence.* Oxford: Blackwell.

Campbell, A. (1984). *The girls in the gang.* Oxford and Boston: Blackwell.

Campbell, A. (1986). Self report of fighting by females. *British Journal of Criminology, 26,* 28–46.

Campbell, A. (1998). Gender and the development of interpersonal orientation. In A. Campbell and S. Muncer (Eds.), *The social child* (pp. 325–52). Hove: Psychology Press.

Campbell, A. (1999). Staying alive: Evolution, culture and intra-female aggression. *Behavioral and Brain Sciences, 22,* 203–52.

Campbell, A. (2006). Sex differences in direct aggression: What are the psychological mediators? *Aggression and Violent Behavior, 11,* 237–64.

Campbell, A. (2008a). The morning after the night before: Affective reactions to one-night stands among mated and unmated women and men. *Human Nature, 19,* 157–73.

Campbell, A. (2008b). Attachment, aggression and affiliation: The role of oxytocin in female social behaviour. *Biological Psychology, 77,* 1–10.

Campbell, A. (2009). What kind of selection? *Behavioral and Brain Sciences, 32,* 272–3.

Campbell, A. (2010). Oxytocin and human social behavior. *Personality and Social Psychology Review, 14,* 281–95.

Campbell, A. (2011). Ladies, choose your weapons. *The Evolutionary Review, 2,* 106–12.

Campbell, A., Muncer, S., & Bibel, D. (1998). Female-female criminal assault: An evolutionary perspective. *Journal of Research in Crime and Delinquency, 35,* 413–28.

Campbell, A., Muncer, S., & Bibel, D. (2001). Women and crime: An evolutionary approach. *Aggression and Violent Behavior, 6,* 481–97.

Campbell, A., Shirley, L., & Candy, J. (2004). A longitudinal study of gender-related cognition and behaviour. *Developmental Science, 7,* 1–9.

Campbell, A., Shirley, L., & Caygill, L. (2002). Sex-typed preferences in three domains: Do two-year-olds need cognitive variables? *British Journal of Psychology, 93,* 203–17.

Campbell, A., Shirley, L., Heywood, C., & Crook, C. (2000). Infants' visual preference for sex-congruent babies, children, toys and activities: A longitudinal study. *British Journal of Developmental Psychology, 18,* 479–98.

Campbell, D.T. (1960). Blind variation and selective retention in creative thought as in other knowledge processes. *Psychological Review, 67,* 380–400.

Campbell, M., & Bedford, K. (2009). The theoretical and political framing of the population factor in development. *Philosophical Transactions of the Royal Society of London, Series B, Biological Sciences, 364,* 3101–13.

Card, N.A., Stucky, B.D., Sawalani, G.M., & Little, T.D. (2008). Direct and indirect aggression during childhood and adolescence: A meta-analytic review of gender differences, intercorrelations, and relations to maladjustment. *Child Development, 79,* 1185–229.

Carey, W.B., & McDevitt, S.C. (1978). Revisions of the infant temperament questionnaire. *Pediatrics, 61,* 735–9.

Carmichael, M.S., Humbert, R., Dixen, J., Palmisano, G., Greenleaf, W., & Davidson, J.M. (1987). Plasma oxytocin increases in the human sexual response. *Journal of Clinical Endocrinology and Metabolism, 64,* 27–31.

Carver, C.S. (2005). Impulse and constraint: Perspectives from personality psychology, convergence with theory in other areas, and potential for integration. *Personality and Social Psychology Review, 9,* 312–33.

Carver, C.S., & Harmon-Jones, E. (2009). Anger is an approach-related affect: Evidence and implications. *Psychological Bulletin, 135,* 183–204.

Carver, C.S., Johnson, S.L., & Joormann, J. (2008). Serotonergic function, two-mode models of self-regulation, and vulnerability to depression: What depression has in common with impulsive aggression. *Psychological Bulletin, 134,* 912–43.

Cashdan, E. (1993). Attracting mates; Effects of paternal investment on mate attraction. *Ethology and Sociobiology, 14,* 1–24.

Cashdan, E. (1996). Women's mating strategies. *Evolutionary Anthropology, 5,* 134–43.

Cashdan, E. (1998). Are men more competitive than women? *British Journal of Social Psychology, 37,* 213–29.

Caspi, A., McClay, J., Moffitt, T.E., Mill, J., Martin, J., Craig, I.W. *et al.* (2002). Role of genotype in the cycle of violence in maltreated children. *Science, 297,* 851–4.

Caspi, A., Sugden, K., Moffitt, T.E., Taylor, A., Craig, I.W., Harrington, L. *et al.* (2003). Influence of life stress on depression: Moderation by a polymorphism in the 5-HTT gene. *Science, 301,* 386–9.

Cayetano, L., Maklakov, A.A., Brooks, R.C., & Bonduriansky, R. (2011). Evolution of male and female genitalia following release from sexual selection. *Evolution, 65,* 2171–83.

Ceci, S.J., Williams, W.M., & Barnett, S.M. (2009). Women's underrepresentation in science: Sociocultural and biological considerations. *Psychological Bulletin, 135,* 218–61.

Center for Disease Control and Prevention. *Unmarried childbearing.* <http://www.cdc.gov/nchs/fastats/unmarry.htm>

Cerda-Flores, R.M., Barton, S.A., Marty-Gonzalez, L.F., Rivas, F., & Cakraborty, R. (1999). Estimation of nonpaternity in the Mexican population of Nuevo Leon: A validation study with blood group markers. *American Journal of Physical Anthropology, 109,* 281–93.

Chagnon, N.A. (1983). *Yanomamo: The fierce people* (3rd ed.). New York, NY: Holt, Rinehart and Winston.

Chagnon, N.A. (1988). Life histories, blood revenge and warfare in a tribal population. *Science, 239,* 985–92.

Chapais, B. (2002). The role of alliances in social inheritance of rank among female primates. In A. Harcourt & F.B.M. de Waal (Eds.), *Coalitions and alliances in humans and other animals* (pp. 29–59). Oxford: Oxford Science Publications.

Chapman, T., Arnqvist, G., Bangham, J., & Rowe, L. (2003). Sexual conflict. *Trends in Ecology and Evolution, 18,* 41–7.

Charlesworth, W.R., & Dzur, C. (1987). Gender comparisons of preschoolers' behavior and resource utilization in group problem solving. *Child Development, 58,* 191–200.

Cherlin, A. (1979). Work life and marital disruption. In G. Levinger & O.C. Moles (Eds.), *Divorce and separation: Context, causes and consequences* (pp. 151–66). New York, NY: Basic Books.

Cherlin, A. (1981). *Marriage, divorce, remarriage.* Cambridge, MA: Harvard University Press.

Chidester, D. (2003). *Salvation and suicide: Jim Jones, the People's Temple and Jonestown.* Bloomington, IN: Indiana University Press.

Chisholm, J.S. (1993). Death, hope, and sex: Life-history theory and the development of reproductive strategies. *Current Anthropology, 34,* 1–24.

Chisholm, J.S., Quinlivan, J.A., Peterson, R.W., & Coall, D.A. (2005). Early stress predicts age at menarche and first birth, adult attachment, and expected lifespan. *Human Nature, 16,* 233–65.

Clark, L., & Tiggemann, M. (2008). Sociocultural and individual psychological predictors of body image in young girls: A prospective study. *Developmental Psychology, 44,* 1124–34.

Clark, R.D., & Hatfield, E. (1989). Gender differences in receptivity to sexual offers. *Journal of Psychology and Human Sexuality, 2,* 39–55.

Clarke, C.A., & Shepherd, P.M. (1971). Further studies of on the genetics of the mimetic butterfly *Papilio memnon. Philosophical Transactions of the Royal Society of London, Series B, Biological Sciences, 263,* 35–70.

Clarke, M., & Reis, H.T. (1988). Interpersonal processes in close relationships. *Annual Review of Psychology, 39,* 609–72.

Closson, L.M. (2009). Status and gender differences in early adolescents' descriptions of popularity. *Social Development, 18,* 412–26.

Clutton-Brock, T. (2007). Sexual selection in males and females. *Science, 318,* 1882–5.

Clutton-Brock, T.H. (2009). Cooperation between non-kin in animal societies. *Nature, 462,* 51–7.

Coan, J.A., & Allen, J.J.B. (2004). Frontal EEG asymmetry as a moderator and mediator of emotion. *Biological Psychology, 67,* 7–49.

Coccaro, E.F., Sripada, C.S., Yanowitch, R.N., & Luan, K. (2011). Corticolimbic function in impulsive aggressive behavior. *Biological Psychiatry, 69,* 1153–9.

Cohen, J.T., Bellinger, D.C., Connor, W.E., & Shaywitz, B.A. (2005). A quantitative analysis of prenatal intake of n-3 polyunsaturated fatty acids and cognitive development. *American Journal of Preventive Medicine, 29,* 366–74.

Cohen, L.J., & Campos, J.J. (1974). Father, mother and strangers as elicitors of attachment behaviors in infancy. *Developmental Psychology, 10,* 146–54.

Cohen, L.L., & Shotland, R.L. (1996). Timing of first sexual intercourse in a relationship: Expectations, experiences, and perceptions of others. *Journal of Sex Research, 33,* 291–9.

Cohen, N.J., Gotlieb, H., Kershner, J., & Wehrspann, W. (1985). Concurrent validity of the internalizing and externalizing profile pattern of the Achenbach Child Behaviors Checklist. *Journal of Consulting and Clinical Psychology, 53,* 724–8.

Colapinto, J. (2000). What the doctor ordered. *The Independent on Sunday,* February 6.

Colletta, N., & Lee, D. (1983). The impact of support for black adolescent mothers. *Journal of Family Issues, 4,* 127–43.

Collier, J. (1974). Women in politics. In M. Rosaldo & L. Lamphere (Eds.), *Women, culture and society* (pp. 89–96). Stanford, CA: Stanford University Press.

Colom, R., Rebello, I., Palacios, A., Juan-Espinosa, M., & Kyllonen, P.C. (2004). Working memory is (almost) perfectly predicted by g. *Intelligence, 32,* 277–96.

Comb, S., Hyman, S.E., & Goodman, H.M. (1987). Mechanisms of trans-synaptic regulation of gene expression. *Trends in Neuroscience, 10,* 473–8.

Constable, J.L., Ashley, M.V., Goodall, J., & Pusey, A.E. (2001). Noninvasive paternity assignment in Gombe chimpanzees. *Molecular Ecology, 10,* 1279–300.

Cooke, L.P. (2004). The gendered division of labor and family outcomes in Germany. *Journal of Marriage and the Family, 66,* 1246–59.

Cooke, L.P. (2007). Policy pathways to gender power: State-level effects on the US division of housework. *Journal of Social Policy, 36,* 239–60.

Cooney, R.E., Joormann, J., Atlas, L.Y., Eugene, F., & Gotlib, I.H. (2007). Remembering the good times: neural correlates of affect regulation. *Neuroreport, 18,* 1771–4.

Cooper, R.M., & Zubek, J.P. (1958). Effects of enriched and restricted environments on the learning ability of bright and dull rats. *Canadian Journal of Psychology, 12,* 159–64.

Cope, W. (1992). "Men and their boring arguments." *Serious Concerns.* London: Faber and Faber.

Copeland, W., Shanahan, L., Miller, S., Costello, E.J., & Angold, A. (2010). Outcomes of early pubertal timing on young women: A prospective population based study. *American Journal of Psychiatry, 167,* 1218–25.

Cosmides, L. (1989). The logic of social exchange: Has natural selection shaped how humans reason? Studies with the Wason selection task. *Cognition, 31,* 187–276.

Cosmides, L., & Tooby, J. (1992). Cognitive adaptations for social exchange. In J.H. Barkow, L. Cosmides & J. Tooby (Eds.), *The adapted mind: Evolutionary psychology and the generation of culture* (pp. 163–228). New York, NY: Oxford University Press.

Costa, P.T., Terracciano, A., & McCrae, R.R. (2001). Gender differences in personality traits across cultures: Robust and surprising findings. *Journal of Personality and Social Psychology, 81,* 322–31.

Cote, S., Tremblay, R.E., Nagin, D., Zoccolillo, M., & Vitaro, F. (2002). The development of impulsivity, fearfulness and helpfulness during childhood: Patterns of consistency and change in the trajectories of boys and girls. *Journal of Child Psychology, Psychiatry and Allied Disciplines, 43,* 609–18.

Craig, S. (2008). *Sports and games of the ancients.* London: Greenwood.

Crawford, C. (1998). Environments and adaptations: Then and now. In C. Crawford & D.L. Krebs (Eds.), *Handbook of evolutionary psychology* (pp. 275–302). Mahwah, NJ: Lawrence Erlbaum.

Crawford, J., Kippax, S., Onyx, J., Gault, U., & Benton, P. (1992). *Emotion and gender: Constructing meaning from memory.* London: Sage.

Crawford, M., & Popp, D. (2003). Sexual double standards: A review and methodological critique of two decades of research. *The Journal of Sex Research, 40,* 13–26.

Cross, C.P., Copping, L.T., & Campbell, A. (2011). Sex differences in impulsivity: A meta-analysis. *Psychological Bulletin, 137,* 97–130.

Cross, C.P., Tee, W., & Campbell, A. (2011). Gender symmetry in intimate aggression: An effect of intimacy or target sex? *Aggressive Behavior, 37,* 268–77.

Cross, S.E., & Madson, L. (1997). Models of the self: Self-construals and gender. *Psychological Review, 122,* 5–37.

Cunningham, A.S. (1995). Breastfeeding: Adaptive behavior for child health and longevity. In P. Stuart-Macadam & K.A. Dettwyler (Eds.), *Breastfeeding: Biocultural pespectives* (pp. 243–64). Hawthorne, NY: Aldine de Gruyter.

Curry, J.F., & Hock, R.A. (1981). Sex differences in sex-role ideals in early adolescence. *Adolescence, 16*, 779–89.

d' Alfonso, A.A.L., van Honk, J., Hermans, E., Postma, A., & de Haan, E.H.F. (2000). Laterality effects in selective attention to threat after repetitive transcranial magnetic stimulation at the prefrontal cortex in female subjects. *Neuroscience Letters, 280*, 195–8.

Daly, M., Salmon, C., & Wilson, M. (1997). Kinship; The conceptual hole in psychological studies of social cognition and close relationships. In J.A. Simpson, & D.T. Kenrick (Eds.), *Evolutionary social psychology* (pp. 265–96). Mahwah, NJ: Erlabaum.

Daly, M., & Wilson, M. (1983). *Sex, evolution and behavior*. Boston, MA: Willard Grant.

Daly, M., & Wilson, M. (1988). *Homicide*. New York, NY: Aldine de Gruyter.

Daly, M., Wilson, M., & Weghorst, S. J. (1982). Male sexual jealousy. *Ethology and Sociobiology, 3*, 11–27.

Darwin, C. (1871). *The descent of man, and selection in relation to sex*. London: John Murray.

Davidovic, A., Bell, K., Ferguson, C., Gorski, E., & Campbell, A. (2011). Impelling and inhibitory forces in aggression: Sex-of-target and relationship effects. *Journal of Interpersonal Violence, 26*, 3098–126.

Davidson, R.J. (2000). Affective style, psychopathology, and resilience: Brain mechanisms and plasticity. *American Psychologist, 55*, 1196–214.

Davies, L. (1984). *Pupil power: Deviance and gender in school*. London: Falmer Press.

Dawkins, R. (1986). *The blind watchmaker*. London: Longman.

Dawkins, R. (1989). *The selfish gene*. Oxford: Oxford University Press.

Dawkins, R., & Carlisle, T.R. (1976). Parental investment, mate desertion and a fallacy. *Nature, 262*, 131–2.

Deary, I. (2012). Intelligence. *Annual Review of Psychology, 63*, 453–82.

Debiec, J. (2007). From affiliative behaviors to romantic feelings: A role of nonapeptides. *Febs Letters, 581*, 2580–6.

De Dreu, C.K.W., Greer, L.L., Handgraaf, M.J.J., Shalvi, S., Van Kleef, G.A., Baas, M., *et al.* (2010). The neuropeptide oxytocin regulates parochial altruism in intergroup conflict among humans. *Science, 328*, 1408–11.

DeKeseredy, W.S. (2011). Feminist contributions to understanding woman abuse: Myths, controversies, and realities. *Aggression and Violent Behavior, 16*, 297–302.

Del Giudice, M. (2009). Sex, attachment, and the development of reproductive strategies. *Behavioral and Brain Sciences, 32*, 1–21.

Del Giudice, M., & Belsky, J. (2010). The development of life history strategies: Toward a multi-stage theory. In D.M. Buss & P.H. Hawley (Eds.), *The evolution of personality and individual differences* (pp. 154–76). Oxford: Oxford University Press.

De Martino, B., Kumaran, D., Seymour, B., & Dolan, R.J. (2006). Frames, biases, and rational decision-making in the human brain. *Science, 313*, 684–7.

Demo, D., & Acock, A. (1988). The impact of divorce on children. *Journal of Marriage and the Family, 50*, 619–48.

Dennett, D. (1995). *Darwin's dangerous idea: Evolution and the meaning of life*. New York, NY: Touchstone.

Dennett, D. (1997). *Kinds of minds: Towards an understanding of consciousness*. London: Phoenix.

Depue, R.A., & Collins, P.F. (1999). Neurobiology of the structure of personality: Dopamine, facilitation of incentive motivation, and extraversion. *Behavioral and Brain Sciences, 22*, 491–569.

Derlega, V., Durham, B., Gockel, B., & Sholis, D. (1981). Sex differences in self-disclosure: Effects of topic content, friendship and partner's sex. *Sex Roles, 7*, 433–47.

DeSteno, D., Bartlett, M.Y., Braverman, J., & Salovey, P. (2002). Sex differences in jealousy: Evolutionary mechanism or artefact of measurement? *Journal of Personality and Social Psychology, 83*, 1103–16.

DeSteno, D.A., & Salovey, P. (1996). Evolutionary origins of sex differences in jealousy? Questioning the fitness of the model. *Psychological Science, 7*, 367–72.

Deutsch, M. (1985). *Distributive justice: A social psychological perspective*. New Haven, CN: Yale University Press.

Devincenzi, I., Ancellepark, R. A., Brunet, J. B., Costigliola, P., Ricchi, E., Chiodo, F., *et al.* (1992). Comparison of female-to-male and male-to-female transmission of HIV in 563 stable couples. *British Medical Journal, 304*, 809–13.

de Waal, F.B.M. (1982). *Chimpanzee politics: Power and sex among the apes*. New York, NY: Harper & Row.

de Waal, F.B.M. (1989). *Peacemaking among primates*. Cambridge, MA: Harvard University Press.

de Waal, F.B.M. (1993). Sex differences in chimpanzee (and human) behaviour: A matter of values? In M. Hechter, L. Nader, & R.E. Michod (Eds.), *The origin of values* (pp. 285–303). New York, NY: Aldine de Gruyter.

DeWall, C.N., MacDonald, G., Webster, G.D., Masten, C.L., Baumeister, R.F., Powell, C., *et al.* (2010). Acetaminophen reduces social pain: Behavioral and neural evidence. *Psychological Science, 21*, 931–7.

De Weerth, C., & Kalma, A. (1993). Female aggression as a response to sexual jealousy: A sex role reversal? *Aggressive Behavior, 19*, 265–79.

Diamond, J. (1991). Borrowed sexual ornaments. *Nature, 349*, 105.

Diamond, J. (1997). *Why sex is fun: The evolution of human sexuality*. London: Weidenfield and Nicholson.

Diamond, M., & Sigmundson, H.K. (1997). Sex reassignment at birth: Long-term review and clinical implications. *Archives of Pediatrics and Adolescent Medicine, 151*, 298–304.

Dickemann, M. (1979). The ecology of mating systems in hypergynous dowry societies. *Social Science Information, 18*, 163–95.

Di Forti, M., Iyegbe, C., Sallis, H., Kolliakou, A., Falcone, M.A., Paparelli, A., *et al.* (2012). Confirmation that the AKT1 (rs2494732) genotype influences risk of psychosis in cannabis users. *Biological Psychiatry, 72*, 811–16.

Dindia K., & Allen, M. (1992). Sex differences in self-disclosure: A meta-analysis. *Psychological Bulletin, 112*, 106–24.

DiPietro, J.A. (1981). Rough and tumble play: A function of gender. *Developmental Psychology, 17*, 50–8.

Ditzen, B., Neumann, I. D., Bodenmann, G., von Dawans, B., Turner, R. A., Ehlert, U., *et al.* (2007). Effects of different kinds of couple interaction on cortisol and heart rate responses to stress in women. *Psychoneuroendocrinology, 32*, 565–74.

Ditzen, B., Schaer, M., Gabriel, B., Bodenmann, G., Ehlert, U., & Heinrichs, M. (2009). Intranasal oxytocin increases positive communication and reduces cortisol levels during couple conflict. *Biological Psychiatry, 65,* 728–31.

Dobash, R.E., & Dobash, R.P. (1979). *Violence against wives: A case against the patriarchy.* New York, NY: Free Press.

Dobash, R.P., Dobash, R.E., Wilson, M., & Daly, M. (1992). The myth of sexual symmetry in marital violence. *Social Problems, 39,* 71–91.

Dodge, K.A., & Coie, J.D. (1987). Social information processing factors in reactive and pro-active aggression in children's peer groups. *Journal of Personality and Social Psychology, 53,* 1146–58.

Domes, G., Schulze, L., Moritiz, B., Grossmann, A., Hauenstein, K., Wirtz, P.H., *et al.* (2010). The neural correlates of sex differences in emotional reactivity and emotion regulation. *Human Brain Mapping, 31,* 758–69.

Donohoe, M.L., von Hippel, W., & Brooks, R.C. (2009). Beyond waist-hip ratio: Experimental multivariate evidence that average women's torsos are most attractive. *Behavioral Ecology, 20,* 716–21.

Dorjahn, V.R. (1958). Fertility, polygyny and their interrelations in Temne society. *American Anthropologist, 60,* 838–60.

Dougherty, D.D., Shin, L.M., Alpert, N.M., Pitman, R.K., Orr, S.P., Lasko, M., *et al.* (1999). Anger in healthy men: A PET study using script-driven imagery. *Biological Psychiatry, 46,* 466–72.

Downey, D.B. (2001). Number of siblings and intellectual development: The resource dilution explanation. *American Psychologist, 56,* 497–504.

Draper, P., & Harpending, H. (1982). Father absence and reproductive strategy: An evolutionary perspective. *Journal of Anthropological Research, 38,* 255–73.

Draper, P., & Harpending, H. (1988). A sociobiological perspective on the development of human reproductive strategies. In K.B. MacDonald (Ed.), *Sociobiological perspectives on human development* (pp. 340–72). New York, NY: Springer-Verlag.

Dreifuss, J.J., Dubois-Dauphin, M., Widmer, H., & Raggenbass, M. (1992). Electrophysiology of oxytocin actions on ventral neurons. *Annals of the New York Academy of Sciences 652,* 46–57.

Dunbar, R.I.M. (1984). *Reproductive decisions: An economic analysis of Gelada baboon social strategy.* Princeton, NJ: Princeton University Press.

Dunbar, R.I.M. (1988). *Primate social systems.* Beckenham: Croom Helm.

Dunbar, R.I.M. (1992). Neocortex size as a constraint on group size in primates. *Journal of Human Evolution, 20,* 469–93.

Dunbar, R.I.M. (1995). Are you lonesome tonight? *New Scientist, 145,* 26–31.

Duncan, N. (1999). *Sexual bullying: Gender conflict and pupil culture in secondary schools.* London: Routlege.

Dunn, S., & Morgan, V. (1987). Nursery and infant school play patterns: Sex-related differences. *British Educational Research Journal, 13,* 271–81.

Durham, W. H. (1991). *Coevolution: Genes, culture, and human diversity.* Stanford, CA: Stanford University Press.

Dykiert, D., Gale, C.G., & Deary, I.J. (2009). Are apparent sex differences in mean IQ scores created in part by sample restriction and increased male variance? *Intelligence, 37,* 42–7.

Eagly, A.H. (1987). *Sex differences in social behavior: A social role interpretation*. Hillsdale, NJ: Erlbaum.

Eagly, A.H. (1995). The science and politics of comparing women and men. *American Psychologist, 50*, 145–58.

Eagly, A.H., Ashmore, R.D., Makhijani, M.G., & Longo, L.C. (1991). What is beautiful is good, but...: A meta-analytic review of research on the physical attractiveness stereotype. *Psychological Bulletin, 110*, 109–28.

Eagly, A.H., & Johnson, B.T. (1990). Gender and leadership style: A meta-analysis. *Psychological Bulletin, 108*, 233–56.

Eagly, A.H., & Karau, S.J. (1991). Gender and the emergence of leaders: A meta-analysis. *Journal of Personality and Social Psychology, 60*, 685–710.

Eagly, A.H., & Karau, S.J. (2002). Role congruity theory of prejudice toward female leaders. *Psychological Review, 109*, 573–98.

Eagly, A.H., Makhijani, M.G., & Klonsky, B.G. (1992). Gender and the evaluation of leaders: A meta-analysis. *Psychological Bulletin, 111*, 3–22.

Eagly, A.H., & Steffen, V. (1986). Gender and aggressive behavior: A meta-analytic review of the social psychological literature. *Psychological Bulletin, 100*, 309–30.

Eagly, A.H., & Wood, W. (1999). The origins of sex differences in human behavior: Evolved dispositions versus social roles. *American Psychologist, 54*, 408–23.

Eagly, A.H., & Wood, W. (2009). Sexual selection does not provide an adequate account of sex differences in aggression. *Behavioral and Brain Sciences, 32*, 276–7.

Eagly, A.H., & Wood, W. (2011). Feminism and the evolution of sex differences and similarities. *Sex Roles, 64*, 758–67.

Eaton, W.O., & Enns, L.R. (1986). Sex differences in human motor activity level. *Psychological Bulletin, 100*, 19–28.

Eberhard, W.G. (1996). *Female control: Sexual selection by cryptic female choice*. Princeton, NJ: Princeton University Press.

Eder, D. (1985). The cycle of popularity: Interpersonal relations among female adolescents. *Sociology of Education, 58*, 154–65.

Eder, D. (1990). Serious and playful disputes: Variations in conflict talk among adolescent females. In A. Grimshaw (Ed.), *Conflict talk: Sociolinguistic investigations of arguments in conversations* (pp. 67–84). Cambridge: Cambridge University Press.

Eder, D., Evans, C.C., & Parker, S. (1995). *Gender and adolescent culture*. New Brunswick, NJ: Rutgers University Press.

Eder, D., & Sandford, S. (1986). The development and maintenance of interactional norms among early adolescents. *Sociological Studies of Child Development, 1*, 283–300.

Edwards, S., & Self, D.W. (2006). Monogamy: Dopamine ties the knot. *Nature Neuroscience, 9*, 7–8.

Egan, S.J., Wade, T.D., & Shafran, R. (2011). Perfectionism as a transdiagnostic process: A clinical review. *Clinical Psychology Review, 31*, 203–12.

Eibl-Eibesfeldt, I. (1989). *Human ethology*. New York, NY: Aldine de Gruyter.

Eisenberg, N., Fabes, R.A., Schaller, M., & Miller, P.A. (1989). Sympathy and personal distress: Development, gender differences and inter-relations of indexes. *New Directions for Child Development, 44*, 107–26.

Eisenberg, N., & Lennon, R. (1983). Sex differences in empathy and related capacities. *Psychological Bulletin, 94,* 100–31.

Eisenberger, N.I., Lieberman, M.D., & Williams, K.D. (2003). Does rejection hurt? An fMRI study of social exclusion. *Science, 302,* 290–2.

Eldredge, N., & Gould, S.J. (1972). Punctuated equilibria: An alternative to phylogenetic gradualism. In T.J.M. Schopf (Ed.), *Models in paleobiology* (pp. 82–115). San Francisco, CA: Freeman, Cooper & Company.

Elliott, D., Huizinga, D., & Morse, B. (1983). Self-reported violent offending: A descriptive analysis of juvenile violent offenders and their offending careers. *Journal of Interpersonal Violence, 1,* 472–514.

Ellis, B.J. (2004). Timing of pubertal maturation in girls. *Psychological Bulletin, 130,* 920–58.

Ellis, B.J. (2010). Toward an evolutionary-developmental explanation of alternative re- productive strategies: The central role of switch-controlled modular systems. In D.M. Buss & P.H. Hawley (Eds.), *The evolution of personality and individual differences* (pp. 177–209). New York, NY: Oxford University Press.

Ellis, B. J., & Garber, J. (2000). Psychosocial antecedents of variation in girls' pubertal timing: Maternal depression, stepfather presence, and marital and family stress. *Child Development, 71,* 485–501.

Ellis, B.J., & Symons, D. (1990). Sex differences in sexual fantasy: An evolutionary psychological approach. *Journal of Sex Research, 27,* 527–55.

Ellis, L. (1995). Dominance and reproductive success among nonhuman animals: A cross-species comparison. *Ethology and Sociobiology, 16,* 257–333.

Ellison, P. (1994). Advances in human reproductive ecology. *Annual Review of Anthropology, 23,* 255–75.

Ellison, P. (1996). Understanding natural variation in human ovarian function. In R.Dunbar (Ed.), *Human reproductive decisions* (pp. 22–51). London: Macmillan.

Else-Quest, N.M., Hyde, J.S., Goldsmith, H.H., & Van Hulle, C.A. (2006). Gender differ- ences in temperament: A meta-analysis. *Psychological Bulletin, 132,* 33–72.

Ember, C. (1981). A cross cultural perspective on sex differences. In R.H. Monroe, R.L. Monroe, & B. Whiting (Eds.), *Handbook of cross cultural human development* (pp. 531–80). New York, NY: Garland.

Ember, C.R. (1974). An evaluation of alternative theories of matrilocal versus patrilocal residence. *Behavior Science Research, 9,* 135–49.

Ember, C.R. (1978). Myths about hunter-gatherers. *Ethnology, 17,* 439–48.

Emery Thompson, M., Kahlenberg, S.M., Gilby, I.C., & Wrangham, R.W. (2007). Core area quality is associated with variance in reproductive success among female chimpanzees at Kanyawara, Kibale National Park. *Animal Behaviour, 73,* 501–12.

Emery Thompson, M., Stumpf, R.M., & Pusey, A.E. (2008). Female reproductive strategies and competition in apes: An introduction. *International Journal of Primatology, 29,* 815–21.

Epstein, C.F. (1997). The multiple realities of sameness and difference: Ideology and prac- tice. *Journal of Social Issues, 53,* 259–78.

Ermer, E., Guerin, S.A., Cosmides, L., Tooby, J., & Miller, M.B. (2006). Theory of mind broad and narrow: Reasoning about social exchange engages ToM areas, precautionary reasoning does not. *Social Neuroscience, 1,* 196–219.

Erskine, M.S., Barfield, R.J., & Goldman, B.D. (1980). Postpartum aggression in rats: II. Dependence on maternal sensitivity to young and effects of experience with pregnancy and parturition. *Journal of Comparative Physiology and Psychology, 94*, 495–505.

Eschenbeck, H., Kohlmann, C., & Lohaus, A. (2007). Gender differences in coping strategies in children and adolescents. *Journal of Individual Differences, 28*, 18–26.

Eshbaugh, E.M., & Gute, G. (2008). Hookups and sexual regret among college women. *The Journal of Social Psychology, 148*, 77–89.

Essock, S., & McGuire, M.T. (1989). Social reproductive histories of depressed and anxious women. In R.W. Bell & N.J. Bell (Eds.), *Interfaces in psychology: Sociobiology and the social sciences* (pp. 63–72). Lubbock, TX: Texas Tech University Press.

Essock-Vitale, S.M., & McGuire, M.T. (1985). Women's lives viewed from an evolutionary perspective. II. Patterns of helping. *Ethology and Sociobiology, 6*, 155–73.

Essock-Vitale, S.M., & McGuire, M.T. (1988). What 70 million years hath wrought: Sexual histories and reproductive success of a random sample of American women. In L. Betzig, M. Borgerhoff Mulder, & P. Turke (Eds.), *Human reproductive behaviour: A Darwinian perspective* (pp. 221–35). Cambridge: Cambridge University Press.

Etaugh, C., Grinnell, K., & Etaugh, A. (1989). Development of gender labeling: Effects of age of pictured children. *Sex Roles, 21*, 769–73.

Etcoff, N. (1999). *Survival of the prettiest*. London: Little, Brown and Company.

Evans, J. St. B.T. (2008). Dual processing accounts of reasoning, judgement and social cognition. *Annual Review of Psychology, 59*, 255–78.

Fabes, R.A., Shepard, S.A., Guthrie, I.K., & Martin, C.L. (1997). Roles of temperamental arousal and gender-segregated play in young children's social adjustment. *Developmental Psychology, 33*, 603–702.

Faer, L.M., Hendriks, A., Abed, R.T., & Figueredo, A.J. (2005). The evolutionary psychology of eating disorders: Female competition for mates or for status? *Psychology and Psychotherapy: Theory, Research and Practice, 78*, 397–417.

Fagot, B.I. (1985). Beyond the reinforcement principle: Another step toward understanding sex role development. *Developmental Psychology, 21*, 1097–104.

Fagot, B. (1991). *Peer relations in boys and girls from two to seven*. Paper presented at the biennial meeting of the Society for Research in Child Development, Seattle.

Fagot, B., & Leinbach, M. (1989). The young child's gender schema: Environmental input, internal organisation. *Child Development, 60*, 663–72.

Fagot, B., & Leinbach, M. (1993). Gender role development in young children: From discrimination to labeling. *Developmental Review, 13*, 205–24.

Fagot, B., Leinbach, M., & Hagan, R. (1986). Gender labeling and the adoption of sex-typed behaviors. *Developmental Psychology, 22*, 440–3.

Faust, M. (1960). Developmental maturity as a determinant of prestige in adolescent girls. *Child Development, 31*, 173–84.

Fausto-Sterling, A. (1992). *Myths of gender: Biological theories about women and men* (2nd ed.). New York, NY: Basic Books.

Fedigan, L.M. (1982). *Primate paradigms: Sex roles and social bonds*. Montreal: Eden Press.

Feingold, A. (1990). Gender differences in effects of physical attractiveness on romantic attraction: A comparison across five paradigms. *Journal of Personality and Social Psychology, 59*, 981–93.

Feingold, A. (1992a). Good-looking people are not what we think. *Psychological Bulletin, 111*, 304–41.

Feingold, A. (1992b). Gender differences in mate selection preferences: A test of the parental investment model. *Psychological Bulletin, 112*, 125–39.

Feingold, A. (1994). Gender differences in personality: A meta-analysis. *Psychological Bulletin, 116*, 429–56.

Feld, S.L., & Felson, R.B. (2008). Gender norms and retaliatory violence against spouses and acquaintances. *Journal of Family Issues, 29*, 692–703.

Feldman, R., Weller, A., Zagoory-Sharon, O., & Levine, A. (2007). Neuroendocrinological foundation of human affiliation: Plasma oxytocin levels across pregnancy and the post-partum period predict mother-infant bonding. *Psychological Science, 18*, 965–70.

Felson, R.B. (2002). *Violence and gender re-examined*. Washington, DC: American Psychological Association.

Felson, R.B. (2008). The legal consequences of intimate partner violence for men and women. *Children and Youth Services Review, 30*, 639–46.

Felson, R.B., & Feld, S.L. (2009). When a man hits a woman: Moral evaluations and report-ing violence to the police. *Aggressive Behavior, 35*, 477–88.

Felson, R.B., Messner, S.F., & Hoskin, A. (1999). The victim-offender relationship and call-ing the police in assaults. *Criminology, 37*, 931–47.

Felson, R.B., & Outlaw, M.C. (2007). The control motive and marital violence. *Violence and Victims, 22*, 387–407.

Felson, R.B., & Pare, P.P. (2007). Does the criminal justice system treat domestic violence and sexual assault offenders leniently? *Justice Quarterly, 24*, 435–59.

Ferguson, C.J., Winegard, B., & Winegard, B.M. (2011). Who is the fairest one of all? How evolution guides peer and media influences on female body dissatisfaction. *Review of General Psychology, 15*, 11–28.

Ferguson, J.N., Young, L.J., & Insel, T.R. (2002). The neuroendocrine basis of social recogni-tion. *Frontiers in Neuroendocrinology, 23*, 200–24.

Fernando Rodriguez, S., & Henderson, V.A. (1995). Intimate homicide: Victim-offender relationship in female-perpetrated homicide. *Deviant Behavior, 16*, 45–57.

Ferreira, A., Hansen, S., Nielson, M., Archer, T., & Minor, B.G. (1989). Behavior of mother rats in conflict tests sensitive to anti-anxiety agents. *Behavioral Neuroscience, 103*, 193–201.

Fiebert, M.S., & Gonzalez, D.M. (1997). College women who initiate assaults on their male partners and the reasons offered for such behavior. *Psychological Reports, 80*, 583–90.

Field, T. (1985). Neonatal perception of people: maturational and individual differences. In T.M. Field & N.A. Fox (Eds.), *Social perception in infants*. Norwood, NJ: Ablex.

Fielder, R.L., & Carey, M.P. (2010). Predictors and consequences of sexual "hookups" among college students: A short-term perspective study. *Archives of Sexual Behavior, 39*, 1105–119.

Figueredo, A.J., Sefcek, J.A., & Jones, D.N. (2006). The ideal romantic partner personality. *Personality and Individual Differences, 41*, 431–41.

Fillion, K. (1997). *Lip service*. London: Pandora.

Fischer, A.H. (1993). Sex differences in emotionality: Fact or stereotype? *Feminism and Psychology, 3*, 303–18.

Fischer, A.H., & Evers, C. (2011). The social costs and benefits of anger as a function of gender and relationship context. *Sex Roles, 65,* 23–34.

Fischer, A.H., & Manstead, A.S.R. (2000). Gender and emotions in different cultures. In A.H. Fischer (Ed.), *Gender and emotion: Social Psychological Perspectives* (pp. 71–94). Cambridge: Cambridge University Press.

Fischer, A.H., Mosquera, P.M.R., van Vianen, A., & Manstead, A.S.R. (2004). Gender and culture differences in emotion. *Emotion, 4,* 87–94.

Fisher, H.E. (1993). *Anatomy of love: A natural history of monogamy, adultery and divorce.* London: Simon and Schuster.

Fisher, H.E., Aron, A., & Brown, L. (2006). Romantic love: A mammalian system for mate choice. *Philosophical Transactions of the Royal Society of London, Series B, Biological Sciences, 361,* 2173–86.

Fisher, K. (2000). Uncertain aims and tacit negotiation: Birth control practices in Britain, 1925–50. *Population and Development Review, 26,* 295–317.

Fisher, R.A. (1930). *The genetical theory of natural selection.* Oxford: Clarendon Press.

Fiske, A.P. (1992). The four elementary forms of sociality: Framework for a unified theory of social relations. *Psychological Review, 99,* 689–723.

Fleming, A.S., & Luebke, C. (1981). Timidity prevents the virgin female rat from being a good mother: Emotionality differences between nulliparous and parturient females. *Physiology and Behavior, 27,* 863–70.

Flory, J.D., Harvey, P.D., Mitropoulou, V., New, A.S., Silverman, J.M., Siever, L.J., & Manuck, S.B. (2006). Dispositional impulsivity in normal and abnormal samples. *Journal of Psychiatric Research, 40,* 438–47.

Fodor, J. (1983). *The modularity of mind.* Cambridge, MA: MIT Press.

Foley, R.A. (1987). *Another unique species.* London: Longman.

Foley, R.A. (1996). An evolutionary and chronological framework for human social behaviour. *Proceedings of the British Academy, 88,* 95–117.

Follingstad, D.R., Wright, S., Lloyd, S., & Sebastian, J.A. (1991). Sex differences in motivations and effects in dating violence. *Family Relations, 40,* 51–7.

Folstad, I., & Karter, A.J. (1992). Parasites, bright males and the immunocompetence handicap. *American Naturalist, 139,* 603–22.

Forgas, J.P. (1995). Mood and judgment: The affect infusion model (AIM). *Psychological Bulletin, 117,* 39–66.

Foster, C. (2000). The limits to low fertility: A biosocial approach. *Population and Development Review, 26,* 202–34.

Fox, N.A., & Davidson, R.J. (1986). Taste-elicited changes in facial signs of emotion and the asymmetry of brain electrical activity in human newborns. *Neuropsychologia, 24,* 417–22.

Franklin, C.A. (2010). Physically forced, alcohol-induced, and verbally coerced sexual victimization: Assessing risk factors among university women. *Journal of Criminal Justice, 38,* 149–59.

Fredrickson, B.L., & Roberts, T.-A. (1997). Objectification theory: Toward understanding women's lived experiences and mental health risks. *Psychology of Women Quarterly, 21,* 173–206.

Fredrikson, M., Annas, P., Fischer, H., & Wik, G. (1996). Gender and age differences in the prevalence of specific fears and phobias. *Behaviour Research and Therapy, 34,* 33–9.

Freedman, D. (1974). *Human infancy: An evolutionary perspective*. Hillsdale, NJ: Erlbaum.

Freedman, M.B., Leary, T.F., Ossorio, A.G., & Coffey, H.S. (1951). The interpersonal dimension of personality. *Journal of Personality, 20,* 143–61.

Freeman, D. (1983). *Margaret Mead and Samoa: The making and unmaking of an anthropological myth*. Cambridge, MA: Harvard University Press.

Frijda, N.H. (1986). *The emotions*. Cambridge: Cambridge University Press.

Frost, W.D., & Averill, J.R. (1982). Differences between men and women in the everyday experience of anger. In J.R. Averill (Ed.), *Anger and aggression: An essay on emotion* (pp. 281–317). New York, NY: Springer-Verlag.

Fry, D.P. (1992). Female aggression among the Zapotec of Oaxaca, Mexico. In K. Björkqvist, & P. Niemela (Eds.), *Of mice and women: Aspects of female aggression* (pp. 187–99). New York, NY: Academic Press.

Fuentes, A. (2002). Patterns and trends in primate pair bonds. *International Journal of Primatology, 23,* 953–78.

Furlow, F.B., Armijo-Prewitt, T., Gangestad, S.W., & Thrornhill, R. (1997). Fluctuating asymmetry and psychometric intelligence. *Proceedings of the Royal Society of London B, 264,* 823–9.

Furnham, A., & Radley, S. (1989). Sex differences in the perception of male and female body shape. *Personality and Individual Differences, 10,* 653–62.

Furuichi, T. (2009). Factors underlying party size differences between chimpanzees and bonobos: A review and hypotheses for future study. *Primates, 50,* 197–209.

Gabriel, K.I., & Williamson, A. (2010). Framing alters risk-taking on a modified Balloon Analogue Risk Task (BART) in a sex-specific manner. *Psychological Reports, 107,* 699–712.

Galen, B.R., & Underwood, M.K. (1997). A developmental investigation of social aggression among children. *Developmental Psychology, 33,* 589–600.

Gallese, V. (2003). The roots of empathy: The shared manifold hypothesis and the neural basis of intersubjectivity. *Psychopathology 36,* 171–80.

Gallup, G.G., & Burch, R.L. (2004). Semen displacement as a sperm competition strategy in humans. *Evolutionary Psychology, 2,* 12–23.

Gammie, S.C., Negron, A., Newman, S.M., & Rhodes, J.S. (2004). Corticotropin releasing factor inhibits maternal aggression in mice. *Behavioral Neuroscience, 118,* 805–14.

Gangestad, S.W., & Buss, D.M. (1993). Pathogen prevalence and human mate preferences. *Ethology and Sociobiology, 14,* 89–96.

Gangestad, S.W., & Simpson, J.A. (1990). Toward an evolutionary history of female sociosexual variation. *Journal of Personality, 58,* 69–96.

Gangestad, S.W., & Simpson, J.A. (2000). The evolution of human mating: Trade-offs and strategic pluralism. *Behavioral and Brain Sciences, 23,* 573–87.

Gangestad, S.W., & Thornhill, R. (1997). The evolutionary psychology of extrapair sex: The role of fluctuating asymmetry. *Evolution and Human Behavior, 18,* 69–88.

Garcia, J. R., & Reiber, C. (2008). Hook-up behavior: A biopsychosocial perspective. *Journal of Social, Evolutionary, and Cultural Psychology, 2,* 192–208.

Gartstein, M.A., & Rothbart, M.K. (2003). Studying infant temperament via the Revised Infant Behavior Questionnaire. *Infant Behavior and Development. 26,* 64–86.

Garver-Apgar, C.E., Gangestad, S.W., Thornhill, R., Miller, R.D., & Olp, J.J. (2006). MHC alleles, sexually responsivity, and unfaithfulness in romantic couples. *Psychological Science, 17,* 830–5.

Geary, D.C. (1995). Sexual selection and sex differences in spatial cognition. *Learning and Individual Differences, 7,* 289–301

Geary, D.C. (1998). *Male, female: The evolution of human sex differences.* Washington, DC: American Psycholog l Association.

Geary, D.C. (2000). Evolution and proximate expressions of human paternal investment. *Psychological Bulletin, 126,* 55–77.

Geary, D.C. (2010). *Male, female: The evolution of human sex differences* (2nd ed.). Washington, DC: American Psychological Association.

Geary, D.C., Rumsey, M., Bow-Thomas, C.C., & Hoard, M.K. (1995). Sexual jealousy as a facultative trait: Evidence from the pattern of sex differences in adults from China and the United States. *Ethology and Sociobiology, 16,* 355–83.

Geerz, C. (1984). Anti anti-relativism. *American Anthropologist 86,* 263–78.

George, M. (1999). A victimisation survey of female-perpetrated assaults in the United Kingdom. *Aggressive Behavior, 25,* 67–79.

Gerloff, U., Hartung, B., Fruth, B., Hohmann, G., & Tautz, D. (1999). Intracommunity relationships, dispersal pattern and paternity success in a wild living community of bonobos (Pan paniscus) determined from DNA analysis of faecal samples. *Proceedings of the Royal Society of London, Series B, 266,* 1189–95.

Gigerenzer, G., & Brighton, H. (2009). Homo heuristicus: Why biased minds make better inferences. *Topics in Cognitive Science, 1,* 107–43.

Gilbert, L.E. (1976). Postmating female odor in Heliconius butterflies: A male contributed aphrodisiac. *Science, 193,* 419–20.

Gilby, I.C., & Wrangham, R.W. (2008). Association patterns among wild chimpanzees (Pan troglodytes schweinfurthii) reflect sex differences in cooperation. *Behavioral Ecology and Sociobiology, 62,* 1831–42.

Gingrich, B., Liu, Y., Cascio, C., Wang, Z.X., & Insel, T.R. (2000). Dopamine D2 receptors in the nucleus accumbens are important for social attachment in the female prairie voles (Microtus ochrogaster). *Behavioral Neuroscience, 114,* 173–83.

Glazer, I. (1992). Interfemale aggression and resource scarcity in a cross-cultural perspective. In K. Björkqvist & P. Niemela (Eds.), *Of mice and women: Aspects of female aggression* (pp. 163–71). New York, NY: Academic Press.

Glenn, N., & Marquardt, E. (2001). *Hooking up, hanging out, and hoping for Mr. Right: College women on dating and mating today.* New York, NY: Institute for American Values.

Goethals, G., Messick, D.M., & Allison, S.T. (1991). The uniqueness bias: Studies of constructive social comparison. In J. Suls & T.A. Wills (Eds.), *Social comparison: Contemporary theory and research* (pp. 149–76). Hillsdale, NJ: Erlbaum.

Goldberg, S. (1973). *The inevitability of patriarchy.* Peru, IL: Open Court.

Goldberg, S. (1993). *Why men rule: A theory of male dominance.* Peru, IL: Open Court.

Goldberg, S., & Lewis, M. (1969). Play behavior in the year-old infant: Early sex differences. *Child Development, 40,* 21–31.

Goldstein, J.M., Seidman, L.J., Horton, N.J., Makris, N., Kennedy, D.N., Caviness, V.S., *et al.* (2001). Normal sexual dimorphism of the adult human brain assessed by in vivo magnetic resonance imaging. *Cerebral Cortex, 11,* 490–7.

Goldstein, K. (1939). *The organism: An holistic approach to biology, derived from pathological data in man.* New York, NY:American Book Company.

Goodall, J. (1986). *The chimpanzees of Gombe: Patterns of behavior.* Cambridge, MA: Harvard University Press.

Goodwin, M.H. (1990). *He-said-she-said: Talk as social organisation among black children.* Bloomington, IN: University of Indiana Press.

Gore, S., Aseltine, R.H., & Colten, M.E. (1993). Gender, social-relational involvement and depression. *Journal of Research on Adolescence, 3,* 101–25.

Gosso, Y., Otta, E., Morais, M.L.S., Ribeiro, F.J.L., & Bussab, V.S.R. (2005). Play in hunter-gatherer society. In A.D. Pellegrini & P.K. Smith (Eds.), *The nature of play* (pp. 213–53). New York, NY:Guilford.

Gottfredson, M., & Hirschi, T. (1990). *A general theory of crime.* Stanford, CA: Stanford University Press.

Gottfredson, L.S. (1997). Mainstream science on intelligence: An editorial with 52 signatories, history, and bibliography. *Intelligence, 24,* 13–23.

Gottfredson, L.S. (2007). Innovation, fatal accidents and the evolution of general intelligence. In M.J. Roberts (Ed.), *Integrating the mind* (pp. 387–425). Hove: Psychology Press.

Gouin, J-P., Carter, C.S., Pournajafi-Nazarloo, H., Glaser, R., Malarkey, W.B., Loving, T.J. *et al.* (2010). Marital behaviour, oxytocin, vasopressin and wound healing. *Psychoneuroendocrinology, 35,* 1082–90.

Gould, S.J. (1991). Exaptation: A crucial tool for evolutionary psychology. *Journal of Social Issues, 47,* 43–65.

Gould, S.J. (1992a). Life in a punctuation. *Natural History, 101,* 10–21.

Gould, S.J. (1992b). Male nipples and clitoral ripples. In S.J. Gould (Ed.), *Bully for brontosaurus: Further reflections in natural history* (pp. 124–38). London: Penguin Books.

Gould, S.J., & Lewontin, R. (1979). The spandrels of San Marco and the panglossian paradigm: A critique of the adaptationist program. *Proceedings of the Royal Society, Series B, 205,* 581–98.

Gouldner, A.W. (1973). The norm of reciprocity: A preliminary statement. In A.W. Gouldner (Ed.), *For sociology: Renewal and critique in sociology today* (pp. 226–59). London: Allen Lane.

Gowaty, P.A. (1992). Evolutionary biology and feminism. *Human Nature, 3,* 217–49.

Grabenhorst, F., & Rolls, E.T. (2011). Value, pleasure and choice in the ventral prefrontal cortex. *Trends in Cognitive Sciences, 15,* 56–67.

Graham-Kevan, N., & Archer, J. (2009). Control tactics and partner violence in heterosexual relationships. *Evolution and Human Behavior, 30,* 445–52.

Grammer, K., & Thornhill, R. (1994). Human (Homo sapiens) facial attractiveness and sexual selection: The role of symmetry and averageness. *Journal of Comparative Psychology, 108,* 233–42.

Grammer, K., Fink, B., Moller, A.P., & Manning, J.T. (2005). Physical attractiveness and health: Comment on Weeden and Sabini. *Psychological Bulletin, 131,* 658–61.

Grant, P.R. (1986). *Ecology and evolution of Darwin's finches.* Princeton, NJ: Princeton University Press.

Graziano, W.G., Jensen-Campbell, L.A., Shebilske, L.J., & Lundgren, S.R. (1993). Social influence, sex differences, and judgements of beauty: Putting the interpersonal back into interpersonal attraction. *Journal of Personality and Social Psychology, 65*, 522–31.

Green, R. (1987). *The "sissy boy" syndrome and the development of homosexuality.* New Haven, CT: Yale University Press.

Greenfeld, L.A. (1997). *Sex offenses and offenders.* Washington, DC: Bureau of Justice Statistics, US Department of Justice.

Greenfeld, L.A., & Snell, T.L. (1999). *Bureau of Justice Statistics Special Report: Women offenders.* Washington, DC: US Department of Justice.

Gregersen, E. (1982). *Sexual practices: The story of human sexuality.* New York, NY: Irvington Press.

Greif, G.L. (1985). *Single fathers.* Lexington, MA: Heath.

Grello, C.M., Welsh, D.P., & Harper, M.S. (2006). No strings attached: The nature of casual sex in college students. *Journal of Sex Research, 43*, 255–67.

Grewen, K. M., Girdler, S. S., Amico, J., & Light, K. (2005). Effects of partner support on resting oxytocin, cortisol, norepinephrine, and blood pressure before and after warm partner contact. *Psychosomatic Medicine, 67*, 531–38.

Griffith, S.C., Owens, I.P.F., & Thuman, K.A. (2002). Extra pair paternity in birds: A review of interpsecific variation and adaptive function. *Molecular Ecology, 11*, 2195–212.

Gross, M.R. (1996). Alternative reproductive strategies and tactics: Diversity within sexes. *Trends in Ecology and Evolution, 11*, 92–8.

Guala, F. (2012). Reciprocity: Weak or strong? What punishment experiments do (and do not) demonstrate. *Behavioural and Brain Sciences, 35*, 1–59.

Gullone, E. (2000). The development of normal fear: A century of research. *Clinical Psychology Review, 20*, 429–51.

Gullone, E., & King, N.J. (1993). The fears of youth in the 1990s: Contemporary normative data. *The Journal of Genetic Psychology, 154*, 137–53.

Gur, R.C., Gunning-Dixon, F., Bilker, W.B., & Gur, R.E. (2002). Sex differences in temporolimbic and frontal brain volumes of healthy adults. *Cerebral Cortex, 12*, 998–1003.

Guttentag, M., & Secord, P. (1983). *Too many women?* Beverly Hills, CA: Sage.

Hacklander, K., Mostl, E., & Arnold, W. (2003). Reproductive suppression in female Alpine marmots, Marmota marmota. *Animal Behaviour, 65*, 1133–40.

Hager, L.D. (Ed.) (1997). *Women in human evolution.* London: Routledge.

Hahn-Holbrook, J., Holbrooke, C., & Haselton, M. (2011). Parental precaution: Neurobiological means and adaptive ends. *Neuroscience and Biobehavioral Reviews, 35*, 1052–66.

Haig, D., & Graham, C. (1991). Genomic imprinting and the strange case of the insulin-like growth factor II receptor. *Cell, 64*, 1045–6.

Haig, D., & Westoby, M. (1989). Parent-specific gene expression and the triploid endosperm. *American Naturalist, 134*, 147–55.

Halcomb, H.R. (1998). Testing evolutionary hypotheses. In C. Crawford & D.L. Krebs (Eds.), *Handbook of evolutionary psychology* (pp. 303–34). Mahwah, NJ: Lawrence Erlbaum.

Hall, J.A. (1984). *Nonverbal sex differences: Communication accuracy and expressive style.* Baltimore, MD: Johns Hopkins University Press.

Hall, J.A., Carter, J.D., & Horgan, T.G. (2000). Gender differences in nonverbal communication of emotion. In A.H. Fischer (Ed.), *Gender and emotion: Social Psychological Perspectives* (pp. 97–117). Cambridge: Cambridge University Press.

Hall, P., & Innes, J. (2010). Violent and sexual crime. In J. Flatley, C. Kershaw, K. Smith, R. Chaplin, & D. Moon (Eds.), *Crime in England and Wales 2009/10* (pp. 43–72). London: Home Office Statistical Bulletin 12/10.

Halpern, D.F. (2000). *Sex differences in cognitive abilities*. Mahwah, NJ: Lawrence Erlbaum.

Hamer, D., & Copeland, P. (1994). *The science of desire: The search for the gay gene and the biology of behavior*. New York, NY: Simon & Schuster.

Hamilton, G., Stoneking, M., & Excoffier, L. (2005). Molecular analysis reveals tighter social regulation of immigration in patrilocal populations than in matrilocal populations. *Proceedings of the National Academy of Sciences of the United States of America, 102,* 7476–80.

Hamilton, W.D. (1964). The genetical evolution of social behaviour I, II. *Journal of Theoretical Biology, 7,* 1–52.

Hamilton, W.D., & Zuk, M. (1982). Heritable true fitness and bright birds: A role for parasites? *Science, 218,* 384–7.

Hammel, E.A. (1996). Demographic constraints on population growth of early humans: Emphasis on the probable role of females in overcoming such constraints. *Human Nature, 7,* 217–55.

Hampton, R.L. (1975). Marital disruption: Some social and economic consequences. In G.J. Duncan & J.N. Morgan (Eds.), *Five thousand American families* (Vol. 3, pp. 163–88). Ann Arbor, MI: Institute for Social Research.

Hankin, B.L., Mermelstein, R., & Roesch, L. (2007). Sex differences in adolescent depression: Stress exposure and reactivity models. *Child Development, 78,* 279–95.

Hankin, B.L., Stone, L., & Wright, P. A. (2010). Corumination, interpersonal stress generation, and internalizing symptoms: Accumulating effects and transactional influences in a multiwave study of adolescents. *Development and Psychopathology, 22,* 217–35.

Hansen, G.L. (1982). Reactions to hypothetical jealousy producing events. *Family Relations, 31,* 513–18.

Hansen, G.L. (1985). Perceived threats and marital jealousy. *Social Psychology Quarterly, 48,* 262–8.

Harcourt, A.H., Harvey, P.H., Larson, S.G., & Short, R.V. (1981). Testis weight, body weight and breeding system in primates. *Nature, 293,* 55–7.

Hard, E., & Hansen, S. (1985). Reduced fearfulness in the lactating rat. *Physiology and Behavior, 35,* 641–3.

Harding, S. (1991). *Whose science? Whose knowledge?* Ithaca, NY: Cornell University Press.

Hareven, T. (1985). Historical changes in the family and the life course: Implications for child development. *Monographs of the Society for Research in Child Development, 50* (4–5), 8–23.

Harmon-Jones, E. (2003). Anger and the behavioural approach system. *Personality and Individual Differences, 35,* 995–1005.

Harmon-Jones, E., Gable, P.A., & Peterson, C.K. (2010). The role of asymmetric frontal cortical activity in emotion-related phenomena: A review and update. *Biological Psychology, 84,* 451–62.

Harmon-Jones, E., & Sigelman, J.D. (2001). State anger and prefrontal brain activity: Evidence that insult-related relative left-prefrontal activation is associated with experienced anger and aggression. *Journal of Personality and Social Psychology, 80,* 797–803.

Harned, M.S. (2001). Abused women or abused men? An examination of the context and outcomes of dating violence. *Violence and Victims*, *16*, 269–85.

Harris, C.R. (2003). A review of sex differences in sexual jealousy, including self-report data, psychophysiological responses, interpersonal violence, and morbid jealousy. *Personality and Social Psychology Review*, *7*, 102–28.

Harris, C.R., & Christenfeld, N. (1996). Gender, jealousy and reason. *Psychological Science*, *7*, 364–6.

Harris, C.R., Jenkins, M., & Glaser, D. (2006). Gender differences in risk assessment: Why do women take fewer risks than men? *Judgment and Decision Making Journal*, *1*, 48–63.

Harris, J.R. (1995). Where is the child's environment? A group socialization theory of development. *Psychological Review*, *102*, 458–89.

Harris, M.B. (1994). Gender of subject and target as mediators of aggression. *Journal of Applied Social Psychology*, *24*, 453–71.

Hasegawa, T., & Hiraiwa, M. (1980). Social interaction of orphans observed in a free-ranging troop of Japanese monkeys. *Folia Primatologica*, *33*, 129–58.

Haslam, N. (1997). Four grammars for primate social relations. In J.A. Simpson, & D.T. Kenrick (Eds.), *Evolutionary social psychology* (pp. 297–316). Mahwah, NJ: Erlbaum.

Hatfield, E., & Rapson, R.L. (1996). *Love and sex: Cross-cultural perspectives*. Boston, MA: Allyn and Bacon.

Hatfield, E., & Sprecher, S. (1995). Men's and women's preferences in marital partners in the United States, Russia and Japan. *Journal of Cross-Cultural Psychology*, *26*, 728–50.

Hausfater, G. (1975). Dominance and reproduction in baboons (Papio cynocephalus). *Contributions to Primatology*, *7*, 1–150.

Hawkes, K. (1990). Why do men hunt? Benefits for risky choices. In E. Cashdan (Ed.), *Risk and uncertainty in tribal and peasant economies* (pp. 145–66). Boulder, CO: Westview Press.

Hawkes, K. (1993). Why hunter-gatherers work: An ancient version of the problem of common goods. *Current Anthropology*, *34*, 341–61.

Hawkes, K., O'Connell, J.F., Blurton-Jones, N.G., Alvarez, H., & Charnov, E.L. (1998). Grandmothering, menopause and the evolution of human life histories. *Proceedings of the National Academy of Sciences of the United States of America*, *95*, 1336–9.

Hayano, D.M. (1973). Sorcery, death, proximity and the perception of out-groups: The Tauna Awa of New Guinea. *Ethnology*, *12*, 179–91.

Heath, C., Bell, C., & Sternberg, E. (2001). Emotional selection in memes: The case of urban legends. *Journal of Personality and Social Psychology*, *81*, 1028–41.

Heinrichs, M., Meinlschmitt, G., Neumann, I., Wagner, S., Kirchbaum, C., Ehlert, U., *et al.* (2001). Effects of suckling on hypothalamic–pituitary–adrenal axis responses to psychosocial stress in postpartum lactating women. *Journal of Clinical Endocrinology and Metabolism*, *86*, 4798–804.

Helmreich, R., Spence, J., & Gibson, R. (1982). Sex role attitudes 1972–1980. *Personality and Social Psychology Bulletin*, *8*, 656–63.

Henrich, J., Boyd, R., & Richerson, P.J. (2012). The puzzle of monogamous marriage. *Philosophical Transactions of the Royal Society of London, Series B, Biological Sciences*, *367*, 657–69.

Hermans, E.J., Putman, P., Baas, J.M., Koppeschaar, H.P., & van Honk, J. (2006). A single dose of testosterone reduces fear-potentiated startle in humans. *Biological Psychiatry, 59,* 872–4.

Hermans, E.J., Ramsey, N.F., & van Honk, J. (2008). Exogenous testosterone enhances responsiveness to social threat in the neural circuitry of social aggression in humans. *Biological Psychiatry, 63,* 263–70.

Herold, E.S., & Mewhinney, D.M.K. (1993). Gender differences in casual sex and Aids prevention: A survey of dating bars. *Journal of Sex Research, 30,* 36–42.

Hersch, J. (1997). Smoking, seat belts and other risky consumer decisions: Differences by gender and race. *Managerial and Decision Economics, 11,* 241–56.

Herzog, A.R., Bachman, J.G., & Johnston, L.D. (1983). Paid work, child care and housework: A national survey of high school seniors' preferences for sharing responsibilities between husband and wife. *Sex Roles, 9,* 109–35.

Hetherington, M. (1972). Effects of paternal absence on personality development in adolescent daughters. *Developmental Psychology, 7,* 313–26.

Hettrich, E.L., & O'Leary, K.D. (2007). Females' reasons for their physical aggression in dating relationships. *Journal of Interpersonal Violence, 22,* 1131–43.

Hewlett, B.S. (1988). Sexual selection and paternal investment among Aka pygmies. In L. Betzig, M. Borgerhoff Mulder, & P. Turke (Eds.), *Human reproductive behaviour: A Darwinian perspective* (pp. 263–76). Cambridge: Cambridge University Press.

Hill, C., Rubin, Z., & Peplau, L. (1976). Breakups before marriage: The end of 103 affairs. *Journal of Social Issues, 32,* 147–68.

Hill, E.M., & Low, B.S. (1992). Contemporary abortion patterns: A life history approach. *Ethology and Sociobiology, 13,* 35–48.

Hill, K., & Hurtado, A.M. (1996). *Ache life history: The ecology and demography of a foraging people.* New York, NY: Aldine de Gruyter.

Hill, K., Hurtado, A.M., & Walker, R.S. (2007). High adult mortality among Hiwi huntergatherers: Implications for human evolution. *Journal of Human Evolution, 52,* 443–54.

Hill, K., & Kaplan, H. (1994). On why male foragers hunt and share food. *Current Anthropology, 34,* 701–6.

Hill, S. (2007). Overestimation bias in mate competition. *Evolution and Human Behavior, 28,* 118–23.

Hines, N.J., & Fry, D.P. (1994). Indirect modes of aggression among women of Buenos Aires, Argentina. *Sex Roles, 30,* 213–36.

Hodgins, H.S., Liebeskind, E., & Schwartz, W. (1996). Getting out of hot water: Facework in social predicaments. *Journal of Personality and Social Psychology, 71,* 300–14.

Hoffman, M.L. (1977). Sex differences in empathy and related behaviors. *Psychological Bulletin, 84,* 712–22.

Hoffman, S.D., & Duncan, G.J. (1995). The effect of incomes, wages and AFDC benefits on marital disruption. *Journal of Human Resources, 30,* 19–41.

Hogan, D.P., & Eggebeen, D.J. (1995). Sources of emergency help and routine assistance in old age. *Social Forces, 73,* 917–36.

Holland, B., & Rice, W.R. (1999). Experimental removal of sexual selection reverses intersexual antagonistic coevolution and removes a reproductive load. *Proceedings of the National Academy of Sciences of the United States of America, 96,* 5083–8.

Hollway, W. (1984). Gender difference and the production of subjectivity. In J. Henriques, W. Hollway, C. Urwin, C. Venn, & V. Walkerdine (Eds.), *Changing the subject: Psychology, social regulation and subjectivity* (pp. 227–63). London: Methuen.

Holmberg, A. (1969). *Nomads of the long bow: The Siriono of Eastern Bolivia*. Garden City, NY: Natural History Press.

Holt-Lunstad, J., Birmingham, W. A., & Light, K. C. (2008). Influence of a "warm touch" support enhancement intervention among married couples on ambulatory blood pressure, oxytocin, alpha amylase, and cortisol. *Psychosomatic Medicine, 70*, 976–85.

Home Office Research and Planning Unit (1993). *The 1992 British Crime Survey*. London: Her Majesty's Stationery Office.

Home Office Statistical Bulletin (1996). *The 1996 British Crime Survey England and Wales*. London: Government Statistical Service.

Hopkins, W.D., Bennett, A.J., Bales, S.L., Lee, J., & Ward, J.P. (1993). Behavioral laterality in captive bonobos (Pan paniscus). *Journal of Comparative Psychology, 107*, 403–10.

Horrocks, J., & Hunt, W. (1983). Maternal rank and offspring rank in vervet monkeys: An appraisal of the mechanisms of rank acquisition. *Animal Behaviour, 31*, 772–82.

Hosken, D.J., & Stockley, P. (2004). Sexual selection and genital evolution. *Trends in Ecology and Evolution, 19*, 87–93.

Howes, C. (1988). Peer interaction of young children. *Monographs of the Society for Research in Child Development, 53* (Serial number 217).

Howes, C., & Eldredge, R. (1985). Responses of abused, neglected and non-maltreated children to the behaviors of peers. *Journal of Applied Developmental Psychology, 6*, 261–70.

Hrdy, S.B. (1979). Infanticide among animals: A review, classification and examination of the implications for the reproductive strategy of females. *Ethology and Sociobiology, 1*, 13–40.

Hrdy, S.B. (1981). *The woman that never evolved*. Cambridge, MA: Harvard University Press.

Hrdy, S.B. (1997). Raising Darwin's consciousness: Female sexuality and the prehominid origins of patriarchy. *Human Nature, 8*, 1–49.

Hrdy, S.B. (1999). *Mother nature: Natural selection and the female of the species*. London: Chatto & Windus.

Hrdy, S.B. (2000). The optimal number of fathers: Evolution, demography and history in the shaping of female mate preferences. *Annals of the New York Academy of Sciences, 907*, 75–96.

Hrdy, S.B. (2009). *Mothers and others: The evolutionary origins of mutual understanding*. London: Belknap Press.

Hsu, C., Soong, W., Stigler, J.W., Hong, C., & Liang, C. (1981). The temperamental characteristics of Chinese babies. *Child Development, 52*, 1337–40.

Hubbard, R. (1990). *The politics of women's biology*. New Brunswick, NJ: Rutgers University Press.

Huber, D., Veinante, P., & Stoop, R. (2005). Vasopressin and oxytocin excite distinct neuronal populations in the central amygdala. *Science 308*, 245–8.

Huber, S., Bookstein, F.L., & Fieder, M. (2010). Socioeconomic status, education, and reproduction in modern women: An evolutionary perspective. *American Journal of Human Biology, 22*, 578–87.

Hughes, J.F., Skaletsky, H., Pyntikova, T., Graves, T.A., Van Daalen, S.K.M., Minx, P.J., et al. (2010). Chimpanzee and human Y chromosomes are remarkably divergent in structure and gene content. *Nature, 463*, 536–9.

Hughes, L.A. (1988). "But that's not really mean": Competing in a cooperative mode. Sex Roles, 19, 669–87.

Hurst, L.D., & McVean, G.T. (1997). Growth effects of uniparental disomies and the conflict theory of genomic imprinting. *Trends in Genetics, 13*, 436–43.

Hurtado, A.M., Hawkes, K., Hill, K., & Kaplan, H. (1985). Female subsistence strategies among Ache hunter-gatherers of eastern Paraguay. *Human Ecology, 13*, 1–28.

Huston, A. (1983). Sex typing. In E.M. Hetherington (Ed.), *Handbook of child psychology: Socialization, personality and social development* (Vol. 4, pp. 387–487). New York, NY: Wiley.

Hyde, J.S. (1986). Gender differences in aggression. In J.S. Hyde & M.C. Linn (Eds.), *The psychology of gender: Advances through meta-analysis*. Baltimore, MD: Johns Hopkins University Press.

Ickes, W., Robertson, E., Tooke, W., & Teng, G. (1986). Naturalistic social cognition: Methodology, assessment and validation. *Journal of Personality and Social Psychology, 51*, 66–82.

Inoue, E., Inoue-Murayama, M., Vigilant, L., Takenaka, O., & Nishida, T. (2008). Relatedness in wild Chimpanzees: influence of paternity, male philopatry, and demographic factors. *American Journal of Physical Anthropology, 137*, 256–62.

Insel, T.R. (2000). Toward a neurobiology of attachment. *Review of General Psychology, 4*, 176–85.

Insel, T.R., Winslow, J.T., Wang, Z.X., & Young, L.J. (1998). Oxytocin, vasopressin and the neuroendocrine basis of pair bond formation. *Advances in Experimental Medicine and Biology, 449*, 215–24.

Ironside, V. (2011). *We paid the price for free love: The flip side of the sexual revolution*. Retrieved from <http://www.dailymail.co.uk/home/you/article-1346813/The-flip-1960s-sexual-revolution-We-paid-price-free-love.html#ixzz1y9LG2Ozm>

Irwing, P., & Lynn, R. (2005). Sex differences in means and variability on the progressive matrices in university students: A meta-analysis. *British Journal of Psychology, 96*, 505–24.

Jacklin, C.N., & Maccoby, E.E. (1978). Social behavior at 33 months in same-sex and mixed-sex dyads. *Child Development, 49*, 557–69.

Jaffee, S.R., Caspi, A., Moffitt, T.E., Dodge, K.A., Rutter, M., Taylor, A., et al. (2005). Nature x nurture: Genetic vulnerabilities interact with child maltreatment to promote behaviour problems. *Development and Psychopathology, 17*, 67–84.

Jankowiak, W.R., & Fischer, E.F. (1992). A cross-cultural perspective on romantic love. *Ethnology, 31*, 149–55.

Jankowiak, W.R., Sudakov, M., & Wilreker, B.C. (2002). Co-wife conflict and co-operation. *Ethnology, 44*, 81–98.

Janoff-Bulman, R. (1985). Criminal vs. non-criminal victimisation: Victim's reactions. *Victimology, 10*, 498–511.

Jarvinen, D.W., & Nicholls, J.G. (1996). Adolescents' social goals, beliefs about the causes of social success and satisfaction in peer relations. *Developmental Psychology, 32*, 435–41.

Jasienska, G., Ziomkiewicz, A., Ellison, P.T., Lipson, S.F., & Thune, I. (2004). Large breasts and narrow waists indicate high reproductive potential in women. *Proceedings of the Royal Society B, 271*, 1213–17.

Jeffreys, S. (1990). *Anticlimax: A feminist perspective on the sexual revolution*. London: The Women's Press.

Jennings, K.D., Stagg, V., & Connors, R.E. (1991). Social networks and mothers' interactions with their preschool children. *Child Development, 62*, 966–78.

Jessor, R., Costa, F., Jessor, L., & Donovan, J. (1983). Time of first intercourse: A prospective study. *Journal of Personality and Social Psychology, 44*, 608–26.

Johanna, A., Forsberg, L., & Tullberg, B.S. (1995). The relationship between cumulative number of cohabiting partners and number of children for men and women in modern Sweden. *Ethology and Sociobiology, 16*, 221–32.

Jokela, M., Rotkirch, A., Rickard, I.J., Pettay, J., & Lummaa, V. (2010). Serial monogamy increases reproductive success in men but not in women. *Behavioral Ecology, 21*, 906–12.

Jolly, A. (1985). *The evolution of primate behavior* (2nd ed.). New York, NY: Macmillan.

Jolly, A. (1999). *Lucy's legacy: Sex and intelligence in human evolution*. Cambridge, MA: Harvard University Press.

Jones, B.C., Little, A.C., Penton-Voak, I.S., Tiddeman, B.P., Burt, D.M., & Perrett, D.I. (2001). Facial symmetry and judgements of apparent health: support for a 'good genes' explanation of the attractiveness–symmetry relationship. *Evolution and Human Behavior, 22*, 417–29.

Jones, D.C., Vigfusdottir, T.H., & Lee, Y. (2004). Body image and the appearance culture among adolescent girls and boys: An examination of friend conversations, peer criticism, appearance magazines, and the internalization of appearance ideals. *Journal of Adolescent Research, 19*, 323–39.

Jones, J.H. (2009). The force of selection on the human life cycle. *Evolution and Human Behavior, 30*, 305–14.

Jones, M., & Mussen, P. (1958). Self-conceptions, motivations and interpersonal attitudes of early and late maturing girls. *Child Development, 29*, 492–501.

Jordan, J.V., Kaplan, A.G., Miller, J.B., Stivey, I.P., & Surrey, J.L. (Eds.) (1991). *Women's growth in connection: Writings from Stone Center*. New York, NY: Guildford Press.

Josephson, S.C. (2002). Does polygyny reduce fertility? *American Journal of Human Biology, 14*, 222–32.

Jouriles, E., Pfiffner, L., & O'Leary, S. (1988). Marital conflict, parenting, and toddler conduct problems. *Journal of Abnormal Child Psychology, 16*, 197–206.

Judge, T.A., & Piccolo, R.F. (2004). Transformational and transactional leadership: A meta-analytic test of their relative validity. *Journal of Applied Psychology, 89*, 901–10.

Kaar, P., Jokela, J., Merila, J., Helle, T., & Kojola, I. (1998). Sexual conflict and remarriage in preindustrial human populations: Causes and fitness consequences. *Evolution and Human Behavior, 19*, 139–51.

Kaeager, D.A., & Staff, J. (2009). The sexual double standard and adolescent peer acceptance. *Social Psychology Quarterly, 72*, 143–64.

Kahlenberg, S., Thompson, M.E., & Wrangham, R.W. (2008). Female competition over core areas in Pan troglodytes schweinfurthii, Kibale National Park, Uganda. *International Journal of Primatology, 29*, 931–47.

Kaighobadi, F., Shackelford, T.K., & Goetz, A.T. (2009). From mate retention to murder: Evolutionary psychological perspectives on men's partner-directed violence. *Review of General Psychology, 13*, 327–34.

Kalmijn, M., Loeve, A., & Manting, D. (2007). Income dynamics and the dissolution of marriage and cohabitation. *Demography, 44*, 159–79.

Kano, T. (1992). *The last ape: Pygmy chimpanzee behavior and ecology*. Stanford, CA: Stanford University Press.

Kaplan, H. (1994). Evolutionary and wealth flow theories of fertility: Empirical tests and new models. *Population and Development Review, 20*, 753–91.

Kaplan, H. (1996). A theory of fertility and parental investment in traditional and modern human societies. *Yearbook of Physical Anthropology, 39*, 91–135.

Kaplan, H., Hill, K., Lancaster, J., & Hurtado, A.M. (2000). A theory of human life history evolution: Diet, intelligence, and longevity. *Evolutionary Anthropology, 9*, 156–85.

Kaplan, H., Lancaster, J. B., Bock, J., & Johnson, S. (1995). Fertility and fitness among Albuquerque men: a competitive labour market theory. In R.I.M. Dunbar (Ed.), *Human reproductive decisions: biological and social perspectives* (pp. 96–136). London: Macmillan.

Kawai, M. (1958). On the system of social ranks in a natural troop of Japanese monkeys. 1. Basic rank and dependent rank. *Primates, 1*, 111–30.

Kawamura, S. (1958). The matriarchal social order in the Minoo-B group. *Primates, 1*, 149–56.

Kaye, W.H., Fudge, J.L., & Paulus, M. (2009). New insights into symptoms and neurocircuit function of anorexia nervosa. *Nature Reviews Neuroscience, 10*, 573–84.

Keister, L.A. (2003). Sharing the wealth: The effect of siblings on adults' wealth ownership. *Demography, 40*, 521–42.

Keister, L.A. (2004). Race, family structure, and wealth: The effect of childhood family on adult asset ownership. *Sociological Perspectives, 47*, 161–87.

Keith, V., & Finlay, B. (1988). The impact of parental divorce on children's educational attainment, marital timing and likelihood of divorce. *Journal of Marriage and the Family, 50*, 797–809.

Keller, E. (1992). *Secrets of life, secrets of death: Essays on language, gender and science*. New York, NY: Routledge.

Kendler, K.S. (1998). Major depression and the environment: A psychiatric genetic perspective. *Pharmacopsychiatry, 31*, 5–9.

Kendrick, K.M. (2000). Oxytocin, motherhood and bonding. *Experimental Physiology, 85S*, 111S–124S.

Kennedy, G.E. (2005). From ape's dilemma to weanling's dilemma: Early weaning and its evolutionary context. *Journal of Human Evolution, 48*, 123–45.

Kenrick, D.T., & Keefe, R.C. (1992). Age preferences in mates reflect sex differences in human reproductive strategies. *Behavioral and Brain Sciences, 15*, 75–133.

Kenrick, D.T., Keefe, R.C., Gabrielidis, C., & Cornelius, J.S. (1996). Adolescents' age preferences for dating partners: Support for an evolutionary model of life-history strategies. *Child Development, 67*, 1499–511.

Kenrick, D.T., Sadalla, E.K., Groth, G., & Trost, M.R. (1990). Evolution, traits and the stages of human courtship: Qualifying the parental investment model. *Journal of Personality, 58*, 97–116.

Keverne, E.B., Fundele, R., Narasimha, M., Braton, S.C., & Surani, M.A. (1996). Genomic imprinting and the differential roles of parental genomes in brain development. *Developmental Brain Research, 92*, 91–100.

Keverne, E.B., Martel, F.L., & Nevison, C.M. (1996). Primate brain evolution: Genetic and functional considerations. *Proceedings of the Royal Society of London, B, 263*, 689–596.

Kiernan, K. (1999). Childbearing outside marriage in Western Europe. *Population Trends, 98*, 11–20.

Kiesler, D.J. (1983). The 1982 interpersonal circle: A taxonomy for complementarity in human transactions. *Psychological Review, 90*, 185–214.

Kim, P., Leckman, J.F., Mayes, L.C., Feldman, R., Wang, X., & Swain, J.E. (2010). The plasticity of human maternal brain: Longitudinal changes in brain anatomy during the early postpartum period. *Behavioral Neuroscience, 124*, 695–700.

Kirsch, P., Esslinger, C., Chen, Q., Mier, D., Lis, S., Siddhanti, S., *et al.* (2005). Oxytocin modulates neural circuitry for social cognition and fear in humans. *Journal of Neuroscience, 25*, 11489–93.

Kitson, G.C. (1992). *Portrait of divorce*. London: Guildford Press.

Kitson, G.C., Babri, K.B., & Roach, M.J. (1985). Who divorces and why: A review. *Journal of Family Issues, 6*, 255–93.

Knight, G.P., Fabes, R.A., & Higgins, D.A. (1996). Concerns about drawing causal inferences from meta-analyses: An example in the study of gender differences in aggression. *Psychological Bulletin, 119*, 410–21.

Knight, G.P., Guthrie, I.L., Page, M.C., & Fabes, R.A. (2002). Emotional arousal and gender differences in aggression: A meta-analysis. *Aggressive Behaviour, 28*, 366–93.

Kochenderfer-Ladd, B., & Skinner, K. (2002). Children's coping strategies: Moderators of the effects of peer victimization? *Developmental Psychology, 38*, 267–78.

Koenig, A.M., Eagly, A.H., Mitchell, A.A., & Ristikari, T. (2011). Are leader stereotypes masculine? A meta-analysis of the three research paradigms. *Psychological Bulletin, 137*, 616–42.

Koenigs, M., & Tranel, D. (2007). Irrational economic decision making after ventromedial prefrontal damage: Evidence from the ultimatum game. *Journal of Neuroscience, 27*, 951–6.

Kohnstamm, G.A. (1989). Temperament in childhood: Cross-cultural and sex differences. In G.A. Kohnstamm, J.E. Bates, & M.K. Rothbart (Eds.), *Temperament in childhood* (pp. 483–508). Chichester: Wiley.

Kokko, H., & Jennions, M.D. (2008). Parental investment, sexual selection and sex ratios. *Journal of Evolutionary Biology, 21*, 919–48.

Komarovsky, M., & Philips, J.H. (1962). *Blue collar marriage*. New Haven, CT: Yale University Press.

Konner, M. (2010). *The evolution of childhood: Relationships, emotion, mind*. Cambridge, MA: Belknap Press.

Konner, M.J. (1975). Relations among infants and juveniles in comparative perspective. In M. Lewis & L.A. Rosenblum (Eds.), *Friendship and peer relations* (pp. 99–129). New York, NY: Wiley.

Koot, H.M., & Verhulst, F.C. (1991). Prevalence of problem behavior in Dutch children aged 2–3. *Acta Psychiatrica Scandinavica, 83*, 1–37.

Korchmaros, J.D., & Kenny, D.A. (2001). Emotional closeness as a mediator of the effect of genetic relatedness on altruism. *Psychological Science, 12,* 262–5.

Kosfeld, M., Heinrichs, M., Zak, P.J., Fischbacher, U., & Fehr, E. (2005). Oxytocin increases trust in humans. *Nature, 435,* 673–6.

Kotelchuck, M. (1976). The infant's relationship to the father: Experimental evidence. In M.E. Lamb (Ed.), *The role of the father in child development* (pp. 329–44). New York, NY: Wiley.

Kreager, D.A., & Staff, J. (2009). The sexual double standard and adolescent peer acceptance. *Social Psychology Quarterly, 72,* 143–64.

Kring, A.M. (2000). Gender and anger. In A.H. Fischer (Ed.), *Gender and emotion: Social psychological perspectives* (pp. 211–31). Cambridge: Cambridge University Press.

Kring, A.M., & Gordon, A.H. (1998). Sex differences in emotion: Expression, experience and physiology. *Journal of Personality and Social Psychology, 74,* 686–703.

Kritz, M.M., Makinwa-Adebusoye, P., & Gurak, D.T. (2000). The role of gender context in shaping reproductive behaviour in Nigeria. In H.B. Presser & G. Sen (Eds.), *Women's empowerment and demographic processes: Moving beyond Cairo* (pp. 239–60). Oxford: Oxford University Press.

Kroeber, A.L., & Kluckhohn, C. (1952). *Culture: A critical review of concepts and definitions.* New York, NY: Vintage Books.

Krones, P., Stice, E., Batres, C., & Orjada, K. (2005). In vivo social comparison to a thin-ideal peer promotes body dissatisfaction: A randomized experiment. *International Journal of Eating Disorders, 38,* 134–42.

Kropotkin, P. (1972). *Mutual aid: A factor of evolution.* New York, NY: New York University Press.

Kross, E., Berman, M.G., Mischel, W., Smith, E.E., & Wager, T.D. (2011). Social rejection shares somatosensory representations with physical pain. *Proceedings of the National Academy of Sciences of the United States of America, 108,* 6270–5.

Kruttschnitt, C. (1994). Gender and interpersonal violence. In A. Reiss & J. Roth (Eds.), *Understanding and Preventing Violence* (Vol. 3, pp. 293–376). Washington, DC: National Academy Press.

Kurzban, R., & Clark Barrett, H. (2006). Modularity in cognition: Framing the debate. *Psychological Review, 113,* 628–47.

Kuschel, R. (1992). Women are women and men are men: How Bellonese women get even. In K. Björkqvist & P. Niemela (Eds.), *Of mice and women: Aspects of female aggression* (pp. 173–85). New York, NY: Academic Press.

Lack, D. (1954). *The natural regulation of animal numbers.* London: Clarendon Press.

LaFontana, K.M., & Cillessen, A.H.N. (2002). Children's stereotypes of popular and unpopular peers: A multi-method assessment. *Developmental Psychology, 38,* 635–47.

Lagerspetz, K., Björkqvist, K., & Peltonen, T. (1988). Is indirect aggression typical of females? Gender differences in aggressiveness in 11- to 12-year old children. *Aggressive Behavior, 14,* 403–14.

Laland, K.N., Odling-Smee, J., & Myles, S. (2010). How culture shaped the human genome: Bringing genetics and the human sciences together. *Nature Reviews Genetics, 11,* 137–48.

Lamb, M.E., Frodi, A.M., Hwang, C.-P., & Frodi, M. (1982). Varying degrees of paternal involvement in infant care: Attitudinal and behavioural correlates. In M.E. Lamb (Ed.),

Nontraditional families: Parenting and child development (pp. 117–37). Hillsdale, NJ: Erlbaum.

Lamb, M.E., Frodi, A.M., Hwang, C.P., Frodi, M., & Steinberg, J. (1982). Mother-infant and father-infant interaction involving play and holding in traditional and non-traditional Swedish families. *Developmental Psychology, 18,* 215–21.

Lambert, T.A., Kahn, A.S., & Apple, K.J. (2003). Pluralistic ignorance and hooking up. *The Journal of Sex Research, 40,* 129–33.

Lamphere, L. (1974). Strategies, cooperation and conflict among women in domestic groups. In M. Rosaldo & L. Lamphere (Eds.), *Women, culture and society* (pp. 97–112). Stanford, CA: Stanford University Press.

Lancaster, C.S., & Lancaster, J.B. (1983). Parental investment: The hominid adaptation. In D. Ortner (Ed.), *How humans adapt* (pp. 33–65). Washington, DC: Smithsonian Institution Press.

Lancaster, J.B. (1989). Evolutionary and cross-cultural perspectives on single-parenthood. In R.W. Bell & N.J. Bell (Eds.), *Interfaces in psychology: Sociobiology and the social sciences* (pp. 63–72). Lubbock, TX: Texas Tech University Press.

Lancaster, J.B. (1991). A feminist and evolutionary biologist looks at women. *Yearbook of Physical Anthropology, 34,* 1–11.

Lancaster, J.B., & Lancaster, C.S. (1983). Parental investment: the hominid adaptation. In D.J. Ortner (Ed.), *How humans adapt: A biocultural odyssey* (pp. 33–69). Washington, DC: Smithsonian Institution Press.

Lang, P.J., Bradley, M.M., & Cuthbert, B.N. (1992). A motivational analysis of emotion: Reflex–cortex connections. *Psychological Science, 3,* 44–9.

Langergraber, K.E., Mitani, J., & Vigilant, L. (2009). Kinship and female bonds in female chimpanzees (Pan troglodytes). *American Journal of Primatology, 71,* 840–51.

Langergraben, K.E., Siedel, H., Mitabni, J.C., Wrangham, R.W., Reynolds, V., Hunt, K., *et al.* (2007). The genetic signature of sex-biased migration in patrilocal chimpanzees and humans. *PlosOne, 10,* e973.

Langhinrichsen-Rohling, J., Neidig, P., & Thorn, G. (1995). Violent marriages: Gender differences in levels of current violence and past abuse. *Journal of Family Violence, 10,* 159–76.

Langlois, J.H., Kalakanis, L., Rubenstein, A.J., Larson, A., Hallam, M., & Smoot, M. (2000). Maxims or myths of beauty? A meta-analytic and theoretical review. *Psychological Bulletin, 126,* 390–423.

Langlois, J.H, & Roggman, L.A. (1990). Attractive faces are only average. *Psychological Science, 1,* 115–21.

Larsen, U., & Hollos, M. (2003). Women's empowerment and fertility decline among the Pare of Kilimanjaro region, Northern Tanzania. *Social Science & Medicine, 57,* 1099–115.

Lassek, W.D., & Gaulin, S.J.C. (2008). Waist-hip ratio and cognitive ability: Is gluteofemoral fat a privileged store of neurodevelopmental resources? *Evolution and Human Behavior, 29,* 26–34

Launhardt, K., Borries, C., Hardt, C., Epplen, J.T., & Winkler, P. (2001). Paternity analysis of alternative male reproductive routes among the langurs (Semnopithecus entellus) of Ramnagar. *Animal Behaviour, 61,* 53–64.

Lavrakas, P.J. (1975). Female preference for male physiques. *Journal of Research in Personality, 9,* 324–34.

Law-Smith, M.J., Perrett, D.I., Jones, B.C., Cornwell, R.E., Moore, F.R., Feinberg, D.R., *et al.* (2006). Facial appearance is a cue to oestrogen levels in women. *Proceedings of the Royal Society B, 273,* 135–40.

Lawson, D.W., & Mace, R. (2009). Trade-offs in modern parenting: a longitudinal study of sibling competition for parental care. *Evolution and Human Behavior, 30,* 170–83.

Lawson, D.W., & Mace, R. (2010). Optimizing modern family size: trade-offs between fertility and the economic costs of reproduction. *Human Nature, 21,* 39–61.

Lawson, D.W., & Mace, R. (2011). Parental investment and the optimization of human family size. *Philosophical Transactions of the Royal Society of London, Series B, Biological Sciences, 366,* 333–43.

Le Roux, A., Beehner, J.C., & Bergman, T.J. (2011). Female philopatry and dominance patterns in wild geladas. *American Journal of Primatology, 73,* 422–30.

Leadbetter, B.J., Blatt, S.J., & Quinlan, D.M. (1995). Gender-linked vulnerabilities to depressive symptoms, stress and problem behaviors in adolescents. *Journal of Research on Adolescence, 5,* 1–29.

Leakey, R., & Lewin, R. (1979). *People of the lake.* London: Collins.

Leaper, C. (1991). Influence and involvement: Age, gender and partner effects. *Child Development, 62,* 797–811.

Leary, M.R., Kowalski, R.M., Smith, L., & Phillips, S. (2003). Teasing, rejection, and violence: Case studies of the school shootings. *Aggressive Behavior, 29,* 202–14.

Lease, A.M., Kennedy, C.A., & Axelrod, J.L. (2002). Children's social constructions of popularity. *Social Development, 11,* 87–109.

Lease, A.M., Musgrove, K.T., & Axelrod, J.L. (2002). Dimensions of social status in preadolescent peer groups: Likability, perceived popularity, and social dominance. *Social Development, 11,* 508–33.

Leckman, J.F., Carter, C.S., Hennessy, M.B., Hrdy, S.B., Kervene, E.B., Klann-Delius, G., *et al.* (2005). Biobehavioral processes in attachment and bonding. In C.S. Carter, L. Ahnert, E. Klaus, S.B. Grossman, S.B. Hrdy, S.W. Lamb, *et al.* (Eds.), *Attachment and bonding: A new synthesis, Dahlem Workshop Report 92* (pp. 301–47). Cambridge, MA: MIT Press.

LeDoux, J. (1998). *The emotional brain.* London: Weidenfeld and Nicholson.

Lee, I.C., Pratto, F., & Johnson, B.Y. (2011). Intergroup consensus/disagreement in support of group-based hierarchies: An examination of socio-structural and psycho-cultural factors. *Psychological Bulletin, 137,* 1029–64.

Lee, R.B. (1979). *The !Kung San: Men, women, and work in a foraging society.* Cambridge: Cambridge University Press.

Leenaars, L.S., Dane, A.V., & Marini, Z. (2008). Evolutionary perspective on indirect victimization in adolescence: the role of attractiveness, dating and sexual behavior. *Aggressive Behavior, 34,* 404–15.

Lees, S. (1993). *Sugar and spice: Sexuality and adolescent girls.* London: Penguin.

Lehmann, J., & Boesch, C. (2008). Sexual differences in chimpanzee sociality. *International Journal of Primatology, 29,* 65–81.

Leibowitz, A., Eisen, M., & Chow, W.K. (1985). An economic model of teenage pregnancy decision making. *Demography, 23,* 67–77.

Leigh, S.R. (1996). Socioecology and the ontogeny of sexual size dimorphism in anthropoid primates. *American Journal of Physical Anthropology, 101*, 455–74.

Lempers, J.D., & Clark-Lempers, D.S. (1993). A functional comparison of same-sex and opposite-sex friendships during adolescence. *Journal of Adolescent Research, 8*, 89–108.

Lerner, J.S., Gonzalez, R.M., Small, D.A., & Fischhoff, B. (2003). Effects of fear and anger on perceived risks of terrorism: A national field experiment. *Psychological Science, 14*, 144–50.

Lerner, J.S., & Keltner, D. (2000). Beyond valence: Toward a model of emotion-specific influences on judgment and choice. *Cognition and Emotion, 14*, 473–93.

Lerner, J.S., & Keltner, D. (2001). Fear, anger and risk. *Journal of Personality and Social Psychology, 81*, 146–59.

Lever, J. (1978). Sex differences in the games children play. *Social Problems, 23*, 478–87.

Leveroni, C.L., & Berenbaum, S.A. (1998). Early androgen effects on interest in infants: Evidence from children with congenital adrenal hyperplasia. *Developmental Neuropsychology, 14*, 321–40.

Levesque, J., Fanny, E., Joanette, Y., Paquette, V., Mensour, B., Beaudoin, G., *et al.* (2003). Neural circuitry underlying voluntary suppression of sadness. *Biological Psychiatry, 53*, 502–10.

Levine, A., Zagoory-Sharon, O., Feldman, R., & Weller, A. (2007). Oxytocin during pregnancy and early postpartum: Individual patterns and maternal-fetal attachment. *Peptides, 28*, 1162–9.

Levi-Strauss, C. (1969). *The elementary structures of kinship*. Boston, MA: Beacon.

Lewin, M., & Tragos, L. (1987). Has the feminist movement influenced adolescent sex role attitudes? A reassessment after a quarter century. *Sex Roles, 16*, 125–35.

Lewontin, R.C. (1994). Women versus the biologists. *New York Review of Books*, April 7.

Li, N., Smith, A.R., Griskevicius, V., Cason, M.J., & Bryan, A. (2010). Intrasexual competition and eating restriction in heterosexual and homosexual individuals. *Evolution and Human Behavior, 31*, 365–72.

Lieberman, M.D. (2003). Reflective and reflexive judgment processes: a social cognitive neuroscience approach. In J.P. Forgas, K.R. Williams, & von Hippel, W. (Eds.), *Social judgments: Implicit and explicit processes* (pp. 44–67). New York, NY: Cambridge University Press.

Lieberman, M.D. (2007). Social cognitive neuroscience: A review of core processes. *Annual Review of Psychology, 58*, 259–89.

Liebow, E. (1967). *Tally's corner*. Boston, MA: Little, Brown.

Liessen, L.T. (2007). Women, behaviour and evolution: Understanding the debate between feminist evolutionists and evolutionary psychology. *Politics and the Life Sciences, 26*, 51–70.

Light, K.C., Grewen, K.M., & Amico, J.A. (2005). More frequent partner hugs and higher oxytocin levels are linked to lower blood pressure and heart rate in premenopausal women. *Biological Psychology, 69*, 5–21.

Light, K.C., Smith, T.E., Johns, J.M., Brownley, K.A., Hofheimer, J.A., & Amico, J.A. (2000). Oxytocin responsivity in mothers of infants: a preliminary study of relationships with blood pressure during laboratory stress and normal ambulatory activity. *Health Psychology, 19*, 560–7.

Lilenfeld, L.R.R., Wonderlich, S., Riso, L.P., Crosby, R., & Mitchell, J. (2006). Eating disorders and personality: A methodological and empirical review. *Clinical Psychology Review, 26*, 299–320.

Lishner, D.A., Nguyen, S., Stocks, E.L., & Zillmer, E.J. (2008). Are sexual and emotional infidelity equally upsetting to men and women? Making sense of forced-choice responses. *Evolutionary Psychology, 6*, 667–75.

Little, A.C., Jones, B.C., & DeBruine, L.M. (2011). Facial attractiveness: evolutionary based research. *Philosophical Transactions of the Royal Society of London, Series B, Biological Sciences, 366*, 1638–59.

Liu, Y., & Wang, X. (2003). Nucleus accumbens oxytocin and dopamine interact to regulate pair bond formation in female prairie voles. *Neuroscience, 121*, 537–44.

Lloyd, B., & Smith, C. (1986). The effects of age and gender on social behaviour in very young children. *British Journal of Social Psychology, 25*, 33–41.

Lloyd, E.A. (2005). *The case of the female orgasm: Bias in the science of evolution*. Cambridge, MA: Harvard University Press.

Loehlin, J.C., Horn, J.M., & Willerman, L. (1989). Modeling IQ change: Evidence from the Texas Adoption Project. *Child Development, 60*, 993–1004.

Loehlin, J.C., & Nichols, R.C. (1976). *Heredity, environment and personality*. Austin, TX: University of Texas Press.

Loewenstein, G.F., Weber, E.U., Hsee, C.K., & Welch, N. (2001). Risk as feelings. *Psychological Bulletin, 127*, 267–86.

Lonstein, J.S. (2005). Resolving apparent contradictions concerning the relationships among fear or anxiety and aggression: theoretical comment on D'Anna, Stevenson and Gammie (2005). *Behavioral Neuroscience 119*, 1165–8.

Lonstein, J.S., Simmons, D.A., & Stern, J.M. (1998). Functions of the caudal periaqueductal gray in lactating rats: Kyphosis, lordosis, maternal aggression and fearfulness. *Behavioral Neuroscience, 112*, 1502–18.

Low, B.S. (1988). Pathogen stress and polygyny in humans. In L. Betzig, M. Borgerhoff Mulder, & P. Turke (Eds.), *Human reproductive behaviour: A Darwinian perspective* (pp. 115–27). Cambridge: Cambridge University Press.

Low, B.S. (1990). Marriage systems and pathogen stress in human societies. *American Zoologist, 30*, 325–39.

Low, B.S. (2000). *Why sex matters: A Darwinian look at human behavior*. Princeton, NJ: Princeton University Press.

Loy, J. (1971). Estrous behavior of free-ranging rhesus monkeys (Macaca mulatta). *Primates, 12*, 1–31.

Lueptow, L.B. (1985). Concepts of masculinity and femininity: 1974–1983. *Psychological Reports, 57*, 859–62.

Lueptow, L.B., Garovich, L., and Lueptow, M.B. (1995). The persistence of gender stereotypes in the face of changing sex roles: Evidence contrary to the socio-cultural model. *Ethology and Sociobiology, 16*, 509–30.

Lueptow, L.B., Garovich-Szabo, L., & Lueptow, M.B. (2001). Social change and the persistence of sex typing: 1974–1997. *Social Forces, 80*, 1–36.

Lumsden, C.J. (1985). Color categorisation: A possible concordance between genes and culture. *Proceedings of the National Academy of Sciences of the United States of America, 82*, 5805–8.

Lynn, M., & Shurgot, B.A. (1984). Responses to lonely hearts advertisements: Effects of reported physical attractiveness, physique and coloration. *Personality and Social Psychology Bulletin, 10,* 349–57.

Lyons-Ruth, K., Connell, D.B., Zoll, D., & Stahl, J. (1987). Infants at social risk: Relations among infant maltreatment, maternal behavior, and infant attachment behavior. *Developmental Psychology, 2,* 223–32.

Lytton, H., & Romney, D. (1991). Parents' differential treatment of boys and girls: A meta-analysis. *Psychological Bulletin, 109,* 267–96.

MacArthur, R., & Wilson, E.O. (1967). *The theory of island biogeography.* Princeton, NJ: Princeton University Press.

Maccoby, E.E. (1988). Gender as a social category. *Developmental Psychology, 24,* 755–65.

Maccoby, E.E. (1990). Gender and relationships: A developmental account. *American Psychologist, 45,* 513–20.

Maccoby, E.E. (1998). *The two sexes: Growing up apart, coming together.* London: Belknap Press.

Maccoby, E.E., & Jacklin, C.N. (1974). *The psychology of sex differences.* Stanford, CA: Stanford University Press.

Maccoby, E.E., & Jacklin, C.N. (1987). Gender segregation in childhood. In H. Reese (Ed.), *Advances in Child Development* (Vol. 20, pp. 239–87). New York, NY: Academic Press.

Macdonald, G., & Leary, M.R. (2005). Why does social exclusion hurt? The relationship between social and physical pain. *Psychological Bulletin, 131,* 202–23.

MacDonald, K. (1997). Life history theory and human reproductive behavior: Environmental/contextual influences and heritable variation. *Human Nature, 8,* 327–59.

MacDonald, K. (1995). Evolution, the five-factor model, and levels of personality. *Journal of Personality. 63,* 525–67.

MacDonald, K. (2008). Effortful control, explicit processing, and the regulation of human evolved dispositions. *Psychological Review, 115,* 1012–31.

Madden, T.E., Feldman Barrett, L., & Pietromonaco, P.R. (2000). Sex differences in anxiety and depression. In A.H. Fischer (Ed.), *Gender and emotion: Social psychological perspectives* (pp. 277–300). Cambridge: Cambridge University Press.

Madhavan, S. (2002). Best of friends and worst of enemies: Competition and collaboration in polygyny. *Ethnology, 41,* 69–84.

Maestripieri, D. (1992). Functional aspects of maternal aggression in mammals. *Canadian Journal of Zoology, 70,* 1069–77.

Maestripieri, D. (1994). Costs and benefits of maternal aggression in lactating female rhesus macaques. *Primates, 35,* 443–53.

Maestripieri, D., Badiani, A., & Puglisiallegra, S. (1991). Prepartal chronic stress increases anxiety and decreases aggression in lactating females. *Behavioral Neuroscience, 105,* 663–8.

Maidment, M.R. (2006). Transgressing boundaries: Feminist perspectives in criminology. In W.S. DeKeseredy, & B. Perry (Eds.), *Advancing critical criminology: Theory and application* (pp. 43–62). Lanham, MD: Lexington Books.

Majerus, M., Amos, W., & Hurst, G. (1996). *Evolution: The four billion year war.* London: Longman.

Maltz, D., & Borker, R. (1982). A cultural approach to male-female miscommunication. In J. Gumperz (Ed.), *Language and social identity* (pp. 196–216). New York, NY: Cambridge University Press.

Manning, J.T. (1995). Fluctuating asymmetry and body weight in men and women: Implications for sexual selection. *Ethology and Sociobiology, 16*, 145–53.

Manning, J.T., Koukourakis, K., & Brodie, D.A. (1997). Fluctuating asymmetry, metabolic rate and sexual selection in human males. *Evolution and Human Behavior, 18*, 15–21.

Manning, J.T., Scutt, D., & Lewis-Jones, D.I. (1998). Developmental stability, ejaculate size, and sperm quality in men. *Evolution and Human Behavior, 19*, 273–82.

Manstead, A.S.R., & Fischer, A.H. (1995). *Gender and emotions: The role of powerlessness.* Paper presented to the meeting of the International Society for Research on Emotion, Toronto, August.

Marks, M.J., & Fraley, R.C. (2005). The sexual double standard: Fact or fiction? *Sex Roles, 52*, 175–86.

Marlowe, F.W. (2003). A critical period for provisioning by Hadza men: Implications for pair bonding. *Evolution and Human Behavior, 24*, 217–29.

Marlowe, F.W. (2004). Is human ovulation concealed? Evidence from conception beliefs in a hunter-gatherer society. *Archives of Sexual Behavior, 33*, 427–32.

Marsh, P., & Paton, R. (1984). Unpublished interview transcripts, Volumes 1–5. Research supported by the Economic and Social Research Council (GOO230113). Oxford: Oxford Brookes University.

Marsh, P., & Paton, R. (1986). Gender, social class and conceptual schemas of aggression. In A. Campbell & J. Gibbs (Eds.), *Violent transactions: The limits of personality* (pp. 59–85). Oxford: Blackwell.

Martin, C.L. (1993). New directions for investigating children's gender knowledge. *Developmental Review, 13*, 184–204.

Martin, C.L. (1994). Cognitive influences on the development and maintenance of gender segregation. In C. Leaper (Ed.), *Childhood gender segregation: Causes and consequences.* San Francisco, CA: Jossey Bass.

Martin, C.L., & Halverson, C.F. (1981). A schematic processing model of sex-typing and stereotyping in children. *Child Development, 52*, 1119–34.

Martin, E.K., Taft, C.T., & Resick, P.A. (2007). A review of marital rape. *Aggression and Violent Behavior, 12*, 329–47.

Martin, R.P., Wisenbaker, J., Baker, J., & Huttunen, M.O. (1997). Gender differences in temperament at six months and five years. *Infant Behavior and Development 20*, 339–47.

Marvin, R.S. (1997). Ethological and general systems perspectives on child-parent attachment during the toddler and preschool years. In N.L. Siegel, G.E. Weisfeld, & C.C. Weisfeld (Eds.), *Uniting psychology and biology: Integrative perspectives on human development* (pp. 189–216). Washington, DC: American Psychological Association.

Mason, K.O., & Smith, H.L. (2000). Husbands' versus wives' fertility goals and contraception use: The influence of gender context in five Asian countries. *Demography, 37*, 299–311.

Mason K.O., & Taj, A.M. (1987). Differences between women's and men's reproductive goals in developing countries. *Population and Development Review, 13*, 611–38.

Massar, K., Buunk, A.P., & Rempt, S. (2012). Age differences in women's tendency to gossip are mediated by their mate value. *Personality and Individual Differences, 52*, 106–9.

Mathes, E.W. (1986). Jealousy and romantic love: A longitudinal study. *Psychological Reports, 58,* 885–6.

Matthiesen, A.-S., Ransjö-Arvidson, A.-B., Nissen, E., & Uvnäs-Moberg, K. (2001). Postpartum maternal oxytocin release by newborns: Effects of infant hand massage and suckling. *Birth, 28,* 13–19.

Maziade, M., Boudreault, M., Thivierge, J., Caperaa, P., & Cote, R. (1984). Infant temperament: SES and gender differences and reliability of measurement in a large Quebec sample. *Merrill-Palmer Quarterly, 30,* 213–26.

Mazur, A., Mazur, J., & Keating, C. (1984). Military rank attainment of a West Point class: Effects of cadet's physical features. *American Journal of Sociology, 90,* 125–50.

McAndrew, F.T., Bell, E.K., & Garcia, C.M. (2007). Who do we tell and whom do we tell on? Gossip as a strategy for status enhancement. *Journal of Applied Social Psychology, 37,* 1562–77.

McAndrew, F.T., & Milenkovic, M.A. (2002). Of tabloids and family secrets: The evolutionary psychology of gossip. *Journal of Applied Social Psychology, 32,* 1064–82.

McCarthy, M.M., McDonald, C.H., Brooks, P.J., & Goldman, D. (1996). An anxiolytic action of oxytocin is enhanced by estrogen in the mouse. *Physiology and Behavior, 60,* 1209–15.

McClure, E.B. (2000). A meta-analytic review of sex differences in facial expression processing and their development in infants, children and adolescents. *Psychological Bulletin, 126,* 424–53.

McClure, E.B., Monk, C.S., Nelson, E.E., Zarahn, E., Leibenluft, E., Bilder, R.M., et al. (2004). A developmental examination of gender differences in brain engagement during evaluation of threat. *Biological Psychiatry, 55,* 1047–55.

McGue, M., & Lykken, D.T. (1992). Genetic influence on risk of divorce. *Psychological Science, 3,* 368–73.

McHenry, H.M. (1994). Tempo and mode in human evolution. *Proceedings of the National Academy of Sciences of the United States of America, 91,* 6780–6.

McIntosh, E.G. (1989). An investigation of romantic jealousy among black undergraduates. *Social Behavior and Personality, 17,* 135–41.

McKibbin, W.F., Shackelford, T.K., Goetz, A.T., Bates, V.M., Starratt, V.G., & Miner, E.J. (2009). Development and initial psychometric assessment of the Rape Avoidance Inventory. *Personality and Individual Differences, 39,* 336–40.

McKibbin, W.F., Shackelford, T.K., Goetz, A.T., & Starratt, V.G. (2008). Why do men rape? An evolutionary psychological perspective. *Review of General Psychology, 12,* 86–97.

McLean, C.P., & Anderson, E.R. (2009). Brave men and timid women? A review of the gender differences in fear and anxiety. *Clinical Psychology Review, 29,* 496–505.

McLean, C.Y., Reno, P.L., Pollen, A.A., Bassan, A.I., Capellini, T.D., Guenther, C., et al. (2011). Human-specific loss of regulatory DNA and the evolution of human-specific traits. *Nature, 471,* 216–19.

McLoyd, V. (1990). The declining fortunes of black children: Psychological distress, parenting, and socioemotional development in the context of economic hardship. *Child Development, 61,* 311–46.

McManis, M.H., Bradley, M.M., Berg, W.K., Cuthbert, B.N., & Lang, P.J. (2001). Emotional reactions in children: Verbal, physiological and behavioral responses to affective pictures. *Psychophysiology, 38,* 222–31.

McWhirter, N., & McWhirter, R. (1975). *Guinness book of world records*. New York, NY: Sterling.

Mead, M. (1935). *Sex and temperament in three primitive societies*. New York, NY: Morrow.

Mealey, L. (1995). The sociobiology of sociopathy: An integrated evolutionary model. *Behavioral and Brain Sciences, 18*, 523–99.

Mealey, L. (2000a). *Sex differences: Developmental and evolutionary strategies*. London: Academic Press.

Mealey, L. (2000b). Anorexia: A 'losing' strategy. *Human Nature, 2*, 31–57.

Meehan, C.L. (2005). The effects of residential locality on parental and alloparental invest-ment among Aka foragers of the Central African Republic. *Human Nature, 16*, 58–80.

Meehan, C.L. (2008). Allomaternal investment and relational uncertainty among Ngandu Farmers of the Central African Republic. *Human Nature, 19*, 211–26.

Mehta, P.H., & Beer, J. (2009). Neural mechanisms of the testosterone–aggression relation: The role of orbitofrontal cortex. *Journal of Cognitive Neuroscience, 22*, 2357–68.

Melson, G.F., Ladd, G.W., & Hsu, H.-C. (1993). Maternal support networks, maternal cognitions, and young children's social and cognitive development. *Child Development, 64*, 1401–17.

Menzel, J.E., Schaefer, L.M., Burke, N.L., Mayhew, L.L., Brannick, M.T., & Thompson, J. K. (2010). Appearance-related teasing, body dissatisfaction, and disordered eating: A meta-analysis. *Body Image, 7*, 261–70.

Mercer, C.H., Copas, A.J., Sonnenberg, P., Johnson, A.M., McManus, S., Erens, B., *et al.* (2009). Who has sex with whom? Characteristics of heterosexual partnerships reported in a national probability survey and implications for STI risk. *International Journal of Epidemiology, 38*, 206–14.

Mesnick, S.L. (1997). Sexual alliances: Evidence and evolutionary implications. In P.A. Gowaty (Ed.), *Feminism and evolutionary biology: Boundaries, intersections and frontiers* (pp. 207–60). New York, NY: Chapman and Hall.

Mesoudi, A. (2009). How cultural evolutionary theory can inform social psychology and vice versa. *Psychological Review, 116*, 929–52.

Mezzacappa, E. S., & Katkin, E. S. (2002). Breast-feeding is associated with reduced perceived stress and negative mood in mothers. *Health Psychology, 21*, 187–93.

Miczek, K.A., & O'Donnell, J.M. (1980). Alcohol and chlordiazepoxide increase suppressed aggression in mice. *Psychopharmacology, 69*, 39–44.

Mikolajczak, M., Pinon, N., Lane, A., de Timary, P., & Luminet, O. (2010).Oxytocin not only increases trust when money is at stake, but also when confidential information is in the balance. *Biological Psychology, 85*, 182–4.

Mikula, G. (1980). *Justice and social interaction*. New York, NY: Springer.

Mildner, V. (2008). *The cognitive neuroscience of human communication*. New York, NY: Lawrence Erlbaum Associates.

Milhausen, R.R., & Herold, E.S. (1999). Does the sexual double standard still exist? Perceptions of university women. *Journal of Sex Research, 36*, 361–8.

Miller, E.M. (1994). Paternal provisioning versus mate seeking in human populations. *Personality and Individual Differences, 17*, 227–55.

Miller, G.A. (2003). The cognitive revolution: A historical perspective. *Trends in Cognitive Sciences, 17*, 141–4.

Miller, G.F. (2000a). *The mating mind*. London: Heinemann.

Miller, G.F. (2000b). Sexual selection for indicators of intelligence. In G. Bock, J. Goode, & K. Webb (Eds.), *The nature of intelligence* (pp. 260–75). New York, NY: John Wiley.

Millett, K. (1969). *Sexual politics*. New York, NY: Ballantine.

Milovchevich, D., Howells, K., Drew, N., & Day, A. (2001). Sex and gender role differences in anger: An Australian community study. *Personality and Individual Differences, 31*, 117–27.

Mirowsky, J., & Ross, C.E. (1995). Sex differences in distress: Real or artifact? *American Sociological Review, 60*, 449–68.

Mithen, S. (1996). *The prehistory of mind*. London: Thames & Hudson.

Mizukami, K., Kobayashi, N., Ishi, T., & Iwata, H. (1990). First selective attachment begins in early infancy: A study using telethermography. *Infant Behavior and Development, 13*, 257–71.

Moely, B., Skarin, K., & Weil, S. (1979). Sex differences in competition-cooperation behaviour of children at two age levels. *Sex Roles, 5*, 329–42.

Moffitt, T. (1993). Adolescence-limited and life-course-persistent antisocial behavior: A developmental taxonomy. *Psychological Review, 100*, 674–701.

Mogg, K., Bradley, B.P., Dixon, C., Fisher, S., Twelftree, H., & McWilliams, A. (2000). Trait anxiety, defensiveness and selective processing of threat: An investigation using two measures of attentional bias. *Personality and Individual Differences, 28*, 1063–77.

Moller, A.P. (1990). Effects of a haematophagous mite on the barn swallow (Hirundo rustica): A test of the Hamilton and Zuk hypothesis. *Evolution, 44*, 771–84.

Moller, A.P. (1992). Female preference for symmetrical male sexual ornaments. *Nature, 357*, 238–40.

Moller, A.P. (1994). Symmetrical male sexual ornaments, paternal care and offspring quality. *Behavioral Ecology, 5*, 188–94.

Moller, A.P., Soler, M., & Thornhill, R. (1995). Breast asymmetry, sexual selection and human reproductive success. *Ethology and Sociobiology, 16*, 207–19.

Moller, A.P., & Thornhill, R. (1998). Bilateral symmetry and sexual selection: A meta-analysis. *American Naturalist, 151*, 174–92.

Moran, P.B., & Eckenrode, J. (1991). Gender differences in the costs and benefits of peer relationships during adolescence. *Journal of Adolescent Research, 6*, 396–409.

Moretti, L., Dragone, D., & di Pellegrino, G. (2008). Reward and social valuation deficits following ventromedial prefrontal damage. *Journal of Cognitive Neuroscience, 21*, 128–40.

Mos, J., & Oliver, B. (1989). Quantitative and comparative analyses of pro-aggressive actions of benzodiazepines in maternal aggression of rats. *Psychopharmacology, 97*, 152–3.

Moskowitz, A. K. (2006). "Scared stiff": Catatonia as an evolutionary-based fear response. *Psychological Review, 111*, 984–1002.

Muehlenbein, M.P., & Bribiescas, R.G. (2005). Testosterone-mediated immune functions and male life histories. *American Journal of Human Biology, 17*, 527–58.

Mueller, U., & Mazur, A. (1996). Facial dominance of West Point cadets as a predictor of later military rank. *Social Forces, 74*, 823–50.

Muldoon, O., & Reilly, J. (1998). Biology. In K. Trew & J. Kremer (Eds.), *Gender and psychology* (pp. 55–65). London: Arnold.

Muller, M.N., Emery Thompson, M., & Wrangham, R. W. (2007). Male chimpanzees prefer mating with older females. *Current Biology, 16*, 2234–8.

Muller, M.N., & Mitani, J.C. (2005). Conflict and cooperation in wild chimpanzees. *Advances in the Study of Behaviour, 35*, 275–331.

Munafo, M.R., Brown, S.M., & Hariri, A.R. (2008). Serotonin transporter (5-HTTLPR) genotype and amygdala activation: A meta-analysis. *Biological Psychiatry, 63*, 852–7.

Muncer, S., Campbell, A., Jervis, V., & Lewis, R. (2001). 'Ladettes', social representations and aggression. *Sex Roles, 44*, 33–44.

Murdock, G.P. (1967). *Ethnographic atlas.* Pittsburgh, PA: Pittsburgh University Press.

Muris, P., du Plessis, M., & Loxton, H. (2008). Origins of common fears in South African children. *Journal of Anxiety Disorders, 22*, 1510–15.

Murphy, F.C., Nimmo-Smith, I., & Lawrence, A.D. (2003). Functional neuroanatomy of emotion: A meta-analysis. *Cognitive, Affective, & Behavioral Neuroscience, 3*, 207–33.

Murphy, Y., & Murphy, R. (1974). *Women of the forest.* New York, NY: Columbia University Press.

Nagy, E., Loveland, K.A., Kopp, M., Orvos, H., Pal, A., & Molnar, P. (2001). Different emergence of fear expressions in infant boys and girls. *Infant Behavior and Development, 24*, 189–94.

National Health Service (2010). *Statistics on obesity, physical activity and diet, England 2010.* London: The Health and Social Care Information Centre.

Nelkin, D. (2000). Less selfish than sacred? Genes and the religious impulse in evolutionary psychology. In H. Rose & S. Rose (Eds.), *Alas poor Darwin: Arguments against evolutionary psychology* (pp. 17–32). London: Jonathan Cape.

Nepomnaschy, P.A., Sheiner, E., Mastorakos, G., & Arck, P.C. (2007). Stress, immune function and women's reproduction. *Annals of the New York Academy of Sciences, 1113*, 350–64.

Ness, C.D. (2004). Why girls fight: Female youth violence in the inner city. *Annals of the American Academy of Political and Social Science, 595*, 32–48.

Nettle, D., & Pollet, T.V. (2008). Natural selection on male wealth in humans. *American Naturalist, 172*, 658–66.

Neumann, I.D. (2002). Involvement of the brain oxytocin system in stress coping: interactions with the hypothalamo–pituitary–adrenal axis. *Progress in Brain Research 139*, 147–62.

Neumann, I.D. (2003). Brain mechanisms underlying emotional alterations in the peripartum period in rats. *Depression and Anxiety 17*, 111–21.

Neumann, I.D. (2008). Brain oxytocin mediates beneficial consequences of close social interactions: From maternal love and sex. In D.W. Pfaff, C. Kordon, P. Chanson, & Y. Christen (Eds.), *Hormones and social behaviour* (pp. 81–102). London: Springer.

Newcomb, A.F., Bukowski, W.M., & Pattee, L. (1993). Children's peer relations: A meta-analytic review of popular, rejected, neglected, controversial, and average sociometric status. *Psychological Bulletin, 113*, 99–128.

Newcomer, S., & Udry, J. (1984). Mothers' influence on the sexual behavior of their teenage children. *Journal of Marriage and the Family, 46*, 477–85.

Newson, L., Postmes, T., Lea, S.E.G., & Webley, P. (2005). Why are modern families small? Toward an evolutionary and cultural explanation for the demographic transition. *Personality and Social Psychology Review, 9*, 360–75.

Newton-Fisher, N.E., Thompson, M.E., Reynolds, V., Boesch, C., & Vigilant, L. (2010). Paternity and social rank in wild chimpanzees *(Pan troglodytes)* from the Budongo Forest, Uganda. *American Journal of Physical Anthropology, 142*, 417–28.

Nichter, M. (2000). *Fat talk: What girls and their parents say about dieting.* Cambridge, MA: Harvard University Press.

Niehoff, D. (1999). *The biology of violence.* New York, NY: Free Press.

Nisbett, R.E., & Wilson, T.D. (1977). Telling more than we can know: Verbal reports on mental processes. *Psychological Review, 84*, 231–59.

Nock, S.L. (1995). Commitment and dependency in marriage. *Journal of Marriage and the Family, 57*, 503–14.

Norton, A.J., & Glick, P.C. (1979). Marital stability in America: Past, present and future. In G. Levinger & O.C. Moles (Eds.), *Divorce and separation: Context, causes and consequences* (pp. 6–19). New York, NY: Basic Books.

O'Brien, M., & Huston, A.C. (1985). Development of sex-typed lay behavior in toddlers. *Developmental Psychology, 21*, 866–71.

O'Dougherty, M., Schmitz, K.H., Hearst, M.O., Covelli, M., & Kurzer, M.S. (2011). Dual conversations: Body talk among young women and their social contacts. *Qualitative Health Research, 21*, 1191–204.

Oberzaucher, D., & Grammer, K. (2011). *The case of Moulay Ismael The Bloodthirsty: Fact or fancy?* Paper delivered to the 23 meeting of the Human Behavior and Evolution Society, Montpelier, France.

Ochsner, K.N., Ray, R.D., Cooper, J.C., Robertson, E.R., Chopra, S., Gabrieli, J.D., *et al.* (2004). For better or for worse: Neural systems supporting the cognitive down- and up-regulation of negative emotion. *NeuroImage, 23*, 483–99.

Office of Population Censuses and Surveys (1995). *Mortality Statistics: Cause.* London: H.M.S.O.

Oliver, M.B., & Hyde, J.S. (1993). Gender differences in sexuality: A meta-analysis. *Psychological Bulletin, 114*, 29–51.

Omark, D.R., Omark, M., & Edelman, M. (1973). Formation of dominance hierarchies in young children. In T.R. Williams (Ed.), *Psychological anthropology* (pp. 289–316). The Hague: Mouton.

Ono, H. (1998). Husbands' and wives' resources and marital dissolution. *Journal of Marriage and the Family, 60*, 674–89.

Orenstein, P. (1994). *Schoolgirls: Young women, self-esteem, and the confidence gap.* New York, NY: Doubleday.

Ostermeyer, M.C. (1983). Maternal aggression. In R.W. Elwood (Ed.), *Parental behavior of rodents* (pp. 151–79). Chichester: Wiley.

Ostovich, J. M., & Sabini, J. (2004). How are sociosexuality, sex drive, and lifetime number of sexual partners related? *Personality and Social Psychology Bulletin, 30*, 1255–66.

Ousley, L., Cordero, E.D., & White, S. (2008). Fat talk among college students: How undergraduates communicate regarding food and body weight, shape and appearance. *Eating Disorders: The Journal of Treatment & Prevention, 16*, 73–84.

Owen, J.J., Rhoades, G.K., Stanley, S.M., & Fincham, F.D. (2010). "Hooking up" among college students: Demographic and psychosocial correlates. *Archives of Sexual Behavior, 39*, 653–63.

Owens, I.P.F. (2002). Sex differences in mortality rate. *Science, 297*, 2008–9.

Owens, L., Shute, R., & Slee, P. (2000). "Guess what I just heard!": Indirect aggression among teenage girls in Australia. *Aggressive Behavior, 26*, 67–83.

Packer, C. (1979). Male dominance and reproductive activity in Papio anubis. *Animal Behaviour, 27*, 37–45.

Pagelow, M. (1984). *Family violence*. New York, NY: Praeger.

Palombit, R.A. (1999). Infanticide and the evolution of pair bonds in nonhuman primates. *Evolutionary Anthropology, 7*, 117–29.

Parish, A. (1996). Female relationships in bonobos (Pan paniscus): Evidence for bonding, cooperation, and female dominance in a male-philopatric species. *Human Nature, 7*, 61–96.

Park, J.H., & Schaller, M. (2005). Does attitude similarity serve as a heuristic cue for kinship? Evidence of an implicit cognitive association. *Evolution and Human Behavior, 26*, 158–70.

Parker, G.A. (1970a). Sperm competition and its evolutionary consequences in the insects. *Biological Reviews, 45*, 525–67.

Parker, G.A. (1970b). The reproductive behaviour and the nature of sexual selection in Scatophaga stercoraria L. (Diptera: Scatophagidae): II. The fertilization rate and the spatial and temporal relationships of each sex around the site of mating and oviposition. *Journal of Animal Ecology, 39*, 205–28.

Parker, G.A., Baker, R.R., & Smith, V.G.F. (1972). The origin and evolution of gamete dimorphism and the male-female phenomenon. *Journal of Theoretical Biology, 36*, 529–53.

Parker, J.G., & Asher, S.R. (1993). Friendship and friendship quality in middle childhood: Links with peer group acceptance and feelings of loneliness and social dissatisfaction. *Developmental Psychology, 29*, 611–21.

Parker, J.G., & Seal, J. (1996). Forming, losing, renewing, and replacing friendships: Applying temporal parameters to the assessment of children's friendship experiences. *Child Development, 67*, 2248–68.

Parkhurst, J.T., & Hopmeyer, A. (1998). Sociometric popularity and peer-perceived popularity: Two distinct dimensions of peer status. *Journal of Early Adolescence, 18*, 125–44.

Parmigiani, S., Brain, P.F., Mainardi, D., & Brunoni, V. (1988). Different patterns of biting attack employed by lactating female mice (Mus domesticus) in encounters with male and female conspecific intruders. *Journal of Comparative Psychology, 102*, 287–93.

Patterson, G.R. (1986). Performance models for antisocial boys. *American Psychologist, 41*, 432–44.

Paul, E.L., & Hayes, K. A. (2002). The casualties of "casual" sex: A qualitative exploration of the phenomenology of college students' hookups. *Journal of Social and Personal Relationships, 19*, 639–61.

Paul, L., Foss, M.A., & Baenninger, M. (1996). Double standards for sexual jealousy: Manipulative morality or a reflection of evolved sex differences? *Human Nature, 7*, 291–321.

Paul, L., Foss, M.A., & Galloway, J. (1993). Sexual jealousy in young women and men: Aggressive responsiveness to partner and rival. *Aggressive Behavior, 19*, 401–20.

Paul, L., & Galloway, J. (1994). Sexual jealousy: Gender differences in response to partner and rival. *Aggressive Behavior, 20*, 203–12.

Pavard, S., Gagnon, A., Desjardins, B., & Heyer, E. (2005). Mother's death and child survival: The case of early Quebec. *Journal of Biosocial Science, 37,* 209–27.

Pearson, P. (1998). *When she was bad.* London: Virago.

Pedersen, C.A., & Boccia, M.L. (2006). Vasopressin interactions with oxytocin in the control of female sexual behavior. *Neuroscience, 139,* 843–51.

Pedersen, C.A., & Prange, A.J. (1979). Induction of maternal behavior in virgin rats after intracerebroventricular administration of oxytocin. *Proceedings of the National Academy of Sciences of the United States of America, 76,* 6661–5.

Pedersen, F.A. (1991). Secular trends in human sex ratios: Their influence on individual and family behavior. *Human Nature, 2,* 271–91.

Pellegrini, A.D., & Perlmutter, J.C. (1989). Classroom context effects on children's play. *Developmental Psychology, 25,* 289–96.

Pemberton, M.B., Insko, C.A., & Schopler, J. (1996). Memory for and experience of differential competitive behavior of individuals and groups. *Journal of Personality and Social Psychology, 71,* 953–66.

Penke, L., Denissen, J.J.A., & Miller, G.F. (2007). The evolutionary genetics of personality. *European Journal of Personality, 21,* 549–87.

Penn, D.J., & Smith, K.R. (2007). Differential fitness costs of reproduction between the sexes. *Proceedings of the National Academy of Sciences of the United States of America, 104,* 553–58.

Percy, C. (1998). Feminism. In K. Trew & J. Kremer (Eds.), *Gender and psychology* (pp. 27–40). London: Arnold.

Perrett, D.I., Lee, K.J., Penton-Voak, I., Rowland, D., Yoshikawa, S., Burt, D.M., et al. (1998). Effects of sexual dimorphism on facial attractiveness. *Nature, 294,* 884–7.

Perry, D., & Bussey, K. (1979). The social learning theory of sex differences: Imitation is alive and well. *Journal of Personality and Social Psychology, 37,* 1699–712.

Perry, G.H., Dominy, N.J., Claw, K.G., Lee, A.S., Fiegler, H., Redon, R., et al. (2007). Diet and the evolution of human amylase gene copy number variation. *Nature Genetics, 39,* 1256–60.

Perusse, D. (1993). Cultural and reproductive success in industrial societies: Testing the relationship at the proximate and ultimate levels. *Behavioral and Brain Sciences, 16,* 267–322.

Petersen, J.L., & Hyde, J.S. (2010). A meta-analytic review of research on gender differences in sexuality, 1993–2007. *Psychological Bulletin, 136,* 21–38.

Peterson, C.K., Gable, P., & Harmon-Jones, E. (2008). Asymmetric frontal ERPs, emotion, and behavioral approach/inhibition sensitivity. *Social Neuroscience, 3,* 113–24.

Peterson, C.K., Shackman, A.J., & Harmon-Jones, E. (2008). The role of asymmetric frontal cortical activity in aggression. *Psychophysiology, 45,* 86–92.

Phinney, V.C., Jenson, L.C., Olsen, J.A., & Cundick, B. (1990). The relationship between early development and psychosexual behaviors in adolescent females. *Adolescence, 25*(98), 321–32.

Pietrini, P., Guazzelli, M., Basso, G., Jaffe, K., & Grafman, J. (2000). Neural correlates of imaginal aggressive behavior assessed by positron emission tomography in healthy subjects. *American Journal of Psychiatry, 157,* 1772–81.

Pines, A.M., & Aronson, E. (1983). Antecedents, correlates and consequences of sexual jealousy. *Journal of Personality, 51,* 108–36.

Pines, A.M., & Friedman, A. (1998). Gender differences in romantic jealousy. *Journal of Social Psychology, 138*, 54–71.

Pinker, S. (1994). *The language instinct.* New York, NY: Morrow.

Pinker, S. (1997). *How the mind works.* New York, NY: Norton.

Pinker, S. (2010). The cognitive niche: Coevolution of intelligence, sociality, and language. *Proceedings of the National Academy of Sciences of the United States of America, 107*, 8993–9.

Piper, E. (1983). *Patterns of violent juvenile recidivism.* PhD dissertation, University of Philadelphia, PA.

Pitkanen-Pulkkinen, L. (1981). Long term studies on the characteristics of aggressive and non-aggressive juveniles. In P.F. Brain & D. Benton (Eds.), *Multidisciplinary approaches to aggression research* (pp. 215–43). Amsterdam: Elsevier/North Holland Biomedical Press.

Pizzari, T., & Birkhead, T.R. (2000). Female feral fowl eject sperm of subdominant males. *Nature, 405*, 787–9.

Pleck, E. (1989). Criminal approaches to family violence 1640–1980. *Crime and Justice: A Review of Research, 11*, 19–58.

Plomin, R. (1994). *Genetics and experience.* London: Sage.

Plomin, R., Asbury, K., & Dunn, J. (2001). Why are children from the same family so different? Nonshared environment a decade later. *Canadian Journal of Psychiatry, 46*, 225–33.

Plomin, R., Corley, R., DeFries, J.C., & Fulker, D.W. (1990). Individual differences in television viewing in early childhood: Nature as well as nurture. *Psychological Science, 1*, 371–7.

Plomin, R., & DeFries, J.C. (1985). *Origins of individual differences in infancy: The Colorado Adoption Project.* New York, NY: Academic Press.

Polanyi, K. (1957). *The great transformation: The political and economic origins of our time.* New York, NY: Rinehart.

Pomiankowski, A., Iwasa, Y., & Nee, S. (1991). The evolution of costly mate preferences 1: Fisher and biased mutation. *Evolution, 45*, 1422–30.

Post, R.M. (1992). Transduction of psychosocial stress into the neurobiology of recurrent affective disorder. *American Journal of Psychiatry, 149*, 999–1010.

Powlishta, K.K. (1995). Intergroup processes in childhood: Social categorisation and sex-role development. *Developmental Psychology, 31*, 781–8.

Pradhan, G.R., & van Schaik, C.P. (2008). Infanticide-driven intersexual conflict over matings in primates and its effects on social organization. *Behaviour, 145*, 251–75.

Pratto, F. (1996). Sexual politics: The gender gap in the bedroom and the cabinet. In D. Buss & N. Malamuth (Eds.), *Sex, power, conflict: Evolutionary and feminist approaches* (pp. 179–230). New York, NY: Oxford University Press.

Prins, K.S., Buunk, B.P., & VanYperen, N.W. (1993). Equity, normative disapproval and extramarital relationships. *Journal of Social and Personal Relationships, 10*, 39–53.

Promislow, D.E.L., & Harvey, P.H. (1990). Living fast and dying young: A comparative analysis of life-history variation among mammals. *Journal of Zoology, 220*, 417–37.

Pulkkinen, L. (1987). Offensive and defensive aggression in humans: A longitudinal perspective. *Aggressive Behavior, 13*, 197–212.

Pusey, A., Murray, C., Wallauer, W., Wilson, M., Wroblewski, E., & Goodall, J. (2008). Severe aggression among female Pan troglodytes schweinfurthii at Gombe National Park, Tanzania. *International Journal of Primatology, 29*, 949–73.

Pusey, A., Williams, J., & Goodall, J. (1997). The influence of dominance rank on the reproductive success of female chimpanzees. *Science, 277*, 828–31.

Pusey, A.E., & Packer, C. (1987). Dispersal and philopatry. In B.B. Smuts, D.L. Cheney, R.M. Seyfarth, R.W. Wrangham, & T.T. Struhsaker (Eds.), *Primate societies* (pp. 250–66). Chicago, IL: University of Chicago Press.

Quinlan, R.J. (2007). Human parental effort and environmental risk. *Proceedings of the Royal Society B, 274*, 121–5.

Quinlan, R.J. (2008). Human pair-bonds: Evolutionary functions, ecological variation, and adaptive development. *Evolutionary Anthropology, 17*, 227–38.

Quinlan, R.J., & Quinlan, M.B. (2007). Evolutionary ecology of human pair-bonds: cross-cultural tests of alternative hypotheses. *Cross-Cultural Research, 41*, 149–69.

Quinlan, R.J., & Quinlan, M.B. (2008). Human lactation, pair-bonds, and alloparents. *Human Nature, 19*, 87–102.

Raine, A., Lencz, T., Bihrle, S., LaCasse, L., & Colletti, P. (2000). Reduced prefrontal gray matter volume and reduced autonomic activity in antisocial personality disorder. *Archives of General Psychiatry, 57*, 119–27.

Raine, A., Yang, Y., Narr, K.L., & Toga, A.W. (2011). Sex differences in orbitofrontal gray as a partial explanation for sex differences in antisocial personality. *Molecular Psychiatry, 16*, 227–36.

Rasmussen, P.K., & Ferraro, K.J. (1979). The divorce process. *Alternative Lifestyles, 2*, 443–60.

Rawls, J. (1971). *A theory of justice.* Cambridge, MA: Belknap Press.

Reader, S.M., Hager, Y., & Laland, K.N. (2011). The evolution of primate general and cultural intelligence. *Philosophical Transactions of the Royal Society of London, Series B, Biological Sciences, 366*, 1017–27.

Reiber, C., & Garcia, J.R. (2010). Hooking up: Gender differences, evolution, and pluralistic ignorance. *Evolutionary Psychology, 8*, 390–414.

Rhode, D.L. (1991). The "no problem" problem: Feminist challenges and cultural change. *Yale Law Review, 100*, 1731–93.

Rhodes, G. (2006). The evolutionary psychology of facial beauty. *Annual Review of Psychology, 57*, 199–226.

Rice, W.R. (1984). Sex chromosomes and the evolution of sexual dimorphism. *Evolution, 38*, 735–42.

Rice, W.R. (1992). Sexually antagonistic genes: Experimental evidence. *Science, 256*, 1436–9.

Rice, W.R. (1996). Sexually antagonistic male evolution triggered by experimental arrest of female evolution. *Nature, 361*, 232–4.

Rich, A. (1976). *Of woman born: Motherhood as experience and institution.* New York, NY: Norton.

Richerson, P.J., & Boyd, R. (2005). *Not by genes alone.* Chicago, IL: University of Chicago Press.

Ridley, M. (1999). *Genome: The autobiography of a species in 23 chapters.* London: Fourth Estate.

Roberts, M.L., Buchanan, K.L., & Evans, M.R. (2004). Testing the immunocompetence handicap hypothesis: A review of the evidence. *Animal Behaviour, 68*, 227–38.

Robertson, K., & Murachver, T. (2007). It takes two to tangle: Gender symmetry in intimate partner violence. *Basic and Applied Social Psychology, 29*, 109–18.

Robinson, I.E., & Jedlicka, D. (1982). Change in sexual attitudes and behavior of college students from 1965 to 1980: A research note. *Journal of Marriage and the Family, 44*, 237–40.

Robinson, I.E., Ziss, K., Ganza, B., & Katz, S. (1991). Twenty years of the sexual revolution, 1965-1985: An update. *Journal of Marriage and Family, 53*, 216–20.

Robinson, M. (2011). The great porn experiment. *The Evolutionary Review, 2*, 98–105.

Rodseth, L., Wrangham, R.W., Harrigan, A.M., & Smuts, B.B. (1991). The human community as a primate society. *Current Anthropology, 32*, 221–54.

Rogers, A.R. (1988). Does biology constrain culture? *American Anthropologist, 90*, 819–31.

Rogers, L. (1999). *Sexing the brain*. London: Weidenfeld & Nicholson.

Roney, J.R. (2009). The role of sex hormones in the initiation of human mating relationships. In P.T. Ellison, & P.B. Gray (Eds.), *Endocrinology of social relationships* (pp. 246–93). London: Harvard University Press.

Rood, L., Roelofs, J., Bögels, S., Nolen-Hoeksema, S., & Schouten, E. (2009). The influence of emotion-focused rumination and distraction on depressive symptoms in non-clinical youth: A meta-analytic review. *Clinical Psychology Review, 29*, 607–16.

Roopnarine, J.L. (1986). Mothers' and fathers' behaviors toward the toy play of infant sons and daughters. *Sex Roles, 14*, 59–68.

Rose, A.J. (2002). Co-rumination in the friendships of girls and boys. *Child Development, 73*, 1830–43.

Rose, A.J., & Rudolph, K.D. (2006). A review of sex differences in peer relationship processes: Potential trade-offs for the emotional and behavioral development of girls and boys. *Psychological Bulletin, 132*, 98–131.

Rosenberg, K., & Trevathan, W. (1996). Bipedalism and human birth: The obstetrical dilemma revisited. *Evolutionary Anthropology, 4*, 161–8.

Rosenblatt, J.S., Factor, E.M., & Mayer, A.D. (1994). Relationship between maternal aggression and maternal care in the rat. *Aggressive Behavior, 20*, 243–56.

Ross, C., & MacLarnon, A. (2000). The evolution of non-maternal care in anthropoid primates: A test of the hypotheses. *Folia Primatogica, 71*, 93–113.

Ross, C.E., & VanWilligen, M. (1996). Gender, parenthood, and anger. *Journal of Marriage and the Family, 58*, 572–84.

Rosser, S.V. (1997). Possible implications of feminist theories for the study of evolution. In P.A. Gowaty (Ed.), *Feminism and evolutionary biology: Boundaries, intersections and frontiers* (pp. 21–41). New York, NY: Chapman & Hall.

Rotermann, M., & McKay, A. (2009). Condom use at last sexual intercourse among unmarried, not living common-law 20 - to 34-year-old Canadian young adults. *The Canadian Journal of Human Sexuality, 18*, 75–88.

Rothbart, M.K. (1988). Temperament and the development of the inhibited approach. *Child Development, 59*, 1241–50.

Rowe, D.C. (1994). *The limits of family influence: Genes, experience and behavior*. London: Guildford Press.

Roy, R., & Benenson, J.F. (2002). Sex and contextual effects on children's use of interference competition. *Developmental Psychology, 38,* 306–12.

Rozen, S., Skaletsky, H., Marszalek, J.D., Minx, P.J., Cordum, H.S., Waterston, R.H., *et al.* (2003). Abundant gene conversion between arms of palindromes in human and ape Y chromosomes. *Nature, 423,* 873–6.

Rozin, P., Millman, L., & Nemeroff, C. (1986). Operation of the laws of sympathetic magic in disgust and other domains. *Journal of Personality and Social Psychology, 50,* 703–12.

Rubia, K. (2011). "Cool" inferior frontostriatal dysfunction in attention-deficit/hyperactivity disorder versus "hot" ventromedial orbitofrontal-limbic dysfunction in conduct disorder: A review. *Biological Psychiatry, 69,* e69–e87.

Rubin, L.B. (1990). *Erotic wars: What happened to the sexual revolution?* New York, NY: Farrar, Straus, & Giroux.

Rubin, L.R., Nemeroff, C.J., & Russo, N.F. (2004). Exploring feminist women's body consciousness. *Psychology of Women Quarterly, 28,* 27–37.

Ruble, D.N., & Martin, C.L. (1998). Gender development. In W. Damon & N. Eisenberg (Eds.), *Handbook of child psychology volume three: Social, emotional and personality development* (pp. 933–1016). New York, NY: John Wiley.

Rushton, J.P., Fulker, D.W., Neale, M.C., Nias, D.K.B., & Eysenck, H.J. (1986). Altruism and aggression: The heritability of individual differences. *Journal of Personality and Social Psychology, 50,* 1192–8.

Rutter, M. (1978). Diagnosis and definition. In M. Tutter and E. Schopler (Eds.), *Autism: A reappraisal of concepts and treatment.* New York, NY: Plenum.

Ryan, M.J. (1991). Sexual selection and communication in frogs. *Trends in Evolution and Ecology, 6,* 351–5.

Sadalla, E.K., Kenrick, D.T., & Vershure, B. (1987). Dominance and heterosexual attraction. *Journal of Personality and Social Psychology, 52,* 730–8.

Sagi, A., Lamb, M., Shoham, R., Duir, R., & Lewkowicz, K. (1985). Parent-infant interaction in families on Israeli Kibbutzim. *International Journal of Behavioral Development, 8,* 273–84.

Salcuni, S., Di Riso, D., Mazzeschi, C., & Lis, A. (2009). Children's fears: A survey of Italian children ages 6 to 10 years. *Psychological Reports, 104,* 971–88.

Salmon, C.A. (1999). *Who's keeping in touch? Sex, birth order and contact with kin.* Paper presented to Human Behavior and Evolution Society, Salt Lake City, June.

Salmon, C.A., & Daly, M. (1996). On the importance of kin relations to Canadian women and men. *Ethology and Sociobiology, 17,* 289–97.

Sandberg, D.E., & Meyer-Bahlberg, H.F.L. (1994). Variability in middle childhood play behaviour: Effects of gender, age and family background. *Archives of Sexual Behavior, 23,* 645–63.

Sander, D., Grafman, J., & Zalla, T. (2003). The human amygdala: an evolved system for relevance detection. *Review of Neuroscience 14,* 303–16.

Sasse, G., Müller, H., Chakraborty, R., & Ott, J. (1994). Estimating the frequency of nonpaternity in Switzerland. *Human Heredity, 44,* 337–43.

Savin-Williams, R.C. (1980). Social interactions of adolescent females in natural groups. In H.C. Foot, A.J. Chapman, & J.R. Smith (Eds.), *Friendship and social relations in children* (pp. 343–64). Chichester: Wiley.

Savin-Williams, R.C. (1987). *Adolescence: An ethological perspective*. New York, NY: Springer Verlag.

Sayer, L.C., & Bianchi, S.M. (2000). Women's economic independence and the probability of divorce: A review and re-examination. *Journal of Family Issues, 21*, 906–43.

Sayers, J. (1982). *Biological politics: Feminist and anti-feminist perspectives*. London: Tavistock.

Scarr, S., & McCartney, K. (1983). How people make their own environments: A theory of genotype-environment interaction effects. *Child Development, 54*, 424–35.

Schaefer, K., Fink, B., Grammer, K., Mitteroecker, P., Gunz, P., & Bookstein, F.L. (2006). Female appearance: Facial and bodily attractiveness as shape. *Psychology Science, 48*, 371–89.

Schaffer, H.R., & Emerson, P.E. (1964). The development of social attachment in infancy. *Monographs of the Society for Research in Child Development, 29*, 1–77.

Schmitt, D.P. (2005). Sociosexuality from Argentina to Zimbabwe: a 48 nation study of sex, culture and strategies of human mating. *Behavioral and Brain Sciences, 28*, 247–311.

Schmookler, T., & Bursik, K. (2007). The value of monogamy in emerging adulthood: A gendered perspective. *Journal of Social and Personal Relationships, 24*, 819–35.

Schneider, D.M., & Cottrell, C.B. (1975). *The American kin universe: A genealogical study*. Chicago, IL: University of Chicago Press.

Schofield, V.W. (1981). Complementarity and conflicting identities: Images of interaction in an interracial school. In S. Asher, & J.M. Gottman (Eds.), *The development of children's friendships* (pp. 53–90). New York, NY: Cambridge University Press.

Schulte-Rüther, M., Markowitsch, H.J., Shah, N.C., Fink, G.R., & Piefkea, M. (2008). Gender differences in brain networks supporting empathy. *NeuroImage, 42*, 393–403.

Schuster, I. (1983). Women's aggression: An African case study. *Aggressive Behavior, 9*, 319–31

Sear, R., & Mace, R. (2008). Who keeps children alive? A review of the effects of kin on child survival. *Evolution and Human Behavior, 29*, 1–18.

Sear, R., Steele, F., McGregor, I.A., & Mace, R. (2002). The effects of kin on child mortality in rural Gambia. *Demography, 39*, 43–63.

Segerstrale, U. (2000). *Defenders of the truth: The battle for science in the sociology debate and beyond*. Oxford: Oxford University Press.

Serbin, L.A., Moller, L.C., Gulko, J., Powlishta, K.K., & Colburne, K.A. (1994). The emergence of gender segregation in toddler playgroups. In C. Leaper (Ed.), *Childhood gender segregation: Causes and consequences* (pp. 7–17). San Francisco, CA: Jossey-Bass.

Serbin, L.A., Tonick, I.J., & Sternglanz, S.H. (1977). Shaping cooperative cross-sex play. *Child Development, 48*, 924–9.

Sergerie, K., Chochol, C., & Armony, J.L. (2008). The role of the amygdala in emotional processing: A quantitative meta-analysis of functional neuroimaging studies. *Neuroscience and Biobehavioral Reviews, 32*, 811–30.

Seyfarth, R.M. (1976). Social relationships among adult female baboons. *Animal Behaviour, 24*, 917–38.

Shackelford, T.K., & Buss, D.N. (1996). Betrayal in mateships, friendships and coalitions. *Personality and Social Psychology Bulletin, 22*, 1151–64.

Shackelford, T.K., & Goetz, A.T. (2007). Adaptation to sperm competition in humans. *Current Directions in Psychological Science, 16*, 47–50.

Shackelford, T.K., Weekes-Shackelford, V.A., LeBlanc, G.J., Bleske, A.L., Euler, H.A., & Holer, S. (2000). Female coital orgasm and male attractiveness. *Human Nature, 11*, 299–306.

Shepher, J. (1971). Mate selection among second generation kibbutz adolescents and adults: Incest avoidance and negative imprinting. *Archives of Sexual Behavior, 1*, 293–307.

Shepher, J. (1983). *Incest: A biosocial view.* New York, NY: Academic Press.

Sherman, P., & Reeve, K. (1997). Forward and backward: Alternative approaches to studying human social evolution. In L. Betzig (Ed.), *Human nature: A critical reader* (pp. 147–58). New York, NY: Oxford University Press.

Shermer, M. (2004). A bounty of science. *Scientific American, 290*, 33.

Sichona, F.J. (1993). The polygyny-fertility hypothesis revisited: The situation in Ghana. *Journal of Biosocial Sciences, 25*, 473–82.

Siever, L.J. (2008). Neurobiology of aggression and violence. *American Journal of Psychiatry, 165*, 429–42.

Sievert, L.L., & Dubois, C.A. (2005). Validating signals of ovulation: Do women who think they know, really know? *American Journal of Human Biology, 17*, 310–20.

Silk, J. (2009). Nepotistic cooperation in non-human primate groups. *Philosophical Transactions of the Royal Society of London, Series B, Biological Sciences, 364*, 3243–54.

Sillen-Tulberg, B., & Moller, A.P. (1993). The relationship between concealed ovulation and mating systems in anthropoid primates: A phylogenetic analysis. *American Naturalist, 141*, 1–25.

Silverman, I., & Eals, M. (1992). Sex differences in spatial ability: Evolutionary theory and data. In J.H. Barkow, L. Cosmides, & J. Tooby (Eds.), *The adapted mind: Evolutionary psychology and the generation of culture* (pp. 533–49). New York, NY: Oxford University Press.

Simmons, R.G. (1987). *Moving into adolescence: The impact of pubertal change and social context.* New York, NY: Aldine de Gruyter.

Simon, R.J., & Baxter, S. (1989). Gender and violent crime. In N.A. Weiner & M.E. Wolfgang (Eds.), *Violent crime, violent criminals* (pp. 171–97). London: Sage.

Simon, R.W., & Nath, L.E. (2004). Gender and emotion in the United States: Do men and women differ in self-reports of feelings and expressive behavior? *American Journal of Sociology, 109*, 1137–76.

Simpson, J.A., & Gangestad, S.W. (1992). Sociosexuality and romantic partner choice. *Journal of Personality, 60*, 31–51.

Singer, T., Seymour, B., O'Doherty, J. P., Stephan, K. E., Dolan, R.J., & Frith, C.D. (2006). Empathic neural responses are modulated by the perceived fairness of others. *Nature 439*, 466–9.

Singh, D. (1993). Adaptive significance of female physical attractiveness: Role of waist to hip ratio. *Journal of Personality and Social Psychology, 65*, 293–307.

Singh, D. (1995a). Female judgement of male attractiveness and desirability for relationships: Role of waist-to-hip ratio and financial status. *Journal of Personality and Social Psychology, 69*, 1089–101.

Singh, D. (1995b). Female health, attractiveness and desirability for relationships: Role of breast asymmetry and waist-to-hip ratio. *Ethology and Sociobiology, 16*, 465–81.

Singh, D. (2002). Female mate value at a glance: Relationship of waist-to-hip ratio to health, fecundity and attractiveness. *Neuroendocrinology Letters, 23*, 81–91.

Skuse, D.H. (2000). Imprinting, the X-chromosome, and the male brain: Explaining sex differences in the liability to autism. *Pediatric Research, 47*, 9–16.

Skuse, D.H., James, R.S., Bishop, DVM, Coppin, B., Dalton, P., Aamodt Leeper, G., *et al.* (1997). Evidence from Turner's syndrome of an imprinted X-linked locus affecting cognitive function. *Nature, 387*, 705–8.

Small, M.F. (1993). *Female choices: Sexual behavior of female primates.* London: Cornell University Press.

Small, M.F., & Smith, D.G. (1985). Sex of infants produced by male rhesus macaques. *American Naturalist, 126*, 354–61.

Smetana, J.G., & Letourneau, K.J. (1984). Development of gender constancy and children's sex-typed free play behaviour. *Developmental Psychology, 20*, 691–6.

Smith, A., Lyons, A., Ferris, J., Richters, J., Pitts, M., Shelley, J., *et al.* (2011). Sexual and relationship satisfaction among heterosexual men and women: The importance of desired frequency of sex. *Journal of Sex and Marital Therapy, 37*, 104–15.

Smith, E., Udry, J., & Morris, N. (1985). Pubertal development and friends: A biosocial explanation of adolescent sexual behavior. *Journal of Health and Social Behavior, 26*, 183–92.

Smith, E.A., Borgerhoff Mulder, M., & Hill, K. (2001). Controversies in the evolutionary social sciences: a guide for the perplexed. *Trends in Ecology and Evolution, 16*, 128–35.

Smith, E.L., & Farole, D.J. (2009). *Profile of intimate partner violence cases in large urban counties.* Washington, DC: Bureau of Justice Statistics Special Report NCJ 228193, US Department of Justice.

Smith, T. (1994). Attitudes toward sexual permissiveness: Trends, correlates, and behavioral connections. In A.S. Rossi (Ed.), *Sexuality across the life course* (pp. 63–97). Chicago, IL: University of Chicago Press.

Smits, D.J.M., & Kuppens, P. (2005). The relations between anger, coping with anger, and aggression, and the BIS/BAS system. *Personality and Individual Differences, 39*, 783–93.

Smuts, B.B. (1985). *Sex and friendship in baboons.* New York, NY: Aldine de Gruyter.

Smuts, B.B. (1987). Gender, aggression and influence. In B.B. Smuts, D.L. Cheney, R.M. Seyfarth, R.W. Wrangham, & T.T. Struhsaker (Eds.), *Primate societies* (pp. 400–12). Chicago, IL: University of Chicago Press.

Smuts, B.B. (1987). Sexual competition and mate choice. In B.B. Smuts, D.L. Cheney, R.M. Seyfarth, R.W. Wrangham, & T.T. Struhsaker (Eds.), *Primate societies* (pp. 385–99). Chicago, IL: University of Chicago Press.

Smuts, B. (1992). Male aggression against women. *Human Nature, 3*, 1–44.

Smuts, B. (1995). The evolutionary origins of patriarchy. *Human Nature, 6*, 1–32.

Snell, W.E., Miller, R.S., Belk, S.S., Garcia-Falcone, R., & Hernandez-Sanchez, J.E. (1989). Men's and women's emotional disclosures: The impact of disclosure recipient, culture and the masculine role. *Sex Roles, 21*, 467–86.

Sommer, V., Bauer, J., Fowler, A., & Ortmann, S. (2010). Patriarchal chimpanzees, matriarchal bonobos: Potential ecological causes of a Pan dichotomy. In V. Sommer & C. Ross (Eds.), *Primates at Gashaka: Socioecology and conservation in Nigeria's biodiversity hotspot* (pp. 417–49). New York, NY: Springer

Sorenson, S.B., & Taylor, C.A. (2005). Female aggression toward male intimate partners: An examination of social norms in a community-based sample. *Psychology of Women Quarterly, 29*, 78–96.

Speizer, I.S. (1999). Are husbands a barrier to women's family planning use? The case of Morocco. *Social Biology*, *46*, 1–16.

Spence, J.T. (1985). Gender identity and its implications for the concepts of masculinity and femininity. In T.B. Sonderegger (Ed.), *Nebraska Symposium on Motivation*, *32*, 59–95. Lincoln: University of Nebraska Press.

Sperber, D. (2002). In defense of massive modularity. In E. Dupoux (Ed.), *Language, brain and cognitive development: Essays in honor of Jacques Mehler* (pp. 47–57). Cambridge, MA: MIT Press.

Sprecher, S., Sullivan, Q., & Hatfield, E. (1994). Mate selection preferences: Gender differences examined in a national sample. *Journal of Personality and Social Psychology*, *66*, 1074–80.

Sroufe, L.A., Bennett, C., Englund, M., Urban, J., & Shulman, S. (1993). The significance of gender boundaries in preadolescence: Contemporary correlates and antecedents of boundary violation and maintenance. *Child Development*, *64*, 455–66.

Stanik, C.E., & Ellsworth, P.C. (2010). Who cares about marrying a rich man? Intelligence and variation in women's mate preferences. *Human Nature*, *21*, 203–17.

Stanovich, K.E. (2004). *The robot's rebellion: Finding meaning in the age of Darwin*. Chicago, IL: Chicago University Press.

Statham, A. (1987). The gender model revisited: Differences in the management styles of men and women. *Sex Roles*, *16*, 409–29.

Steelman, L., Powell, B., Werum, R., & Carter, S. (2002). Reconsidering the effects of sibling configuration: Recent advances and challenges. *Annual Review of Sociology*, *28*, 243–69.

Stein, J.A., Newcomb, M.D., & Bentler, P.M. (1992). The effect of agency and communality on self-esteem: Gender differences in longitudinal data. *Sex Roles*, *26*, 465–81.

Sterelny, K. (2001). *Dawkins vs. Gould: Survival of the fittest*. Cambridge: Icon Books.

Stern, M., & Karraker, K.H. (1989). Sex stereotyping of infants; A review of gender labeling studies. *Sex Roles*, *20*, 501–22.

Stevens, J.M.G., Vervaecke, H., de Vries, H., & van Elsacker, L. (2007). Sex differences in the steepness of dominance hierarchies in captive bonobo groups. *International Journal of Primatology*, *28*, 1417–30.

Stice, E. (2002). Risk and maintenance factors for eating pathology: A meta-analytic review. *Psychological Bulletin*, *128*, 825–48.

Stiegel-Moore, R. H., Tucker, N., & Hsu, J. (1990). Body image dissatisfaction and disordered eating in lesbian college students. *International Journal of Eating Disorders*, *9*, 493–500.

Stockley, P., & Bro-Jorgensen, J. (2011). Female competition and its evolutionary consequences in mammals. *Biological Reviews*, *86*, 341–66.

Strassmann, B.I. (1997). Polygamy as a risk factor for child mortality in the Dogon. *Current Anthropology*, *38*, 688–95.

Strathearn, L., Li, J., Fonagy, P., & Montague, P.R. (2008). What's in a smile? Maternal brain responses to infant facial cues. *Pediatrics*, *122*, 40–51.

Straus, M.A., & Ramirez, I.L. (2007). Gender symmetry in prevalence, severity, and chronicity of physical aggression against dating partners by university students in Mexico and USA. *Aggressive Behavior*, *33*, 281–90.

Stroud, L.R., Salovey, P., & Epel, E.S. (2002). Sex differences in stress responses: Social rejection versus achievement stress. *Biological Psychiatry, 52,* 318–27.

Strube, M.J. (1981). Meta-analysis and cross-cultural comparison: Sex differences in child competitiveness. *Journal of Cross-Cultural Psychology, 3,* 15–6.

Stumpf, R.M., & Boesch, C. (2006). The efficacy of female choice in chimpanzees of the Taï Forest, Côte d'Ivoire. *Behavioral Ecology and Sociobiology, 60,* 749–65.

Sussman, R.W. (1999). *Primate ecology and social structure: Vol. 1. Lorises, lemurs and tarsiers.* Needham Heights, MA: Pearson Custom Publishing.

Sutton-Smith, B., Rosenberg, B.G., & Morgan, E.E. (1963). Development of sex differences in play choice during preadolescence. *Child Development, 34,* 119–26.

Swain, J.E., Lorderbaum, J.P., Kose, S., & Strathearn, L. (2007). Brain basis of early parent–infant interactions: Psychology, physiology, and in vivo functional neuroimaging studies. *Journal of Child Psychology and Psychiatry, 48,* 262–87.

Swami, V., Frederick, D.A., Aavik, T., Alcalay, L., Allik, J., Anderson, D., *et al.*, (2010). The attractive female body weight and female body dissatisfaction in 26 countries across 10 world regions: Results of the international body project I. *Personality and Social Psychology Bulletin, 36,* 309–25.

Swim, J. (1994). Perceived versus meta-analytic effect sizes: An assessment of the accuracy of gender stereotypes. *Journal of Personality and Social Psychology, 66,* 21–36.

Symons, D. (1979). *The evolution of human sexuality.* Oxford: Oxford University Press.

Symons, D. (1992). On the use and misuse of Darwinism in the study of human behavior. In J. Barkow, L. Cosmides, & J. Tooby (Eds.), *The adapted mind* (pp. 137–59). New York, NY: Oxford University Press.

Tajfel, H. (1982). Social psychology of intergroup relations. *Annual Review of Psychology, 33,* 1–39.

Takagi, T., Tanizawa, O., Otsuki, Y., Haruta, M., & Yamaji, K. (1985). Oxytocin in the cerebrospinal fluid and plasma of pregnant and non-pregnant subjects. *Hormone and Metabolism Research, 17,* 308–10.

Talmud, P.J. (2004). How to identify gene-environment interactions in a multi-factorial disease: CHD as an example. *Proceedings of the Nutrition Society, 63,* 5–10.

Tannen, D. (1996). *Talking from nine to five.* London: Virago.

Tanner, J.M. (1990). *Foetus into man: Physical growth from conception to maturity* (Revised ed.). Cambridge, MA: Harvard University Press.

Taylor, C. (1993). *Girls, gangs, women and drugs.* East Lansing, MI: Michigan State University Press.

Taylor, S.E. (2006). Tend and befriend: Biobehavioral bases of affiliation under stress. *Current Directions in Psychological Science, 15,* 273–7.

Taylor, S.E., Gonzago, G.C., Klein, L.C., Hu, P., Greendale, G.A., & Seeman, T.E. (2006). Relation of oxytocin to psychological stress response and hypothalamic-pituitary-adrenocortical axis activity in older women. *Psychosomatic Medicine, 68,* 238–45.

Taylor, S.E., Klein, L.C., Lewis, B.P., Gruenewald, T.L., Gurung, R.A.R., & Updegraff, J.A. (2000). Biobehavioral responses to tress in females: Tend-and-befriend, not fight-or-flight. *Psychological Review, 107,* 411–29.

Taylor, S.E., Saphire-Bernstein, S., & Seeman, T.E. (2010). Are plasma oxytocin in women and plasma vasopressin in men biomarkers of distressed pair-bond relationships? *Psychological Science, 21,* 3–7.

Taylor, S.P., & Epstein, S. (1967). Aggression as a function of interaction of sex of aggressor and sex of victim. *Journal of Personality, 35*, 474–86.

Teachman, J. (2010). Wives' economic resources and risk of divorce. *Journal of Family Issues, 31*, 1305–23.

Tesser, A. (1980). Self-esteem maintenance in family dynamics. *Journal of Personality and Social Psychology, 39*, 77–91.

Tesser, A. (1993). The importance of heritability in psychological research: The case of attitudes. *Psychological Review, 100*, 129–42.

Tesser, A., Campbell, J., & Smith, M. (1984). Friendship choice and performance: Self-evaluation maintenance in children. *Journal of Personality and Social Psychology, 46*, 561–74.

Tharp, R. (1963). Psychological patterning in marriage. *Psychological Bulletin, 60*, 97–117.

Theokas, C., Ramsey, P.G., & Sweeney, B. (1993). *The effects of classroom interventions on young children's cross-sex contacts and perceptions.* Paper presented to the Society for Research in Child Development, New Orleans.

Thoits, P.A. (1992). Identity structures and psychological well-being: Gender and marital status comparisons. *Social Psychology Quarterly, 55*, 236–56.

Thompson, S.K. (1975). Gender labels and early sex role development. *Child Development, 46*, 339–47.

Thorne, B. (1986). Girls and boys together but mostly apart: Gender arrangements in elementary schools. In W.W. Hartup & Z. Rubin (Eds.), *Relationships and development* (pp. 167–84). Hillsdale, NJ: Erlbaum.

Thornhill, R., & Gangestad, S.W. (1993). Human facial beauty: Averageness, symmetry and parasite resistance. *Human Nature, 4*, 237–69.

Thornhill, R., & Gangestad, S.W. (1994). Human fluctuating asymmetry and sexual behavior. *Psychological Science, 5*, 297–302.

Thornhill, R., & Gangestad, S.W. (2006). Facial sexual dimorphism, developmental stability, and susceptibility to disease in men and women. *Evolution and Human Behavior, 27*, 131–44.

Thornhill, R., & Gangestad, S.W. (2008). *The evolutionary biology of human female sexuality.* Oxford: Oxford University Press.

Thornhill, R., Gangestad, S.W., & Comer, R. (1995). Human female orgasm and mate fluctuating asymmetry. *Animal Behaviour, 50*, 1601–5.

Thornhill, N.W., & Thornhill, R. (1990). An evolutionary analysis of psychological pain following rape: 1. The effects of victim's age and marital status. *Ethology and Sociobiology, 11*, 155–76.

Thornton, A.J.V., Graham-Kevan, N., & Archer, J. (2010). Adaptive and maladaptive personality traits as predictors of violent and nonviolent offending behavior in men and women. *Aggressive Behavior, 36*, 177–86.

Tiesman, M., & Mosher, D. (1978). Jealous conflict in dating couples. *Psychological Reports, 42*, 1211–16.

Tinbergen, N. (1963). On aims and methods in ethology. *Zeitschrift fur Tierpsychologie, 20*, 410–33.

Tobin-Richards, M., Boxer, A., & Peterson, A. (1983). The psychological significance of pubertal change: Sex differences in the perception of self during early adolescence. In J. Brooks-Gunn & A. Peterson (Eds.), *Girls at puberty: Biological and psychosocial perspectives* (pp. 127–54). New York, NY: Plenum.

Tooby, J. (1982). Pathogens, polymorphisms and the evolution of sex. *Journal of Theoretical Biology, 97*, 557–76.

Tooby, J., & Cosmides, L. (1990a). The past explains the present: Emotional adaptations and the structure of ancestral environments. *Ethology and Sociobiology, 11*, 375–424.

Tooby, J., & Cosmides, L. (1990b). On the universality of human nature and the uniqueness of the individual: The role of genetics and adaptation. *Journal of Personality, 58*, 17–67.

Tooby, J., & Cosmides, L. (1992). The psychological foundations of culture. In J.H. Barkow, L. Cosmides & J. Tooby (Eds.), *The adapted mind: Evolutionary psychology and the generation of culture* (pp. 19–136). New York, NY: Oxford University Press.

Tooke, W., & Camire, L. (1991). Patterns of deception in intersexual and intrasexual mating strategies. *Ethology and Sociobiology, 12*, 345–64.

Townsend, J.M. (1995). Sex without emotional involvement: An evolutionary interpretation of sex differences. *Archives of Sexual Behavior, 24*, 171–204.

Townsend, J.M., Kline, J., & Wasserman, T.H. (1995). Low-investment copulation: Sex differences in motivations and emotional reactions. *Ethology and Sociobiology, 16*, 25–51.

Townsend, J.M., & Wasserman, T.H. (2011). Sexual hook-ups among college students: Sex differences in emotional reaction. *Archives of Sexual Behavior, 40*, 1173–81.

Townsend, S.W., Slocombe, K.E., Thompson, M.E., & Zuberbuhler, K. (2007). Female-led infanticide in wild chimpanzees. *Current Biology, 17*, R355–6.

Trivers, R. (1971). The evolution of reciprocal altruism. *Quarterly Review of Biology, 46*, 35–56.

Trivers, R.L. (1972). Parental investment and sexual selection. In B. Campbell (Ed.), *Sexual selection and the descent of man 1871–1971* (pp. 136–79). Chicago, IL: Aldine.

Trivers, R.L. (1985). *Social evolution.* Menlo Park, CA: Benjamin/Cummings.

Troisi, A., & Carosi, M. (1998). Female orgasm rate increases with male dominance in Japanese macaques. *Animal Behaviour, 56*, 1261–6.

Troisi, A., D'Amato, F.R., Carnera, A., & Trinca, L. (1989). Maternal aggression by lactating group-living Japanese macaque females. *Hormones and Behavior, 22*, 444–52.

Tronick, E.Z., Morelli, G.A., & Winn, S. (1987). Multiple caretaking of Efe (Pygmy) infants. *American Anthropologist, 89*, 96–106.

Turner, R.A., Altemus, M., Enos, T., Cooper, B., & McGuiness, T. (1999). Preliminary research on plasma oxytocin in normal cycling women: Investigating emotion and interpersonal distress. *Psychiatry: Interpersonal and Biological Processes, 62*, 97–113.

Turner, R.A., Altemus, M., Yip, D.N., Kupferman, E., Fletcher, D., Bostromn, A., *et al.* (2002). Effects of emotion on oxytocin, prolactin and ACTH in women. *Stress, 5*, 269–76.

Tutin, C.E. (1979). Mating patterns and reproductive strategies in a community of wild chimpanzees (Pan troglodytes schweinfurthii). *Behavioral Ecology and Sociobiology, 6*, 29–38.

Tversky, A., & Kahneman, D. (1974). Judgment under uncertainty: Heuristics and biases. *Science, 185*, 1123–31.

Twenge, J.M., Catanese, K.R., & Baumeister, R.F. (2003). Social exclusion and the deconstructed state: Time perception, meaninglessness, lethargy, lack of emotion, and self-awareness. *Journal of Personality and Social Psychology, 85*, 409–23.

Tybur, J.M., Lieberman, D., & Griskevicius, V. (2009). Microbes, mating, and morality: Individual differences in three functional domains of disgust. *Journal of Personality and Social Psychology, 97*, 103–22.

Tybur, J.M., Miller, G.F., & Gangestad, S.W. (2007). Testing the controversy: An empirical examination of adaptationists' attitudes toward politics and science. *Human Nature, 18*, 313–28.

Uvnäs-Moberg, K. (1997). Physiological and endocrine effects of social contact. *Annals of the New York Academy of Sciences, 807*, 146–63.

Uvnäs-Moberg, K. (1998). Oxytocin may mediate the benefits of positive social interaction and contact. *Psychoneuroendocrinology, 23*, 819–35.

Vacquier, V.D., Swanson, W.J., & Hellberg, M. (1995). What have we learned about sea-urchin sperm bindin? *Development Growth and Differentiation, 37*, 1–10.

Van Honk, J., Peper, J.S., & Schutter, D.J. (2005). Testosterone reduces unconscious fear but not consciously experienced anxiety: Implications for the disorders of fear and anxiety. *Biological Psychiatry, 58*, 218–25.

Van Honk, J., Tuiten, A., Hermans, E.J., Putman, P., Kopeschaar, H., Thijssen, J., *et al.* (2001). A single administration of testosterone induces cardiac accelerative responses to angry faces in healthy young women. *Behavioural Neuroscience, 115*, 238–42.

van Hoof, J.A., & van Schaik, C.P. (1992). Cooperation in competition: The ecology of primate bonds. In A. Harcourt & F.B.M. de Waal (Eds.), *Coalitions and alliances in humans and other animals* (pp. 357–89). Oxford: Oxford University Press.

van Schaik, C.P. (1989). The ecology of social relationships amongst female primates. In V. Standen & G.R.A. Foley (Eds.), *Comparative socioecology: Behavioral biology of humans and other mammals* (pp. 195–218). Oxford: Blackwell.

van Schaik, C.P., & Burkart, J.M. (2011). Social learning and evolution: the cultural intelligence hypothesis. *Philosophical Transactions of the Royal Society of London, Series B, Biological Sciences, 366*, 1008–16.

van Schaik, C., & Dunbar, R.I.M. (1990). The evolution of monogamy in large primates: A new hypothesis and some crucial tests. *Behaviour, 115*, 30–62.

van Schaik, C.P., Pradhan, G.R., & van Noordwijk, M.A. (2004). Mating conflict in primates: infanticide, sexual harassment and female sexuality. In P.M. Kappeler & C.P. van Schaik (Eds.), *Sexual selection in primates* (pp. 131–50). Cambridge: Cambridge University Press.

Van Vugt, M., De Cremer, D., & Janssen, D.P. (2007). Gender differences in cooperation and competition: The male-warrior hypothesis. *Psychological Science, 18*, 19–23.

Van Wingen, G., Mattern, C., Verkes, R.J., Buitelaar, J., & Fernandez, G. (2010). Testosterone reduces amygdala-orbitofrontal cortex coupling. *Psychoneuroendocrinology, 35*, 105–13.

Vandermassen, G. (2005). *Who's afraid of Charles Darwin? Debating feminism and evolutionary theory.* Lanham, MD: Rowman & Littlefield.

Verona, E., & Curtin, J.J. (2006). Gender differences in the negative affective priming of aggressive behavior. *Emotion, 6*, 115–24.

Verona, E., & Kilmer, A. (2007). Stress exposure and affective modulation of aggressive behavior in men and women. *Journal of Abnormal Psychology, 116*, 410–21.

Verona, E., Sadeh, N., & Curtin, J.J. (2009). Stress-induced asymmetric frontal brain activity and aggression risk. *Journal of Abnormal Psychology, 118*, 131–45.

Vigil, J.M. (2007). Asymmetries in the social styles and friendship preferences of men and women. *Human Nature, 18*, 143–61.

Villarreal, Y. (2009, March 30). Reality TV is in a big-family way. *Los Angeles Times.*

Voland, E. (1988). Differential infant and child mortality in evolutionary perspective: Data from late 17th to 19th century Ostfrieland (Germany). In L. Betzig, M. Borgerhoff Mulder, & P. Turke (Eds.), *Human reproductive behaviour: A Darwinian perspective* (pp. 253–62). Cambridge: Cambridge University Press.

Von Rueden, C., Gurven, M., & Kaplan, H. (2011). Why do men seek status? Fitness payoffs to dominance and prestige. *Proceedings of the Royal Society B, 278*, 2223–32.

von Schantz, T., Wittzell, H., Goransson, G., Grahn, M., & Persson, K. (1996). MHC genotype and male ornamentation: Genetic evidence for the Hamilton-Zuk model. *Proceedings of the Royal Society of London B, 263*, 265–71.

Vukovic, J., Jones, B.C., DeBruine, L.M., Little, A.C., Feinberg, D.R., & Welling, L.L.M. (2009). Circum-menopausal effects on women's judgements of facial attractiveness. *Biology Letters, 5*, 62–4.

Wagner, H.L., Buck, R., & Winterbotham, M. (1993). Communication of specific emotions: Gender differences in sending accuracy and communication measures. *Journal of Nonverbal Behavior, 17*, 29–53.

Wagner, S., Winner, E., Cicchetti, D., & Gardner H. (1981). "Metaphorical" mapping in human infants. *Child Development, 52*, 728–31.

Waguespack, N. (2005). What do women do in large-game hunting societies? The organization of male and female labor in foraging societies: Implications for early paleoindian archaeology. *American Anthropology, 107*, 666–76.

Wakefield, M.L. (2008). Grouping patterns and competition among female Pan troglodytes schweinfurthii at Ngogo, Kibale National Park, Uganda. *International Journal of Primatology, 29*, 907–29.

Walden, T.A., & Ogan, T.A. (1988). The development of social referencing. *Child Development, 59*, 1230–40.

Walker, K. (1994). Men, women, and friendship: What they say, what they do. *Gender and Society, 8*, 246–65.

Walker, L.E. (1979). *The battered woman.* New York, NY: Harper and Row.

Walker, L.E. (1984). *The battered woman syndrome.* New York, NY: Springer.

Walters, J. (1980). Interventions and the development of dominance relationships in female baboons. *Folia Primatologica, 34*, 61–89.

Walters, J., & Seyfarth, R.M. (1987). Conflict and cooperation. In B.B. Smuts, D.L. Cheney, R.M. Seyfarth, R.W. Wrangham, & T.T. Struhsaker (Eds.), *Primate societies* (pp. 306–17). Chicago, IL: University of Chicago Press.

Walters, S., & Crawford, C. (1994). The importance of mate attraction for intrasexual competition in men and women. *Ethology and Sociobiology, 15*, 5–30.

Wasilenko, K., Kulik, J., & Wanic, R. (2007). Effects of social comparisons with peers on women's body satisfaction and exercise behavior. *International Journal of Eating Disorders, 40*, 740–5.

Watkins, S.C. (1990). From local to national communities: The transformation of demographic regimes in Western Europe, 1870–1960. *Population and Development Review, 16*, 241–72.

Watson, D., Wiese, D., Vaidya, J., & Tellegen, A. (1999). The two general activation systems of affect: Structural findings, evolutionary considerations, and psychobiological evidence. *Journal of Personality and Social Psychology, 76*, 820–38.

Wedekind, C. (1992). Detailed information about parasites revealed by sexual ornamentation. *Proceedings of the Royal Society of London B, 247*, 169–74.

Wedekind, C., Seebeck, T., Bettens, F., & Paepke, A.J. (1995). MHC-dependent mate preferences in humans. *Proceedings of the Royal Society B, 260*, 245–9.

Weeden, J., Abrams, M.J., Green, M.C., & Sabini, J. (2006). Do high-status people really have fewer children? *Human Nature, 17*, 377–92.

Weinraub, M., Clements, L.P., Sockloff, A., Ethridge, T.E., & Myers, B. (1984). The development of sex role stereotypes in the third year: Relationships to gender labeling, gender identity, sex-typed toy preference and family characteristics. *Child Development, 55*, 1493–503.

Weinraub, M., & Gringlas, M.B. (1995). Single parenthood. In M.H. Bornstein (Ed.), *Handbook of parenting* (Vol. 3, pp. 65–87). Mahwah, NJ: Lawrence Erlbaum.

Weisfeld, G.E., Muczenski, D., Weisfeld, C.C., & Omark, D.R. (1987). Stability of boys' social success among peers over an eleven year period. *Contributions to Human Development, 18*, 58–80.

Welborn, B.L., Papademetris, X., Reis, D.L., Rajeevan, N., Bloise, S.M., & Gray, J.R. (2009). Variation in orbitofrontal cortex volume: Relation to sex, emotional regulation and affect. *Social Cognitive and Affective Neuroscience, 4*, 328–39.

Wellcome Trust (2001). Variation in the genome. *Wellcome News (Supplement 4: Unveiling the human genome)*. London: Wellcome Trust.

Wells, B.E., & Twenge, J.M. (2005). Changes in young people's sexual behavior and attitudes, 1943–1999: A cross-temporal meta-analysis. *Review of General Psychology, 9*, 249–61.

Wert, S.R., & Salovey, P. (2004). A social comparison account of gossip. *Review of General Psychology, 8*, 122–37.

West, M.M., & Konner, M.J. (1976). The role of the father: An anthropological perspective. In M.E. Lamb (Ed.), *The role of the father in child development.* (pp. 185–217). New York, NY: Wiley.

Westermarck, E. (1891). *The history of human marriage*. London: Macmillan.

Wheeler, L., & Miyake, K. (1992). Social comparison in everyday life. *Journal of Personality and Social Psychology, 62*, 760–74.

Whitaker, D.J., Haileyesus, T., Swahn, M., & Saltzman, L.S. (2007). Differences in frequency of violence and reported injury between relationships with reciprocal and nonreciprocal intimate partner violence. *American Journal of Public Health, 97*, 941–7.

White, F.J., & Wood, K.D. (2007). Female feeding priority in bonobos, Pan paniscus, and the question of female dominance. *American Journal of Primatology, 69*, 837–50.

White, G.L. (1981). A model of romantic jealousy. *Motivation and Emotion, 5*, 295–310.

Whiteside, S.P., & Lynam, D.R. (2001). The five factor model and impulsivity: Using a structural model of personality to understand impulsivity. *Personality and Individual Differences, 30*, 669–89.

Whiting, B.B., & Edwards, C.P. (1988). *Children of different worlds: The formation of social behavior.* Cambridge, MA: Harvard University Press.

Whiting, B.B., & Whiting, J.W.M. (1975). *Children of six cultures: A psycho-cultural analysis.* Cambridge, MA; Harvard University Press.

Whittle, S., Yap, M.B.H., Yucel, M., Fornito, A., Simmons, J.G., Barrett, A., *et al.* (2008). Prefrontal and amygdala volumes are related to adolescents' affective behaviors during parent-adolescent interactions. *Proceedings of the National Academy of Sciences of the United States of America, 105,* 3652–7.

Widdig, A., Bercovitch, F. B., Jurgen Streich, W., Sauermann, U., Nurnberg, P., & Krawczak, M. (2004). A longitudinal analysis of reproductive skew in male rhesus macaques. *Proceedings of the Royal Society of London B, 271,* 819–26.

Wiederman, M.W., & Allgeier, E.R. (1993). Gender differences in sexual jealousy: Adaptionist or social learning explanation? *Ethology and Sociobiology, 14,* 115–40.

Wiederman, M.W., & Kendall, E. (1999). Evolution, sex and jealousy: Investigation with a sample from Sweden. *Evolution and Human Behavior, 20,* 121–8.

Wiesenfeld, A.R., & Klorman, R. (1978). The mother's psychophysiological reactions to contrasting affective expressions by her own and an unfamiliar infant. *Developmental Psychology, 14,* 294–304.

Wiggins. J.S. (1979). A psychological taxonomy of trait descriptive terms: The interpersonal domain. *Journal of Personality and Social Psychology, 37,* 395–412.

Wiggins, J.S. (1991). Agency and communion as conceptual coordinates for the understanding and measurement of interpersonal behavior. In W.M. Grove & D. Cicchetti (Eds.), *Thinking clearly about psychology, Volume 2: Personality and psychopathology* (pp. 89–113). Minneapolis, MN: University of Minnesota Press.

Wilkstrom, S., Gunnarsson, T., & Nordin, C. (2003). Tactile stimulus and neurohormonal response: A pilot study. *International Journal of Neuroscience, 113,* 787–93.

Will, J.A., Self, P.A., & Datan, M. (1976). Maternal behavior and perceived sex of infant. *American Journal of Orthopsychiatry, 46,* 135–9.

Willbanks, W. (1984). *Murder in Miami.* Lanham, MD: University Press of America.

Williams, G.C. (1966). *Adaptation and natural selection.* Princeton, NJ: Princeton University Press.

Williams, G.C. (1996). *Plan and purpose in nature.* London: Phoenix.

Williams, J., & Best, D. (1982). *Measuring sex stereotypes: A thirty nation study.* Beverly Hills, CA: Sage.

Williams, K.D. (2007). Ostracism. *Annual Review of Psychology, 58,* 425–52.

Williams, K.D., & Sommer, K.L. (1997). Social ostracism by one's coworkers: Does rejection lead to loafing or compensation? *Personality and Social Psychology Bulletin, 23,* 693–706.

Wills, C. (1995). *The runaway brain.* London: Flamingo.

Wilson, D. (1978). Sexual codes and conduct: A study of teenage girls. In C. Smart & B. Smart (Eds.), *Women, sexuality and social control.* London: Routledge and Kegan Paul.

Wilson, D.S. (1994). Adaptive genetic variation and human evolutionary psychology. *Ethology and Sociobiology, 15,* 219–35.

Wilson, E.O. (1978). *On human nature.* Cambridge, MA: Harvard University Press.

Wilson, M., & Daly, M. (1992). The man who mistook his wife for a chattel. In J.H. Barkow, L. Cosmides, and J. Tooby (Eds.), *The adapted mind: Evolutionary psychology and the generation of culture* (pp. 289–322). New York, NY: Oxford University Press.

Wilson, M., & Daly, M. (1993). Spousal homicide risk and estrangement. *Violence and Victims, 8*, 3–16.

Wilson, M., & Daly, M. (1996). Male sexual proprietariness and violence against wives. *Current Directions in Psychological Science, 5*, 2–7.

Wilson, M., & Daly, M. (1997). Life expectancy, economic inequality, homicide, and reproductive timing in Chicago neighbourhoods. *British Medical Journal, 314*, 1271–4.

Wilson, M., Daly, M., & Scheib, J.E. (1997). Femicide: An evolutionary psychological perspective. In P.A. Gowaty (Ed.), *Feminism and evolutionary biology: Boundaries, intersections and frontiers* (pp. 431–65). New York, NY: Chapman & Hall.

Wilson, M., Daly, M., & Wright, C. (1993). Uxoricide in Canada: Demographic risk patterns. *Canadian Journal of Criminology, 35*, 263–91.

Wilson, M., & Mesnick, S.L. (1997). An empirical test of the bodyguard hypothesis. In P.A. Gowaty (Ed.), *Feminism and evolutionary biology: Boundaries, intersections and frontiers* (pp. 505–11). New York, NY: Chapman and Hall.

Windle, R.J., Kershaw, Y.M., Shanks, N., Wood, S.A., Lightman, S.L., & Ingram, C.D. (2004). Oxytocin attenuates stress-induced c-fos mRNA expression of forebrain regions associated with modulation of the hypothalamo–pituitary–adrenal activity. *Journal of Neuroscience, 24*, 2974–82.

Wing, L. (1981). Asperger syndrome: A clinical account. *Psychological Medicine, 11*, 115–30.

Winking, J., Gurven, M., & Kaplan, H. (2011). Father death and adult success among the Tsimane: Implications for marriage and divorce. *Evolution and Human Behavior, 32*, 79–89.

Winking, J., Gurven, M., Kaplan, H., & Stieglitz, J. (2009). The goals of direct paternal care among a South Amerindian population. *American Journal of Anthropology, 139*, 295–304.

Winstok, Z. (2007). Perceptions, emotions, and behavioral decisions in conflicts that escalate to violence. *Motivation and Emotion, 31*, 125–36.

Wong, P.T.P., Kettlewell, G., & Sproule, C.F. (1985). On the importance of being masculine: Sex role, attribution and women's career achievements. *Sex Roles, 12*, 757–69.

Wood, J.L., Heitmiller, D., Andreasen, N.C., & Nopoulos, P. (2008). Morphology of the ventral frontal cortex: relationship to femininity and social cognition. *Cerebral Cortex, 18*, 534–40.

Wood, W., & Eagly, A.H. (2002). A cross-cultural analysis of the behaviour of women and men: Implications for the origins of sex differences. *Psychological Bulletin, 128*, 699–727.

Woolgar, S. (1996). Psychology, qualitative methods and the ideas of science. In J.T.E. Richardson (Ed.), *Handbook of qualitative research methods for psychology and the social sciences* (pp. 11–24). Leicester: British Psychological Society.

Worthman, C.M., Jenkins, C.L., Stallings, J.F., & Daina, N.L. (1993). Attenuation of nursing-related ovarian suppression and high fertility in well-nourished, intensively breast-feeding Amele women of lowland Papua New Guinea. *Journal of Biosocial Science, 25*, 425–43.

Wrangham, R.W. (1997). Subtle, secret female chimpanzees. *Science, 277*, 774–5.

Wrangham, R.W., Jones, J.H., Laden, G., Pilbeam, D., & Conklin-Brittain, N. (1999). The raw and the stolen: Cooking and the ecology of human origins. *Current Anthropology, 40*, 567–94.

Wrangham, R., & Peterson, D. (1996). *Demonic males*. New York, NY: Houghton Mifflin.

Wright, R. (1994). *The moral animal*. New York, NY: Pantheon.

Wright, S. (1922). Coefficients of inbreeding and relationship. *American Naturalist, 56,* 330–8.

Wroblewski, E.E., Murray, C.M., Keele, B.F., Schumacher-Stankey, J.C., Hahn, B.H., & Pusey, A.E. (2009). Male dominance rank and reproductive success in chimpanzees, Pan troglodytes schweinfurthii. *Animal Behaviour, 77,* 873–85.

Wylie, R.C. (1974). *The self-concept*. Lincoln, NE: University of Nebraska Press.

Xu, F., & Carey, S. (1996). Infants metaphysics: The case of numerical identity. *Cognitive Psychology, 30,* 111–53.

Yarab, P.E., Allgeier, E.R., & Sensibaugh, C.C. (1999). Looking deeper: Extradyadic behaviors, jealousy and perceived unfaithfulness in hypothetical dating relationships. *Personal Relationships, 6,* 305–16.

Young, A.J., Carlson, A.A., Monfort, S.L., Russell, A.F., Bennett, N.C., & Clutton-Brock, T.H. (2006). Stress and the suppression of subordinate reproduction in cooperatively breeding meerkats. *Proceedings of the National Academy of Sciences of the United States of America, 103,* 12005–10.

Young, K.A., Gobrogge, K.L., Liu, Y., & Wang, Z. (2011). The neurobiology of pair bonding: Insights from a socially monogamous rodent. *Frontiers in Neuroendcrinology, 32,* 53–69.

Young, L.J., Nilsen, R., Waymire, K.G., MacGregor, G.R., & Insel, T.R. (1999). Increased affiliative response to vasopressin in mice expressing the V-1a receptor from a monogamous vole. *Nature, 400,* 766–8.

Young, L.J., & Wang, Z. (2004). The neurobiology of pair bonding. *Nature Neuroscience, 7,* 1048–54.

Younger, B.A., & Cohen, L.B. (1983). Infant perception of correlations among attributes. *Child Development, 54,* 858–67.

Youniss, J., & Smollar, J. (1985). *Adolescent relations with mothers, fathers and friends*. Chicago, IL: University of Chicago Press.

Zahavi, A. (1975). Mate selection: A selection for handicap. *Journal of Theoretical Biology, 53,* 205–14.

Zahn-Waxler, C., Radke-Yarrow, M., Wagner, E., & Chapman, M. (1992). Development of concern for others. *Developmental Psychology, 28,* 126–36.

Zucker, K.J. (1990). Gender identity disorders in children: Clinical descriptions and natural history. In R. Blanchard and B.W. Steiner (Eds.), *Clinical management of gender identity disorders in children and adults* (pp. 1–23). Washington, DC: American Psychiatric Press.

Subject Index

Author Index